Max and Marjorie

The Correspondence between
Maxwell E. Perkins and
Marjorie Kinnan Rawlings

University Press of Florida

Gainesville · Tallahassee

Tampa · Boca Raton

Pensacola · Orlando

Miami · Jacksonville

Edited by Rodger L. Tarr

The Correspondence between

Maxwell E. Perkins and

Marjorie Kinnan Rawlings

. . . .

04   03   02   01   00   99   6   5   4   3   2   1

Library of Congress Cataloging-in-Publication Data
Perkins, Maxwell E. (Maxwell Evarts), 1884–1947.
Max and Marjorie: the correspondence between
Maxwell E. Perkins and Marjorie Kinnan Rawlings /
edited by Rodger L. Tarr.
p. cm.
Includes bibliographical references and index.
ISBN 0-8130-1691-6 (alk. paper)
1. Perkins, Maxwell E. (Maxwell Evarts), 1884–1947—
Correspondence. 2. Rawlings, Marjorie Kinnan, 1896–
1953—Correspondence. 3. Women authors, Ameri-
can—20th century Correspondence. I. Rawlings,
Marjorie, 1896–1953. II. Tarr, Rodger L. III. Title.
PN149.9.P4A4   1999
070.4'1'092—dc21
[B]   99-34772

The University Press of Florida is the scholarly
publishing agency for the State University System of
Florida, comprising Florida A&M University, Florida
Atlantic University, Florida International University,
Florida State University, University of Central
Florida, University of Florida, University of North
Florida, University of South Florida, and University
of West Florida.

University Press of Florida
15 Northwest 15th Street
Gainesville, FL 32611–2079
http://www.upf.com

For Matthew and Arlyn Bruccoli

MARJORIE RAWLINGS was a frequent visitor, and her book, *The Yearling,* was one of Scribners' great successes. Marjorie became an intimate friend of the family, and . . . eventually appointed my sister as her executor. Marjorie was as pleasant and down to earth as her books would suggest, even though on one occasion I remember her saying at lunch that "art transmogrifies life." It was out of character for her to use such a jawbreaker; she may have felt that the occasion demanded something profound.

That she was a tough-minded woman was clear when she met Ernest Hemingway; they hit it off wonderfully. She later made a penetrating analysis of Hemingway's character, weighing his sensitivity against his braggadocio, and putting into words what is probably one of the best characterizations of Hemingway. She understood that Hemingway was divided between two worlds: the world of sporting things, in which he had to be tough and a great sportsman, and the world of literature, in which he was a truly sensitive artist. She was a very perceptive woman and a formidable writer.

—Charles Scribner, Jr. (1921–1995)
In the Company of Writers: A Life in Publishing (Scribners, 1991)

Contents

· ·

Acknowledgments

. . . .

I am especially indebted to the late Norton S. Baskin, who as executor of the Rawlings estate granted me permission to publish the Rawlings letters. His support, encouragement, and generosity will not be forgotten. To Charles Scribner, III, I owe not only the debt of permission to publish from the Scribner Archive, but also the kindness of offering the reminiscence of his father, Charles Scribner, Jr., for the epigraph. I here gratefully acknowledge the Manuscripts Division, Department of Rare Books and Special Collections, Princeton University Library; letters and photographs from this collection are published with the permission of the Princeton University Library. To the staff at Princeton University, but especially Margaret M. Sherry, Ben Primer, AnnaLee Pauls, and Don C. Skemer, who facilitated my use of the correspondence, I am most grateful. I am similarly grateful to the Department of Special Collections, George A. Smathers Libraries, University of Florida. To Carla Summers and Jeffrey A. Barr of the University of Florida, I owe a special thanks. For their unwavering support and attention to my seemingly endless requests, I owe a significant debt to John Ingram and Frank Orser. To Philip S. May, Jr., who owns documents represented here, I am particularly grateful.

To Jackson Bryer and David Nordloh, my thanks for their support and advice. To Meredith Morris-Babb, Susan Fernandez, and all the other wonderful folks at the University Press of Florida, my special acknowledgment—particularly my divine editor over the years, Deidre Bryan, copyeditor Sharon Damoff, editorial assistant Lucinda Treadwell, and designer Louise OFarrell. To Kevin M. McCarthy and Webb Salmon, for their expert reading of the manuscript, my indebtedness. To Amanda Yurick Muzzarelli, who not only typed in the letters but sat through the torturous collation, while maintaining her sense of humor, I owe an enormous debt. To Louise Freeman-Toole, who proofed the whole and helped compile the index, I owe an equal debt. To Brent Kinser, who ran down sources, I am most grateful. To Paul Schollaert, dean of the College of Arts and Sciences, and Ronald Fortune, chair of the Department of English,

Illinois State University, I acknowledge both support and grants-in-aid. To Carol Anita Tarr, whose patience, help, and understanding made this project possible, I owe my gratitude. And to Matthew J. Bruccoli, whose scholarly presence, able assistance, and valued friendship inform this work, I owe a profound debt.

Editorial Note

This volume comprises the entire correspondence known to the editor, most of which is housed in the Scribner Archive at Princeton University. Important documents held in the Rawlings Collection at the University of Florida and in private hands are also represented here. Some letters, not many, are missing, and some parts of letters are lost. Yet it seems safe to say that virtually all of the correspondence is published here. As the introduction to this volume details, the correspondence, 698 located letters, notes, and wires, is remarkable, both in its size and in its quality. Perkins was first Rawlings's editor, then her mentor, and finally her close personal friend. This volume presents a seventeen-year epistolary history of the friendship, which eventually grew to include the Scribner family as well. And as a history it reveals a great deal about the current literature, publishing practices, and evolving politics during the period it covers, from 1930 to 1947.

Every effort has been made to preserve the integrity of the letters. Nearly all of Perkins's letters are typescripts and thus are relatively consistent in form. Perkins's habits of writing are protected, such as the comma-hyphen (,-) or period-hyphen (.-), both hallmarks of his style. In the case of Rawlings also, most letters are typed, producing few problems in transcription. Her handwritten letters are quite another matter. She employs, depending upon her mood, various lengths of the dash. In an effort to represent her style, I have used a short dash (–), a medium dash (—), and a long dash (——). This system is entirely arbitrary.

There are also idiosyncrasies common to both writers. It was the habit of the day to place book titles in quotation marks rather than italics; this habit has been preserved. Both on occasion misspell words. Because most misspellings are not in any manner part of the fabric of the letters, these—few that they are—have been silently corrected. Indeed, Rawlings's miscues were often the result, as she freely admits, of alcohol or anger or both, which caused her to type "weeek" for "week," or to fail to use a capital at the beginning of a sentence. Such mistakes are also silently corrected. However, mistakes that clearly contribute to the flavor of the letter are retained and are indicated by [*sic*].

The editor's notes and emendations appear in *square* brackets. Punctuation is supplied only where it is necessary to convey clear meaning, and always within brackets to indicate editorial intrusion. Underlining is indicated by italics; double or triple underlining is noted in brackets. Wires, or telegrams, are printed in capital letters, and "STOP" is provided in brackets if necessary to make the meaning clear. Notes at the ends of the letters explain peculiarities in the text, such as inserted commentary in the margins. Authorial excision is indicated by *angle* brackets (< >).

In the heading at the beginning of each letter, "UF" means the Rawlings Collection, Smathers Library, University of Florida. If no location is indicated, the letter is at Princeton University. The letters are numbered consecutively, with the type and the length of the letter in parentheses. The following abbreviations are used:

ALS	Autograph letter, signed	TLS	Typed letter, signed
ANS	Autograph note, signed	CC	Carbon copy

Dates and places are supplied when it is possible to reconstruct them. Salutations and closings are retained, although on occasion a letter does not have one or the other. Many of Perkins's letters are reproduced from carbon copies and hence have no signature. However, on a few of the carbon copies "MEP" appears, which means that Perkins signed the original over the carbon. To conserve space, signatures have not been reproduced. Early in the correspondence, Perkins signed his letters "Maxwell E. Perkins"; later, "MEP" or "Max," almost always underlined. Rawlings signed her letters "Marjorie Kinnan Rawlings," then the more familiar "Marjorie K. R.," and later "MKR" or "Marjorie."

In the Charles Scribner lineage, various numbers have been adopted by the family over the years. The following is an accurate chronological enumeration: Charles Scribner I (1821–1871), Charles Scribner II (1854–1930), Charles Scribner III (1890–1952), Charles Scribner IV, aka Jr. (1921–1995), Charles Scribner V, aka III (1951–).

To conserve space, the letterheads on Perkins's stationery, either "Charles Scribner's Sons / Publishers / Fifth Avenue at 48th Street" (or later variations) or "Maxwell Evarts Perkins / 597 Fifth Avenue / New York," have not been reproduced. The Rawlings headers are preserved, for they indicate the myriad origins of her letters. The Scribner convention in typescript of putting the addressee's name at the end of the letter on the bottom left has been dropped, also as a compromise to space restrictions. The explanatory notes are deliberately brief, again because of space restrictions.

Introduction

The correspondence of Maxwell E. Perkins and Marjorie Kinnan Rawlings comprises 698 letters, notes, and telegrams. Its size is astonishing, even when compared to other Scribner writers of the period, such as Ernest Hemingway and F. Scott Fitzgerald. Why is it that so much was written from that first letter in 1930 to the last in 1947, on average nearly forty exchanges a year, nearly one per week for seventeen and a half years? What was it about this friendship that survived not only the passing of time but the fickleness of human nature? The two could not have been more *un*alike. Perkins, the sophisticated, urbane editor, had little in common with Rawlings, the earthy, remote orange grower. The former was given to reading uncommon books and the latter to telling ribald stories. One was a graduate of Harvard, the other of Wisconsin. One was a socialite, the other eschewed social preoccupations. It is, indeed, difficult to understand the attraction, but the attraction was there nevertheless, almost magnetic in quality, certainly magic in substance.

Life was particularly difficult for the female author in 1930, when Rawlings first came to Perkins's attention. In spite of the image of the "new woman" of the 1920s, women still confronted inequalities. Rawlings was a product of these new times, often an outspoken advocate in the feminist movement. She was graduated with honors in English from the University of Wisconsin in 1918, and was immediately thrust into the competitive world of unemployed writers. For a year, she walked the streets of New York, hawking her manuscripts to unreceptive editors. To survive, she worked as a publicist for the YWCA. In the early 1920s she moved to Louisville, Kentucky, and took a job as a feature writer for the *Courier-Journal* and then moved to Rochester, New York, to write for the *Times-Union*. Her columns were decidedly feminist in character. She even wrote a short-lived society column for the equally short-lived fashion rag *Five O'Clock*. Yet the bitter truth to her was that such writing was hack work, done out of necessity rather than from commitment.

A stormy marriage to Charles Rawlings, her Wisconsin sweetheart, himself a struggling writer, exacerbated the situation. In 1926, nearly breaking under the strain, she proposed to the editor of the *Times-Union* that she write a column of newspaper poetry called "Songs of a Housewife." For the next two and one-half years, she wrote nearly five hundred of these stylish poems, which were syndicated throughout the United States. She became famous, but not rich. She wrote an as yet unpublished autobiographical novel, *Blood of My Blood,* which she called "poor Jane Austen." Yet, in spite of the success of "Songs of a Housewife," her fiction continued to be rejected. In 1928, despondent, somehow aware that she needed a new venue, a new outlook, she convinced her husband to move to Cross Creek in remote central Florida, where she hoped to run an orange grove by day and to write, one must presume, by night. This idealistic vision proved a fantasy, of course. Yet, as she began to turn her attention to her new surroundings and new-found Cracker friends, her creative impulses quickened. She discovered her strength—narrative description.

Perkins's urban world could not have been farther removed from Rawlings's remote Cross Creek. As a young editor with Charles Scribner's Sons, he was already successful as the 1920s drew to a close. His special talent for spotting potential writers and then nourishing them into fame soon led him to the top of the publishing house. In the fall of 1930, Rawlings sent to Scribners her first manuscript inspired by Florida, entitled *High Winds,* later retitled *Jacob's Ladder.* This short novel first brought her to the attention of the brilliant editor who saw something different, almost unique, in Rawlings's descriptive narratives of life among the Florida Crackers. Coming to the attention of Perkins was the single most important event in Rawlings's literary life. To become his protégée was beyond her wildest imagination. That she even knew who Perkins was when she first wrote to Scribners is in itself unlikely. Perkins had already guided Fitzgerald and Hemingway to literary success, and when he took Rawlings under his wing, he was developing the talents of Thomas Wolfe. The situation was idyllic for the thirty-four-year-old Rawlings, who had yet to sell a story. Her first story, "Cracker Chidlings," was published in *Scribner's Magazine* in February 1931. What transpired in the next sixteen years is legendary in Scribner circles. In their constellation of stars, Rawlings became one of the brightest.

From the outset Perkins realized he had a gem in the rough. Rawlings conveyed the passion and the sensitivity Perkins felt were requisite to fine writing. His first letter to her, on November 19, 1930, is typical of what was to become a constant litany. "We are very much inclined to publish your novel," he wrote, "but would you consider certain suggestions for the revision, . . . excellent as we think it is as it stands." The fledgling but fiercely stubborn artist Rawlings was quick to accept Perkins's suggestions, largely because they were framed in the form of generous praise. The pattern was always the same. Perkins would begin with a compliment, then follow with a host of suggestions to make the work acceptable. The suggestions ranged from the choice of language, to the use of metaphor, to the arrangement of plot. In effect, with subtle urging Perkins was able to convince Rawlings to revise.

Early on she had very little sense of audience, or at least of the Scribner audience. She laced her work with a mixture of intellectualism and bawdiness that often defeated her purpose. She always captured essence but seldom fully grasped form. Perkins became her framer, a function Rawlings came increasingly to appreciate. And through it all, she always betrayed her lack of self-confidence. Perkins accepted *Jacob's Ladder* for publication in *Scribner's Magazine* in April 1931, but not before he convinced Alfred Dashiell to publish her first work, a series of sketches entitled "Cracker Chidlings" in February. Rawlings responded by saying that *Jacob's Ladder,* a novella, was "over-written," but "if you will be patient with me, I can do better work" (March 31, 1931). Patience was Perkins's virtue.

The better work quickly followed. After another story, "A Plumb Clare Conscience," appeared in *Scribner's Magazine* in December, Rawlings reported that she was already at work on a novel about the "scrub country" (March 31), later to become *South Moon Under.* As always, Perkins was patient. He knew when to leave Rawlings to her own devices, and he would only occasionally write to ask how her work was progressing. Caught between her perfectionist artistic nature and the very real need to run her orange grove, Rawlings suffered both delays and setbacks. She did manage, however, to write a number of short stories, one of them (about a woman's self-realization) having a decidedly feminist perspective and the teasing title "Gal Young Un." Dashiell, who had just published her "A Crop of Beans" in *Scribner's Magazine* in May, thought "Gal Young Un" was too anti-male, too strident, and declined to publish it. Rawlings's agent, Carl Brandt, sold it immediately to the rival *Harper's Magazine,* and it was subsequently awarded the O. Henry Prize for the best short story of 1932. Scribners never made another mistake of this magnitude. From then on, all of Rawlings's submissions were handled by Perkins.

Perkins encouraged Rawlings throughout the writing of *South Moon Under.* In early August 1932, she mailed the manuscript to him with the usual complaint that it was not ready and with the usual appeal for him to sort it out for her. She was especially concerned that her "episodic treatment" of narrative contributed to disunity of design. In mid-August Rawlings made her first sojourn to New York to meet Perkins and to receive his verdict. Perkins, to her relief, thought the manuscript "excellent." As was his habit when he discussed matters with Rawlings in person, Perkins gave her his thoughts on general revisions. In a letter of August 23, he outlined in precise detail what would have to be done to make the novel unified, beginning the letter as always with a compliment about the "highly interesting material, truly valuable material."

Perkins was more than an editor. He was her second voice, one might almost say her silent voice. In response to his gentle persuasions, she wrote, "I can't tell you how deeply I appreciate your helpfulness——your thoughtfulness and sympathy. You make it very easy for me to go at it again" (August 31, 1932). Before receiving Rawlings's letter of gratitude, Perkins "worried for fear what I suggested might seem to you to be asking a great deal" (September 1, 1932), and the next day, after receiving her response, he was relieved to write that he was "delighted . . . to find that you did not think my suggestions were too difficult." He then added the prophetic line "I think we shall have a splendid novel."

South Moon Under was published in 1933 with as much fanfare as Scribners could give it. The bleak financial picture made marketing especially difficult. The reading public, recoiling from the Depression, was not buying books. Scribners was not immune. Almost apologetically, Perkins assured Rawlings of his goodwill and then offered her "10% royalty on the first 5,000 copies, and 15% thereafter" (November 15, 1932). Rawlings, fifteen hundred miles away, overseeing an orange grove that had yet to make a profit, was stunned and could only muster the understatement that the terms were "fair enough" (November 18, 1932). Having not yet received Rawlings's assent, and sensing her naiveté and financial predicament, Perkins sweetened the offer to "15% after a sale of 3,000" (November 21, 1932), with the recommendation that Rawlings not pay Brandt and Brandt, her agents, 10 percent commission on her royalty percentage because they had "nothing whatever to do with its publication." At this juncture Perkins assumed another role. He now was not only her literary editor but her financial advisor as well. For Rawlings this was a very important moment. From then on Perkins became her chief negotiator between Brandt and Brandt and Charles Scribner's Sons, especially on the subject of foreign rights, a role that only the expert diplomat Perkins could play.

The initial sales of *South Moon Under* were disappointing to Perkins. In contrast, Rawlings was thrilled to have the income, and was especially grateful when Perkins sold the novel to the Book-of-the-Month Club for $8,000— "$4,000 for you, and $4,000 for us" (January 17, 1933). Rawlings feigned a sort of artist's indifference as she wrote to Perkins: "I think, really, you are taking the most beautiful care of me. The Book of the Month business is very nice indeed. As far as I was concerned, I had washed my hands of 'South Moon Under'. The book doesn't suit me at all . . ." (January 19). As if aware of her false bravado, Rawlings added a note at the end of the letter about the importance of the Book-of-the-Month Club sale: "It means I can have a new cypress shingle roof, by God."

Perkins never lost the knack for addressing Rawlings's peculiar needs and wishes. He sent copies of *South Moon Under* to the established stars like Willa Cather, Scott Fitzgerald, and James Branch Cabell. He introduced her to Charles Scribner, III, who became her champion and later her close friend. He invited her to New York to meet the literati, to bask in the glamour surrounding Scribner novelists. Rawlings was most grateful, although at first overwhelmed. The friendship quietly grew beyond the editor-artist relationship. Perkins began to trust and to confide in Rawlings, and she reciprocated in kind.

Meanwhile, the reception and the sales of *South Moon Under* perked up. It was nominated for the Prix Femina Americain, an important event for such an unheralded writer. The sales were steady, although continuing to disappoint Perkins. "The actual royalty sale to date is a little bit short of 5,000," Perkins wrote to Rawlings on April 1, 1933. On April 10 he wrote, "We have sold over 6,000 now, but the book business was never anything like so bad." Even so, the novel was listed as the "third best seller" in the *New York Herald Tribune.*

Insofar as Rawlings the writer was concerned, Perkins's encouragement redoubled. He wanted her to continue to write more about life in rural Florida among the Crackers. Rawlings suddenly became recalcitrant. She had other ideas and wanted to broaden her vista. Perkins continued to lay foundations, at one point suggesting that she write a "boys' book." Rawlings bristled. A minor conflict erupted between novelist and editor. Perkins knew exactly what Rawlings was capable of. Rawlings, not surprisingly, thought otherwise. She insisted upon writing a novel with the incongruous plot of an alienated Englishman finding grace in the Ocklawaha scrub. Perkins had little choice but to give Rawlings the room she demanded. In August she departed for England to do research for the book, but not before meeting with Perkins in New York to demand that he tell her the "truth" about his ideas for the "child's book" (July 15). It was also a difficult period in her personal life; her marriage to Charles Rawlings ended in divorce in late 1933.

Perkins's patience paid off. On October 4, upon returning from England, Rawlings wrote to Perkins, "I'm strongly considering the desirability of doing, before the novel [*Hamaca*], the boys' book of the scrub." Although Rawlings eventually decided to continue with *Hamaca* first, Perkins could little have imagined the victory he had won in persuading her to consider his suggestion, for this "boys' book" was to become *The Yearling*, which was awarded the Pulitzer Prize in 1939. Meanwhile, Perkins was cautious, as in this response on October 10: "I am distinctly in favor of your doing the boys' book on the scrub. You do have to do what you want to do in writing, but if you could put off the novel . . . I think it would be the better course." Always proud, and increasingly stubborn, Rawlings did not heed Perkins's advice to write that book first, but the seed had been planted and it continued to be nourished. As she worked on *Hamaca,* she worried openly about whether the boys' book should be an "out-and-out boy's juvenile" (October 23). Perkins continued his subtle pressure, suggesting that she should and could write a book to rival *Huckleberry Finn.* Rawlings was more than flattered, but stuck to her determination to finish *Hamaca* first. Perkins capitulated, with his usual offer of encouragement and help: "I was mighty glad to hear that you had got underway with 'Hamaca'. If ever you should want to show me any of it, remember how eagerly I should read it" (December 18). Rawlings could not have received a more generous Christmas present.

Hamaca, later retitled *Golden Apples,* proved a difficult book to write. Rawlings was out of her element. She was writing about an Englishman she could know only from a distance. Gone was the intensity of observation she displayed so well in her Cracker stories. Perkins knew she would have trouble, but in the end he was powerless to stop her. He could only offer his guidance and hope that all would turn out for the best. Rawlings's problems were complicated by yet another disastrous year for citrus. She wrote to inform Perkins that she was "broke." He responded with advances on her royalties. But, more important, he responded with encouragement. "I am sure you will do a fine book, and you ought to have trouble in getting under way with a fine book," he wrote on February 1, 1934.

Recognizing the fragility of her ego, he then told her that Scott Fitzgerald thought her *South Moon Under* was a "beautiful book." Rawlings was sustained and further buoyed by the knowledge that *South Moon Under* had been nominated for the Pulitzer Prize. Whatever his encouragements were, they never seemed enough. Rawlings, who lacked the hubris to believe she had the talent to join the stars, would fall into moods of artistic depression, often tearing up whole sections of manuscript. Through these periods of distress, Perkins's support never wavered. "You tend to underrate your abilities," he wrote her, "as the best writers almost always do" (February 28), an observation he offered in the context of discussing the start-up trials experienced by Hemingway. Later, in discussing the similar trials of Thomas Wolfe, he wrote, "I really have no anxiety about your book. I am certain it will be good" (June 14).

Golden Apples was published in 1935, but not before nearly another year of false beginnings, torn manuscripts, and claims of inability. As the manuscript reached the polishing stage in 1934, Perkins seemed to manifest a new-found ardor. He genuinely liked what Rawlings had written, and he offered page-by-page analysis of both plot and style. How he could do this and attend to the equally difficult Wolfe attests to the legendary abilities upon which his reputation is founded. He stayed close to Rawlings. Indeed, it would not be an overstatement to say that Rawlings's book was in a real sense *his* book. *Golden Apples,* like *South Moon Under,* took on the silent voice of Perkins, a voice that harnessed the wind to make an articulate melody. Through it all he was instructing her on writing, including sending her James's *The Art of the Novel,* although he cautioned, "Don't take Henry James too seriously" (November 23, 1934). In the end, Perkins even chose the title *Golden Apples* from a list of possibilities offered to him by Rawlings. When the manuscript went to proof, there were still defects, and as was his usual and costly procedure with Rawlings, Perkins encouraged substantive emendation in proof. His feeling was that one could not really visualize a novel until it was in proof. In Rawlings's case, her manuscripts often went through several stages of proof. The novel was published in 1935, with a more generous contract of 10 percent on 2,000 copies, 12.5 percent on the next 3,000, 15 percent after 5,000, and 20 percent after 10,000. Clearly Scribners anticipated large sales. It was at this point that "Mr. Perkins" became "Max" and "Mrs. Rawlings" became "Marjorie." The friendship never waned.

Golden Apples itself was a dud, at least insofar as sales were concerned. No one was more shocked than Perkins. His intellectual and emotional investment in the novel had been immense. Rawlings, typical of her self-effacing personality, wrote that she did not "blame anyone but myself for 'Golden Apples' being interesting trash instead of literature" and was "astonished" at the generosity of the reviews (October 15, 1935). Perkins acknowledged that the reviews were "favorable," although "they tend to talk about the wrong things." With unerring instinct, Perkins added, "Do you plan to do the boy's book?" (November 2). Perkins did not want Rawlings to sulk. Two weeks later he promised, "I won't say anything more about the boy book, but that I greatly hope you will do it, and in the way you wish" (November 15). In an undated letter, written in late November or early December, Rawlings responded, "The feeling for the boy's book, the particular thing I want to say, came to me. It will not be a story for boys, though some of them might enjoy it. It will be a story *about* a boy—a brief and tragic idyll of boyhood. I think it cannot help but be very beautiful." With these words the celebrated *The Yearling* was born, words that owe their impetus to the sensitivity and sensibility of Perkins.

In 1936, Rawlings's personal and literary fortunes brightened. The oranges were "beautiful and delicious" and the "boy's book well thought out" (March 26). The only concern seemed to be the title. Rawlings first proposed *The Sinkhole,* but this was quickly nixed by Perkins for fear it conveyed the wrong message. *The Fawn* was considered, but it too did not convey the book's subject. Rawlings worried and Perkins pondered. "I do not believe the boy's story is going to be what you have in your own mind, at all," Rawlings wrote on May 20. Perkins, on the other hand, kept Rawlings distracted by writing anecdotal letters about Hemingway and Wolfe, sending her nonfiction books to read, and seeking her opinions and judgments. Such diversion kept Rawlings from the ever-persistent questioning of her own talents. So comfortable was Rawlings that she was able to announce that the anticipated short work would now have to be a "full-length novel" to be finished in a "cottage in the Carolina mountains" (July 14). Perkins continued to keep names like Hemingway and Fitzgerald before her. During this period Rawlings was also able to write a number of important short stories, not the least of which was the widely popular "A Mother from Mannville," the story of a boy and his dog, later to be adapted by MGM for the Lassie movie *The Sun Comes Up.* By the fall she was proposing more titles to Perkins: "Do you like either / The Flutter-Mill / The Yearling / Do you like a place name, such as Juniper Creek?" (September 22). Perkins chose *The Yearling.*

Rawlings left the mountains in early November, carrying not only her manuscript but also her memories of a meeting with Fitzgerald in Asheville in October. The beginning of the new year was not as rewarding. In late January Rawlings wrote to Perkins, "I had to discard everything of 'The Yearling' ——which we may call it for the time being——back to the first chapter." Perkins responded immediately, "I wish you would send me chapters. I would not care if they were very much in the rough too, for I know now enough about how you do to be able to understand what the later development would be" (February 2, 1937).

Two months passed with little news on the progress of the manuscript, a fact that frustrated Perkins to the point of asking the question "Have you been able to get back to 'The Yearling' and is it going well?" (March 24). Rawlings assured him that she hoped to complete the work in North Carolina in "the late summer or early fall" (March 26). She interjected a bit of wit when she confided to Perkins that she was putting off her too curious agent Carl Brandt by assuring him that there was "no love interest" in the novel and that "All women characters [were] past the menopause." Perkins must have been relieved to learn that Rawlings was ignoring Brandt, who wanted to sell the novel as a serial to *Cos-*

mopolitan, but he also was anxious enough to ask, "Can you now make a pretty definite prophecy as to when 'Yearling' will be done?" (April 21).

Rawlings understood that Perkins had to make definite plans for publication. But what creeps into her letters for the first time is the teasing knowledge that she is no longer a literary supplicant, financially dependent upon the house of Charles Scribner's Sons. Rawlings was incorrect, of course, but this new-found illusion of freedom of expression sustained her through the final months of preparation. She was not above playing Perkins off against Brandt, rival suitors for her manuscripts. Perkins became frustrated, if not annoyed. "The sooner we get 'The Yearling' the better," he wrote, with the immediate apologia, "you never were a delinquent author. . . . My impatience about 'The Yearling' is mostly that of being extremely anxious to read it" (May 7, 1937). Rawlings's response is indicative of her increasing confidence. "'The Yearling' progresses," in spite of an "insane maid [who] left me out of a clear sky" (May 10). It is clear from such banter that Rawlings came to realize that she was a celebrity, that she was a writer of importance. She had earned the full respect of Perkins. She had become what she wanted to be, one of Scribner's stars. As if to accentuate her status, and perhaps to frustrate his timetable, she sent Perkins manuscripts of poems, with instructions to publish them if he saw fit. Finally, in late June, she forwarded a draft of *The Yearling.* Perkins was relieved, almost grateful.

On the other hand, Rawlings was careful not to go too far. She knew more than anyone how important Perkins was to her. She wrote the following in a letter of June 24, 1937: "I should like very much to have a really quiet bit of talk with you. . . . You give me so much mentally, are so stimulating and understanding, that I long for free talk with you, and we have almost never had it. You have much more than I of satisfying intellectual interchange, and I have a certain need of you that you do not have of me." Perhaps a psychoanalyst could make much of this passage, with its hints of desire couched in the language of intellectual fulfillment. After all, Rawlings was a divorcée of forty-two. However, within the context of the correspondence as a whole, Rawlings's words convey quite another meaning. She viewed Perkins more in Wordsworthian terms: "The anchor of my purest thoughts, the nurse, / The guide, the guardian of my heart, and soul, / Of all my moral being." Whether Perkins recognized this clearly is another matter. Unwittingly, he expressed his own doubts to Hemingway on November 28:

> Maybe I might come down to Key West. I would like to do it mighty well. I'd like to spend an afternoon on the dock looking at those lazy turtles swim-

ming around. The trouble is there is another author in Florida,- Marjorie Rawlings. She is a fine author too, and a fine woman. But I never did feel comfortable alone with women (I suppose there is some complex involved in it) and the idea of visiting one with nobody else around (she is divorced) scares me to death. She is one of the best as a person, and a mighty good writer too, and she is just finishing a book. She has asked me to come down a lot of times, and if she ever knew I went to Key West and did not stop there, it would be mighty bad. (Hemingway and Perkins 217)

Perkins never visited Cross Creek.

In the fall of 1937, Rawlings wrote a letter to assure Perkins that she had "finished the writing" of *The Yearling* "last week-end and am well into the editing" (October 20), and then she followed it with an undated note saying, "Copying the manuscript for some reason is a nightmare. It goes as slowly as walking in quicksand, and I am getting something of the same desperate feeling. . . . Pray for my sanity." On December 2, 1937, Rawlings mailed the manuscript with the request that Perkins prune out what makes him "*uncomfortable.*" Perkins assured her on December 10 that he was reading the manuscript with the "very greatest pleasure," and on December 13 he added, "It is a very beautiful book." By December 23 he informed Rawlings that Scribners had hired the artist Edward Shenton to draw "head pieces" for the chapters: "We must give this book individuality so that it will stand apart, and not be thought of as just the ordinary novel." This time Perkins asked for only minor adjustments in the text, arguing at one point that the "unseemly incident" of Grandma Hutto on the chamber pot in full view of family members might hurt sales. Rawlings acquiesced, with the comment that she took "perverse pleasure" in worrying Perkins about such potentially explosive scenes that she knew would eventually be removed. And, once again, Perkins accorded Rawlings the privilege of substantial correction in proof. Perkins also negotiated a 15 percent royalty, an offer Rawlings could hardly refuse.

The Yearling became an instant best-seller. The long hours of work and the sheer persistence had paid off. Perkins wrote enthusiastically, "I never knew a book that had such universal liking" (April 26, 1938). Of all the praise, the comment that was assuredly most satisfying to Rawlings came from Fitzgerald through Perkins: "The Marjorie Rawlings book fascinated me. I thought it was even better than 'South Moon Under' and I envy her the ease with which she does those action scenes, such as the tremendously complicated hunt sequence, which I would have to stake off in advance and which would probably turn out to be a stilted business in the end. Hers just simply flows; the characters keep thinking, talking, feeling, and don't stop, and you think and talk and feel with them" (Fitzgerald, *Dear Scott/Dear Max* 244). Rawlings's reaction was appropriately low-keyed. "People's response to the book amazes me," she wrote to Perkins on May 14, 1938. "I am getting the most wonderful and touching letters. . . . It is fine to have the book stirring as many people as it seems to, but . . . the so-called 'success' seems to have nothing to do with me." Rawlings is not being artful here. She recognized that if it were not for the foundation laid by Scribners, if it were not for the genius of Perkins, *The Yearling* would not have enjoyed such acclaim. She had become wise enough to know that writing was, in the end, a business. But what a business!

Within the space of two years, the trade edition of *The Yearling* went through twenty-five editions, selling 265,000 copies in 1938 alone. In addition, 200,000 copies were marketed through the Book-of-the-Month Club, and 190,000 more for the Armed Services Edition. By 1946, the year of the filming of the MGM blockbuster starring Gregory Peck and Jane Wyman, Scribners boasted that sales were in excess of 700,000, including the special edition illustrated by N. C. Wyeth. In 1939, *The Yearling* was awarded the Pulitzer Prize. Rawlings became an international celebrity. Of those proudest of her success, Perkins was paramount. He flooded her with copies of reviews from America and abroad, nearly all of which were positive to the point of discipleship. Perkins had asked Rawlings to write a *Huckleberry Finn,* and she had responded. But neither could have anticipated the sensation created by *The Yearling.* The letters Rawlings received at Cross Creek from admiring readers were in the thousands. The ones that particularly struck her she would attempt to answer. Being a celebrity was difficult for her. She tried to be stoic. She was, of course, especially grateful to Perkins, and once again acknowledged his influence: "Max, what a blessing we didn't cut the book any. Half the letters I receive complain that it isn't long enough. . . . But it proved right to leave it alone" (May 21, 1938). When it came to her Scribners work, Rawlings was always wise enough with Perkins to use the collective "we."

Perkins, true to character, continued to push Rawlings. He asked her to write a collection of stories gathered around her fictional alter ego, Quincey Dover, a character in several of her stories. They must strike while the iron is hot, he advised. Rawlings agreed, but she wanted to write a novel about northeast Florida in the period 1790–1840 (May 22, 1938). Perkins saw the dangers of her stepping outside her element. But Rawlings saved him the need to caution when she decided to revive her earlier, and largely unpublished, Cross Creek chronicles (June 8). Perkins was delighted. There were interruptions, however, not the least of which were Rawlings's recurring bouts of severe diverticulitis.

Operations were scheduled, only to be canceled by second opinions. Rawlings managed to survive. She sought relaxation instead of surgery, which in turn led her to Bimini and fishing trips with Hemingway, among others.

Perkins was ever vigilant, ever attentive, assuring her it was a "privilege" to be her editor: "cooperating with you as an Editor has been one of the happiest & most satisfying experiences I have ever had,- & ever shall- & I am most grateful for it" (June 10). To brighten her spirits, he inundated her with books to read and wrote gossipy letters about the Scribner writers. A special topic of conversation was Thomas Wolfe. Rawlings appreciated such attention and returned it in kind. She assured Perkins that she would be all right as long as she kept to a "rigid diet" (July 28). She did not obey reason, of course. Her one constant love in life was cooking and eating. Perkins's response was always the same when it came to Rawlings's health: "I do hope everything will go well" (June 20), followed by her assurances that it would, in time.

By the fall of 1938 Rawlings was significantly improved, so much so that she was once again able to turn her attention to writing. Then came the news that Thomas Wolfe had died suddenly. Perkins was devastated. Rawlings was particularly helpful, offering sympathy to Perkins ("I have grieved for you ever since I heard of Tom's death") and musing about Wolfe's awareness that "he had come to the great wall. He must have felt far beyond most of us that withdrawing of the cosmic force from his individual unit of life" (September 21). Perkins fully appreciated Rawlings's sentiments: "I was most grateful for what you wrote about Tom" (October 21).

At this juncture, the letters shift focus toward Rawlings's next project, which, because of her social commitments and endless lectures, she did not seem to have time to begin. Perkins is there again to tell her: "I think your work ought to come before anything else in the world"; lecturing is "very exhausting and unrewarding" (December 12). Just after Christmas, Perkins urged Rawlings to come to New York because of the "difficulties that are besetting you. The most important thing is your work, and so it is the one thing that you should think of seriously" (December 29). As if to bolster Rawlings's flagging belief in herself, Perkins wrote the next day to quote what Ellen Glasgow had written to him: "Few books have ever moved me more deeply than 'The Yearling'. . . . It is a perfect thing of its kind, with the accent of inevitability that tempts me to use the word 'genius'" (December 30).

By New Year's Day 1939, however, Rawlings was again beset with more domestic problems, reporting to Perkins that her "domestic arrangements have been again disturbed by another of the explosions that seem always to occur here . . ." (January 2). Her grove man, the husband of her favorite maid, was shot, and Rawlings was saddled with the consequences. As always, Perkins was there to sympathize, also complimenting her about the "wonderful picture you gave of the old negress" (January 25). He clearly saw a story developing from the incident, a short story for the volume he had been pushing Rawlings to write around the character of Quincey Dover. In the meantime, Perkins was editing a collection of Rawlings's previously published stories under the title *When the Whippoorwill—*. Then there was the Wyeth-illustrated edition of *The Yearling* to proof. The burgeoning sales of the trade edition of *The Yearling* ensured a certain tranquility. Rawlings was able to approach all these projects at a more leisurely pace. Perkins seemed almost hurt by her lack of communication, pleading in a letter on April 20: "I'll write you lots of news if you'll soon send me a postcard," and then asking: "Have you scratched the old Fox off your list altogether that you won't answer his letters?!" Yet by May 13, having rejected the idea of a "girl's book on the scrub," Rawlings was sufficiently convinced by Perkins to pursue the fresh collection of stories under the title *Cross Creek*, perhaps with Quincey Dover as a focus. The year 1939 was not a good one for Scribners, however, owing, Perkins thought, to the "repeated war scares" (July 7) preceding World War II.

Rawlings and Florida seemed somehow removed from the debates on the war. So confident was she of the future that she rented a "delightful modern cottage right on the ocean" (July 31) to get the manuscript of *Cross Creek* into shape. Except for brief spats with Scribners about the royalties being paid for the Wyeth edition of *The Yearling*, the fall came and went with Perkins and Rawlings exchanging various letters of pleasantry. Among other things, Perkins kept the name of Ellen Glasgow before her, and it was not long before Glasgow invited Rawlings to Virginia for a visit. Rawlings could not, however, escape her persistent physical setbacks. "Getting the stories done is like walking up a windy hill in a nightmare. I finished the first drafts . . . [when a] perfectly vicious intestinal attack hit me" (August 29), Rawlings wrote from her hospital bed in Jacksonville. Perkins was duly concerned and offered several medical contacts in Boston. The poor reviews of the first British edition of *Golden Apples* did not help matters. Perkins was ever optimistic, however. By October, Rawlings was back on the lecture circuit, being treated like the "Queen of Sheba" in Louisville and the "lowliest of Sheba's slaves" at the "icy" University of Chicago (October 18). The increasingly anxious Perkins responded, "Any time you are willing to send me the stories that will be in the book, I'd love to read them, if only just for the pleasure of it" (October 26).

Rawlings in more regal fashion complained about the "goddamned proofreader" of the Wyeth *Yearling*, whose mistake "almost completely ruined" the edition for her (October 28, 1939). Then two weeks later she apologized for her fit of ill-temper: "It was cruel of me to be snappish about it, for I know that a publishing house like yours must take such errors even more seriously than do the authors." She then apologetically admits to missigning deliberately one of the signature sheets "Dora Rolley Dooflickit," under which Wyeth signed, "I always suspected she did" (November 14).

By 1940, the Perkins-Rawlings correspondence was punctuated more and more with such humor. They were by then close friends and thus were able to write to each other as close friends write. Perkins would send business letters, such as appeals for the proof of *When the Whippoorwill*— to the tardy Rawlings, but always with a paragraph or two about matters personal, not the least of which were his growing problems with his wife, Louise. As early as 1938, Rawlings had been offering advice, but none more frank than her perception of Louise's lack of judgment regarding Catholicism: "She is very sweet and a little pathetic, and I understand her. You are so much wiser than she—you must not be intolerant" (May 14, 1938). Even Perkins, used to such frankness from Rawlings, must have been taken aback. As was typical when she spoke imprudently, Rawlings apologized later. In keeping with both their growing friendship and his genuine interest in her writing, Perkins continued to encourage Rawlings: "I am delighted that some of 'Cross Creek' will come soon" (July 26, 1940). Rawlings as always asked for patience.

The rest of 1940 was dominated by such exchanges, with the important development that Julia Scribner had become a favorite of Rawlings; hence, the letters are laced with personal references to the Scribner family. Charles Scribner, III, had long been a friend, but with the entrance of Julia that friendship inevitably became closer. At first Perkins was pleased by the new association, but there seems silent evidence that he began to resist—*resent* is too strong—Rawlings's effusive references to Julia. It was as if the Scribner friendship took Rawlings from her assigned task—writing. She would write drafts and forward them for Perkins's commentary and editing.

Cross Creek went slowly for quite another reason, however. Rawlings was falling in love with and would soon marry her longtime friend Norton Baskin. Baskin, the consummate raconteur, was a breath of fresh air for Rawlings. He diverted her attention from her problems and told her stories that refreshed her soul and nourished her own story-telling spirit. Perkins, always noble, wrote to Rawlings when he learned of the marriage: "Anything that makes you happy makes me happy" (October 29, 1941). Still, there was the impending war. Both Perkins and Rawlings were isolationists at first—especially Rawlings, who openly complained about the "flood of literature asking for money and cooperation for everything connected with the world's mess" (undated letter, early January 1941).

"John Barleycorn," as Rawlings called it, was ever present. Both Rawlings and Perkins had drinking problems. Rawlings drank heavily, then would sober up to write. Perkins drank to relieve the increasing pressures of his position. Neither admitted to alcoholism, but both knew their health was affected by alcohol. Drinking was to Rawlings a way of life; to Perkins it was a form of escape. In the early 1940s, they managed the problem, but that was soon to change. Rawlings's health worsened by the mid-1940s, forcing her on a strict diet, and Perkins was ordered by his doctor to restrict his drinking. Both were unhappy at the prospect of altering their lifestyles. Yet, even their health problems did not get in the way of their friendship. The letters continued to flow at a steady pace as Rawlings finished *Cross Creek*. Perkins remained a positive inspiration, always knowing how to handle Rawlings, depending upon her mood or whim. If anything, his nurturing increased, almost in proportion to her lagging creative abilities. Once, while she was struggling with the opening of the book, he counseled her that "it is generally the books that worry good authors that do turn out to be the best ones" (May 20, 1941). And then six weeks later he wrote, "I think 'Cross Creek' will be a very fine book indeed" (June 30).

Perkins was correct. *Cross Creek* did, indeed, prove to be a very fine book, but only after it was carefully edited by Perkins. Rawlings complained that she had "suffered" in the writing (undated letter, early August), having particular difficulty with the lack of "straight narrative" and the "sharp variance of style" (September 15). To allay her fears, Perkins sent a telegram: "Think Cross Creek will make very fine unusual book. Revision not difficult but needs some days study. Will write fully" (September 22). The revisions Perkins finally suggested were extensive, but not overwhelming, and helped Rawlings to find her voice. And, as usual, Perkins sent the manuscript directly to galley proof, where the revisions were then made, and finally to page proof, where additional revisions were accomplished. This was an expensive method, to be sure, but one he felt worked best for Rawlings. When she could see her work in proof, it always gave her the added incentive to see the project to its end. Interestingly, as Rawlings's semi-autobiographical documentary unfolded, Perkins worried about libel (November 12) and edited the material accordingly. As fate would have it, he overlooked the description of Zelma Cason, whose subsequent lawsuit kept Rawlings tied up in court for years. The "Cross Creek Trial," as it was called, exhausted the participants.

On January 5, 1942, Perkins informed Rawlings that *Cross Creek* was in page proofs. Once again, Rawlings's spirits were buoyed by the knowledge that the

Book-of-the-Month Club had put the book on its list, for the profits would thus be greater. Perkins reminded her, "So now three of your books, out of four, have been taken by the Book of the Month Club, and I don't believe that has happened to anyone else" (January 14).

Cross Creek, like The Yearling, was an instant best-seller. Perkins was pleased to report to Rawlings that by March 1942 400,000 copies had been printed, 300,000 of which were for the Book-of-the-Month Club. In April, Reader's Digest asked to condense it. Rawlings was again a celebrity. Cross Creek enjoyed an even larger initial audience than The Yearling. To take advantage of this audience, Rawlings suggested that she do a cookbook with the fetching title Cross Creek Cookery. Both Perkins and Charles Scribner thought it a novel idea, and while the presses were still printing copies of Cross Creek, Rawlings completed Cross Creek Cookery. The cookbook was also a hit. Readers loved the Cracker recipes, such as cooter soup, pan-fried alligator, and bourbon-laced pecan pie. But what they liked even more was Rawlings's homespun narrative interspersed among the recipes. In many respects, Cross Creek Cookery was an extension of the "Songs of a Housewife" column she had done fifteen years earlier.

At this point, after the publication of Cross Creek and Cross Creek Cookery, the correspondence of Perkins and Rawlings begins to wane slightly. There are the obvious reasons: Perkins was overwhelmed with work while his health continued to deteriorate, and Rawlings was overcome with personal trials, not the least of which was Norton Baskin's entrance into the war as an ambulance driver in Burma. His volunteering for the American Field Service caught her by surprise. "I feel utterly flattened out about it," she wrote Perkins (June 17, 1942). The letters at this point shift focus. Rawlings's overriding concern was the war she once opposed but now supported publicly as a patriot. Because of the popularity of her books among service personnel—South Moon Under, The Yearling, and Cross Creek were each printed in an Armed Services Edition—she found herself answering hundreds of letters from those in or about to go to war, a task she felt to be her duty. She eschewed public pronouncement, as she told Perkins: "I cannot turn out the sort of thing that Wrigley's chewing gum and Pepsi-cola use on the radio for 'morale' " (July 23).

Rawlings's personal commitment and the constant worry about the safety of her husband left her little quiet time for reflection. Her writing suffered. She began her ill-fated novel The Sojourner, but the inspiration was simply not there, a problem that tore at her. Perkins offered his support at every moment, but it was no longer enough. Rather than disappoint him, she would not answer his letters of encouragement for several months at a time. She was absorbed in something far greater, the fate of her husband and the fate of the United States of America.

As grim as 1943 was, it did have a salutary moment: Rawlings won at the local level the lawsuit filed against her in the famous Cross Creek trial, a verdict that was later overturned by the Florida Supreme Court, which ordered Rawlings to pay one dollar in damages for "invasion of privacy." For the time being, however, the news was uplifting: "Wasn't that fine news about the lawsuit?" she wrote Perkins on August 11. With the trial behind her, Rawlings returned once more to *The Sojourner,* her novel about Michigan farm life. Perkins was delighted, although he could not know that she would not finish it while he was alive. There were also moments of personal triumph, as when she introduced to Perkins the struggling writer Edith Pope, who under Perkins's guidance was later to write the best-selling novel *Colcorton.*

However, among the many writers that Rawlings recommended to Perkins the most celebrated was Zora Neale Hurston, a close friend. On one occasion Rawlings sent to Perkins a letter of Hurston's. Perkins responded that she "certainly writes good letters, and is obviously a very unusual person" (August 16). So close were Rawlings and Hurston that at one point, when Rawlings's maid Idella Parker had "gone Harlem" (married suddenly and went to New York), Hurston offered to come to Cross Creek to "keep me comfortable until I finished my book. That seems a truly big thing to me" (August 26). Such personal commentary continued well into 1944. Rawlings would write of Baskin's experiences, of her frustrations with *The Sojourner,* and of her domestic trials and tribulations. Perkins would always offer support, although his letters became more infrequent. His comment to her on November 1 is typical: "I am sure you are having a hard time,- not only because Norton is way off Heaven knows where, but also because you are going through those agonizing stages of trying to begin a novel."

Perkins's unwavering encouragement clearly kept Rawlings from abandoning writing altogether. As she wrote on November 13, "Your letter was a great consolation to me, and on the strength of it, I took myself by the nape of the neck, lifted myself by my boot-straps, and began the book." No words could more effectively express the impact that Perkins had upon Rawlings at this point and throughout her career. That he took a personal as well as literary interest in her compounded the influence. If she failed to write after a reasonable period, he would pen a newsy note headed by "How are you making out?" (March 15, 1944). Rawlings would write equally newsy replies, informing Perkins of the visits of Julia Scribner, by then a Rawlings favorite, almost a daughter in absentia.

Embedded in her remarks, however, was an ever-present lamentation: "I am afraid that I won't be able to write until Norton is safe home, or if that worst happens, for a year or two after—" (March 29). Perkins was sympathetic, but the editor in him caused him to push her in spite of her personal travails: "But I suppose it is possible you may hit your stride at any moment" (April 10). To be sure, there were amusing moments of distraction, as when the myopic Edith Pope held a deadly coral snake close to her face to see if its head was black, or when the comedic Dessie Smith suggested that Rawlings join her in the WACs to shift the focus of her troubles (May 3). The stoic Perkins could only respond: "I am glad you are not a WAC, and I hope you can go ahead with the novel" (June 8).

Through the summer of 1944 the correspondence picked up at a lively pace and with it the confession by Perkins that his health was in jeopardy because of "John Barleycorn." "It wasn't that I was really drinking heavily," he confessed to Rawlings on June 23, "but that I was not eating nearly enough, and wouldn't if I didn't cut down." Perkins's doctor ordered him not to drink more than "two cocktails a day," an order difficult to follow. Drinking, he added, "makes[s] one less aware of the passage of time, and let[s] one think and ponder in a leisurely way. Everything moves too fast nowadays, and John Barleycorn slows things up. I had always thought that if I got very old, I would take up hashish, which completely destroys the sense of time, so that you can sit in eternity." The poignancy (and humor) of this confession was not lost on Rawlings. She knew exactly what Perkins meant and how he felt. She responded with a lavishly humorous letter about the repeated malapropisms of her visiting Aunt Ida, who would announce that a friend recently died, "after lying for a week in a semi-comma," or that *The Grapes of Wrath* was a "wonderful book for anyone to read, that's moving" (July 10).

The fall of 1944 came without progress on either the personal or the literary front. Baskin, who almost died from malaria, was recovering in a field hospital in India, but she knew little of his condition in spite of repeated inquiries. The trauma was severe for her, and consequently *The Sojourner* startups became less frequent. "My book will have to wait for some sort of security of my personal life," she wrote to Perkins on October 11. In turn Perkins announced that he was "laid up with the most idiotic and utterly unknown ailment. . . . I keep getting worse, and worse, and worse" (October 17). Six months passed before another letter came from Perkins, this time saying that he had not written because he did not want to leave the impression that he was "checking up" on Rawlings (March 6, 1945).

The letters continue through 1945 with literary gossip, domestic situation, and humorous anecdote. It is as if Rawlings sensed that the roles had shifted, and it was now her responsibility to aid her dear friend. She wrote openly of the Scribner family and defended Julia's choice of husband, even though she had had someone else in mind for her. She exchanged gossip about the current giants of literature. She offered ribald humor to entertain. And she always sent what Perkins called the "most wonderful oranges ever." Throughout this period, Rawlings continued to write and to publish short fiction, including several pieces in the prestigious *New Yorker*. But she had nothing for Scribners. Perkins knew that she was struggling, but he never let on. When she stalled on *The Sojourner*, he would suggest that she compile a book of Quincey Dover stories; when she got stuck on her short fiction, he would suggest that she return to the novel.

In October 1945 came the word of the tragic death of N. C. Wyeth, whose car had been hit by a train. The death of Wyeth, whose lavish illustrations of *The Yearling* had given new popularity to the novel, shook both Rawlings and Perkins and gave warning again about the fragility of life. Rawlings went to North Carolina in the fall of 1946 to adapt her haunting short story "A Mother in Mannville" for MGM, while at the same time attempting to expand it to novel length under a different title for Scribners. On November 7, 1946, came what had to be stunning news from Perkins: "I do not think that A FAMILY FOR JOCK should be published as a book." For the first time, Perkins had rejected her work. That he suggested magazine serialization was little consolation. The *Saturday Evening Post* did finally publish the serial under the title "Mountain Prelude." However, her movie script was also rejected. It simply did not work. The final script was nothing like what she had suggested. MGM decided to turn her "Lassie movie" into a musical, *The Sun Comes Up*, starring Jeanette MacDonald. Rawlings was paid generously, even given screen credit, but such money and fame were not what she desired. She already had both. What she wanted was to recapture her artistic integrity.

In early 1947, Rawlings expressed her frustrations to Perkins: "For myself, I have never felt more inadequate. The time between books has been so unreasonably long that I feel a true writer would not, could not, have let it happen" (February 13). There were moments of creativity, of course, most notable among them her "child's story of the little Negro girl," *The Secret River*. Perkins continued to encourage her: "I believe you could write a sad and lovely story of a negro child" (February 25). When Rawlings sent the draft of the story to Perkins in March, his editorial role returned as he offered extensive revisions, both in plot and characterization. He suggested that she employ the "wild logic" of *Alice in Wonderland*. Rawlings, as if the past were now the present, responded, "I think you are absolutely right . . ." (April 4). Several more letters were exchanged as Rawlings worked to perfect the story, which was published posthumously under the editorial eyes of Julia Scribner. On June 7 she wrote to inform Perkins that the Florida Supreme Court had indeed ruled against her in what the justices termed an "invasion of privacy." It was Rawlings's last letter to her beloved Perkins.

On June 17 the following wire from Charles Scribner was forwarded to her at her new summer residence in Van Hornesville, New York:

MAX DIED OF PNEUMONIA EARLY THIS MORNING AFTER TWO DAYS ILLNESS CHARLIE

Scribner then wrote a letter, as he did to Hemingway and others, asking Rawlings not to abandon Scribners—that they would cope with this tragedy somehow. Rawlings rose above her personal grief to comfort of her close friend Charlie, writing on July 3: "Any author who could be lured away from you because Max is gone, would be overlooking a vital factor: Max would always have been Max, but only with Scribner's would he have had such a free hand, with the integrity of the house backing up his own integrity. The almost indefinable quality of your firm is as important to a writer as Max's rare editorial judgment. This is safe at least during your life-time and that of young Charlie." On July 9 Scribner responded, "It is good to read of your regard for Charles Scribner's Sons, apart from the personal affection you bore for Max. I know that he would have been happy that you felt this way." True to her word, Rawlings never parted from the house of Charles Scribner or her "Magnificent Editor." Writing to Bernice Gilkyson on July 9, she described the shock upon receiving the news at Van Hornesville of Perkins's death: "It was startling to realize . . . how much we wrote *for* him, and certainly with his judgment constantly in mind. I dream about him often and wake up in tears" (*Selected Letters* 300).

Insofar as Rawlings is concerned, the end of the story is not a happy one. She had become so dependent upon Perkins for personal inspiration and editorial guidance that she became increasingly despondent. Her literary career declined rapidly. Once one of Scribners' most celebrated novelists, considered in the company of Hemingway, Fitzgerald, and Wolfe, she now found writing a chore, almost debilitating, without the encouragement and expertise of Perkins. To be sure, she managed in 1953 to finish the novel *The Sojourner*, begun under Perkins's nurturing guidance, but it was a hollow victory.

That Rawlings died a few months after the long struggle to publish *The Sojourner* says a great deal. In the end, she simply lacked the ego of Hemingway who, although shaken, hastened to assure Charles Scribner that he could and would continue on without Perkins. Rawlings could not offer such assurances. Without the unique talents of Perkins, she became a shell whose echo was silenced. The extent of her dependence upon Perkins is expressed in her 1950 review "Portrait of a Magnificent Editor as Seen in His Letters": "In the case of Max Perkins himself, it seems undeniable that no editor has ever so influenced and 'helped to realize themselves' so impressive a number of writers. . . . It is likely that the name Maxwell E. Perkins will outlive many of the authors to whom he addressed himself so generously" (1573–74).

The value of the Perkins-Rawlings correspondence seems beyond question. Not only is it, until now, an untold story of Perkins the editor and Rawlings the writer, it also offers a fresh insight into the firm of Charles Scribner's Sons. Beyond the editor-writer personality of the letters is a larger subtext. Perkins came to trust Rawlings as a friend, a confidante. Indeed, what is most striking about the letters is their progressive intimacy.

At first Rawlings was to Perkins a potential novelist whose fiction about rural Florida he found compelling. Perkins was to Rawlings a guardian, one who charted her course through the art of novel-writing. The early part of their relationship was especially dynamic. Rawlings questioned, Perkins answered; Rawlings veered, Perkins straightened. Offering more than general advice, Perkins improved the plot, fixed the metaphors, and enhanced the language. For example, he censored whole episodes and proposed others in *The Yearling,* and he suggested the clothes metaphor that binds the whole in *Cross Creek,* all the time making Rawlings feel like she was the editor.

In many respects the correspondence as a whole tells us as much that is important about Perkins the editor as it does about Rawlings the writer. Perkins is the prism through which Rawlings's words are refracted. Even when her work was not a commercial success, as with *Golden Apples,* Perkins was by her side, writing eloquently about the novel's artistic achievement, comparing it to the work of Faulkner. Rawlings responded that she did not like Faulkner ("too dense"), but the importance of Perkins's comparison was not lost on her. From this point, they addressed each other as "Max" and "Marjorie." Rawlings and Perkins soon became intimates, sharing both trial and tribulation. As biographer A. Scott Berg puts it, "Max felt easy with her" (211).

There is no doubt that one of the most important points of the correspondence is the impact of Perkins upon Rawlings's art. Yet there is more—something richer, something deeper. It is the sheer confidence that each developed in the other. Perkins seemed quite willing to share not only his own personal feelings but the day-to-day operations of Charles Scribner's Sons as well. The letters provide a chronicle of the "Scribner writers." Perkins discusses in detail the literary lives and personal travails of his most celebrated writers. Hemingway, or "Hem" as Perkins referred to him, is dissected repeatedly, with substantive comments made about his life as a craftsman and as a man. At first, Rawlings hesitated to respond, so in awe was she of Hemingway's myriad talents. But she soon waded in and offered pointed critical appraisal. Later, Hemingway became her personal friend, and on occasion she went fishing with him at Bimini. Norton Baskin, her second husband, on occasion entertained Hemingway at his hotel in St. Augustine, which added yet another dimension to the friendship.

Then there is Scott Fitzgerald. Perkins pressed Rawlings into different action in his case, prevailing upon her to visit the psychologically and physically ailing Fitzgerald in North Carolina. Rawlings, with some reluctance, addressed Fitzgerald on his own terms. The two liked each other instantly. For one thing Rawlings was willing to drink with Fitzgerald; for another she was willing to listen and to sympathize. As Perkins's letters convey, he credited Rawlings with stabilizing Fitzgerald at a crucial moment in his life. Perkins also used Rawlings to help with Thomas Wolfe, whose incessant delays and matchless verbosity were an endless nemesis for Perkins. When Wolfe left Scribners, Rawlings was there to offer encouragement. Perkins's and Rawlings's critical assessments of Wolfe are particularly engaging. And it was Rawlings who recommended Zora Neale Hurston, among others, to Perkins. Beyond assessment of individual writers, both Perkins and Rawlings wrote extensively about the responsibilities of authorship, and especially how these responsibilities impact female writers.

The Perkins-Rawlings correspondence goes beyond the "Scribner writers," of course. In sharing all manner of personal problems with each other, it was inevitable that they became close, abiding friends. Perkins was especially defensive of Rawlings. He protected her, acting in many respects like her literary agent, even though this caused complications with her actual agent, Brandt and Brandt. He helped arrange the sale of *The Yearling* to MGM, which forever secured Rawlings's financial affairs.

Yet any final evaluation of the Perkins-Rawlings correspondence will inevitably turn to Rawlings's reputation as a writer. Perkins's immortality as an editor is not questioned. Rawlings, sadly, is the one on trial. "Is she worth all this effort?" some will ask. "Is she deserving?" Such questions creep more and more into academe, where much less substantive heroes are created daily. To be sure, fame without an audience is fleeting. Today, Rawlings's major audience is made up of the thousands who each year purchase *The Yearling* and *Cross Creek,* and the thousands more who seek her spirit at Cross Creek. But this is a popular, not an academic audience. Academics are far less charitable. What they did to Scott Fitzgerald until he was "rediscovered" in 1953 is testimony to intellectual fickleness. The plain truth is that Rawlings is a popular writer whose audience was and still is the popular audience. Her works sell because they are enduring records of time past and present.

Rawlings's creations owe a great deal to the narrative strength and moral legacy of Romanticism. She believed in what she called "cosmic consciousness," what we call Transcendentalism. She was a reformer, she thought. Her friend Margaret Mitchell once wrote to her, "Your versatility is a marvelous thing. There is no one today writing the way you write or the type of things you write. There have been all too few writers like you in the past. Yours is truly an American gift. You are just a born perfect storyteller . . ." (June 12, 1940). Indeed, it is the magical quality of the story that makes the Perkins-Rawlings correspondence an important and enduring moment in American letters.

Bibliography

Acton, Patricia N. *The Cross Creek Trial of Marjorie Kinnan Rawlings.* Gainesville: University of Florida Press, 1988.

Berg, A. Scott. *Max Perkins: Editor of Genius.* New York: E. P. Dutton, 1978.

Fitzgerald, F. Scott. *Correspondence.* Ed. Matthew J. Bruccoli and Margaret M. Duggan. New York: Random House, 1980.

———. *Dear Scott/Dear Max: The Fitzgerald-Perkins Correspondence.* Ed. John Kuehl and Jackson R. Bryer. New York: Scribners, 1971.

Hemingway, Ernest, and Maxwell E. Perkins. *The Only Thing That Counts: The Ernest Hemingway/Maxwell Perkins Correspondence, 1925–1947.* Ed. Matthew J. Bruccoli. New York: Scribners, 1996.

Mitchell, Margaret. Personal correspondence, Mitchell to Rawlings, June 12, 1940. Copy, Tarr Rawlings Collection.

Parker, Idella. *Idella: Marjorie Rawlings' "Perfect Maid."* Gainesville: University Press of Florida, 1992.

Perkins, Maxwell E. *Editor to Author: The Letters of Maxwell E. Perkins.* New York: Scribners, 1950.

Rawlings, Marjorie Kinnan. *Poems by Marjorie Kinnan Rawlings: Songs of a Housewife.* Ed. Rodger L. Tarr. Gainesville: University Press of Florida, 1997.

———. "Portrait of a Magnificent Editor as Seen in His Letters." *Publishers' Weekly* 157 (April 1950): 1573–74.

———. *Selected Letters.* Ed. Gordon E. Bigelow and Laura V. Monti. Gainesville: University Presses of Florida, 1983.

———. *Short Stories by Marjorie Kinnan Rawlings.* Ed. Rodger L. Tarr. Gainesville: University Press of Florida, 1994.

Scribner, Charles, Jr. *In the Company of Writers: A Life in Publishing.* New York: Scribners, 1990.

Tarr, Rodger L. *Marjorie Kinnan Rawlings: A Descriptive Bibliography.* Pittsburgh: University of Pittsburgh Press, 1996.

———. "Marjorie Kinnan Rawlings and the Rochester (NY) Magazine *Five O'Clock.*" *American Periodicals* 1.1 (Fall 1991): 83–85.

———. "Marjorie Kinnan Rawlings and the *Washington Post.*" *Analytical and Enumerative Bibliography* n.s. 4.4 (1990): 163–68.

1930

1. MEP to MKR (TLS: UF, 3 pp.)

Nov. 19, 1930

Dear Mrs. Rawlings:

We are very much inclined to publish your novel, "High Winds"[1] in the magazine, but would you consider certain suggestions for the revision of it, to that end, which we think might very much improve it,- excellent as we think it is as it stands.

Two of these suggestions are superficial,- one is that the title be changed to some synonymous term, simply for the reason that Arthur Train[2] has used the phrase "High Winds" on a successful novel. The other is that titles to the sections be simply omitted, and that numbers be substituted for them.

This second <section> suggestion really does reach below the surface because it has to do with the motive of the story. In this motive there must have been a desire to show the varied forms in which the struggle for existence presents itself in Florida;- and the different aspects of this struggle are suggested by the titles to the parts. We think that this element in the motive is a good one, but that it should be a subordinate one — as it would tend to be simply by eliminating the subtitles — and that the main motive should be simply the story of these two people.

As a story, your manuscript is a little disappointing in not completely fulfilling the great promise of the opening. One expects at the start that Florry at least, will more completely transcend typicality,- that her individuality would make her more of a *character* in her own right than she is, apart from her value as a representative of the Florida Cracker.- And anything that you might do in way of revision in this respect, would be advantageous.

But our principal, specific suggestion relates to the last section of the book.

Nov. 19, 1930

Dear Mrs. Rawlings:

We are very much inclined to publish your novel, "High Winds"
in the magazine, but would you consider certain suggestions for revision
of it,to that end,which we think might very much improve it,- excellent
as we think it is as it stands.

Two of these suggestions are superficial,- one is that the
title be changed to some synonymous term, simply for the reason that
Arthur Train has used the phrase "High Winds" on a successful novel.
The other is that titles to the sections be simply omitted, and that
numbers be substituted for them.

This second suggestion really does reach below the surface because
it has to do with the motive of the story. In this motive there must
have been a desire to show the varied forms in which the struggle for
existence presents itself in Florida;- and the different aspects of this
struggle are suggested by the titles to the parts. We think that this
element in the motive is a good one, but that it should be a subordinate
one -- as it would tend to be simply by eliminating the subtitles -- and
that the main motive should be simply the story of these two people.

As a story, your manuscript is a little disappointing in not
completely fulfilling the great promise of the opening. One expects
at the start that Florry at least, will more completely transcend typicality,-
that her individuality would make her more of a character in her own right
than she is, apart from her value as a representative of the Florida Cracker.-
And anything that you might do in way of revision in this respect, would

No. 1 (MEP's first letter to MKR). By permission of Princeton University Library.

26

be advantageous.

But our principal, specific suggestion relates to the last section of the book. The Florida Crackers have always been looked upon as a low people, and have been despised. One great quality in what you have written is that you enable the reader to see them from a new point of view, by which he can sympathize with them. He understands the nature of these two people, identifies himself with one or the other of them, and shares their experiences. This is the point of view of the story, and it is one of its virtues. But in the last section you change the point of view. One comes to see Mart as nothing but a miserable Cracker, as the Yankee does. It seems to us that this unnecessarily breaks the right conception which the reader has hitherto had, and that there is nothing in the character of the narrative that requires that it be broken. We wondered if you could possibly give another last section which brought the story to some conclusion, not necessarily a tragic one. Might these two people not in some way find a permanent resting place? Anyway, we thought we would suggest the possibility of this. If the last section were more consistent with the opening, in concerning itself more with the individual characters, sympathetically, we believe that the narrative would be better artistically, as well as more pleasing to the casual reader.

There is one other suggestion. Florry appears in the story and does and says certain things, and her character reveals itself to the reader in her acts and speech. This, it seems to us, is the right method. It is required of the writer that she sometimes reinforce this method by herself telling things about the characters, but she should avoid doing it, in this sort of story anyhow, so far as possible. There

are places in this story where it seems to us the writer intrudes to
tell things that would be imparted simply by the action and speech in
the story. On page 7 the first paragraph seems to us an intrusion of
the writer. It does not reveal more of the character of Florry than
comes out in the preceding and succeeding paragraphs, and although it
is well done itself, it is also a digression. There is no reason for
taking the reader from the scene before him,- Florry and Mart sitting
on the steps, to some place in the hammock where a man was struck by
a rattler. The reader's mind is fixed on this meeting of these two
lovers, and it should be allowed to concentrate upon that alone. We
would suggest omitting this paragraph, and some other places in the story
of a *digressive* character.

If, after reading this letter, you feel inclined to reconsider
the manuscript in the light of these suggestions, we shall return it.
It will be considered for the prize we offer, by the judges, but apart
from that matter, we should like to arrange to publish it, but should
greatly hope that you might think well of revising it for that purpose.

Ever sincerely yours,

MEP.

To Mrs. Marjorie K. Rawlings

The Florida Crackers have always been looked upon as a low people, and have
been despised. One great quality in what you have written is that you enable
the reader to see them from a new point of view, by which he can sympathize
with them. He understands the nature of these two people, identifies himself
with one or the other of them, and shares their experiences. This is the point of
view of the story, and it is one of its virtues. But in the last section you change

the point of view. One comes to see Mart as nothing but a miserable Cracker, as the Yankee does. It seems to us that this unnecessarily breaks the right conception which the reader has hitherto had, and that there is nothing in the character of the narrative that requires that it be broken. We wondered if you could possibly give another last section which brought the story to some other conclusion, not necessarily a tragic one. Might these two people not in some way find a permanent resting place? Anyway, we thought we would suggest the possibility of this. If the last section were more consistent with the opening, in concerning itself more with the individual characters, sympathetically, we believe that the narrative would be better artistically, as well as more pleasing to the casual reader.

There is one other suggestion. Florry appears in the story and does and says certain things, and her character reveals itself to the reader in her acts and speech. This, it seems to us, is the right method. It is required of the writer that she sometimes reinforce this method by herself telling things about the characters, but she should avoid doing it, in this sort of story anyhow, so far as possible. There are places in this story where it seems to us the writer intrudes to tell things that would be imparted simply by the action and speech in the story. On page 7 the first paragraph seems to us an intrusion of the writer. It does not reveal more of the character of Florry than comes out in the preceding and succeeding paragraphs, and although it is well done itself, it is also a digression. There is no reason for taking the reader from the scene before him,- Florry and Mart sitting on the steps,- to some place in the hammock where a man was struck by a rattler. The reader's mind is fixed on this meeting of these two lovers, and it should be allowed to concentrate upon that alone. We would suggest omitting this paragraph, and some other places in the story of a <similar> digressive character.

If, after reading this letter, you feel inclined to reconsider the manuscript in the light of these suggestions, we shall return it. It will be considered for the prize we offer, by the judges, but apart from that matter, we should like to arrange to publish it, but should greatly hope that you might think well of revising it for that purpose.

Ever sincerely yours,

1. Later retitled "Jacob's Ladder," *Scribner's Magazine* 89.4 (April 1931): 351–66, 446–64.
2. Arthur C. Train (1875–1945), *High Winds* (New York: Scribners, 1927).

Cross Creek
Hawthorn, Route 1
Florida
Nov. 25, 1930

To the Contest Editor
SCRIBNER'S MAGAZINE
New York City

Dear Sir:

It is extremely considerate of *Scribner's* to give me an opportunity to improve my story of the Cracker interior of Florida, "High Winds". I appreciate your painstaking criticism and the story can only profit by your editorial suggestions. There is no question but that you are right about the minor changes you suggest. I can make them easily. You are probably right about the major one——

I had a choice of three endings, all logical as concerns the characters and their environment. (I grant at once the point you make that for a moment, and unnecessarily, Mart is presented as the petty-thief Cracker of careless general conception; even using the present ending, that could be overcome.) The ending I used showed Florry, if not defeated by "the high winds of change", at least with her last shred of security swept from under her by them. The ultimate violence has been done to her.

A second ending would be one which took her a step beyond the present one. She could be shown, unchanged, with nothing more than she has ever had——her courage——between her gaunt body and the cyclic sweep of natural violence which is the background of this life. She could be shown living like a rabbit in the brush, as it were, self-sufficing, building her own security out of her fearlessness, making her own isolated nest. I rejected this as anti-climax. I imagine you would find it objectionable on the same grounds as you do the present conclusion.

The third ending, along the lines you have in mind, might indeed be more satisfying. Although Florry is perhaps the more vital character, it is true that I have made Mart and Florry a unit, and I suppose they should stand or fall together. And there is certainly no point to be made in annihilating both of them. I cannot convince myself that the third ending would be as strong, but your feeling as to its artistic value is perhaps more to be trusted than mine. If one chose to have Mart and Florry survive their batterings, I believe it would work out this way:

Cross Creek
Hawthorn, Route I
Florida
Nov. 25, 1930

To the Contest Editor
SCRIBNER'S MAGAZINE
New York City

Dear Sir:

It is extremely considerate of _Scribner's_ to give me an
opportunity to improve my story of the Cracker interior of Florida,
"High Winds". I appreciate your painstaking criticism and the story can
only profit by your editorial suggestions. There is no question but that
you are right about the minor changes you suggest. I can make them
easily. You are probably right about the major one---

I had a choice of three endings, all logical as concerns the
characters and their environment. (I grant at once the point you make that
for a moment, and unnecessarily, Mart is presented as the petty-thief
Cracker of careless general conception; even using the present ending, that
could be overcome.) The ending I used showed Florry, if not defeated by
"the high winds of change", at least with her last shred of security swept
from under her by them. The ultimate violence has been done to her.

A second ending would be one which took her a step beyond the
present one. She could be shown, unchanged, with nothing more than she has
ever had---her courage---between her gaunt body and the cyclic sweep of
natural violence which is the background of this life. She could be shown
living like a rabbit in the brush, as it were, self-sufficing, building
her own security out of her fearlessness, making her own isolated nest.
I rejected this as anti-climax. I imagine you would find it objectionable
on the same grounds as you do the present conclusion.

No. 2 (MKR's first letter to MEP). By permission of Princeton University Library.

The third ending, along the lines you have in mind, might indeed be more satisfying. Although Florry is perhaps the more vital character, iti is true that I have made Mart and Florry a unit, and I suppose they should stand or fall together. And there is certainly no point to be made in annihilating both of them. I cannot convince myself that the third ending would be as strong, but your feeling as to its artistic value is perhaps more to be trusted than mine. If one chose to have Mart and Florry survive their batterings, I believe it would work out this way:

Florry's instinct would naturally draw her back, in a circle, to the one sure thing she knew---the clearing in the piney-woods, the patch of ground her father owned. I would want to keep the summer of heat, much as I have it. It is one of the things here to be fought. The close of the summer would find Mart at the end of the tether. Florry, who has followed him unquestioning, leaving behind at each move something precious to her, would be moved in her wisdom to lead Mart back to what she knows of permanence.

Old Joe's age and character have paved the way for any suitable disposition of him as a danger. The man and woman would return to the cabin in the piney-woods to find that he has died, or been crippled at his drunken logging---whatever worked out best to remove his ancient menace. Here they would not be aliens, or trespassers, or outcasts. The seasonal hurricane would be impending. The two would be subject, as they have ever been, as they must always be, to the danger of the elements; but the human factor would be solved.

This is necessarily sketchy, but you can judge whether the logic of such an ending conforms with what you sense as the artistic logic. If you feel that the satisfaction of it outweighs what I consider the greater strength of the tragic ending, I shall be perfectly willing to work it out.

How much time may I have for the revision?

Are you particular that I should return a fresh, new copy of the whole revised manuscript, or is it desirable to save time by editing on parts of the original manuscript?

And shall I return both the original and the revised versions of the last section?

Very sincerely,

Marjorie Kinnan Rawlings

Florry's instinct would naturally draw her back, in a circle, to the one sure thing she knew——the clearing in the piney-woods, the patch of ground her father owned. I would want to keep the summer of heat, much as I have it. It is one of the things here to be fought. The close of the summer would find Mart at the end of the tether. Florry, who has followed him unquestioning, leaving behind at each move something precious to her, would be moved in her wisdom to lead Mart back to what she knows of permanence.

Old Joe's age and character have paved the way for any suitable disposition of him as a danger. The man and woman would return to the cabin in the piney-woods to find that he has died, or been crippled at his drunken logging ——whatever worked out best to remove his ancient menace. Here they would not be aliens, or trespassers, or outcasts. The seasonal hurricane would be impending. The two would be subject, as they have ever been, as they must always be, to the danger of the elements; but the human factor would be solved.

This is necessarily sketchy, but you can judge whether the logic of such an ending conforms with what you sense as the artistic logic. If you feel that the satisfaction of it outweighs what I consider the greater strength of the tragic ending, I shall be perfectly willing to work it out.

How much time may I have for the revision?

Are you particular that I should return a fresh, new copy of the whole revised manuscript, or is it desirable to save time by editing on parts of the original manuscript?

And shall I return both the original and the revised versions of the last section?

Very sincerely,

. . . .

3. MEP to MKR (TLS: UF, 3 pp.)

Nov. 29, 1930

Dear Mrs. Rawlings:

I think you could safely take three weeks or a month in revising your Long Story.- And you need not have the whole manuscript copied, but only the last part which you will presumably rewrite.

Our inclination is toward the third ending you suggest by which Florry and Mart are brought back to the clearing in the piney woods. Our great aim is to intensify the human element in the story by strengthening the interest in the characters, and by bringing out the individuality of the characters, so that it will be a story of two people primarily, and only in an underlying sense a story of two Crackers with the sociological significance. It seems to us you will not lose the value of a sociological significance by the new ending.- You will show the natural human perseverance and courage of the two Crackers who have been driven from one place to another, but in the end are back where they started, and just naturally go on with the struggle against nature.

Perhaps when you work on this section you may give it more meaning and do it differently even from what you planned. At any rate, we must not persuade you against your convictions. If only you agree with us in the desire to make it rather more a story of characters, and only fundamentally a story representative of a species of humanity, I think all will come out well.

Ever sincerely yours,

· ·

4. MKR to MEP (TLS, 1 p.)

Cross Creek
Hawthorn, Route 1
Florida
December 24, 1930

Contest Editor
SCRIBNER'S MAGAZINE
New York City
Attention of Mr. Maxwell E. Perkins

Dear Sir:

I am thoroughly convinced that you were right about the desirability of increasing the character interest in my Florida Cracker story. The ending I have worked out does, I believe, make a rounder unit. You see, I began with my mind full of the power of this environment——and after all, from the human if not the cosmic point of view, the courage of these people is more important.

Mart and Florry rather got away from me. Perhaps I was fortunate enough to have given them more vitality than I really intended, so that I did them an injustice in not more fully developing their characters and carrying out their story to a more consistent conclusion. They do indeed deserve more dignity than I originally allowed them.

I do hope you find the revised story satisfying.

Sincerely,

Dec. 30, 1930

Dear Mrs. Rawlings:

    The story came back and we think it very greatly improved. I do not know exactly when we can publish it, though I think within the next several months, but we believe it will be liked and admired.

                              Ever sincerely yours,

CHARLES SCRIBNER'S SONS
PUBLISHERS
FIFTH AVENUE AT 48 TH STREET

NEW YORK   Dec. 30, 1930

Dear Mrs. Rawlings:

    The story came back and we think it very greatly improved. I do not know exactly when we can publish it, though I think within the next several months, but we believe it will be liked and admired.

        Ever sincerely yours

[signature: Maxwell E. Perkins]

To Mrs. Marjorie K. Rawlings

No. 5. By permission of University of Florida Libraries.

1931

Feb. 3, 1931

Dear Mrs. Rawlings:

Mr. Dashiell[1] has shown me the clippings you sent him from Florida news-papers.- I hope you won't be troubled by their attacks upon your sketches.- They should — but they won't — like your "Jacob's Ladder", for there you certainly show people what one must admire and sympathize with. Of course, in the sketches too, these papers completely misunderstand you,- but that is what a writer must expect.[2]

Dashiell has probably written you how very much your "Jacob's Ladder" was admired by the judges of the contest.- We believe it will also be greatly admired by the public, and look forward to its appearance in the magazine.

I am writing now chiefly for the purpose of saying that we want to assure you of our great interest in your work in the general editorial department of the house, as well as in the magazine.- Is there any chance that you will write a novel? If you do, you can depend upon a very eager and prompt consideration of it from us.

Ever sincerely yours,

1. Alfred Dashiell, associate editor of *Scribner's Magazine*.
2. In an editorial, G. B. E. of the *Ocala Weekly Star* (June 30, 1931) criticized MKR for her portrayal of the life and the dialect of the Florida Cracker in "Cracker Chidlings," *Scribner's Magazine* 89.2 (February 1931): 127–34. MKR protested the editorial in a letter to the editor on February 2, 1931.

Cross Creek
Hawthorn, Route 1, Fla.
March 31, 1931

Mr. Maxwell E. Perkins
CHARLES SCRIBNER AND SONS
New York City

My dear Mr. Perkins:

Your recent question as to the possibility of my doing a novel makes me wish I might talk with you, for I am vibrating with material like a hive of bees in swarm. It would take pages of necessarily vague ramblings to discuss it. At present I see four books very definitely. Two of them need several more years of note-taking. Of the two I am about ready to begin on, one would be a novel of the scrub country. I managed to get lost in <it> the scrub, the first day of the hunting season——and I encountered for the first time the palpability of silence.

So isolated a section gives a value to the scattered inhabitants. There is a handful of fascinating characters ready to be woven into the fabric of the story. So far, I have not come on the necessary thread of continuity. When it occurs to me, I think it will force me to drop whatever else I may be doing. Once I know where I am going, the book will almost write itself.

The novel that I should like to postpone a little, but that I shall probably begin on, will be called "Hammock".[1] A few miles away, on the road to Micanopy, we cross a strange, unearthly stream that has overflowed into the hammock itself. It is called, inexplicably, the River Styx. It seemed to me that it might well have been so named by one of the young Englishmen, remittance men, who colonized a section around Orange Lake in the middle and late '80's——younger sons in disgrace, subsidized to stay away. Some of them planted orange groves; others, I am told, pretended to, sending home mythical accounts of their development.

There took shape in my mind one of these young men, to whom, coming into this jungle hammock, an embittered exile, the strange small river would indeed seem another Styx, transporting him from life into death. To his nature as I conceived it, this country would be intolerable. This region is beautiful, but it is not pretty. It is like a beautiful woman capable of a deep evil and a great treachery. Back of the lushness is something stark and sinister.

This man, in a desperate moment, would take a Cracker girl for wife; father a Cracker son. Both wife and son would be relegated to the kitchen almost at once, offensive to him in speech and habits. Against the one background, then, would run the two threads: the man in spiritual and physical torment, immersing himself fitfully and cynically in the social life that flourished here for a few brief years just before and after the Big Freeze of '95:[2] fitfully in this, habitually in his liquor and his books; and the growing boy, finding exultation and beauty in all the elements that, to the other, are the essence of horror. The major characters and some of the minor ones are as sharply etched before me as though I could call them by name—and have them answer. The outline of the story is also comparatively clear to me. The book could become, incidentally, one of several things: possibly something of a study in the relativity of beauty.

I am hesitant about it, because it will be such an impossible mess if I bungle it. The characters are sufficiently complicated, psychologically——the young Englishman, at least——to make me feel as a surgeon must feel the first time he tackles a major operation. The scrub story contains no more than the ordinary pit-falls, and for that reason I should feel a little more sure of myself in doing it first.

Out of the welter of equally indiscriminate praise and abuse that I have received, I am sending on three letters of favorable comment that may interest you as they did me, for they are from three of the comparatively rare souls who have seen the Florida I see. The comments of the elderly man from Massachusetts, who saw this Florida in his youth, I found quite touching. May I have the letters back, if you don't mind, for out of my gratitude for their genuine understanding, I want to answer them.

"Jacob's Ladder" was, of course, over-written. If you will be patient with me, I can do better work.

I wish you would thank for me the proof-reader who worked on the story. He has an eye like a sharp-shooter, and did an amazing piece of work. With anything short of such perfection of accuracy, he could have ruined the whole story.

Sincerely,

1. Retitled *Golden Apples* (1935), this was the second novel MKR wrote for Scribners, the first being *South Moon Under* (1933).
2. The freeze of 1895, which devastated the citrus and other agricultural crops, soon took on mythic proportions in the oral and written literature about Florida. It became one of MKR's favorite metaphors.

April 10, 1931

Dear Mrs. Rawlings:

I have read your letter with very great interest indeed. Your story, "Jacob's Ladder" by the way, is being greatly admired,- it is a question if it is not the best liked of all the stories we have run. I am returning the letters you enclosed, but I shall not answer you in detail until I have thought over the matter of the novel,- though whatever you do we shall have great hopes for. I was very glad to get your letter, and to hear from you because I had been afraid that you were being greatly troubled by the Floridians who objected to your writing. Their objections were inevitable, as perhaps you foresaw. Anything written about a given region, even in a tone of highest compliment, is always objected to. We might have warned you.

I shall write you shortly, after considering more carefully your very interesting plans.

Ever sincerely yours,

. . . .

April 13, 1931

Dear Mrs. Rawlings:

I had not spoken in my letter about the question of a novel, and now after reading your letter over again I doubt if there is any occasion for my speaking of it. You would be by far the best judge, of course, and apparently you intend to be the judge, and to write when you come to that point where you feel the necessary confidence, and that compulsion which is the best indication that the book should be done.

I do think that the theme which you outline, about the young Englishman who comes into the hammock is interesting. It would be very difficult psychologically, I should think, so far as the Englishman is concerned, but I should think too, that your own judgment would in the end instruct you as to whether you were equal to it.- But the only way in which I should think you might not be, would come from the fact that Englishmen are peculiar, and particularly remittance men. But it may well be that you have had a chance to observe them sufficiently to know them. By the way, did you ever read that very fine story of Owen Wister's called, "The Honorable Strawberries"[1] about one of them in the West? I merely speak of it because I thought it so very fine a story, and not, of course, with any application to what you plan. Anyhow, will you let me know when you do decide to begin? The last thing I want to do is become troublesome to [remainder of letter missing].

1. Owen Wister (1860–1938), best known for the novel *The Virginian* (1902).

. . . .

10. MEP to MKR (TLS: UF, 1 p.)

June 26, 1931

Dear Mrs. Rawlings:

I really ought not to trouble you with this enquiry because you would inform me when you are ready, but I'm very anxious to know if your plans for a novel, or for other writings, have advanced since last you wrote. Could you send us a line?

Ever sincerely yours,

. . . .

11. MKR to MEP (TLS, 3 pp.)

Cross Creek
Hawthorn, Route 1, Fla.
June 30, 1931

My dear Mr. Perkins:

My plans for a novel have advanced, since I wrote you, to this extent: that there is no question now in my mind, but that the story of the scrub country must come next. As soon as I have finished the several shorter things I am working on now, and stolen a very brief vacation on the coast, I have arranged to go over into the scrub and live, for as long as I need to gather up the intimate, accurate details that make up the background. Three of the handful of Cracker families in that section, are my good friends. The family with which I will spend most of my time, a boy as indigenous to the scrub as the deer, and his ninety-pound wisp of a white-haired mother, who ploughs, and last week with an axe cut a sapling and killed a rattlesnake in her field, is 'shining. Leonard[1] says that when I come to board with his mother, I've got to help him run his 'shine at night. The federal agents have been very active lately, so don't be too surprised if your correspondent has the misfortune to be run in! If it should happen, please don't bail me out, because the jail-house would be a splendid place for quiet work!

I still do not know along what line of thought I mean to co-ordinate the story. I feel sure that will come to me when I am sufficiently immersed in the life. It is very possible that the simpler the narrative, the better. An absence of formal motivation may be exactly what it needs. It is a temptation, of course, to stress the 'shining. My husband,[2] whose judgment I trust, warns me against this, saying that it is a relatively unimportant element. I suppose, if it were not handled with the most exquisite care, it could be cheapening——the Saturday Post taint. I don't know.

The actual writing of this story will only take a few months. When I return from the scrub, I am sure the story will be in such shape in my mind that I can feel safe in naming an actual date for its completion. My stuff always goes through a long gestation period, but once I begin the actual writing, the first draft goes quite rapidly.

These are the shorter things I am working on now:

A short story, probably six to eight thousand words, "A Crop of Beans".[3] My material, basically true, is vital, and it will be my own fault if the story isn't good. I am well into it now, and I think two <or three> weeks will see it done.

A narrative about which I wrote Mr. Dashiell last week, "'Gators".[4] As it stands, it is a 3,000-word true yarn told me by one Cracker friend. I keep coming across so many more awfully funny Cracker alligator experiences, that I decided at the last minute not to enter it in the contest, but to amplify it from time to time, until I have a really comprehensive study of the Florida Cracker in humorous relation to that fast-vanishing and utterly preposterous reptile.

A short story, about 3,000 words. "Ol' Mule",[5] half fact and half fancy, in which the most important character, and a true one, is a highly individual mule, owned jointly and quarreled over for nearly thirty years by two Cracker farmers. The first draft is done——badly done——and I have to do it all over again.

Then I have a dozen or so completed sketches about which I also questioned Mr. Dashiell. They are really "Cracker Chidlings", but if the magazine doesn't care to repeat the title, six or seven of them, perhaps more, could be grouped under some such heading as "Cracker Town" indicating the village psychology.[6]

I submitted a manuscript in the contest, "Lord Bill of the Suwannee River,"[7] modestly addressing it only to the Contest Editor. Mr. Crichton[8] informs me that it is absolutely lost in the snowstorm that has filled the offices. I should really have gone over into the scrub before the heat and the mosquitoes and the rattlesnakes began to appear, but I spent the late spring weeks on my contest narrative.

What an amazing response you have had. The office must feel like the old woman whose magic kettle kept on boiling, so that she had to eat her way through a village of soup.

I am reminded of the sad remark of a friend of mine,[9] who had novel aspirations, and who wrote tremendously well. She was a reader for Houghton Mifflin, and after nearly completing a novel, she suddenly stopped writing altogether. When I asked her the reason, she said:

"I was astonished at the number of people who are writing, and writing well. I decided that the greatest contribution I could make to contemporary literature, was to get out of it."

I am not so high-minded. You have given me a fatal encouragement. I am like the old Cracker whose story I will write up some day, who fiddled in ecstasy as long as a single soul would listen to him.

Very sincerely,

I wonder if you would mind passing on to the proper quarter, an advance C.O.D. order for Waldo Frank's "America Hispana",[10] which I see announced for the near future? His "Ordeal of Cuba" in the current Magazine is one of the most stirring things I have read——gorgeously written.

1. Leonard Fiddia, whose family was a constant source of Cracker lore for MKR.
2. Charles A. Rawlings, Jr., whom MKR married in 1919.
3. "A Crop of Beans," *Scribner's Magazine* 91.5 (May 1932): 283–90.
4. "Alligators," *Saturday Evening Post* 23 (September 1933): 16–17, 36, 38. Although MKR wrote the narrative, she gave co-authorship to Fred Tompkins, who took her on alligator hunts.
5. "Varmints," *Scribner's Magazine* 100.6 (December 1936): 26–32, 84–85.
6. The sketches were never published as a whole. MKR later rewrote some into what were called her "Quincey Dover" stories, the most famous of which was "Benny and the Bird Dogs," *Scribner's Magazine* 94.4 (October 1933): 193–200. Others became the fabric of *Cross Creek* (1942).
7. "Lord Bill of the Suwannee River," published posthumously in *Southern Folklore Quarterly* 27.2 (June 1963): 113–31.
8. Kyle Crichton, editor at Scribners, who wrote under the pen name Robert Forsythe.
9. Perhaps Esther Forbes, a Wisconsin friend of MKR, who in fact wrote a number of novels and who won the Pulitzer Prize in 1942 for her biography of Paul Revere.
10. Waldo Frank (1889–1967), *America Hispaña* (New York: Scribners, 1931), a history of South America. "Ordeal of Cuba," *Scribner's Magazine* 90.1 (July 1931): 15–23.

12. MEP to MKR (TLS: UF, 1 p.)

July 7, 1931

Dear Mrs. Rawlings:

We have put you down for a copy of "America Hispana",- and a very fine book it will be.

I am delighted to know that you are definitely planning for work on a novel now, and shall look forward eagerly to seeing some of it. Everything you say about your work is very interesting, including the shorter pieces. I knew we had a narrative here, and have tried to have it found,- for it is quite possibly buried under a couple of thousand of others.- But when we do find it, you may be sure it will be instantly read. Please let me know sometime how you get on.

Always sincerely yours,

. . . .

13. MKR to MEP (TLS, 1 p.)

Cross Creek
Hawthorn, Route 1, Fla.
October 13, 1931

My dear Mr. Perkins:

It was most gracious of you to make me a present of "America Hispana".

It is a spectacular piece of work and will undoubtedly have rather profound reverberations. It isn't every writer or scholar who can hold the Andes in the hollow of his hand. Mr. Frank gives you an understanding of peoples in flux, as though he were presenting the unified drama of individual lives.

The actual writing is of course thrilling. The man makes history flamboyant; ethnology, voluptuous.

I am grateful and indebted to Mr. Frank, and to you. Many thanks.

Most sincerely,

. . . .

14. MEP to MKR (CC, 1 p.)

Oct. 15, 1931

Dear Mrs. Rawlings:

I was delighted to get a letter from you, but although I read with great pleasure what you said about Waldo Frank's book, I was a little disappointed because you said nothing about your own work. I must not keep pressing you, but do remember that whenever you have anything to tell, it will be heard with great interest.

Ever sincerely yours,

Cross Creek
Hawthorn, Route 1, Florida
November 4, 1931

Dear Mr. Perkins:

About my novel of the scrub country——

I came back recently from very absorbing weeks lived with the old woman[1] and her 'shiner son, of whom I believe I wrote you. I have voluminous notes of the intimate type, for which the most prolific imagination is no substitute. I have also, well as I thought I knew the people of this particular section, an entirely new conception of them. I knew they were gentle; honest. I knew that living was precarious, but just how hand-to-mouth it is, surprised me. I was also astonished by the *utter lack of bleakness or despair,* in a group living momentarily on the very edge of starvation and danger. Whatever else my story turns out to be, it will not be a gloomy, morose "novel of the soil". I found a zestfulness in living, a humor, an alertness to beauty, quite unexpected, and of definite value to record, if I can "get" it.

These people are "lawless" by an anomaly. They are living an entirely natural, and very hard, life, disturbing no one. Civilization has no concern with them, except to buy their excellent corn liquor and to hunt, in season, across their territory with an alarming abandon. Yet almost everything they do is illegal. And everything they do is necessary to sustain life in that place. The old clearings have been farmed out and will not "make" good crops any more. The big timber is gone. The trapping is poor. They 'shine, because 'shining is the only business they know that can be carried on in the country they know, and would be unwilling to leave.

The 'shining will have to be the main thread in my story. But I want to make it dramatic by an entire absence of melodrama. It is quite simply a part of the background; a part of the whole resistance of the scrub country to the civilizing process. The scrub, as a matter of fact, has defeated civilization. It is one of the few areas where settlements have disappeared and the scanty population is constantly thinning. Just this side of the Ocklawaha River, in the open range cattle country, the old-timers have recently heard their doom pronounced. The cattle must be fenced, which means the end of the old regime. A grand row has been raging there the past year, a Yankee family being whipped by the cattle men for not minding their own business, and I shall use the situation. Several of the old cattle men are "kin" to the 'shiner families just across the river.[2]

There is no human habitation——there never has been and probably never will be——in the scrub itself. As far as I can determine, there is no similar section anywhere in the world. The scrub is a silent stretch enclosed by two rivers, deeply forested with Southern spruce (almost valueless), scrub oak, scrub myrtle and ti-ti, occasional gall-berry and black-jack and a few specialized shrubs and flowers, with "islands" of long-leaf yellow pine. There is an occasional small lake with its attendant marsh or "prairie". The only settlement is here and there on these bodies of water, and along the river edges, where the natural hammock growth has been bitten into by the settlers' clearings. It is a fringe of life, following the waterways. The scrub is a vast wall, keeping out the timid and the alien.

I have to go back again to stay another couple of weeks, for I need more information about the 'shining on the river of forty or fifty years ago, and the sources are of course scanty. I don't intend to dwell at any length on the past— –the story will be one of the present——but I want to take the old woman of the book briefly through two or three generations of 'shining; it will indicate, as nothing else could do, the profound instincts that motivate the present generation. The 'shiner boy will be the chief protagonist.

When I facetiously urged you not to bail me out if I was caught at the still, I wasn't too far off. Just the week before I went over to stay, a cousin of my 'shiner friend betrayed him, with two others, to the federal agents, and his still was torn up and burned. I had one experience I would not have missed for a great deal——a discussion of a group of the 'shiners and their friends, of various plans for dealing with the traitor. Nothing definite has been done to him yet, for reasons too involved to go into, but in one way and another they are closing in on him, and some day he will simply disappear.[3]

Possibly you wonder how I gain the confidence of these people without being a cold-blooded spy who intends to "use" them. It is so easy for me to live their life with them, that I am in some danger of losing all sophistication and perspective. I feel hurried sometimes, as though I must get "written out" in this country within the next few years, because so much is no longer strange or unusual to me. The life in the scrub is peculiarly right. While I was there, I did all the illegal things too; stalked deer with a light at night, out of season, kept the family in squirrels, paddled the boat while my friend dynamited mullet, shot limpkin on the river edge and had to wade waist deep in cypress swamp to get him (if you haven't eaten roast limpkin, you just haven't eaten, but you can go to county, state and federal jails for shooting them). But with food scarce, these people kill, quite correctly, I think, what they need. Incidentally, *only* what they need for food. The hunters with their licenses, on the other hand, kill a greater quantity during the legal season, and much of it is absolutely wasted——all of it entirely un-needed.

I helped the old lady do her work, helped her wash her heavy quilts that had gone two years without washing, to her despair, because she had no help with them, and can no longer lift them alone from the water and get them on the line. She cried when I left! They live cleanly and decently, and have one sheet on the bottom of the bed. For cover, they use quilts, hand-pieced, of course, summer or winter. One bed had a counterpane instead, which the occupant used over him in place of sheet or quilt, and the phrase was used, "to quilt with the counterpane."

Innumerable phrases are fascinating. The verb "to use" is passive, not active. My friend, finding deer-tracks in the sweet potato patch, said, "Marge, let's you an' me come about moon-down tonight an' kill us the son-of-a-bitch been *usin' in* this field." The deer *use in* the hammock, as do the hammock rabbits ——"them whistlin' bastards". Many expressions are very beautiful. The fish and deer, in fact most of the game, feed "on the moon"——at moon-rise, moon-down, south-moon-over and south-moon-under. The people are conscious at all times of the position of the sun and moon and stars and wind. They *feel* the moon under the earth——south-moon-under. The simplicity of speech is most effective. Old Granny Brinson, whom we went to visit one night by way of row-boat down the river, described what you might call the state of consciousness between life and death. She answered the old lady's inquiry about her health, with the true and simple statement, "I'm sick, Piety, an' dyin'", and told us of her "spells": "I go off into the twilight; into some lonesome-looking place."

The story is clear in my mind, and I am beginning the actual writing this week. Its success will depend, I should say, almost altogether on how real, how vivid, I am able to make the individuals whose lives move along with the 'shiner boy's. The background and small details are fool-proof, but tremendously hard work in delineating each character will be necessary to make the story anything like a reality. The final effect should be one of utter absorption in the people and their lives. For that reason, the title is giving me some difficulty. I don't like to call it "Yonder in the Scrub", as the Crackers in my own section do, for the title is detached, looking at the scrub from the outside. I want a complete submersion from the very beginning. An objective treatment, of course, but submersion. And I can't call it "The Scrub" or "Big Scrub," simply, for the word to any reader in the country outside of Florida suggests football! It annoys me to work without a definite heading.

Shall I let you know when I am, say, half-done?

I was interested in Lewis Gannett's criticism of Galsworthy's American idiom,[4] remembering your asking me, when I discussed my other embryonic novel with you, "Hammock", whether I knew enough about young English-men! Gannett seems to think Galsworthy doesn't know enough about young Americans! I haven't read "Maid in Waiting", but if Galsworthy has erred, I should say it was because he made too deliberate an attempt to use an Ameri-can idiom. It is my belief that there is a common academic speech, used nor-mally by the intellectual classes, intelligible to both nations. Conspicuous idiom, particularly when used by the cultured, is a social affectation in any case—an effort at sprightliness. When I do my young Englishman, he will use a simple Anglo-Saxon that is always, to my idea, more effective than colloquial-isms. The simple speech of the Scandinavian novels, for instance, creates a cer-tain timelessness, dignifies the characters.

Of course, you were questioning more than that—my knowledge of young Englishmen psychologically. He isn't going to be entirely normal, which gives me some leeway! I have recently come across a track that will help me, I think. There is still alive, in late middle-life, an Englishman who came with his two brothers to the scrub country, establishing by their own effort a prosperous orange grove on the river edge, which was killed to the ground by the big freeze. The man went to Jacksonville and was recently retired with honors as a Clyde Steamship Line agent. If he proves to be a man of ordinarily sensitive perceptions, I can ask him innumerable "lead" questions, whose answers should keep me on the right track. I have a superficial knowledge of young Englishmen, besides.

A fascinating assortment of people is being born into that book. One of our Florida friends has been strangely reticent about one of his grandmothers, but an uncle of his, with a deeper appreciation of character, told us of a hard-riding, hard-drinking woman who left her weak husband in the house and over-saw the plantation and orange groves herself. She carried mint juleps in a canteen at her saddle, and careened down sometimes on astonished strangers jogging along the sand roads in a buckboard, offering them a julep!

But that is a year or two away.

By the way, if any of your staff should come to Florida this winter, send them on to us for a few days' visit, if they're not too aesthetic. I don't mean to imply extreme aestheticism on SCRIBNER's, for the virility of the magazine is one of its most striking features. I mean, for example, just what would I do with William Lyon Phelps.[5] We aren't entirely primitive——we set a good civi-lized table and have a bathroom. And we do have a powerful good time——so good that one would scarcely notice the state of our exchequer. Do you sup-pose the millionaires will eat oranges this winter? We begin to doubt it. But it really makes very little difference. We have a fine stand of broccoli, thick cream, home-cured hams superior to Smithfield, friends from mayors and university professors on up to sheriffs and Cracker constables, comfortable access to both sea-coasts and a charge account at a gas station. As the old French valentine verse has it, "Que voulez-vous encore?"

Very sincerely,

1. Piety Fiddia, mother of Leonard.
2. MKR later used this range war as the plot for her story "The Enemy," *Saturday Evening Post* 212 (January 20, 1940): 12–13, 32, 36.
3. MKR recast this incident in "A Plumb Clare Conscience," *Scribner's Magazine* 90.6 (December 1931): 622–26.
4. Lewis S. Gannett, reviewer for the *New York Herald Tribune*. John Galsworthy (1867–1933), British novelist and playwright, best known for a group of novels entitled *The Forsyte Saga*, one of which is *Maid in Waiting* (New York: Scribners, 1931).
5. William Lyon Phelps (1865–1943) wrote the "As I Like It" column for *Scribner's Magazine*.

. . . .

16. MEP to MKR (TLS: UF, 1 p.)

Nov. 19, 1931

Dear Mrs. Rawlings:

I think your letter is one of the most interesting I ever read. It made me feel very anxious to see that novel done. I showed it also to Mr. Scribner[1] and to Crichton, and they felt as I do. May nothing interrupt the writing so that we can look forward to it before very long.- And at the same time I do not want to hurry you for such things must be done according to the demands of the subject and the material. But that I need not tell you, for you clearly know what you are about.

Always sincerely yours,

1. Charles Scribner, III. MKR eventually became a favorite of the Scribner family, once describing herself as the "godmother" of Julia Scribner. The unpublished Scribner-MKR correspondence is in itself significant.

1932

17. MEP to MKR (TLS: UF, 1 p.)

May 13, 1932.

Dear Mrs. Rawlings:

May I ask you again how your novel progresses? Be sure that we look forward to reading it eagerly the moment you are ready to send it.

Ever sincerely yours,

· ·

18. MKR to MEP (TLS, 1 p.)

Cross Creek
Hawthorn, Route 1
Florida
May 14, 1932

Mr. Maxwell E. Perkins
CHARLES SCRIBNER'S SONS
New York City

My dear Mr. Perkins:

I thought perhaps you might like to know how I am getting on with the novel. I had hoped to have it for you by this time, but circumstances ruined most of my winter for work. At the rate at which I am now steadily going, I think I can safely say that I shall have the first draft for you to see at the end of July. It is tentatively titled "South Moon Under".[1]

The story in the May *Scribner's*, "A Crop of Beans", seems to have been generously received. I am enclosing two of the comments that may interest you. I noticed that Mr. Dashiell very kindly let it stand almost intact. As I read it over

in print, it did seem to me that it would have been improved by some condensation of the first third.

By the way, the fifteen-thousand-word story, "Gal Young Un,"[2] that you and
Mr. Dashiell and I didn't consider so good, Carl Brandt[3] sold to *Harper's*, to my
surprise. They are using it in June and July. I sent it to Brandt thinking it might
be suitable for two-part use in one of the women's magazines, and he thought
more highly of it than we did.

I shall be interested in the prize short novel result——"A Portrait of Bascom
Hawke"[4] is my candidate.

Thank you for your patience about the novel.

1. *South Moon Under* (1933), MKR's first novel.
2. "Gal Young Un" was rejected by Dashiell as too stridently feminist. It was published in *Harper's
   Monthly Magazine* 165 (June 1932): 21–33, 225–34, and was awarded the O. Henry Memorial
   Prize for the best short story of 1932.
3. Carl Brandt, MKR's literary agent, head of the firm of Brandt and Brandt, New York.
4. Thomas Wolfe (1900–1938), "A Portrait of Bascom Hawke," *Scribner's Magazine* 91.4 (April
   1932): 193–98, 239–56.

. . . .

19. MEP to MKR (CC, 2 pp.)

May 18, 1932

Dear Mrs. Rawlings:

You must have written me on the very day I wrote you. I was delighted with
your letter and "South Moon Under" is an excellent title. "A Crop of Beans"
was a fine story, and I think you will be getting an inquiry about your novel
from Ray Long, ex-editor of the Cosmopolitan,[1] for he asked for a copy of the
Scribner's that has your long story[2] in it. He will certainly like that too. I suppose he was impressed with "A Crop of Beans" and had not seen that other,
and now he will be sure to write you.

As to "Gal Young Un", we may have been wrong in not thinking it as good as
the other, but anyhow it is a good thing to spread around a bit, and I am glad it
is in Harper's. I am delighted you liked "Bascom Hawke", and be sure that your
novel will be eagerly read at the end of July.

Ever sincerely yours,

1. MKR rejected the offer from *Cosmopolitan* magazine to serialize *South Moon Under*.
2. "Jacob's Ladder."

20. MEP to MKR (TLS: UF, 1 p.)

July 27, 1932

Dear Mrs. Rawlings:

Is everything going well with the novel? I don't mean to hurry you, but I am impatient to see it.- But don't bother to write if you too busy [last sentence script].

Ever sincerely yours,

. . . .

21. MKR to MEP (TLS, 2 pp.)

Cross Creek
Hawthorn, Florida
August first

My dear Mr. Perkins:

I had expected to be mailing you my manuscript this morning, but the editing and pruning proved a more tedious job than I had counted on. The novel, "SOUTH MOON UNDER", is finished, and I am reasonably sure I can have it in the mail a week from today. I am forced to copy it myself, principally because no typist could decipher the changes and corrections.

There is no point in raising too many questions until you have read it, but I should like to ask you to be on the look-out for two things. One is a comparatively minor matter: I wanted to take the narrative in its first few pages smoothly along from the human angle, and create an impression of the scrub country from time and time as it showed through the eyes of its inhabitants. I decided that this was hopelessly confusing to the reader, and that there was nothing for it but to give an absolutely definite and geographical description of the physical background of the story, at the very beginning. Note whether this seems to come as an interruption or not, and whether it is dull enough to turn the reader from the narrative. It may be perfectly all right.

The other question involves the book as a unit. I have given the story quite decidedly an episodic treatment. I did it deliberately, and such treatment seemed to me necessary, if the story, covering a period of forty-five years, was not to run to an inordinate length. The day-to-day treatment I considered highly unsuitable. Now: if my chronology is perfectly clear, the episodic handling should be effective, and tend to keep reader-interest at a pitch. If the chronology is not sufficiently smooth and clear, the narrative will be confusing. I have an exact table of dates that I followed for my own guidance, and everything is of course clear to me, but I cannot judge from the outside whether the chronological progression is plain. If necessary, I can make more obvious links between chapter and chapter.

I am prepared to work on the book as much as is needed. Bobbs-Merrill and Harper[1] have asked to see it if you don't like it, but I should prefer to try to bring it up to meet your high critical standards than to have it brought out at once in an imperfect form. In other words, I want the book as good as possible, rather than published as soon as possible.

There is no question in my mind but that the material and the characters have value. The impression *in toto* made on the reader when he turns the last page, is probably something that very few writers can gauge for themselves.

If you feel, after reading the manuscript, that it would be desirable to go over it with me personally, rather than writing me about it, I should be free to come up to New York.

Very sincerely,

1. The publishers Bobbs-Merrill and Harper and Brothers.

. . . .

22. MEP to MKR (TLS: UF, 1 p.)

Aug. 3, 1932

Dear Mrs. Rawlings:

Thanks ever so much for your letter. I hope you will be able to send "South Moon Under" so that it will get here in a week.- And I shall read it as you say, and look forward to it impatiently. Many thanks.

Ever sincerely yours,

. . . .

23. MKR to MEP (TLS, 1 p.)

Cross Creek

Hawthorn, Route 1

Florida

August 11, 1932

My dear Mr. Perkins:

I thought perhaps I had better let you know that I planned to be with an aunt[1] in New Rochelle next week, so that you might not write me about the novel here at the Creek, expecting possibly an immediate answer about something.

My husband has been on Lake Ontario covering the international yacht races for the Canada's Cup, and the Lake Yacht Racing Association Regatta, etc., and will be returning about the end of the week. So I am hopping an excursion boat to New York and will return with him by water. I will drop you a note or telephone you from New Rochelle, and if you should care to see me, we can arrange a meeting.

By the way, my husband's Greek sponger material is proving very entertaining, and he has just sold what I consider a delightful story, "The Dance of the Bends", to the Saturday Evening Post.[2] Really too good a story for the Post, and yet not literary enough for the "intellectual" magazines, if I make myself clear.

I'm hoping that whoever is reading "South Moon Under" about now is liking it——

Very sincerely,

1. Wilmer Kinnan, a teacher in New Rochelle, who later retired to Phoenix.
2. Charles A. Rawlings, Jr., "The Dance of the Bends," *Saturday Evening Post* 205.17 (October 22, 1932): 10–11, 80–81, 83–84. The story is about the sponge fishing industry in Tarpon Springs, Florida.

· ·

24. MEP to MKR (TLS: UF, 8 pp.)

August 23, 1932

Dear Mrs. Rawlings:

After our talks about "Half Moon Under" [*South Moon Under*] a good deal of what I have now to say will be superfluous.- But I'll say everything that has occurred to me, and then you can make use of any suggestions you think worthwhile. The book consists of highly interesting material,- truly valuable material - very effectively presented.- And my suggestions come only from the fact that the material is presented rather from the point of view of a social chronicle than from that of a novel. For instance, the narrative is in episodic form, as it has to be in order to cover so much ground, and as social chronicle no criticism of this is justifiable; but to form a novel these episodes should be woven together by fictional devices, which arouse expectation in the reader as to the outcome of certain complications which have arisen between the principal characters and enforce a continuity of interest. If the reader comes early to feel that there is some strong attraction between Kizzy and Lant which is likely to lead to something, he will be drawn on through the book to find out, and his interest will not lapse at the end of each episode; and this will be true also if he becomes early aware of hostility between Lant and Cleve,- if it becomes apparent to him that Cleve is not really true to his type, that there is something wrong with him that will lead to trouble.

It seems to me therefore that these two elements should be greatly emphasized in the story,- that Kizzy should be brought in very much sooner, and her sympathy with the boy Lant, on account of her love of hunting, and all, should be salient; and that in the same way the lack of sympathy between Cleve and Lant should also be emphasized, and that the reader should throughout be kept aware of these two relationships, in such a way that he will feel that they will result in something important. If these two strands of interest were woven through the episodes of the story, I think it would be greatly to its advantage.

But these two relationships could not develop until the reader is pretty far into the story, because Lant is not born. Before that, the relationship of supreme interest is one between Piety and her father. This shift of interest from that relationship to the others presents a considerable problem. The story does drop off in interest after the death of old Lantry because there is nothing to take its place until Lant, the boy, begins to grow up, when Piety transfers her affection for her father to him. I think it is very important, therefore, to find a way to get Lant along faster so that this relationship between mother and son will more quickly take the place of the old one.

This intensification of relationships and emphasis of these principal characters seems to me the great thing to be done, and in fact, to be all that is needed — (though I think that if you will introduce that other girl early, it will do a great deal to bring forward Lant's character sooner) — and the following suggestions are all intended to be to that end.

The first two chapters of the book are extremely well done.- The fence raising is equal to episodes of a similar kind that are classic, certainly. But in some degree the fence raising chapter, and the first chapter, are in the nature of a prologue, and if you could reduce them somewhat without injuring them, it would be an advantage.- But for Heaven's sake, don't do this unless you find it easy and are sure that you will not impair their quality. But I do think that the development of Piety's character in that second chapter is very important, and it could be accomplished by having the fence raising considerably presented as seen through Piety's eyes. Instead of simply telling the reader directly about Annie Wilson, couldn't it be presented as something that Piety saw, and how she thought of it? It is almost always more effective anyhow to present a scene through the eyes of one of the characters because that takes the reader into the story by his tendency to identify himself with that character. You should do everything possible to get Piety to the front, and I think that by presenting things as seen by her, you would do this. At the end of this chapter would it be out of place to have old Lantry dance with Piety, as he did with the older girl, or instead of with Sarah? If she could be brought forward in that way — if it would be natural for him to dance with a child in fun, as it would be hereabouts, of course, — it would be well to do it.

(In this chapter I have marked two passages which I think could be omitted. The first is on pages 15 and 16. In the first place, I think Lantry does not need this explanation, and in the second place, I think that you tend to destroy the reader's illusion of being present by breaking in with exposition.- And there are other places where you do this in the book, and I think unnecessarily, and harmfully.

The second pas[sage] is on pages 22 and 23. I think this sort of generalization about the women also tends to destroy the reader's illusion somewhat and besides, all that you tell is better imparted to the reader by the specific instances of talk, etc., that you give.- And these specific instances, like the one just before this passage, intensify the illusion.)

In Chapter iii I have suggested the omission of passages I have thought superfluous.- A good deal of what Lantry feels can be left to inference.

On page 42 I suggest the omission of an explanatory sentence because the reader will understand without it, from the dialogue.- And such interpolated comments by the author tend to weaken the reader's illusion of <being> hearing actual dialogue.- I think your dialogue and narrative can be trusted to do what you want without the help of comment and explanation.

In Chapter iv I suggest the omission of the first several pages. What happened to the other children comes along well enough with the story to which they are only incidental.- Deletion of such material as this does in itself put emphasis on the principal characters. You might combine Chapters iv and v, and so get sooner to Kizzy, and on with Piety's story.

Page 62, suggest omitting this anticipatory comment, "Lantry *was* to feel, etc." A number of times in the book you do this, but I think it is always harmful.- It takes the reader out of this story. He has no natural means of looking ahead, and if you anticipate, you weaken his illusion.

Chapter vii. I think you could tell about the timber outfit much more briefly and casually.- The reader will infer much of pages 70 and 71 for himself, and the rest will come out in the narrative.

Chapter viii. Could you shorten this chapter? Would it be possible to introduce Kizzy hereabouts in some way?

Chapter x. This first sentence is one of those in which you anticipate and thereby (I think) destroy the illusion of reality. I'd say, make it straight narrative.

Chapters xi and xii. Could you get Kizzy in at about this point? Perhaps you could interpolate a chapter between xi and xii, in which she was conspicuous.

Chapter XIII. Suggest omitting the incident of the wolf.- If the wolf came to figure in some important way in the story it would be different, but as it is, though interesting as an incident, it makes no contribution to the story. It merely introduces something that one would like to hear more of, but there is no more to hear, and therefore it seems superfluous. The incident of the Alabaman is valuable because Lant figures so prominently in it, and is revealed by it. I do not think though, that you ought to interrupt the narrative and take the reader out of it for that story about Marsh,- good though it is as an anecdote.

Chapter XIV. The book is half way done now, and Lant is only fifteen. Couldn't you make him grow up more rapidly? Couldn't chapters XIV and XV be combined? A good deal of what is in XIV might be shortened because the relation between Piety and Sarah is not very important. The talk in the chapter is good, and it leads up to Cleve's coming.

Chapter XVI. I think most of this about Ramrod could be omitted. His character comes out and you might interpolate a little of his history elsewhere. You might have him actually talk to Lant on the way down the river, for I think that a trip down the river might actually be described, directly. It is wonderfully good material, as good as Huckleberry Finn. Instead of generalizing it, sometimes give specific instances.- Present the thing not as something that used to happen, but as happening. I think a great deal might be made of this chapter if you could put it directly and specifically.

Chapter XVII. Then comes the gatoring. (Incidentally, on page 170 you make one of those references outside the story about what happened "years later".- I think these are bad for they destroy the illusion by taking the reader outside what is happening.) In this gatoring chapter you tend to generalize too much. The giving of one incident as actually happening is worth more than any amount of generalizing about what happened *sometimes*.

Chapter XVIII. It is in this chapter that Kizzy first appears. The book is almost two-thirds done, and she is one of the very most important people. She must be brought in much earlier. She appears here remarkably well, and that is one reason why she ought to appear sooner. She is mighty good.

I think you might intensify the relations between Piety, Kizzy, and Lant, in this chapter. (On page 190 you have another of the instances of referring beyond the narrative — "He was soon to use ash". The reader should be absorbed in what he was doing *now* only)[.]

Chapter XX. I think you could cut out most of this chapter and combine XX and XXI. People do not have to be informed very specifically and fully about these changes.- They only have to be made aware of them. The changes are only important, of course, in so far as they affect the characters, and they can be inferred almost by the reader from the characters. I would believe in omitting the Streeters entirely, and all that about the lawsuits.

In Chapter xxiii Cleve comes to work for Lant. Couldn't the order of the chapters here by [be] changed so that he came to work for Lant before the cane grinding? That cane grinding, which is very good, would then stand in the middle of the episode in which Cleve betrays his people and gets killed. The delay in this episode by the interpolation of the cane grinding would add to the suspense, and it might in some way be used to intensify the relationship between Kizzy, Lant, and Cleve.

The very ending of the book is splendid.

All these suggestions are simply to weave through the episodes of the narrative — and so bind them all tightly together — the elements of the various stories which are in the book and should be its main purpose,- the story of Piety and her relationship with her father which should evolve into that with Lant; the story of Lant which should take over the reader's interest in the father, when the father dies; and the story of Kizzy which is so much a part of that of Lant, and that of Cleve. These three stories should be always in the reader's mind, and should be always growing throughout the book.- And the reader should be wanting to know the end of them so that there will be always continuity of interest, as well as that great interest which is in the material itself as you beautifully present it. But the more you can do, I think, to intensify all these stories and emphasize all these leading characters, the finer will be the book.

Ever sincerely yours,

. . . .

25. MKR to MEP (TLS, 2 pp.)

Cross Creek
Hawthorn, Route 1, Fla.
August 31, 1932

Dear Mr. Perkins:

Your letter is tremendously helpful. Your diagnosis and prescription are so specific, that I think between us we can have the patient on his feet in no great while. You have a truly amazing genius for taking the product of another's imagination in the hollow of your hand. It is the height, I suppose, of critical sympathy and understanding.

Reading over the manuscript of "South Moon Under", I am astonished at how far I went out of my way to be random and rambling. The direct narrative form throughout is so patently required——and through so much of the book I seem perversely to have avoided it. Looking back to my earliest conception of the book, I do not believe that I ever planned it as a true novel, but, as you express it, as "a social chronicle." But I agree heartily that the true novel form will be much more effective, and will convey the truth beyond truth, by making the characters more vital. I believe that I was afraid of two things: first, of getting into too great length in the straight narrative form, which always takes more space than a few paragraphs of generalization; and second, of not being detached enough. But I think I can lay both ghosts.

I plan to re-write altogether most of the central third to half of the book, considering what now stands as simply a collection of coherent notes. I remember I didn't answer you when you asked how long it would take me. I hate to say too definitely——it makes one nervous in spite of oneself——but if the end of October is reasonable for your requirements, I think that only an untoward interruption would prevent my having the work done by that time. I could <probably> do it in a month if necessary. I probably work better under pressure. The bad part of the book is the part I dawdled over.

You asked me what Carl Brandt said about it. I did not see him again after I left a carbon copy for him, although I found out later that he had wanted to talk with me about it. Miss Baumgartner (spelling?)[1] had read it and talked with my husband about it. She considered it "fascinating" material, and made a general comment similar to yours, saying that it lacked "a backbone" to hold it together. Her principal suggestion toward unifying it was to urge an emphasizing of the boy's inherited fear. To a minor degree I shall do this, but to carry it very far I should consider artificial, tending to make a book with too obtrusive a "theme" or "motif", which, when too much dwelled on, I find abhorrent. Miss Baumgartner thought his fear should be brought out in his dealings with the girl Kezzy. That would be all tommy-rot, as I conceived of her as very much a harbor of refuge for him, at all times. However, when I bring in the other girl, it will automatically be his hidden fears that will keep him from her. She will be too much a part of the civilized world he does not know, and mistrusts; the game warden will be <a> an habitue of her father's house; the sheriff will be her father's friend. Everything about her, except her physical appeal for him, will <make> chill the very marrow in his bones, and make it impossible for him to do anything but run from her and from his desire; his instinct for self-preservation being more profound, in such a situation, than the sex-instinct.

I can't tell you how deeply I appreciate your helpfulness——your thoughtfulness and sympathy. You make it very easy for me to go at it again. You have only asked one hard thing of me——to give up the wolf!

Very sincerely,

1. Bernice Baumgarten, Carl Brandt's secretary.

26. MEP to MKR (TLS: UF, 2 pp.)

Sept. 1, 1932

Dear Mrs. Rawlings:

Ever since I wrote you I have been worried for fear what I suggested might seem to you to be asking a great deal. When you have thought it over, and decided what to do, I should be very grateful to hear from you. Anyhow, you may think of better ways of developing the story, and giving it a continuity throughout the book, and so drawing the whole book into a more perfect unity.- What I suggested was perhaps more by way of example, to show what it seemed to us was required. Will you write me soon, and tell me how the matter looks to you? I have great hopes for the book.

Ever sincerely yours,

. . . .

27. MEP to MKR (TLS: UF, 2 pp.)

Sept. 2, 1932

Dear Mrs. Rawlings:

I was delighted to get your letter, and to find that you did not think my suggestions were too difficult and that you were going on with the revision so speedily. This letter of yours answers the one I wrote you yesterday. I think we shall have a splendid novel.

Ever sincerely yours,

P.S. Perhaps you might get the wolf in because in the revision he might come to have some greater significance than the fact that he just appears and then disappears completely without doing anything to the development of the story.- But if he did serve to bring out Lant's character, this would not be so.

. . . .

28. MKR to MEP (TLS, 4 pp.)

Cross Creek
Hawthorn, Route 1, Fla.
October 6, 1932

Dear Mr. Perkins:

You are most thoughtful, as usual.

I have just finished "Death in the Afternoon",[1] and I find it quite insane and entirely stirring. It is one of those books on which you can see the mark of an inner compulsion in the writer. This seems to make, not necessarily for a finished artistry, even in the hands of so true an artist as Hemingway, but for a terrific vitality. I could wish that he had not felt it necessary to apologize for his style and his subject. When he puts aside his self-consciousness and lets go, he moves me as profoundly as anyone, including himself, has done in a long time.

It will be intensely interesting to see what the critics say, lifting their coyote-noses to sense which way the wind blows. I think the book is almost certain to cause a furore, both in literary circles (Is it or isn't it a work of art?) and among such people as belong to women's clubs, book societies, etc. (Is it or isn't it shocking and indecent?) There can't help but be passionate attacks and still more passionate defenses.

I haven't had a chance to get any outside reactions, but the battle *en famille* shook the walls of the Rawlings shack, and blows were dealt that will be perhaps too long remembered.[2] To borrow Hemingway's type of dialogue with his Old Lady, part of the row went like this:

He: This book is a symbol to me that our civilization is going to Hell.

I: It had never occurred to me that our civilization had reached a point high enough from which it could descend to Hell. Your distress is touching. What do you mean?

He: I mean that it is a sign of decadence that one of our finest American artists, perhaps our finest, should absorb himself with a personal enthusiasm with a cruel and decadent subject.

I: You, a hunter of game, (although a poor one), are defining cruelty and decadence ——

He: From the civilized point of view. The Anglo-Saxon view has always been——

I: And the question has been raised whether I know anything about an Englishman who remains English even after two generations —— merciful Heaven, I am living with one! You are doing precisely what Hemingway begs you not to do —— you are approaching bull-fighting with preconceived prejudices.

He: But they are sound. The Anglo-Saxon point of view has always been——

I: Mother of God!

He: ——that bull-fighting inflicts deliberate and sadistic torture, while game-shooting is quick and clean and decent.

I: Is it quick and clean and decent, then, when a quail or squirrel or dove is wounded and not retrieved and lies dying in the brush? When a wounded deer gets away and takes hours and days of great agony, without food and water, to die?

He: (Loftily) When such a thing happens, it is accident and not intent.

I: You consider yourself morally intact, then, when, setting out deliberately to kill, you end by causing suffering?

He: In ethics, it is customary to take account of the intention.

I: And in law, it is customary to consider an accidental harming of another, if engaged at the time in the commission of a crime or a felony, a most serious offense. You are smug, hypocritical and inconsistent. It is not possible to draw a logical line between bull-fighting and any other sport that ends in death.

He: But the Anglo-Saxon point of view has always been that bull-fighting is not a sport. You do not understand, nor does Hemingway, the civilized conception of a sport.

I: Hemingway understands. I understand only too well that you are the most offensive sort of Anglophile. You exhibit this objectionable quality in many ways: in your passionate devotion —— simply because it is English —— to black-currant roly-poly, which resembles in sight, smell and texture nothing more than crushed bed-bugs wrapped in a wet blanket ——

He: You are going too far. You are a vulgar woman with an obscene tongue, without fineness of taste or perception. If you are damning black-currant roly-poly and defending bull-fighting, you too are decadent. I have long suspected it.

I: I am not decadent. I am only detached. Life is not to me the intensely personal matter that it is to such people as you, with your fixed ideas. I accept all of life as an abstract phenomenon, and nothing in it shocks me nor too greatly concerns me. I am interested in ideas as ideas, in facts as facts, in emotions as emotions. I really have the advantage of you ——. I too had conceived of bull-fighting as cruel and vicious, but Hemingway passes on to me a terrific emotion that he has felt; reveals a beauty he has seen. I know what he means. He makes me understand what he means. I remember, in my journalistic days, I was mad about wrestling matches. Men and women hooted with laughter when I said in all simplicity and innocence that I found wrestling beautiful. Oddly, I think "Strangler" Lewis[3] himself, when I said something of the sort to him, knew what I meant. I meant, the beauty of plastic line. If architecture is frozen music, then good wrestling and good bull-fighting are rhythmic sculpture. Add to the beauty of line in good wrestling, the emotional and spiritual climax of death in bull-fighting —— a certain abstraction of death, as Hemingway writes of it —— and I can share with him an overpowering cosmic excitement.

He: You can jolly well share. The book in style and subject is abominable. (Grudgingly and thoughtfully). The decadent idiot makes me want to see a bull-fight——

# # # # #

It was nice of you to send it to me. Did you sense that I was suffering? I am getting along almost as fast as I planned, with the revision of my own book, but it's not a bit of fun —— won't be, until I get to the new girl. I have the grandfather killed off about thirty pages earlier, and the girl Kezzy introduced at the end of Chapter vii, instead of Chapter xviii, a difference of a hundred pages earlier. I am making the boy's uncle who had the moonshining mishap when the boy was young, the foster-father of the girl Kezzy, so that she will fit in with more of what happens to him (the boy). And as far as I have gone, I have re-written everything that was generalized, and made direct, specific narrative of it. It is a dull torment, or course, like a toothache, to do this kind of work, but if it comes out all right I sha'n't mind. In another couple of weeks I can tell you how I'm coming out, as to time and results.

Very sincerely,

1. Ernest Hemingway (1898–1961), *Death in the Afternoon* (New York: Scribners, 1932).
2. The confrontations, often physical, between MKR and her husband finally led to divorce in 1933. His maltreatment of her becomes the subject of her autobiographical story "The Pelican's Shadow," *New Yorker* 15 (6 January 1940): 17–19.
3. Lewis, a famous wrestler, known for his staged villainy. MKR wrote a satire on wrestling for *Five O'Clock* 1 (May 13, 1924): 7.

. . . .

29. MEP to MKR (TLS: UF, 2 pp.)

Oct. 19, 1932

Dear Mrs. Rawlings:

I very much enjoyed your letter.- I showed the dialogue to others here who appreciated it. But I should think though, that "He" being a sportsman, would think that the intensity with which E. H. writes of the technique of a sport, looking at that alone, was a remarkable contribution.- And this book made me think that Hemingway could write a wonderful book on any sport with which he was familiar, as for instance, fishing. Having fished with him, and seen the waters off the coast of Florida, and all the life in them and around them, and Ernest's great love of all the equipment of fishing and everything about it, I can imagine him writing such a book on that sport as would make all the others look trivial.

I hope you have got to the girl now so that there is more fun in it, but what you say about getting on faster, and getting Kezzy in earlier and all, sounds exactly right. I am eager to see the revision. If you could let half of it go before you finish all of it, I would welcome reading it in that way.- But it may be you would not be able to let the first part go until you have finished.

Ever sincerely yours,

Oct. 26, 1932

Dear Mrs. Rawlings:

We had the pleasure of publishing in Scribner's Magazine your "A Plumb Clare Conscience" which came to us in connection with the contest we held for articles representing "Life in the United States".[1]

This series attracted considerable attention, and brought the comment that if all these representations of life in the United States were published together, the total effect would be impressive. We frankly could not expect in the face of the present business conditions, a very considerable sale for such a book, but we do think that these contributions are entitled to a better form of publication than only that in the magazine, and we have been working on a plan to publish them in book form if the authors will consent to it.

The difficulty is that we can offer them very slight hope of any substantial remuneration, so that there would not be much advantage to them beyond that which would come from the recognition the contribution should get when put in the more permanent form of a volume. All that we can propose is that after a sale of 5,000 copies we shall divide a 15% royalty between thirty authors. It will be necessary for us to sell as many copies as that on account of costs of manufacturing and advertising, etc., and the introduction, which Laurence Stallings[2] has agreed to do.

On the other hand, we should not ask for any rights to your article beyond that of publishing it in this form. If you had any opportunity to publish it in any other form, to include it in a book of your own, for instance, we should have no right or reason to object.

Would you be willing to have us publish your article on that basis, in a book to be called "Life in the United States"?

Ever truly yours,

[Postscript in MEP's hand] Forgive me for writing you a form letter in this matter.- We're very impatient to see any or all of South Moon Under.

1. A human interest section in *Scribner's Magazine*.
2. Laurence Stallings (1894–1968), novelist, dramatist, and scriptwriter.

Cross Creek
Hawthorn, Route 1
Florida
November 2, 1932

Dear Mr. Perkins:

About the "Plumb Clare Conscience" for "Life in the United States" —— of course, use it. I'm delighted to have representation for the section and people that interest me so much. I can't take it as a personal compliment, for the story is very little more than a piece of accurate reporting.

As to the novel, "South Moon Under," I'm glad to report that the rest of this week will see it entirely finished, and another week, ready to mail, so that the complete manuscript can be in your hands, say, November 14. I can let you have the first half several days earlier if it is a matter of greater convenience to you in reading. Or, if you really need to have a look at it for purely business reasons — if by chance you are making up your spring list and need to know at once whether or not the book is going to suit you —— do say so, better, wire me at Island Grove (not Hawthorn) —— and I'll get it to you.[1]

I can't keep the promise I made to report on "results." That doesn't matter anyway, as a writer's opinion of his own stuff must be valueless, nine times out of ten. I can't tell whether the total impression is effective or not. I can see that the narrative moves much more simply and directly. It still seems to me that some of the transitions are jerky, and much of the book still seems over-written to me. Perhaps I can prune it down in a final editing. The line, plain enough to others, is often unfortunately almost invisible to the writer, between what is telling or moving and what is —— well, flagrant. I am rather counting on you to catch anything of the sort for me.

The new girl is maddeningly insipid. I conceived of her that way —— obviously unsuitable for Lant, obviously a painful contrast to Kezzy —— simply an object for a first love, as girls in general usually are. If she annoys you as much as she does me, I'll have a try at making her more vital. Of course, in a way it is desirable to have her a somewhat unsympathetic character —— you will know whether or not she serves her purpose.

I have been unable to do two of the things you asked, or suggested. So far, I haven't found any way of shortening the first two chapters without taking out material that, unimportant in itself, yet seemed to me of value in setting my scene; placing my people in their background. If you find anything there that you think definitely superfluous, I should be glad to have you point it out.

It was absolutely impossible to take out the episode of the row about the cattle, for this reason: the under-current of fear through the boy's life, powerful and hidden (the south-moon-under motif) reaches its climax in the fear of his treacherous cousin that sweeps over him, at the end. It is necessary to have that fear suggested to him, implanted in his mind. His uncle who had the cattle trouble seemed to me the logical one to do this, serving his own interests through fear that Cleve would tattle about his, the uncle's, share in the beating of the anti-cattle men. However, I have made the young man a closer participant in the row, and have woven the girl business in with it, but having her family on the anti-cattle side. This leads directly to his revulsion against her as representing a life, a point of view, alien to his own, and dangerous to him. If the writing is all right, I think you won't object to the episode as it is now used.

The book runs, I should estimate, about fifteen thousand words longer than the first version. I imagine you were prepared for this, knowing the greater space required to tell of a matter specifically, rather than in a few generalizations. I should hazard a guess that the book is better balanced than before, the first parts, about old Lantry and the very young boy, not being now so disproportionate.

If you like the book, I shall drink a quart of Bacardi in celebration. If you don't like it, I shall drink a quart of Bacardi.

Very sincerely,

I forgot to tell you before how gorgeous the physical make-up of Hemingway's book strikes everyone as being. You, of course, are responsible for that. I encountered a terrific enthusiasm for the book from a most interesting friend, a Tampa surgeon[2] who alternates three or four years of foot-loose soldier-of-fortuneing [sic], with three or four years of utterly brilliant operative work. He is a bit of an aesthete as well, and I thought his admiration was worth passing on. He considers the book "wonderful". He has seen some fifteen bull-fights, some in Mexico City, most of them in Madrid, and never understood them. Hemingway's book absolutely draws back a curtain, he says, and all the pieces of the puzzle-picture jump together into a stirring, comprehended whole. He insists that Hemingway's description of the Spanish prostitute is one of the most wonderful things he has ever read. He said, "The man is a finished dissector," which seems to me *mot juste* from an expert with the knife.

---

1. Island Grove and Hawthorne (generally misspelled "Hawthorn" by MKR) are both villages, Island Grove the smaller and closer to Cross Creek.
2. J. C. Vinson, MKR's Tampa doctor and friend.

32. MEP to MKR (TS for wire, I p.)

NOV. 4, 1932
MRS. MARJORIE K. RAWLINGS
ISLAND GROVE
FLORIDA
PLEASE DO SEND FIRST HALF TO EXPEDITE PUBLICATION MANY THANKS

· ·

33. MKR to MEP (TLS, 2 pp.)

Cross Creek
Hawthorn, Route 1
November 7, 1932

Dear Mr. Perkins:

I'm sending you almost the first half of the manuscript for, I imagine, a decision on its desirability —— in answer to your wire.

The rest of the manuscript, in rough form, is almost the whole story. The remaining few chapters that I am keeping represent the trouble with the traitor, the killing, etc. and are a matter of rearrangement, not re-writing. I am sending you my first draft for your own private reading —— a little against my better judgment, for I find, at least, that I do not get so favorable an impression from a manuscript that is hard to read. But you are so familiar with it, and will be able so easily to see what I have done, and changed, that I am risking it. Do as you wish, of course, about letting anyone else see the rough part. As far as I am concerned, it is just for you. I will send you the remainder in two or three days. I have been handicapped by having to do my own copying; my manuscripts seem to be beyond the local typists. By the way, this is my only copy of the new form.

I realize that I allowed myself too short a time for the revision. My own fault, for if I had told you I needed a year, you would not have questioned it. If it should happen that you find the substance now satisfactory, or nearly so, and decide to put out the book —— I *must* have three or four weeks before the manuscript goes to the printer's hands. The style is crying out for the free use of axe, hatchet, saw, to say nothing of anything so delicate as a manicure set. My demand is presumptuous, of course, when I don't even know how the revision is going to strike you. I'm just speaking up in your private ear in plenty of time, so that you can take care of me in the matter. I *must* have a chance to edit, all other revision aside.

If you find you are going to want the book, you will of course let me have the manuscript back as soon as possible. I didn't mean to mislead you when I called it "finished". I meant matter, not form.

Very sincerely,

· ·

34. MEP to MKR (TS for wire, I p.)

NOV. 9, 1932
MRS. MARJORIE K. RAWLINGS
ISLAND GROVE
FLORIDA
MANUSCRIPT RECEIVED STOP NEVER HAD DOUBT ABOUT PUBLICATION
BUT WISHED TO PREPARE SINCE MUST BEGIN SELLING BY JANUARY FIRST
STOP SHALL RETURN MANUSCRIPT SATURDAY RETAINING FIRST CHAPTER
FOR DUMMIES

· ·

35. MKR to MEP (TLS, I p.)

[Cross Creek]
[November 1932]

Dear Mr. Perkins:

Do you think the first 4 1/2 pages of chapter XII are *dangerously* dull? The information given there is necessary, of course. If you think it can and should be conveyed in two or three sentences, turn somebody like Crichton loose on it to cut. Just be sure no necessary point is left out. You may think it is all right as it stands.

· ·

36. MEP to MKR (TLS: UF, 2 pp.)

Nov. 12, 1932

Dear Mrs. Rawlings:

I am sending back the manuscript. Do work as fast as you can on it. We can take another look in the galley proof, anyhow. I have only spent a half an hour or so going over it, but it seems to me that all is well, and I believe it is a fine book. It certainly has a very appealing quality, and I can see that you have done a number of the things we talked of. I could not give it more time because I had to let the art department read it. They have removed a certain few pages for the sake of basing a jacket on them, or at any rate giving the artist some suggestions and sense of the character of the book. We have also withheld the first two chapters which must be set up for the dummy. It looks like a mighty good book to me, and I would have liked to have gone through it with care.- But we shall have a fresh eye on it in the galleys anyhow.

Always yours,

· ·

37. MKR to MEP (TLS, 3 pp.)

Cross Creek
Hawthorn, Route 1
Florida
November 12, 1932

Dear Mr. Perkins:

There will almost certainly be a note from you in with my manuscript, perhaps giving counter instructions to what I am doing. If so, just ignore the manuscript that will reach you with this letter.

I had no idea that you planned to move so fast on the book, "South Moon Under." As a matter of fact, you have had more confidence in the outcome than I have had. You have been so awfully decent about everything——you really are a dear, you know——that I do want to cooperate in every way. Unless you have suggested changes in the first 152 pages, it occurred to me that I could make quite a bit of time by doing my editing on my carbon copy of that much of the manuscript. So I am sending it on to you, ready to set from——unless, as I say, you want something changed. If they are minor changes, perhaps you could make them yourself.

I should suggest——perhaps you are making the same suggestion——that I send you the rest of it day by day as I get it done. If the 152-page start does you any good, I think I can almost keep up with your printer.

When I talked with you in New York, you spoke of the possible desirability of a map of the scrub and river. I am going over to the Ocklawaha tomorrow to check up on the position of various of the river landings with picturesque names that are not on the map. I will put these on the Forest Preserve map I got hold of. I shall also indicate <the> a few such things as the wild-cat hunt, the home of old man Paine the hunter, the imaginary location of the Lantry clearing, etc. If you had in mind using some such thing for a decorative inside book-cover, it will be very simple for a draughtsman (I don't think you even need an out-and-out artist) to trace the outline of as much of the section as you want to indicate, putting in the desired names in decorative letters, or something of the sort. Little crosses for the pine trees across it might be effective. Anyway, I'm mailing you the map on Monday so that you should get it Wednesday morning for any use you may care to make of it.

I am anxious to know just how the revision strikes you. Now that it is done, I realize that it is not the book I wanted to write——not the picture I wanted to give. Very possibly it is a better book——probably more readable——but <somewhere> somehow or other the emotion I intended to convey, has escaped me. Probably it is always so with any writer except a true genius. The thing that sweeps across you, clamoring for expression, is probably always more powerful than the flabby words and phrases you begin to trot out about it. The profound reality, the essence, of an idea or a feeling, manages to slip away in the shuffle. I wonder what <excision> proportion of books gives the thing the writer wanted so much to give.

Do feel assured that you can count on me to work as fast <and> as possible and not hold you up. I'll even promise good behavior to the extent of not raising the devil with the proofs.

Very sincerely,

Giving you "Island Grove" as a wiring address may have been confusing, as if I had moved or something. It is only that while Island Grove is our nearest village, four miles away, it has no rural delivery. Our ordinary mail is delivered every morning from Hawthorn, fourteen miles away. Telegrams to Hawthorn reach us, much belated, in the mail. Telegrams to Island Grove are always gotten to us, somehow, by friends in the village.

. . . .

38. MKR to MEP (TLS, 3 pp.)

[Cross Creek]
[November 1932]

Dear Mr. Perkins:

Here's the map of the scrub and river, in case your artist wants to make use of it.

Am also enclosing the note we spoke of, to take care of possible complaints about dates from men who know the scrub from hunting in it. I should suggest having it as unobtrusive as possible. <illegible excision>

I'm really quite put out with you for not reading the manuscript.

You have one swell guarantee of my hurrying with my editing —— hunting season opens November 20th. I was in the scrub yesterday and saw bear tracks the size and shape of a Georgia nigger's foot, with claws beyond that as long as my fingers. Also bear cub tracks and deer-tracks thick as chicken-scratchings. The game warden told me he saw the bear cubs the other day and would have shot one, but "I says to him, No, I'll leave you in the scrub and let you scare some hunter."

The more I think about it, the more put-out I am at you. You did go back on me, after all. I don't give a damn about Scribner's wanting to hurry to get the book published —— I wanted it as good as possible —— and you didn't even read it. ——

[Enclosure]
Map of the scrub & the Ocklawaha river, as it concerns Lant. (Lantry Jacklin)
X marks Lantry clearing in hammock at top of bluff above river, between river and scrub. O marks Otter Landing on river at foot of clearing.
A marks site of Lant's still in swamp below Lantry clearing
Y marks Zeke Lantry's clearing (Kezzy lived there)
B marks Taylor's Dread on W. side of river, site of Zeke's still
Z marks property of the Alabaman
Property of Martha Lantry Jacklin and Syl Jacklin would lie 3/4" on the map above Y, and property of Thad Lantry anywhere between that point and Z.
Landings on river, passed by Lant at his rafting:
1. The Lady Slipper
2. Indian Bluff
3. Hog-thief Creek
4. Hard Scramble Creek
5. Double S Cut-off
6. The Needle's Eye
7. The Gallopin' Reaches
8. Turkey-foot Landing
    Note: Apparent narrowing of the river in between Orange Springs and Deep Creek is merely indication of county line. "The Scrub" is the entire area on this map bounded on the west and north by the Ocklawaha River, on the east by the St. John's and Lake George. The area covered by the action of the story of "South Moon Under" is the northern portion lying between Eureka and the junction of the Ocklawaha and the St. John's. If <this map is used, or> the northern portion only of the map is used, an arrow pointing to the S.W. from the Lantry clearing would be sufficient to indicate the direction of the clearing of old Man Paine the hunter. The scrub is composed of scrub pine. Other names are sand pine and Southern spruce. A little black-jack oak, much

scrub oak, low bushes. The hammock fringe that lies in a thin strip between river and scrub is composed of live oak, magnolia, sweet gum, ironwood, several kinds of bay, holly, ash, dogwood, hickory, cabbage palm (palmetto). The swamp at the foot of the hammock has dense cypress, palmetto, ash, intertwined with briers and rattan.

The river is from fifty feet to three hundred wide, deep, swift, cypress brown in color.

"Islands" on map are "pine islands" —— sections of slash pine and some long-leaf yellow pine.

A "prairie" is a low marshy place, wet, grass-filled, boggy.

Editor's note: Copy of map enclosed.

. . . .

39. MEP to MKR (CC, I p.)

Nov. 14, 1932

Dear Mrs. Rawlings:

I return herewith the pages of "South Moon Under" which we held out to use in connection with the jacket.

Sincerely yours,

. . . .

40. MEP to MKR (TLS: UF, 2 pp.)

Nov. 15, 1932

Dear Mrs. Rawlings:

If you could, without disadvantage, send us the manuscript in sections, every other day or so, it would help.- I have put what has come to us in hand, and told the printer we would supply him with more as fast as he used what he had. But he won't use it so very fast, so don't let that worry you. The main thing is to get the book right. I think it probably is right now, though as you will have heard from me, I did not really read it, but just skimmed through it. We can do a good deal, even a great deal, in the galleys if we have to, you know. And when one reads a book in type it gives quite a new impression and a fresh opportunity to judge it.

We have got a wrap planned out, and I hope it may turn out well. You have a very effective title, and that will be made very strong on the jacket.

We have never discussed terms. It is true that with a book for which we had hopes in the boom days we might have offered a 15% royalty after the first two or three thousand copies, but now that is much more difficult, and if you would be willing to do it, we should rather publish on a 10% royalty on the first 5,000 copies, and 15% thereafter.

Ever sincerely yours,

. . . .

41. MEP to MKR (TLS: UF, 3 pp.)

Nov. 18, 1932

Dear Mrs. Rawlings:

I have just read those chapters (they just came) which end with the one about going down the river. I think these chapters are excellent, and that you have done most beautifully with the river trip. Don't you think it is much better than it was? I am very much pleased myself.

As for not reading the manuscript before.- I would have done it if it had been possible, but we had the book on the list and had started all the preliminaries and prepared everything so that we could not put it off without doing damage; and in order properly to publish it, we had to get on with it. I should have read it if I had not felt sure of it, but as it was, the important thing was to get the artist to work. So I gave it to the art department, and then got it right off to you. I shall read all the galleys, you can be sure of that, and I expect to enjoy them.

Ever sincerely yours,

P.S. I did not think the 4 1/2 pages of chapter XII were dull at all. Looked at alone they ought not to be compressed. It may be, of course, that when one reads the whole book through, it will seem wise that they should be. We can tell in the galleys.

. . . .

42. MKR to MEP (TLS, 5 pp.)

Cross Creek
Hawthorn, Route 1
Florida
November 18, 1932

Dear Mr. Perkins:

I was bullying my husband last night into reading some of my chapters of "South Moon Under" as I worked on them. He threw down the manuscript and said, "I'm going to make a suggestion that will infuriate you, and I'm possibly wrong about it. Take out all your profanity. If you do this, you automatically open up a wide and continuous market for the book *among boys,* entirely distinct, an accidental by-product, from your mature appeal."

Of course, I was as shocked as if he'd suggested that I sell myself into slavery. I remember, out of the red fog that enveloped me, remarking caustically that possibly the book could become the first of a series, "The Rover Boys in Florida."[1] I remember being soothed with copious draughts of native rye. When I came to, he went on to explain that he meant nothing of the sort. He said that the book, as an accurate picture of one of the last strips of American frontier, contains so much woods and river lore that would appeal to boys in the way Huckleberry Finn, Treasure Island, and some of Kipling, appeal to them,[2] that it would be a pity to cut off the book from such a group by what he considers the casual excrescence of the profanity of Lant. He didn't mean, he said, to impugn the artistic quality of the book at all; that far greater, more artistic and mature books than I will ever write, happen here and there to contain a picture or a quality that makes boys devour them, ignoring the mature angle altogether. Then I remembered your speaking of Huckleberry Finn in connection with the possibilities you saw in the river chapter, and I am ready to admit there may be something in the idea.

It sounds like an affectation to say that I don't particularly care whether or not the book sells. I just happen to mean it. I should rather have it considered good by people of discernment, than popular. But I do have common sense enough to be willing to broaden its appeal if the book is not harmed in so doing. I have possibly already fallen between two stools as to its artistic unity. The mass of out-of-the-ordinary detail and native lore, may, if I am lucky, slip naturally along with the narrative. Or, it may obscure and defeat my basic conception of the cosmic conflict of man in general struggling against an obscure law and destiny. So for Heaven's sake, since this menace is already present, don't let me bring in a new one unless we're pretty sure of our ground. I mean, don't let's "purify" the book for an adolescent consumption that might never materialize, and ruin the book at the same time for the discriminating adult palate.

Now: I want you to think it over very carefully from both the publisher's and the artist's standpoint. I don't know you well enough to know which is dominant in you. But in spite of your betrayal of me by handing over the manuscript to the printer without being sure that it contained no atrocities, I trust you implicitly as an artist and a critic, and I shall accept your judgment in the matter without further question. I want you to answer two questions:

Is Lant's profanity extraneous and meaningless, as my husband claims it is in 75% of the instances? (He admits the effectiveness of such phrases as "the ring-tailed bastard," the "skew-tailed bastard" and such.) Or is the profanity, as of course I intended it to be, an amusing and vigorous part of my character? Typical changes occasioned by the deletion would be, for instance, when Lant is trying to roll the big dead alligator in his boat, "He sobbed, 'God damn you, you stinkin' bastard, I'll not leave go'." This would become, "He sobbed, 'I'll not leave go——.'" Substitutes for "son of a bitch" and "bastard" would be "booger", "scaper", "scoundrel", "jay-bird", "buzzard" and "jessie". There are <two> three places that occur to me <also> where Lant's profanity is an integral part of the story; where his mother accepts his son of a bitch and bastard without question, but objects violently to his "I'll beat your butt"; where she objects to his calling her sister's son a son of a bitch or a bastard but agrees with enthusiasm to the epithet taken up by the whole vicinity, "the pimp"; and where Lant objects to Kezzy's roughness of speech in front of the girl, Ardis. (About page 302).

The other question: is there so much else in the book that would be objectionable for boys from a parent's standpoint, that nothing is to be gained by toning down one character's language? I have already been talked into deleting one or two of the more medical bits of folk lore. I think such bits of lore as the doctor's comment on women in relation to child-bearing and the moon, Zeke's remark that "a woman in the house ain't a woman in the bed"——that type of thing would simply, I should think, go right over an adolescent's head and not be objected to by a Puritan parent. I may be quite wrong about that. That leaves such things as the quarrel about the out-house and the quarrel of the crazy man, Ramrod Simpson, with "ol' Desus Chwist." My husband thinks that since the crazy man is not very much developed anyway, in the story, that it would be as effective to replace Jesus with the devil——(always a neat and tasty change.)

Well, you figure it out. Mechanically, the changes would be quite simple. *Don't* let me emasculate either character or story to a very problematical end. *Don't* let me turn a rough woodsman into a Boy Scout! But you will see the thing absolutely clear, and I have a queer feeling there may be something in it.

This is the last time I'll be tugging at your coat-tails to have you answer questions. I hope to be quite done this week and go off hunting on the 20th with the whole thing off my mind. You will receive the last installment not later than Wednesday the 23rd.

About the terms. The arrangement you suggest of 10% on the first 5,000, and 15% thereafter, is fair enough with conditions as they are. If the book doesn't go up to or over the first 5,000, the difference isn't worth squabbling about. There is a chance, of course, it may catch on and be something more than just another novel, because of the undeniable freshness of the material. However, you're the last person in the world to whom I need to remark that it's all a grand gamble.

Brandt seems to think (I haven't been in touch with him for some months) that he can "be of use in the general field". What does he want? I wish he had showed you the letter I wrote him, saying that I preferred to sign my own contract with you, letting you name the terms, at least for the American rights. I told him that if he wanted to handle the foreign rights, movies and what-have-you, that would be all right with me.

Very sincerely,

1. A series of books for boys by Edward Stratemeyer (1863–1930).
2. Mark Twain (1835–1910), *The Adventures of Huckleberry Finn* (1884); Robert Louis Stevenson (1850–1894), *Treasure Island* (1883); Rudyard Kipling (1865–1936), whose most famous novel is *Kim* (1901).

. . . .

43. MEP to MKR (TLS: UF, 4 pp.)

Nov. 21, 1932

Dear Mrs. Rawlings:

I am enclosing the contract herewith. I have had it drawn somewhat more favorably, so that it gets to 15% after a sale of 3,000. That certainly is a fair contract, and if the book goes well, we ought to be warranted in coming to the 15% that much sooner.

I just read your letter about the profanity, etc. This is an old issue for me, fought over many times; but I think in the case of "South Moon Under" the best way to do is simply to leave it to the proof. Then we shall both read it again, and maybe have a third person read it, and see how it all looks. I think that where a character might have used one of two expletives or adjectives, <as well as> it would be better to use the one that could not be objected to. Sometimes you know for sure that he would only use one of them, and then there is a compromise of conscience in making the change. When Lant has killed the old grand-daddy alligator, I think you have him say exactly what he would have said, and unless you can think of some other way of getting around it, than the one you suggest, it would be hard not to use the words you have given. As a matter of fact there is not much in this book in the way of words that would be objected to. The most likely thing is in old Ramrod's speeches.- But you would lose the point if you change it to "devil".

I don't really think though that there is much in the book that is injurious to a wide popular sale. There is a good deal in the material of "The Good Earth"[1] that would have been objected to a few years ago, and yet nothing interfered with it. On the other hand, there is no doubt but that Hemingway has sacrificed thousands in his sales by the use of what we have come to call the "four-letter words", and I do not think he need have done it. The truth is that words that are objected to have a suggestive power for the reader which is quite other than that which they have to those who use them; and therefore they are not right artistically. They should have exactly that meaning and implication which they have when uttered. But they have an altogether different one when they strike unaccustomed ears and eyes. But I think most of the words you use are hardly in that class now. At the same time, those that can be honestly spared, might be, and we shall consider it in the proof.

As for Brandt, I think you are doing exactly right by him. There is no reason he should take his 10% commission on the sales of this book, since he had nothing whatever to do with its publication. But it might well bring the sale of movie rights, and there he should come in very useful. Foreign rights too, he could handle well. If he were the agent he would be satisfied with the terms we proposed. Certainly he would think well of the ones we have embodied in the contract. But there is one thing I might tell you he would ask for, and that is a small advance. All agents ask for an advance, because they can deduct their commission from it, and make something right away. But these times are very adverse to advances, and generally speaking, there is no occasion to pay one on a first novel, and we try to avoid even small ones under present conditions when so much credit has to be extended to the book trade all over the country.

Ever sincerely yours,

1. Pearl S. Buck (1892–1973), *The Good Earth* (New York: Day, 1931).

. . . .

44. MKR to MEP (TLS, 1 p.)

[Cross Creek]

[November 1932]

[No greeting]

This is the rest of it. I lost track of page and chapter number from the part I sent you, so I numbered chapters at random and just began numbering pages all over again.

I do hope you're getting a mild kick out of the manuscript, because the way I feel about the damn thing today, I'd swap it for a hunting license.

45. Charles A. Rawlings to MEP (TS, 1 p.)

November 23, 1932
Hawthorne, Florida

Mr. Maxwell E. Perkins,
Charles Scribner's Sons
597 Fifth Avenue
New York City

Dear Mr. Perkins; - Mrs. Rawlings has contracted a rather violent attack of influenza. It is just that, the doctor states, but right this minute she is feeling very badly. The fever is expected to abate tomorrow.

This is the remainder of her manuscript. Four chapters are in a crude state. The remaining chapters are in fair condition. I am sending them all on knowing that your plans call for copy. What few errors creep in can be rectified in the galleys.

Sincerely,
Charles A. Rawlings

Editor's note: At bottom of letter in MEP's handwriting: "Thanks Ms. received. Very sorry for illness Hope for good news soon MP"

. . . .

46. MEP to Charles A. Rawlings (TS for wire, 1 p.)

NOV. 25, 1932
MR. CHARLES A. RAWLINGS
ISLAND GROVE, FLORIDA
THANKS MANUSCRIPT RECEIVED VERY SORRY FOR ILLNESS HOPE FOR
GOOD NEWS SOON

. . . .

47. MEP to MKR (TLS: UF, 1 p.)

Dec. 1, 1932

Dear Mrs. Rawlings:

I hope you are no longer ill. I think you did wonders in getting the manuscript to us so rapidly. Has this spoiled your hunting? I am now sending you the first twelve galleys of "South Moon Under" and I hope to send others in daily, or almost daily, batches.- And I must say I think that the first part reads excellently well.

Ever sincerely yours,

December 1, 1932

Hawthorne, Florida

Mr. Maxwell E. Perkins,

Charles Scribner's Sons,

597 Fifth Avenue

New York City.

Dear Mr. Perkins; - Mrs. Rawlings' ailment proved to be a double malaria. She has had a rather hard time of it with high temperatures; - 105 1/5 [i.e., one-half] at one peak. We broke the fever two days ago and she has made the usual rapid recovery. She should be out of bed shortly.

If you have been holding any questions or answers back I believe you can safely send them on. She will be able to exert herself considerably by the time they could arrive.

"Island Grove" rather than "Hawthorne" will save a day in express. Our mail is delivered out of Hawthorne but the nearest express depot is at Island Grove.

Sincerely,

Charles A. Rawlings

. . . .

Dec. 3, 1932

Dear Mr. Rawlings:

Thanks for writing me. I am delighted to know that Mrs. Rawlings is getting on. I know that malaria is a mighty bad business, but I guess they all understand it down there and know how to deal with it. I hope so anyhow.

I am sending "South Moon" galleys through 43, and I shall have about 20 more by Monday. I don't want to tell Mrs. Rawlings too much about the book because publication is always a speculation, and in these times everything is against success. But if it can be between you and me, I should like to say that I think it is a very remarkable piece of work. It is most uncommon to find a book which is good through and through. You find people who can do excellent dialogue, or excellent description, or have a sense of character, or any one, or two, or three, of the half dozen requirements of a truly fine thing. But this book is good in all those respects.

Ever sincerely yours,

Cross Creek
Hawthorn, Route 1, Fla.
Dec. 3, 1932

Dear Mr. Perkins:

I have my Portable on the bed-tray——so you see my world is reasonably normal again. I have taken a bit of a beating, but I'm on top again. My hunting has been spoiled, of course, but it doesn't matter especially.

This letter will be rather scrappy and assorted, but I want to gather up the loose ends in our correspondence.

I am returning the contract with my signature. I think you have drawn it very favorably for me. I knew of course that publishers sometimes paid an advance, but I have never been able to see any reason for their doing so, unless a writer had depleted his resources in doing a book, and was actually destitute.

I don't quite understand the section "Provided nevertheless that one-half the above-named royalty shall be paid on all copies sold outside the United States." Am I correct in interpreting it to mean that if a book-seller in England or Canada, say, should order and sell some copies of your edition of the novel, that my royalty on such copies would be only half of the ten or fifteen percent paid on American sales?

Your Mr. Henry Hart[1] wrote for a photograph and biographical note for a catalogue, and sounded in a hurry. I'm not quite up to another letter, and I wonder if I might trouble you to send him a memorandum explaining what is holding it up. I haven't had a studio photograph in six years, and even that one proved impossible to run down. I had hopes of some shots made recently on a river trip, but when the owner and picture were finally run to earth yesterday, the picture of me was found to be an excellent camera study of a presumably totally uninhabited pair of riding breeches. It would be at least another week before I could get to town to a studio, and a friend with a Graflex is coming out to get a couple of informal outdoor shots that ought to be more suitable in any case than posed photographs. I despise pictures of writers, anyway. The women smirk and the men look fatuous and you search in vain for any connection with their work. Tell your Mr. Hart a week should see a usable photo in his hands. The biographical note will be just a few lines.

I am so glad that the revision is pleasing you—especially glad you like the river part. I tried very hard to give it what I felt you wanted in it. And I am happy that you get a feeling of vitality. I was afraid about that, of course. There is no question but that the book is improved— the original version was quite impossible. I knew I hadn't made the most of it, and the line of thought you opened up to me was exactly what I needed to go on.

A word about the profanity——I think we shall end by making substitutions for many of the "sons of bitches", otherwise not doing much. I had misgivings as soon as I wrote you, for bit after bit came to memory that could be called unsuitable if a fine tooth comb was going to be used.

I should like to ask one more question, and then I should be done with bothering you. In what status does this contract leave my foreign rights? I imagine a foreign publisher would have to deal with you about a release of copyright.

Many thanks for your patience.

1. Henry Hart, an editor at Scribners.

· ·

51. MEP to MKR (TLS: UF, 3 pp.)

Dec. 5, 1932

Dear Mrs. Rawlings:

I was mighty glad to get your letter and to see that everything was going right with you. I want now only to speak about two points in the galleys that are important. Wasn't it a winter's night that Kezzy was lost in the scrub? I think maybe in the revision you changed the seasons. It was cold the next night apparently, and the cold might have been a very serious element in the situation. The other point is quite a serious one:- a tentative reader ought to understand that Kezzy wanted to marry Lant, and that she was thrown off by Piety's repeating Lant's remark that he wasn't interested in any damn girl, but I think you handle this too cleverly, and that the casual and not very perceptive reader might not understand the situation fully, and that pointing up the text here and there so as to emphasize Kezzy's feelings would be effective.

I wanted to write you this immediately so that you could consider it in the galleys. There are several places where a little emphasis on how Kezzy looked, and what she said, would make it all plain.

The rights to publication in countries other than this one and Canada are entirely yours, and the clause about half royalty probably would have no practical application at all. It is intended as you surmise. You could arrange for publication in England yourself, or through Brandt & Brandt.- Ordinarily we would present the book to English publishers through an agent there, generally Curtis Brown.[1] But this can wait for a time and be taken up on the basis of a finished book.

We shall have these books a good many weeks before publication. It is because of the desire to do this that we have been hurrying into type.

We have got what we think is an excellent jacket. I shall send you a proof soon.

Hoping there will be no more malaria, I am,

Ever sincerely yours,

1. Curtis Brown, Ltd., London literary agents.

. . . .

52. MEP to MKR (CC, I p.)

Dec. 9, 1932

Dear Mrs. Rawlings:

The first of the proofs have come back to us, but you did not return the original copy. The printer always requires this copy before he puts the proof into pages, so can you send it back?

Sincerely yours,

. . . .

53. MEP to MKR (TLS: UF, 2 pp.)

Dec. 13, 1932

Dear Mrs. Rawlings:

I think you have rightly intensified Kezzy's emotion with regard to Lant. You have also covered the weather element in the episode of her night in the scrub. Now other people here have read the book, and I can tell you they like it immensely. This question has been raised, though I bring it to you with some hesitation:- whether Cleve's weaknesses and faults are sufficiently emphasized so that his final betrayal seems right. It did seem so to me, but I think when you begin to read the page proof you might consider the possibility of intensifying a little his inclination which resulted in his final downfall.

I hope there has been no more malaria.

Ever sincerely yours,

Cross Creek
Hawthorn, Route 1
Florida
[December 1932]

Dear Mr. Perkins:

I'm very glad if my touching up of Kezzy's feeling for Lant came out all right——my judgment is none too sound these days and I rather picked phrases out of the air. I seem to do everything that I do, with a perfectly point-less intensity, and the malaria is a case in point. It seems there are several vari-eties, and I chose the most vicious and persistent type, and I have at least two months more to go, of the most absurd quantities of quinine. It does outland-ish things to one's nerves and balance—both physical and mental. I think it's rather a piece of luck that the thing didn't hit a month or two earlier, for the book just did get "under the wire" as it was. I don't see how your type-setter ever made out some of that last copy.

About the matter of Cleve and his treachery. Unless some fresh angle strikes me as I read the proofs, I do not see that anything further can be done. I have indicated throughout his physical laziness and unwillingness to work, which leads to two things——a feeling of being abused, of jealousy, as he sees Lant and the other 'shiners prosper——and the theft of the whiskey from the Poseys. The theft in turn leads to Lem Posey's hasty cutting of Cleve——which gives Cleve his motive for turning him up. In his sullenness, which I think I have made clear throughout, Cleve includes the Saunders and Lant in his betrayal. By this time, he hates everybody. I don't see what more I can do. I could introduce an element of jealousy of Lant as far as Kezzy is concerned, but I should consider such an element undesirable and would not be willing to do it. I do not care to have any undue hidden desire for Lant on Kezzy's part——she deliberately dis-misses such thoughts when she actually marries Cleve——and I do not care to introduce any such element on Lant's part. He goes to Kezzy at the end, as his one harbor of refuge in an increasingly dangerous world. I do not want any possible suggestion that Lant's killing of Cleve could be motivated in any way through Kezzy. It is a spontaneous reaction against the dangers of which he has always been conscious since childhood.

Cleve's ultimate and wholesale betrayal of Lant and the others is a surprise to everyone. It is his final crumbling of character. Unless you have something in mind that does not occur to me, I scarcely even see or understand what is questioned. I shall keep the question in mind, however. If you have any specific suggestions, I should be glad to have them.

Very sincerely,

If Cleve is made too patently a renegade, a potential traitor, you throw suspicion on him too soon, and lose the whole point of Lant's long-expected danger coming from a totally unexpected source. Am I right? Aren't you calling for an out-and-out violation of Hemingway's rule-of-restraint, which impressed me greatly——I can't quote exactly, for DEATH IN THE AFTERNOON is loaned out; it's to the effect that if the writer has a thing clearly in his own mind, that thing comes through into his copy without his needing to make it obvious. The unsaid reads itself between the lines and the reader "gets" it.

. . . .

55. MKR to MEP (TLS, with holograph postscript, 1 p.)

Cross Creek
Hawthorn, Route 1, Fla.
December 18, 1932

Dear Mr. Perkins:

In your last letter you spoke of my watching for something in the page proofs of "South Moon Under". I have received no galley proofs for a week. The last galley I corrected was number 75. This came part way through chapter XXVIII. I think there are about XXXIII chapters, if I remember correctly. I estimate there should be one or possibly two more sets of galley proofs still to come.

I am just wondering if this is all right. If anything has gone astray, I thought I had better be speaking of it.

Sincerely,

Editor's note: In MKR's handwriting at bottom of page: "I sent Miss Wyckoff[1] the manuscript as requested, last week——"

1. Irma Wyckoff, MEP's secretary.

. . . .

56. MEP's secretary to MKR (CC, 1 p.)

Dec. 22, 1932

Dear Mrs. Rawlings:

Your two letters have come in the absence of Mr. Perkins who has been away for a week. I think he will be back sometime this week, and I am sure you will hear from him soon. In the meantime I write to tell you that the balance of your galley proof on "South Moon Under" was sent on the 15th, and the first of the page proof has also gone to you. You have no doubt received them before this.

We received the manuscript back safely. Many thanks.

Sincerely yours,

Sec. to Mr. Perkins

. . . .

57. MEP to MKR (TLS: UF, 2 pp.)

Dec. 23, 1932

Dear Mrs. Rawlings:

I was afraid you had that kind of malaria.- I know about it because a cousin of mine had it. It is too bad.- What makes it worse is that I, who never do such things, went off and did your shooting down in Arkansas on the White River, with Hemingway. Nearly froze to death, too.

I wrote you just before I left, and I felt uneasy about the Cleve matter a good many times while crouching in the snow waiting for ducks. I guess you are right about Cleve. I never felt the need of anything myself, but only those who read the book afterward here, and I think they are wrong about it. Don't do anything unless you feel like it. A very slight emphasis might be good, but I do not really think it is needed.

I hope you will have a good Christmas and holiday season in spite of the miserable malaria.

Ever sincerely yours,

. . . .

58. MKR to MEP (TLS, with holograph insertions, 3 pp.)

Cross Creek
Hawthorn, Route 1, Fla.
December 24, 1932

Dear Mr. Perkins:

I sent you corrected page proofs by parcel post, special, this morning, in which I deleted only the second hyphen in the phrases "south-moon-under" and "south-moon-over."

Now, as I look at the entirely unhyphenated title, I realize that <it> the absence of hyphens is much to be preferred as far as the eye is concerned, and is probably technically correct as well. The phrases are so local in character that I had no precedent to follow in putting them down. It is probable that they have never been in type before.

I am sorry to trouble your proof-reader with my second thoughts, but it is rather an important point. So, if you agree with me about it, would you mind having him check this on the page proofs which should reach you in the same mail as this, asking him to delete both hyphens in the phrases "south moon over" and "south moon under"? The phrases do not occur very often and are pretty well bunched within a few pages; <from> page 100, page 108 and page 109 being the only places I am able to find them on my uncorrected copy of the proofs. "Moon-rise" and "moon-down" should, I am sure, remain hyphenated. I <will> shall watch carefully for the phrases in the remainder of the proofs.

I found a spot, which you may notice, pages 151, 152, 153 where I gave unintentionally something of a pathetic picture of Cleve. I have tried to change this, in accordance with your suggestion, to indicate that he is <illegible excision> putting on something of a show in order to have Piety and Lant insist on his staying with them, so that he will not have to get out and hustle for himself. I hope it is clear that <illegible excision> when he does go to work, it is under the temporary stimulus of the desire to have Kezzy marry him; then, after he gets her, he drops back to his normal reluctance to work.

Very sincerely,

If you have never known anything but bitter cold Florida weather, you should be here for this Christmas with us——it's absolutely stifling hot. It makes a farce of the Christmas egg-nog!

Editor's note: Typed note of galley corrections accompanying letter:

Galley 21 Insert 1
    and stroking the head of Lantry's small mongrel dog.
Galley 22 Insert 2
    The dog whined at the door and went unheeded.

1933

[Cross Creek]
January 1, 1933

Dear Mr. Perkins:

I think we'd all better renounce duck-shooting for the new year——

I came in the other morning from futile hours with my husband at the sport, to find your pitiful story waiting for me. It seems to me that Hemingway drags you the most preposterous distances just to freeze you to the marrow. I remember your telling me that an icy norther had blown every time you went to Key West to fish with him. At least we were warm and comfortable on Orange Lake. Our lake is black with ducks, but they're all "in the clare", and to get a shot you need to sit in the marsh up to your neck, or have more beaters than we have ever been able to assemble. I'm no good at hitting anything on the wing, anyway.

Thank you, yes, I had a grand Christmas. We spent it at the log hunting lodge of our Tampa surgeon friend and were able to do full justice to his very good Burgundy and the Chauvet 1920 for whose vintage he apologized. Vintages become minor matters after more than four years on corn liquor.

What a fiendish conscience you have! You paint the most devastating picture of yourself, crouched in the Arkansas snow, worrying about as yet unborn characters in books you're publishing——. To my ignorance, Arkansas is so God-forsaken a place that of course there's no telling what one would be forced to worry about there. If you could live through Arkansas, the Rawlings needn't hesitate to try to get you to sample Cross Creek some time.

Anyway, many thanks for your sympathy, and with the best of wishes for the year——

Jan. 5, 1933

Dear Mrs. Rawlings:

You have had the last of the page proofs now, and I suppose you will have sent it back before this letter gets to you, and then we shall be able to go ahead.

I judge that you are all over the malaria,- or does it have to recur in diminishing degrees for certain periods. I hope not. I suppose they know how to deal with it pretty well down there.

I really had a grand time out in Arkansas. It is a wonderful looking country. The forests along the banks are entirely untouched. It is melancholy and monotonous, but I like that too. As for pleasure, I have always found that it consisted considerably in relief from pain. Warmth does not amount to anything when you have it all the time, but there is nothing so wonderful as warmth is after you have shivered for three or four hours. It was wonderful when we got back in the evening and were perfectly comfortable again. Besides, the country and the people and everything about it all was exactly like in the days Mark Twain wrote about. But I know I would have a better time down where you are. If you ever feel it indispensable that you should consult me about a novel I shall then have the right to come.

Ever sincerely yours,

. . . .

Jan. 17, 1933

Dear Mrs. Rawlings:

We have just had definite news that that had happened to "South Moon Under" which I had been praying for,- not so much because of the money involved as because of the very great advertising value for a first novel.- The Book of the Month Club[1] has chosen it for their March book, although there is some possibility that it will be coupled with a very slight book by Bernard Shaw,[2] hardly more than a pamphlet, though it is a sort of fable. If it is coupled with this book, the amount you will receive and we, will be somewhat smaller, but at worst it should be $4,000 for you, and $4,000 for us.- I [page or pages of letter missing] book — of which we here are all so fond — of a real chance for success. That is much the best thing about it.

Hoping that you will be as much pleased as we are, I am,

Always sincerely yours,

1. The Book-of-the-Month Club adopted three of MKR's novels: *South Moon Under, The Yearling*, and *Cross Creek*. MEP claimed that to be a record.
2. Bernard Shaw (1856–1913), *Androcles and the Lion* (London: n.p., 1913).

Cross Creek

Hawthorn, Route 1, Fla.

January 19, 1933

Dear Mr. Perkins:

I think, really, you are taking the most beautiful care of me. The Book of the Month business is very nice indeed. As far as I was concerned, I had washed my hands of "South Moon Under". The book doesn't suit me at all, but I had done the best I could for the moment, and I had the feeling that it was your affliction now, not mine. And when you wrote of my consulting with you about a novel, I had the guilty thought that if SCRIBNER's lost every cent they had invested in my first book, you'd never want to see me again, to say nothing of talking about another novel.

A queer thing happens to me whenever I am all through with one piece of work, and I have wondered if it was common to all writers. Before I go to work on something else, I drop into the most terrific despair. It has always been so. I feel that I have no pretensions to artistry, that I have my bally nerve ever to sit down to the typewriter again. Then when the new work takes hold of my mind, nothing exists but the necessity for working it out. I have been in that distressing mid-way state of mind for some weeks——hating everything and everybody in sight——and have been worrying, as I say, about your house taking a loss on the book——so the news that it will not be entirely lost in the scramble is a welcome mental lift.

Of course, make any financial arrangements that are customary and that are acceptable to you.

It goes without saying that you are "indispensable" to my plans for another novel, and if you refuse to visit Cross Creek without my wringing my hands and calling for help, very well, I shall wring my hands and scream for help. By the way, the other book[1] in my mind, which I discussed with you somewhat, will be called, not "Hammock", as I said, (as a title, too hard to dissociate from the Victorian petting implement) but "Hamaca", the Spanish word. Almost all the land in this section of Florida goes back to not too far distant Spanish grants, so the Spanish word for the type of land is perfectly suitable.

The book will be absolutely impossible, horrible, if I don't find out, before I begin, what fault of technique I have that makes me give a certain atmosphere I do not intend to give. It is a style fault of some sort. I am going to have to ask you to read the story Dashiell rejected and Harper's accepted, last summer, "Gal Young Un". (Not yet, for I am not ready to profit by your analysis.) I think that the thing that wants to be the matter with the new book, is the same thing that is the matter with that story. You can find the trouble if anyone can. It has me licked. I shall S.O.S. at the necessary moment.

Many thanks for your note.

Very sincerely,

Don't tell me the profitable angle of the Book of the Month is unimportant. It means I can have a new cypress shingle roof, by God.

1. *Golden Apples.*

. . . .

63. MEP to MKR (TLS: UF, 3 pp.)

Jan. 23, 1933

Dear Mrs. Rawlings:

I am getting a copy of Harper's containing "Gal Young Un". I shall read it right away. I am delighted that you are thinking so hard about the novel you spoke of. I won't say anything though, even in criticism of "Gal Young Un" until you ask me to, because you may find your way to what you want yourself. In fact I am almost sure you will because you have the instinct for it. It is all well enough to criticize details afterward, but I won't do more than that unless you call for it.

I sent a set of the sheets of "South Moon Under" to Miss Baumgartner, of Brandt & Brandt, who had heard of the Book of the Month Club choice, and I daresay you will hear from her. If you do correspond with her, I hope you will tell her that we suggest an equal division from the Book of the Month Club because, although I can personally tell you that you will never receive anything but the rightest kind of dealing from us, you really ought to be informed, seeing it is a matter of business, by somebody outside.

I received a letter from Mr. Powers of the Ocala Banner.[1] I am sure you must know him, and so I told him I would send him the first advance copy I could get of "South Moon Under" and that I would let him know when he could make an announcement of the selection of the Book Club. I am taking it for granted this will seem right to you.

Looking forward to hearing more about "Hamaca" I am,

Ever sincerely yours,

1. Harris Powers, editor of the *Ocala Morning Banner.*

64. MEP to MKR (TS for wire, 1 p.)

JAN. 26, 1933
MRS. MARJORIE K. RAWLINGS
ISLAND GROVE
FLORIDA
LENGTH OF ALLIGATOR ON PAGE 184 QUESTIONED AS TOO GREAT STOP
IS THIRTY AN ERROR FOR THIRTEEN QUESTION CAN CORRECT

. . . .

65. MKR to MEP (wire, 1 p.)

1933 JAN 28 PM 4 38
MAXWELL PERKINS, CARE CHARLES SCRIBNERS SONS
597 FIFTH AVE
THIRTY INTENTIONAL BUT MAKE IT TWENTY TO AVOID QUESTIONING

. . . .

66. MKR to MEP (TLS, 3 pp.)

Cross Creek
Hawthorn, Route 1, Fla.
February 4, 1933

Dear Mr. Perkins:

A very gracious note from Mr. Scribner this morning informs me that the confusion over the English rights of "South Moon Under" has been straightened out. I have felt awfully guilty at making you bear the brunt of the mix-up by holding the house of Scribner in general to your statement to me about subsidiary rights. But you interpreted my contract exactly as I did when I signed it——as I still interpret it——and I just couldn't see any other way out. I have a passion for abstract justice that is my only inheritance from a long line of Scotch preachers, and I'll be damned if I know why I let it bother me, because whenever I find myself between two opposed persons or points of view and make a strenuous effort to be square, I end up by making a grand mess of everything.

I have meant to write you that I thought the catalogue summary of the novel very understanding, and the trade publicity generous and not at all objectionable. You are quite right——the day has long since passed when I'd get any pleasure out of being advertised. Not that I'm in the least bashful——only that it is my conviction that the personality of a writer has nothing to do with the literate product of his mind. And publicity in this case embarrasses me because I am acutely conscious of how far short the book falls of the artistry I am struggling to achieve. It's like being caught half-dressed.

By the way, I wonder if you mind asking the person at Scribner's who has charge of newspaper publicity to see that a mistake in the catalogue copy isn't repeated? It has Lant hunting *crocodiles,* and the Florida papers would simply hoot. I had thought that even the strange-customed natives of Fifth Avenue knew the difference between crocodiles and alligators. It made me feel awfully shaggy to find they didn't. It was established some thirty years ago that the true crocodile does exist in the extreme southern part of Florida, but it is very rare and quite distinct from the alligator common to almost all Florida waterways. It gives as mythical an aspect to "South Moon Under" to say that crocodiles are hunted, as to announce the duck-billed platypus as the Cracker's favorite article of diet.

About my thirty-foot alligator: thirty feet is the size of about the biggest alligator caught on the Ocklawaha of late years. At the time I wrote of it, I asked an expert alligator hunter if one man could get a thirty-footer in a boat alone. After long thought, he decided that if the 'gator was on a bank level with the gunwales of the boat, a strong man could just possibly manage it. But it does strain credulity, doesn't it? As long as it was questioned, I'm glad you changed it. You see, an alligator's tail makes up so much of his length, that the body part of a big one isn't as formidable as the over-all length would indicate. It's the same way with a panther. People see panthers six or seven feet long from nose to tail——but the tail is a good half of the total.

My husband is on the Gulf of Mexico again with his Greek sailor friends, and I have been having a mental rest by prowling about the state. I've never seen it more gorgeous——simply riotous with the flame vine and the bougainvillea. I took in the Bok Tower[1] solely because I happened to be near it——and I was bowled over by the beauty of the thing, and the setting. It's on top of a mountain and possesses, to me, at least, the sort of loveliness that tears you to pieces. When you come next to Florida to see the Rawlings or Hemingway, you mustn't miss it. And then maybe you'd be disappointed——. It struck me so, perhaps, because I was taken totally unawares. I had thought of it as a memorial to Bok's conceit, well publicized on picture post cards.

Please don't trouble to comment on the agent-tangle. It's over and done with and was quite unimportant anyway. I only wanted you to know that I have been sorry to contribute to any discomfort you may have felt in the matter.

Sincerely,

1. A carillon with gardens near Lakeland, Fla., donated by Edward Bok, longtime editor of *Ladies' Home Journal.*

[Cross Creek]
February 6, 1933

Dear Mr. Perkins:

Just a note to thank you for the Book of the Month folder and the advance copy of "South Moon Under". The book looks very well, I think. I like the inside cloth cover particularly.

I'm off again this morning for two or three days' rambling along the east coast. Expect to spend tonight at a rickety old rum-running hotel on the beach at Matanzas, outside St. Augustine. The St. Augustine beach isn't cluttered up with tourists, so when I want ocean and nothing else, I go there.

Many thanks for the nice make-up of the book. Carl Brandt told me last summer, "If Max brings you out, he'll do a swell job." Hope I'll have something better for you to work on next time.

Sincerely,

. . . .

Feb. 8, 1933

Dear Mrs. Rawlings:

Thanks very much for writing me. I have no idea about the geography of Florida, but if you are accustomed to being not so very far from St. Augustine, I would hope to enable Van Wyck Brooks[1] to meet you as he is staying in St. Augustine, and would I know be most sympathetic with you because of his intense interest in all American life and its ways of speech, and all that.

I know the trouble about the English rights was my fault. I had simply got it so firmly into my head that the agents had nothing to do with the book itself that I never thought of confusion arising, and though I sent Miss Baumgarten a set of sheets for her to make use of as agent, I was thinking only of motion picture rights. I am sorry it caused trouble, but it was not so very much, for we did turn over to them all the foreign language rights. The book is now in the hands of Faber & Faber[2] who are very good publishers. If they take it in England, you will have done very well, and of course we do not participate in the commission or profit in any way.- It is only that having so especially recommended it to Curtis Brown, the English agent, we could not very well withdraw it from them.

Everyone who has read "South Moon Under" is greatly taken with it. I sent copies to two old-timers,- Owen Wister and Professor Copeland[3] of Harvard. I want to send one to Willa Cather[4] as soon as I can get her address.

I sent you a poster yesterday. Everything goes well.

Always yours,

1. Van Wyck Brooks, literary critic, MEP's classmate at Harvard University.
2. Faber and Faber, London publisher.
3. Charles Townsend Copeland, MEP's rhetoric professor at Harvard University.
4. Willa Cather (1873–1947), American novelist.

. . . .

69. MEP to MKR (TS for wire, I p.)

FEB. 28, 1933

MRS. MARJORIE K. RAWLINGS

ISLAND GROVE, FLORIDA

FABER AND FABER EXCELLENT ENGLISH PUBLISHERS OFFER FORTY POUNDS ADVANCE TEN PERCENT TO TWO THOUSAND TWELVE AND A HALF TO FIVE FIFTEEN TO TEN THEN TWENTY OPTION NEXT THREE NOVELS WISH TO ACCEPT IMMEDIATELY IF YOU WIRE APPROVAL EXCELLENT REVIEWS IN NEXT SUNDAY TIMES AND TRIBUNE[1]

1. *New York Times* and *New York Herald Tribune.*

. . . .

70. MEP to MKR (TLS: UF, 2 pp.)

March 1, 1933

Dear Mrs. Rawlings:

I am sending you the first two reviews we have had, though I know there are to be others over the week-end. The one that is not obviously from the Times is from the Tribune.

I hope I shall have a telegram from you today about the English proposal, but it has been somewhat changed in your favor, by limiting the option to the next two novels, and by proposing in the case of each of them an advance of two-thirds of the royalties earned on the previous novel in the first six months or forty pounds, whichever is greater. They would also change the royalty on the second and third books to accord with the percentage earned by the previous novel in the first six months. You might therefore get a 15%, or conceivably even higher, royalty from the beginning. It seems to us a very fair contract now. At the start it seemed unreasonable to ask an option on three more novels.

I hope everything goes well with you, and that I shall hear from you soon.

Ever sincerely yours,

. . . .

71. MKR to MEP (TLS, 4 pp.)

Cross Creek
Hawthorn, Route 1, Fla.
March 3, 1933

Dear Mr. Perkins:

Am I the only one who is still mixed up about the English agent for "South Moon Under"? The last I knew, Mr. Scribner had called off his dogs and the whole British business had been put unqualifiedly in the hands of the Brandt people. Now your wire and letter would seem to indicate that the matter is being handled through your office. I have had no answer from Brandt to my wire. I can't make sense out of it to save me. Who is British agent for the book? Have I failed to receive some communication about the matter?

The suggestion for royalties on the present book seems fair and reasonable, but I don't think an option on future books is desirable. I suppose it can be taken as something of a compliment, but I shouldn't think Faber and Faber would especially want it without knowing how the present book will go; and certainly the quality of forthcoming novels is a bit of a gamble. And I think it is very definitely unfair to an author to ask him to commit himself so far ahead.

I am so at sea as to why the English proposal is coming through you, that I don't know what to tell you about going ahead. I hate to hold up anyone's plans, but I don't see what I can do but ask you to straighten me out on the agent business before going any further. I shall write Miss Baumgarten on this mail. If the Brandt people are acting as agents, whatever they advise is acceptable to me.

Many thanks for the reviews. They are more generous than I had expected, but they sadden me. I feel quite cheap, quite the Judas, at having apparently delivered the Cracker into the hands of the Philistines. You may remember my telling you that I dreaded the thought of making the Crackers seem utterly wild and woolly, when they are not. You comforted me by saying that they didn't seem so to you; no more queer, I believe you said, than a Maine woodsman. Well——. The country I hoped to present as stirring and beautiful, emerges under Percy Hutchison's [sic][1] well manicured touch as "repellant".

Good old Piety ends up "a blind and toothless hag". It's his privilege to think of her as a hag but God knows I never even mentioned her teeth! I thought I was getting in quite a nice little touch as to the sheer relativity of social viewpoints when I had Kezzy say of the Moslems, "It makes me faint-hearted to think there's sich people with sich ways," (incidentally, a remark I really heard made) but it seems to have gone quite by without leaving any claw marks. Anyway, the feeling that I have written a wild animal book removes any lingering doubt as to future subject matter. No more Crackers. I have two or three humorous short things in mind, but no more Cracker novels. I gave as accurate a picture as possible of a way of life and a group of people—so that's that.

What did please me in the reviews I've seen, particularly the Phila. Public Ledger (naturally, I suppose, as it was the most enthusiastic) was favorable comment on style, because that tends to relieve my mind somewhat of the fear that my seemingly *outré* material was carrying me along. Any good journalist, able to get the material, could have made a readable book out of the scrub stuff. The "Hamaca" will have to stand on its own feet. I'll write you about it later.

I plan to take possibly a very foolish trip, beginning this coming Wednesday or Thursday. Another woman——an amazingly capable sportswoman——and I are going down the St. John's river by rowboat with outboard motor.[2] We put our boat into the water at its source, which is, ominously enough, Lake Hellenblazes——about on a line with Melbourne on the east coast. I know that the first 100 miles at least lie through an utterly forsaken marsh country dotted with palm islands, and I can't help being a little afraid that false channels may get us into trouble until the river broadens and develops definite banks. But as a Cracker friend says, "No fool, no fun." All this strenuous out-door stuff is new to me since coming to Florida. I've taken to it naturally, but my chief claim to capability in such matters lies only in being game for anything. So wish me luck.

You should receive this Monday morning. If you need to get in touch with me in a hurry about the English business, you can reach me Monday by wire:

Care of Dr. J. C. Vinson

Embassy Apts.

Tampa, Fla.

Tuesday and Wednesday the Island Grove address will reach me by telegram. (Or if you write me Monday, I will get the letter Wednesday morning by the regular Hawthorn route, before I leave.) Then, leaving Thursday, I'll be gone on the river trip for ten days if all goes well.

Do things look any brighter financially in New York? A Tampa friend in with the politicians and such got us word on the Q. T. today to get our fifty cents out of our Ocala bank in a hurry——the inside word is that 26 Florida banks are folding on Monday. It may be just one of those absurd rumors, but it's reasonable enough so that I'm going to take out the amount of our last orange check at least. The world infection is beginning to spread even to our peaceful backwater.

Very sincerely,

1. Percy Hutchinson, "Backwater Life in Florida's 'Scrub,'" *New York Times Book Review* (March 5, 1933): 7.
2. Dessie Vinson Smith. The trip is described by MKR in "Hyacinth Drift," *Scribner's Magazine* 94.3 (September 1933): 169–73, and expanded in *Cross Creek*, chapter 22.

· ·

72. MEP to MKR (TLS: UF, 2 pp.)

March 6, 1933

Dear Mrs. Rawlings:

Everything is right about the contract. It was made through Curtis Brown, the British agents. We had no interest in it at all except on your account, but having started with them, we could not break off on Brandt & Brandt's request very well. Brandt & Brandt have heard the terms of the contract, and think it perfectly fair.- The truth is I think we are the only publisher there now is who does not take an option on the next two novels after the first one. We do not do it because we do not think we ought to publish for a writer who hasn't confidence in us.- We hope very much that you will have, and that we shall be able to continue to publish for you right along.

I know Percy Hutchinson went off the track, but I do not think that is general. The reviews in general (and even his in the main) express the opinion that these are good people who live a good life in a good place.- That is the final feeling that they get from the book. I know that that is what everyone feels who reads it.

That trip down the river sounds mighty dangerous, but also fascinating.

Ever sincerely yours,

P.S. I thought the review by Ernest L. Meyer[1] might please, and would certainly amuse you.

1. Ernest L. Meyer, "*[South Moon Under]*," *Madison Capitol-Times* (March 2, 1933). Meyer later wrote for the *New York Post*.

The Embassy

Tampa, Florida

March 7 [1933]

Dear Mr. Perkins——

A wire today from Miss Baumgarten of Brandt & Brandt straightens out the English rights business on "South Moon Under".

I think Mr. Scribner rode rough-shod over everyone——including me—— and I don't like it at all. But if Brandt & Brandt retired from the field in the matter, of course it makes no practical difference to me.

Go ahead and fix me up the best contract you can.

Rather amusing, for me, to bring out a first novel the day the financial system of the country goes to pot!

Florida seems to be receiving the book very well——of course, sales are something else again.

I'm really awfully sorry Brandts got such a raw deal from Scribner's. I hope you can make it up to them some way. The money involved is probably no great amount, but Mr. Scribner's attitude was needlessly ruthless and I do resent it.

Everything is set for the river-trip I mentioned. Mrs. Vinson & I leave our section Thursday morning, as well equipped as possible. The water hyacinths are bad in the upper reaches of the St. John's, and everyone predicts a rather wild time. Our one gamble is whether we can carry enough gasoline for the first 300 miles——we will probably not be able to get any for that distance.

All the men we've talked to who know anything about Florida rivers (we can't find a living soul who's ever made the trip, altho' U.S. Engineers have surveyed it) envy us the trip and say "you'll undoubtedly get lost——but if your supplies hold out, you'll get back to the main current again. I wish to god I were going with you!" All the women think we're crazy!

If we don't show up again——well, working on "South Moon Under" was fun, wasn't it? That's the only fun there is in anything——before it's been finished.

Sincerely,

Sorry to scrawl so——I never write long-hand, and I'm almost illiterate.

74. MKR to MEP (ALS, 2 pp.)

[Cross Creek]
Thursday morning
[March 9, 1933]

Dear Mr. Perkins:——

Please don't ever again suggest such a thing as my not having complete confidence in you and the Scribner house. I shall feel very badly if my footstampings about Brandt and the English business have made you think I've lost my perspective as to the value to me of Scribner support. *Believe me*——I appreciate it.

I'm counting on you personally to see me through in the next novel. It's going to be very difficult going——and I've been conscious from my earliest contact with you, of a mental sympathy and understanding that I should feel quite lost to do without.

Thanks for the reviews. The column from the Wisconsin chap did amuse me. There was something very tender and touching about it, wasn't there?

Off for the river——may be unable to go to the extreme source for water hyacinths are bad.

. . . .

75. MEP to MKR (TLS: UF, 2 pp.)

March 9, 1933

Dear Mrs. Rawlings:

I want to write you personally about this Brandt matter, as myself alone, and not as an editor or officer of Scribner's; and I want you to believe me. I cannot allow blame to fall upon the *house* or anyone in it but myself since what happened was wholly my fault. The house merely followed the regular procedure: the contract gave us the right to act for you and so the book was sent to the best English agent, Curtis Brown, and he submitted it to Faber & Faber, very good publishers. The house did not know that I had told you anything about English rights,- which are of no interest to us except that we wish to serve the interest of an author for whom we publish. It did happen though, that when Mr. Brown was over here Mr. Scribner told him that "South Moon" was a very fine book, so that he—knowing we were not financially interested in the English outcome—was especially interested in the book.

When Mr. Scribner heard of the confusion then, the book had been submitted to Faber & Faber by Curtis Brown. It had not been submitted to anyone by Brandt & Brandt, though it was on the way to Longmans Green.[1] How would we recall it? How could we call upon Curtis Brown to do it? It was a bad situation, but what could we do? Curtis Brown would then have been in a much more embarrassing position than Brandt was in.- He was not much involved,- and we had no valid excuse to offer Curtis Brown. Besides, it seemed to us that you would be vastly better off with Faber & Faber than with Longmans Green.

Anyhow, the whole trouble came from me alone, and I'm mighty sorry for it. You spoke to me about Brandt and the desirability of an agent when you were in New York, and I said I thought that you would need an agent on account of all the trouble of serial and movie-rights, and that Brandt was a good agent. From then on I thought of them as acting for those rights, and as having nothing to do with book rights,- which as publishing practice goes was not unnatural. But I'm not so interested now in defending myself. <I am certainly the one at fault.> What I am concerned about is that you should get so totally wrong an impression of Mr. Scribner who is quixotically, almost, fair and true and considerate.- You would know it if you saw him. Please do believe me. I never meant anything more.

I do hope you'll come safely out of that trip. I wish you'd let me know.

Always sincerely yours,

1. London publisher.

. . . .

77. MKR to MEP (from *Selected Letters of Marjorie Kinnan Rawlings,* ed. Gordon E. Bigelow and Laura V. Monti [Gainesville: University of Florida Press, 1983], 63; original not seen)

Cross Creek
[March 18, 1933]

Dear Abbé:

Now what can I say to you? When you put me in such a corner? You say, in implication, "You trust me, don't you?" And I say, "Yes, Abbé, I have publicly professed my faith." And you say, "Very well, then, you must be entirely dutiful and think as I tell you to think."

Ordinarily I love a good argument for its own sake—and I think a pair of lawyers could work up a lively one over the interpretation of that contract. But I intended you to draw it up to suit yourself in the first place—so if you've decided to back up Mr. Scribner (when he wouldn't back you up) in his insistence that the English rights always were—or at any rate always should have been—in Scribner's hands—I sha'n't quarrel about it ever again. At the risk of being vulgar, I tell you of an incident that illustrates my point of view about not calling Mr. Scribner names. One of our good friends is the Cracker constable of a nearby village.[1] He had taken both my husband and me in hand from the beginning, trying to make hunters and fishermen of us. I often go off alone with him for a day's sport. One of his minor vices is a mania for attempting to stroke a woman's legs. A woman like myself is as safe with him as with a ten-year-old-boy—as a matter of fact, this tendency is, I believe more mischievous than evil—the last woman he tried it on was a woman evangelist, sitting next to him in church, bowed in prayer—so that it annoyed, rather than disturbed me. I had cracked his knuckles with the butt of a revolver and this had pleased, rather than dissuaded him. Finally I had it out with him when fishing one day. I told him that it interfered with our honest sport and spoiled all my pleasure in being with him; that if he ever put his hand on me again, I should never fish or hunt with him from that day on. He knew I meant it.

"Well," he conceded, "you can keep me from pettin' them purty legs—but you can't keep me from wantin' to."

But really—if you knew how little the English business means to me, or bothers me——. I spoke my piece about it—the Brandt people have been very decent and have made no complaint—and as far as I'm concerned, that's the end of it. It doesn't interfere with my conviction that you are my friend and my support in time of trouble, and that the house of Scribner is quite the noblest and most dignified with which a (comparatively) young author could hope to be associated. I'm an old woman of 36, you know, and after having been buffeted a bit by life and circumstance and what-not (which accounts for my changed character and physique from my co-ed days), I'm deeply appreciative of kindness and goodness in any form.

Which reminds me of the river trip, from which Mrs. Vinson and I returned yesterday. It was gorgeous. Two impressions stay with me. One is of the just-mentioned kindness and goodness of simple people. Somehow or other, I understand such people. I also understand lunatics. The people in between are quite beyond me. Water is, after all, an unfamiliar element, yet our only life, our only safety, lay in continued progress down a flowing stream. The poor fishermen we met along the way were helpful and concerned as none of my sophisticated friends have ever been. The first one we encountered, who gave us channel information, begged us to send him a card when we reached home and civilization. He said, "I don't want to keep on worryin' about you." And when we reached Lake George, we found that news of our passage had preceded us. The fishermen had sent word down the river to watch for us, to see if we got through all right . . .

Our correspondence is frightfully one-sided. I think sometimes—usually at the end of a letter, like this, when it's too late to do anything about it without going to a lot of trouble—that the ramblings of writers about themselves to you must be very wearisome. You know a great deal about me, about my way of life, and so forth, and I know nothing at all about you, except that you have a magnificently lucid mind that contrives also to be sympathetic.

Very sincerely,

P.S. On my last day up the river a great deal about "Hamaca" suddenly straightened itself out in my mind. I am desperately afraid of several things—one, that the first part of the book may be too raw and disgusting—and I am so weary of the Faulkner[2] school of filth that I should almost prefer to be a Harold Bell Wright,[3] than to contribute to it. Yet my character and my plot require some things that in themselves are revolting—they are all part of the horror of an alien background, from which my man finally emerges—rather, with which he finally identifies himself.

Of course, I shouldn't think of anything so selfish as insisting that you come to Florida for the sole purpose of talking about an unwritten book, when we are both perfectly literate and able to work things out on paper. When I said that I should like you to come, I only wanted to make very sure that you understood the certainty of your welcome if your affairs should bring you near us. Until you crouched in the snow with Hemingway, I had felt a little uneasily that our life here might strike you as—I don't know—random—messy—a little shabby. But once I realized you were entirely adaptable, I felt you would enjoy it, as widely varying persons seem to have done. So if you should plan to come south this spring any time after the next two weeks—my husband will then be home from the Gulf—please stop off with us for a week at least. I'll show you the scrub and a couple of lovely rivers.

If you're not coming, I'll take up the book in detail later. I plan several months of research, just to have my period firmly fixed. Then I feel I must get away during the worst of the summer, as another dose of malaria would be too devastating.

In all seriousness, all is forgiven and forgotten about the Brandt mix-up—I understand your viewpoint and quite harmlessly disagree with it. I'll be glad to assign "Hamaca" to you right now, if you want it.

P.S. Use your engraved stationery some time when you're not solemnly taking me to task! It's not fair to use your dressiest stuff for purposes of chastisement!

1. Fred Tompkins, whom MKR wrote about in the satiric "Benny and the Bird Dogs," *Scribner's Magazine* 94.4 (October 1933): 193–200, and who was a source for much of the Cracker material she used in her stories.
2. William Faulkner (1897–1962), who MKR felt "makes you sick at your stomach" (*Selected Letters of Marjorie Kinnan Rawlings,* 164).
3. Harold Bell Wright (1872–1944), American novelist, who emphasized moral earnestness.

78. MKR to MEP (TLS, I p.)

> Cross Creek
> Sunday
> [March 19, 1933]

Dear Mr. Perkins:

I wrote you yesterday——out of pure high spirits, because I came in from the river trip really happy for the first time in months——a very flippant letter in answer to your awfully decent and earnest one. It just came over me that the matter in question is one you don't care to jest about.

I can only plead that, with Stevenson——is it in *Virginibus Puerisque* or some of the *Letters?*——"Down life's great cathedral aisle" (that's not quite accurate)[1]

> "I love to scamper, love to race;
> To swing by my irreverent tail
> All over the most sacred place."

And if I've treated the thing so lightly as to hurt you——please forgive me. I'm probably being exactly like Mr. Scribner——seemingly bland and ruthless, but with the most honorable intentions!

1. Robert Louis Stevenson, *Virginibus Puerisque and Other Papers* (1881).

. . . .

79. MEP to MKR (TLS: UF, I p.)

> March 21, 1933

Dear Mrs. Rawlings:

I only wanted to get the matter right. I used my own note paper because I wanted to write ex-officio. I guess you understood that. I certainly enjoyed your long letter, and I do hope you will do that article.

I should love to come down there but I see no prospect of it. Like everyone else, I am all knotted up in problems, but I am led to hope from what you say of planning to leave in the summer, that you will be up this way, and if you are, please keep enough time open so that we can have lunch. I would greatly like to have you meet Charles Scribner, and then you'd see.

> Always yours,

[Cross Creek]

[late March 1933]

Dear Mr. Perkins:

I thought possibly you might like to know what sort of reader reaction I'm getting on South Moon Under——here are some letters that for obvious reasons interest me particularly. I was delighted with the one from the literary lumberman——the Wilson Cypress Co. president——for it was like having the river itself rise and approve of the book. I was only dimly aware that the company was still in existence. I intend to make the man's acquaintance and take him up on his offer to visit the Dixie County logging camps. I guess it's sure-enough wild country up there.

What's the news on the book, from your end? It's a rather queer feeling to be sitting here in the swamp and having the merest dribbles of information come in. From personal sources I hear, here and there, of its selling. Somebody is wild about it and somebody else writes to the Tampa Tribune asking if they don't consider it obscene in spots.

I had an amusing reaction from the family[1] in the scrub where I stay off and on. I gave them a copy, suitably and gratefully inscribed, and the man of the family says "You done a damn good job, for a Yankee." He is being tormented by friends and relatives who want to borrow the book, and he's being very choosy in the loaning. He refuses point blank to lend it to his uncle to take home, because he's afraid his uncle's wife would tear up the book or burn it. I asked, astonished, why she might do such a thing. He said, "Well, she's one o' them Christian-hearted sons o' bitches, and peculiar as Hell, to boot. You got right smart o' cussin' in the book, and she might be scairt her boy Lester'd learn to cuss by it. Now Lester kin out-cuss the book right now——but his Mammy don't know it."

By the way, don't be puzzled when your sales sheets show two or three copies disposed of in Ocala. It's not a boycott. The whole town is standing in line to read the copy donated to the public library, and the copy in the circulating library. Everyone tells me with great pride, "I've got my name on the list to read your book. I can hardly wait." I say politely, "I do hope you'll enjoy it," and I'm bursting, like Cabell[2] with his letter answers, to say something such as, "Do you think I'm a damn orchid, that I can live on air?"

What is one supposed to do about answering letters, anyway? I have a whole swarm about Jacob's Ladder that I never answered because it seems so futile. I tried to keep up for a while and found it almost impossible to hit a cordial but distant medium. I either sounded cold and heard later I was considered high-hat——or sounded too big-hearted and had the correspondents on my neck. You just can't be bothered with only men in Boston who send you candy. Do you think it matters in the least if you don't answer mail at all? Of course several of those I'm sending you today I shall very much want to answer, because the contact appeals to me. So send me back this batch, please.

Very sincerely,

1. The Fiddias.
2. James Branch Cabell (1879–1958), American novelist, who later was instrumental in bringing together MKR and Ellen Glasgow.

· ·

81. MEP to MKR (TLS: UF, 2 pp.)

April 1, 1933

Dear Mrs. Rawlings:

I very much enjoyed the letters you sent, but I am sending them back quickly so that none will be lost by any chance. Do you think we could quote what you tell about in your letter, in literary notes? I would not do it without permission because the notes might get printed in Florida, and that might offend the people. These quotations though, would be very effective.

Are you doing the article on the river trip?[1] I am sure it would be very good.

One hates to think of sales nowadays. Everything was bad enough anyway, and then the bank holiday simply put a stop to the publishing business for a couple of weeks. Now there is a little more life in it, and eternal hope is fixed upon the fall. The actual royalty sale to date is a little bit short of 5,000.

Please do go on with the river article.

Ever sincerely yours,

1. "Hyacinth Drift."

· ·

82. MKR to MEP (TLS, 3 pp.)

Cross Creek
Hawthorn, Route 1, Fla.
[April 1933]

Dear Mr. Perkins:

I've had to stop and think just what it was I wrote you that sounded quotable for publicity. It must have been what my friend of the scrub said——"You done a damn good job, for a Yankee", and his statement as to why he wouldn't lend the book to his uncle, describing his aunt as "one of them Christian-hearted sons of bitches", etc. Is that what you mean?

Now——. If what you want is to be able to quote the reaction of the scrub inhabitants, the prototypes of the characters in the book, I'm frightfully sorry, but it just can't be done. On the other hand, if you want to use the remarks as coming from Florida Crackers in some other section, that would be perfectly all right.

You have been awfully careful from the beginning in taking care of me from the local angle, and I appreciate it a lot. I scarcely need to go into detail about the present situation, because I'm sure you understand pretty well, but I'll be briefly specific. It's not a question, as it was in the "Cracker Chidlings", of hurting people's feelings by writing them up, and of bothering the Chamber of Commerce type of person as well by bringing to public notice a class of natives considered by many no special asset to the state. It would be a matter of actually getting a definite family in trouble with the law by identifying them too publicly with my book-characters. I have been nervous about that part of it from the beginning. As you know, as my friends here and elsewhere know, I have spent a good deal of time with a family[1] in the scrub whose living is made by moonshining. The young man also hunts as he pleases, very much as Lant does in the book. My character of Piety in her latter years is drawn very closely from life, from the mother of this family. Lant is a composite portrait, but many of the small details of his life are those of the life of my scrub friend. He understood all this perfectly, knew I was writing the book, that I was using all the things he told me. I checked over a great mass of detail with him, from the manuscript. He has recognized in the book the parts that are photographic—— told a mutual friend "It's a good thing she didn't tell no more'n she did about my huntin'——she'd of had the game warden on my neck, shore." He seemed rather indifferent to danger about the illicit distilling, I think because he feels so safe about the present location of his still. So far, so good.

You keyed your publicity about the book very nicely, and there has been no public mention anywhere that I have seen of my having done any more than work from life in a general way. Now——. There are so few families in the scrub, that if any public mention is made of my connection with any one of them, people hereabouts will go even beyond the truth and it would be quite conceivable that "one of them Christian-hearted sons of bitches" would raise a great row about moonshining in Marion County being so common and public that a Yankee writer could make a book about it. You are no doubt familiar with the depths of depravity in the reforming type of mind. Of course, the new political slant on liquor makes interference improbable, but I just couldn't run the risk of getting my friends in trouble to make a Roman holiday.

Would it answer your purpose to use the quotations as coming from Cracker friends of mine in Gulf Hammock? It would all sound alike to anyone in the north, and if the quotation were picked up here in Florida, it would be harmless, since Gulf Hammock is on the opposite side of the state. But they *can't* [underlined twice] be quoted as coming out of the scrub itself. If you use them, I'll have to ask you to let me see the notes before they are released, just to make sure they're all right from my point of view.

Very sincerely,

1. The Fiddias.

· ·

83. MEP to MKR (TLS: UF, 2 pp.)

April 10, 1933

Dear Mrs. Rawlings:

Thanks very much for your letter. I suppose it would be safer not to quote any of those people. It would be hard to do it without running the risk of some harm coming from it.

We have sold over 6,000 now, but the book business was never anything like so bad. You were listed as the third best seller yesterday in the New York Tribune.

I am mighty curious to know how the article is coming along, but we shall just wait and see. I hope it won't take you away from the novel for too long.

Always sincerely yours,

P.S. Are you going to be up here in May? If you are to be, you will find it difficult to escape going to a big dinner given by "the friends of the Princeton library". We are mixed up in this dinner for various reasons, and we shall plead with you to sit at our table. Would you do it? If your husband is about, we should want him too.- I believe that you hate public dinners as profoundly as I do, and will evade this one if you can. I cannot, and I should not try to if you were to be there. It really will be better than most dinners. Willa Cather, for instance, will be there. I just thought you might be in this neighborhood then, and if so might come.

84. MKR to MEP (TLS, 1 p.)

Cross Creek
Hawthorn, Route 1, Fla.
April 10, 1933

Dear Mr. Perkins:

Can you tell me when I may expect my Book-of-the-Month-Club check? I
don't imagine it is subject to the six-months accounting of regular royalties.
Our orange year was bad, as you can imagine, and I have to know when I can
expect my next considerable amount of money. If anything is going to hold
that money up, I shall have to arrange to sell some securities, or borrow on
them, and with the market so low it's a bad time to do that, and I don't want to
if it isn't going to be necessary. Thanks a lot.

Very sincerely,

Editor's note: At bottom of letter in MEP's hand: "Sending cheque for thousand
will send balance if needed. MP"

. . . .

85. MEP to MKR (TS for wire, 1 p.)

APRIL 12, 1933
MRS. MARJORIE RAWLINGS
ISLAND GROVE, FLORIDA
SENDING CHECK FOR THOUSAND WILL SEND BALANCE IF NEEDED

. . . .

86. MEP to MKR (TLS: UF, 1 p.)

April 12, 1933

Dear Mrs. Rawlings:

Immediately on getting your letter I had this check drawn and am sending
it as quickly as I can. If it is not enough, we can send you the remainder. Be sure
to tell me if you want more. The money belongs to you but payments are so
slow on everything that we do try to go easy.

Always yours,

Cross Creek
Hawthorn, Route 1, Fla.
April 15, 1933

Dear Mr. Perkins:

Many thanks for the thousand-dollar reinforcements. But it is more than a matter of immediate tiding over in a small way——rather more a matter of planning six months to a year ahead. I know you wouldn't care to be embarrassed with private details, but there are such things as long over-due notes, a four-year-old car falling to pieces, and so forth, that have been waiting for some such thing as a good orange year or such an accidental quick income as the Book of the Month business represents.

Now, you didn't answer my question as to when the Book of the Month money is due me. I don't know whether they make a cash settlement with a publisher within a couple of months, or whether their payments come in slowly and the publisher "gets his" as the Book of the Month people "get theirs." Is a writer supposed to be kept in a mystical ignorance of all financial dealings, like a child waiting for Santa Claus? I suppose it is all the more fun when the checks do come in! But I should like to know my exact status on that Book of the Month deal. By the 56,000 copies figure I should imagine the Book of the Month sale itself must have been about 50,000 instead of the minimum 30,000 to 40,000 you estimated when the deal first came off. What will be the total figure, and the total cash settlement?

If the Book of the Month money is in, I do need and want it. If it is not, or is only in, in part, I want to know, as I said, when it will be in and how much it will amount to. Then I can plan accordingly. If I know that I can count on it on a certain date, I'll go ahead and dispose of the reserve capital I've hung on to through these lean times, or borrow on it, knowing that I'm perfectly safe in doing so. I can make better cash deals right now in clearing up old obligations than perhaps ever again.

If that money is not in, I do not want Scribner's to advance it as a favor—— that wouldn't be fair to the house. But I must know dates and figures.

Very sincerely,

P.S. No, I don't expect to be in New York in May, for which, after your threats about the dinner, I can't say I'm sorry. I can well imagine that, as you say, the dinner will be better than most such, but even so, can you imagine anything more revolting than a large room crawling with authors!

April 17, 1933

Dear Mrs. Rawlings:

The Book of the Month Club did pay us, and I am sending you now the remainder. They pay a flat sum, $8,000. When I wrote you about it I could not be positive at the moment about their having paid, and was trying to be cautious because I had once paid an author in a similar case about two years ago.- And even now we have not ourselves yet been paid anything.

If you find difficulty even now in working out your problem, the probability is that we shall be perfectly willing to pay you what has been earned by the regular trade book sale on the date when the first report is due,- six months after the date of publication. Our practice always was to pay in that way, and not to take advantage of the four months' latitude the contract gives; but in this depression with our own collections so difficult and so often delayed, we have been taking advantage of that clause.- But the Book of the Month has always paid promptly.

I hope you will soon be sending the article about the river trip.

I did not suppose the dinner would appeal to you, but I wish you were coming, nevertheless. I know you would have enjoyed talking to Tom Wolfe.

Ever sincerely yours,

. . . .

April 18, 1933

Dear Mrs. Rawlings:

I am sending you herewith a copy of a letter we have just received with regard to the Prix Femina Americain.[1] I should rather dislike to tell you of it if I thought you were much affected by such things as prizes because we have no idea what the outcome of the competition is likely to be, but you must decide whether you wish to defer the French translation as this letter shows would be necessary. My opinion would be in favor of doing it.

At any rate I am writing Brandt & Brandt about the matter so that they may be informed even before they hear from you; and we are sending the copies they ask for.

Always yours,

1. Prix Femina Americain, a fiction prize, usually for novels.

Cross Creek
Hawthorn, Route 1, Fla.
April 20, 1933

Dear Mr. Perkins:

Many thanks for the check. It will be put promptly to work to get a few annoyances off my mind. The chances are that I shall be all right now. We'll wait and see what September brings.

How very relative this "best-seller" business is! The term really shouldn't be used, for it connotes things that simply aren't so! We should all probably have done very nicely on "South Moon Under" if we'd hit a better period with it. It may still survive, but I've learned never to count on anything, or even to bother very much. It is possibly a type of book that will continue to sell along with some steadiness, but I do think the tendency now is to buy the book that is being talked of for the moment, and to pass up possibly the better books that were missed a year or two before. For that reason, I was glad to see in an advertisement for the retail booksellers that either you or Mr. Hart sent me, that you're going to go ahead with your advertising on the book. I'm sure a capitalization on recent favorable publicity will pay. Incidentally, interfering in what is really none of my business, I think you would find that it would pay to place some very small ads in the sporting magazines mentioning the hunting and wild life angle of the book. Most of my response on the book has been from men.

About the *Prix Femina Americain* submission: of course, the thing to do is to hold off on any other French publication possibilities——which have not as yet been mentioned. Before anybody puts over another fast one, let me say in time to you, in case at any time you should have anything to say about French rights, that I should want the privilege of correcting the translation myself. I am no longer capable of making the translation itself, for some thirteen years of disuse have dissipated my vocabulary, but I still have the "feel" of the French language and an ear for its rhythms. I was so deep in the language at the end of college that I thought in French a good deal of the time, and was doing French verses——so you see I should want a hand in any translation.

However, I shouldn't think the *Prix Femina* people would consider my book very seriously, for two reasons. The dialect speech they would feel, I should imagine, a deterrent to French translation. And then the book is so peculiarly *locally* American, set in so circumscribed a space and sphere, that I shouldn't think they'd feel justified in taking it for their purpose, even if they like it otherwise. I certainly shan't lose any sleep over the <illegible excision> matter.

Don't ever worry about me and the prize business, or any of that sort of thing. Like the best-selling, it's too utterly relative. To have a book picked as the best of the month, or of the year, or anything like that, over a group of very dreadful books, is surely a dubious honor! All that concerns me is to come as close as my limitations allow, to re-creating the thing that stirs me.

This has turned into another one of those fearfully miscellaneous letters I seem to dote on writing you, so I might as well go on, and give you my tentative plans. It has been my increasing conviction that I must go to England this summer for the express purpose of knowing what the English countryside looks like, in relation to my young Englishman exiled in Florida. When the whole key to the book lies in his revulsion <to> against a physical background, it would be perfectly absurd not to know, with my own eyes, the background he had come from——the thing against which he contrasts the new and, to him, disagreeable country. I should scarcely use it at all, but having the picture in my own mind would represent just the difference between bluff and honesty. This won't be at all the vacation I wanted——I had wanted so much to take a grand cruise on the new Grace Liner[1] from Havana, Cuba to Seattle, Washington, to see my only close relative, my brother,[2] who thinks, and says, shamelessly and without apology, that I'm the one perfect woman in the world (the only living human being to think so), and I could have taken the whole round trip for the price of English passage alone. So do bolster me up in my decision by agreeing with me that I'm doing the wise thing. I plan to go to England in mid- or late July. I'll have my local research done before I go, then I can get right into my writing when I come back in the fall.[3]

Very Sincerely,

1. Grace Steamship Line.
2. Arthur H. Kinnan.
3. On *Golden Apples*.

· ·

91. MEP to MKR (TLS: UF, 3 pp.)

April 27, 1933

Dear Mrs. Rawlings:

I had to go down to Washington and was away several days and found your letter on returning. You are right about sales,- best sellers are very far from being what they once were. But we shall keep "South Moon Under" to the front in every way through the season, in so far as it can be done in these days, not only for its own sake, but also because the extent of its success will have a bearing on your next novel too, because it will tend to give you a public. That was one of the reasons why we regarded the Book of the Month Club adoption as important, and it was because I thought we could get that for "South Moon Under" by the way, that I rather hurried you. I could not give you the reason at the time because the odds are always so much against an adoption.

I do not know what to guess about the Prix Femina. I thought of the disadvantages you spoke of, but one could think of them almost as advantages. But it is best not to think about the outcome at all in those matters.

I hope you have not given up that article on the river trip. I am sure it would be a fine one. People would be so glad to read such a thing as that in place of these dreadful economic problems. I do think you are right about going to England, and what is more, you will enjoy it immensely because it is a wonderfully restful place. You feel that everything is all right the moment you get there,- partly because you are entirely surrounded by people of the same race. You feel much more at home there than in New York.

Ever sincerely yours,

. . . .

92. MEP to MKR (TLS: UF, 1 p.)

May 18, 1933

Dear Mrs. Rawlings:

I guess Dashiell will have written you about the article.- It is true that it is rather uneventful, but it has a great deal of quality and a peaceful charm, and we thought it would go very well as a Life in the United States article.

If you are going to England will that mean that you will be hereabouts before very long? I hope it may.

Ever sincerely yours,

. . . .

93. MKR to MEP (TLS, 2 pp.)

Cross Creek
Hawthorn, Route 1, Fla.
May 21, 1933

Dear Mr. Perkins:

I'm glad you felt that the river article had enough of value to redeem it from dullness. I couldn't judge of that, and I was very mistrustful.

I plan now to spend about all of August and the first week or two of September in England. That will put me in New York for a few days' shopping the last week in July or the first week in August. Will you be there then? I should hate to pass near your habitat and not see you.

I am limiting myself to the several English shires from which I expect, unless they are very different from my conception, to choose a locale for my young Englishman of "Hamaca". These are Lancaster (which I expect to reject), Sussex, Devon and Somerset. I should like to have you help me decide on the exact social class that fits my requirements, and that will be consistent with a particular locale. I don't want an out-and-out aristocrat. Upper middle class—rather scholarly *landed* people. They won't come into the story at all, but I want to be accurate.

I'm having better luck than I ever dared hope for in tracking down the remnants of the English colonists of the period I'm using——the hey-day of the orange industry from 1880 to <1800> 1895, the year of the Big Freeze, and then five years more after that, bringing it to 1900. I've found some adorable old Englishmen and Englishwomen in varying stages of prosperity and poverty. They're being most cooperative. I'm unearthing all kinds of interesting stuff, including a 50-year-old scandal about the former Duke of Sutherland, whose heirs still own land on the Florida Gulf coast. One old lady (a solitary cup-bearer for the Church of England in the most desolate small Florida village you ever laid eyes on) is sending to England for some diaries of the period for me, and is making a contact for me (if her family proves as agreeable as she) with two sisters who lived in Florida at that time and went back to Lancaster after the disastrous freeze.

I'm going to Jacksonville tomorrow to keep a date with an Englishman who came to the Riverside colony on the Ocklawaha in the scrub that I mentioned in "South Moon Under". Next week I'm going to Miami and intermediate points where I've located some very promising English folk. I don't think I'll have any trouble in getting together all I need for my setting, from that angle.

Very sincerely,

. . . .

94. MEP to MKR (TLS: UF, 2 pp.)

May 25, 1933

Dear Mrs. Rawlings:

I think I am sure to be here the last week in July and the first in August. I might get a vacation later. The trouble is with Tom Wolfe. I cannot tell when, or whether, he will come through with his magnificent but stupendous manuscript, and if it is to come this summer, I cannot go away until it does. I waited all last summer in vain, and the same thing may happen this time. I hope you will see though what he is writing in the magazine,- there have been two stories (so-called),- "Train in [and] the City" and "Death the Proud Brother" and there is to be another, "No Door" in the next issue.[1]

I think everything you say about your novel sounds as if it would be very fine. I won't be hurrying you with it, either. The reason I was pressing at the end with "South Moon Under" was that I thought we could get a Month Club adoption, but I could not tell you that in advance, of course. We did get that, but then we had the bad luck to come out when we did. We could not have found a worse moment in a century. But it is selling along.

Ever sincerely yours,

1. Thomas Wolfe, "The Train and the City," *Scribner's Magazine* 93.5 (May 1933): 288–94; "Death the Proud Brother," *Scribner's Magazine* 93.6 (June 1933): 332–38, 378–88; "No Door," *Scribner's Magazine* 94.1 (July 1933): 7–12, 46–56.

. . . .

95. MEP to MKR (TLS: UF, 1 p.)

June 1, 1933

Dear Mrs. Rawlings:

We should like to see the work of Mr. Hawkins.[1] Could you send us some of his material? I am afraid we could not make use of them in connection with "South Moon Under", but we might make use of them later on, and I should be most interested to see the picture of the boy Lant.

When you come on, I do wish to talk to you about another possible plan for you in connection with writing, though I suppose you would not be able to do much about it until after the next novel is done.

Ever sincerely yours,

1. Edward Meredith Hawkins, an artist, sent sample illustrations of *South Moon Under* to MEP on June 8, 1933.

. . . .

96. MKR to MEP (TLS, 2 pp.)

Hawthorn, Route 1, Fla.
June 7, 1933

Dear Mr. Perkins:

I've sent to Mr. Hawkins for some of the "South Moon Under" illustrations, and will send them on to you. Occasional details are not precisely accurate——

in the still picture, for instance, the cooker should be rectangular—but the look of the figures, the characterization and most particularly the backgrounds——scrub, hammock, river——I consider very good.

The only possible plan I can conceive of your having for me that answers the rather strange description of being "in connection with" writing, would be that you'd like to have me do a text-book for your educational department on "The Principle and Practice of Moonshine Liquor."

The difficulties you're having with Wolfe make me think I've been quite a model author. I only worried you crouched in the snow with Hemingway—certainly I never cost you a whole vacation.

Yes, I've been following the Wolfe stories. It was rather startling to have the first one in the same issue of the magazine with the Hemingway story——you couldn't get a wider variance in technique if you culled over the whole field of American writers. I read the <Wolfe> Hemingway story[1] first and then turned immediately to the Wolfe story——and I was totally unable to read the Wolfe. Two days later I picked it up again, and read and enjoyed it. I didn't like "The Train and the City" nearly so well as "Death the Proud Brother", however. When Wolfe hits it right with his very gorgeous style, the effect is tremendously satisfying emotionally, like a symphony at its best. When he beats his chest and tears his hair and pounds on the drums too lavishly, as I thought he did in the first story, you get more the effect of an awfully enthusiastic German band, and you rather long to empty pitchers of water from the third story, to shut up the tumult. I imagine he's the sort of person who has to get his effects that way or not at all, and that there's no such thing as safely toning him down.

Hemingway, damn his soul, makes everything he writes terrifically exciting (and incidentally makes all us second-raters seem positively adolescent) by the seemingly simple expedient of the iceberg principle——three-fourths of the substance under the surface. He comes closer that way to retaining the magic of the original, unexpressed idea or emotion, which is always more stirring than any words. But just try and do it!

Very sincerely,

I was amused the other day to come across a most domestic photograph of Hemingway and his progeny, in "Vogue"[2] and someone had scrawled across it, "What do you suppose is the opium of the literati?"

1. Ernest Hemingway, "Give Us a Prescription, Doctor," *Scribner's Magazine* 93.5 (May 1933): 272–78.
2. *Vogue* magazine.

June 10, 1933

Dear Mrs. Rawlings:

Now I shall have to tell you what it was in connection with writing.- I was simply going to suggest that you do a book about a child in the scrub, which would be designed for what we have to call younger readers. You remember your husband spoke of how excellent parts of "South Moon Under" were for boys. It was true. If you wrote about a child's life, either a girl or a boy, or both, it would certainly be a fine publication, and such books have a way of out-doing even the most successful novels in the long run, though they do not sell many in a given season except now and then. Such a book would require very little plot.- Its interest would simply be that of character and that of the peculiar & adventurous life. You may have thought of doing this yourself. You ought not to let it interfere with the novel, anyhow, but when one plans a thing of that kind, the mind works on it, even if unconsciously. What brought the idea back to me was your speaking of Mr. Hawkins' illustrations. A child's book would require illustrations, and I am very curious to see what his are like. He writes me they have been sent.

The next story by Tom Wolfe is the best one of all, called "No Door" in the next number.

Hemingway is one of the most domestic people in the world, with an extraordinarily domestic wife, though very intelligent, and three magnificent sons.[1]

Ever sincerely yours,

1. Hemingway's wife: Pauline Pfeiffer; sons: John, Patrick, and Gregory.

. . . .

Cross Creek
Hawthorn, Route 1, Fla.
June 10, 1933

Dear Mr. Perkins:

I am both surprised and pleased to find that Curtis Brown, Ltd. have been watching my work with interest and admiration for some time and are wondering if now is the moment at which an agent could be useful to me.

I thought Curtis Brown and his playmates were supposed to be handling the English contract for "South Moon Under". Perhaps this letter just concerns itself with magazine stuff, but in any case I have been wondering for some time where that English contract was. I should really write to Curtis Brown, but if I'm dawning on their horizon for the first time, as this letter would seem to indicate, and as the absence of my name from their list of American authors they've dealt with recently would indicate, I wouldn't get anywhere.

So I'm asking you about it—you're the only person who ever sounds coherent. If it weren't for you, I'd wish to Heaven I'd turned the damn book over to Brandt at the very beginning. These mixed-up business details are terribly annoying. I hope "Hamaca" is a complete mess, and then I'll be relieved of any compulsion ever to write another word.

Editor's note: At top of page in MEP's hand: "Mr. Lowe" [underlined twice][1]

1. William G. Lowe, III, editor at *Look* magazine.

. . . .

99. MKR to MEP (TLS, 2 pp.)

Hawthorn, Route 1, Fla.

June 12, 1933

Dear Mr. Perkins:

I really didn't intend to bait you into telling me about your plan for me "in connection with" writing——which, incidentally, is an entirely accurate phrase for what you have in mind! Such a book had never occurred to me. My first reaction was one of sheer distress, and then on second thought I was quite intrigued.

Your suggestion has brought back a whole train of memories of my Washington childhood,[1] that I hadn't thought of in years and years. They are memories of spring and summer evenings and nights when I sat on the cool stone steps of a Baptist church and told stories to other children. We'd usually play our strenuous running games in the long twilight, and then when Tony the Italian lamp-lighter had lit the red-glass gas lamps all along our street, we'd gather deliciously close together on the church steps and I'd "cut loose". I can remember very distinctly the feeling of smugness that came over me when one of the youngsters would run up the street calling to any stragglers, "Marjorie's going to tell stories!" and the hauteur with which I refused to begin until everyone was there. There was a tumultuous Irish child that shrieked and screamed if any of the details depressed him—particularly what I realize now must have been my very celebrated imitation of a wolf howl. He got to be such a nuisance that I recall saying sternly, "You'll have to take Jimmy home now ——there's going to be a wolf in the next one."

It comes over me that I have always had a predilection for wolves in a story. I believe I protested so your making me take a wolf out of the scrub book, because it was really quite a serious repression! I think I should almost be willing to do the book you speak of for the sole purpose of getting in that wolf again.

It really would be interesting to see if I could recapture whatever quality it is that gives glamor to stories for the young mind. We'll certainly have to talk about it.

If you haven't already made inquiries about my English contract, please don't bother to do it. I shouldn't have troubled you about it——I should have written directly to Curtis Brown. You're always so helpful and forbearing, that it's very easy to impose on you.

Thanks for your note,
Very sincerely,

1. Rawlings grew up in Washington, D.C., where her father, Arthur Kinnan, worked for the U.S. Patent Office.

. . . .

100. MEP to MKR (TLS: UF, 2 pp.)

June 13, 1933

Dear Mrs. Rawlings:

We expect those few English pounds will be picked up very soon,- but there is one good thing about it. Pounds have been growing in terms of dollars.- But the delay was caused by our having to get that contract redrawn, although it is certainly unwarranted even then. The letter you received is from the New York office of Curtis Brown, which operates as a semi-independent agency. It has a new manager who should, of course, be familiar with what the main office in London is doing.

Mr. Hawkins' pictures have just come. They are good particularly, I should think, in the feeling he has for the nature of the country, and the background. I am showing them to the art editors.

Ever sincerely yours,

July 6, 1933

Dear Mrs. Rawlings:

If you have not changed your plans you will be coming up soon. Then if you are willing, we can talk about the "younger readers" book.[1] I am absolutely positive you could do it. The only question would be whether it would interfere with your doing something more important,- the novel, for instance. Anyhow, please don't write me that you won't be here after all. I shall not go on a vacation until you come.

We have been doing quite a lot of advertising lately on "South Moon Under", whether you have seen it or not. And the sale has continued, but not in large numbers. There were several orders for it today, for instance.

Ever sincerely yours,

1. The book that eventually would be *The Yearling*.

. . . .

Cross Creek
Hawthorn, Route 1, Fla.
July 15, 1933

Dear Mr. Perkins:

I'll be along, if nothing queer happens, as I planned. I plan to get into New York, by boat, early Wednesday morning, July 26. I'm taking the Red Star *Westernland*[1] at 5 P.M. Friday July 28. Any time between those hours I'll be at your disposal, so, since you're busy and I'm vacationing, I'll let you suggest any meeting convenient to you.

I'll be stopping at a mid-town hotel, probably the Barbizon-Plaza. I have nothing planned for my New York time except talk with you about the two books. A painful thought is in my mind as to why you may have brought up the matter of the child's book. I give you fair warning that I'm going to make you tell me the truth.

Did I mention to you that I found exactly what I've been hunting for, from the English people now in Jacksonville, who were at the Riverside settlement in the scrub in the late '80's and early '90's? There are two couples of them, people in their sixties. They spent a week-end with me here. I'll tell you about them when I see you.

Very sincerely,

'No Door' is completely magnificent. I've read it three times—parts of it four—and it was more stirring the last time than the first. Does Wolfe talk with the same quality? I'd imagine so.

1. Red Star Steam Lines.

....

103. MEP to MKR (CC, 1 p.)

July 18, 1933

Dear Mrs. Rawlings:

I'll call you on July 26th at the Barbizon-Plaza. I'll tell you why I suggested a child's book,- for reasons very simple. There is nothing that would give any pain in it.- Far from it.

Tom does sometimes talk wonderfully, but incoherently. It's quite an experience when it gets going. He agonizes in trying to express himself, and you do in trying to grasp what he means. If you'd like we might manage so that he could meet you.

Ever sincerely yours,

....

104. MEP to MKR (TLS: UF, 2 pp.)

Aug. 10, 1933

Dear Mrs. Rawlings:

Thanks ever so much for your letter from the boat. I hope this one will get to you,- I suppose it will eventually.

I just heard from Lorimer of The Saturday Evening Post.[1] He says, "We have just received a grand humorous article from her," her being you. I spoke to him about you a long time ago, before "South Moon" was published, and that is why he wrote me. Then the magazine is taking the other story, so all that will help financially. I wrote Kingsley[2] about giving you any money you might need, and there is also the advance due you from the English publisher.

I hope you did enjoy the voyage, and it won't be so long before you are back here, really. If you do get time, I should love to hear how things go over there, and how it seems to you.

I have been thinking about what might have happened to send the young Englishman to Florida. It is a hard problem. I don't know that what we talked of can be worked out to fit it.

Tom Wolfe turned up just after you left with a pretty good alibi. He was mighty sorry to have missed you, but he swore he would be on hand when you get back.

Always yours,

1. George H. Lorimer, editor of the *Saturday Evening Post*.
2. Charles Kingsley of Charles Scribner's Sons, London.

. . . .

105. MKR to MEP (ALS, Wotton Hatch Hotel stationery, 2 pp. frag.)

Wotton Hatch Hotel

Wotton

Nr. Dorking

Surrey

[England]

[August 1933]

Dear Mr. Perkins:——

You don't need to worry any more about the circumstances precipitating the exile of my young Englishman. I have a grand situation that I'm sure will satisfy you as well as it does me.

Every thing has been going splendidly.

I rented a car in London and am prowling about the South-England by-ways. It's devilishly lonely, but the beauty is always a compensation. It is really incredibly beautiful——almost [remainder of letter missing]

. . . .

106. MEP to MKR (CC, 2 pp.)

Aug. 28, 1933

Dear Mrs. Rawlings:

I was mighty glad to get your letter, and was relieved to hear that you had found a solution with regard to the opening situation.- Though I did feel sure you would in the end. Everything I could think of was rather melodramatic, or heroic.

Kingsley wrote us of your arrival and said you had set out in a motor and that he hoped you could remember to keep to the left of the road. But by now you must have become accustomed to that, and will have difficulty in keeping to the right when you get home.

I knew you would think England beautiful. It won't now be so very long before you are back, and I am looking forward to it.

Always yours,

South Western Hotel,
Southampton.
[England]
[September 1933]

Dear Mr. Perkins:——

Just a line to say that I'll be in New York about the 26th of September and will 'phone you or drop into your office then.

. . . .

108. MKR to MEP (TLS, 2 pp.)

[Cross Creek]
October 4, 1933

Dear Mr. Perkins:

I'm strongly considering the desirability of doing, before the novel, the boys' book of the scrub. I found old man Long,[1] the hunter, still alive, and his wife very reproachful because I hadn't come two years ago to stay with them as I promised. I am going over next week to stay, as long as necessary to get what stories I need from the old man. I hope you can see his place some day——in the very core of the scrub, where he has lived since 1872——falling into decay under the exquisite mantle of flowering vines. They are hard put to it to make a living, principally because the deer and foxes eat their crops almost faster than they can raise them. They are in the forest preserve, and are not allowed to kill the game. When I asked Mrs. Long what to bring with me when I came, she chuckled and said, "Something to eat——".

The notes will be fresh in my mind——the book will certainly be a comparatively simple matter, and a not too long one. I happen to be in a rather distressed mental condition, and while I don't think personal happiness or unhappiness makes a scrap of difference in writing, it might be just as well to have my thinking a bit clearer for so complicated a piece of work as my Englishman's psychology. (Entirely by the way, I have come to the conclusion I shall have to begin the novel in England and move along more directly than I had planned. His whole viewpoint takes its substance from the English background and the English injustice, and it would only make for incoherence to treat it as a casual incidental, part-way through the book.)

Of course, you will tell me to do as my judgment dictates in this matter of precedence. A few months one way or the other wouldn't, I should think, make much difference in interest in the novel. If it is bad, the first book's having been liked will not save it. And if it's good, it wouldn't matter, would it, how soon or how late it had followed a previous novel?

I am undecided in this matter, and wish you would throw your opinion in the balance for me. Then I'll go ahead, either way, without any further indecision.

Did you happen to see the review of South Moon Under in the London Times Literary Supplement?[2] It was more benign than I had expected from an English source, but interested me particularly because the reviewer emphasized the cosmic pattern I had in mind, and which I felt I had failed to "put over", because the American reviewers weren't particularly conscious of it.

The orange grove is, more than ever, home. I doubt whether I can ever bear to leave it permanently.

Very sincerely,

Forgive the stationery——I despise people's names sprawled across their writing paper. It was a gift, and is a convenient size——.

1. Cal Long, the prototype for Jody in *The Yearling*. The Long family supplied an endless stream of Cracker lore for MKR.
2. *Times Literary Supplement* (September 21, 1933): 628.

. . . .

109. MEP to MKR (CC, 1 p.)

Oct. 10, 1933

Dear Mrs. Rawlings:

I have sent the copy of "Life in the United States" to W. Birtwistle, London, and have just now found the English paper bound copy of "South Moon Under" and am sending it to Mr. Bohnenberger.[1]

Sincerely yours,

1. Carl Bohnenberger of the *Jacksonville Times-Union*.

. . . .

110. MEP to MKR (CC, 3 pp.)

Oct. 10, 1933

Dear Mrs. Rawlings:

I was mighty glad to hear from you. I hope it was pleasant to get back,- and I judge that it was by your saying that you doubt if you can ever leave the orange grove permanently. In some ways places are better friends than people,- if they are places that do not change, as they always do in the East now.

I am distinctly in favor of your doing the boys' book on the scrub. You do have to do what you want to do in writing, but if you could put off the novel (and it would be growing in your <conscience> consciousness all the time) for a long enough time to do this, I think it would be the better course. Then too, it would be in the same field as "South Moon Under" and it is a field that you may be permanently leaving.- Although I should hope myself that you might get back to it sometime in a novel, perhaps.- Then too, there is the great value of being with Long the hunter while there is still time for it. Altogether, I wish you would do the boys' book first. It might be that you would not even need much more time in getting the novel completed by the delay in beginning, be- cause of the inevitable, if wholly unconscious reflection you will have been doing on the material.

I have not seen the London Times review. I shall look it up immediately. The English do have much more intelligent reviewers than we. I would expect them to understand what you were driving at, even if they might be less sym- pathetic with the characters and the detail.

Always yours,

. . . .

111. MEP to MKR (CC, 1 p.)

Oct. 16, 1933

Dear Mrs. Rawlings:

The enclosed lot of reviews have just come and I am sending them to you, though most of them are in little papers, and of small account. I am sending also the Times review. We have a copy of it anyhow, and it is the best. I hope you will tell me soon that you are going to go on with the boys' book.

We are just on the point of selling a thousand sheets of "Life in the United States" to an English publisher, Cape;- so maybe there will be a tiny bit of roy- alty coming out of that after all.[1]

Always yours,

1. Jonathan Cape, London publisher.

Hawthorn, Fla.

[October 1933]

Dear Mr. Perkins:

Thank you for the very helpful comment. I have had an interesting week at the old hunter's, but will have to go back again. His stories come slowly. May I trouble you with another question? Two more, rather. What age of boy would you aim for? And how careful do I need to be to avoid the suggestion of cruelty (about which people are very touchy these days) in the hunting of the game? Hunting was for the table, and to sell as a means of livelihood. I don't want to encourage young male bloodthirstiness, nor do I want to be sentimental in the matter.

I wonder if I might have five hundred dollars right away? If so, might it be sent direct, to be deposited to my account, as follows:

Marjorie K. Rawlings

Commercial Bank and Trust Co.

Ocala, Fla.

I ran completely out of money——to my astonishment!

Very sincerely,

· ·

Hawthorn, Fla.

[October 1933]

Dear Mr. Perkins:

Can you say definitely whether you are likely to want young Hawkins (whose illustrations for South Moon Under were sent you in the spring) to do any illustrating for the boys' book? Does your art department think his stuff is "finished" enough? His animals are bad——his human figures moderately good (catching the *spirit* of the look of the people, however, if you know what I mean)——his background excellent. By working from stuffed models—— about the only way he could get it—he could probably do the animals better ——he has drawn them from imagination so far.

The reason I ask, I had a note from Hawkins asking if he might see me, and I thought that if he was still planning to go to New York this fall, I ought to know now whether you are going to want to use him. If you are, I can send him into the scrub to do some sketching, and from his sketches he can do finished stuff later. If you have someone better in mind, let me know, please.

Sincerely,

Oct. 20, 1933

Dear Mrs. Rawlings:

I have been in Baltimore with Scott Fitzgerald.[1] That is why I did not answer you sooner;- but the check has been deposited today, five hundred dollars in the Commercial Bank and Trust Co., and charged against your account.

As to the age of the boy, I do not think it makes very much difference because a boy who lives that simple kind of outdoor life, fishing and shooting and all, is about the same whether he is twelve, or sixteen, or even perhaps eighteen. Lant was about the right kind of a boy until he got to the age where he assumed all the responsibility and fell in love. I think the way to fix his age would be simply for you to follow your inclination. The book would probably be one anyhow that men would read as well as boys. But its interests would be those of a boy, in the woods and fishing and hunting, and all that. In other words, he ought not to be what they used to call a small boy, but a boy, and that might make him even eighteen if it suited you.

I have looked again at the Hawkins pictures, and had them looked at. If he comes to New York, we should like to see him, and I think he might go a good way. But I do not believe he would be the right man to do this book. In fact, I have the man in mind if it turns out that he is available, and if you like him.- I am sending you a copy of "Two Little Confederates". Even that is not so good as he has done. He has done illustrations for "The Adventures of Davy Crockett by Himself"[2] which we are to publish.- But all we have now is originals so I cannot show them to you. I shall when you come to New York,- better come fairly soon, after you get all you want from the old hunter. But I wish you would have Mr. Hawkins come in here if he comes to New York, for I think it might result to his advantage.

I keep meeting people who admire "South Moon Under". Both the Burts, Struthers Burt and his wife,[3] whom I saw yesterday, were full of it. I am also sending a copy to Scott.- It is not his *kind* of book, for he likes indoors better than out, but I know he will like "South Moon".

Always yours,

1. F. Scott Fitzgerald (1896–1940), who particularly admired *South Moon Under* and *The Yearling*.
2. John W. Thomason (1893–1944) illustrated *The Adventures of Davy Crockett by Himself* (New York: Scribners, 1934) and, by Thomas Nelson Page (1853–1922), *Two Little Confederates* (New York: Scribners, 1932).
3. Maxwell Struthers Burt (1882–1954), author, and Katherine Newlin Burt (1882–1977), fiction editor of *Ladies' Home Journal* who wrote under the name Rebecca Scarlett.

Hawthorn, Route 1, Fla.

Oct. 23, 1933

Dear Mr. Perkins:

I think we must come to a much clearer understanding of what you are expecting of me as to the boys' book. By "you", in this case, I mean the house of Scribner. (I dote on infuriating you by speaking of "the house", as contraposed to you personally.) You say "The book would probably be one anyhow that men would read as well as boys", and in the same mail Mr. Darrow writes, having talked with you, of "a book which anyone might enjoy but which would possibly ultimately become a Juvenile".

Do you by any wild chance think that once I get into it, I will automatically find myself doing another Cracker book for mature consumption? Are you hoping for that? I can't say too emphatically that that is not the case. In the first place, the material simply is not there. And in the second place, if it were, <I> or if it could be induced, I have neither the taste nor the heart for such a book. It is not impossible that in a few years I should turn again to the backwoods field——there is an untouched locale I know of that might some day prove fertile——but right now I will not, under any circumstances, consider it. I will not consider anything but an out-and-out boy's juvenile——written without condescension, and an attempt at a simple artistry. If that will satisfy you——if you will promise to publish it (if good enough to publish at all) only as a juvenile, I'll go ahead with it.

The principal reason, aside from my personal feeling in the matter, I could not agree to an adult book, or any pretense at an adult book, is that for the present at least I have nothing to say for mature people along the South-Moon-Under line. A book in the same general locale could only be compared with the first book, could only be called its sequal [*sic*] or successor at best, and, at worst, would be considered an attempt to capitalize on what earlier interest there was in such characters in such a setting. It would be ruinous. Incidentally, for the boys' book, I should prefer to use, if not a pseudonym, at least some variation of my name that would keep them from realizing the writer was a woman, say, "M. Kinnan Rawlings". Boys I have found very touchy about that. Sex antagonism is rampant in the 'teens.

Don't think I'm taking myself too seriously about all this, but it is important that we understand each other perfectly. There will be then less likelihood of my disappointing you.

A question I'd like answered specifically, if you don't mind——We discussed it rather vaguely before. The book being strictly a juvenile, is it legitimate to lift three or four incidents from South Moon, particularly those of the deer playing in the sink-hole in the moonlight, and the cat-hunt?

"Two Little Confederates" has just come. The Thomason illustrations are charming. He has a feeling for boys and animals that I should think would be priceless for our purpose. And he is, of course, a true and finished artist. The Gainesville youngster, Hawkins, of course as yet is not——though I agree with you as to his possibilities. He is progressing rapidly, and the other day brought over an illustration that shows a tremendous advance. If he goes to New York, I'll send him to you——he is young and shy——and I think you can do something with him. Meanwhile, Thomason would be splendid for the scrub book, if you can get him. If you can, do as you please about having him see the scrub, etc. If you want to wait for the manuscript, all right——also, all right if he should care to drop down this winter and look the ground over and do some sketching.

And please make a mental note of it that I should get a great deal of pleasure out of entertaining anyone like that, or any Scribner or personal friends who enjoy out-of-the-way and simple things. I have a roomy, if unpretentious, place, with adequate help, and I love to feed people.

Did I give you the impression that I expected to come to New York this fall or winter? I didn't intend to, at all. I considered myself "put" for a couple of years. Do you consider it necessary or desirable to talk over the boys' book when it is further along, or for me to talk with the illustrator? If the latter, it would surely, I should think, be much more to the point for him to come here.

Thank you for taking care of the money matter. Am I right in thinking of the first six months' royalty, from March 1 to Sept. 1, being due me Dec. 1? Beastly nuisance——money. I think I shall spend my royalties as soon as possible and settle down to grits and greens.

And you will make your point of view about this book clear to me, won't you?

Very Sincerely,

As you love me, please don't go about inflicting S.M.U. on people like Scott Fitzgerald. You will have a huge group of sophisticates actively hating me. True, I have had some delightful correspondence with Robert W. Chambers,[1] than whom there is no one who goes in more for drawing room literature—— but his secret vice is the diurnal and nocturnal lepidoptera of Florida, so you see it was his baser nature that I appealed to.

1. Robert W. Chambers (1865–1933), novelist, painter, and illustrator.

Oct. 27, 1933

Dear Mrs. Rawlings:

I did not expect you to come back to New York, or understand that you intended to; but I hoped you would and thought you might, because that often happens with people who say they won't. Perhaps you may, too.

As to the book, it is too bad we should be getting into a tangle about it because the idea is really perfectly simple to me. I am thinking of a book about a boy, but his age is not important. Every boy between twelve and eighteen who lives an outdoor life is interested in the same things. In a general way (though your book would of course not be supposed to resemble them, and could not resemble all of them because they do not resemble each other), I associate with it such books as "Huckleberry Finn," Kipling's "Kim," David Crockett's Memoirs, "Treasure Island," and "The Hoosier School Boy."[1] All these books are primarily *for boys*. All of them are read by men, and they are the favorite books of some men. The truth is the best part of a man is a boy. It is subject matter that counts, and the fact that the hero is a boy. I do not know what Darrow is thinking about, and it does not make much difference, but of course the sales department always wants a novel. They want to turn everything into a novel. They would have turned the New Testament into one if it had come to us for publication, and they could have. But I am right about it, and a book about a boy and the life of the scrub is the thing we want. Anyhow, the thing for you to do is to write it as you feel it and want it, without regard to anybody at all. It is those wonderful river trips, and the hunting, and the dogs and guns, and the companionship of simple people who care about the same things which were included in "South Moon Under" that we are thinking about. It is all simple, not complicated,- don't let anything make it complicated to you.

I don't think though, that you can lift out any of the actual words in "South Moon Under". Probably you did not mean that, you meant to retell the incidents. That you could do, and I do hope you will have something about going down a river because the rivers there are so good, and the journey element in a narrative is always a fine one, particularly to youth.

There would be no use in doing anything about the illustrations until the manuscript is pretty far on.- The first thing would be for the artist to read the manuscript. Wait until I send you the David Crockett pictures, which I will the moment I can get proofs, but not for quite a while. I wish John would go down there. He would enjoy it and I know would get the greatest pleasure from talking to you. You would have to keep the corn, etc., under your own control.

The royalties on "South Moon Under" are not strictly due until four months after September first. But I think we could at any time send you payments from them, or even all of them if you wanted.

Sincerely yours,

1. Edward Eggleston (1837–1902), *Hoosier Schoolboy* (1883).

. . . .

117. MEP to MKR (CC, 1 p.)

Nov. 8, 1933

Dear Mrs. Rawlings:

I was delighted to see that you had won the O. Henry prize.[1] Won't they make you come up here for a dinner when they award it? I also have hopes that you may win the Prix Femina with "South Moon Under" which will be announced in a week or so. I was just talking with Madame Dauban,[2] the Secretary here, who says the book has been much admired by the readers in France.

Is everything right now about the boys' book in your mind? You are always the one who must finally decide any question, and your instinct would make you decide it rightly.

Ever sincerely yours,

1. "Gal Young Un" won the O. Henry Memorial Prize for the best short story of 1932.
2. Jeanne Cune-Dauban Rieffel, chair of Prix Femina Americain.

. . . .

118. MKR to MEP (ALS, 10 pp.)

Hawthorn, Route 1, Fla.
Nov. 11 [1933]

Dear Mr. Perkins:——

I'll have to ask you to put up with my almost illegible hand-writing while my typewriter is being cleaned and oiled for the next siege.

I imagine——fear——that I may have to come up to New York to collect the O. Henry thing, although I haven't had a blessed word from anyone connected with the matter——just a copy of the book of stories from Doubleday Doran.[1] I know that Marjory Stoneman Douglas[2] of Miami won 2nd award one year and had to go up to get it——and naturally it cost the lion's share of the $250. to make the trip——and she had to get up, unknown and almost unannounced, no one knowing she had won a prize——and make a speech on "The Art of the Short Story"! She said she never felt quite so imbecilic in her life.

I suppose it makes a little necessary publicity for the awards and for the book, to make some fuss about the awarding, etc. and if I have to go through with it, I'll try not to be ungracious about it. But I hate to take the time——and you know how I feel about that particular story—it's like being handed a medal for committing murder——and I'd have to keep still about that!

You must be reasonably sure about the Prix Femina to have mentioned it to me at all. "There is a tide in the affairs of men", etc. and it has *nothing* [underlined twice] to do with merit! The moment simply arrives when material things go astonishingly right for a while——then, as astonishingly and unreasonably, they go wrong——and the trick is not to let either road fool you into thinking it will continue in the same direction forever!

I'm hoping the same favorable stars are at work on my private affairs—— I was granted a divorce yesterday from my husband. The end, simply——I hope——of fourteen years of Hell——of a fourteen-year struggle to adjust myself to, and accept, a most interesting but difficult——impossible——personality. It was a question, finally, of breaking free from the feeling of a vicious hand always at my throat, or of going down in complete physical and mental collapse. That was one reason I wanted to go as far away as rural England——to be sure I had perspective on it, and to make up my mind what was best to do .

I am not riotously happy, not being interested in freedom for its own sake ——I could have been a *slave* to a man who could be at least a *benevolent* despot——but I feel a terrific relief——I can wake up in the morning conscious of the sunshine, and thinking, "How wonderful! Nobody is going to give me Hell today!"

But enough of such nonsense——

I have almost definitely decided that I will have to get into the novel right away without stopping for the boys' book.

Do you realize how calmly you sat up there in your office and announced that you were expecting a boy's *classic* of me? I could toss off a 50–75,000-word simple boy's story of the scrub, without too much interfering with the novel ——but I can't do a really decent boy's book quite so casually. There is more fine material to be gotten for it, that will have to come slowly, and it would be a pity to toss off a pot-boiler when by letting it go until my material has increased, and until I can give it my undivided attention, we might get something really decent out of it. A boy's mind is really too sacred a responsibility just to flip crumbs at it——

If the novel is any good, I can feel reassured as to the desirability of going on writing (that sounds hypocritical—but you know, what I mean) and can draw a breath and not feel hurried——and do the boy's book leisurely.

If it is bad——the novel——I can plunge for relief into the other, thinking "At least I can please the adolescent!" I hope you're not disappointed at my deciding this way——almost the last kindness my husband did me was to try to convince me that you were so certain that the novel would be an impossible mess, that you were doing all you could to divert my mind from it, in the hope you could steer me away from it altogether.

But I asked you that question, and I believe you would have told me honestly if you felt so. We certainly have enough mutual confidence and trust so that you would have felt free to warn me of any specific dangers you feared for me.

If you get any advance information on the necessity for my coming to New York, I'd appreciate greatly your tipping me off. I have my hands full, as you can imagine, with the grove etc., and I'm having long-needed repairs made to my shack. My new hand-hewn cypress shingle roof is just completed——but it took 2 men 5 weeks instead of the estimated 1.

The local carpenter lined a clothes closet the one day I was away——my only access to the attic——and I came home to find that he had completely sealed up ten gallons of liquor I had up in the attic, aging! I didn't want the local folk to know where I kept my stores——or that I had that much——and the reasons I had to think up to get him to cut a hatch big enough to get the keg down when I need it!

As ever,

I promise *never* [underlined twice] to write you such a long letter in long-hand again!

1. Doubleday, Doran, publishers.
2. Marjory Stoneman Douglas (1890–1998), Florida novelist, newspaper writer, and environmentalist (in particular, a defender of the Everglades).

. . . .

119. MKR to MEP (ALS, 1 p.)

Hawthorn, Fla.

Nov. 13, 1933

Dear Mr. Perkins:——

I had a note——and $500. check—from Doubleday, Doran this morning——and gather that it won't be necessary for me to come to New York in connection with the O. Henry award.

But you will slip me any advance information, won't you, if it should seem likely?

Many thanks.

Nov. 15, 1933

Dear Mrs. Rawlings:

Thanks ever so much for writing me. I think your handwriting is as easy to read as anybody's I ever saw, so don't ever let the absence of a typewriter keep you from writing me if you have the inclination.

I am glad things have worked out the way you want to have them, and I'll say no more about that. If it is all right for you, it is right.

But what is all this mystery about your writing a novel? You wrote one very fine novel, and I know of no reason to feel anxious about another, except that I can understand your feeling anxious because a good writer always does, and ought to. What such a one wants to do is very hard, and perhaps unattainable even, but no one who wrote "South Moon Under" ought to be doubted by other people. Certainly I have no doubts, and the only reason I favored your doing the boys' book was, first, the fact that the old hunter was available now and might not be later, and then that I do think when one is to do a difficult novel a long period of meditation, mostly unconscious, is helpful. But you have probably had that long period anyway. Of course all our sales force, etc., etc., would be delighted to have you do the novel first. I would not have wanted to hurry you into the boys' book either, but I thought that having done so well by Lant, and having thought so much about the scrub, and the rivers, and alligators, and all, from the point of view of Lant, you would be pretty well primed for a book about another boy. But it is all right that you should do the way you think best.

I am glad you do not have to come up here to get the five hundred, except that I had hoped we would see you again. Maybe something will bring you. Anyhow, please let me know how things come on.

Always yours,

. . . .

Dec. 6, 1933

Dear Mrs. Rawlings:

I thought you might like to read Alice Longworth's book,[1] which is entertaining enough anyhow, because of your associations with Washington. So I am sending that down. I wish you would let me know if you see anything we publish that you do want.- And when you have time I hope you may also have the inclination to write how things go. I hope they go well.

Always yours,

1. Alice Longworth (1884–1980), *Crowded Hours: Reminiscences of Alice Longworth Roosevelt* (New York: Scribners, 1933).

. . . .

122. MKR to MEP (ALS, 3 pp.)

[Cross Creek]
Dec. 11, 1933

Dear Mr. Perkins:——

Many thanks for the Alice Longworth book——it looks delightful. I was a high school girl——in school with Bob and Phil La Follette, "Kit" Williams (son of Senator Williams from Mississippi) Dick Herron (Taft's nephew) Dick [illegible] etc, when she was in her glory, and she has always been a glamorous figure to me.[1]

Things are going well. I've been working out some personal problems and rather neglecting the writing, but last week I began "Hamaca". I began with the English scene and we'll see how we like it that way. I would prefer to begin it in Florida, and it will be easy enough to do so if the English opening seems to detract from the intensity of the American setting. Nothing, I begin to know, is ever wasted.

I do wish I could feel that my work mattered. It seems to me that I have nothing to give but a certain emotional response to life and beauty and feeling——and that because it is emotional and not intellectual it can so easily be without substance or validity. But never mind——what of it!

I've been doing lots of hunting and camping——went down the Suwanee River[2] last week. So many of the Florida rivers are peculiarly detached from life——they flow from nowhere to nowhere, with very little life, human or bird or animal, along their courses.

Again——many thanks for the book,

1. Bob La Follette, classmate of MKR at Western High School, Washington, D.C., and Phil La Follette, sons of Robert La Follette, senator from Wisconsin.
2. The Suwannee River was made famous by Stephen Collins Foster (1826–1864).

Dec. 18, 1933

Dear Mrs. Rawlings:

I was mighty glad to hear that you had got under way with "Hamaca". If ever you should want to show me any of it, remember how eagerly I should read it.

This I am in hopes will get to you in time to wish you a happy Christmas season.

Always yours,

1934

Jan. 8, 1934

Dear Mrs. Rawlings:

I am enclosing a check for the amount due on the last royalty report, to-gether with a memorandum showing certain deductions from what had actu-ally been earned.

I hope the book goes on well. Everyone here asks me if I have heard about it.- But don't let that tend to hurry you. Do it the way you want to do it. And I do not know many people who should have as few doubts as to whether it was worth doing, in view of what you have done already.

We have had, as you will have read, the coldest weather in years, and it looks now as if we were going to have some more of it. I hope Florida has not been unseasonable.

Always yours,

. . . .

Hawthorn, Route 1, Fla.
January 20, 1934

Dear Mr. Perkins:

I've been frightfully delinquent in not acknowledging the thoughtful things you've done lately. "Brazilian Adventure"[1] is still waiting to tide me over some bad moment——it looks delightful.

I came in Thursday night late from a four-day rattlesnake hunt——my house and grove were devastatingly lonely——and I found "Such is My Beloved"[2] here and sat down and read it through. At first the style annoyed me——it had a peculiar childishness and formlessness. Then I began to realize that it was absolutely the proper medium for the story. The thing is exquisitely touching and I would not be surprised if it becomes something of a classic. Callaghan did a very subtle thing in using the two street-walkers instead of just one, as would have seemed off-hand the logical thing to do. It makes valid the sublimation of the "carnal" instinct. I mean to read it again more carefully for it is well worth it. Taken at a gulp, it is very very beautiful.

I am ashamed to write you about my own work. "Hamaca" should have been a quarter or a half done by now——and instead, I have only made the *third* beginning. Even now, the beginning does not please me at all, but I am going to stick to it this time and go on, and if necessary re-write once it is completed. The whole thing, the whole effect I want to get, is so clear in my mind that it is absurd for me to have allowed the tumult in my own personal emotions to have kept me from working——but I simply could not concentrate. Some day when we're old I'll sit with you by a fire somewhere and give you a good evening's entertainment telling you my own story. Maybe twenty-five years from now I can look at it with an amused detachment. Just now I can't quite. My favorite confessor, the only person to know my complete story—— the Tampa surgeon I've mentioned to you, who knows bull-fighting and got such a kick out of Death in the Afternoon——infuriates me by his laboratory attitude. He'll say, "Your story is gorgeous—deMaupassant[3] never did anything half so fascinating. The things you've done and gone through will be the making of you as a writer. You'll come out of it an artist." But how can anyone expect the beetle on the pin to take a scientific interest in his *own* struggles? "Emotion remembered in tranquillity"[4] may be literary material and all that ——but perspective is badly needed.

You must say "Thank you" to me for not deluging you with my personal details that are on my mind more than my work——I've noticed that the personal angle tends to embarrass you——you like your writers to be neatly boxed in their workshops.

I have begun a terrific effort to box myself, and hope to report progress soon. <illegible excision> I'll write you some time about the rattlesnake hunt, <illegible excision> with Florida's best herpetologist.[5] We got eighteen—— he let me catch one. It was tremendously interesting, and in fascinating country——the north-west corner of the Everglades, Big Prairie, west of Lake Okeechobee.

If I can once hit my stride on the book, it will go fast. Be patient with me, as always, and perhaps we can make something out of it. I want it to be an intense and *disturbing* book, with a bitter and beautiful emotional quality. It may not be the kind of thing I can do successfully. If not, it won't particularly matter, because I have to get it out of my system before I could do anything else anyway.

Many thanks for both books. It was awfully nice of you to send them.

I have kept forgetting to subscribe to a New York paper since I got back, and haven't followed the news at all. What happened to the Prix Femina——to whom and what was it awarded? Some other things have come up so that—— now there seems likely to be nothing to bring me——I should have welcomed a reason for coming to New York!

1. Peter Fleming (1907–1971), *Brazilian Adventure* (New York: Scribners, 1933).
2. Morley Callaghan (1903–1990), *Such Is My Beloved* (New York: Scribners, 1934). Callaghan was a Canadian writer influenced by Hemingway.
3. Guy de Maupassant (1850–1893), French fiction writer.
4. Cf. William Wordsworth, preface to *Lyrical Ballads* (1800): ". . . poetry is the spontaneous overflow of powerful feelings . . . recollected in tranquillity."
5. Ross Allen of Silver Springs, Florida. The snake story found its way into the plot of *The Yearling* and then into the chapter "The Ancient Enmity" in *Cross Creek*.

. . . .

126. MEP to MKR (TLS: UF, 3 pp.)

Feb. 1, 1934

Dear Mrs. Rawlings:

I am sure you will do a fine book, and you ought to have trouble in getting under way with a fine book. Incidentally you once remarked upon my having sent "South Moon" to Scott Fitzgerald as not being very apt because it was not his sort of book. He had never said anything about it to me, but last night in talking about his own book by long distance, he referred to yours, and in the highest terms. It is not his kind of book either, but he knew it was a beautiful book. I shall be patient, but you ought not to get discouraged if it goes hard. I know you won't be.

As for the Prix Femina, I have tried to find out about it, but I do not know how to get hold of the French woman who now and then calls up about it. But apparently it has not been awarded. I do not understand how they do, for I was informed that it lay between your book and one other, a long time ago. But I shall let you know the moment I hear, and I hope things will turn out so that you will come to New York.

I do not want you to be neatly boxed in a workshop at all, and if personal angles seem to you to tend to embarrass me, remember that I am a Yankee on both sides of my family, and I suppose I shall never get over it altogether.

Couldn't you sometime do an account of the rattlesnake hunt for an article?

I am struggling with Tom Wolfe for a couple of hours every night now, and he is going to get his book done for the fall.[1] But it is the most difficult work I was ever engaged in. I feel that Scott, having got his done is a good omen, for that seemed perfectly hopeless many times.[2] Now he has done it, and it is a very fine thing, and will restore him to the position he held after "The Great Gatsby"[3] if not put him in a higher one. I was down with him for three days last week in Baltimore.

If ever you want to show me any fragments of "Hamaca" even, please do it. You must not let my Yankee reticence ever make you feel that there is any book in which I should [not] be so interested.

Always yours,

1. Thomas Wolfe, *Of Time and the River* (New York: Scribners, 1935).
2. F. Scott Fitzgerald, *Tender Is the Night* (New York: Scribners, 1934).
3. F. Scott Fitzgerald, *The Great Gatsby* (New York: Scribners, 1925).

. . . .

127. MKR to MEP (TLS, with holograph postscript, 3 pp.)

Hawthorn, Fla.
Feb. 11, 1934

Dear Mr. Perkins:

You do encourage me by indicating that difficulty in "getting going" is not necessarily a sign of complete incompetence. But I had long held the theory that to allow personal turbulence to interfere with one's work was a fatal weakness, and a sure sign that the artistic impulse was not valid. Physical obstacles never bother me——I can work just as well in pain, in fearful heat——in any place. But when I am emotionally torn up I find myself submerged in a miasma, with clear thought seemingly impossible. It is a maddening thing to have happen, for several reasons. When you really *want* to be working, it gives you the nightmare sensation of trying to run and not being able to lift your feet. You are torn between the reality of yourself and your relations to other people, and the reality of the thing you wish to create, and you cannot give your mind to both at the same time. I find when I *force* myself to write, in this fog, that I produce un-true rubbish that has to be thrown out. There is no alternative but to put your own problems totally out of your mind, and that proves difficult when all your most intimate happiness is at stake.

I didn't intend to expatiate on this——I set out principally to remark on the enclosed extract, copied for me from an old book of Lord Northcliffe's,[1] I think, by the English friend who helped me work out a satisfactory disgrace for my young Englishman in "Hamaca". I am delighted with the quotation, as I think you will be, as I could certainly find no better authority to verify my theories, pre-conceived in ignorance, on the effect of the Florida backwoods on a sensitive young man. I knew that regardless of what the Galsworthian Englishman does or does not do under given conditions, that my basic conception of his psychology and his reactions, under the circumstances I lay down, was *sound*.

I hear much talk already of "Tender is the Night." I thought, beginning to read it after I had written you, that Fitzgerald had filled the contract I was setting up for myself——a book disturbing, bitter and beautiful. I am totally unable to analyze the almost over-powering effect that some of his passages create——some of them about quite trivial people and dealing with trivial situations. There is something terrifying about it when it happens, and the closest I can come to understanding it is to think that he does, successfully at such times, what I want to do——that is, visualizes people not in their immediate setting, from the human point of view——but in time and space——almost, you might say, with the divine detachment. The effect is very weird when he does it with unimportant people moving in a superficial and sophisticated setting. I shouldn't put it that way, for of course importance and un-importance are relative——if they exist at all.

People to whom I have loaned "Such is My Beloved"——(I realize it's disloyal to loan a book instead of making them buy it!) have been much touched by it.

Thank you for writing me.

[Postscript] This is an absolutely perfect picture of many small English "pubs" I drank ale in, and a marvelous assortment of rural "types".

It is also to my notion a very nice piece of English satire——and an amusing "dig" from the Englishman who sent it, and who took me into pubs where I could not have gone alone. He is referring, in reminding me of the red beret, to a hat I had to stop wearing when I went into certain types of places. Some day I will tell you the rather amazing story of the entirely different reactions I got in different kinds of English hotels, inns and pubs according to the kind of clothes——especially hats——I had on.

[Holograph postscript] You might pass this on to Whitney Darrow. I think it would amuse him.

1. Alfred Charles William Harmsworth, Lord Northcliffe (1865–1922), British journalist. Book not identified.

128. MEP to MKR (TLS: UF, 2 pp.)

Feb. 23, 1934

Dear Mrs. Rawlings:

I am returning the very amusing picture from Punch,[1] and the letter that goes with it. I wish something would bring you to New York for a while. It must be harder to have things the way they are and be in so solitary a place;- For though solitude is a state that greatly appeals to me, I do not think it is good when things seem bad.

I showed the cartoon and the letter to Darrow. He is always asking how I think the book is getting on, and will certainly put the sales department behind it to the very limit when it does come. Maybe you will be willing to show me something of it when not much is done. I shall be mighty careful not to say anything more than one has a right to on the basis of a part.

I am going to send you a set of proofs of the last installment of Fitzgerald,[2] which is very fine.

Always yours,

1. *Punch,* British satiric periodical, founded in 1841, known especially for its caricatures.
2. *Tender Is the Night.*

. . . .

129. MKR to MEP (wire)

1934 FEB 27 PM 5 09
MAXWELL PERKINS—
597 FIFTH AVE NYC—
ROBERT HERRICK[1] IS MUCH INTERESTED IN MY WORK AFTER GIVING HIM SKETCHY IDEA OF NEXT BOOK HE IS FEARFUL FOR ME BEGS COMPLETE SUMMARY OF BOOK WITH HOPE OF HELPING ME AVOID DANGERS HE FORESEES   FIND HIM HELPFUL AM IGNORANT OF HIS CONNECTIONS IS THERE ANY OBJECTION TO SUCH COOPERATION—

1. Robert Herrick (1868–1938), American novelist.

. . . .

130. MEP to MKR (TS for wire)

FEB. 28, 1934
MRS. MARJORIE K. RAWLINGS
ISLAND GROVE, FLORIDA
DISTRUSTFUL OF ASSISTANCE SUGGESTED WRITING

Hawthorn, Fla.
Wednesday
[February 28, 1934]

Dear Mr. Perkins:

Thank you for answering my wire. Our letters will probably cross and the chances are we will automatically answer each other's questions. I'll tell you what was back of the question in my wire to you, and why I was so precipitous about it.

Saturday night in Winter Park, where I went to read on a program at Rollins College, I met Robert Herrick at a supper Dr. Albert Shaw[1] gave for me. Mr. Herrick has something of your peculiarly understanding quality, and we disgraced ourselves by getting in a far corner and talking to please ourselves and ignoring the party all evening. He had an amazing enthusiasm for South Moon Under and had come to the party just to meet the writer of it. It appears he had told his brother-in-law, who is on the Pulitzer prize committee, before leaving the north, that "You should give the Pulitzer to S.M.U., but of course you won't." He asked me, as many people do, on what I was working——and I told him just a little of the book, in quite hazy fashion. As you know, I have a reasonably clear conception of what I want to do. He expressed some concern at the time and pointed out one or two obvious pit-falls. As a matter of fact, I doubt whether anyone could indicate to me a danger in it over which I have not already sweat blood in anticipation. He said he should like to go into it further with me——that as a teacher of many years, working with young writers, he might possibly have some concrete and practical help for me.

Meantime, Mr. Herrick and Mr. and Mrs. Winston Churchill,[2] with whom he is staying, accepted my invitation to spend a day and night with me at my place, probably this week-end. On receiving Mr. Herrick's note yesterday morning, my first impulse, in response to his sympathy and interest, was to do as he suggested in it, taking advantage in due time of any help he might give me. Then it occurred to me that on more counts than one I could get into embarrassment on it. As I said in my wire, I know nothing of his connections, really nothing of him, except that his name strikes familiarly. Personally, he is everything wise and charming. He may be a very great editor and teacher, with a great deal to give. On the other hand, as a novelist himself, he may have set ideas of his own as to how things should be done, and it would be impossible for me to profit by his experience. On the whole, it is easier for me to work with you as I did on the other book and on Jacob's Ladder——making my mistakes my own way, then going at it fresh and re-writing after you have showed me the trouble.

It also occurred to me that he might have definite publishing connections, and being pleasantly and satisfactorily associated with Scribner's, I would find myself embarrassed by being under some obligation to anyone who had helped me. I didn't want to cause any mix-up by accepting a seemingly desirable offer of cooperation. It was necessary to get your reaction at once, as I must write him and the Churchills today about the time of their visit, and I needed to know at once how to respond to his offer——which I feel sure is purely kindly and unselfish. Your wire confirms my <feeling> second thought of avoiding this assistance, and I presume your letter will give me the reason. Unless you knew that Mr. Herrick has a special gift for such things, to be accepted gratefully, I should have preferred in any case just to bungle along as usual and count on you to straighten me out after the writing was done.

You do have your hands full. I pity you with Tom Wolfe's gorgeous bedlam. As I see it, he *must* discipline himself. Please don't spare the blue-pencil, as far as he will stand for it without shooting you on sight. He repeats and repeats, and says in four magnificent ways, what could have been said more magnificently in any one. His own sonorousness betrays him. If you could only give him Hemingway's restraint!

I have finally satisfied myself, why, aside from my difficulty in concentrating on any work at all, I have had so much trouble in getting going. The English beginning is wrong, all wrong. It is impossible to key it to the main part of the book——it makes a totally undesirable transition in characters and locale. The English portion has no meaning, no value, *except as it exists in the man's mind in Florida.* So I have thrown out <the> what I had done once again——and the Florida beginning, while it does not please me as to the writing, is in the mood, the key, that I want, and I am much better satisfied to go on from there. I had been forcing myself to work on something I knew inherently was off-key.

1. Albert Shaw (1857–1947), editor and historian, member of the Rollins College faculty.
2. Winston S. Churchill (1871–1947), American novelist noted for his historical romances.

. . . .

132. MEP to MKR (CC, 4 pp.)

Feb. 28, 1934

Dear Mrs. Rawlings:

Whatever your perplexities about the book, I am sure you are the better judge of it, and I should be very fearful of your consulting Robert Herrick deeply about it, and I say this flatly. I have always understood that he was an extremely interesting man, and I should think it would be very pleasant to talk to him, but I do not think his advice would be good. He has written fine novels, but they belong to a time that we have entirely left behind. I do not think his ideas of technique, or anything of that sort would be really consonant with your own, and trying to adjust yourself to them might do great damage. I think it is a bad thing to talk to anyone very much about a novel. That is why I myself have not tried to find out more about it, and to get a summary or anything of that sort. Sometimes when one talks about a novel, they give it a degree of expression that makes it impossible for them to write it even.

I have no doubt whatever that Robert Herrick is an extremely intelligent man—though I thought he was extremely misunderstanding in denouncing as rubbish Hemingway's "A Farewell to Arms"[1]—but he is also a professor, and has rather fixed ideas, I gather. In fact, it makes me very anxious to hear of your considering him as an intimate adviser in this book. We have here in the office one who knew all about him as a teacher in Chicago, because he was there. I simply asked him his opinion of Robert Herrick—and he is a young man of very excellent judgment—and it completely confirmed my own. I dislike to seem to be critical of him in any way at all because I know that he is an exceptional person, but I still more dislike the idea of this cooperation. If you do, in spite of everything, make the summary, I hope you will send it also to me. I naturally would be very greatly interested to see a summary, very greatly, but I do think too, that a book comes out of the author, and that it cannot be artificially criticized; if I saw a summary, I should be very careful in discussing it for fear of influencing an author toward doing what was not, for her, right.

You tend to underrate your abilities,- as the best writers almost always do. You can do this book by yourself, and the fact that it is hard, means that it is good, I believe. You do beautiful work, and I am terribly afraid of it being marred if you do not do it yourself. There are plenty of writers—we have one, a notable one—who writes his books with the help of criticism and never could get a book done without it. He brings in version after version, and we go over it, or I do, several times and talk hours with him about it. But he is a second-rate writer, and never could be anything else. But a first-rate writer ought not to do it that way in the beginning, but should only take criticism in the late stages of the book. It must be his book, and being that is what makes it good.

Ever yours,

1. Ernest Hemingway, *A Farewell to Arms* (New York: Scribners, 1929).

Hawthorn, Fla.
Saturday
[March 3, 1934]

Dear Mr. Perkins:

Just a note in answer to your letter. Even before receiving it——after your wire——I wrote Mr. Herrick what I *trust* was a gracious and tactful letter, excusing myself from the summary or any deep discussion of *Hamaca,* on the grounds that it was easier for me to make my own mistakes and then accept help later, when I had something tangible to work on.

I also dropped what I hope, again, was a tactful hint, that I already had a "sympathetic mind" or whatever it was he called [it], to work with, by remarking casually that I had twice worked closely with you, to my great satisfaction, after a piece of work was in concrete form; that you had asked to see pieces of the new book, and even with you, I found it impossible to work too closely on anything in process of conception.

Mr. Herrick and Mrs. Churchill are coming up tomorrow or Monday, and I hope I have handled the situation adequately, because his interest was too genuine, the gift of his own personality too generous, for me to care to offer him anything in the nature of an obvious rebuff.

I should have felt a peculiar sense of betraying you if I had worked deeply with anyone else on the book, because you have more to give than anyone else could possibly have. Not knowing but that you might feel Mr. Herrick, immediately at hand, could be of help, I wanted you to have the say-so on accepting his offer. I was prepared to accept any judgment you might have about it. Your wire and your letter confirmed, fortunately, my impulse to go slow.

. . . .

March 5, 1934

Dear Mrs. Rawlings:

I enclose a review from Australia,- simply because it is from Australia and shows that "South Moon Under" was published there, through the English publisher.[1]

I am returning Mr. Herrick's letter. I think it a very nice letter, and an intelligent one. But I am very firmly of the opinion that you ought not to do as he suggests, for the reasons I gave you. He did speak rightly of "South Moon Under",- and also of "As the Earth Turns".[2] I think one of the best things he says in a good letter is that about "going ahead and bringing it forth whatever it may prove to be". I know it will prove to be something notable anyhow, and I do not think you are one to be deterred by the anxiety of not equalling, or excelling your first book. But I have known it often to happen, and in strict confidence, I do believe that one reason Scott could not get his book finished for so long was on account of the great success of "The Great Gatsby"; and I think Tom Wolfe too, has been held back unconsciously by the fear that his second book would not be thought so highly of as "The Angel".[3]

I can see the difficulty you have had about the first part. It would have been hard actually to narrate what occurred in England directly, without making that part a sort of prologue or interlude;- and if you can find a way to weave it into the actual scene in Florida, through the "hero's" thoughts or conversation, it might be very much better to do that.

It may be that "South Moon Under" and your stories have put you in a position where agents will wish to have you serialize this new novel in a popular magazine where you will get a high price;- but I have had a secret plan myself that we might be able to serialize it in Scribner's. It might well be of too high quality for the popular magazine, and just exactly what we are searching for.

Always yours,

1. Faber and Faber. Review not located.
2. Gladys Hasty Carroll (1904–1999), *As the Earth Turns* (New York: Macmillan, 1933).
3. Thomas Wolfe, *Look Homeward, Angel* (New York: Scribners, 1929).

. . . .

135. MEP to MKR (CC, 2 pp.)

March 24, 1934

Dear Mrs. Rawlings:

I am just writing in great haste to get the enclosed letter to you. It comes down to a matter of personal feelings. You might not like having "South Moon Under" serialized in this paper. If the idea did seem to you a good one, it would be purely personal too because plainly it would not be remunerative. On the other hand, it would certainly do no harm at all. If you will send the letter back with Yes or No on it, I'll deal with Mr. Powers.[1]

Darrow told me that you had written that things were going much better, and I believe once you get over the first difficulty, they will go well. I hope they are better in every way, and not only in respect to the novel.

Always yours,

1. Harris Powers.

Hawthorn

[March 1934]

Dear Mr. Perkins:

I am being, frankly, very cowardly, about the matter of serializing South Moon in the Ocala paper. If you don't mind taking all the blame for it, and keeping my skirts entirely clear, I don't want to do it. Harris Powers has been very nice to me and given me the best of treatment, but there has been as much local reading of the book, and discussion of it, as I care for. The people I should want to read it about here, have already done so. The mass of his subscribers, as he said, are pretty much Crackers. Serializing it in his paper would only, as far as I'm concerned, stir up a lot of unprofitable talk about the book, and carry still further the business of identifying, often with painful incorrectness, often with painful correctness!, various of the characters. The whole thing would be so localized there would be no publicity gain for any of us, and I should not enjoy the new discussion at all.

I imagine it<'s> makes no difference to you one way or the other, so if you can, and will, preserve my innocence, I'd like to say No.

Many thanks for About Levy and Davy Crockett.[1] The Thomason drawings are literally priceless.

1. Arthur Calder-Marshall (1908–1992), *About Levy* (London: Jonathan Cape, 1933); John W. Thomason, illus., *The Adventures of Davy Crockett* (New York: Scribners, 1934).

. . . .

April 2, 1934

Dear Mrs. Rawlings:

I have written to the Ocala Banner. It is exactly as I thought was probable, and I wanted to take all the responsibility of course.

I am sending you a copy of the Fitzgerald.[1]

Always yours,

1. *Tender Is the Night.*

138. MEP to MKR (CC, 1 p.)

April 23, 1934

Dear Mrs. Rawlings:

I wanted you to see some more of John Thomason's pictures and so I am sending you his new book of stories,- the stories are good too if you have time for them.[1]

I hope I shall hear from you how things go before long, but not until you are ready to tell me.

Always yours,

1. John W. Thomason, *Salt Winds and Gobi Dust* (New York: Scribners, 1934).

. . . .

139. MKR to MEP (TLS, with holograph additions and postscript, 2 pp.)

Hawthorn, Florida
June 8. [1934]

Dear Mr. Perkins:

Just a hurried note, since you must be wondering what progress I'm making. Can't say I'm exactly satisfied, but at least I can report 3 chapters finished, and that the new conception of the book as I discussed it with you is indubitably *right*.

I believe I have a rather touching pair of characters in my Cracker brother and sister who are squatters on the young Englishman's undeveloped hammock property. I plunged into the thing at the point where they were expecting the arrival of the Englishman to take possession, but decided it was desirable, probably even necessary, to go further back in their lives to the point where they were thrown on their own in the world. Have done this & think it is sound.

The young Cracker will unquestionably dominate the book, but I think the situation will work out interestingly, as he will have to express himself through the Englishman's land——and in turn, the Englishman will be peculiarly dependent on him.

Are you going to Key West in July, as you planned? If you do, I think I can safely promise, barring accidents, that I will have enough of the book done to make it worth your while to stop off here on your way and go over it with me. I will be grateful for your help at just about that time, because you will know at once whether I am headed right or not.

You might feel some reticence at stopping here alone——if you will be alone——and if you will stop, I will either arrange to have someone else stay with me while you are here, or, my friend Dr. Vinson extends you his invitation to stay at his hunting lodge if you prefer not to stop with me. The lodge is about 15 miles from me; [missing material?][1]

If by any chance Hemingway is on his way back from abroad and will be traveling with you, by all means ask him to stop off too. Tell him, for God's sake, that I'm not the typical female author, "dragging", as Dorothy Parker put it, "her petticoats through literature".[2] This country is different from any other Florida and would probably interest him briefly. He wouldn't be bothered with other people, or anything. He could get tight on the 5-gallon keg of good rye that has lain in a charred keg for over a year in an attic that must hit 140 degrees at times, or he can run around Cross Creek naked or anything that amuses him. And if his grand family is with him, I have sleeping capacity for 9 people and 30 spring chickens crying to be boiled. My Jersey cow has just come fresh, producing over 3 gallons a day, butter beans are ready, etc.

This is just to urge you to stop off, and to report some progress.

As ever,

Many thanks for the new Thomason book. His *Davy Crockett* illustrations are infinitely better, don't you think? I am saving notes for the boy's book.

1. In spite of repeated invitations, MEP never visited Cross Creek. He was particularly sensitive on the subject of visiting MKR. On November 28, 1934, he wrote to Hemingway: "Maybe I might come down to Key West. . . . The trouble is there is another author in Florida,- Marjorie Kinnan Rawlings. She is a fine author too, and a fine woman. But I never did feel comfortable alone with women (I suppose there is some complex involved in it) and the idea of visiting one with nobody else around (she is divorced) scares me to death. She is one of the best as a person, and a mighty good writer too, and she is just finishing a book. She has asked me to come down a lot of times, and if she ever knew I went to Key West and did not stop there, it would be mighty bad" (*The Only Thing That Counts: The Ernest Hemingway/Maxwell Perkins Correspondence*, ed. Matthew J. Bruccoli [New York: Scribners, 1996], 217).
2. Dorothy Parker (1893–1967), American satirist.

· · · · · · ——· ·

140. MEP to MKR (CC, 2 pp.)

June 14, 1934

Dear Mrs. Rawlings:

I really have no anxiety about your book. I am certain it will be good. It is only a matter of your getting going on the right line, and I felt sure after talking to you that you had found the right line. I am afraid there is no chance of my getting down to Key West in July. I am engaged in a kind of life and death struggle with Mr. Thomas Wolfe still, and it is likely to last through the summer. I cannot stop while he will go on, and if he will go on for six weeks more at the present rate, the book will be virtually done. I could even now, if I dared, send a third of it to the printer. But Tom is always threatening to go back to the early part, and if he does that, I do not know what the result will be. We might have to go through the whole struggle over again. It has become an obsession with me now,- one of those things that you get to feel you have got to do even if it costs your life.

But when I do go to Key West, which may not be until winter, I shall certainly take advantage of your invitation. I know I should rather be in the country there and see the places you have written of than be on the sea.

Always yours,

. . . .

141. MKR to MEP (TLS, with holograph header, 1 p.)

[Cross Creek]
[June 1934]

Dear Mr. Perkins:

As you know, I would prefer to show you a completed manuscript——I'm even a little superstitious about showing part of one!——but I am wondering if it would afford you any particular satisfaction to see the present manuscript as far as it has gone——about 10,000 words, bringing the thing up to the arrival of the Englishman. If you read it and consider it at all promising, of course, I would be much encouraged. On the other hand, if it sounds bad to you, you would be pretty much "on the spot", because if it was totally without quality, you would hate to say so, knowing that in such a case I would be inclined to call quits on the whole thing——. Yet better that way, than to go on——. What do you say? Of course, I am just now at the beginning of the really difficult part, yet it is perhaps a good point at which to determine whether my Cracker brother and sister are a sufficiently touching or appealing pair of characters to go on with, into the situation you know I am building up.

If you think the thing is worth going on with, I think I can pretty safely promise the completed manuscript by the end of November. Short of accidents I see no reason now why I cannot average at least a steady thousand words a day.

I don't want any comparatively detailed criticism now, just a broad statement as to how promising you consider it.

Sincerely,

Editor's note: In MKR's handwriting at top of page: "Have decided to let you see it anyway——no use being Cowardly about it."

. . . .

142. MEP to MKR (TS for wire)

JUNE 27, 1934
MRS. MARJORIE K. RAWLINGS
ISLAND GROVE, FLORIDA
THINK MANUSCRIPT EXTREMELY PROMISING DELIGHTED AND EAGER
TO SEE MORE

. . . .

143. MEP to MKR (TLS: UF, 2 pp.)

June 27, 1934

Dear Mrs. Rawlings:

I telegraphed you how much I liked the beginning of the book. I really had a mighty pleasant morning in spite of interruptions reading it, and I could have gone on reading a manuscript of that quality all day and counted it a holiday. I think you have done splendidly, and a reader would be very much in suspense about the coming of the stranger. You have managed it all admirably well. I only thought that when you first mentioned that house there might have been a suggestion that there was some mystery about it, and some expectation that it might some day be claimed by a foreigner. That is a matter easily fixed if it is right, and everything else certainly is right. I do greatly hope that you will push on now. It is true that the difficulty will come when the Englishman comes, but I am sure you will get over it. This pair of Crackers will carry a book through almost alone. I would not try to subordinate them too much — as you have decided not to do anyhow — and you are certainly right, now that I know them, in presenting things largely through their eyes. This has been a good day for me, to know that you are going on so well.

Always yours,

144. MKR to MEP (ALS, 2 pp.)

[Cross Creek]
July 6. [1934]

Dear Mr. Perkins:—

Can't tell you how encouraging your feeling about the manuscript has been to me.

Have about 7,000 words more done. The Englishman is settled on the place. Will do another chapter or two and let you see it, to see if I have keyed him right. Then I'd rather not send you any more until it is completed.

I hope you haven't thrown away the 35 pages I sent you——that was my first draft and only copy.

Thanks a lot for your wire and note——I feel a lot better about everything.

. . . .

145. MEP to MKR (CC, 1 p.)

July 9, 1934

Dear Mrs. Rawlings:

I just got your letter and if the copy I have is the only one there is, you had better have it.- So I am sending it back directly. I would not need it to go on with the next 7,000 words because I can remember perfectly well where it ended, almost the words of it. It is splendid that things are working out so well.

Always yours,

. . . .

146. MKR to MEP (TLS, with holograph additions and postscript, 3 pp.)

Hawthorn, Florida
July 31, 1934

Dear Mr. Perkins:

Here is the next section of the book, the one I need most help on, because it must be keyed right in every way to make the rest build up properly. I should like quite specific and detailed criticism, if you can give it to me now, because I think a large part of the battle is won or lost right here. I'm not even going to ask you questions. You know about what I want to do.

This section ends at what to me is the end of the downward curve——the bottom point of the young Englishman's futility and despair——a complete miasmic blackness as he collapses in his malarial fever. From this point I expect to build up and out. The feeling I spoke of to you of the man climbing a precipice step by step. Only now that I have built things so largely around Luke and his relation to the hammock, it will be a matter of the two of them climbing up, with Luke in his firmness and ignorance, the steady one of the two. Probably the more important of the two.

Luke goes to the other side of the lake for the old doctor I had always planned to bring in, who brings Tordell through his fever. Also the doctor arranges to bring Tordell in contact with people of his own world at the high-class settlement across the lake. The doctor takes Luke back there with him for him to learn the minutiae of orange grove development and care. I have decided not to have Tordell's affair with the Cracker sister Allie a cold-blooded seduction, but a rather delicate and groping tenderness. But never mind the rest of the "plot"——I despise working out an outline. The rest is all clear in my mind and all I need to go ahead rapidly is to get this part keyed right.

I ought to be whipped, when I only do simple things well, for tackling anything as involved and difficult as this. The Crackers are so earthy in their way, and the Englishman's struggle is so definitely a spiritual thing, that there is danger of falling between the two and not achieving reality for any of them. I may need a greater emphasis on one or the other, less of what seems now a balance. I want drama and emotional excitement, and a shade in the wrong direction will produce melodrama and tommy-rot. Of course I have made practically no attempt to edit. Time and again I find that just taking out an adjective or an adverb takes away a florid effect.

If desirable, I can work out a little richer pattern here. I think I want a pet crane in here for Allie. I have known of a big gray heron that was a pet and followed its owner in a rowboat across a lake and waited in the marsh while the owner did business, then flew back home over the boat again. It did a wild queer dance when the owner came back from a few hours' absence.

From now on, there will be lots more people. If it doesn't seem boring and flat, I prefer to keep no more than these people so far. I ran into a problem I hadn't expected——the fact that an Englishman coming among such people would have felt and shown a sharp sense of social difference. Just another complication! I was prepared for the difficulty of the two kinds of speech, his and the Crackers', and my aim——don't know whether I have succeeded——is to keep both as simple and un-queer as possible, so that the reader is not painfully conscious of an affected dialect in either case.

I imagine it is clear already that I intend to have Luke and Tordell complement each other, each dependent on the other to work out his destiny.

Well, I don't envy you your job. Don't spare me. You know I don't mind work and it is hard to hurt my feelings. Anything to get it right. Thanks a lot.

[Holograph postscript, underlined] *This is still just a first draft so please send it back. Perhaps I should have made a carbon, but it seems pretentious to do that with something more or less abortive.*

[Typed postscript] Do you think "Hammock" would carry as a title, or can I do better? It seems to me that "Hamaca", which I wanted, would be forced—dragged in by the heels, without relation to anything. I could have Tordell have his old Spanish map, of course, yet it doesn't seem to go with anything else. What do you think?

. . . .

147. MEP to MKR (TLS: UF, 2 pp.)

Aug. 7, 1934

Dear Mrs. Rawlings:

I have read this new section, but I would rather not write to you about it before reading it over again except to say that while it does not seem to be quite right in every respect, it is certainly part of a very fine book. It is toward the end of this section that I felt some doubts, but they are certainly not of a serious kind. I have no doubts about the piece in a large sense, so I am sure you ought to go on in the meantime. The most important point is gained.- The Englishman is already a definite person, a real one. It is only in his actions and reactions toward the end of this section that he did not seem quite right to me,- possibly there are little matters earlier, but I shall read it all over and then write in detail.

I am enclosing excerpts from a couple of letters I have received, and they are not the only thing I have heard either, about your story.[1]

Always yours,

1. "The Pardon," *Scribner's Magazine* 96.2 (August 1934): 95–98.

. . . .

148. MKR to MEP (TLS, 3 pp.)

Hawthorn, Fla.

Aug. 9 [1934]

Dear Mr. Perkins:

I can't tell you how relieved I am at your note indicating that you think things can be worked out all right. When I didn't hear from you I was sure you thought it all hopeless and were struggling to figure a way out. As you evidently guessed, I have found myself unable to go ahead without hearing from you, but now I shall go on into what cannot help but be firmer ground, because it will deal with real people doing real things without too great an undercurrent of implications.

I knew of course the part I just sent you wasn't right, but as long as it isn't inherently impossible, I am not too worried. I have complete confidence in your ability to show me what is wrong and what to do about it. I do a very peculiar thing sometimes in my writing, and I did it in that section——I get definitely *off-key*, into a queer plane that is without reality. I simply do not know how or why I do it. My only hope is that I have become reasonably able at least to recognize it once it has happened. If I can ever figure out what it is I do, and why, I feel I will be capable of going ahead with my writing[,] speaking in general. Perhaps I just let a haze of words, of imperfect conceptions, carry me along, without focussing sharply and accurately enough. I simply don't know.

Two of the places I'll guarantee you found unconvincing——one where the white bird with the black band flies over the mule and wagon and the Englishman says "Oh God." He wouldn't say "Oh God." That whole several paragraphs in there is cock-eyed. Then when he is drunk at the end of chapter eight I think it is, and looks at the palm trees after the rain, he wouldn't have made, even drunk and feverish the remarks he made. That part isn't sound and I know it. The part about the negress you will be a better judge of than I——the way the fever gathers you up and hurls you into oblivion is accurate. I want to use the negress to carry out the feeling of his dropping into the bottom of the pit, spiritually and physically. I want to accentuate the blackness in every way. Then as I told you, from there he climbs up and out, in contact with all sorts of people.

Keep the manuscript <and ta> as long as you wish to work on it. Now that I know you haven't thrown up your hands in sheer despair, I can go on and work again. You must not ever be polite, you know. I will bring up a live rattlesnake and drop it on your desk if you are ever polite about my stuff and I catch you at it. The truth is the most difficult thing in the world to get at, and I have always felt that the closest approach to truth is the greatest kindness.

I am very happy that you hear favorable comment of "The Pardon". Except for the present novel, it is my first piece of pure creation, with no facts to suggest the story, so I am glad <that> to feel that I am not entirely dependent on the nature of my material. You don't know what a nightmare that has been.

Thanks a lot and take your time about the criticism.

[Postscript] A thousand thanks for "So Red the Rose".[1] It meant as much to me as almost any book I've ever read. I've always felt a vicarious nostalgia for that old plantation life. The book is infinitely better than "Balisand", which to now had stood to me for a re-creation of the pre-war South. Young does one brand new thing here——he brings out the larger implications of the Civil War, the meaning that will probably go into the next century's history books——the fact that the old plantation south went down, not so much under the Union armies, as under the sweep of a hypocritical industrial civilization.

Also many thanks for the last Thomason book. He must be a delightful sort of person. Some day I should love to have his "Jeb Stuart".[2]

You spoke once to me of what you thought the baneful influence of the Middle-west on Scott Fitzgerald. If you ever have time to do any reading that isn't connected with your work, I do wish you would try to read "The Farm" by Louis Bromfield.[3] It will drive you crazy, as an editor, because it goes backward and forward, backward and forward, without any form, and is not a novel at all. I am sure it is not intended to be, because Bromfield can do a coherent novel as well as anyone. As a study of a way of life, I found it magnificent. If you have a closed mind on the Middle-West, you really should read it.

1. Stark Young (1881–1963), *So Red the Rose* (New York: Scribners, 1934).
2. John W. Thomason, *Jeb Stuart* (New York: Scribners, 1934).
3. Louis Bromfield (1896–1956), *The Farm* (New York: Collier, 1933).

· ·

149. MEP to MKR (TLS: UF, 4 pp.)

Aug. 10, 1934

Dear Mrs. Rawlings:

I am sure you need have no anxiety about this second part of the book. I have read it through three times, and each time with greater pleasure. The Englishman is excellent, and there was your only danger. You have done everything that you aimed to do. You have made the hammock seem beautiful, and yet you have made the reader understand how it seems horrible to Tordell. The only criticism that I could make — and I do not do that with any great confidence — is in the matter of timing; the way he takes to drinking is excellent. The widow's visit is a very good scene indeed, and might be lengthened a little with good effect;- for you are never in danger of over-stressing, but perhaps just a little bit the other way. When she says "Don't let him git to Allie" the idea of that element is first introduced. It seems to me that perhaps his beginning to talk about the advantage of being a eunuch in Florida comes a little too quickly after that, and that his stumbling upon Rhea in the woods when he has fever comes perhaps too quickly after he has drunkenly talked to the Queen of Sheeba [*sic*]. Perhaps you ought to separate these incidents further by developing the intervals between them, or by putting in other incidents, of a different kind. But I think that in every large and serious sense you are absolutely right, and the Englishman is coming out excellently well.

Now from what you tell me of the doctor, and from the general turn the story is to take, I can imagine how beautifully it will go on. The truth is you are a writer, and no one need have any anxiety about what you do. The other story was the first novel you wrote, and it did seem to be wrong in construction in the beginning. But I never saw anybody so quick to understand what a book needed. You have always given me great credit for helping you, but all you needed almost was a hint. I believe now that having done that one book, you have learned vastly from it, and that everything will go well.

I started marking little trifles but there were so few that I thought anything like that might wait for proof. I did mark on page 36 the phrase "in a tone of anxiety". If Luke could hear the tone, would he not also have gained a sense of its foreignness? I know you do not want to, and should not overstress little English peculiarities like accent, but it must have struck Luke as a strange way of speaking and might be mentioned that once. I think you have had him use the way of speech of an Englishman always well, without forcing. On page 53 it seemed a little artificial and unnatural when he spoke of the Lancashire Hills and of having been a boy at the time of the Civil War. This is a trifle, but I think it would be better not to fix the time of the story at all. I supposed this would put it in the 80's, but it could as well have been in the 90's, and there is no need of calling attention to the fact that it was a score of years in the past.

I did see a few other little things, but they were so small as not to be worth mentioning, and particularly as you have not revised, and may easily change them. Otherwise I would leave them to the proof when one gets a new view of the book anyhow.

I am returning this part of the ms. by registered mail, and with many thanks. I look forward to reading anything you write, and I hope some more may come pretty soon.

Always yours,

P.S. Quite a bit of Tom's book is in proof, and we are having a great struggle over it. Stark Young's book is selling astonishingly well for these times.

August 27, 1934.

Dear Mrs. Rawlings:

I can't write you properly because my secretary is away on a vacation and everyone else seems to be away too. I was so busy all last week in a kind of labyrinth of difficulties that I couldn't write.

I know that the point you spoke of is untrue and I notice a number of places like that as I read,— but these seem to me to be details. Once you get the character right you'll see this and correct them, and I am sure he is right and will be very distinct when you finish the book. I'd even rather leave any such matters as that which you point to for the proof, when a book is read anew. I hope soon some more will come.

Always yours,

. . . .

Hawthorn, Fla.
Aug. 29. [1934]

Dear Mr. Perkins:

You really didn't need to write me, but thank you. I hope to catch most of the false notes such as we have spoken of before the manuscript goes into proof. I can do a much better job before things have gone so far. I get nervous and hurried when I have proofs to work on. It will make me much happier to get the "dirty work" done first, then the editing of proof will be almost in the nature of a pleasure.

I was surprised (and faintly mistrustful) that you had so little fault to find with the second section. Naturally, much relieved. I am going ahead steadily ——I should say, on a guess, the book is half done——the worst half. For the rest, I have only to keep myself at it. I think you will like the old doctor.

Unless you want particularly to see it as it goes along, I should much prefer not to send you any more until it is all done. I can scarcely go too far wrong now. I am aiming for the end of October, to finish, allowing the first three weeks of November for revision. I do want very much to have you work on it with me before it actually goes into proof.

Many thanks for the Jeb Stuart. I couldn't see Thomason (didn't get a thing out of his "Salt Winds") until I loaned that book to a man who was charmed with it and insisted on reading aloud from it. Hearing it read, I got at once the quality and was equally delighted——an odd experience for me, because I usually get the oral texture of anything myself. Now I am a Thomason enthusiast. He is distinctly a man's writer.

. . . .

152. MKR to MEP (TLS, 3 pp.)

Hawthorn, Fla.

Oct. 2, 1934

Dear Mr. Perkins:

I know you must be wondering whether I'm coming along on the book according to schedule. Glad to report that I am. Things seem to be coordinating themselves a bit; the inter-weaving of lives and so on seems to be following a convincing pattern. It seems to be a queer sort of book and I don't know what to make of it. It seems to be rather violent.

Lots of questions are in my mind, of course. In my fear of making melodrama of the violent parts, I may have under-done it, and may have to go back and put in more detail. On the other hand, the part I am working on just now contains much conversation between the Englishman and the old doctor, and I may have said too obviously, in too set and stiff a form, some of the things that I want to say. A technical difficulty is bothering me a little——the necessity for switching back and forth between the life with Luke and Allie in the hammock, and the <life> contact with the more civilized life of the doctor's community. I may have to do some coordinating along that line when we see the book as a whole, and see definitely whether it is Luke's or Tordell's story. The two are complementary, of course, and yet one must dominate. The Englishman is becoming a stronger character, and more important than I had thought at first. The thing that I thought would weaken him, drag him down in his spiritual progress, that is, the whipping by the local community for his affair with Allie, turned out to be a strengthening <character> element, when he finds, to his own surprise and satisfaction, as he says to the doctor, "Something within me was untouched by the whip."

It is going to be a much longer book than South Moon, and that may make it take me longer than I planned. If it were the length of the other, the end would be already in sight, but it is not. But I am going very steadily, sometimes as much as 3,000 words a day, never less than 1,000.

I wish you would give me your reaction to the word "Hammock" as a title. That is actually the title, as far as the substance of the book is concerned, but as

I have said to you before, the word seems objectionable simply because to everyone it means something ridiculously different from what it means in this part of Florida. Of course, a few pages <in the book explain it> after the opening of the book, explain it, but that doesn't help it as a title. I love the "Hamaca" but have not tried to use it, as it would have to be pretty much dragged in by the heels. I could have the natives call this particular hammock "Black Hammock", or "Dark Hammock", or "Palm Hammock", something like that, as most of the individual hammocks here have their own names. Would that help? If Hergesheimer[1] had not used the title, I should have liked, I think, "Wild Oranges", because the background of the story is the clearing of the wild orange grove in the hammock.

If it didn't come to your notice, it might interest you to look up an article by Ida Tarbell in the September Delineator, "The Cure for Too Much", in which she speaks very beautifully of South Moon Under to illustrate a point.[2] Coming from her, it pleased me very much.

I do wish you thought of coming to Florida about the end of November to go over the manuscript. If you can't, or don't care to, I'll get it in as good shape as possible to send you.

As ever,

1. Joseph Hergesheimer (1880–1954), *Wild Oranges* (New York: Grosset and Dunlap, 1918).
2. Ida M. Tarbell, "The Cure for Too Much," *Delineator* 125 (September 4, 1934): 4, 41.

. . . .

153. MEP to MKR (CC, 2 pp.)

Oct. 9, 1934

Dear Mrs. Rawlings:

Thanks ever so much for your letter. The story as you tell about it sounds extremely interesting. As to the word "hammock" I do not believe it is good. I have tried it on lots of people outside the office to ask them if they knew its meaning, or what its connotation was, and it misses fire every time. "Wild Oranges" would have been good. Isn't there some other highly characteristic thing like that that would do to put into the title?

I shall get Ida Tarbell's article. She is good, and also influential.

I wish I could think of coming down there in November, but I doubt that it will be possible. I have so many things and people to look after that it is mighty hard for me to get away. Maybe I might make it, but I don't dare to believe it.

Always yours,

Hawthorn, Fla.

October 18, 1934

Dear Mr. Perkins:

I've just written Mr. Darrow, in answer to a recent letter of his, that it looks just now as though I shouldn't be able to finish the manuscript by the end of November. I'm going ahead as rapidly as I planned, and if the book were the length of the other one, I would be through the first draft in another ten days or two weeks.

There is going to be a difficulty anyway about the proportions of the book. If the new people in the Englishman's life, the doctor's son, the woman orange-grower, Camilla, are at all good or convincing, the reader is going to resent in any case their appearing so late in the book. It is impossible and meaningless, I am convinced, to have them in any earlier, and the only way to balance things at all is to let them work out their part in his life with almost as much leisure as the earlier people take.

I am not particularly happy over the part I'm working on now, but there's no point in my raising prejudices in your mind. You will see what's wrong without my calling attention to it, and I might only distract you with my own criticism. I had to destroy entirely two important key chapters and begin all over again. I find as usual, much that is bad can be remedied by sharp pruning or even elimination.

I am using a tentative title in my own mind that may not stand, or that you may not like at all, "The Intruder". The book is proving unquestionably to be the Englishman's story. The Cracker, Luke, is the human element, you might say, of the natural background, and as such is important, but the struggle, the development, <are Tordell> the assimilation, are Tordell's. I began using the title in my own mind when it seemed to me that there was no apparent connection between his life with the Brinley's and his life with the more sophisticated people of the settlement where the doctor lives. Yet I knew the connection was there. Tordell does as much damage in the doctor's family as to the Brinley's, and "The Intruder" occurred to me as linking everything together, making him definitely the alien, filled with hate and despair, who finally joins his destiny with this people and this land. I hope to hit on something perhaps more colorful to suggest this, yet I am reasonably sure that the basic idea back of this is what I will work into a title. The definite turn the story has taken, to Tordell, takes me away a little from trying to use the type of country, or its meaning, as a title.

I am going so fast that it is still remotely possible I can keep my dates, but you never know when you're going to hit a bad snag to slow things up. The whole rest of it seems perfectly clear in my mind, but you can't ever be sure. So don't let the business office get any fixed date in mind. We may have to re-write half of it, and what then? I'm not a bit satisfied with a lot of it.

Many thanks for the Calder-Marshall book.[1] I hated most of it. I hate English upper-class slang, anyway, and it annoys me so, as a medium, that it stands between me and the meaning of what I'm reading. I hated it in Galsworthy.[2] English upper class people, well educated people, professors and such, who aren't trying to be "smart" in the society sense, don't jabber that cheap temporary dialect. If I were <an> a serious English writer, I should not want to "date" what I wrote that way. I still claim that only what I call *basic English* has dignity. Of course, I'm having trouble with my Englishman and with the upper class Americans for the very reason that I'm trying to use it, yet make it informal and free and natural enough so that the people sound real. I ran out of anything to read last night, and picked up "Jane Eyre", which I had happened never to read——and the worst of that sounds exactly like some of my stuff now, when I get stilted. At least I know what I'm trying to avoid!

But I liked what Calder-Marshall was trying to do, and did, and I thought he lifted it to a very high plane by the time he was done.

I hope next time I write it will be to say the manuscript is done. I will have to copy it myself——it's easier than correcting a typist's errors. My manuscripts look as if ink-footed chickens had scratched over them.

1. Arthur Calder-Marshall, *At Sea: A Novel* (London: Cape, 1934).
2. John Galsworthy.

. . . .

155. MEP to MKR (CC, 2 pp.)

Nov. 1, 1934

Dear Mrs. Rawlings:

I feel exactly the way you do about British slang. Absolutely repulsive. I have turned down a good many manuscripts on account of it,- several stories by this Calder-Marshall himself. But he is a man of talent. I am sending you a book you might enjoy on account of its subject which is largely fishing and shooting. It is called "Aleck Maury, Sportsman",- not a very good title.[1]

Everything you say about your book makes it sound very very interesting. I do not think "The Intruder" is a good title, but it did occur to me that there might be a local word which would still be understood in general, used in those parts to designate such a person,- like the word used in the mountains, "Furriner". The story is working out to be what you originally intended, and feared it might not be, if the Englishman is becoming definitely the protagonist and the Crackers part of the environment. Pretty soon I shall be asking you to send some pages for advance material. But I shall ask you a few days ahead of our need for them.

Always yours,

1. Caroline Gordon (1895–1981), *Aleck Maury, Sportsman* (New York: Scribners, 1934).

. . . .

156. MKR to MEP (TLS, 3 pp.)

Hawthorn, Florida
November 9, 1934

Dear Mr. Perkins:

I'd so much rather be able to send the completed manuscript—. Do you mind telling me what you need "a few pages" for? I'm not crying "Wolf!" when I say that a great deal of work may have to be done over again on the latter half. I do really think, if I can make the more civilized characters real, that the book should be interesting. And there are things I do want to say in it. But whether it is of value or not, God knows. But even through my intense dissatisfaction with this manuscript, a conviction comes to me that even if it is very bad indeed, some day I shall write a good book.

It is too early to tell whether the completed manuscript will be good enough for your purposes or not, but if it should be, luckily, do you still have any idea of serialization in the Magazine? It doesn't seem likely to me that it will be suitable for the average run of popular magazines, but if you don't want to use it that way, I'd like to send Carl Brandt a copy when I send you yours, just on the off-chance of his being able to do something with it that way. It seems to me all thought of any such thing should wait until we see the quality of the book, but I suppose plans have to be made ahead, and gambled on.

The Caroline Gordon book came and I am sure I shall enjoy it tremendously. The Copeland Translations[1] are a gorgeous thing, and I can't tell you how much I appreciate your sending me a copy. I shall treasure it. I was delighted to see the dedication to you. You see, more important people than I recognize your genius as critic and editor. I knew I was correct in the emphasis I put on the help you have given me.

By the way, I have just seen Robert Herrick off after a few hours' stop with me on his way south. He has proved a delightful friend——and after reading some of his books, I have thanked my stars that I was dubious enough to query you about the advantage of letting him see my stuff, and that you were honest enough to warn me against it. His personality is infinitely beyond his literary gifts. (Entre nous.) I had a good argument with him about "Farewell to Arms." I felt he had only a superficial understanding of it, and of Hemingway. I was impudent enough to tell him so. I told him that to me the point of the thing was that there is no "Farewell to Arms." The man thought he could turn his back on the silly turmoil and confusion of the war. He sunk himself in what to him represented peace and ecstasy; and the casual slap in the face of circumstance, of destiny, of death, destroyed all security, all happiness, for him. There is, simply, no escape. Herrick said, astonished, "But that gives the book dignity and meaning!" I said, "Precisely." Then he questioned whether Hemingway had that in mind or whether I had read it into what to Herrick was merely a love story. I said I was sure it was in Hemingway's mind, that all his stuff had that undercurrent. The old gentleman grew very thoughtful and said he should like me to interpret some of the other younger writers!

I became entirely exhausted and had to stop work a few days. I'm going at it again today. I simply can't give you a date. It all depends on whether I get that very desirable spurt, that keeps you at the job ten hours at a stretch. If that hits, well and good. If it doesn't, it will be well into December before I can quite finish. So say a brief prayer for me.

Again, thanks for the sporting book and many thanks indeed for the magnificent Copeland.

And please don't hurry me unless you have the best of reasons. I trust you so implicitly that if you wired me that it was absolutely necessary to finish the book in a week, I should believe you, and do it if it killed me.

1. Charles Townsend Copeland (1860–1952), *The Copeland Translations; Mainly in Prose from French, German, Italian and Russian* (New York: Scribners, 1934).

. . . .

157. MKR to MEP (TLS, 2 pp.)

Hawthorn, Fla.
Nov. 17, 1934

Dear Mr. Perkins:

"The Art of the Novel"[1] comes to me from you——I suppose something of an answer to my letter.

It is rather uncanny, but I find this, the thing I had begun to feel as the fault, basically, with the latter part of my manuscript:

"It stared me in the face that the time-scheme of the story is quite inadequate, and positively to that degree that the fault but just fails to wreck it. *************** Everything occurs, nonetheless, too punctually and moves too fast: Roderick's disintegration (in the case of Hamaca, the Englishman's achievement of his personal integrity and union with his surroundings) a gradual process, and of which the exhibitional interest is exactly that it *is* gradual and occasional, and thereby traceable and watchable, swallows two years (in Hamaca, very little over a year) in a mouthful, proceeds quite *not* by years, but by weeks and months, and thus renders the whole view the disservice of appearing to present him as a morbidly special case."

In my manuscript, the too-swift action of the latter part also serves to make the new characters, who are violent enough in any case, spectacular without being convincing. My great fear is that what should and could be authentic drama, becomes melodrama, without reality. I like to write in a series of dramatic scenes, building each chapter up to its own little climax. If it works, it gives the emotional intensity I want to achieve above everything else. If it doesn't work——we might as well tear up the manuscript and be done with it. Or else I'll have to go back and create more slowly, with greater detail, and more convincingly.

Again, I find my aim expressed in James: "——the question here was that of producing the maximum of intensity with the minimum of strain."

Well, what shall I do? Go ahead and finish——with the copying, a matter of three weeks? Or shall I take a week and copy what I have ready and send it to you? If it makes very little difference to you, I should prefer the former. If the latter would be of very definite help to you in planning your schedules, I'll be glad to cooperate. Or, if you don't think the risk is too great, I'll send the original manuscript.

[Postscript] I find too an expression <or definition> of what I have always felt was your own critical genius: "To criticize is to appreciate, to appropriate, to take intellectual possession, to establish in fine a relation with the criticized thing and make it one's own."

1. Henry James (1843–1916), *The Art of the Novel* (New York: Scribners, 1934).

. . . .

158. MEP to MKR (CC, 4 pp.)

Nov. 19, 1934

Dear Mrs. Rawlings:

I very much enjoyed what you had to say about Robert Herrick. I knew, of course, that he was capable of understanding that book, but belonging to a so much earlier generation, and having given his allegiance to many things that are opposed, he was not in a mood to understand a new way of expression, and a new point of view. He could have done it all right if he had made the effort, and probably after your talk with him he will sometime read "A Farewell" again and understand it fully, or at least enough to appreciate its importance.

Are the Churchills down there now too? I know they headed for Florida some time ago.

I do not want to hurry you at all about the novel, however long it may take you to finish it. The difficulty is that we are up against the same old problem about the time of publication. If we are to publish this spring which would be preferable, because it is not a good thing to have too long a lapse between novels, we ought fully to inform the salesmen by the middle of December, and to send them out armed with dummies.- To do this we should need a few pages of the text which need not be in finished form.

There is no doubt that we could prepare them with this material, and there is no doubt you could have the novel ready for spring publication, I should say,- because it would not need to be completed for a couple of months to do that. But the serial question is a complication. Scribner's has been forced to conclude that they haven't the space to run any serials except very short ones. We tried it out thoroughly with the Fitzgerald and the Boyd,[1] and we found that although they attracted a good deal of attention, they were not justified on account of the amount of space they take up in the magazine, which made it all lopsided.- After trying it with two such different stories, we decided that only very short serials were possible,- ones that we could get in two or three numbers, and with not more than 15,000 words or so in each installment. Besides, we cannot compete in price with the popular magazines under present conditions. Although I had always from the beginning hoped we could run a serial by you, and even considered our doing it at the last minute with "South Moon Under" until the Book of the Month Club became so interested, I think that possibility is out for a full length novel.

There certainly is a good possibility elsewhere, and in fact the editor of Pictorial Review[2] came in to say that she was much interested in the possibility if you wrote another novel. Even so, the availability of any particular story for serialization is always a guess. I think we had better proceed as though we were to publish this spring, but Brandt & Brandt should be furnished with a duplicate of the manuscript. I shall tell them of the interest of Pictorial. It is so great a disadvantage though, to publish a book without giving it the full benefit of advance salesmanship, that I should like to set up a few pages for the dummy, and get ready for spring publication. You understand that these pages are not read, but are merely used to give the look of the type page. The bookstore buyer merely glances at the text.- It can be in the roughest sort of form and serve the purpose, but to get up a dummy we must know the title. Did you think there was anything in the possibility that I suggested, that of using some word in the local vernacular to designate an intruder?

Always yours,

1. James Boyd (1888–1944), famous for his novels about the frontier.
2. *Pictorial Review* absorbed *Delineator*.

. . . .

159. MEP to MKR (CC, 2 pp.)

Nov. 23, 1934

Dear Mrs. Rawlings:

I would say go ahead and finish,- even with the copying a matter of three weeks. Only, if you can, do send some fifteen pages or so of the manuscript for us to set up a dummy from. We must not bring out a book by you without complete preparation for it. If publication is put off by serialization, we shall be none the worse off for having made this preliminary preparation;- but if it is not, the book's chances would be injured. You can believe me fully when I say that this manuscript need not be in finished form — just a rough copy of the first twenty pages would do even if you are going to rewrite every word of it,- which I do not think you will do anyhow.

I would love to see the manuscript as early as I can, but I think it would be better for you to do as you prefer,- which seems to me the better way anyhow.

Don't take Henry James too seriously though. I think you have a right diagnosis of your own weaknesses in the matter of writing a novel, but I think you exaggerate them very much, and that knowing them, you will also know how to correct them. I am terribly impatient to get forward with the book for the pleasure of publishing it.

Always yours,

. . . .

160. MKR to MEP (wire)

1934 NOV 27 PM 4 37
MAXWELL PERKINS—
597 FIFTH AVE—
MANUSCRIPT HAMACA COMPLETED MAILING TWENTY PAGES TOMORROW REMAINDER IN WEEK—

Hawthorn
Wednesday
[November 28, 1934]

Dear Mr. Perkins:——

The copying goes *so slowly* [both words underlined twice]——it will be another week before I'll have the manuscript entirely done. I simply cannot turn it over to a typist because it is so hard to decipher in places, and because I do a great deal of editing as I go. I leave off whole tails of sentences——most beneficially!

I am certain it will *not do* [both words underlined twice] for serialization. My editorial judgment is usually worthless, but in this case I think there is no question but that it's unsuitable in every way for magazine use.

I hate to lose the fat sum they pay, but otherwise I'm better pleased. Serialization is somehow cheapening.

. . . .

Dec. 7, 1934

Dear Mrs. Rawlings:

Don't hurry too much. Another week is certainly well within the time limit since we now have the dummy material, which by the way, seemed extremely good to me when I read it over. What does worry me is the title. I doubt if "Hamaca" ought to be used. Do you think "The Furriner" is common-place?

Always yours,

. . . .

[Cross Creek]
Dec. 12, 1934 [postmarked]

Mr. Maxwell Perkins
597 Fifth Ave.
New York City

Mss. of "Hamaca" sent you today American Express. Letter Enclosed with discussion of title etc.

Hawthorn, Fla.

Dec. 13. [1934]

Dear Mr. Perkins:

Here's the manuscript. I am tempted of course to pitch in and tell you how lousy it seems to me, and what I think is the matter here and there and so forth, but I'll restrain my general disgust and let you come to your own conclusions without the added handicap of my own ideas. In a later mail I am sending a résumé of my own criticism and questionings, and if you don't mind, I'll ask you not to read it until after you've read the manuscript and thought it over.

I am so sure that it won't do for serialization that I'm sending Carl Brandt the carbon instead of the original, but if by any wild chance I am mistaken about this, I'll ask you as a favor to me to swap copies with him so that he'll have a legible one to submit. But I'm positive it's no go for a magazine.

About the title——. Carl dislikes "Hamaca", as you do, but calls it "musical and arresting". I don't think it matters if it is not immediately understood by a book-buying public. I have never before been in trouble about a title, for I usually get my title *first*, and build around it——which of course I did, mentally, in this case, "Hammock" being the title in my own mind——unfortunately its connotation making the word out of the question.

If, after reading the Mss., you still object to "Hamaca", my choice would be "Beyond Darkness". I have a vague feeling such a title has been used before, however. What I want is a title as a *general background,* against which the people, the actions, the originally conflicting but ultimately harmonious philosophies, work themselves out. There are half a dozen *specific* titles that would be apropos, but none of them appeals to me. Some of them, in something of the order of my own preference, would be:

Bud-Wood (to me, this is too specific, too narrowing, and, if you'll pardon the language, too God-damned *pat.*)

The Betrayal

The River Styx

The Grove

The Clearing

Sweet Oranges

Sour Oranges

The Intruder

Golden Apples

I do not like "The Furriner" because there is condescension in the use of a dialect title, it's self-conscious, and besides, so much of the action absorbs itself with people who would not use the dialect expression, that it seems to me entirely unsuitable.

I feel I need help badly on the last third of the Mss.

Please let me know your *general* reaction as soon as possible, so that I may either

——.

If we eliminate "Hamaca" as a title, I will take out all references to the word in the text.

Editor's note: The number 2, in MEP's handwriting, appears before *Sweet Oranges;* the number 1, before *Golden Apples.*

. . . .

165. MEP to MKR (CC, 1 p.)

Dec. 14, 1934

Dear Mrs. Rawlings:

I just got your postcard saying the manuscript was on the way. I hope it won't be held back by the Christmas rush. If I could only get it tomorrow, I could read it over the weekend. I shall write you as soon as I possibly can about everything concerned with it, and I am enclosing herewith a contract. The title "Hamaca" will do anyway for that purpose. Our jacket is already designed though it needed some more work in detail. It will be very good indeed.

Always yours,

. . . .

166. MEP to MKR (TS for wire)

DEC. 17, 1934

MRS. MARJORIE K. RAWLINGS

ISLAND GROVE, FLORIDA

GREATLY ENJOYED NOVEL STOP THINK EXTRAORDINARILY FINE THROUGH WHIPPING STOP WILL SEND CRITICISMS OF SECOND HALF AFTER TWO OR THREE DAYS STOP STRONGLY URGE TITLE GOLDEN APPLES FOR ITS APPEAL

167. MEP to MKR (TS for wire)

DEC. 19, 1934
MRS. MARJORIE K. RAWLINGS
ISLAND GROVE, FLORIDA
MAILING LETTER TOMORROW BUT NEED TITLE BADLY FOR DUMMY

. . . .

168. MEP to MKR (TLS: UF, 7 pp.)

December 20, 1934

Dear Mrs. Rawlings:

I took your manuscript home the day it came, which was Saturday, and I read it all through the next day, and had a mighty fine day doing it. I cannot say too much for it up to page 250. Thereafter I have criticisms to make that seem to me important. But you are the only one to decide,- you are the only judge of their validity, and you must not be beguiled into anything that you do not think is right. There is also the complication that comes from possible—and I think Carl thinks probable—magazine publication. The popular magazine prefers qualities other than those favored by the book publishers. What might seem too crowded with happenings, too melodramatic and romantic to the book publisher (as the last third of this book does to me), would seem desirable to the magazine publisher. In fact, Carl, I rather thought from a short talk on the telephone, did not agree with me, or did only partially. But I will tell you what I think, and if it seems to you untrue, it probably is. Anyhow, it is your book and must be made as you want it.

As for the background, and the whole layout in the house and region where Luke and Allie and Tordell live, it is magnificently given;- in fact I think it is even better in all that part than "South Moon Under," — though comparisons are always irrelevant. The life of these three people together, and of Tordell and Allie alone, is admirably suggested, and very movingly. Allie wins the reader from the start, and yet his sympathy is with Tordell too. The idea you wanted to give of the changing effect upon Tordell of the environment has succeeded perfectly, when one thinks of the environment as being that of his own land and the region around it.

It seems to me that when Tordell goes to the other side of the lake to the doctor's, you write with a different point of view and set up an environment there which is at variance with that one which you have created before. It is not simply that it is different in being so much more civilized: it is that the way it is treated is not objective and realistic, but romantic. The very fact that there is this region peopled by rather romantic, and one might almost say finished characters, so near, does in itself an injury to the effect of the other environment which is so essential a part of the story. I would hope that you might modify this in certain ways which would prevent what seems to me a kind of incongruity in view of the motive of the book.

To take it in a purely obvious way: if Tordell was so near to a region and a group of people of that sort, he was truly not in so desperate a situation as seemed at first when he came into a kind of wilderness. But it is not only the superficial and obvious objection that I mean, but rather it is a difference in tone and quality. I would hope that you might modify this by leaving out the dinner party where several characters, including DeVigny, are introduced who have no later place in the book, but merely seem to me to break the mold of environment you have created; and also by making very little of the horse element, and concentrating the whole effect upon the orange groves,- and by the way this is a most lovely description you give of the forest of orange trees. That is in every sense a right part of the book.- What I am trying to express is the idea that the spirit and quality of the life you picture in Camilla's house and thereabouts, does do an injury to your motives. It is romantic. The treatment of the other part is not romantic, and neither is your natural writing in your stories, or in "South Moon". It seems to me that in dealing with Camilla and the doctor's son, your point of view has been modified from its natural objectiveness into romanticism. If the whole book were in that method, it might be a very fine book of that kind, but I do not think that these two elements combine. Each one is hurt by the other, and the first element in which everything is treated more objectively and realistically, is certainly the right one for this book, and in fact characterizes all but this last part of it, and even a large part of that.

The major characters in this book are Luke and Allie, Tordell, the doctor, and Camilla. It seems to me that you have been completely successful with her. In Camilla it seems to me only that you have verged on the too romantic. But even if that is so, she is a fine character. Her introduction into the story with her mint juleps is dramatic and rightly effective. But when you have her there with the invalid husband hidden away, and behaving with a kind of Byronic promiscuity, I think you are moving into that melodramatic and romantic vein which seems to me to belong in some other mine than this. I wish she could just be a widow who was not promiscuous though she was strong, and that she was kept away from Tordell by those natural things that came from the complications of his life, and her own interest in the doctor's son,- which I should think need not go to such extremes. It seems to me that the incident of Tordell blundering into the husband's room and being asked for the penknife for purposes of suicide, is melodramatic and does not belong in a book like this one. But I am not sure that Camilla ought not to be spoken of by the Crackers or glimpsed earlier in the book, so that the reader would be aware of her for a long time before she actually appears.

As for Tordell, who is the most important character in the whole book, I think you have succeeded wonderfully. The ordeal and shame of that whipping was enough to account for his sudden development into greater maturity, since he took it as he did. His marriage to Allie, which seemed to me, before I read it to be impossible, turns out to be completely convincing. And so does Camilla's first reaction to it. The only thing that troubled me about all this was that Tordell should seem completely to have forgotten the whipping after he came back from the doctor's. Even though they could not touch his innermost self, the mere fact of their having laid a whip upon him would in itself have made him shudder, I should think, for many many days. Camilla would have known of it too, and it would have affected her,- for surely nothing of that sort would happen without everyone knowing of it. It seems to me that something ought to be made of this, and that perhaps if you changed some of the steps by which Tordell and Camilla eventually came together, this might be one of the influences on the course of their story: the very fact of the thing having happened would have affected their relationship if she knew it had happened.

Another character who comes very near being a major one, is the doctor's son. The plain truth is I do not think he is a success. It seems to me that he is a character out of romance, and not convincing. I would hope that he might be greatly toned down into a more real kind of person. It is true that he was somewhat mad, but he must still be real, and I honestly do not think he is. Apart altogether from the artificiality of the book's coming to its conclusion through the not inevitable deaths of three people, I think that the death of Claudius and Camilla's husband is melodramatic and therefore unconvincing. I should hope that there could be no husband, and that Claudius should not die. You have got to get him killed if you leave him as he is, but if he were much toned down and were not engaged in an active love affair with Camilla, he could still live. I do not even think that the doctor has his earlier reality in the incident following the death of Claudius.- But the truth is that all these characters and incidents might be successful and effective in a sheer romance such as the Brontes wrote, but it does not go, if I am right, with the general stuff and texture of this book.

All the time that Tordell is on his own ground, even when Camilla is also there, everything is right and fine. The account of the fox hunt is so. But when you take Tordell into the other region, especially into Camilla's house, the quality is different, and there is a sort of unreality which is not necessary,- for it does not inevitably come from the character of Camilla. It comes from the romantic way of treatment, and the not convincing incidents, rather.

I think the very ending of the book is splendid. Luke's marriage and everything about him and his life and his relationship with Tordell, and his struggle for the orange trees, and Tordell's growing interest in it, and the widow Raynes,- all these things and people are beautifully managed. The book as a whole is very fine indeed — I could not have hoped for anything better, but to my mind it is marred by these elements of melodrama and romance. You have always asked me to be downright in criticism, and so I must do it. Besides, while the questions raised are all ones for you to answer as you wish, I have the highest regard for your talent, and the greatest interest in its full realization, and I could not but make a strong appeal for the consideration of changes to eliminate these qualities I speak of.

After you have decided about the criticisms I made, and we get the manuscript into proof, I might make a few suggestions on the galleys for changes in detail. There are still two points of relative detail that I might speak of.

The first and most important is that concerning the story Tordell told the doctor. I see no reason for the game keeper's boy element. In fact, I think it makes the scene less convincing: any father would react violently against that accusation. On the other hand, no husband would want to disbelieve the accusation made by the young wife. He would want to believe it, and he could do it easily on the support of the maid. Didn't Potiphar's wife get away with it? A man would believe that more quickly against his son, I think, than against his friend, because he would hate more to believe the truth if the man were his son. I think if the accusation were made, and the boy in horror and anger referred to the wife in the terms he used, and his father knocked him down, that his exile would be completely accounted for without any testimony from the game keeper. Nobody would question the exile, but with the boy element brought in, they almost begin to. It is a case of protesting too much. Any elderly man would rather believe that his son had betrayed him than that his young wife had.- At least that is what I regretfully think.

Another is the incident of the young negress. It is well done and I do not know whether it ought to be questioned or not. If it should, the only reason is a commercial one.- It would be resented by many readers of a kind who run into large numbers, and who ought greatly to like this book. I think it is a question to consider, but it is not essential to the story. It could be left out. The only thing is that we then should lose a striking and moving happening.

I was delighted to see you getting into a wider field than that represented by "South Moon". The whole business of orange growing and the beauty of the orange groves, and the struggle against the cold and all that, is excellent, and new. I was glad also to see so fine a character as Camilla (not to mention Tordell) come into this book. That is all very much to the good, and my objections are only those stated about with regard to the treatment and incompatibility of tone.

As the story stands I think it moves too rapidly after page 250. Too much happens. At the same time, I do not think it should be longer, but if anything shorter. Allie dies very near the end, but she faded out before that, and all the readers loved her. She must fade out, I suppose, but when she begins to go out of the story you have passed its high point, I think. You ought to get more quickly to the end if it can be managed, then. It could be managed if it seemed to you that there was merit in what I have argued,- for that would mean a considerable number of excisions, and a somewhat simpler treatment of other parts.

Anyhow, I never read a book with more personal interest, and I hope you will let me know how all this strikes you.

Always yours,

. . . .

169. MKR to MEP (wire)

1934 DEC 21 AM 9 57
MAXWELL PERKINS—
597 FIFTH AVE—
GOLDEN APPLES—

. . . .

170. MKR to MEP (TLS, with holograph postscript, 7 pp.)

Hawthorn, Fla.

[December 1934]

Dear Mr. Perkins:

I am staying home from a deer-hunt to write you, because I am so much stirred by your letter of criticism about the book.

I agree with you almost entirely, with the most enormous feeling of relief, since once again you have clarified for me what I recognized as a muddle. I should have said however that it was almost impossible to tell what precisely was wrong, but you have done this. I do not see how Carl or anyone could question your reaction to the things you speak of. I have been telling you myself that I sensed a theatricality that was most offensive to me, but I could not seem to prevent its happening at the time, or tell, afterward, what to do about it. But you gave me a perspective, or vision, as though you had put an immense magnifying glass on the thing, so that I believe I can eliminate much of the taint. I have told you that I knew I got off-key, knew when it happened, but was at a loss how to change it. I think in time I shall be able to prevent this, at least to such an objectionable degree. It is odd, but I am much happier to have had you find this particular fault with a portion of the manuscript, than if you had accepted it more or less in toto, as Carl did, because those people, those relations, that life, made me so desperately unhappy in reading over those parts, and I felt so acutely that much was wrong, that if you had found it acceptable I should always have had a more blurred feeling in judging what I was doing than I think I shall ever have again, because now I know that that sick feeling, actually a physical revulsion, is an authentic warning.

I do fear that it is always going to be difficult for me to handle sophisticated or complicated people with an impression of reality, and I may always be somewhat limited in subject matter for that reason. But I feel on more solid ground at this moment than ever before, because of the nature of your criticism.

I should have said that I was wrung dry of all ability to deal with these characters over again, but you stimulate me so intensely that it will be possible, even pleasurable, to do it, since now I have a feeling of hope about it. I do hope you don't mind my saying again what a prodigious genius I feel you have for getting inside a writer's mind and judging absolutely from the inside; for making the incoherent, coherent. I wish I might add the lucidity of your mind to my own often hazy imaginative processes, and it is like such an addition to have you work with me this way. Frankly, I could not endure the thought of having to get along without your help, and I hope no circumstance ever deprives me of it.

No thought of serialization must be allowed to interfere for one moment with doing the best possible job on this. I have worked too hard to achieve an inner satisfaction to let the question of a profitable sale bother me now. I need money as badly as anyone——I have serious grove injury from the freeze—— but I am searching in all of my work and living for the elements that bring me happiness, and self-respect, and a sliding over the taint in this manuscript simply because it was acceptable or preferable to a magazine editor, would affect me as uncomfortably as any other kind of prostitution——not that it really matters to anyone except myself. So we will ignore that aspect of it and let the serialization take care of itself.

Except that a sizable flat sum of money would be so very usable, I am disinterested in the idea in any case, and almost regret having allowed it to go so far. I should really hope for rejections. I think I shall tell Carl that I will have to have a high figure so that if it goes through, it would be at a price I couldn't afford to pass by. Otherwise, I actually feel that serialization hurts rather than helps the sale of a book. When I sounded you out on your plans for the book, before I told Carl he might try to place it, I had hoped that if the book was likely to be at all good, you might say another Book of the Month sale was possible. In that case I should have passed up the other thing. While I think of it, since I am rather thinking aloud in a rambling fashion, I don't think the contract you sent me is fair, if the book proves worth publishing at all. It is the same terms as the first one, and it seems to me a publishing house does not run the same kind of risk on a second book that is run on the first one, since the first few thousand copies will positively be sold on the strength of the previous book, and I think the author should profit to a greater extent for that reason. But that again is a minor matter and I know no such question will ever interfere with our mutual work and plans. Now to the main questions:

You are entirely right about Camilla's husband. He goes out of the book at once, and that in itself will be an enormous help.

Claudius Albury was never real even to me. There is taking shape in my mind now an entirely different sort of person, who will come out with greater reality. The horse-breeding will go out altogether but I think I shall keep his music. Make him a sulkier, more brooding sort of person, with almost a suggestion of his being the spiritual failure that it seemed at the beginning Tordell must be, as though to say, "Here is the way two different men react to the inner despair." I think it is necessary to have Claudius <die> kill himself, because it makes two points I feel I must make: one, the frightful vulnerability of the doctor in his love for his son; the other, the point I try to make in other connections, that is, the peace that is to be found in losing oneself in something greater than the individual——when he turns from his grief back to the service of his profession. I think when I get a better Claudius, the doctor will be better afterward, because as it stands we have the doctor interested in a person who actually has no existence. I intend to take out an early remark about the doctor, I think, about his having prowled freely among women in his earlier days. I think the predatory suggestion (while I intended it merely as a character touch) is inconsistent with the picture I try to give of his general beneficence.

As I conceive of it now, while I shall eliminate from Camilla the promiscuity, I see no other way but to have Claudius actually her lover. I think if I take away this element entirely, take away her vulgarity and some of her violence in her relations with him, you would find her a rather flat person. Since much of the book concerns itself with the struggles of people to lift themselves out of darkness of one sort and another, I am reasonably sure I want to suggest progress for her, too, so that in the end Tordell, who began so deep in the mire himself, has a helpful and spiritual effect on her. But we will see how that works out when we get a new Claudius.

The dinner party is out of the book at once. I am wondering if it might be less artificial not to try to have Camilla's house so pretentious, although as a matter of fact people with large groves at that time made a great deal of money. While I think of it, the date of the book is of no importance except that I needed a time of such isolation and the time of the Big Freeze for dramatic purposes. (And it looks as though the Big Freeze is going to be repeated this year. I shall re-write some of the freeze part, now that I have actually seen the phenomenon, which is very rare.) And this brings us to the proximity of the civilized life to Tordell's hammock. To a certain extent, this is and has been, from the 1870's to the present time, a peculiarity of Florida that we shall have more or less to accept. The two kinds of life exist side by side, each one scarcely conscious of the other. That is one reason the Florida papers set up a howl about my early stuff. The people living an urban life are actually unconscious of the existence of the remaining backwoods life. As for Tordell, I meant to suggest that the hopelessness of his wilderness situation was a great deal in his own mind, and that when he had won his battles, his junction with what was good of life about him followed as a natural thing. I have made the life on the doctor's side of the lake seem too accessible, however. I think if an expert checked up on me, he would find me having the horses doing some pretty quick traveling. I think I need to have everyone take a longer time to get back and forth, to emphasize, in every such piece of travel, the distance and so on. Yet as I say, the coincidence of the two ways of living is something scarcely to be gotten away from. Although we had a car, you have no idea how remote my own place seemed to me the first year. The urban life, where I knew no one, seemed incredibly far away and different. I shall have to point this up better in the manuscript.

About the black girl Rhea. Since you admit her elimination would be for commercial reasons, you won't mind my saying that we should both be inconsistent if we did everything possible in taking out the melodramatic superficiality, which would appeal to large numbers of people who feed on that kind of thing, and then took out something necessary, as a sop to buyers. If we're going to try for artistic unity, we can't make any exceptions. To me, the episode, while grantedly revolting, is <completely> necessary, in order to give Tordell a completely be-mired condition from which to rise. Nothing else could so suggest heat and blackness and muck and fever. It is the low point of his spiritual life, and I feel it is needed vitally for a foundation from which to proceed.

As to the pederasty, you are of course right about that. It is unnecessary and confusing and needlessly unpleasant. I very nearly left it out when I copied the Mss.

You are right, too, about following through on the whipping episode. I was somewhat conscious of a gap there myself. It would be possible for Camilla not to have heard of it, but it will be much better probably to have Tordell tell her of it himself, or perhaps have Claudius do so maliciously, and as you say, it will certainly be a shaping element in the development of their relations. I rather dodged that whole issue.

I shall try to have more of the later action take place in Tordell's territory. That ought to help. Did you object to Dr. Albury's establishment? I did not. It seemed to me a natural enough sort of place, except that <this> the entrance of Claudius anywhere is an immediate signal for the disintegration of all quality in the writing. I think he alone has done an enormous amount of harm, tainting all the episodes where he figures. I am surprised you liked Camilla as well as you did. I do not like her, although she is very real to me as she stands. I shouldn't like her in real life.

I can't tell you how happy I am that you like the general fabric of the book. I have put up a pretty stiff fight against despair of one sort and another, and the feeling you gave me that I have accomplished something of what I set out to do, and that the thing is not utterly impossible, is like firm ground under my feet after struggling in quick-sand. So many times the effort to keep the grove going properly, the struggle to build some personal happiness, and so on, have seemed absurdly hopeless, and if the book had come out a total failure, things would have been difficult for me mentally. As it is, I feel great hope in all directions.

Thank you again for your good help. I'll welcome any further ideas.

[Postscript] Is your copy of the manuscript complete? I do hope so, for I believe the part missing from Carl's copy is a section I rewrote as I copied, a foolish thing to do without any other record. I cannot imagine what happened to it. Do let me know whether you have it all properly. It positively is not here.

"Golden Apples" does not entirely please me, but it has a certain appeal and glamour. I'll try to close my mind on the subject so as not to hit on a title I'm enthused about at the moment of going to press!

· ·

171. MEP to MKR (TS for wire)

DEC. 27, 1934
MRS. MARJORIE RAWLINGS
ISLAND GROVE, FLORIDA
READ <YOUR> LETTER WITH GREAT PLEASURE STOP BELIEVE <YOUR>
OUR COMPLETE AGREEMENT SHOWS WE ARE RIGHT STOP SHOULD SUBMIT
TO CLUB BUT OUTCOME ALWAYS SHEER SPECULATION STOP ASHAMED
OF CARELESSNESS ABOUT CONTRACT STOP WILL OF COURSE PAY FIF-
TEEN PERCENT FROM <THE> START [STOP] WRITING

· ·

172. MEP to MKR (TLS: UF, 5 pp.)

Dec. 31, 1934

Dear Mrs. Rawlings:

I am terribly sorry about the contract. I did not give the matter much thought. Of course you ought to have the highest royalty we can give,- 15% from the start. We are not by way of suggesting advances in these times (and as a matter of fact they are not such good things for an author who can do with-out them) but if you want one, you can have that too. We might make it that you should receive on publication whatever had been earned in royalties on the advance sale. The way in which authors have a hard time is that according to a publisher's contract they have to wait (as, of course, the publisher himself does) for so long before receiving anything on a book,- six months at least, and generally ten. This payment of what the English call accrued royalties on pub-lication, is certainly reasonable enough. But tell us what you want and I guess you shall have it.

I cannot tell you how much relieved and delighted I was by your letter. I had had in mind some rather specific suggestions to make, but I think that you cover every one of them.- For instance, I thought that you could make the orange grove region more remote but still accessible, and that if you reduced the difference in that life by simply reducing the emphasis, as you would if you eliminated the dinner party, you would greatly gain. These things you yourself suggest, and they were exactly what I would have suggested. I did realize that Claudius was important in connection with your idea of the doctor's character, and I think your plan of treatment for him now is right. I think you have thought out also the way in which Camilla and Tordell act upon each other, and I did suppose you could not prevent Claudius from being her lover. I would also not have the elaborateness of Camilla's house emphasized. I guess we shall have to keep Rhea. I recognized that she was important. Perhaps she ought in some way to be heard about later in the story, since she was in a way part of the landscape. But all the rest beyond what we have discussed I think are matters of detail, and we can take care of them easily in the proof. It seems as if I saw the book exactly now as you do. I like Camilla greatly as a character, but if she charged up to me with a mint julep, I think I should take to the bushes. But she is fine in the book,- at bottom a fine character.

As for the Book of the Month Club, I had talked about this book to the people we see there, and in the highest terms, and they expressed themselves very emphatically as wishing to see it, but you never can count on that, of course. They have hundreds of books offered each month. There are all kinds of elements that govern their selection which we cannot calculate upon.

I am sorry about the oranges. After reading the book I can imagine how tragical cold spells can be down there. Perhaps on that account you may want an advance.

I recognize that the title "Golden Apples" is a concession, but it seems to me it is legitimate to make a concession in a title, and the truth is a title takes its meaning in the end from a book, and if we can do with the book what we hope, it will seem to have been exactly the right title in every way.

Always yours,

P.S. What I did was to give Carl the original typescript, and to keep the carbon here. Then we gave him the pages missing from the original in the carbon. He seems to be very hopeful, and perfectly satisfied.

1935

173. MEP to MKR (TS for wire)

JAN. 14, 1935
MRS. MARJORIE RAWLINGS
ISLAND GROVE, FLORIDA
DISLIKE BEING TROUBLESOME BUT ANXIOUS TO KNOW IF YOU COULD
ROUGHLY ESTIMATE TIME NECESSARY TO COMPLETE REVISION

· ·

174. MKR to MEP (wire)

1935 JAN 15 PM 10 56
MAXWELL PERKINS—
597 FIFTH AVE NYC—
WHEN WOULD YOU LIKE REVISION COMPLETED WILL TRY TO ACCOM-
MODATE

· ·

175. MKR to MEP (TLS, with holograph postscript, 4 pp.)

Hawthorn, Fla.
Jan. 15, 1935

Dear Mr. Perkins:

I hope you haven't been picturing me working busily on the book revision, because I haven't been giving it a thought, more than the unavoidable night-thinking. I really should have back again the carbon to work from——I made so many changes as I went along with the typing. If you are using the carbon for necessary purposes at your end, then I'll trouble you to call Carl and ask him to send me back the fifty or so pages from the original manuscript that I sent him when we were trying to get together on the few pages missing from the finished copy. The pages I sent him cover a very important part of the revising, and I must have them, if you can't spare the carbon.

I have your wire asking about time needed for revision. I haven't the faintest idea. My conception of Claudius Albury has taken definite shape, and it will work out convincingly, but the new character plays hell with my conception of Camilla as she stands, and with implications between her and Tordell. This will probably be all to the good, but I am furious about it. There will be implications from this change reaching far backwards, perhaps, into the book. The new Claudius couldn't possibly be the woman's lover——he's just not man enough——he would appeal more to her maternal instinct than anything else, and this invalidates all the vulgarity and violence of her, that I formerly had as responsive to, and influenced by, his vulgarity and violence. This again gets involved with Tordell's character, in that, as I mentioned before, I want his good influence over Camilla to come as a high point in the development of his own character. I liked the progress made, from a man so far gone in despair that he would lose himself, with his last conscious breath, in union with a nigger woman——to a man who, finding a woman who is everything he wants and who offers herself frankly, will not take her on her terms because he rejects them as not good enough, spiritually. You may say that in the new arrangement he would reject her for perhaps other spiritual reasons, connected with his marriage to Allie. To hell with that <illegible excision>. A man who'd made <an unfortunate> a liaison with a girl his inferior might see her through decently, as I have him do, but he wouldn't be so noble he'd consider his marriage a bar to the woman he really wanted, and if he did he'd be a damn <illegible excision> fool. I want the obstacles between him and Camilla her own arrogance and what seems to him, not quite understanding her, a taint in her own standards. I may have to solve this by keeping her violent, with the suggestion of other lovers. I'll be damned <illegible excision> if I'll make her noble too. I mean altogether and disgustingly noble. I like pitiful people and loving people and hard people and people who have any elements of strength and put up a fight, but nobility turns my stomach.

However, you probably know me well enough to know that I stamp my foot and curse and rave and then go ahead and do the job to be done, so don't let what seems to be a swell mess bother you. If you agree with me that the unreality of the present Claudius is the key to the whole melodramatic falseness in the book, I can only go ahead with him from the moment he enters, and let the rest <as exists> shape itself as it must, fighting as I go along to keep it real, and clearly visualized, and in key.

Carl puts up another plea to take out Rhea, even in the book. I haven't the faintest desire to be pornographic or nauseating, you know that, and you know why I used the episode as I did. If you can think of any acceptable substitute to do what I wanted, I don't have a closed mind on it. Mind you, I will not be pure just to be pure——this book is going to lose me all my friends and readers among sporting men as it is, and if I finish up with something that old women read in their rockers and think is "too sweet", I'll never write another word as long as I live. However, here is an idea that occurs to me. Would it convey the same feeling if I carried this episode as it is to the point where Tordell discovers Rhea naked and asleep, removes the magnolia petal from over the black breast——I think that's a gorgeous picture——but not to have union occur—— possibly the idea vaguely in his mind in his fever, but perhaps have him simply collapse with his head on her breast. It might be as effective to have her half-drag, half[-]carry him, to the house, like a black nurse or mother. Luke could meet her coming in with the man, and could drive her off in mistrust. This would accentuate his torment in connection with Tordell and Allie as well as if it had actually happened. If this would convey the feeling of Tordell's lost-ness as well, I have no objection to eliminating the actual union. But I will not invalidate the whole structure of his spiritual progress by being fussy. I'd hate to estimate how many white men have had relations with negresses. Where do people think our rapidly increasing numbers of mulattoes have come from? The negro race is being absorbed so rapidly that a hundred years from now people will wonder why on earth there was talk, in our day, of the race problem in America.

As you can see, I'm in a rather vicious mood. I'm in bed, have been for nearly a week, not having missed bronchial pneumonia by too wide a margin. I was having the most marvelous time hunting, without a thing on my mind. I have no business getting myself stirred up right now over things I've been deliberately forgetting for a breathing spell, but I can't have any peace with all these questions up in the air anyway.

I thought things were sort of waiting on whether Carl makes a magazine sale. I'll guarantee he can't do it.

Suppose you tell me when you would like the revision completed. You evidently have some date in mind. Let me know what you would like and I can probably tell you whether it's possible or impossible. There's no use wiring you. Just tell me what you want.

Thank you for offering the advance. I know publishers hate them. I'd rather get along without it if I possibly can. I had a fifty per cent or more loss on my citrus, and the remainder I have been able to sell has not brought much, but I can get along for a while.

Just get me my material of one sort or another, the carbon or the fifty pages I sent Carl, and I'll get to work again.

[Postscript] Another thing I'm furious about is not being able to *talk* [underlined twice] with you about these things. I need to talk to somebody for hours and hours, to help clarify my ideas!

· ·

176. MEP to MKR (CC, 2 pp.)

Jan. 16, 1935

Dear Mrs. Rawlings:

I do not want to press you into working faster than you ought to do, however long you need. There is also the question of serialization, for if that is to take place we shall not, I suppose, be able to publish until the fall. Carl Brandt must have told you that he feels very hopeful, but has no final word as yet. If serialization should not go through, we should want to publish as soon as we can, and could not have the manuscript too soon. If we had it by the 7th of February, which might perhaps give you time enough, we could publish in May, which seems now to be a good season. But the truth is we cannot have it too soon and yet we ought not to have it sooner than you are ready.

If I knew that there was to be no serialization, I should put the first two-thirds of the manuscript in hand now. But it seems very probable, and so we may as well wait until we hear from Carl.

I sent you a book yesterday that I am sure you will enjoy called "The Islandman".[1]

We are in no hurry to draw up the contract, but when you want us to do it we shall do it in the idea of meeting your wishes.

I hope the orange situation looks more favorable.

Always yours,

1. Tomas O Crohan (1856–1937), *The Islandman* (New York: Scribners, 1934).

January 22, 1935

Dear Mrs. Rawlings:

I waited to answer your letter of the 15th until the Cosmopolitan question was cleared up.[1] I have just at this moment heard from Carl that serialization had been arranged, and that we shall not be able to publish until about the 10th of July. An editor is always impatient to publish a book he is deeply interested in, of course, but in every other respect I think this has worked out well. You will now have plenty of time for revision since we shall not have to begin to set up until the first of April, though if we can do it sooner we shall wish to. And while mid-summer used to be thought a bad time to publish, it has not seemed to be so lately, notably in the case of Stark Young's great success.[2] Carl told me you were very glad too about the serial, and I hope you are also well. This may all have worked out to relieve your mind from the worry about the oranges. We returned the duplicate manuscript so that you could work from that, and I am now drawing up a contract,- for the straight 15% royalty. You will probably not want an advance now, but if for some reason you should, the fact that none is stipulated in the contract will make no difference, of course.

The question of revision is rather confused in detail, but it does not seem to me that it is at all confused in principle. I completely agree with your fundamental feeling about it. The last thing I want you to do is to have the people "noble" or any part of the book what anyone could call "too sweet"; and while popular magazines are inclined to work that way, I would hope, if I were not sure, that you would not yield much to them.- I do truly think that while the Rhea episode is really right, and not in the faintest degree pornographic, the change that you suggest would be perfectly justifiable: it would not in reality be changed, but you would enable those who are technical in their ideas of morality — and it is funny, but most of the objectors are entirely technical, these pure-minded people — to find an alibi for Tordell. That is all they want, and I do not think you would be modifying the real truth of the situation described at all. I know the magazine will make a big fight on that point, but it is also true that while your books appeal to the big public of readers, they have a great emotional power and a very sympathetic quality which might give them also a very wide sale. A writer is lost if he writes falsely for the sake of a wide sale, but if one can be had without deviating from the actual truth, it is certainly worth having.

I do think that the key to the situation turns on Claudius and I would be for your following your new conception. Of course I do not know exactly what it is, but I do feel sure that after this reflection upon the whole matter, and from the way in which you have looked at it all as shown in your letters, you will have it right. I hope it won't reduce the strength of what you call the vulgarity of Camilla who is a fine character, but those big-natured people of strong feelings are often the ones who also have the maternal instinct strongly in them. I do not mind Camilla having a lover or two, but I don't want her to get to the point of promiscuity, that's all. I feel very happy and confident about the book. I wish we could talk it all over, but anyhow all this new arrangement will give us all more time. Isn't there some possibility of your coming up early in the spring?

Always yours,

P.S. Tom Wolfe's book[3] is now virtually all in plates and it seems as though there were nothing more that could be done about it. We had one last struggle a few days ago, but it was the final one so far as this book is concerned. I have been involved in it for so long that I shall hardly know what to think of it until I can read it over again. There has been so much in it that has come out, and so much that was not originally in it that has gone in, that it is hard for me to remember all its parts, and Tom himself does not know what is in or out, I am sure. It is the queerest way to have done a book, but it was the only way it could be done.

Editor's note: At top of letter in MEP's hand: "Cross Creek / Route / Hawthorne / Florida."

1. *Golden Apples* was serialized in *Cosmopolitan* 98–99 (April–August 1935).
2. Stark Young, *So Red the Rose.*
3. Thomas Wolfe, *Of Time and the River.*

. . . .

178. MKR to MEP (ALS, 7 pp. frag.)

[n.p.]
Wednesday
[January 23, 1935]

Dear Mr. Perkins:——

I do hope my violent letter last week didn't offend you——I was feeling most frustrated at being ill and at not being able to discuss at length various aspects of the novel that have been disturbing me—— It's simply too much of a job to write a thousand rambling ideas and questions, so since I can't talk to you, you'll have to trust me to go ahead as best as I can.

Had a helpful talk with the physician friend I've mentioned to you, who is such a good critic.[1] Had him read the manuscript. He says I came very close to giving a striking picture, recognizable to any trained psychologist, of dementia praecox with a paranoiac tendency, in Claudius. He showed me from a medical angle where I failed in it. For one thing, he said suicide is not in character for that type. Claudius would meet his end as an accidentally inevitable result of his own violence.

The doctor said Camilla has a touch of the same thing——said she is a savagely maternal type, not quite normal, with a certain definite deficiency of certain sexual hormones.

As I see it now, I think for book purposes anyway I shall not have a culmination of the romance between Camilla and Tordell. Leave it with the suggestion that she is like the lush, savage hammock——still something he must tame & wrestle with. That will help take away the Laura Jean Libbey[2] aspect of the romance as it stands——

Had a phone call yesterday from the editor of Cosmopolitan & they are buying the manuscript. I'm not enthused, but with my grove as it is, I can't afford to pass up the $7200, especially since they're not asking anything damaging to my self-respect.

They are rushing it into print, 4 issues beginning April, so that doesn't put us so far behind on publication. [remainder of letter missing]

1. J. C. Vinson.
2. Laura J. Libbey (1862–1924), a writer of romances about girls and women.

. . . .

179. MEP to MKR (CC, 1 p.)

Jan. 24, 1935

Dear Mrs. Rawlings:

I am sending herewith the contract for "Golden Apples" and if there is anything wrong about it, tell us. It is meant to be exactly like the other except for the change in royalty.

Always yours,

. . . .

180. MEP to MKR (CC, 2 pp.)

Feb. 5, 1935

Dear Mrs. Rawlings:

I think the idea in your last letter, by which there would be no conclusion to the love between Tordell and Camilla but that it would be implied for the future, is a fine one. I think Camilla is at bottom a very good character indeed. I am not worried about her. Claudius is the troublesome one.

This is evidently another hard winter, and I hope you won't come out too badly in the end with the orange grove. About all I know on the subject is what I have learned from this novel. I am mighty glad you sold the serial in the circumstances, and July will be a good time to publish the book. Sometime let me know how you get on with the revision.

Always yours,

P.S. I am sending you a book I have liked since boyhood that we are to publish next fall.

....

181. MKR to MEP (TLS, 3 pp.)

Hawthorn, Fla.
Feb. 11, 1935

Dear Max Perkins:

(We agreed that if you liked the next novel I would call you "Max.")

A thousand thanks for "The Adventures of General Marbot"——it's magnificent.[1] The pictures are the best Thomason has done. The style, increasingly firm and stirring.

Having read it and delighted in it, I'm doing a possibly ungracious thing ——I'm giving it away, to a good friend, Major Otto F. Lange.[2] I've hunted with the Major this winter, <his> duck, dove and quail, and shivering in a duck blind one winter day in the middle of Orange Lake, when the ducks had stopped coming over, somehow or other I happened to mention Thomason, and recommend him. And he said he had known him in France! He told me of a night when he and another chap were with Thomason in a cafe in Paris. Thomason drove the waiters and proprietors absolutely insane by drawing pictures with the burnt ends of matches on the tablecloths——. Thomason's leave was up, and along with his companions, he was agreeably high. He was all for telling the whole war to go to Hell, but responsibility rode sternly in the other two—probably because their leave was *not* up—and they called a taxi and ordered the driver to deposit Thomason safely on his train. Thomason balked again and they bundled him head first through the taxi window. The taxi drove off and they returned to the cafe feeling nobly like *enfants de la patrie* etc. They were nicely settled with their drinks when Thomason appeared beside them——still indifferent to the war——still hell-bent on drawing pictures on the table cloth.

Major Lange's sense of responsibility has not been so high in relation to me. I was at his home in Gainesville for cocktails last Friday, before going on to a dinner party at the house of Dr. Tigert, president of the University of Florida.[3] Dr. Tigert is a prig and a fanatical dry, and the Major deliberately set in to get me high, saying that his ambition was to deposit me on the Tigert door-step and say, "Here's your guest." Then, he said, if Dr. Tigert asked me where I had been, I was to say, "I've been out with the Army." He accomplished his purpose. My dinner partner was an inoffensive preacher, and I disgraced myself thoroughly by asking my hostess what the devil she meant by putting me next to a parson, and announcing in a clear voice, "The hell with all preachers."

So on the handsome yellow frontispiece of "General Marbot," I have inscribed:

Pour Otto F. Lange——

Bon soldat, sans doute, mais homme méchant——

Meilleur ami de Thomason, soldat, que de moi,

femme——

If I get my bear material together for the boys' book, do you think Thomason really would condescend to do the sketches? How much longer is his Washington hitch to last? If not long, do suggest to him that he run down here and make sketches on the ground——my old hunter living in the Scrub can't live much longer. Major Lange (I don't know whether he was Captain then or Major) said Thomason might not remember him and our hunting season is over this week, but if Thomason likes fishing, we could give him deep-sea fishing or inland bass fishing and give him a swell time. Do suggest it, anyway.

Cosmopolitan is running me ragged on the shortening for them (the original 130,000 will have to come to 80,000 for them) but they're very considerate and aren't asking anything terrible. Shall I send you on the first quarter to third to get into proof? I can get you that at any time. I am trying to get the second installment off to them today.

"Island Fisherman," frankly, seemed tame and stupid after O'Sullivan's "Twenty Years A-Growing",[4] laid in the same place.

I'll write again when I get a breathing spell.

And again, many thanks for the new Thomason.

1. John W. Thomason, *The Adventures of General Marbot* (New York: Scribners, 1935).
2. Major Otto F. Lange, professor of military science at the University of Florida, close friend and hunting companion of MKR.
3. John J. Tigert.
4. Maurice O'Sullivan (1904–1950), *Twenty Years A-Growing* (New York: Viking, 1933).

Feb. 19, 1935

Dear Marjorie:

I was very much amused to hear about John Thomason. I wish you could see him. He is now very deep, as I may have said, in a story of the army of Northern Virginia, a large full book with many illustrations. I do not suppose it will be ready until Fall, and he is going to be busy if I can keep him so, up until then. But if you get that material together, I am sure it would interest him. I think to show it to him would have to be the first step. He is indefinitely tied to his post in Washington, although I do not think he likes it much, but he could get away on leave.

As to "Golden Apples" we could not begin to set up until we have an accurate idea of the total length, and much more than a third of the copy. But I would like to have any part of the copy that you can spare in order to read it again and get ready for what will come later. How much later will it come? Tell me, if you can do it without it bothering you, how your ideas are working out about the last part.- I am sure they are right in principle now, and am only asking from interest, and not from any anxiety whatever. This should be a grand book, and should make a great success too, and I hope nothing will interfere with your getting along with it. The serial people often get things confused by forcing a writer to do so much that does not have to be done for the book.- But that cannot be helped.

Always yours,

. . . .

Hawthorn, Florida
Feb. 19. [1935]

Dear Mr. Perkins:

If you like the enclosed verse well enough to pass it on to Dashiell, do so.[1] If not, don't bother to return it.

I don't dare read "Of Time and the River" until I've finished my own wretched job.

I think I have the character of Claudius pretty well straightened out. But a melodramatic taint keeps creeping in, with him and Camilla, that will drive me mad before I'm done with it. A lot of the material, even Tordell, is badly blurred toward the last part. I've just got to keep focussing sharply to obtain the reality. My God, it's so sickening at this stage of the game. And I wish the

Cosmopolitan sale was at the bottom of the sea. But that's literally biting the hand that feeds me and is probably a bit hypocritical to boot, because the next year or two will be much simpler because of the added income.

I think the quicker we can get the whole thing into proof the better off we'll be. If you'll plan to do quite a bit of work with me then, it may come easier in that form. I told you, I think, that about 50,000 words are having to come out for the magazine. I'm going to try to have the revision done, for the time being, in two or three weeks, counting on hard work again on it after that.

You must feel out of jail with the Wolfe thing done.

1. "Having Left Cities Behind Me," *Scribner's Magazine* 98.4 (October 1935): 246.

. . . .

184. MEP to MKR (TLS: UF, 2 pp.)

March 9, 1935

Dear Mrs. Rawlings:

I thought that poem was very good, and Dashiell has written you that we want it. I hope you will do more poetry. I have been delayed in writing you about this, or about anything else, by the great turmoil involved in getting Tom out of the country before his book was out and the reviews began to come, and then with all the things that arise on the publication of a book of that sort. But now it is out, and I am looking eagerly forward to another great interest, which is "Golden Apples". Some of the things you write make me feel as if it were getting altogether too gay down there, and might interfere with your work. I hope not. We are counting greatly on "Golden Apples". We are going to make every kind of effort to give it the chance it ought to have.

I gather from all I see about the weather that it goes on being bad. Did you manage to save the oranges at all?

I can tell you that no book will be more emphasized, or more strongly put forward by us in the fall than "Golden Apples."

Always yours,

. . . .

185. MEP to MKR (CC, 1 p.)

March 19, 1935

Dear Marjorie:

I hope everything is all right with you. So many people seem to have flu that one always feels apprehensive. If you have the time for it, I wish you could give me a line or two to tell me what progress you are making. I do not want to be troublesome, but we are anxious to make the most of "Golden Apples" in every sort of way.

Always yours,

· ·

186. MKR to MEP (wire)

1935 MAR 22 PM 4 30
MAXWELL PERKINS—
597 FIFTH AVE—
SO SORRY YOUVE WORRIED REVISION GOING FAIRLY WELL ALMOST FIN-
ISHED CLAUDIUS SATISFACTORY CAMILLA STILL TROUBLESOME STILL
MELODRAMATIC TRACES TO BE ELIMINATED BEFORE PUBLICATION WORK-
ING VERY HARD NOT AT ALL GAY MAY COME NEW YORK APRIL TWENTY
FIFTH WILL MAIL YOU PRESENT REVISION IN ABOUT TEN DAYS NEED
ADVICE—

· ·

187. MKR to MEP (ALS, on Embassy Apartments stationery, 2 pp. frag.)

The Embassy
Tampa, Florida
Saturday
[March 30, 1935]

Dear Max——

I've gone and done an absurd thing——but will hurry to reassure you that there is no permanent damage——

Two weeks ago I was thrown off a horse I was riding——thought it was only muscular injury, but the pain kept getting more severe. Last Monday I came to Tampa to be x-rayed & the x-rays showed a chip off the cervicle (sp.?) vertebra and a fracture of the skull. It seems that type of injury is common, and easily taken care of when gotten early. They put me in a brace at once, devilishly uncomfortable, but you get used to anything. I'll have to be in it another week or two, then by being moderately careful will have no more trouble and no aftereffects. Silly sort of thing to do, & I'm lucky it wasn't serious.

Fortunately, just before I came to Tampa I mailed to Cosmopolitan the revision of "Golden Apples" through the 3^d installment, which they're ending with Chapter xxx-, & I have until April 20–25 to finish the revision on the last few chapters. [remainder of letter missing]

. . . .

188. MEP to MKR (CC, 1 p.)

April 1, 1935

Dear Marjorie:

I am mighty glad you began by telling me that there was no permanent damage. I hope you are not very uncomfortable, and that everything will soon be right. I have known a good many people in Virginia and Southern Pines who have had similar accidents, and sometimes they have been very troublesome.

I am calling up Carl now. If you get a chance to tell me how things go, I hope you will do it, if only by postcard.- And we shall be counting on seeing you toward the end of April.

Always yours,

. . . .

189. MKR to MEP (ALS, 2 pp.)

Hawthorn
Friday
[April 5, 1935]

Dear Max——

Just to report that I'm home from Tampa & getting on nicely but the doctor says I can't think of going to New York. I have another month on the brace. I find there's no point in jeopardizing future health, so I'll be very meek & careful for a time. I'm quite comfortable.

As ever,

. . . .

190. MEP to MKR (TLS: UF, 1 p.)

April 8, 1935

Dear Marjorie:

I never did think you would get up for that dinner. I know that kind of accident very well, and that it means one has to be quiet for quite a long time. But if you do that, you ought to be all right. I think I have some occult power that enables me to foresee things because when I wrote to ask if you had flu, I had an uneasy feeling that something was going to happen. But now it has happened, and everything ought to be right. Maybe you could come in May when the weather would be better, and we could go to the Mayfair Yacht Club and see the big boats come up the East River.

Always yours,

. . . .

191. MEP to MKR (CC, 2 pp.)

April 24, 1935

Dear Marjorie:

I hope things are going along all right, and that you are not too uncomfortable. I am sending a copy of James Boyd's "Roll River"[1] which I believe you will enjoy, and which may help you through the last few days of wearing the brace. It is the kind of book you could read even when you are writing, a very mature, civilized book without any peculiarities of style.- I know one cannot read a book of strongly marked superficial characteristics when writing, without picking up the same thing.

If it were not for the accident now, we should see you tomorrow. I look forward to sitting through a long dinner and speeches with dread, but it would have been different if you had come. I suppose writing is not too easy, but I should be mighty glad to see your handwriting, if only a little bit of it.

Always yours,

1. James Boyd, *Roll River* (New York: Scribners, 1934).

. . . .

192. MKR to MEP (TLS, 3 pp.)

Hawthorn, Florida
Apr. 26, 1935

Dear Max:

The typewriter was permitted me a week or so ago, which kept me from going violently insane in the bad-enough hurrying of the Golden Apples revision for Cosmopolitan's fourth installment. Max, I'd gladly be broke again, not to have sold the serial rights, at least until I had the revision more nearly to my taste. Actually, I never in the world expected Carl to be able to sell it——then when the sale was made without warning, there still seemed time enough to get it right. It has gone so slowly and so badly. A fatal taint creeps in that I seem to be able to avoid only by setting my teeth and writing one word at a time, focussing my characters with an almost hypnotic intensity that is immensely difficult to achieve. And even then, nine times out of ten, it is still wrong. I'm not mistaken about this, either. The thing is still so bad in the magazine, to say nothing of their having cut it to the point of mutilation, that it makes me ill to have people reading it. This isn't constituting any mental hazard in the revision, because I <illegible excision> just <try to> forget my shameful condition.

I think the book is going to be "popular". For some reason it seems to excite people, and everyone who has spoken of it says they like it better than South Moon——but they're the kind of people who would. But whether the thing is going to emerge with the slightest literary value or any soundness at all, is a most dubious matter. The very worst happened——one of my virgin aunts wrote me that it was "just dear". But I'm hoping that she had only read the first installment and that after that she hated it. You'd do anything in the world to keep people like that from liking your stuff, because if they like it, you know it's bad. You can understand Faulknerism, and Hemingway's bomb-shell intrusions of obscenity——anything to drive away the fluttering hands and the genteel, ecstatic voices.

You can't imagine how desperate I am to get the whole manuscript into your hands. Claudius is almost all right. Camilla has come out a rather nicer person. The *speech* of these people is still, a lot of it, very very bad. I don't think I'll ever again start with so many *preconceived* characters. I think it works better for me to feel my way more, so that each step is true, according to the slow progress of a principal character, or of the situation. It won't be long now before I send the revision to you. We'll go over the contract matter then. Carl wrote me that they had inquiries from almost all the major movie companies, and I wired him that no movie sale must be made without the rigid agreement that *production* was not to *begin* until some stated time *after* book publication——that I would not further invalidate the book's chances of serious literary consideration.

Can you, and can the type-setting people, work from my messed-up but typed draft of the revision? I dread copying the whole thing, it's so tedious, and local stenographers are so poor that if one of them could make out the manuscript, I'm sure you could.

Many thanks for the "Gray Owl" [sic] book and for "Puzzled America."[1]

The Gray Owl thing is spoiled by the writer's pretensions to style. It would be splendid if told simply. I haven't yet read Anderson but it looks interesting.

The new Hemingway narrative is *delightful*.[2] I'll be much pleased to have the Boyd book. The title sounds as if it were more his type of thing again. I thought The Dark Shore was not his special stamping ground. I suppose, like me, he hates the thought of limiting himself to one specialized kind of writing.

I'm quite comfortable in my brace and in no hurry to discard it, because the longer I keep my head and neck in one position, the surer I am of a solid knitting of bone. I'm being very careful.

Thank you for writing——I hoped you wouldn't wait for me to write. The Princeton Library dinner would have been only an excuse for working with you on my manuscript, I rather doubt whether I'll try for New York this spring.

As ever,

1. Grey Owl (1888–1938), *Pilgrims of the Wild* (New York: Scribners, 1935); Sherwood Anderson (1876–1941), *Puzzled America* (New York: Scribners, 1935).
2. Ernest Hemingway, *Green Hills of Africa* (New York: Scribners, 1935).

. . . .

193. MEP to MKR (CC, 3 pp.)

May 8, 1935

Dear Marjorie:

I was very glad to get your letter, and especially with the whole tone of it, because it seemed to me to show that things must be going all right with you. There is one thing, though perhaps I ought not to emphasize it since you are doing all you possibly can, and under trying circumstances. But the truth is, the sooner we can publish "Golden Apples" after the end of the serialization, the better. It is then fresh in the minds of thousands who have read parts of it, or even perhaps only seen it, and thought they would read it later,- and also of those who have read it and want to read it again as a book. So we cannot have the manuscript too soon, and any manuscript you think will be suitable, however much corrected, will serve the purpose. It must be legible, but your writing is easily legible, and I believe anything you thought right to send would do for the printer. You speak of being desperate to get the whole manuscript into my hands. Well, I am desperate to get it too. I shall enjoy whatever work has to be done in connection with it,- and that is more than can be said for all but a small fraction of what work one has to do.

Having to keep one's head and neck in exactly the same position, even with the help of a brace, does not sound very comfortable.- I hope it won't have to go on much longer.

Always yours,

194. MKR to MEP (TLS, 1 p.)

Hawthorn, Fla.
May 18, 1935

Dear Max:

I'm mailing to Cosmopolitan today the last of the revision. I don't know whether you knew they are running Golden Apples in five installments instead of the originally planned four. That was partly because they felt they were losing too much of the flavor by cutting so drastically, and partly to give me more time when I broke my neck. So that puts the end of the serial appearance in their August issue, appearing July 10. Don't you think we can hit pretty close to that with book publication? August first, say?

I have come fairly close to doing as much as I can do with the revision, at least as far as <drastic> major changes are concerned. It is greatly improved. There are still lots of places with an emetic quality, but if you will point these out with suggestions for making them more palatable, I can do a lot more work in a hurry. Do hope you haven't inflicted needless suffering on yourself by reading the thing in the magazine. I told them to do their own cutting as long as they didn't add or change. It never occurred to me they'd cut sentences in half! I looked over the first installment but haven't even looked at it since.

It won't take me more than a day or two to get your copy in shape to send you. It's all typewritten, but you see it's all in carbon, and the older manuscript is sometimes pretty faint. I've asked Cosmopolitan to send me the whole revised manuscript after they've got this last installment in proof, and if they will do that, I'll send it right on to you, as it's entirely legible, of course.

Hope you're free to get right at your criticism.

· ·

195. MEP to MKR (CC, 2 pp.)

May 22, 1935

Dear Marjorie:

I am glad you got the last of the copy off to the Cosmop. It has been our wish to publish as early as we possibly can, but the earliest we can hope for is sometime in the first half of August. It takes two months, generally speaking, simply to make a book, and we should have to have copies of your book on hand at least two weeks before publication, for the sake of giving the right proportion. If we were not aiming at anything special, it would not make much difference, but we have great hopes in this case, and do not want to take chances, or neglect possibilities.- So do send the manuscript at the earliest possible moment. I shall read it instantly. I am in hopes though — and I should think it was probable — that we could put it right in hand, and make any further changes in the proof. I too looked at the Cosmop enough not to want to read the story in that form. But serialization has only one real advantage,- that it pays well.

Anyhow, send the manuscript when you can, and I shall put off anything else to take it right up.

Always yours,

. . . .

196. MKR to MEP (postcard)

[Cross Creek]
[May 1935]

Revised copy "Golden Apples" was expressed to you last night. Should reach you Friday or Saturday at latest.

. . . .

197. MEP to MKR (TLS: UF, 3 pp.)

May 28, 1935

Dear Marjorie:

I read "Golden Apples" through yesterday, and though I had to go more rapidly than I wanted to, I enjoyed the re-reading very much indeed. I think every single change you have made in it has been right, and while it seems to me that perhaps a good many more changes should be made, I thought we could make them in the proof (we to bear the expense) when also there would be changes in detail.- So I have sent the manuscript to the printer with the idea of reading it carefully as the proofs begin to come through. There would be no changes of any real moment until within the last 60 or 70 pages.

The changes there might be then, if you thought well of them, would be entirely in the nature of those that I have already spoken of, and that you thought were right, and took steps to meet. But I think even now that those parts of the book toward the end which are so much about Claudius and Camilla, are in a romantic tone not compatible with the book in general, and that at times they run even into melodrama. Probably now this is chiefly true, after the changes you have made, because of the way in which you have written them. The death of Claudius is very much better now than it was in the first version, but I think (though it is very hard to explain) that there is something in the way in which you write it that puts it out of tune, and gives it unreality.

In that part of the book you get into a way of speaking of "the woman Camilla" instead of just Camilla, and there are other things of that sort. I think maybe when we get to that, you might rewrite that chapter in as simple and objective a manner as that in which you have written the early chapters in the book, and in fact all the chapters that relate to Allie and Luke alone and in their relations to Tordell. I think the unreality extends also to the doctor. I would have thought him the kind of man to accept Claudius's death when it came to him, more simply and readily. You may prize that part of the book highly, but I must tell you how it seems to me. It is as if you had written it in a different attitude of mind from the greater part of the book, which is so beautifully done. For instance, you have the doctor in final lamentation paraphrase King David at the death of Absalom. Probably you do not recall the biblical passage, but it must have stayed in your mind from childhood unknown to you, and although when it happens in the Bible, it is one of the most telling things that was ever written, it is one of those things that cannot be used again. It is a small matter to change it, but it seemed to me to show that these parts of the book relating to the doctor, Camilla, and Claudius, were not directly written from looking right at the thing itself as were the other parts. It would not make so much difference if the whole book were written that way, as many fine books have been, but it does mar the unity of this book.

I guess Carl Brandt and the Cosmop people do not think there is much in this idea. I do not myself believe there is anything in it that would interfere with the sale of this book. It might even be that this strong romantic strain, and these passages, would be most popular with a larger public. But you are not thinking of this book only, nor am I,- but of your place as a writer. You could not help being popular, because your writing is full of human qualities, as it most certainly should be. But it is also writing that in the strictest sense takes its roots in direct observation, in presenting things and people the way they are. Mighty few people can truly do that. You can, and you ought not ever to diverge from it, as I think you do tend to do it in these parts of the book even now.

I bring up this point at this time so that you can think about it in the interval before the proofs come, when, if you are willing, we can examine those passages carefully once more. It is too fine a book not to have every advantage of thought and work.

Always yours,

Hawthorn, Fla.

May 31. [1935]

Dear Max:

Just a word of mingled relief and despair in reply to your letter after reading the revised manuscript. Relief that your feeling is the same as my own——despair, because I'll be damned if I know how to correct the fault. I sense the unreality and am helpless to change it. It's going to take all your critical ability to get me straight. I'm counting on you painfully, because I feel just about licked. I can point out to you every chapter, every paragraph, every sentence, every word, that's melodramatic or off-key or false. And I don't know how to make it different. I most certainly do not prize that part of the book——it makes me ill.

I have discovered one thing that makes trouble for me often. It did in the first version of South Moon Under. And that is a building up to some preconceived point or idea that is carried over from real life, but that for the purpose of fiction may not prove to have the reality of an imagined thing. The doctor's reaction to his son's death may be an instance. When I first talked with you of this book I told you of an old doctor in real life who had suggested the character of Albury to me, who cried out in grieving for his son, "Lucius, Lucius, oh my son Lucius!" I remember the Biblical expression, and thought it legitimate to use this way, since it had been so used actually. But it may be that to a religious person such a paraphrase of a familiar expression would be a natural thing, yet not legitimate as I use it. And my whole thought in the doctor's reaction to the death was a building up to this thing.

Do Claudius and Camilla themselves seem more convincing to you now? I wish I might have most of the proofs all at once, to see the thing as a unit, which I have not been able to do. I had to work for the magazine so jerkily (and with such a feeling of the thing's being spotty and yet, for serial use, not mattering if it was) that the manuscript is not unified in my mind, except in that dim region where the story was conceived, and where it still lies in its totally unexpressed and unexpressable perfection.

Help me to keep in mind my fundamental conception of the struggle of the foreigner to merge himself with the larger thing, the important and natural and overwhelming background. Luke and Allie should be a part of that background, Luke solid like the earth itself, somehow, like the earth, past harming. Camilla and Claudius and the doctor are simply the people who cross his life and that background and express philosophies at variance with his own, or that accent his own——other people working out their difficulties, often similar to his, in their own ways. Camilla should suggest a little the nature of the hammock itself. Yet I have not done this successfully, perhaps should not try to do it. Perhaps my very sense of symbolism in connection with her helps to make her unreal.

No, the Cosmopolitan people are not conscious of all this, but you wouldn't expect them to be, would you? My last letter from the editor, asking just a few lines in the last chapter to associate Camilla romantically with Tordell's thoughts, calls the whole thing "great literature as well as a magnificent magazine serial". I cannot see how anyone can be so unperceptive. I'm a little angry with you for thinking that I might think everything was all right. I sense it as acutely as you do, but as I say, I lose my grip and can't get it right. Please don't spare any criticism in any way. Your only unkindness would be in letting the false slip by, if reality was at all possible. I wish Camilla and possibly <the> Claudius were out of the book altogether. Yet I must learn to handle them if I'm to be at all capable.

Do you think we can get most of the proofs at once?

Don't put it up to me to think about these things in the interval. Unless lightning strikes, I can't think any further without help. *You* think! Any stray ideas that come to you from time to time, I'd appreciate your passing them on for me to absorb. Some random thought from you might point the way out.

. . . .

199. MKR to MEP (TLS, with holograph additions, 2 pp.)

Hawthorn, Fla.

June 10, 1935

Dear Max:

I'm afraid I floored you with my demand that you do my thinking for me, and figure out how to do my re-writing. But do send me any stray thoughts on obviating the present difficulties.

About the contract. I can't see why Scribner's should collect anything at all on a possible movie sale or on a second serialization. Any such extra outlets would come as more of a result of the magazine appearance than of the book, and I can't see any reason for the publishers having anything to do with them. I think just the straight sale of the book in the United States and Canada is all Scribner's could make claims on.

How does that troublesome English contract stand? I never received a contract from Curtis Brown to sign. Did Scribner's sign one with him? Of course there's almost nothing involved except whatever advance the English publishers would make, because by the time the British government takes its whopping income tax cut, there's precious little left for the author but satisfaction. But this particular book ought really to have something of a sale in England, if they haven't lost all interest in colonization and its implications.

There are two favors I'd like to ask. One is that my full name, Marjorie Kinnan Rawlings, be used throughout in advertising and on the end of the jacket. Just "Rawlings" was used on the end of the jacket and of the book-cover itself before, and "Marjorie K. Rawlings" was used in the Herald-Tribune's announcement of spring and summer books. I discussed the matter of my name with Mr. Darrow,[1] wanting to drop the Rawlings if practicable, but he showed me it was not. But I do want to keep the "Kinnan". There are lots of three-name writers who don't seem handicapped by the length.

The other favor is that I be given a chance to pass on the jacket blurb, and if possible, the jacket design. The blurb last time made an utter fool of me, through the *typographical* error, an error in Mr. Hart's office, not an error of mine, which quoted me in a letter to Scribner's as speaking of the "typography" of the scrub, when I wrote "topography". I had the most disagreeable reverberations from this, and was much humiliated, and never understood why it went uncorrected. I wrote Mr. Darrow some months ago about this, when the mistake was repeated in the Grosset and Dunlap[2] edition, and told him that I thought Scribner proof-reading was the worst of any publishing house in the country. Also because silly things are sometimes said in the blurbs, I'd like to see this one. <And I'd> The jacket design of course is your affair and not mine, but when "South Moon Under" meant that the moon was invisible under the earth, it was very silly to have a large quarter-moon behind some pine trees.

Please do pass on anything even remotely helpful about the re-writing.

As ever,

Editor's note: At top of letter in MEP's hand: "Noted Weber."[3] In left margin opposite third paragraph in MEP's hand: "Faber & Faber."

1. Whitney Darrow, sales manager for Scribners.
2. Grosset and Dunlap published cheaper printings of MKR's works, using the Scribner plates.
3. William C. Weber, the head of Scribners' advertising department.

June 11, 1935

Dear Marjorie:

This is just to tell you that your book will all be in type by tomorrow, and I shall send it to you after the next weekend. I should like to keep it until after that in order to read it all carefully at once. Then I shall do the best I can by way of suggestion.

Always yours,

. . . .

June 12, 1935

Dear Marjorie:

We are in complete agreement on the question of moving picture rights which we have never claimed on any book, including "South Moon Under" and so I suppose it is rather superfluous to dispute your statement as to what the movie sales result from. I believe it is a well known fact that they never result from serial publication, and almost always result from big success with a novel. That is our experience here certainly, with books which have been published after serialization. It is success in book sales that impresses movie people most, and a good many publishers base their claim for movie rights on that ground. But we never have dreamed of doing so, and there is nothing in the contract I sent you to that effect. When it comes to second serialization, although the matter is such a small one that we should not make any great issue of it, we do believe the publisher should be in control. Second serialization is chiefly an advertising matter. It is done more for the sake of helping the book than for the money that is in it, which is never much, and the publisher's share of the money that comes from it—unless serialization takes place long after the appearance of the book—goes into the advertising. It is therefore a matter that the publisher really should control and is entitled to share in it. I do not know which form we have used in the case of your contract,- the one which leaves it to mutual agreement or the one which specifies a fifty-fifty division. We should be perfectly willing to change it so as to leave it to mutual agreement if the question arises. It is very much a secondary question, and it is linked with the promotion and success of the book.

I have given orders to have the name used in the way you want it, and although confusion and delay often result from sending an author the blurb, etc., we shall do that too. It was too bad about the use of the word "typography" for "topography" but there was one fortunate thing about it,- that anyone would have realized that it was a typographical error, and what the word ought to have been, and could not have been misled by it. It is the errors which confuse the sense that are the worst. Typographical errors are very hard to avoid but at least we have the honor—so a very distinguished and experienced proofreader tells us—of having published the only recent book which had no typographical error in it.- He said, the only book he had ever read without one. There is a race of experts which goes through every important book for typographical errors just for the fun of it. They praise as well as blame, and in the case of the "R. E. Lee"[1] which was an enormously large book, we got many compliments.

You have a contract with Faber & Faber for "South Moon Under" on the following terms:

A royalty of 10% (Ten percent) of the published price of all copies sold up to 2,000 (Two Thousand); 12 1/2% (Twelve and one-half per cent) of the published price of all copies so sold from 2,000 (Two Thousand) and up to 5,000 (Five Thousand); 15% (Fifteen per cent) of the published price of all copies so sold from 5,000 (Five Thousand) and up to 10,000 (Ten Thousand) and 20% (Twenty per cent) of the published price of all copies so sold beyond 10,000 (Ten Thousand).

And this contract gives them also an option on the next two full length novels. We therefore have nothing to do with any sale but that in the United States and Canada, but if you would like to put that phrase into the contract, we have no objection whatever to it.

I shall send you a jacket as soon as we can get one in effective proofs. We have been struggling to get a good jacket. The one we originally had, which was made a year ago, did not seem to be satisfactory, and we are trying for another. I think we'll get a good one. I am sorry you did not like the "South Moon" one altogether. The moon did seem necessary to give a right effect from the artistic standpoint, and the idea was that it was in its last quarter.

I expect the last of the galley proofs today. The story certainly reads beautifully up to date.

Always yours,

---

1. Douglas S. Freeman (1886–1953), *R. E. Lee: A Biography* (New York: Scribners, 1934).

202. MEP to MKR (CC, I p.)

June 14, 1935

Dear Marjorie:

I just want to ask you if you can send us a new picture. The one we have has been used a good deal and we want one for the back of the jacket if we can possibly get it.

I have got complete galleys of your book now, and I think I shall send you a large part of them tomorrow. There is nothing of much importance until the last third of the book, and there I think it is mostly a matter of tone.

Always yours,

· ·

203. MEP to MKR (TLS: UF, 7 pp.)

June 18, 1935

Dear <Mrs. Rawlings> Marjorie [in longhand]:

I am now sending you all the rest of the galleys, that is, from 62 to the end. It is in that part where whatever difficulties there are occur. I have indicated some of them by suggesting omissions, and in other ways, but what I have done is done in the idea that it will give you the direction of the changes. That is all you would accept anyway, being the kind of writer you are, but even if you would accept more, it would be dangerous because a book to be good must be done wholly upon the conviction of the author. I only say this to explain because I know that you would only write a book that way. In this proof, as in the earlier proof, you will find typographical errors — I caught a number myself — but don't let that trouble you.- They are due to the pressure we put on the printers to get the book into type.

Whatever revisions are advisable are all due to the same thing: the relative incongruity in the material itself; that is between that part of it which is all in the hammock, and that part which is across the lake, or which is concerned with the people across the lake. It is this incongruity that presented the great problem in the book, such a problem as every novelist has to face. Tordell himself was also in character incongruous with the hammock and with the Crackers, but you mastered that problem which was the greatest one you had to meet. I think that the chief difficulty with regard to the remaining problem comes from the fact that your treatment is in some degree incongruous. It seems as though you looked at the two sets of people differently,- one set romantically, and the other realistically. I think in the revision you should try to treat the people on the other side of the lake realistically too, to as nearly the same degree as you can, to the way you treat Luke and Allie. The question of congruity of treatment comes even down to the use of words. For instance, there is one place where you say Claudius *strode* about the room. I would change this word to *walked*. He did stride, of course, in reality and if it were not for the sake of trying to bring the texture of the book into unity, the word would be a perfectly proper one to use.- But you do not want to make these lake people seem a different race from the Crackers, partly because they really are not so different except in a superficial way, but mostly because the book should have unity in texture. When you write of Camilla and Claudius you do tend to write of them in a different kind of language, and when they are contrasted, as they must be with Allie and Luke who are so absolutely natural, these characters come to seem almost theatrical. Even your first description of Camilla—though I do think you have made her much better in the respects in question—ought, I think, to be toned down,- so that you would write of her just as you would of an equally beautiful Cracker, assuming that one could be found. I think little changes in that respect would make a great difference. Then you have the tendency to refer to Camilla as "the woman Camilla" and Claudius as "the man Claudius" (you also refer in that way to Luke) and I think this, applying to Camilla and Claudius, does tend to give the feeling of unreality.- And wherever it is used, it also tends to push the reader away, and make the characters more remote, for he has become acquainted with them, and thinks of them simply as Camilla, Claudius, and Luke. <So far as>

So far as any extensive changes are concerned, they apply particularly to the two scenes where Claudius is in Camilla's house. In both cases I think you ought to try to reduce the length, particularly in the first, in respect to Claudius's piano playing. I think there is too much made of it,- it makes him seem romanticized and unreal. In the second scene there, there is a sensational quality that comes from the negro's wrestling with him and carrying him out. This is effective in itself, and it is all because of the old element of congruity. In reality the background of the hammock and the Crackers are the big part of the story. In such a scene as this, one completely forgets that they exist <almost>, and this scene, and the circumstances, have a strangeness which they would not have in a book which was entirely concerned with such people as Claudius, and not with Crackers. I think it would be much better to sacrifice the excitement and sensationalism of this incident by simply having Claudius "pass out" as they say—which he might very naturally do after such a drink as you describe, on top of what he has had before—and be carried out by the negroes.

The same kind of reasoning applies somewhat in the place where Tordell tells of his marriage. I would not have Camilla hurl the whole glass at Claudius. But she had a right to be angry, and she might easily have tossed what was in the glass in his face, perhaps. As it is, it seems too theatrical, and the effect could be got without making it so much so. Otherwise that whole scene is very good, and Tordell does rightly, and quite naturally. It was a great feat to get Tordell into compatibility with the background of the story, and if you can do that, you can certainly do much with respect to Camilla and Claudius.- And Camilla is pretty successful anyway, and will be more so if toned down.

The only other crucial part of the book is the very important scene where the stallion kills Claudius. I think you should go through this very carefully and tell it as simply as you possibly can. It does not require rewriting, but only a scrutiny of the language, and certain excisions. For instance, you have a way of going out of the story with phrases and comments such as that which you use when you say that the death of this man represented all death to them, and they looked upon his body in that way. That is what happens always in the case of a natural death. I doubt if in the case of so sensational and violent a one the horror would not exclude even that natural feeling. But even if I am wrong in that matter, I would leave out such comments because they take you away from the story and make it less real. And after the death I think you should shorten as much as you can the account of taking the body to the doctor. I have suggested places where you could cut it. The climax has come in his death. I think the effectiveness both in the fight with the stallion, and even what went before that, and in taking the body to the doctor and telling him of the death, all should come from understatement,- and that it would be heightened by following that method.

The possible changes I have indicated on the proof are intended to show the way in which these things can be done. But don't hesitate to do whatever you want to do, however extensive it may be. From the mechanical point of view it is not important because all the changes come very close together and could mean nothing more than resetting certain relatively short parts of the book. For example, on Galley 63, when you tell of Camilla and Claudius walking together, you say, "arm brushed arm, thigh touched thigh." I doubt if arm brushed arm, thigh could touch thigh,- especially with a big man like Claudius whose shoulders would have breadth. I think that this is an example of the way in which you are treating these people incongruously with the other part of the material. People can write books in that way, and at<tention> a tension, and filled with strong emotion, but it does not go well in this book with the other and greater, and perhaps more important parts.

In the very next paragraph, where you speak of her "hard splendor" and "wind across the treetops" I think you are overdoing it for the reasons given. In fact that paragraph contains the element which I think should be avoided.

On the next galley occurs an instance of "the woman Camilla". Tordell has just met her, of course, but even so, she is Camilla to the reader.- She is the only woman present anyhow so it would not be necessary to refer to her as both "the woman" and "Camilla". I would be for "Camilla".

On galley 67 you refer to Dr. Aubrey's expression while his son played. It is true that Aubrey does not speak, but I do think there is danger of your making him seem unpleasantly soft, almost sentimental about his son, in places where he does speak of him and in applying such thoughts as this to him. I think the effect would be better if you stop by saying his face held the ecstasy, etc., and omitted the last sentence. I have also indicated once or twice places where it seems to me he speaks of his son in a way that would not be characteristic of such a man, or almost of any man.- One is on the next galley, 68.

On galley 69 where you tell how Camilla looked as Tordell went away, I think that the word "heroic" is out of place for the reasons given. The reader anyhow could visualize how she looked now for he knows her, and if you just left her standing, solitary, between the pillars of the verandah, it would be enough. The effect would be greater I believe, than when you put in the word "heroic". The reader can put that in for himself if it should be there.

This letter is <going> getting to be so huge that I won't go on to enumerate any other points because what I have said will give my idea and you will understand why other places are marked.- And all the criticism runs in exactly the same direction, all of it is to bring the two elements of the story into a greater compatibility. It is a very skillfully constructed story, and in that respect the only thing I would have to say is that the end does seem pretty crowded with striking events. But I think that the tendency will be to correct that if they are somewhat toned down in these ways, so that Camilla and her group are in somewhat less sensational contrast with the hammock and the Crackers.

One little point.- There are places where Claudius is referred to as Claud, and I would be in favor of that change being made more frequently. I think even in the name Claudius there is somehow something a little unnatural in contrast.

It also occurred to me that at the very end of the story where Luke and Tordell have been brought pretty close together, and do understand each other, he might come to use Luke's first name, according to the custom of the country. It would indicate still further that he was being absorbed into his environment, and had come to feel rightly there.

It is a very fine book, and I have it greatly at heart, and that is why I go into all these things.

Always yours,

Hawthorn

June 18. [1935]

Dear Max:

The first proofs came, but I have resisted the temptation to open them until the rest come. It is very necessary that I read the thing through at one sitting to get it as a whole. I will come closer that way to eliminating the change in tone in some of the chapters. Hope the rest come tomorrow, as I am anxious to get at it.

Never mind about sending me the blurb on the jacket if it makes trouble on a rush job, if you will look it over carefully yourself. You know the kind of thing that would make me feel foolish, and I trust your judgment and good taste as well as my own. So take care of it at your end and let it go at this.

I wish I had done as I wanted to long ago and asked permission to have an artist friend of mine here in Florida submit a jacket design to you.[1] He is the real thing, and has a gift for the decorative element besides, and could have turned out a stunning design. But I felt so sure you always had your jackets done by your own art department that I didn't like to suggest it. I liked the jacket for "Of Time and the River". You got the sense of mystic sweep that Wolfe intended. I know just what I would have liked for "Golden Apples", but felt it was out of my province to make any suggestions. But don't let's accept anything banal even though time presses, for I don't think you can underestimate the effect of the jacket on the average book buyer.

The reason I was so fussy about the contract was that good old Carl Brandt did so want me to turn over the whole thing to him——he could save me so much, etc. But it would be very unpleasant to me to have my Scribner dealings go through intermediary hands——I enjoy the personal contact with you and Mr. Darrow <and Dashiell>, and the feeling of confidence I have in you. So to justify my action in refusing Carl, I wanted to make sure I was getting just as good a contract as he could have gotten for me. I'd hate to think he or any other agent could bully anything out of you that you wouldn't give me just by my mentioning it.

You are painfully right about the necessity for my writing from the point of view of direct observation. I got restless waiting for the proofs, and began a short story whose theme excites me very much. I began it in a style that I love to read myself——the style, actually, of Balzac's "A Passion in the Desert"—— the style of the *conte*.[2] Told in the first person in the intimate and casual manner. I had a grand time. Then I began to be uneasy. I thought, "This is going to be bad. This must be bad, or it would [not] be going so devilishly *easy*, and I wouldn't be enjoying myself so much." I stopped, although I could have written all night and perhaps finished it. This morning I read it over. I am totally unable to convey a sense of reality in any way except by a very intense, sharply focussed direct narration of what is happening <now> and being thought *now*. It is definitely harder writing and must be sweat out a little at a time. But that, or nothing, I am afraid is my job. Doing the story the <othe[r]> hard way makes it necessary to drop it now. I'll go at it when the book is done.

Cosmopolitan has been very generous in comment on the serial. They wrote the other day that they thought I had done "a masterly job" and their readers were "vociferously agreeing." Which is a good augur for the book. I also heard from a helpful source that many people are waiting for the book, not liking to read anything serially, which again is good.

As ever,

Editor's note: At top of letter: "Will have pictures taken in Tampa Saturday morning <and get> both formal and informal, and get them off to you early in the week."

1. Robert Camp, who later did the illustrations for *Cross Creek Cookery* (New York: Scribners, 1942).
2. Honoré de Balzac (1799–1850), *Les Chouans* (1829) and *Contes Drolatiques* (1832–37).

. . . .

205. MKR to MEP (ANS on letter to MKR from Brandt and Brandt)

Brandt & Brandt
101 Park Avenue
New York
June 20, 1935.

Mrs. Marjorie Kinnan Rawlings,
Cross Creek,
Hawthorne, Route 1,
Florida.

Dear Mrs. Rawlings:

As the final installment of GOLDEN APPLES is out today, I am writing to ask whether you wish us to secure an assignment of copyright from Cosmopolitan to your name. This is practically an automatic thing with us, when a serial is completed, and as there is considerable interest in the motion picture rights, it would seem advisable to have this in hand to save any delay in completing a contract. We would, of course, be glad to turn this over to your publisher for the book use when the time arrives.

Will you please let me hear from you?

Sincerely yours,
Elizabeth Kilday
Brandt & Brandt.

Editor's note: At bottom of letter in MKR's handwriting: "Max:— I answered this at the time, authorizing the assignment. Imagine it's all a matter of routine form. Marjorie K. R."

. . . .

206. MEP to MKR (TS for wire)

JULY 1, 1935
MRS. MARJORIE RAWLINGS
ISLAND GROVE, FLORIDA
EXTREMELY ANXIOUS TO KNOW HOW WORK GOES AND WHAT YOU THINK
WILL YOU WIRE ME SOME WORD COLLECT

. . . .

207. MKR to MEP (wire)

1935 JUL 2 PM 12 37
MAXWELL PERKINS—
597 FIFTH AVE—
RETURNING TODAY FIRST SIXTY ONE GALLEYS READY FOR PRINTER TO GO AHEAD STOP AGREE WITH ALL YOU WROTE STOP COPIOUS DELETIONS IN LATTER PART PROVING VALUABLE STOP ALSO REWRITING MANY SECTIONS WITH CONSIDERABLE IMPROVEMENT STOP PLEASE NAME DEAD LINE ON REMAINDER STOP CANNOT SEEM TO GET DECENT PHOTOGRAPH [STOP] SUGGEST USING ENGLISH ONE OR PERHAPS PREFERABLY NONE AT ALL STOP WHAT IS DEADLINE ON PHOTOGRAPH STOP OUGHT BLACK GIRL RHEA APPEAR LATER BRIEFLY—

JULY 2, 1935
MRS. MARJORIE K. RAWLINGS
ISLAND GROVE, <FLOR[IDA]>
FLORIDA

DELIGHTED [STOP] THINK PERHAPS RHEA SHOULD REAPPEAR IF IT CAN
BE DONE PERFECTLY NATURALLY AS PART OF THE LANDSCAPE ALMOST
STOP COULD YOU MAIL REMAINDER IN TEN DAYS STOP COULD THEN
PUBLISH <LATE AUGUST OR EARLY> IN SEPTEMBER STOP WILL RECONSIDER
PHOTOGRAPHS [STOP] NO HURRY

. . . .

209. MKR to MEP (TLS, with holograph additions, 2 pp.)

Hawthorn, Fla.

July 4 [1935]

Dear Max:

I believe I'm safe in promising the rest of the corrected proofs and revision in your hands a week from Monday, (July 15).

I think I'm getting somewhere——the substitutions nothing marvelous, but at least more in tone with the rest of the book. Max, there were two books in this material, in the original conception. I should have worked out Tordell's story in the hammock, without any outside characters at all except possibly the doctor. Then there was another story, probably a good one, in such a group of people in that life at the Landing. In my revising, Camilla is toned down to more of an ordinary person. I wanted to make something very violent of her, I wanted Claude Albury more violent, I wanted the old doctor a pathetic but almost ridiculous character——but that conception simply does not fit with the atmosphere of the main substance of the book. But how is one to know? It's too late now, so I'm fitting them in as best I can with the rest of it. I wish I'd left out Claude's music altogether. Made more of his stables. I suppose it's too late on that, too. Oh well.

I can bring Rhea across the picture toward the end, easily.

I'm changing the name to Claude through-out. Have the proof-reader watch closely for any place I may have failed to make the change. I think your printers did an amazingly accurate job with that poor manuscript, and working under pressure.

Do you have a copy of the proofs? If so, let me know now—if not, check it when I return mine——but what do you think of ending Chapter xxviii, Galley 73, with the line "He said, 'Cap'n, you're a white man.'"?

The reason I wanted Claude to have the violent scene with the negroes carrying him out, was to give some indication of the *violence of his rages, to prepare the way for his fighting the* stallion. [The preceding italic phrase is underlined by hand, and written at the top of the page is: "Later in day——have eliminated as you suggested. You were right."] But I shall tone it all down one way or another. What do you think?

No, I don't think an Englishman would ever, at any time, call such a man as Luke Brinley by his first name. It would be "Brinley" always. He wouldn't even think anything of it, or mean it as drawing any line in their relations. I'm sure I'm right about this.

The dictionary gives a choice of "sweat" or "sweated" and I just like the sound of "sweat" better.

I object to *negro* being upper-cased. It looks terribly queer in print to me. I'm not sure of my ground here, so do as you please, but I prefer lower-case if permissible.

Your letter of criticism was everything helpful, as usual. How can I do such sheer *bad writing,* when I know better?

I have no great urge to see my face smirking from the back of the bookjacket. There's something offensive about female authors at best. Why emphasize it? If the picture is fairly good-looking you feel the work can't be sincere. If it's ugly, or a bit stark, or terribly earnest, it turns your stomach. That English picture you've been using is the least objectionable of any I've had in some time, so use it if you insist, but I don't believe you gain anything by it. Tom Wolfe's picture was effective because his face expresses some of the ecstasy and torment of his work. I'm no genius and my picture, to my notion, looks like nothing but just another she-writer. But again, suit yourself. I'll make one more try with a good out-door man in a week or so, to get you something for other publicity use.

Hurriedly,

. . . .

210. MKR to MEP (wire)

1935 JUL 8 AM 10 38
MAXWELL PERKINS—
597 FIFTH AVE—
HAVE TONED DOWN CLAUDES MUSIC BUT WHAT WOULD YOU THINK
OF ELIMINATING IT ALTOGETHER STOP INCLINED TO IT MYSELF STOP

IF IT IS NOT TOO LATE TO MAKE NECESSARY DELETIONS ON GALLEYS
FORTY AND FORTY ONE STOP WIRE TODAY CITRA—

. . . .

211. MEP to MKR (TS for wire)

JULY 8, 1935
MRS. MARJORIE K. RAWLINGS
CITRA, FLORIDA
FAVOUR CUTTING OUT CLAUDES MUSIC DELIGHTED BY YOUR LETTER

. . . .

212. MKR to MEP (TLS, 1 p.)

[Cross Creek]
[July 1935]

Dear Max:

I will write down a question that comes to me now and then as I work on the proofs.

Do you feel that Camilla would and should make some mention to Tordell of Allie's death, at their first meeting in the reader's presence, the fox-hunt? Or can one assume that that was taken care of in the brief meeting Tordell speaks of to Luke, referring to his having seen Camilla and the doctor and making the engagement for the fox-hunt? You will remember Camilla offered to take care of Allie when the time came. Ought she speak of her regret at having not been at home to do so? Or ought Tordell quote her on the subject, perhaps, to Luke, when he speaks of the recent brief meeting? This is Chapter xxxix, Galley 97.

Cosmopolitan asked me to insert some tie-up with Camilla in the very last scene, where Luke and Tordell inspect the successful buds. They said it would be natural for some thought of her to come to him in connection with the grove she helped to make possible. I did as they asked, but did not add the interpolation to your copy, as I did not consider it in any way necessary. What do you think?

I see little checks in ink from Galley 87 on to the end. Do they mean you consider *all* that material bad, to be re-written, or are they just checks to keep track of the reading?

Did the scene of Allie's death seem over-done in any way to you? Do you like or dislike Luke's impulse to kill Tordell? It seems to me a natural thing, yet it may register melodramatically.

213. MEP to MKR (CC, 2 pp.)

July 10, 1935

Dear Marjorie:

I did like Luke's impulse to kill Tordell and I thought that seemed very effective and right as to the character of both men. The only thing that bothered me about it was that it was another sensational incident at a time when the book was rather crowded with sensationalism.- But I didn't speak of it because I did believe in it and the only thing that ought to be done, if it were possible, would be somehow to reduce the rapidity of sensational incident at the end. I dare say you will find a way in the management of it,- perhaps just in the re-writing you are now doing. Anyhow, I do believe in keeping the incident. Luke acts on a sudden impulse. It is natural.

The little checks on the galley were some of them only about typographical matters, and others were points that I had covered in the general comment. I don't think they amount to anything now.

I don't think that Camilla should make mention to Tordell of Allie's death.- I think the assumption can be that it has been referred to outside in the scene presented in the store.

I'll be mighty glad to see the revision.

Always yours,

. . . .

214. MKR to MEP (wire)

1935 JUL 11 PM 4 07
MAXWELL PERKINS—
597 5 AVE—
PLEASE BE SURE TO AIR MAIL ME ANSWERS TO MY VARIOUS QUESTIONS TO REACH ME SATURDAY MORNING STOP CLAUDE ACHIEVES MUCH GREATER REALITY BUT BECOMES SO MUCH THE PETULANT AND DEMENTED BOY THAT I HAVE TO ELIMINATE HIS BEING CAMILLAS LOVER WILL SOON HAVE HAVE [SIC] GOLDEN APPLES A BIBLE TRACT—

. . . .

215. MKR to MEP (wire)

1935 JUL 15 PM 4 13
MAXWELL PERKINS—
597 FIFTH AVE—
PROOFS IN AIR MAIL DELAY NOT WORTH WHILE GOT RESULTS—

216. MEP to MKR (TS for wire)

JULY 16, 1935
MRS. MARJORIE K. RAWLINGS
ISLAND GROVE, FLORIDA
THINK REVISION SPLENDID WORK HAVE SENT TO PRINTER

. . . .

217. MKR to MEP (TLS, 2 pp.)

Hawthorn, Fla
July 17 [1935]

Dear Max:

You don't know what relief your wire brought me. I do think, whatever the other faults, the worst of the melodrama is out. The thing is still faintly saccharine and noble, but that was inevitable once I decided not to make the story one of outright defeat. By the way, did you receive the wire I sent you from Tampa the day before the corrected proofs arrived? We have had trouble with Western Union boys not delivering telegrams entrusted to them for sending.

I will check over that contract in a day or so and get it back to you. But I'm sure there is not, and could never be, any misunderstanding between us.

Max, I am due to go west to spend a month or so with my brother in Seattle.[1] He has a small power yacht and has arranged to take me in it to Alaska by the inland passage for a three or four weeks' jaunt. We will hit southeastern Alaska as soon as possible and go in for some intensive hunting and fishing. He promises deer, bear, moose, elk, quail, geese and grouse. Fog sets in, in Alaska and Puget Sound, the last of August. I want to go by way of Los Angeles to spend a couple of days with an old school friend,[2] and I should like to leave Florida if possible July 30 or 31. I will get the page proofs already sent me, checked over this week. Can you get me the rest of the corrections and any other material I need so that I can get away then? I can give you a Los Angeles address where you can reach me, and any last corrections could be sent me to Seattle. I want to reach Seattle August 7th or 8th.

Let me know, please, how soon you will be through with me.

As ever,

1. Arthur H. Kinnan.
2. Beatrice H. McNeil, MKR's classmate and close friend from the University of Wisconsin.

July 19, 1935

Dear Marjorie:

I am glad you are going West anyhow. You have been in one place perhaps too long, and had too much trouble in it,- what with the frost and all, and the expedition sounds like a wonderful one. Maybe there will be copy in it too.

As to the proof, I have a promise that all of it will be here by Wednesday. I shall send it by air mail. Wednesday will be the 24th. You will just have to read it as fast as you can and get it back as soon as you can. The only trouble is that I must be away the three last days of next week, and so I may not be able to read the proof carefully before sending it. But I do not think that matters so very much, for I have a pretty clear idea of it, and can run through it rapidly myself, and if there were anything very serious we could take it up at long distance somehow. So plan for the trip.

Always yours,

. . . .

July 24, 1935

Dear Marjorie:

I have just sent off the proof. I read it very fast, but it is my belief that you have done wonderfully well by the revision, and it is a very fine book indeed. It is not page proof,- you will have to trust us with the pages, but we shall be very careful. It is revised galley proof and ought to serve the purpose just as well.

I am glad you are going on the trip, and I hope it will be a very happy and successful one, and adventurous enough.

Always yours,

P.S. I do not know exactly what is bothering you about the contract, but we want it to be the way you wish to have it. The only point I can think of is an advance. I have always told you that we would gladly give one if you wanted it. As long as we are your publishers it would seem to me perfectly ludicrous to have an agent for your books. I cannot see how anyone would argue that you should. Why should you turn over ten percent to somebody else who has done nothing to deserve it?

Hawthorn, Fla.

July 25 [1935]

Dear Max:

I'll try to mention as many details as I can think of, that we need to discuss.

I plan to leave here Wednesday July 31. I go direct to Los Angeles, via the Santa Fe. My California address for a week, from about August 6 to August 13, will be:

Care of Mrs. William McNeil

    2373 Mariscal Lane

    Laurel Canyon

    Hollywood, Calif.

My Seattle address from August 14 on, will be:

Care of Arthur H. Kinnan

    1100 Vance Bldg.

    Seattle, Wash.

On South Moon Under, you asked me for the names of any journalistic or literary people to whom the book should be sent. The list I gave you then is a bit outmoded.

Ernest L. Meyer, who was then editorial writer on the Capitol Times, Madison, Wis., and who gave me such a delightful personal review, is now on the N.Y. Post. I do not know in what capacity. You might have Miss Wyckoff check him, and if he does any book work on the Post, a copy of Golden Apples should of course go to him personally, or if he does any type of writing that would be helpful.

I suggest sending a copy to the playwright, Sidney Howard.[1] His N.Y. address is somewhere in the East '80's. He wrote me a grand letter about South Moon.

Elizabeth Shepley Sergeant[2] (I noticed you had an article by her lately) gave me such a nice story in the Herald-Tribune, if you'll remember (very lush and not quite "getting" me, but still very kind) that it might be a good idea to send her a copy personally.

I suggest sending a copy to Sigrid Arne,[3] Associated Press Headquarters, Washington, D.C. She is a friend of mine, and you may consider this my own obligation, but she is one of the women journalists assigned to trailing Mrs. Roosevelt, and she did a lot of boosting in Washington on South Moon, bringing it to the attention of Ruth Bryan Owen,[4] for instance.

Incidentally, being a Florida book, it might not be a bad idea to send a copy to Mrs. Owen. What about Ida Tarbell, who wrote so beautifully of South Moon?

What about a copy to Governor David Sholtz, Tallahassee, Fla.? I know him personally, but wouldn't send him the book myself, unless you thought it desirable from a publicity angle. Or would it be better after all for me to send him an autographed copy?

A copy should go without fail to Marjory Stoneman Douglas, Miami Herald, Miami, Fla.

Please send copies to the following at my expense:

> Robert Herrick, Esquire
> Administration Secretary
> St. Thomas
> Virgin Islands

> Major Otto F. Lange
> 707 East Columbia St.
> Gainesville,
> Florida

Copies at my expense to:

Mrs. Ida Tarrant[5]	Dr. J. C. Vinson
1616 Pullan Ave.	First Nat'l Bank Bldg.
Cincinnati	Tampa
Ohio	Fla.

Send the copies I am entitled to, to me at my brother's address.

<If the book> (Unless, of course, I leave the west before the book is out. I hope to stay away most of September.)

I am sending you a photograph I believe you will find usable. It has a kind and intelligent expression——. Wherever desirable, I still advise using the English photo in preference.

About the proofs. I did not check the sequence of the Chapter numbers, nor the sequence of the page numbers. Having changed the chapter arrangement, this should be checked very carefully.

I have already sent back to you the revised corrections on Galleys 40 and 41, pages 148–165. On the latter part of this, I don't have a copy of any of my previous corrections, but I noticed one place (a period missing) where a previous correction had not been made. Be sure some proof-reader gets *those two sets of corrections together* [*together* underlined three times] on pages 148–165, for I cannot be sure I remember all the first ones.

Max, I have just received a batch of letters forwarded by Cosmopolitan.

Some of them are as fine, from intelligent people, as a writer could possibly receive. I shed a few tears of humility and gratitude. One was wonderful, from what must have been a very high type of Englishman, written from Paris but giving a swanky London address. Aside from his deep understanding of what I tried to do, I was especially pleased at his making no criticism of Tordell's character or speech, as another Englishman. I don't see how he could have resisted making a comment at least, if anything was off-key along that line. He mentioned the strangeness of finding <such> work from "such a type of mind as yours" in "the ordinary American, or rather, Anglo-Saxon, magazine".

Am mailing Contract tomorrow, with the explicit phrasing added that you suggested. Nothing has worried me about it——I just haven't gotten around to going over it again since we last discussed it.

If you need to write me about anything, air mail will reach me Wednesday morning before I leave.

As ever,

1. Sidney Howard (1891–1939).
2. Elizabeth S. Sergeant, "Literary Profile: Marjorie Kinnan Rawlings," *New York Herald Tribune* (18 June 1933): 7.
3. Sigrid Arne, journalist with the Associated Press.
4. Ruth Bryan Owen (1885–1954).
5. Ida Tarrant, known as "Aunt Ida," Charles Rawlings's great-aunt.

· ·

221. MEP to MKR (CC, 2 pp.)

July 29, 1935

Dear Marjorie:

The picture came—but it is not as good as the English one—and your letter with the list of persons to whom "Golden Apples" should go. We have already taken down the list and given orders that early copies shall be sent to those names. The proof is all here and everything seems to me right about it. We shall go over the final proof to see that all the corrections are made. I did not send you the foul proof with the revise because it made so heavy a package for the air mail, and I thought you would not need them. I do not think you need worry about anything now, and least of all about the book's reception. I shall keep you informed as best I can about anything that comes up, but you would do well to forget it all as completely as possible, and enjoy this trip. I hope it will be a happy one.

Always yours,

222. MEP to MKR (CC, 2 pp.)

July 31, 1935

Dear Marjorie:

You had not seen the proof of the front matter, and I thought you should. So I am sending it to California. The Cosmopolitan copyright will be inserted.

Always yours,

. . . .

223. MKR to MEP (ALS, 4 pp.)

St. Louis
Aug. 2 [1935]

Dear Max:——

Didn't hear from you before I left, but left word to have my mail forwarded to me in Seattle. Presume all was well or you'd have wired or 'phoned.

Did a careless thing——packed to leave in a grand rush and gathered up the Scribner contract to mail en route. Glanced at it just now and see it needs a witness to my signature. Nobody knows me here, so I'll have to wait until I reach Los Angeles this coming Tuesday. But I'm sure everything is all right. Don't want an advance if I can manage without it, on account of 1935 income tax running high because of the Cosmopolitan sale. Had to spend nearly half of it on grove and living expenses, and have invested the rest to keep from throwing it away. Am running a little close and may need a little money in the fall. But it won't be much in any case.

I did need to get away from Florida, for the reasons you mentioned, but I'm homesick as a cat right now. If my grand brother weren't waiting so anxiously at the other end, I'd turn around and go home.

This part of the world is *awful* [underlined three times]. But the people are peculiarly sweet and child-like and friendly. The mid-west accent, after many years' absence, hits as strange and staccato as some foreign tongue.

As ever,

. . . .

224. MKR to MEP (ALS, 4 pp.)

2373 Mariscal Lane
Laurel Canyon
Hollywood, Cal.
[August 1935]

Dear Max:——

Thanks for the proofs of the front matter——I'm returning them. Also enclosing the contract and if I haven't made the proper corrections, let me know and we'll change them.

Also, will you please have sent *at once, air mail,* a gloss print of that English photograph of me, to:—

Arthur H. Kinnan

1100 Vance Bldg.

Seattle, Wash.

My brother has newspaper friends who want a picture and a story, and since the book will be out so soon, all such things are probably desirable publicity. I'd appreciate this being sent at once, so that it will reach Seattle about the time I do.

I stopped off at the Grand Canyon for 2 days and took the mule trip down into the bottom of the canyon, spending the night at the ranch down there. It was most impressive. The descent from a mile in the air down those awful, narrow trails, was a bit spooky, especially since it was the first time I'd been on horseback since my spill in the spring. But I had the comfort of knowing that if I broke my neck again, it would be among noble surroundings!

Expect to reach Seattle August 12th. My brother has his yacht all ready for the Alaskan trip and is chafing at the bit for me to get there so we can start a couple of days later.

The trip itself will take six days up and six days back, and we're allowing two or three weeks for the hunting and fishing in between.

If the Golden Apples reviews are too bad, I'll just stay in Alaska!

Thanks for everything.

This part of the world is *gorgeous* [underlined twice].

. . . .

225. MKR to MEP (TLS, 1 p.)

> c/o A. H. Kinnan
> 1100 Vance Bldg.
> Seattle, Wash.
> August 14, 1935

Dear Max:

Just a note to thank you for your own considerate one.

My brother and I are leaving on his boat Friday for British Columbia and Alaska. I can be reached, if it is necessary, by addressing your letter to Gen. Delivery, hold Ketchikan, Alaska.

I shall expect to be away three or four weeks, but of course, will return to Seattle again before leaving for home.

> As ever,

226. MKR to MEP (postcard, signed)

Mr. Maxwell Perkins
597 Fifth Ave
New York City

[Seattle?]

[September 1935]

Have had a fascinating trip. I'll write you on my way East in a couple of weeks.

. . . .

227. MKR to MEP (ALS, Empire Builder railroad stationery, 3 pp.)

The Empire Builder
via Glacier National Park
Sept. 28 [1935]
Saturday

Dear Max:—

I should have written you my whereabouts earlier——hope you haven't sent any "Golden Apples" to the coast.

I'll be home this coming Thursday. I'm anxious to see the jacket——someone spoke of seeing an advance copy and said the jacket was very attractive.

The trip was gorgeous. I'll write you about it when I reach my typewriter. There may possibly be a short narrative for "Life in the United States" in it, called something on the order of "Tidal Highway." It would be much in the mood of "Hyacinth Drift."

As ever,

. . . .

228. MEP to MKR (CC, 1 p.)

Sept. 30, 1935

Dear Marjorie:

I only sent one copy to the coast, and six to Florida. I hope you will do that "Tidal Highway". I know it would be good, and that the magazine would want it. If you write me, your letter will be forwarded, but I am off today for a two weeks' vacation. I have got to take it though I do not want to. I shall be in Vermont. I am delighted you have had such a fine trip.

We are publishing on October fourth.

Always yours,

Hawthorn, Florida

Oct. 15, 1935

Dear Max:

I hope your forced vacation wasn't because of your health. You have had your share of worries with authors-in-need-of-editing, and I should think sooner or later it would wear you down.

But Max, in spite of your great conscientiousness and honesty, you are too lenient a critic. You should simply raise hell with Thomas Wolfe, to *make* him do the artistic thing and not the chest-beating thing. You should make him understand that it is better to say a thing once, superbly, than to scream it hysterically half a dozen times. You have too much sympathy with the torment of the writer's mind. A writer was born to be tormented. It is his destiny. You should torment us still further, when you see, as surely, you must see, the inadequate thing emerging.

I don't blame anyone but myself for "Golden Apples" being interesting trash instead of literature. But you should have bullied me and shamed me further. I can do better than that and you know it. I wish to Heaven I could take the book as I now see it, and re-write the last half of it. There are two or three things I could have done to make a better book. One would have been to work out the story with only Luke and Allie and Tordell and the Doctor. Another would have been to have taken a much greater space to handle the latter part, so that there would not be that staccato and violent effect. To be as leisurely about Camilla and the freeze and so on as I was in the early part. That would have made a book probably in two parts; the two phases of Tordell's life in Florida. Actually, two books in one.

When I read the book the other day, from cover to cover, I was astonished. It never occurred to me it would seem so violent. The "story" was the last thing in the world that concerned me, yet the thing seemed solid "story." No quietness at all. And I had been afraid that it would be too quiet; that Tordell's struggles with his background would seem stupid and without eventfulness. If I had set out to plan a "plot" I could not have done it. The characters were to me all part of his struggle. Yet the book reads as though I had charted an artificial plotting. My only key to this, is my old difficulty with actual truth. When I use characters (like Camilla and the doctor and Claude) suggested, if ever so vaguely, by true characters; when I build on actual events (like the Big Freeze); I deviate somehow from Absolute Truth. Or else the fictitious groundwork I lay does not fit in with the previous true one. I may try, next time, to begin with a simple situation and one dominant character, and let it work itself out as it seems to want to, without any pre-conceptions——and see what happens.

I have only seen three or four of the reviews.

October 16.

A large batch of reviews came in this morning. I am astonished at their generosity. I should not have been nearly so kind with the book! It is amusing to see the reviewers contradict one another, isn't it? One says the book has an unsatisfactory ending, up in the air. Another says the ending is "too perfect"—— managed. Henry Seidel Canby[1] comes closer than anyone, except Carl Bohnenberger in the Jacksonville Times-Union, to understanding what I was trying to do. But Max, *no one*, (least of all your abominable blurb writer on the back of the jacket!) makes note of the one point that was important to me. That is the struggle of a man against a natural background. One paragraph is the key to it, the one beginning, "The relation of a man to a natural background was profound. It completed him as no other human could complete him. It was dispassionate and stable". The Englishman who wrote me some time ago is the only person to pounce on that. He called it the crux of the story. How can people miss it? I was afraid my "message" would be too blatant! Yet everyone is concerned with the characters, the plot, the technique, the "background", using the word in the theatrical sense. To me, that point dignifies and validates all the characters. Otherwise, it would be indeed, as TIME said, "dull melodrama."[2] (I think the JEW on TIME who wrote that review got annoyed with Tordell mid-way and never even finished the book!) At least, this point, that is the one thing I have to say in most of what interests me to write, has gone so unnoticed that I shall dare to say the same thing again, with other characters! The prospect of that pleases me, for I have never been satisfied with the way I said it here. But for no one to give it a thought! It is beyond me.

I do wish I could talk with you occasionally. I need to spill out half-formed ideas, to be shaped later or rejected. I believe, from the reaction, I should go on with the Florida vein in one form or another, a little longer. One hates to be localized. Yet there is still much fascinating material here. And if real and true and honest characters can be made to move across a little-known setting, I suppose it is foolish for me to long for wider worlds to conquer. And I still think I shall write a good book some day——.

Do hope you're well. Hope the book sells to suit all of you who have been so very good to me. Whitney Darrow is a darling, isn't he?

My best, as ever,

PS. Please return the Englishman's letter. He is the only reader to "get" my point.

1. Henry Seidel Canby, "Wild Oranges," *Saturday Review of Literature* 12 (October 5, 1935): 6.

2. "Florida Scrub," *Time* 26 (October 1935): 77–78.

. . . .

230. MEP to MKR (TLS: UF, 4 pp.)

Oct. 18, 1935

Dear Marjorie:

I was mighty glad to get a letter from you. I saw three reviews of "Golden Apples" while I was away in Vermont, and two of them spoke of it as being better than "South Moon Under". Since I got back I have been too crowded to read the other reviews. I do not see how people could miss the point about the man and the environment, but it is very hard indeed to get an advertising man to present abstract or general ideas because he is convinced that what sticks in the minds of people is the specific, and that it is the story that first catches the attention, and that the underlying ideas can only be imparted by the book. I am glad though, that you think there is plenty of material for another Florida novel, and I should think there would easily be. It often passed through my mind to suggest confining this story to Luke, Allie, and Tordell and the doctor, but I really could not see it. I think you did need more story than that would have given you. I thought of raising the question, but it seemed also to me that the serialization had committed you to the lines followed there in a general sense. Personally, I think you did express the meaning of the book very fully, and that readers know it, but that most readers are not of a sort who know that kind of thing consciously, so that they can speak of it. They know it, and feel it, when they read it.

Everything seems to be going well, but I have not got enough in touch to be in command of all the details yet. I shall write you about everything soon.

Are you likely to write to Tom about his book and put a little hell into the letter? It would do good. The criticisms he received have evidently at last impressed him with the truth of what we have been telling him, and often with very great violence, for years. But now when we are about to start on the next book is the time he should be told and if you felt like it, it might be very effective.- But there must be no collusion between us. Let me tell you though, for my own sake, that there was nothing lenient in my dealings with Tom in the matter of this book, and that several times he departed with the emphatic statement that he never wanted to see me again. He is, as the hat check girl said to me after his sudden and violent departure from the cafe, "a very nervous gentleman".

Always yours,

P.S. I studied the hurricane course with care and judged it never got anywhere near your part of Florida, though I suppose it must have been windy everywhere.

Editor's note: In an enclosed note: "Oct. 23, 1935 / Correction for 'Golden Apples' - Rawlings / Page 236, line 9 from bottom, 'Atlanta' should be 'Atalanta'."

· ·

231. MEP to MKR (TLS: UF, 4 pp.)

Nov. 2, 1935

Dear Marjorie:

I have just gone through all the reviews. Do you want to see them? There are many, a good many from the South which are not, of course, important. In fact only a small number of reviews are important, and I think probably those were among the ones that were sent you.- The Times, Tribune, Saturday Review, etc.[1] The reviews here are favorable, though they do tend to talk about the wrong things. I shall send them if you want them.

I have sent you a copy of T. Wolfe's book of stories, though I know you will have read some of them.[2] Those from the magazine are better than when they appeared there, as a result of cutting and some reorganization, but "The Web of Earth" which constitutes a third of the book, is exactly the same. Curiously enough, he did in that story, it seemed to me, achieve a high degree of form, and nothing was ever done to it. It stands now exactly as he first wrote it.

I thought that you might do the boy's book soon, and so I inquired about John Thomason. But there is no possibility, I guess, of his being available, because his military work is exacting,- partly on account of his popularity which causes these Admirals and Secretaries to want him to go all over the country with them, even to Honolulu. On top of that, he is doing a large book to be called, "Lee's Men,"[3] about the Army of Northern Virginia, which will have many pictures and sketches, and a series of stories for The Saturday Evening Post, about a U.S. marine and his adventures.

There is a plan afoot for him and Tom Wolfe and me to go over the battlefield of Chancellorsville. Tom has to do it on account of a book which I suppose won't be finished for years, and John knows every foot of the battlefield and can talk wonderfully about it. This won't be until spring though, and if you could be in this part of the country then, we would try to make you go, and have a fine party. There is a wonderful old house within motoring distance of the battlefield where everything is exactly as it was before the war. We all know the Miss Lemmon[4] who owns it and would also be in the party.- I hope this will all happen.

Do you plan to do the boy's book? It would not be what we call a "juvenile," but one of those books which could show almost to the full, the quality of the region and of the life there, as has always been true of the really fine books written primarily for boys. Some of the great books are among them, and their readers are men and women as well as boys.

Always yours,

1. *New York Times* (October 6, 1935): 3; Mary Ross, "When Pride Meets Pride," *New York Herald Tribune Books* (October 6, 1935): 6; and Henry S. Canby, "Wild Oranges," *Saturday Review* 12 (October 5, 1935): 6.
2. Thomas Wolfe, *From Death to Morning* (New York: Scribners, 1935).
3. Not identified.
4. Elizabeth Lemmon, Middleburg, Va., owned the "Church House."

· ·

232. MEP to MKR (CC, I p.)

Nov. 4, 1935

Dear Marjorie:

On account of the date on which "Golden Apples" appeared, it did not get into the October Book of the Month Club recommendations. It is in the number which I am now sending you, the November, with a note by Dr. Canby.

Always yours,

· ·

233. MKR to MEP (TLS, with holograph additions, 4 pp.)

Hawthorn, Florida
Nov. 5, 1935

Dear Max:

I'm glad to have the Wolfe book of stories. The book form means something a magazine never can, and I'm glad to have the "Web of Earth"——one of my favorites——in permanent form. I believe the reason Wolfe was so successful with that, speaking so much to the point, was because he allowed his character to absorb him. He was no more redundant than the old woman would have been. It was truly her story——not Tom Wolfe perorating——and it had as great a reality as anything he has done. Hemingway wonders, I believe, whether Wolfe would be a great writer if he should serve a term of exile in Siberia. I do not think Wolfe is tainted, as Hemingway is, by any shadow-boxing with the sophisticated world. I do not think he is particularly on the defensive.

As a writer who has always had to fight overwriting, it seems to me that his fault as an artist lies in *indulging himself* in the deliciousness of piling word on word, phrase on phrase, rhythm on rhythm. Used judiciously, his cumulative effect is prodigious, of course. Over-done, it is like too much poetry, or too much symphony music, or too much passion——cloying; surfeiting. I have often been tempted to write him, but being entirely inferior as an artist, it would be presumptuous, so I have never done so.

It would be delightful to meet you and Wolfe and Major Thomason at Chancellorsville. You can count on me at a moment's notice. I have been over several of the battlefields and there were no ghosts there. It seemed to me that the markers and the tourists had driven them all away. I tried to induce them with my own pity, but it was no go. I have always wanted to be there with someone who knew something about <the> it. But are you sure I would be acceptable to your two historians? Can you convince them that I am not a "lady" author? You don't need to worry about the chaperon for me. I can't think of anything safer or more respectable than being with three men.

I have begun the "Tidal Highway." I can't tell yet whether it will be usable or not. But if it isn't, it will serve to give you most of the story, which to me at least was fascinating. I hate to tell you, Max, but I am afraid that some time in the next three or four years I shall have to go to Alaska to spend a year or so and write a novel. A whole set of characters, a motif, suggested themselves to me, irresistibly, requiring that setting and no other. I had to fight staying there, to do it right then. You see, with the acute feeling I have for the relation of man to his natural background, that dark and forbidding and mountainous country offers a setting for the theme of betrayal. Human treachery is the most appalling thing. You have to learn to expect to be betrayed. Yet you must learn never to betray. So I give you fair warning, if things get too thick for me here, or too unhappy, I shall have to clear out for that part of the world. The story is already almost a unit.

Meantime, about the Florida vein, I don't know. Lots of short stuff waiting to be done. Just a matter of keeping myself at it.

I don't know what to say about the boy's book of the scrub. At present, I don't have the enthusiasm. Looking over my notes, and remembering all the bear stories of the northwest, my material seems very thin. There was a time, about two years ago, when I believe I might have done something with it, but the "Golden Apples" material was so deep-rooted it wouldn't let me alone. I'll have to let it take its course. My thought of a further Florida novel is vague. Yet the material is here. The old days of sugar cane, of timbering, are very stirring. I think a great deal about a character who opened up a large part of Florida with a railroad and so on, about whom I wrote a sketch <of> for the "Life in the United States" contest, which was rejected because it didn't carry conviction. A story could be built around that period. There is a story, too, in the period of the Indian Wars in Florida, but it leaves me cold, somehow. Just let me putter along this winter with the short stuff and we'll see. The boy's thing may hit me all of a sudden.

There is one Florida book that will surely be done, I don't know how soon. One I had thought would not be possible because I hadn't done it when the material struck me freshly. Yet mellowness, not freshness, is the requisite. It will be non-fiction, called "Cross Creek: a Chronicle."[1] It will not be a confluent narrative, (for the reason that I do not wish to write my personal story) but made up into chapters. Some of the chapter headings are: "The Sixteen Acres"; "Old Boss"; "'Geechee"; "Black Shadows"; "The Pickers of Magnolia Leaves"; "Toady-Frogs, Snakes and Antses." It will be as quiet in tone as anyone could wish for! Some of the material is violent, but it will be interesting to tell it in a matter of fact and quiet way. It will not be a book to sit down and "do", but one accumulated. Some of the material has been done several years, needing re-writing, of course. Sketches, stories, narratives, essays, laid here at the Creek, done with no special use in mind. But all with a certain, what shall I say, out of the world flavor, catching, I hope, the quality that has made me cling so desperately and against great odds to this place. How it will fit into your publishing schedule, I don't know. It is possible it will be ready in a year or two and will fill in until I have a novel ready for you. Or it may be several years more before I feel I have caught what I want to. I thought I would speak of it to you, since I am sure you wonder what may be shaping itself in my mind.

Nov. 6

I just had a letter from Robert Herrick, whose reaction to the book is much like everyone else's. He finds the simpler people and the setting sound; feels a distaste for the "Hamlet" Englishman; does not find Camilla successful for the great reason, he thinks, that she does not have a good chance in the book. He asks, "Why not do a book about *her*?" Off-hand, having given it no thought at all, it is an interesting suggestion. If I ever did such a thing, I suppose a great deal of my own struggle would go into it. It might have value for the reason that my response to the terrain has value; it would be something thoroughly understood by me. I do not think I shall ever be able to present a convincing picture of anything from the outside. I never got inside Camilla; never even tried to. I presented her as she appeared to other people. <Just have patience with me> Why Tordell is not completely successful, I do not know. I understood him thoroughly. It comes to me sometimes that I violated the truth in having him achieve <the> unity with his background. I am almost afraid that his basic character was such that defeat was inevitable for him; perhaps with understanding. I think it might have been better to do as I first planned; have him go down in his despair; probably into death; with a glimmer of vision before him. Letting Luke express the soundness of union with the particular land.

That is the hell of publishing exigencies; of personal ambition, which makes you want to "produce". If I had put the manuscript aside for a year or two, I might have made a more artistic unit of it. But it annoyed me so, fretted me, and I could get nothing else done with it in me. I took it for granted it would not be quite right. And perhaps the inherent disharmonies were so great that it could never have been. In the end I believe I shall learn a great deal from it; much more than from the first book.

Don't bother about the reviews. As you say, I've seen the more important ones. They were kinder than I should have been. I'm not in the least interested. They said nothing I didn't know. I am only pleased that after all there is as much stimulation in the book as there seems to be.

As ever,

1. Published later as *Cross Creek* (New York: Scribners, 1942).

. . . .

234. MEP to MKR (TLS: UF, 3 pp.)

Nov. 15, 1935

Dear Marjorie:

I did show Tom what you said and he took it very well, and said the only trouble was that people like you were not the ones who wrote reviews. I think he was very much impressed,- and in fact he is more and more impressed with the validity of the criticisms on certain lines that are made against him. Many adverse criticisms are made though that are unjustified — some of the elements in his writing that give its greatest value are not appreciated by reviewers — and I am sometimes a little fearful that he will listen now too much to what is said. But what you said in your last letter was very acute, and it made its mark upon him.

I won't say anything more about the boy book, but that I greatly hope you will do it, and in the way you wish. And the book "Cross Creek" would "fit into our publishing schedule" excellently well. I won't urge you. I know you know what you want to do, and that is what you should do. I think "Cross Creek" might be a beautiful and successful book. One hearing about these plans cannot but be eager to see them carried out, but I know that you should not hurry to produce, and I won't be impatient.- I have no right to be, anyway.

I am going to send you, just as soon as I can get an advance copy, a book that you will like immensely,- it is called "The Last Puritan," a memoir in the form of a novel by George Santayana.[1]

Always yours,

1. George Santayana (1863–1952), *The Last Puritan* (New York: Scribners, 1936).

. . . .

235. MKR to MEP (ALS, 2 pp.)

[Cross Creek]
[November–December 1935]

Dear Max:——

The feeling for the boy's book, the particular thing I want to say, came to me. It will not be a story for boys, though some of them might enjoy it. It will be a story *about* a boy——a brief and tragic idyll of boyhood. I think it cannot help but be very beautiful.

It would be a long story——say, 50,000 words. But don't ask me about it yet. When I have begun to catch what I want, I'll send it on, or tell you about it.

. . . .

236. MKR to MEP (TLS, 2 pp.)

Hawthorn, Fla.
December 18 [1935]

Dear Max:

I am immensely puzzled by the fact that absolutely no mention is made of "Golden Apples" in either last Sunday's or this Sunday's Scribner advertisement in the N.Y. Herald-Tribune. The Tribune is the only New York paper I see and it is possible you have divided your advertising. Yet in a general listing I should think the book would at least be mentioned. If it had been a complete failure I could understand it, but with as many books as there are published, it seems to me that one that has held a place on the general best-seller list for two months, deserves more consideration, especially for Christmas gift-selling. The Magazine never carried an announcement of the book until a full month after publication. What is wrong? I have always felt that you have all been very generous with me, but this omission is really distressing.

The writing has been going very badly. I have done several pieces of verse, but have finished nothing else. The "Tidal Highway" I do not think will work out. It is stilted and without value. After the first of the year I shall "take the veil" again——I cannot write, even short things, and do *anything* else——and get something done.

233

I went last week to the strange and remote place in the scrub, Pat's Island (a pine "island" in the heart of the lower scrub growth) where I stayed with the old hunter who was old man Payne in South Moon Under.[1] The old man is dead, his wife moved away with her children——she was a second wife——and the house that he had lived in for sixty years is beginning to cave in under the pressure of that peculiar despairing frailty that seems to possess uninhabited places, as though the supporting breath had left the body of the house, along with the human occupants. I think I shall take some camping stuff and my typewriter and slip away over there without anyone's knowing where I am, to do the boy's story (based on material I got from the old man) in peace and quiet. The location is one of the strangest and most beautiful places I have ever seen. There is a moonshiner four miles away in one direction, a hunting camp four miles in another, and nothing at all for nearly twenty miles anywhere else. Does "The Sink-Hole" sound at all interesting for a title, or is it phonetically unattractive? There is a large sink-hole near the place, grown up in dog-wood and holly and bay and magnolias, that would have meant something very fascinating to a boy.

Robert Herrick is encouraging me strongly on the verse. I sometimes send him a sonnet I've done instead of writing a letter, and of one lately he wrote that "the firm sure phrasing shows a master's hand". Shall I send anything to the Magazine, or is it just as well not to cross the track of my fiction there?

I hope you have a fine Christmas and that all is well. And do see if something shouldn't be done about my being dropped entirely from your list at this time.

As ever,

Editor's note: At top of letter in MEP's hand: "Oct 4 — Publ. / Sept 20 / Heur [?] / Van D[oran]. / Sullivan / More than Wolfe."

1. Barney Dillard.

· ·

237. MEP to MKR (CC, 4 pp.)

Dec. 20, 1935

Dear Marjorie:

We advertised your book steadily through December 8th. We were not getting reorders then, and as it was one of our earliest books and had been advertised for so long, we turned our attention to books for which we were getting last minute reorders. That is the whole explanation. Campaigns on a book have to be laid out differently according to the length of time in which the money is to be spent. For instance, although Mark Sullivan's book[1] came out quite late, we have spent almost as much on it as we have on yours, partly because of its higher price. But four books we have advertised neck and neck in respect to the appropriation made this season:- Hemingway, Van Dine, Sullivan, and yours.[2] We have spent much more on "Europa" but that had an extraordinary sale which we followed steadily.[3] "Golden Apples" has sold approximately 10,000 copies. It has not kept up well although the trade were all very much in favor of it as we know because we sent out 200 extra copies for them to read. People who read it do like it, but there seems to have come a very strong reaction, the booksellers say, which I suppose we owe chiefly to Mr. Caldwell,[4] against "poor white" literature as they call it. It will only be temporary, and must not be considered in connection with the boys' book. It is ridiculous to put your book in that class and we fought against it, but Americans seem to have a tendency toward classification in the book business. You spoke about "Golden Apples" not being advertised in the Scribner's current at the time it appeared. It was published October 4th and was advertised in the Scribner's that followed that date, about the 18th of October. But it is bad to advertise a book as if it were out two weeks in advance, as we would have had to do if we had put it in the preceding Scribner's.

I do not like the title "The Sink Hole" for it seems to have an unattractive connotation. Isn't there some other name for such a phenomenon? I imagine the difficulty about writing is just one of those which a genuine writer has to go through with, or most people. They say it is not true of Ellen Glasgow,- but I was never one of her admirers and have not read her for a long time.[5] It is true of every real writer I ever knew.

I hope this year you are not going to have bad luck again with the oranges. We have had very warm weather here so far, and very depressing,- hardly a glance at the sun for the last eight or ten weeks.

I shall soon be sending you a copy of the Santayana. I know Dashiell would want to see your poetry for the magazine.

Always yours,

1. Mark Sullivan (1874–1952), *Our Times* (New York: Scribners, 1935).
2. Hemingway, *Green Hills of Africa* (New York: Scribners, 1935), and S. S. Van Dine [W. H. Wright] (1888–1939), *The Garden Murder Case* (New York: Scribners, 1935).
3. Robert Briffault (1876–1948), *Europa* (New York: Scribners, 1935).
4. Erskine P. Caldwell (1903–1987), noted for his novels about poverty in rural Georgia and North Carolina.
5. Ellen Glasgow (1874–1945), who later authorized MKR to write her biography. The work was not completed.

1936

238. MEP to MKR (CC, 1 p.)

March 5, 1936

Dear Marjorie:

I am sending you a book that I think you will enjoy,- the greater part of it is very fine. It is by a new writer.[1]

I am enclosing a royalty report on "South Moon Under" but of course it does not amount to much of anything in money now. I'll tell you exactly how "Golden Apples" came out, and write you at length about it very soon, but it is still impossible to know the situation in the case of a good many stores where books are on sale.

I hope all goes well with the oranges this winter, and with you.

Always yours,

1. John G. Lockhart (1891–), *Great Sea Mystery* (London: Allan, 1930).

. . . .

239. MKR to MEP (TLS, with holograph addition, 4 pp.)

Hawthorn, Florida
March 9. [1936]

Dear Max:

You are good not to reproach me. I have not intended to let so much time go by without writing you and thanking you for "The Last Puritan". I don't need to add my encomiums to the accumulation. It is easily the most stimulating book I have read in years. It gave the exhilaration we used to feel in our college days, when new ideas hit us with almost physical force. I enjoyed the book as much as <I> you knew I should. But how amazing for it to be popular!

I have come to the conclusion that it is useless for me to try to get any work done in the winters here. If you will remember, all my work has been done through the springs and summers. The strenuous hunting season, the comings and goings of people, the activity of my grove work and orange picking, all combine to shatter the stillness and solitude I seem to need for the writing. Yet I have an idea the time is not actually wasted. Ideas gestate, and the very impatience I begin to feel after a time, is good for hard work. As I mentioned before, I have done quite a bit of verse, and have been getting something done on a humorous story that may or may not be your kind. The boy's story is shaping clearly in my mind, and I shall soon go to the deserted cabin to spend what time is necessary. Do you like the title, "The Fawn"?

Some unbelievably exciting material has come to my notice, for a long novel. I should like to talk it over with you in person if it can be worked out. I don't get much satisfaction out of correspondence along such lines, though I think you prefer it. I haven't dared let my imagination go on the subject, for it has great difficulties, and I want to answer many questions before I allow myself to get, as I made the mistake of doing in "Golden Apples", too set a pattern in advance. I have the feeling that if I had been able to talk with you, between us we should have seen the key to harmony in the book——which was to make it Luke's story. Of course the Cosmopolitan sale was what put the monkey wrench in the works. The subsequent sense of hurry was fatal.

Has anything come of your plan to meet Wolfe and Thomason at the Pennsylvania battle field? If so, and you still want me, I'd enjoy driving up if only for a day with you. It would give me a chance to talk over the new subject with you in peace and quiet. Your nice offices and restaurant and so on drive me mad with their racket, and interruptions.

I had a very short crop of oranges this year, due to last year's cold hurting the bloom. My net return was fair considering the shortage. The bloom is just coming now, and everything looks promising for next year's crop. There is no danger of cold now. I wish you could be down here next week or the week after. It will be lovely then.

The "Sea-Mary" just arrived. Many thanks.

I have been carrying your home address and that of Whitney Darrow, around in my car for weeks, to send you oranges. There was a gap in good fruit, and now that my shipper has some good oranges ready again, I can't find the addresses. Please send them to me, and in the meantime I may locate Mr. Darrow's note again.

By the way, I never received the advance $125. guarantee on the cheap edition of South Moon. On the first statement and check I received, the amount was $116., presumably for actual sales over and above the original 2500 printing. I assumed this, since I could account for nothing to make a $9. deduction.

Will you have Miss Wyckoff send me 3 copies of South Moon, (2 of the cheap edition and 1, for my own use, of the regular) and 2 copies of Golden Apples?

There are a number of books I have been wanting to order for my library. How big an order would I have to give to get the trade discount?

Sorry to mix business and pleasure in my letters!

Thank you for everything.

. . . .

240. MEP to MKR (TLS: UF, 2 pp.)

March 26, 1936

Dear Marjorie:

The oranges are beautiful and delicious, and I thank you for them on my own part, and that of my family. I think I should be happy with an orange grove.

I am glad you have the boy's book well thought out. I think "The Fawn" is a good title, but I am not sure that it would be a wise one for it might seem too poetic, or even a little sentimental. I hope you will send the humorous story to us.- People still talk about Bennie.[1]

Wolfe has got himself into another lawsuit,[2] and is so much off the reservation and unable even to sit still, that I cannot make any definite plans about him, but I am to see John Thomason next week, and maybe we shall work something out. If you ever came up though, as far as Washington, I could easily see you there where it is quieter. I cannot get away for some little time because other people are away, but later in the spring it will be different.

The Santayana is really having the most amazing sale. I do not know that you care for things of a philosophical kind, but I thought I would send you anyway, a copy of his "Obiter Scripta".[3] If you read the first flap it will point you to a paper which is supposed by him to give his whole idea.

Always yours,

1. "Benny and the Bird Dogs."
2. An agent, who misrepresented Wolfe in the sale of his manuscripts, then threatened to sue Wolfe for services rendered.
3. George Santayana, *Obiter Scripta* (New York: Scribners, 1936).

April 6, 1936

Dear Marjorie:

I am just getting off this royalty report on "Golden Apples". I shall send you the check on August 4th,- and if you need some of it sooner, tell us. Ten thousand is a good sale for these days, but we do want to have you sell much more because we think you should.

Always yours,

. . . .

Hawthorn, Florida
May 20, 1936

Dear Max:

I was especially glad to have the "Obiter Scripta". Of course I like philosophical things! The abstract is usually more exciting to me than the concrete. I have had to fight that very thing in writing fiction, where nothing much registers distinctly except the specific.

The Santayana success simply doesn't make sense. Nothing but the title, "The Last Puritan", has any appeal to the mind which buys best-sellers. The thing has been a snow-ball, of course, rolling down-hill. A librarian tells me it is the "smart" book to read. I doubt whether the "smart" people finish it. I think the vast publicity given it by TIME did more than anything else. There was a peculiar flavor to that review, hinting at things that, actually, weren't there. Yet as I remember, the flood had begun before TIME reviewed it. It is a gorgeous book——but only for those with sensitive and acute minds. It must leave the masses puzzled, once they've bought it. And what an utterly astonish[ed] old gentleman Santayana himself must be!

I couldn't "see" "Sea-Mary" at all. It was to me, one of those utterly futile books that made you wonder why someone didn't deflect the writer into building a trellis, or a foot-scraper.

I thought the same of "Sally"[1] when I began it. Having just finished it, I cannot be so sure. As the jacket I think said, it has the cumulative effect of "An American Tragedy".[2] It is even more valid than the American thing, because at no point can you see any escape for Sally from the net of circumstance. It is completely convincing as to the inevitability of her actions. On the other hand, Dreiser's Clyde was not forced by society as far as Dreiser wanted to suppose him to be. The character's own weakness and selfishness were infinitely more to blame than any superimposition of social standards from the outside.

Max, I *must* have Wolfe's Story of a Novel,[3] particularly because I am interested in the workings of your own mind in your problem of getting into the writer's mind, and yet keeping a necessary detachment. Would you object terribly to autographing it for me? Please don't mind, if you'd in the least rather not. If I've already had my share of Scribner books for the time being, please have it charged to my account. I do appreciate your sending me these books.

I finished the humorous mule story[4] and since I had promised it to Carl Brandt long ago, felt obliged to send it to him. I wrote him that you had said you would like to see it. He will know whether it's a Scribner type of story or a more "popular" type. I used for a narrator the same character that I used to tell "Benny and the Bird Dogs"——Mis' Dover becomes, in the mule story, Quincey Dover. She grew on me as a personality, and in using her, the thought was in the back of my mind that eventually there will probably be enough of a Quincey Dover series to make a very readable book——which of course would go to you, if you wanted it. I had a wire from Carl that he considered the story "swell", but what he is doing with it, I don't know. I read it aloud the other day to a librarian whose critical judgment I trust, and without telling him what I had in the back of my mind about a book, he commented that I had very possibly there, in Quincey Dover, a great American character. Carl may feel that the story is most desirable for you, and submit it to you in any case, but if he should sell it to somebody like the Post, I'd like your reaction on the possibility of a volume, eventually. Another story is shaping in mind, using this woman and her small timid husband, based on cock-fighting here.

I do not believe the boy's story is going to be what you have in your own mind, at all. But if it comes out in harmony with the feeling I have about it, it will be very touching. Otherwise, just a bad nothing to be torn up. I shall hope to have it done by October, say, when I should like to talk with you about the long and very exciting and very dangerous novel that is beginning to possess me.

It is cold potatoes now, as far as sales etc., are concerned, but I have had some recent favorable comment on "Golden Apples" that has made me feel a lot better about it. Dr. Albert Shaw considers it a better book than South Moon. He called it "a very wise book" and found no disharmony in it. I met the Englishman whose very beautiful letter I sent you. He called here with his wife——by the way, they were good friends of John Galsworthy. He had gotten South Moon in London, and reading it *after* Golden Apples, felt only a mild interest in it. To him, it was only a study of a way of life, authentic and touching, but it did not stir him as Golden Apples did. Max, I really believe that if Golden Apples had appeared first, people would have been interested by the novelty of the setting and its exoticism, just as they were by the same things in South Moon——and that if South Moon had appeared second, they would have been disappointed at, say, a lack of drama! On the strength of several such recent comments, I have had the courage to look at the book, and it is much better than I thought. I am much encouraged. But no more serial mutilations! I hope you won't let Golden Apples disappear entirely, if it can be helped, through a cheap edition perhaps. I believe it would be bought quite a bit at 75¢.

Another novel is complete in my mind as to character, motivation and general pattern. It is very simple, almost too much so, but I was afraid of the same thing with Luke and Allie, and then they were more liked than anyone else. It is hard for me to realize that anyone else can be interested in those very simple details, yet they are. Anyway, when the short book is done, as I say, I hope in early fall, I must talk with you about these two things.

1. Elizabeth Coatsworth (1893–1986), *Away Goes Sally* (New York: Macmillan, 1934).
2. Theodore Dreiser (1871–1945), *An American Tragedy* (New York: Boni and Liveright, 1925).
3. Thomas Wolfe, *The Story of a Novel* (New York: Scribners, 1936).
4. "Varmints," *Scribner's Magazine* 100.6 (December 1936): 26–32, 84–85.

. . . .

243. MEP to MKR (TLS: UF, 4 pp.)

May 29, 1936

Dear Marjorie:

I did send you a copy of "The Story of a Novel".- It will have reached you before this. I called up Brandt & Brandt about the story, but Carl was not there, and I only asked if it came within the reach of our magazine prices, we get a chance at it. I am afraid it has been placed elsewhere by now, but that is in the nature of things, and altogether reasonable. I wish we could have such another one as "Benny and the Bird Dogs" which has never been forgotten, and I think that a collection of such stories would find a public. I wish I knew what the long novel was that you speak about, but I'll wait until October. I knew you were exaggerating your reaction against "Golden Apples". Several of the best reviewers said it was better than "South Moon". I think that both for you and for me it was hard to judge it because of all the changes that went on when it was being written. For me it is always hard to get a real perspective on a book when I have read it in various stages and in sections. I doubt for one thing, if it moved too rapidly toward the end, and Luke and Allie were quite as good as the people in "South Moon".- But "South Moon" was more all of one fabric, and had a greater unity and completeness.- That was due to the nature of the material you used. A real difficulty, and one which went against "Golden Apples" is the popular opposition to books about poor whites. This resulted from the work of Faulkner, Stribling,[1] and Caldwell, and has been very apparent in the bookstores. A large part of the sale of a novel comes from people who know little about the writer when they buy, but ask the clerk what the story is about, and if they gather that it is about poor whites, they think of it in terms of "Tobacco Road" etc. This is one of those currents of feeling that get to moving and generally soon die out because everything changes so rapidly.- But this popular feeling against a subject does also affect a more intelligent level of readers, or a more discriminating one, and even extends to critics and reviewers. It did militate though, against the sale of "Golden Apples".

I am sending you a book I think you will enjoy now,- "Heads and Tails" by Malvina Hoffman.[2]

Always yours,

1. Thomas S. Stribling (1881–1965).
2. Malvina Hoffman (1887–1966), *Heads and Tails* (New York: Scribners, 1936).

. . . .

244. MKR to MEP (ALS, 2 pp.)

[Cross Creek]
[June 1, 1936]

Dear Max:—

Wolfe's "Story of a Novel" is unbearable. I have just finished it. It's unbearable—its honesty,—its fierceness,—its beauty of expression. And for another writer——.

There is no damnation for such a man. Don't be concerned——I know you are not——that he goes "completely off the reservation". He is his own torment and his own strength.

He is so young! When a little of the torment has expended itself, you will have the greatest artist America has ever produced.

My thanks and my gratitude for autographing the book as you did——

When all of us are done for, the chances are that literary history will find you the greatest————certainly the wisest——of us all——

To Marjorie
with admiration & affection
from
Maxwell Perkins

May 22nd 1936

MEP presentation copy of Thomas Wolfe's *The Story of a Novel.* From the collection of Philip May, Jr.

[Bimini, Bahamas]

10 June 1936

Maxwell Perkins

597 Fifth Ave

New York City

U.S.A.

Having a marvelous big-game fishing trip at Bimini with Mrs. Oliver Grinnell.[1] Met Hemingway here. Will settle down to boy's book on return at end of week.

1. Mrs. Oliver Cromwell Grinnell, MKR's Miami fishing companion.

. . . .

246. MKR to MEP (TLS, 4 pp.)

Hawthorn, Florida

June 18 [1936]

Dear Max:

I've had an unbelievably good time. It was somehow without reality. Even while I was being terribly happy, it seemed to be someone else who was being gay. I could live that sporting life forever, and love it, but I should never touch paper if I did it. My friend Robert Herrick——who, by the way, is desperately ill——once told me that if I were happy, the chances were that I shouldn't write. But why should torment be a pre-requisite? I find that Malvina Hoffman first called her group "The Sacrifice," by the title "Sorrow is the Mother of Beauty." I can't quite accede to this. The exquisite sensitiveness which makes sorrow strike deep is of course necessary. Otherwise, I agree with Masefield when he says "The days that make us happy make us wise."[1]

I was glad to meet Hemingway, and wished we could have had time for more than a brief talk. My hostess, Mrs. Oliver Grinnell, was the former president of the Salt Water Anglers of America, and she still works with people like Zane Grey[2] and Hemingway on conservation. He came to call on her on her yacht, and she was privately furious that he talked far more about literary things than fishing! The man astonished me. I should have known, from your affection for him, that he was not a fire-spitting ogre, but I'd heard so many tales in Bimini of his going around knocking people down, that I half-expected him to announce in a loud voice that he never accepted introductions to female novelists. Instead, a most lovable, nervous and sensitive person took my hand in a big gentle paw and remarked that he was a great admirer of my work. He is immensely popular with the anglers, and the natives adore him. The day before I left, he battled six hours and fifty minutes with a 514-lb. tuna, and when his "Pilar" came into harbor at 9:30 at night, the whole population turned out to see his fish and hear his story[.] There was such a mob on the rotten dock that a post gave way, and his Cuban mate was precipitated into Bimini Bay, coming to the surface with a profanity that was intelligible even to one who speaks no Spanish. A fatuous old man with a new yacht and a young bride had arrived not long previously, announcing that tuna-fishing, of whose difficulties he had heard, was easy. So as the "Pilar" was made fast, Hemingway came swimming up from below-decks, gloriously drunk, roaring, "Where's the son of a bitch who said it was easy?" The last anyone saw of him that night, he was standing alone on the dock where his giant tuna hung from the stays—— using it for a punching bag.

A story, told and re-told in Bimini, is of Hemingway's knocking down a man named Platt, for calling him a big fat slob. "You can call me a slob," Hemingway said, "but you can't call me a big fat slob", and he laid him out. Now the natives have a song which they will sing to you if they are sure Hemingway isn't about——"The big fat slob's in the harbor".

<Bimini caught at my throat the way the scrub does. The struggle there for life> There is, obviously, some inner conflict in Hemingway which makes him go about his work with a chip on his shoulder, and which makes him want to knock people down. He is so great an artist that he does not need to be ever on the defensive. He is so vast, so virile, that he does not need ever to hit anybody. Yet he is constantly defending something that he, at least, must consider vulnerable. It seems to me that there is a clue to it in the conflict between the sporting life and the literary life; between sporting people and the artist. That life on the water, with its excitement, which almost nothing that I have experienced can equal, is a self-containing entity. When you are a part of it, nothing else seems valid. Yet occasionally a knife would go through me, and I became conscious of treachery to my own, and when I put it behind me, I felt a great guilt. The sporting people are delightful. They have your soul. You feel clean and natural when you are with them. Then when you leave them, you are overcome with the knowledge that you are worlds away from them. You know things they will never know. Yet they wear an armor that is denied you. They are somehow blunted. It is not so much their money, for some of them are not unduly prosperous, but their reaction to living. They enjoy life hugely, yet they are not sensitive to it.

Hemingway is among these people a great deal, and they like him and admire him——his personality, his sporting prowess, and his literary prestige. It seems to me that unconsciously he must value their opinion. He must be afraid of laying bare before them the agony that tears the artist. He must be afraid of lifting before them the curtain that veils the beauty that should be exposed only to reverent eyes. So, as in "Death in the Afternoon", he writes beautifully, and then immediately turns it off with a flippant comment, or a deliberate obscenity. His sporting friends would not understand the beauty. They would roar with delight at the flippancy. They are the only people who would be pleased by the things in his work that distress all the rest of us. He injects those painfully foreign elements, not as an artist, but as a sportsman, and a sportsman of a particular type.

Bimini caught at my throat the way the scrub does. The struggle there for existence is terrific. Last summer's hurricane swept it almost bare——most of the roofs, most of the coconut palms, the shrubs. Typhoid and malaria followed. A little white girl who followed me like a dog one morning when I got up before dawn to walk along the high crest of the island, told me that her whole family except herself and her mother had been wiped out by the fever. A six-foot West Indian nigger with a beautiful, tender face who caught our bonefish bait for us, had not tasted meat for a year and a half. There are about five hundred blacks, and some thirty or forty whites. The whites, I think, are all a bit batty. There is a nightmare quality about their lives. And the beauty of the waters about them is incredible. The color close to the island, in full sunlight, is the palest jade-green. At a little distance, it is aquamarine. Across the horizon, it deepens into a purple for which I know no name. And when you are out on the deep water, it is the purest indigo.

Unless someone really good, like Hemingway, does something about it, I'd like to go and live there a while some day. There is a stirring novel there. I can see its outlines and most of its people, very plainly.

The Malvina Hoffman book was waiting for me. It is a magnificent document in every way. I am reading it slowly, not to lose anything. I remember being taken off my feet by the quality of the Pavolowa [sic] "Gavotte" in the Metropolitan,[3] some years ago. I thought at the time it was in pink marble, but it seems to have been the colored wax. My deepest thanks for the book and for your thoughtfulness.

I couldn't have liked anyone as much as I liked Hemingway, without his liking me a little. So perhaps now he and his family will stop off with me some time on one of those long drives——I am most conveniently located for it—— and perhaps you would be willing to come too, then, and see my part of Florida.

Thank you for sending the check. I came home to find my account over-drawn.

Always with my best,

1. John Masefield (1878–1967), British poet, dramatist, and novelist.
2. Zane Grey (1875–1939) wrote about the western frontier.
3. "La Gavotte," a colored wax statuette of Russian ballerina Anna Pavlova, by Malvina Hoffman.

. . . .

247. MEP to MKR (TS for wire)

JUNE 18, 1936
MRS. MARJORIE RAWLINGS
ISLAND GROVE, FLORIDA
AIR MAILING CHECK TO BANK GLAD YOU ARE SAFELY HOME

Editor's note: Enclosed is the following deposit slip, addressed to the Commercial Bank and Trust Co., Ocala, Florida: "Dear Sirs: We enclose herewith a check for seven hundred dollars to be deposited to the account of Marjorie K. Rawlings. Will you please acknowledge receipt to her. Very truly yours."

. . . .

248. MEP to MKR (TLS: UF, 2 pp.)

July 8, 1936

Dear Marjorie:

I read your letter with the greatest pleasure. I am delighted to know that you have been at Bimini (I never have, and have always wanted to get there) and that you have seen Hem and enjoyed it. I am anxious for Hem to write to tell me about it.

I am sorry about the Brandt & Brandt matter. We should have let them handle the book, and we shall now, but first we must hear from Curtis Brown. We communicated with them the moment you brought the matter to my attention, and I spoke to Miss Baumgarten about it.

What happened to the humorous story you wrote and sent to Brandt? I hoped it might come here, but they of course must try for the high prices. I wish we could get another story in the general field of Benny and the Bird Dogs. I agreed with a great deal you said about Hem. It is an odd thing, but he has always felt that in being unable to play on a college football team he was deprived of his birthright. I have often noticed that when college and football have been spoken of. He would have been a magnificent player, of course, but probably both college and football would have ruined him as a writer. We'll talk about him sometime.

Always yours,

. . . .

249. MKR to MEP (TLS, 3 pp.)

Hawthorn, Florida
July 14 [1936]

Dear Max:

I'm just back from a week in North Carolina, where I gave a talk at the Blowing Rock School of English, run by the Rollins College people.

I had the great pleasure there of coming to know Herschel Brickell——the principal reason I stayed longer than the day of my talk, for contact with such a personality and spirit as his, is an experience that doesn't come often.[1]

I came very close to going on up to New York to talk with you, but didn't have a car——and too, the reports of your heat were intimidating. Carolina was for the most part, cool, and Florida has been lovely——20 degrees cooler than most of the country. It was 76 on my big porch yesterday.

I wanted to tell you that the material for the boy's story has been mounting. On two grand bear-hunts I have met another old pioneer who is full of animal and nature stories, and I have a growing pile of fascinating material. It lacks only the introduction of a few more characters than I had already conceived, who will make their own "plot" as they go along——and I have had to resist them in the back of my mind, as it was——to make a full book. It will still be <tol[d]> seen through the boy's eyes, and the unit I had conceived of as the story, will make a perfectly grand climax. I don't want to write you too much about it——I could talk about it, and not do harm——but to be coherent enough on paper, would be to try to express too much that should be expressed in final form. I am very happy in the material, Max, and by taking my time feel sure I can do a very moving and harmonious piece of work.

I am sure you are wrong about the reason for Golden Apples' not doing better. People recognized unconsciously its disharmony——and everyone is hungry for harmony and unity. It was not valid to give Tordell the union I made him achieve. It should have been Luke's story, and his being a poor white would not have bothered readers at all. Luke and Allie were more real to casual readers than Tordell. I find lots of people who like the second book better, but you know in your heart, as I do, that <it> the book isn't right.

Anyway, the story of the boy will simply have to be a full-length novel. I shall spend some more time this summer gathering priceless material. I think the writing will go reasonably fast. I think I may take a cottage in the Carolina mountains in September and part of October. That is our beastly time here, and I would be away from <my> the distraction of my friends and my good times and my grove, and could do very steady writing. The material and what I want to do are so impelling that I can work on it anywhere, so I shan't force my location one way or the other. That means that Spring, probably, would be the time it will be done. I can't tell exactly yet. If I go to Carolina in the early fall, I'll certainly come to New York then to talk with you.

About the humorous story.[2] Its length made the POST shy off, and I am revising it now, unifying it better and trying to shorten it. Logically, it should go to you, for as I think I told you, I have a grand character in Quincey Dover, the narrator in "Benny", and there will some day be a book of her stories. But of course the difference in price tempts both Carl and me——though I should never write *for* money——but if the revised form doesn't suit the POST, I imagine Carl will be willing to show it to you——and I know you will like it. It is absolutely a Scribner story. I hear you have a new editor and a new policy. Do you care to tell me something about it?

Let me know your feeling about the change in length of the boy story. My best.

1. Herschel Brickell, book critic for the *New York Post*. MKR read at the Blowing Rock School of English, and while there met the novelist and poet James Still.
2. "Varmints."

. . . .

250. MEP to MKR (TLS: UF, 2 pp.)

July 29, 1936

Dear Marjorie:

Let the boy's book, as we call it—though I can see it may turn out not really to be that—take the form it ought to have, and then we'll study how it should be handled. I feel sure it will be good anyway,- and better for being done according to the way you feel its nature requires, of course.

Did you read Hem's "Snows of Kilimanjaro" in the last Esquire?[1] In the first place it is an extraordinarily fine story, but it is also interesting psychologically, in an autobiographical sense, but try only to think about that part of it after you have read it for itself. And Hem is doing a novel now about Key West and Havana, and the waters between.[2]

As for the story, I hope that the outcome may be that we shall have a chance at it, but I realize perfectly well the reasons why we may not. I'll tell you all I can about the new magazine when we get to the first number, which will be the October number,- but we want to have much more fiction, and to illustrate it.

Always yours,

1. Ernest Hemingway, "The Snows of Kilimanjaro," *Esquire* 6 (August 1936): 27–30, 194–201.
2. Ernest Hemingway, *To Have and Have Not* (New York: Scribners, 1937).

· ·

251. MKR to MEP (TLS, 4 pp.)

Hawthorn, Florida
July 31 [1936]

Dear Max:

I can see that you're disturbed about my feeling that I had better take \<a\> full-length for the boy's book.

It will positively be as we both first conceived of it. I have in front of me your letter of October 27, 1933. You say, "I am thinking of a book about a boy. ———A book about a boy and the life of the scrub is the thing we want.——It is those wonderful river trips and the hunting and the dogs and guns and the companionship of simple people who care about the same things which were included in 'South Moon Under.' "

Until lately, I have had in mind one incident, almost, that would make a complete long-story in itself, about a boy. I wanted a bear-hunt in the story, for it fitted in with the other, and I have been prowling all over trying to find somebody who was actually bear-hunting, for I felt I had to see one to get what I want from it. By the merest accident, I met, and was taken into the confidence of, a perfectly marvelous old pioneer living on the St. Johns river——the beautiful broad river I took the trip on, and which borders the scrub on the east side. This old man, a famous "bad man", but honorable and respected and at one time prosperous, too, took me bear-hunting twice, and in a few days I am going over to live a while with him and his wife and go hunting and fishing with him.[1] So much material has come from my contact with him, and there is so much more there——anecdotes, hunting incidents, people——that I realized before I went to North Carolina that I had at hand a mass of stuff——and as always, the facts have suggested imaginary characters to me who fit in with the true ones——that couldn't possibly go in the simple 50,000 word narrative that I was ready to do. I had to resist constantly the thought of all these other things.

The day before I left Carolina, I told just about this much——I didn't want to go very deeply into it with anyone——to Herschel Brickell and said that I was going home reluctantly instead of on to New York to talk with you about it. He said, "I can tell you what any publisher would say. From a publishing standpoint, there's no question of choice between a short book, which has to sell at almost the price of a full one, and a full-length book. It is only the rare thing, like 'Good-bye, Mr. Chips',[2] that sells in brief form. People want to read about that scrub life you write about, and if you have the material, you would be very foolish to put out a short thing instead of taking all the room you need to tell a real story. And unless a short book happened to have a rare and enormous success, booksellers would not be enthusiastic, and you would harm yourself immensely on your next full-length book."

It was just one of those straws that settle a thing, for I had been having a battle to keep down the thought of taking more room to it.

He said, "See Max, or think it over very carefully before you pass up any chance to do a full-length thing with that wonderful scrub material."

I said, "It's all settled." I don't want to write you about the actual stuff——I could talk to you for hours about it and not do harm. But if I try to express in a few sentences in a letter what I mean to do, it has a paralyzing effect-making the stuff *congeal* in a quickly-said form, when I want to take all those pages and pages of a book to say it. I can't sum it up like a review, without spoiling my pleasure in working it out right. But the short narrative I had in mind will make my culminating point——my climax and my point, and a very stirring point it is, too.

It will be absolutely all told through the boy's eyes. He will be about twelve, and the period will not be a long one——not more than two years. I want it through his eyes before the age of puberty brings in any of the other factors to confuse the simplicity of viewpoint. It will be a book boys will love, and if it is done well enough otherwise, the people who liked South Moon will like it too. It is only since Golden Apples that I realize what it is about my writing that people like. I don't mean that I am writing *for* anyone, but now I feel free to luxuriate in the simple details that interest me, and that I have been so amazed to find interested other people—probably just from the element of sincerity given by my own interest and sympathy.

I have a mass of animal material that will be fascinating to anyone at all interested. I have to laugh at Carl Brandt. I have told him again and again that the short thing I was ready to do was not for any magazine. I wrote him that the short thing would have to be full-length. He wrote back blandly, "Such good news. Cosmo will be delighted." I refuse to tell Carl what I have in mind, but what a shock it will be when all the stuff about bear-hunts and so on comes before him!

I think I will burst sometimes at your not coming to Florida and letting me show you some of the places that I shall use for background. If Hemingway is at a place where he wants you in the early fall, for Heaven's sake come down, and let me talk with you on the ground. A few words here and there and you will see just what I'm after. If you still won't, I'll come up in say, October and show you what I have in hand and as much writing as I may have done by then. If by any chance it wasn't good I could still do the short narrative, but I don't see how what I have in mind could fail me.

Of course, I am up against the technical problem now of working out "plot" and inter-play of characters, but once I have decided on the people who will be in the book, I think the narrative will flow naturally of its own accord. The basic theme is clear in my mind the same as for the short thing——and it should be very moving. I *cannot* write about it.

Yes, I read Hemingway's story in Esquire. It is *gorgeous*. It stirred me deeply as story. Then I thought about it as autobiography and it was illuminating. Also most encouraging, for I had the feeling of his having taken a hurdle, faced facts with courage, and being ready to go. I can't tell you how glad I am about the novel laid in that section. If he doesn't see the Bahamas as I saw them, someday I'll do you a book about them.

I'm feeling happier than in a long time. Desolation doesn't strike so often or last so long; and I'm not being bothered, this time of year, with the frivolous diversions that make life bearable when it's too black, but that interfere with me when I'm ready or trying to work. I have two jolly new pets——and you can always shut them up when you don't want them around, as you can't do with your good friends!-a highly pedigreed and marvelous pointer puppy, 6 months old, and a pet baby raccoon who is great fun.[3]

I'm enclosing what Herschel Brickell wrote after I talked with him. Send it back to me, if not too much trouble.

Now please don't write me another of those restrained "You must do it as seems right to you" notes. Tell me what is really in your mind.

And I *must* talk to you not later than October, here or in New York.

My best,

1. Barney Dillard.
2. James Hilton (1900–1954), *Goodbye, Mr. Chips* (Boston: Little, Brown, 1934).
3. MKR's pointer named Pat and raccoon named Racket.

252. MEP to MKR (CC, 3 pp.)

Aug. 5, 1936

Dear Marjorie:

Here is a check for the amount due in royalty according to the last report. We seem to have got into confusion about the boy's book. Those sentences from my letter that you quote are exactly the way I have always thought of it, but when I write in the do-as-it-seems-right-to-you way, it is because it has always been my conviction—and I do not see how anyone could dispute the rightness of it—that a book must be done according to the writer's conception of it as nearly perfectly as possible, and that the publishing problems begin then.- That is, the publisher must not try to get a writer to fit the book to the conditions of the trade, etc. It must be the other way around. I know that you think this yourself. Everything that Herschel said was absolutely true. But I do feel sure that you have the best possible idea of the book, and I do think that the rivers, the hunting adventures, the characters, and the ways of life, ought all to be in. I know that a writer ought not to give summaries of what he means to do, and that with some, even telling the story and talking about it, makes it so that they cannot write it. It is often that way, and it is not hard to see why. But I have the most complete confidence in the quality of this book. I would not be a bit surprised if it were not the best book you have done, and it might well be the most successful.

I should love to come to Florida sometime, but it always seems just impossible for me to get away from here. It is not so bad here either. But if you cannot come here in October, we'll meet somehow.

Always yours,

. . . .

253. MKR to MEP (wire)

1936 AUG 19 PM 10 15

MAXWELL PERKINS—

597 5 AVE NYC—

DELIGHTED TO REPORT POST HAS REFUSED VERSION OF HUMOROUS MULE STORY HAVE WIRED CARL TO OFFER IT TO YOU WITHOUT TRYING OTHER POPULAR MAGAZINES STOP STORY IS DEFINITELY UNCLE BENNY TYPE AND SHOULD BE ONE OF SERIES WITH EYE TO BOOK PUBLICATION [STOP] HOPE YOU LIKE IT—

254. MEP to MKR (TS for wire)

AUG. 26, 1936
MRS. MARJORIE RAWLINGS
ISLAND GROVE, FLORIDA
DELIGHTED WITH STORY STOP MAGAZINE IS MAKING OFFER THROUGH
BRANDT [STOP] MANY THANKS

. . . .

255. MKR to MEP (TLS, 3 pp.)

Hawthorn, Florida
August 27 [1936]

Dear Max:

I was glad to have your wire and know you liked the mule story. I haven't heard from Carl yet, but any reasonable price will be all right as far as I'm concerned. I feel much better about Scribner's using it, for it really has a more substantial quality than a "popular" story. And it will be wise to have them all in the one magazine. I thoroughly enjoy doing that kind of story, and I imagine it's as much of a relief to most readers, after solemn fiction, as it is to me. The way Uncle Benny has been re-printed and talked of has amazed me, and yet it's understandable enough.

Max, I am going perfectly delirious with delight in my material as the boy's book takes shape in my mind. The most delicious people are in it. Wait until you see Grandma Hutto. A little impudent, infidel, sharp-spoken thing with gold circle ear-rings and Spanish or Minorcan blood who scandalizes the staid <Crackers> residents of the scrub and who tells the boy wise and impudent things. She doesn't want to go to Heaven because they live on milk and honey, and she likes a piece of fried mullet <and> now and again. She likes music made from a harp and a bass violin and an octave flute, and she couldn't get along listening to just a harp. I intend to be careful about not over-stepping any boundaries, so that the book won't be spoiled for boys. But oh Max, the stuff is going to be grand. I've been spending a lot of time over on the St. John's river, which is the eastern boundary of the scrub, if you'll remember. And the people of the east scrub have never even heard of the ones on the west side. I'll use the St. John's river a good deal in the story. You and I are going to love the book [even] if nobody else in the world reads it. I am very happy and confident about it as it forms. None of the fear and torment of "Golden Apples". Then the following book will be hell again——. By the way, do you still have that map of the scrub I sent you? I'd like it back, if you do.

I had a grand letter from Ernest Hemingway. I wrote him how much I liked the Snows of Kilimanjaro, and asked him to stop off here with his family any time they passed through. He said he would like to stop this fall late if he comes back then to Florida. I can give him some good bird hunting of various kinds then. I told him to try to get you here some time, that I had been a miserable failure at it. But you might be disappointed, at that. Hemingway's letter was very remarkable——most revealing in many ways.

My ex-husband has just married again, which takes a burden off my mind. I had a tragic letter from his mother, hoping I'd do something about it while there was yet time. She wrote that the girl (much younger than he, only 26) was very gentle and lovable, but said "It's you I want." It was so hard to write her that I wouldn't be back in the hell I lived in with him, without hurting her, because after all, a son is a son, even though, as she herself once said, "Nobody could live with him that didn't love him." But it is a great relief to me to know he is taken care of. I've never wanted anything at the expense of anyone else ——even peace.

I don't know yet whether I'll get north or not. If I can work here when I begin the actual writing, I'd rather, but if the September heat is too bad I'll go to the Carolina mountains and come to New York from there. I'd rather see you when I have a start made.

Tell Whitney Darrow I love him even though I don't write to him.

Had an amusing experience. I've spent a good deal of time with the marvelous old pioneer I've been bear-hunting with. Several of his fifteen grown children raised a howl about his telling me stories etc. He is a famous character with a really brilliant but self-tutored mind, and they thought of what he had to give me as something tangible, with a cash value to him and to them—— sheer illusion, of course. They thought I was working up his own life-story— which is of no use to me at all. One of his sons followed me around whenever I was at their house with the suspicious eye of a police dog. The other morning I was taking notes from the old man on the various herbs that were used locally for medicines and "remedies"——such stuff as "mullein tea", and dried pomegranate peelings brewed for fever. The son asked in amazement, (he seldom spoke to me directly), "She writing up sich as that?" The old man said, "That's just the kind of thing she's writing. She's not like you sorry, no-account things. She's interested in the old days and the old ways. Why, I never heard a woman cuss like she cussed this morning when we went to Juniper Springs and she found the government had cleaned out the Springs and put up picnic tables." The son said, "Well, I'll be dogged." When I left, he followed me rather sheepishly to the car and handed me a very handsome ram's horn. He said, "You get you some old-timer to put you a mouth-piece on this and polish it up, and you'll have you the finest blowing-horn in the county."

I have a pet baby raccoon that is lots of fun. He sleeps with the dogs and makes a strange, chirring sound that a damn mocking-bird has learned to imitate, so that we're always thinking Racket is lost in the grove! I don't know how long it will work, for baby that he is, he can bite like the dickens.

All my best,

. . . .

256. MEP to MKR (TLS: UF, 2 pp.)

Sept. 1, 1936

Dear Marjorie:

I fully expect that the book you are doing will be one that I shall delight in. It is just the sort of book that I do most enjoy, and it is probably a better means for you to tell all about the life of the country than even "South Moon Under". I would put in everything you want to. And if a book is as good as it can be of its kind, it is a book for everyone.

I am off tonight for a couple of weeks' vacation. I am just going to Quebec, the Chateau Frontenac, which has been sending me circulars for years as they do everybody. I always wanted to see the St. Lawrence. Just the same, I wish I had done it and were back.

Hemingway will certainly find a million things to interest him if he makes the visit, and I guess he will do it too. Everything that you care about there, he will care about. I'll write you as soon as I get back, and by then there will be some interesting books.

Always yours,

. . . .

257. MEP's secretary to MKR (CC, 1 p.)

Sept. 2, 1936

Dear Mrs. Rawlings:

You will have had Mr. Perkins' letter telling you that he was going on a vacation. The copy of your story with your deletions marked on it came just after he had left, and so I have turned it over to Marian Ives, of the Magazine. She will write you about it.

Sincerely yours,
Sec. to Mr. Perkins

Pinnacle Inn Cottages
Banner Elk, North Carolina
Sept. 22 [1936]

Dear Max:

A hurried note to say that I am here for a month at least. I simply could not get going on the book, although it was clear as daylight in my mind. Things were on my nerves——mosquitoes bad, heat sticky and depressing, grove responsibilities wearing, and a drugged lassitude besides. Decided just to bolt for the mountains to see if I couldn't take the hurdle that way. Saw my doctor before I left and found there was a very good reason for my being in such shape——full of malaria, and running a steady temperature of 100 all through the day. The doctor laughed when I said I couldn't work. He said no wonder, with a steady temperature. I'm on quinine, reached North Carolina last Friday and feel like a new person already.

After a search, found simply an ideal cabin and location. A new, attractive cabin of undressed white oak, hand made furniture, big fireplace, electric lights, bathroom, electric stove and water heater, and a gorgeous mountain view. A village within walking distance. Just enough isolation. Brought my Proust[1] and my pointer—perfect company for work! Just got settled today, but can tell I'll have no further difficulty, more than the ordinary ones, with the work. Am having my mail forwarded, and hope there'll be a letter from you telling me your vacation did you lots of good.

My best,

Any book you want to send me, would love to have it here.

Still can't settle on a title to suit me——you can't judge very well without knowing more of my theme, but I'll keep suggesting titles to you, and give me your opinion on any that do or do not appeal, just on their own value.

Do you like either

The Flutter-Mill

The Yearling

Do you like a place name, such as Juniper Creek? Would use perhaps Juniper Island—the pine "island" in the scrub, but the word would be too deceptive.

---

1. Marcel Proust (1871–1922), French novelist.

Sept. 24, 1936

Dear Marjorie:

I just got back, several days ago, and have been crowded ever since. Are you near Asheville? If you are, I should like to have Scott Fitzgerald see you, for I think you would do him a great deal of good. He is in a very defeatist state of mind, has been for years, and his tendency to dramatize however he feels, makes him more so than he should be, even though he has a good deal to discourage him. He has just inherited enough money to live on for a couple of years, and I begged him to take this chance—the first he has had since he started, to be free of worry and of the pressure of potboiling, and to make his great effort now. If you are near Asheville and tell me so, and are willing to see Scott, and perhaps be somewhat depressed by it at first, I'll send him.

The books I had in mind for you have not quite come through yet, but I am sending a book of excellent stories of Africa by Grace Flandrau, and Sherwood Anderson's novel.- Probably it is easier for you to read stories than any other sort of fiction when you are working.[1]

As to the title, I would think one which carried the meaning of "The Yearling" was probably right. I like the name "Juniper Creek" as a name, but I do not think place names are good for a book. There is not enough human suggestion in them. There might be some other word than Yearling that would carry the same meaning and connotation but would be better.

By the way, one of the Flandrau stories has a vivid account of a very bad attack of malaria. It should be a warning to you to be careful. Maybe you read it when it was in Scribner's.

I was very much interested in a book we are to publish on "The Lordly Hudson"[2] until I saw the St. Lawrence, which is incomparably finer, except that it hasn't the Palisades. It has mountains though, and the better for being not too close, and a beautiful island with the descendants of the original French settlers on it,- Orleans. We went on a trip up the Saguenay River which is different from anything I ever saw,- very deep and narrow, so that the water is black, and bordered on both sides by small mountains with rounded tops bristling with firs, but with their sides almost bare. The whole thing must look as it has always looked from the very beginning. Sometimes there are great cliffs. Canada is an extraordinary country of huge dimensions that you feel, for some reason, more than you feel the great spaces in America. Quebec itself is in some parts almost medieval and always charming on account of the French traditions.- The French movies are beyond anything we have, though much less elaborate. You do not have to understand French speech to follow them because everyone of the actors is always good. I do not know that the vacation did me any particular good, except that it showed me scenes I shall always remember.

Always yours,

1. Grace Flandrau (1889–1971), *Under the Sun* (New York: Harcourt, Brace, 1936); Sherwood Anderson, *Kit Brandon* (New York: Scribners, 1936).
2. Paul Goodman (1911–1972), *The Lordly Hudson* (New York: Scribners, 1937).

. . . .

260. MKR to MEP (TLS, with holograph additions and postscript, 3 pp.)

> Pinnacle Inn Cottages
> Banner Elk, N.C.
> Sept. 30 [1936]

Dear Max:

Thank you for your interesting letter and for the books. The Sherwood Anderson thing looks far beyond anything he's done lately. Yes, I remember Grace Flandrau's story "One Way of Love" in the magazine, and with "Portrait of Bascom Hawke" it was my pick of that series.[1] I like her stuff immensely. But as for being "careful" about the malaria, there's no way to do it. It is so insidious, and you can be bitten by the Anophiles mosquito without knowing it, even with all the precautions we take in summer about spraying and screening. Then too the kind of malaria I had is the sort that settles in the spleen and flares up under favorable tropical conditions. The symptoms are very hard to check, and often the malarial parasite doesn't even show in the blood tests. I am foolish ever to spend a full summer in Florida as long as I can afford to get away. Living is so cheap in the mountains, especially this time of year, I shall come again. I am feeling tremendously well now and enjoying every minute of it.

I am 85 miles north and east of Asheville. That is far or close according to one's notions of distance. It seems like nothing at all to me, but it might seem an impossible distance to Fitzgerald. Of course I will see him if he cares to come and if you think I can be of any help. I was deeply shocked at the feature story about his condition plastered across the front page of the N.Y. Post last Friday.[2] <Even to> I don't see how any journalist could do such a cruel thing. It might easily be the last straw for Fitzgerald. It is a temptation to damn Fitzgerald without sympathy, but I know how that state of mind creeps up on you and I have had to fight it myself. It comes usually when one's personal background is unstable or unsatisfying or empty. Nothing, no work, takes the place of the right human contacts. Of course he has indulged himself, wallowed in self-pity. He is evidently not truly interested in anything but Scott Fitzgerald. Then too he evidently has no contact with anything sound and vital. The Grove Park Inn is the worst place in the world for him. Yet without resources within himself, he would be sunk in such a place as I am working in. I feel very sorry for anyone who finds no comfort in the earth and hills and wind and stars. "The world is too much with him."[3]

At this distance, I don't know how it could be managed for him to see me. I want to go to two or three places in the state while I am here, among them Pisgah Forest, 43 miles beyond Asheville where I want to see a potter to have him make me some things. I could pick him, Fitzgerald, up in Asheville and take him with me, to Pisgah Forest and then if he wished, bring him back here and have him spend the evening with me. My cabin is too intimate to put him up here, but there is a very quaint little country hotel in Banner Elk where he could spend the night. I could take him for a drive or walk again in the morning and then put him on a bus for Asheville. I'd like to take him with me to call on a mountain family with which I've made friends, and he might have the grace to be ashamed of himself. It might shame him, too, to talk with a friend of mine, an orphan boy 12 years old who lives at the Grandfather Orphanage near here.[4] The stamina and integrity of the child tear my heart, and I'll do well if I can go back to Florida without him. The boy comes every day to visit with me and chop wood, and his courage and his loneliness are bound inextricably together.

But Max, if you send Fitzgerald, or arrange for me to take him on such a trip, you must write me explicitly and in detail, beforehand, just what you think it is I have to give him. You know him well and you know me, I don't know how well, but there must be some particular quality in me that you feel would nourish him, or some particular point of view. I should need to know, in order not to get off on the wrong foot. The only thing that occurs to me that you might mean, is that the man has taken a licking, and that you must know that I too have been through a great deal but that I refuse to be licked.

I took time off over the week-end to go up Mt. Mitchell, the highest point east of the Rockies. Nearly to the top by car, and devilish driving it was, too, then the peak on foot. And by the way, in the next two weeks would be the time for me to contact Fitzgerald, and I should have to have a choice of dates. Let me know how you want it handled. I'll write him or wire him as you suggest. He would probably be free to go any time. But after that feature story, I shouldn't be surprised any moment to hear that he'd blown his brains out.

I'm not too sure he's worth anyone's bothering about, but you must think so, or you wouldn't be concerned about him. And "The Great Gatsby" really had something.

Would you mind passing on word to Miss Ives that if proofs on "Varmints" are ready any time in the next month, they should come here.

My best.

Actually, non-fiction is all I can enjoy when I'm working. I love *biography* then.

1. Grace Flandrau, "One Way of Love," *Scribner's Magazine* 88.4 (October 1930): 345–52, 444–56.
2. Michel Mok, "The Other Side of Paradise: Scott Fitzgerald, 40, Engulfed in Despair," *New York Post* (September 25, 1936): 1, 15.
3. Allusion to William Wordsworth's "The World Is Too Much with Us."
4. This boy, Dale Wills, became the subject of MKR's "A Mother in Mannville," *Saturday Evening Post* 209 (December 12, 1936): 7, 33.

. . . .

261. MEP to MKR (TLS: UF, 4 pp.)

Oct. 7, 1936

Dear Marjorie:

I did greatly wish Scott to see you, but not with any direct object.- Only that I thought that you would make him feel better and restore his courage, because you do seem to have that power. I did not want you to take any particular line with him, but I thought that something might develop which would enable you to speak directly. Of course he knows nothing about your own life. He only knows you from what I have told him, and from "South Moon Under" which he was very much taken with,- although it was altogether out of his field of interest. As you say, he is very much concentrated upon himself, and always has been, and has no love of simple things at all. He cares nothing about the country, or the people in it, or animals, or anything of that sort whatever. That is a bad thing because so many people are able to rest and draw strength just from being in quiet places and among simple people. Scott cannot get any good even out of the companionship of people except by talking. There are many people who almost communicate with you by being with you without saying anything. Some of those people are intellectually rather dull, but have something else that is just as important, or even more important.- Scott thinks all such people are just stupid and scorns them. I have spent an evening which I thought was most pleasant at a house in Baltimore where he was, and where nobody said anything brilliant and people talked very little at all, but where everybody liked everyone else.- But Scott afterward said he could not have stood it a moment longer, and we must immediately get a drink to revive ourselves. He got all sorts of wrong notions as a boy, and I am afraid he will never get rid of them. What I hoped to do was to persuade him to write an objective book of reminiscences of the period between 1920 and now. He knew all sorts of interesting people, quite as many as Gertrude Stein[1] did. I thought that by doing this he might throw off all the bad old past that holds him,- get rid of it for good. But what you yourself say about him is very near the truth, and I too was frightened to death when I saw the story in the Post. How in the world did you see it out there? At present though, he is more or less prostrated with a broken shoulder and one thing or another, and I cannot get a word out of him. I shall write you when I do. It was mighty good of you to be willing to see him because there would be a strong chance that it would be depressing. I am going to make a final effort to get him to stand on his feet when I next see him.

I do not believe that "The Flutter Mill" would be a good title. Too few people have any idea what it is. It does have a certain amount of appeal in the words themselves, but not many people seem to respond to that. I am delighted to know that you have such a grasp of the book. "Yearling" might be a good title. Proofs of the story will not be ready till November.- They say they have fine pictures for it.

Always yours,

1. Gertrude Stein (1874–1946), American expatriate novelist, poet, and critic, who lived in Paris. The reference is to *The Autobiography of Alice B. Toklas* (1933).

. . . .

262. MKR to MEP (TLS, 2 pp.)

Pinnacle Inn Cottages
Banner Elk, N.C.
Oct. 16 [1936]

Dear Max:

So many thanks for the good books. They have been a great treat, and except for the Flandrau book, which I am saving, just what I enjoy when I'm doing work of my own. I got a great deal out of the Anderson book, and was much stirred by it——the woman with whom I took the river trip is a Kit Brandon, high-powered rum-running and all——but I'm sorry I read it just now. The disjointed but effective style is contagious, and gave me some trouble, shaking it off.

I took the bull by the horns and dropped a gay and natural note to Fitzgerald, just as I should to anyone in a normal mood, saying that you wanted us to meet and I was willing to risk it if he was. Said I should be passing through Asheville to go to the potter at Pisgah Forest, and wouldn't he drive with me. The note was so exactly what I should write anyone——the type that brought me a perfectly grand answer from Hemingway for instance, when I wrote asking him to use me for a stop-off with his family, that if it hits him wrong there is no ultimate loss, for it would mean I myself would hit him wrong. With my time passing so fast, thought I had better chance it. Will let you know what response I get.

The book moves slowly but steadily. Have already made a mistake, I think, as to angle. The first chapter will have to be rewritten just for style, but as for material, is about as I want it. It begins, as it should, with the boy himself, since it is to be his book. Then I found it necessary to give a background, in the reasons for his father's having gone to the scrub in the first place, but I am afraid I have lost reality and effectiveness by making a shot backward. It is real enough as far as the father is concerned, for he is a very real person and you will [word missing] him and be touched by him, but it makes an aside from the direct narrative, although at the end of the chapter I manage, how cleverly I can't tell, to tie it back to where I left the boy at the end of the first chapter. If it were not necessary to tell the story throughout from the boy's point of view, at least more or less through his eyes, I should enjoy beginning the story as direct narrative with the father. But I dare not switch the interest that way; that is, begin from the father's point of view; then take it up from the boy's; for the father continues throughout the narrative, but it must be as the boy's father, not as the chief protagonist, which too detailed an introduction might tend to make him, and so give the fatally divided interest that we got in Golden Apples when I made Luke and Allie so real that the Englishman didn't matter. There will have to be a re-writing through that part, I believe, but it is purely a technical problem and between us we can take care of it later. I shall not let it slow me up, for the rich material tempts me constantly forward. I do not know when I have ever enjoyed my material so much, unless it was in Jacob's Ladder. I hate terribly to go home, to the interruptions of grove responsibilities and of beloved but intruding friends. I have just moved an elderly aunt[1] who had been very good to me, to Ocala——against my wishes, she came before my own return, and her arrival was not comfortable. So I feel obligated to get back soon. But it is a pity for the work, for I have a peace of mind here, a pleasure in the uninterrupted work, that is not possible at home, much as I love being there.

Again, thanks for the book. I want to write you when I have more time about the Grant book, which fascinated me, and about the whole matter of attitude toward the Civil War. Grant became a touching and sympathetic character for the first time—and I took a most violent personal antipathy to Horace Green![2] The framework of the book, for which I see he gives you credit, is admirable. Green himself slops over at the most annoying moments.

1. Aunt Ida Tarrant.
2. Horace Green (1885–1943), *General Grant's Last Stand: A Biography* (New York: Scribners, 1936).

....

263. MKR to MEP (TLS, with holograph additions and postscript, 4 pp.)

Banner Elk, N. C.
Oct. 25 [1936]

Dear Max:

I had a strange answer from Scott Fitzgerald, refusing my invitation to drive to the Pisgah Forest Pottery, but saying with what I could only take as sincerity, that he wanted to meet me and hoped I could make him a stop when I did go through Asheville. So Friday afternoon late I wired him that I'd be in Asheville at seven that night, and I barged along. I ran into the most beastly driving, storms and detours and those vicious mountain roads, and finally, thick fog for the last thirty miles into Asheville. I was all but babbling by the time I got in, alone, and I thought I'd have to climb in bed beside Fitzgerald and send for another psychiatrist. So it was almost with relief that first his nurse's voice, and then his own, very faint, informed me that his arthritis had been bad and he had run a high temperature all day and couldn't see me. He was doubtful of his health the next day and I was very dubious about pressing the matter. But again I felt sure he really did care about a meeting. So the next morning I wrote him a very nice long note and said he needn't get out of bed if he felt badly but wanted a bit of a chat, and I went along to the potter's and took care of my business there, came back to Asheville and telephoned him again at one o'clock. Something in the note must have hit right, for when he found I hadn't had luncheon, he insisted on my coming right over and having it with him in his room.

Max, we had a perfectly delightful time. Far from being depressing, I enjoyed him thoroughly, and I'm sure he enjoyed it as much. He was as nervous as a cat, but had not been drinking—had had his nurse put his liquor away. We had only sherry and a table wine, and talked our heads off. His reaction to the

Dear Max:

I had a strange answer from Scott Fitzgerald, refusing my
invitation to drive to the Pisgah Forest Pottery, but saying with what
I could only take as sincerity, that he wanted to meet me and hoped I
could make him a stop when I did go through Asheville. So Friday afternoon
late I wired him that I'd be in Asheville at seven that night, and I
barged along. I ran into the most beastly driving, storms and detours
and those vicious mountain roads, and finally, thick fog for the last
thirty miles into Asheville. I was all but babbling by the time I got in,
alone, and I thought I'd have to climb in bed beside Fitzgerald and send
for another psychiatrist. So it was almost with relief that first his
nurse's voice, and then his own, very faint, informed me that his arthritis
had been bad and he had run a high temperature all day and couldn't see me.
He was doubtful of his health the next day and I was very dubious about
pressing the matter. But again I felt sure he really did care about a
meeting. So the next morning I wrote him a very nice long note and said
he needn't get out of bed if he felt badly but wanted a bit of a chat,
and I went along to the potter's and took care of my business there,
came back to Asheville and telephoned him again at one o'clock. Something
in the note must have hit right, for when he found I hadn't had luncheon,
he insisted on my coming right over and having it with him in his room.

Max, we had a perfectly delightful time. Far from being
depressing, I enjoyed him thoroughly, and I'm sure he enjoyed it as much.
He was as nervous as a cat, but had not been drinking--had had his nurse
put his liquor away. We had only sherry and a table wine, and talked our
heads off. His reaction to the N.Y. Post story had been to go to New York
and kill the German Jew, Mok, until he decided that would be a silly gesture
with one arm disabled. He was terribly hurt about it, of course, for he

No. 263 (MKR on F. Scott Fitzgerald). By permission of Princeton University Library.

had listened to a sob story from ~~the man~~, to let him in at all, and had
responded to a lot of things theman told him---possibly spurious---about
his own maladjusted wife, ~~knxk~~ by talking more freely than he should have
done But he has taken the thing very gracefully and is not unduly bitter
or upset about it He was also more forgiving and reasonable than I
think I should havebeen, about Hemingway's unnecessary crack at him in
"The Snows of Kilimanjaro " We agreed that it was a part of Hemingway's
own sadistic maladjustment, which makes him go around knocking people down
Scott said that Hemingway had written him very violently, ~~xmpxnaxkinx~~
damning him for his revealing self-searchings in Esquire, and expressed
the ~~ixgikimaxm~~ idea that it was just as legitimate to get one's grievances
against life off the chest that way, as by giving an upper-cut to some
harmless weakling He resented Hemingway's calling him "ruined", and from
other things he said, it was plain to me that he does not himself consider
himself "ruined", by a long shot

      I am firmly convinced that theman is all right I know
just what his state of mind has been The same kind of panic hits anyone
like me, with no one dependent on me With an ill and expensive wife,
a child bought up to luxury, and then one thing after another going
wrong---all on top of the inevitable revulsion, almost, against writing---
"the times", as Hemingway wrote me, "when you can't do it"---it was natural
enough for him to go into a very black mood It lasted longer and he
publicized it more, than with most of us---I am always ashamed to let
anyone know about mine---but I should lay a heavy wager that he's safely
on the way out

      We disagreed heartily about many things, of course Principally
as to what we expect of life. I expect the crest of the wave to have a
consequent and inevitable trough, and whenever I'm at the bottom, I know
there will be an up-turn sooner and later Then when I'm at the top, I
don't expect it to last indefinitely---he said that he did!---but know
there will have to be less pleasant things coming along sooner or later

He said, "You're not as much of an egotist as I am!" Then he said
and more or less correctly, too, that a writer almost had to be an egotist,
to the point of megolomania, because everything was filtered through his
own universe

His point of view lets him in for much desperate unhappiness
and disillusion, because he simply cannot expect the consistent perfection
and magnificence of life that he does, frankly, expect! But as a writer,
except for the times such as this one has been , when his misery holds
him up too long, his masochism will not interfere with his work! We talked
from a little after one, until five-thirty, when his nurse came back and
fussed about his not resting, but we never reached talk of our plans for
the future in any detail He did say that he had a plan---and he spoke
with every sign of the secret pleasure that is an indication of work in
the brewing!

He spoke of the autobiographical thing, but said he could not
do it with most of the poeple alive! That he could only do it now in a
pleasant way, and it wouldn't be any fun without a little malice!

I wrote him that I felt he had a great gift as a social
historian, and I do---that he had Thackeray's feeling for a period, but
a finer literary style than Thackeray's, and that I thought he would some
day do something very stirring as a record of our confused generation!

I feel I had no tangible help for him---he is in no truly
desperate need of help- --and our points of view are very different---
but there is a most helpful stimulation in talk between two people who
are trying to do something of the same thing---a stimulation I miss and
do not have enough of, at Cross Creek! And I am sure that stimulation
was good for him! I may be able to have another visit with him when I
return to Pisgah Forest in a couple of weeks, if the dishes I ordered are
ready before I drive home! He may go to a quiet place on one of the Florida
coasts, this winter, and if he does, we shall have some good talks

So certainly I can report that the contact was very pleasant

And I do not think you need to worry about him, physically or psychologically

He has thrown himself on the floor and shrieked himself black in the
face and pounded his heels---as ~~xxxxxx~~ lots of us do in one way or another---but
when it's over, he'll go back to his building blocks again   Have you
ever felt what I call the cosmic despair? It's no joke. And if you slip
a little too deep in it, as he did, it's one devilish job getting out
again But he's well on the way out and I think deserves lots of credit
for getting himself so well in hand again There will perhaps be relapses,
but I don't think he feels the abyss so inescapably under him

Mayne

When we had our sherry,
we lifted our glasses,
as you might know,
" To Max "

The period has broke off my typewriter. (over)

I didn't realize I was ——
such a violent user of
decisiveness !

N.Y. Post story had been to go to New York and kill the German Jew, Mok, un-til he decided that would be a silly gesture with one arm disabled. He was terri-bly hurt about it, of course, for he had listened to a sob story from <the man> Mok, to let him in at all, and had responded to a lot of things the man told him——possibly spurious——about his own maladjusted wife, <to t> by talk-ing more freely than he should have done. But he has taken the thing very gracefully and is not unduly bitter or upset about it. He was also more forgiv-ing and reasonable than I think I should have been, about Hemingway's un-necessary crack at him in "The Snows of Kilimanjaro." We agreed that it was a part of Hemingway's own sadistic maladjustment, which makes him go around knocking people down. Scott said that Hemingway had written him very violently, <reproaching> damning him for his revealing self-searchings in *Esquire,* and Scott expressed the <legitimate> idea that it was just as legitimate to get one's grievances against life off the chest that way, as by giving an upper-cut to some harmless weakling. He resented Hemingway's calling him "ru-ined", and from other things he said, it was plain to me that he does not him-self consider himself "ruined", by a long shot.

I am firmly convinced that the man is all right. I know just what his state of mind has been. The same kind of panic hits anyone like me, with no one de-pendent on me. With an ill and expensive wife, a child brought up to luxury, and then one thing after another going wrong——all on top of the inevitable revulsion, almost, against writing——"the times", as Hemingway wrote me, "when you can't do it"——it was natural enough for him to go into a very black mood. It lasted longer and he publicized it more, than with most of us——I am always ashamed to let anyone know about mine——but I should lay a heavy wager that he's safely on the way out.

We disagreed heartily about many things, of course. Principally as to what we expect of life. I expect the crest of the wave to have a consequent and inevi-table trough, and whenever I'm at the bottom, I know there will be an up-turn sooner or later. Then when I'm at the top, I don't expect it to last indefinitely ——he said that he did!——but know there will have to be less pleasant things coming along sooner or later.

He said, "You're not as much of an egotist as I am." Then he said and more or less correctly, too, that a writer almost had to be an egotist, to the point of megalomania, because everything was filtered through his own universe.

His point of view lets him in for much desperate unhappiness and disillu-sion, because he simply cannot expect the consistent perfection and magnifi-cence of life that he does, frankly, expect. But as a writer, except for the times such as this one has been, when his misery holds him up too long, his masochism will not interfere with his work. We talked from a little after one, until five-thirty, when his nurse came back and fussed about his not resting, but we never reached talk of our plans for the future in any detail. He did say that he had a plan——and he spoke with every sign of the secret pleasure that is an indication of work in the brewing.

He spoke of the autobiographical thing, but said he could not do it with most of the people alive. That he could only do it now in a pleasant way, and it wouldn't be any fun without a little malice.

I wrote him that I felt he had a great gift as a social historian, and I do——that he had Thackeray's[1] feeling for a period, but a finer literary style than Thackeray's, and that I thought he would some day do something very stirring as a record of our confused generation.

I feel I had no tangible help for him——he is in no truly desperate need of help——and our points of view are very different——but there is a most helpful stimulation in talk between two people who are trying to do something of the same thing——a stimulation I miss and do not have enough of, at Cross Creek. And I am sure that stimulation was good for him. I may be able to have another visit with him when I return to Pisgah Forest in a couple of weeks, if the dishes I ordered are ready before I drive home. He may go to a quiet place on one of the Florida coasts, this winter, and if he does, we shall have some good talks.

So certainly I can report that the contact was very pleasant. And I do not think you need to worry about him, physically or psychologically. He has thrown himself on the floor and shrieked himself black in the face and pounded his heels——as <we all> lots of us do in one way or another——but when it's over, he'll go back to his building blocks again. Have you ever felt what I call the cosmic despair? It's no joke. And if you slip a little too deep in it, as he did, it's one devilish job getting out again. But he's well on the way out and I think deserves lots of credit for getting himself so well in hand again. There will perhaps be relapses, but I don't think he feels the abyss so inescapably under him.

[Postscript] When we had our sherry, we lifted our glasses, as you might know, "To Max."
The period has broken off my typewriter.[2] (over)
I didn't realize I was such a violent user of decisiveness!

1. William Makepeace Thackeray (1811–1863), Victorian novelist.
2. Periods have been added to the present text.

264. MKR to MEP (postcard)

[Banner Elk]

[October 1936]

Dear Max:

Forgot to answer your question as to how I saw the Post feature story about Fitzgerald down here. I was so charmed with Herschel Brickell when I met him at Blowing Rock this summer, subscribed to the Post to follow his reviews.

Found my old Wisconsin friend Ernest L. Meyer was also doing a column in the Post. Had my subscription sent here while I was here.

But between you and me, Herschel's personal charm does not show up in his reviews, which are too cautious and without his own magnetism—he talks better than he writes——and Ernie has such rabid social prejudices, that, coupled with the Post's tabloid air, I shall have to go back to the Tribune. How I miss the old N.Y. World!

. . . .

265. MKR to MEP (ALS, 2 pp.)

Banner Elk

Wednesday

[November 4, 1936]

Dear Max:—

Just a note to say that I am returning to Florida tomorrow, arriving there Saturday.

Was distressed to have Whitney Darrow say you told him I was doing a juvenile——I did not intend it as such—only a book so simple and elemental and full of natural stuff, that it would naturally appeal to boys——more of this later——but please do not announce a "juvenile" until I am done——I do not believe it will be a juvenile at all.

. . . .

266. MEP to MKR (TLS: UF, 2 pp.)

Nov. 5, 1936

Dear Marjorie:

A bad cold and election day have kept me from writing you sooner, but thank you deeply for your fine long letter about Scott. I have known him so long, and have liked him so much that his welfare is very much a personal matter with me too. I would do anything to see him recover himself.- Of course drinking is the most dreadful thing to overcome, but I have had an idea that Scott is slowly working out of it. He once told me that the only way he could get out was in the way he went in.- Although I never fully understood why he thought this, it may be he was right. I knew that he would get good from seeing you, and am mighty glad that he did see you.

Always yours,

. . . .

267. MEP to MKR (TLS: UF, I p.)

Nov. 7, 1936

Dear Marjorie:

What I told Darrow was that you were writing a book about a boy, and that I thought it would have in it some of those qualities, and the kind of adventure, that was in the early parts of "South Moon". It is a problem about that word "juvenile" which I always hated anyhow, and we shall have to meet it when the time comes.

I hope you are going to have a good winter for oranges. The law of averages ought to bring one this year.

Always yours,

. . . .

268. MKR to MEP (ALS, 5 pp.)

Cross Creek

Nov. 10 [1936]

Dear Max:——

The touchiness of writers and the fixed ideas of publishing as a business, must keep you constantly "on the spot." I knew the chances were that you had been a little misunderstood, but you are the logical wailing wall, you know, because you always understand.

What I am concerned about, is that the forthcoming book should not be labeled a "juvenile", because I think it will only *incidentally* be a book *for* [underlined twice] boys. I hope there will be nostalgic implications for mature people, for we never *feel* [underlined twice] more sensitively than in extreme youth, and the color and drama of the scrub can be well conveyed through the eyes and mind of a boy. I believe, I hope, that the book will be able to stand on its own feet. The only thing different I am doing, with the market, or appeal, for boys in mind, is avoiding the psychological (usually sexual) involvements

Cross Creek
Nov. 16 [1936]

Dear Max:—

The touchiness of writers and the fixed ideas of publishing as a business, must keep you constantly "on the spot." I knew the chances were that you had been a little misunderstood, but you are the logical wailing wall, you know, because you always understand.

What I am concerned about, is that the forthcoming book should not be labeled a "juvenile", because I think it

No. 268 (MKR on *The Yearling*). By permission of Princeton University Library.

will only incidentally be a —— book for boys. I hope there will be —— nostalgic implications for —— mature people, for we never *feel* more sensitively than in extreme youth, and the color and drama of the —— scout can be —— well conveyed through the eyes and mind of a boy. I believe, I hope, that the book will be able to stand on its own feet. The only thing different I am doing, with the market, a appeal, for boys.

in mind, is avoiding the psychological
(usually sexual) involvements
of maturity. But a boy's
reaction to the mature world
is a valid one, and has value
for anyone. The adventure,
and simplicity, will carry it,
quite secondarily, for boys' use.
But it is important that no
announcement ever be made, anywhere,
that the book is a "juvenile."
Walter de la Mare's "Memoirs of a
Midget" is from the point of view
of the midget but no one could
call it a book "for" little people.

4

He simply shared a phase of the world through a sensitive mind.

I run a danger, I know, of ending up with what is neither fish, flesh nor fowl, but I really feel I have that angle of the thing firmly in hand.

I reached here Saturday and found completely disorganized darkies, whom I had to fire. My vacations always cost me dear that way, but I consider it just part of the price. My place is in complete confusion, and it irks me to have to stop and look after domestic details, and break in a brand – new grove man and house woman, when I should like to sit down in tranquillity and go ahead with the book.

I get so tired of carrying such a complete responsibility, but my place here offers the only security that is at all tangible, so I cling to it.

I believe it will be a good orange year, and I plan to sell my fruit by Christmas, to be free of the anxiety about freezes.

I wrote a story while I was in the mountains that Carl sold to the Post— but it's not a Scribner type at all, so you didn't miss a thing. I think the new magazine is immensely thrilling.

Marjorie

of maturity. But a boy's reaction to the mature world is a valid one, and has value for anyone. The adventure, and simplicity, will carry it, quite secondarily, for boys' use. But it is important that no announcement ever be made, anywhere, that the book is a "juvenile". Walter de la Mare's "Memoirs of a Midget"[1] is from the point of view of the midget, but no one could call it a book "for" little people. He simply showed a phase of the world through a sensitive mind.

I run a danger, I know, of ending up with what is neither fish, flesh nor fowl, but I really feel I have that <part> angle of the thing firmly in hand.

I reached home Saturday and found completely disorganized darkies, whom I had to fire. My vacations always cost me dear that way, but I consider it just part of the price. My place is in complete confusion, and it irks me to have to stop and look after domestic details and break in a brand-new grove man and house woman, when I should like to sit down in tranquility and go ahead with the book.

I get so tired of carrying such a complete responsibility, but my place here offers the only security that is at all tangible, so I cling to it.

I believe it will be a good orange year, and I plan to sell my fruit by Christmas, to be free of the anxiety about freezes.

I wrote a story[2] while I was in the mountains that Carl sold to the Post—— but it's not a Scribner type at all, so you didn't miss a thing. I think the new magazine is immensely thrilling.

1. Walter de la Mare (1873–1956), *Memoirs of a Midget* (London: Collins, 1921).
2. "A Mother in Mannville."

. . . .

269. MKR to MEP (TLS, with holograph additions and postscript, 2 pp.)

[Cross Creek]
[November 1936]

Dear Max:—

I should have told you what is a flutter-mill, for I am more and more inclined to the title. It is a toy the backwoods boys make here; two forked twigs placed in a shallow stream, or branch——a straight twig laid across them, through which has been inserted two strips of palmetto leaf, <so that> at angles, so that the running water turns the fragments of leaf like a water-mill. The straight twig rotates. A boy and I placed one in Juniper Creek, and a month later it was still turning. Only leaves accumulating against it, or high water to wash it away, would destroy it. I shall have to tell you something of the theme. At the beginning of the book the boy Jody builds himself a flutter-mill on an April afternoon. It always delights him. Everything for him is young and safe, and the world is good and beautiful. A year of time progresses for him, with all the free natural life of the scrub; the interest in the doings of other people; the outlaw bear, the predatory wolves, the storm and flood that destroy the game with a plague, the fighting Forresters, his neighbors, making trouble ——it all fascinates him, but none of it is a menace. He is safe. Toward the end of the book, his mother forces him to kill his pet yearling deer which he has raised from a spotted fawn. The yearling destroys their meagre crops as fast as they plant them, and no fence is high enough to keep him out. Food is too hard to come by to allow the boy's pet to destroy it at its source. His frail father is ill and he is ordered to do the job himself. He manages it, but cannot return home. He wanders half-starved several days. He has been betrayed.

He had loved the yearling as only a boy can love an animal he has raised and tamed. His own mother has betrayed him. There is no safety any more. Life itself has impinged on him with its harshness and its necessities and its treachery. Then a curtain is lifted, and for a moment he has an understanding of the unavoidable treachery of all life; of the things that force people to betray. On his way home, he stops to build another flutter-mill to replace the one that had been carried away in the past year. But for the first time it does not comfort him. He takes up the responsibilities that his father's illness impose on him, with understanding and gravity. It is the moment that comes, sooner or later, young or perhaps in maturity, when one steps over the threshold of youth. He is no longer a boy, but a man.

I have hated to sum up the story, for it may sound sentimental or too symbolical to make a good story. But that is only the underlying theme, and I can assure you the fabric of the story will carry it. I have no fear of it at all, and I shall be careful never to sentimentalize. The style will be very simple and direct, and the material is fascinating. "The Yearling" states quite well what I mean to do, but it is so stark a title, that I thought perhaps "The Flutter-Mill" would be more intriguing. Too much emphasis cannot be placed on the proper and appealing title.

Tell me what you think.

[Postscript] I am aware too of the danger of attributing too-mature thoughts to the boy. I shall be very careful about it.

Editor's note: Enclosed is a memorandum from Whitney Darrow dated November 21, 1936, assuring Perkins that "Boys read MOBY DICK. So do you and I."

270. MEP to MKR (TLS: UF, 2 pp.)

Dec. 22, 1936

Dear Marjorie:

I want to tell you that I have heard a great many enthusiastic comments on your story in Scribner's.[1] The magazine gave a party too, on Saturday afternoon, and there it was much talked of. If you could write stories something of that kind from time to time, they might in the end make a collection,- for such a book would have much more unity than a book of stories usually does.

I am really only writing to you to wish that this will be a happy Christmas for you, and I hope it won't be far into the new year before you will be willing and able to show me something of your new book.

Scott seems still to be in North Carolina, but I hear rather favorable reports of him, and I think Christmas must bring him up this way. Hem is finishing a long novel[2] about the part of the world where he lives.- When it is done, which will be very soon, he is bent upon going to Spain. I hope something will keep him from it.

Always yours,

1. "Varmints."
2. *To Have and Have Not.*

. . . .

271. MKR to MEP (TLS, 3 pp.)

Hawthorn, Florida
Dec. 31, 1936

Dear Max:

I'm glad the mule story was liked. The magazine was so generous in its display and illustrations, that I'm pleased that you had a response on it. Miss Ives did a difficult and creditable job in cutting it——but a certain leisureliness that was of value was inevitably lost, and I don't think I shall ever agree again to a cutting of a manuscript that I have myself pared down as far as possible. When I turned the story over to Carl Brandt, I told him, and thought I had told you, that I had a series in mind——humorous stories told by the same woman, Quincey Dover. They would have a definite continuity. Ordinarily a book of stories is poor business for everyone, I know.

I have had the happiest Christmas of many years, for my beloved brother has been here with me from Seattle, since the opening of hunting season. The duck-hunting was really magnificent. I have eaten duck until I am afraid that when I speak a drake will circle around me, recognizing the mating call. I can't hit them myself, but my brother did nobly. I had a perfect set-up—we used small frog-hunting boats and made our blinds, and I hired a man with a motor boat to circle about and keep the ducks in motion. I shouldn't say "hired" because all my arrangements with my Cracker neighbors are peculiar. I had loaned this man money to take his baby to the doctor, had fed his wife while she was convalescing from child-birth and so on, and I simply took out the debt in the duck-hunting. But anyway, everyone who hunted with us said we had the best duck-hunting in the state. Tell Hemingway for me that I thought of him when we were having such good luck. He passed me up cold in November, putting up nearby in Gainesville. I was sorry he didn't come out here, even if he had a party, because my place is wide open to people for whom I have infinitely less respect than for him.

We went for turkey last week, but they had left the island in the marsh where we had them located, evidently the day before we got there. We've had top-notch quail-shooting. I enjoy that the most of any of the hunting, probably because I can hit them.

My brother returns to Seattle Monday, and I shall be quite desolate. We are devoted to each other, and it seems silly for us to be separated by a diagonal line across the continent. Yet ties of one sort and another keep us in our respective sections.

Needless to say, the book, begun nicely in Carolina, stopped short. Not entirely because of his visit, but largely because I returned from the mountains to a pair of completely demoralized niggers, whom I had to fire. My grove work and my house-hold have been so disorganized that I have had to take responsibilities and do actual work that I usually delegate to my help. If things had been running as smoothly as usual, we could have put in part of each day hunting, and I could still have done some work—which we planned. I have stop-gap help now which will do for a while, and one thing the enforced separation from the book has done, is to make me terribly keen to be at it again. I may not be out any time in the end, because I shall sink myself in it completely. I hope that mid-Spring will see it done.

I haven't heard from Scott since I left Carolina. I want to send him a book I promised him. Do you have an address that might reach him? He spoke of Florida this winter, for work, but since he didn't go north at Thanksgiving, as he planned, he may have changed his whole program.

Why do you hope Hemingway won't go to Spain? A grand book might come of it. He writes with so much color of the terrain——he would lose himself in the situation there—and his writing is best when it is objective. If he's killed in the mêlée, what of it? He must go where his feeling impels him.

I sent you some of my oranges——still rather acid. If you use them much, I can send you some better ones a little later in the season when they're sweeter.

Thank you for writing me. There is always comfort in hearing from you.

1937

272. MEP to MKR (TLS: UF, 3 pp.)

Jan. 28, 1937

Dear Marjorie:

I must tell you that the oranges did come and were not at all acid, but very fine, and that we all enjoyed them.- And many thanks for them. I have seen rumors that conditions are bad for oranges this year, but you foresaw trouble, I think you wrote me, and took steps to ward it off. Or didn't you? I suppose that any year may be the beginning of a cycle of good years, but the orange people in Florida do seem to have had a terrible run of luck in the last few.

I hope you get back to the book. I do look forward so to reading it. I am sure of its giving me that kind of pleasure that takes you away from all the usual troubles of life while you read.- But I rather think that such interruptions as you describe, which are happy ones, do not do harm to the writing, but good.

Hem was here for a week arranging about his Spanish expedition,- looking over hospital supplies, etc. He has already persuaded one of our other authors to go along who ought to be here finishing a novel,- and Dos Passos goes too, apparently.[1] I am glad other people are beyond his persuasive reach. Anyhow, he is bent upon going, for good or bad, so there is no use arguing.- I can see that he cannot help going. He began life adventurously, and must live it that way. And it is true that he will get his own kind of material to write about.

I am sending you a life of Whitman,[2] but there are a couple of books coming later that you will like very greatly,- one called "Cruise of the Conrad" a beautiful book by Villiers, much better than any he has done, and with fine pictures in it.[3]

Always yours,

1. John Dos Passos (1896–1970), novelist.
2. Edgar Lee Masters (1868–1950), *Whitman* (New York: Scribners, 1937).
3. Alan J. Villiers (1903–1982), *Cruise of the Conrad* (New York: Scribners, 1937).

[Cross Creek]

[January 1937]

Dear Max:

I had a sheet of paper in the typewriter ready to finish a paragraph, when your welcome letter came. I was beginning to have visions of Hemingway's dragging you about, packing cartridges and guns and bandages. I am glad you are reconciled to his going. It is one of those inevitable things, and, death for him, or no, is somehow right. I only hope for myself that if I ever become too firmly entrenched in a meaningless safety, that something as fatal and as luminous will drag me out.

I am one of your duties, you know, Max, and you really must write to me at least every couple of weeks. Sometimes a letter from you is the only thing that bucks me up. When everything else fails, I can know that it really matters to you whether or not I get a piece of work done, and how well.

I had to discard everything of "The Yearling"——which we may call it for the time being——back to the first chapter. I had to go a little farther back, to give it cohesion. My first thought had been to plunge into more or less exciting events. Then I realized that they were not exciting unless the boy, and his father, and his surroundings, were so real, so familiar, that the things that happened to him took on color because it all came close to home, in its very familiarity. Just as the Louisville flood meant nothing to me until I found that the factory and beautiful home of my dearest friends were under water, and I was unable to contact them. The whole sweep of water and devastation became at once a true and unbearable thing. That is perhaps the whole secret of fiction. When the people written about move in reality before our eyes, touch us, then anything they do becomes vivid and important.

I shall perhaps send you a few chapters after a while, just to give you the flavor of the book. It is terribly slow going. The worst of my interruptions are behind me, but even with all my time and energy given to it, it goes slowly for the very reason that I have to visualize, to feel, with great clarity, every moment, allowing no looseness, no unawareness, in order to show the boy's world through the sensitive medium of adolescent being. If it is not dull, or of too limited an interest, I still think it may be something beautiful and moving.

You didn't send me an address where I might reach Scott Fitzgerald with the book I promised him, Granberry's "The Erl King".[1]

Thanks for writing.

---

1. Edwin Granberry (1897–), *The Erl King* (New York: Macaulay, 1930).

Feb. 2, 1937

Dear Marjorie:

I haven't got Scott's address in full, but I know he is in Tryon, N.C., and I have been simply addressing letters that way.- And they have not come back. He was here too a while ago and seemed in many ways to be in pretty good shape, though he was drinking.- But not in the reckless way that he used to do. He does seem, though, to have lost all ambition, and the only hope is that he may be gradually filling up his reserve of strength which has been for so long exhausted. Now there is somebody who ought to go to Spain for the sake of seeing something totally different from what he ever did see.

I sent you yesterday a Life of Whitman which is a good book, and about the only unprejudiced life that has been written,- that is, the only one that is not based on some particular psychological theory of the author's. But there will be some better books later on in non-fiction, like Villier's book and "The Saga of American Society".[1]

I wish you would send me chapters. I would not care if they were very much in the rough too, for I know now enough about how you do to be able to understand what the later development would be, I think. I know you have to look at everything until you can extract from it its own actual quality,- and it isn't easy!

T. Wolfe has returned from a tour of the South which extended over about six weeks. The principal point was New Orleans, and he talks wonderfully about that and the strange country thereabouts down to the Gulf.

Always yours,

1. Dixon Wector (1906–1950), *The Saga of the American Society* (New York: Scribners, 1937).

. . . .

Feb. 18, 1937

Dear Marjorie:

I went last night to one of those parties that an editor cannot always avoid, to a Spanish restaurant down below Washington Square, and sat next to one of those nice simple southern girls, who was among your great admirers,- and so was her husband. They were the Hamilton Bassos.[1] She said she had read "South Moon" through many times, and asked if you were ever going to do one like it,- and I said you were doing one, though not like it, that would certainly be as much of a pleasure to anyone like her who loved "South Moon".

Well, the reason I mention it is that these two lived not very far from where you were in North Carolina, and if you go there again, you would enjoy seeing them because they are both first rate, and he has the makings of an exceptionally good writer in him,- and in fact, has done very fine work in two novels, "Cinnamon Seed" and "Courthouse Square".- But neither of them have succeeded in point of sales.[2] I won't send them to you though now, because you prefer non-fiction when you are writing, and I do hope that you are writing well again.

Always yours,

1. Hamilton Basso (1904–1964), novelist. Etolia Simmons Basso.
2. Hamilton Basso, *Cinnamon Seed* (New York: Scribners, 1934) and *Court-house Square* (New York: Scribners, 1936).

. . . .

276. MKR to MEP (TLS, 3 pp.)

Hawthorn, Florida

Feb. 25 [1937]

Dear Max:

Thanks so much for both books and the good letters. I don't think I could like anything Edgar Lee Masters wrote, "not even if it was good." And unless a biographer has a luminosity of interpretation to bring to his subject, so that the book itself is creative and stimulating, and can stand on its own feet as a thing of value, I resent a mere probing into the life and mind of a great artist. It is too much like worms feeding on a corpse.

"Dusk of Empire",[1] on the other hand, took me off my feet. I could not put it down. If Williams is as thoroughly honest as the context would indicate, it seems to me the book cannot help but have an international effect. Certainly it should give this whole country a jolt. It saddens me, for I am one of those who rather tend to ignore painful facts, and I have been taking peace for granted. Williams leaves no doubt but that the vast percentage takes war for granted. Admitting that, there is probably no course for the United States but to acquire the whip hand. Among nations, tolerance and generosity and simple goodness, as with our negroes in the south, are not held a sign of strength, but of weakness, and are, slyly or boldly, to be taken advantage of. Williams' title is gorgeous.

The book filled in a vacuum of questions in my mind at this particular moment, for I found it waiting for me on my return from a week-end at Rollins College, where I appeared on the Animated Magazine. The program was keyed by Dr. Hamilton Holt, a lifelong and patient League of Nations advocate, as you know, to the international flavor. Our own Thomas J. Watson was a noble representative of American altruism, and I burst with pride over his fineness. The other two principal guests of honor were Lord David Davies, <who made p> who persisted, with superlative diplomacy, in labeling himself a Welshman, "a citizen of a very small country", and Dr. F. H. F. Van Vlissingen, of the Netherlands, president of the international Chamber of Commerce, and head of the international rayon industry.[2] Lord Davies made precisely the charming and irresistible appeal for British-American cooperation that Williams warns us against, unless we are prepared to give ourselves to it wisely. He went so far as to use the old Wilson shibboleths, and asked whether, having helped fight to preserve democracy, we meant to go back on the job now. He said, "Federalism is the child of the United States. Instead of holding aloof, you should be going up and down the earth, preaching the worth of your progeny." The thought came to me, even in my ignorance of, and actually indifference to, world matters, "England, speaking through the poise and calm of that man, is frightened to death. They are on their knees, begging us to fight with their gang." So you can imagine what a revelation the Williams book was for me.

The Hollander spoke with a magnificent detachment. He was thoroughly sincere, <illegible excision> and he was fighting for free trade. There is of course nothing objectionable in an honest statement of aim. It is only hypocrisy that offends. There was on the face of the man the mark of sorrow, of tragedy. He may see, probably must see, Holland as Williams sees her——the next Belgium. I should have given my orange grove for a long talk with him, for he interested me more than any man I have ever met. I am writing you with a thoroughly broken heart, for while I had a most delightful contact with both Lord Davies and Thomas Watson, Van Vlissingen bowed politely——and was unaware of my existence.

About "The Yearling". I am on the point of exploding with frustration. The work stopped short, as you know, on my return from the mountains, because of my beloved brother's visit. That was worth while. Then servant trouble prevented my getting at the book again. I am peculiarly at the mercy of reliable help. I don't in the least mind doing all my own work, even to feeding the chickens and milking the cow and driving the truck on grove-work, but there is such a mass of detail here on the shabby old lovely place, that I simply cannot do it and do anything else. My nervous energy burns fiercely about so long and then the current just stops. There are at least six hours of hard work here every day, aside from the grove work. And a new or incompetent servant requires all my time and effort to break in. The Lord sent me, or so I was fatuous enough to think, not long ago a most capable and settled woman of intelligence, clean, hard-working, a good cook.[3] She came to me at the time I had a houseful of flood refugees from Louisville——a dear friend and her children.[4] They left on Tuesday, and I prepared to settle back with a sigh of delight, forswearing all human contact. I took the woman to the doctor yesterday and find she has either a tumor or, more likely, a cancer, and operative work is necessary at once. Humanitarianism requires my seeing her through, but leaves unsolved all over again the question as to who shall do the manual labor while I write. It will all work out in the end, but I shall go mad if I can't soon have peace in which to do concentrated work.

Scott Fitzgerald told me that Hamilton Basso was a charming person. His "Cinnamon Seed", which you sent me at time of publication, infuriated me. There is a taint in his viewpoint which I haven't quite analyzed, but he does write well. I had the feeling, in the "Cinnamon Seed," of a good picture's being under a dirty blanket. The thing was definitely *muffled* and a little soiled.

I hope to have better news when next I write.

1. Wythe Williams (1881–1956), *Dusk of Empire: The Decline of Europe and the Rise of the United States* (New York: Scribners, 1937).
2. MKR gave a dramatic reading of "A Mother in Mannville" at Rollins College, a report of which appeared in the *Animated Magazine,* which did not print stories and lectures, but only reported them. Hamilton Holt, president of Rollins College; Thomas J. Watson, American industrialist; Lord David Davies, British author and politician; F. H. F. Van Vlissingen, Dutch industrialist.
3. Martha Mickens.
4. Lois Clark Hardy, a sorority sister at the University of Wisconsin.

. . . .

277. MEP to MKR (TLS: UF, 4 pp.)

March 3, 1937

Dear Marjorie:

There is one thing about it, the more we speak of "The Yearling" the better that seems to be as a title. It seems to have a quality even more than a meaning that fits the book. Maybe something will come up that seems better, but that is very good. I hope things will clear up so you can work steadily on the book.- I can see how disconcerting is such a thing as that which happened with the woman you found. Maybe being held up this way will enable you to go on faster because you will be so eager to do it, and anyhow, unconscious reflection is perhaps the greatest part of the writing of a book.

We are publishing Wythe Williams' book on March 12th. He has always been in a great hurry to get it out because he thought war might begin at any moment. We wanted finished copies three or four weeks before publication so as to get them around and have them read by journalists and reviewers, and he could hardly endure the delay. But I think even he begins to think that war will be put off for a year, and that there is even a slight chance of avoiding it altogether. And there do seem to be favorable developments on the lines referred to in the enclosed Foreign Letter which I have marked.- But we are publishing a book later on called "Floodlight on Europe: A Guide to the Next War"[1] which is almost as pessimistic as Williams' is.

I had a letter from Scott which was very encouraging because he sounded much stronger and saner—as in fact he seemed when he was here several weeks ago, even though he was drinking then. I feel distinctly that he is developing into a better condition,- but he does have this great trouble: he has lost all ambition, all desire to succeed. It comes partly from his always adopting a role, and his role of late has been that of the man burned out at forty. But as he gets stronger he may take a different direction and come up faster than anyone foresees. He is back there in Tryon, and hasn't had a drop since he was here some weeks ago.

I feel much the way you do about biographies, but there never had been a good straightaway biography of Whitman. All the other books of any note have been written from some particular angle, with some special theory about him.- What Masters wants to show, and always does want to show—and as Van Wyck argued in his "Ordeal of Mark Twain"[2]—is that American artists do not realize their possibilities, ever— especially poets— because they do not have a sympathetic audience in this country. But it is not the fault of the country exactly. It is due to a stage of development. He showed that quite pitifully in his life of Vachel Lindsay.[3]

There is a very good story, full of warmth and human feeling in the March Scribner's by Jo Pagano.[4] He is trying to write a novel about those people. You have probably read other stories by him in the magazine. He has very fine material, I think, but he is having a great struggle to do a novel because it is his first. There are several other good stories in that number too. I hope it won't be so very long before they will have another by you.

Always yours,

1. Felix Wittmer (1902–), *Flood-light on Europe: A Guide to the Next War* (New York: Scribners, 1937).
2. Van Wyck Brooks, *The Ordeal of Mark Twain* (New York: Dutton, 1920).
3. Edgar Lee Masters, *Vachel Lindsay: A Poet in America* (New York: Scribners, 1935).
4. Jo Pagano, "Caesar at the Feast," *Scribner's Magazine* 101.3 (March 1937): 52–58.

278. MEP to MKR (TLS: UF, 2 pp.)

March 24, 1937

Dear Marjorie:

I thought you might be interested to read Wolfe's story, "I Have a Thing to Tell You" in the New Republic,[1] and so I am sending you the three numbers containing it. And since these numbers are completely sold out now, you had better keep them for they will have value, in fact have already.

Ham Basso and his wife are back at Pisgah Forest.- If anything takes you again to North Carolina, remember them. I think you would like them both, and surely her;- she's a botanist of some note by the way, and a good cook, I'm told. Scott is also in North Carolina and doing well so far as health goes. There's ground for hope too that he may find a way to clear off his heavy load of debt.- If that were done I think he might move forward into a new field.

Have you been able to get back to "The Yearling" and is it going well?

Always yours,

1. Thomas Wolfe, "I Have a Thing to Tell You," *New Republic* 90 (March 10, 17, 24, 1937): 132–36, 159–64, 202–7.

. . . .

279. MKR to MEP (TLS, 2 pp.)

Hawthorn, Florida
March 26, 1937

Max you dear:

The two new books are a delight. I am saving the animal book, but have started the Villiers, found myself unable to leave it alone. Not so much for the subject matter, but for pleasure in his style. I had read short bits of his, but had no idea he wrote so beautifully. The book will certainly take its place with the great sea voyage books, and justifies the trip——which nothing else, to my no-tion, could do. It all seemed needlessly heroic——. I am fascinated with the be-hind-the-curtain study of the man himself, as revealed in chance comments he makes. He must be a strange person, very young——and very old; very wise—— and very hard and intolerant; a mixture of humility and arrogance.

I shall be so glad to have the new Wolfe thing. I know he is making a violent effort at self-discipline, or rather, disciplined artistry, in his work, and <it> I shall be interested to watch his progress after "Of Time and the River".

I plan definitely to go to North Carolina again in the late summer or early fall——hoping either to be quite done with "The Yearling" or to be doing whatever revising is necessary, or even proof-reading, up there. It is going along again, very slowly, but I think, very surely, and with not much to be undone so far. I had to go back and write a new second chapter——for the third time—— changing the sequence again, but most of what was discarded will fit in later, so very little work was actually wasted. Except for routine, to-be-expected barriers, I cannot see any great hurdles ahead to be taken. It should go along smoothly now, for I have a month-by-month chart of the events for the year that is covered by the book.

I don't know whether Carl Brandt is shocked, angered or amused——. He wired me the other day that Cosmopolitan was in straits for a new serial and insisted on seeing what I had done on the new book. I had told Carl again and again that the book was not their kind, but told him nothing of the type or context. So I wired him that it was so unsuitable there was no use in anyone's looking at it——it was about a twelve-year-old boy in the scrub——it had no love interest. In desperation, to convince him, I finished, "All women characters past the menopause".

I handed the wire to the village telegraph operator——. He pushed down his spectacles and began to count the words. "——48, 49——this word here——." I thought, "Oh damn the Western Union——I suppose I can't say it." "This word here——menopause——is that all one word?"

. . . .

280. MEP to MKR (TLS: UF, 1 p.)

April 21, 1937

Dear Marjorie:

Can you now make a pretty definite prophecy as to when "Yearling" will be done? I am afraid it won't be for some time, but I thought you might have had a streak of good luck, when the writing went well, and free of domestic obstacles. I wish you would get it done,- not that time is so very important, but I know I am going to really enjoy that manuscript very much,- find it a real "escape".

Always yours,

Hawthorn, Florida
April 22, 1937

Dear Max:

"The Yearling" will be done by the end of August or mid-September——or you will publish the fragmentary manuscript posthumously. I shall explode if I don't finish it by that time.

I did have a peaceful period in which it went swimmingly. Then relatives descended on me the very day my insane (literally) maid had to go to the hospital for a minor operation, and I lost my hard-won abstraction again. Last night I sat on my porch in the moonlight with no other light, waiting for the maid to bring me my supper tray. I heard her stop in the living room and say aloud to herself, "I don't know where Mrs. Rawlings is."

I thought, "Sometimes I'm not sure myself——."

Actually, when such halts come, it is because I am organizing the material in my mind. I have learned not to force myself too far, for when I do, that is the work that most likely must be done over again. I am about ready to move ahead. Each time the stops are shorter, for the whole swing of the thing stays with me.

I question the good taste of the incident where I stopped work. But it is really very funny, if you can stomach it. There are some gorgeous characters, Max. They not only breathe, but bellow. The book is quiet, in a way, but violent too. God, if I can only get down what I sense, and see.

Carl of course is fighting to see it. It is barely possible that the POST would be interested in it, but there isn't another magazine in the world that would touch it. And I do not think it is keyed in any way to the POST, except that they like outdoor stuff. If it is good at all, it will simply be too damn good for them. And I shall not damage my hard-won fragment of prestige again by improper presentation, cutting, etc. But if it accidentally hit them right and they offered some large sum, I'd be very much upset. I'd probably feel much the way Mrs. Simpson felt——being perfectly happy with Ernest, I understand——the first time Windsor made improper proposals![1] Perhaps I can be saved from my worst self——by the book's not appealing to <anybody!> any magazine!

Speaking of questionable taste, the Corey Ford[2] parodies were immensely clever, especially the Hemingway take-off. Yet the subject matter offended me.

But how good, how excitingly good, the new Scribner's has become. Some of the ultra-modern painters annoy me, but the old Scribner's, or rather the Scribner's of a couple of years ago, had become so dull that there was nothing in it to annoy!

The Thomas Wolfe "I Have a Thing to Tell You" was sheer triumph. He has gained immeasurably by the self-imposed restraint, and all the old beauty and rhythm and emotion are enhanced by it. Then when he does break loose with one of his magnificent lyricisms, the effect is heart-breaking, like an exquisite melody in the sternness of a symphony. Thank you so much for sending it. It is indeed an important document, both as a milestone in Wolfe's work, and as a social document.

Well, Max——pray for me——

1. Mrs. Wallis Warfield Simpson, twice-divorced wife of Edward VIII, Duke of Windsor, who abdicated the throne to marry her in 1937. Ernest A. Simpson was her second husband.
2. Corey Ford (1902–1969), ". . . And So They Lived Happily Ever After," *Scribner's Magazine* 101.5 (May 1937): 27–31. The parody of *Death in the Afternoon* is entitled "Death Without Women."

. . . .

282. MKR to MEP (ALS, I p.)

Cross Creek
[May 1937]

Dear Max:——

I should have given you more of a ray of hope in your black world of delinquent authors——

Of course, I *hope* [underlined twice] to have "The Yearling" finished long before the end of August, but since you have to be able to make some definite publishing plans, I gave you the date of the ultimate dead-line in case I am much slowed up.

I'm moving along quite satisfactorily. I get badly "off key" at times but that is a matter of editing.

. . . .

283. MEP to MKR (TLS: UF, 2 pp.)

May 7, 1937

Dear Marjorie:

It is not because I was disappointed by your letter that I had not answered you,- for I had not thought you could do the work in time for Fall publication, and also it seems to me not unlikely that the Post will want to serialize. The trouble was that my secretary went off on a vacation and it was practically impossible to get letters written for a couple of weeks.

The sooner we get "The Yearling" the better, for then we can take our time in manufacturing it and have copies all made far in advance of publication, and make people acquainted with the book.- I think this will be important with "The Yearling" because there will be that dreadful inclination to think a book about a boy is a book for "younger readers" only. That we must overcome.

Anyhow, you never were a delinquent author at all, but it is true that many authors are so delinquent that you can only understand it by thinking of yourself as an author,- and how lazy and irresponsible one would be without the discipline of a regular job.- I mean I would be.- But it does often seem as if they deliberately allowed victory to slip between their fingers. My impatience about "The Yearling" is mostly that of being extremely anxious to read it.

Always yours,

. . . .

284. MKR to MEP (TLS, 1 p.)

Hawthorn, Florida

May 10 [1937]

Dear Max:

Thank you for your letter. I did think you had given up all hope of my finishing "The Yearling".

You do have to imagine yourself in the writer's shoes to understand the peculiar and unreasonable procrastinations; the torment of the thing that has only an inner compulsion behind it. You see, the inner compulsion so often fails. One questions everything; the ultimate value; the immediate quality. None of one's friends——or almost none——understands——human relations impinge.

What seemed to me a week ago a misfortune, is proving a bit of good luck. My insane maid left me out of a clear sky. I have dozens of baby ducks, chickens, turkeys, to take care of——but it doesn't take too much time. And I find that I have the perfect alibi for not going places or having guests. "I have no help on the place". People understand the horror of that, when they do not understand the agony of wanting to work, and being interrupted.

Has the short story I wrote lately come to your attention? I thought of Scribner's of course as the logical place for it, but sent it to Carl, more as a courtesy than anything else. He is so sweet about everything, when the commissions he makes from my work are very slight. The story, "Black Secret,"[1] as I wrote him, is not a pretty one, but it tormented me into being written. He wrote me that it was not, truly, a pretty story, but that it was a beautiful one, and he was sending it direct to Scribner's. I hope you like it.

"The Yearling" progresses. The principal difficulty at present is in keeping a steady flow of narrative, rather than falling into the disjointed abyss of mere episodes.

1. "Black Secret," *New Yorker* 21 (September 8, 1945): 20–23.

. . . .

285. MKR to MEP (ALS, 2 pp.)

Hawthorn, Florida
May 31 [1937]

Dear Max:——

I am driving up to New York with Mrs. Grinnell, arriving there probably some time Friday of this week.

I'll only stay a few days, but it will be a welcome break——and I'll bring what is ready of "The Yearling" for you to look at.

I had about decided it was stupid and no good, and it will be helpful for you to say whether I am on the right track, or badly off.

. . . .

286. MKR to MEP (TLS, 4 pp.)

[Bayshore, Long Island]
Sunday
[June 13?, 1937]

Dear Max:

When you do your memoirs, I should suggest for a title, "The Perils of an Editor; or Days and Nights with the Authors". And I hope a brief chapter will include Tom Wolfe plowing his way among the vegetables in a drizzle of rain at four o'clock in the morning, while you and I followed like pieces broken off from a meteor in transit. I shouldn't have started the argument about suicide in the Chinese dive if I'd known he would take it so personally! I have always found suicide a delightful abstraction for discussion, but when I found that he thought I was urging him to do it, and refused at the top of his lungs, "even to satisfy his publishers", I wished I had argued about something simple, like transcendentalism. But it was grand, and I wouldn't have missed it. I should love to feed him some time. If I go to North Carolina, and you go down to see him, I'll drive over to his cabin and cook you both a Ritz dinner.

The outlook for work here is not, at the moment, promising. I can work here as far as adaptation and surroundings are concerned. I am writing now in my room, isolated in the center of the house, overlooking a broad lawn full of flowers and birds, with seven miles of blue bay beyond, and Fire Island just visible across it. But in spite of Mrs. Grinnell's earnest intention to do for me exactly what I may need or want, her social demands are impinging. Her friends are finding that she is at home, and my hope that she would go ahead and play with them and leave me to work, is fading a bit. As a guest, I am helpless. But I'll keep an open mind a few more days. I should love to stay awhile, but I dare not stop the work too long.

Mrs. Grinnell will come in for cocktails with us anytime, as desired, but she has an alternative suggestion, an invitation which seems infinitely more pleasant to me, and I'm hoping that it will to you. She wishes me to ask you to come out here for a brief respite from heat and confusion, either during the day, or to stay over-night. I told her that I didn't think it would make you happy to stay away over-night, and she said I must never take too much for granted what would make anyone else happy or unhappy.

Her place is huge and old-fashioned, the house itself not artistic, but solid ease and freedom, with acres of grounds and gardens. There would of course be no one else here while you were here. There are two morning trains leaving the Pennsylvania Station at 10:30 and at 11:30, getting into Babylon, where her car and chauffeur would meet you, an hour later. There are trains returning to New York in the afternoon at 4:56, at 5:49 and about every hour through the evening. Mrs. Grinnell thinks it might be most comfortable for you to come in the afternoon, giving you practically your whole day for work, taking, say, a train from Pa. Station at 3:45 P.M. or 4:47, having dinner and the evening here——which is very beautiful on the water——and taking any of the many convenient trains back in the morning. But if you will come, it is entirely up to you to say what time appeals to you.

Will you drop me a note or 'phone me? A long wire from a most considerate friend at home informs me that everything is all right there, including the livestock.

Selfishly, I hope you will accept Mrs. Grinnell's invitation. But don't come if you don't really want to. I can give you enough misery with a manuscript, without making you go places and do things you don't want to. I have an infinite capacity for abnegation.

Editor's note: Written at the bottom left: "Bayshore 766."

287. MEP to MKR (TLS: UF, 1 p.)

June 15, 1937

Dear Marjorie:

I hoped you would be in town before this and would let me know. But much as I should like to go down to Mrs. Grinnell's, it really is impossible for me to get away. I know a man who hasn't leisure is supposed to be very incompetent, and that has often worried me, but I cannot help it. But if Mrs. Grinnell will only come to New York and have tea, or a cocktail, on any day but Wednesday, it would certainly be a great pleasure to me to meet her. Couldn't it be managed that way? I hope anyhow to see you soon.

Always yours,

. . . .

288. MKR to MEP (TLS, 1 p.)

[Bayshore, Long Island]
[June 1937]

Dear Max

Just want to be sure you understand this is only a rough first draft. I mean to give a greater richness in many places to the narrative. There may be too much straight description——won't try to cover any ground until you have read it. I dread having you read it, but if I'm off the track, now is a good moment for me to know it.

I shall phone Monday to see when you are ready to talk about it, and for me to give you a résumé of the rest of the book.

Don't let anyone else read it, please. And this is my only copy.

. . . .

289. MKR to MEP (TLS, 2 pp.)

[Bayshore, Long Island]
Friday
[June 18, 1937]

Dear Max:

Sorry you won't come out to this lovely place. I was afraid you wouldn't. You have my own peculiarity of disliking to disturb my roots, even for a little while. But I assure you, once the distress of making the move is over, I am almost always glad to have done it.

Mrs. Grinnell and I will be in New York Tuesday. So if you will save about an hour that afternoon, I'll 'phone you in town to arrange a definite time of meeting. If it's a pleasant day, I <thought> think the terrace of the Hotel Chatham <was> would be very nice. But any place that is convenient for you will be all right.

Why didn't you tell me how *sappy* "The Yearling" was? It has a saccharine stupidity of style and movement. On reading over the manuscript early in the week, I thought it was hopeless, and I'd just have to drop it in Mrs. Grinnell's private canal where her gardener dumps the too-full-blown roses. On second thought, I can probably fix it, but it will be the devil of a job. But you should have told me.

I am still afraid I'll have to go home to get any work done. But even so, the trip, the change, have been worth while in giving me a fresh perspective. I don't want to go home at all——I'm very happy here. But the job has to be done. I haven't earned a vacation yet and I feel guilty. Not that any of it makes a damn bit of difference——.

We're having a gorgeous gale here this afternoon. All the fishing boats are scurrying in for shelter, right under my window. The wind is crying with the same strange sound it has over the English chalk downs. It makes me homesick for something I can't even remember.

. . . .

290. MEP to MKR (TLS: UF, 3 pp.)

June 23, 1937

Dear Marjorie:

I did not feel as if I could talk to you about your poems in the car under the circumstances, but I very much liked them,- especially "And Does My Voice" and "I Did Not Break the Mayhew Bough".- The only one I did not like is called "To A Lover" which did not seem to me to succeed. All the others had utterly sincere feeling. "The Faithless to the Unfaithful" would be one of the best excepting that so many poems of somewhat that kind are written by women.- That is a publisher's point of view, and perhaps has no value, but he gets in the habit of seeing things in relation to what else has been written so much. It does not really affect the intrinsic quality of anything. "Mountain Rain" is beautiful.[1] It only seemed to me that the last stanza, or the last two lines of it, did not justify themselves quite,- or rather fall below what was expected.

I think there is a lovely quality in all the poems, and it is only because the magazine practically publishes no poetry that I am doubtful about their taking anything,- we would have taken one or two of these in past years.- But I am sending all of them over to Logan excepting "To A Lover".

Why don't you come in sometime by yourself. We always seem to be accompanied by very strong personalities when we meet. We could talk quietly, if you would do it, in the Chatham place, or the Park Lane garden.

Always yours,

1. "Mountain Rain," *Scribner's Magazine* 104.1 (July 1938): 63. The other poems were not published.

. . . .

291. MKR to MEP (TLS, 3 pp.)

[Bayshore, Long Island]
Thursday
[June 24, 1937]

Dear Max:

Thank you for your good note. You reacted to the verses much as I hoped, and almost expected, that you would. Sara Teasdale[1] has of course put a stamp on the essentially female type of poetry, so that "The Faithless to the Unfaithful" necessarily seems faintly reminiscent. Yet women will continue to write lyrics, and the only test is whether they are good or bad. I do not like anything in which the sex of the writer is obvious. The creative imagination, fortunately, is sexless. Yet poetry is profoundly personal, and man or woman, impelled by the poetic impulse, which is the most compelling and desperate of all creative impulses, can only speak in terms and images of the personal and so, sexed, response to love and living.

You did not like "To a Lover" for the same reason that I do not like it. It is venomous and not beautiful.

I think that possibly you are wrong about "Mountain Rain". I am sure the last two lines are good and moving. In my opinion, it is the first two lines of the last stanza that spoil the poem, and I was reluctant to include it because they have never pleased me. But we agree that something is wrong in the last stanza, and I shall work it out some day. My poetry matters much more to me than my fiction, on the whole, and I shall probably do more of it as time goes on.

I was much shocked at the audacity of Thomas Moult who, in including the <verse> sonnet you used last year, (or was it two years ago) "Having Left Cities Behind Me", in his anthology, changed two pieces of punctuation, changed "those" to "these", and capitalized "Certain City".[2] I did not know an editor ever took such liberties, certainly not without consultation.

I should like very much to have a really quiet bit of talk with you. That is one reason, the principal reason, I have so often asked you to come to Florida.

You give me so much mentally, are so stimulating and understanding, that I long for free talk with you, and we have almost never had it. You have much more than I of satisfying intellectual interchange, and I have a certain need of you that you do not have of me. Any time that you are (comparatively) free, I should be most happy to talk without alien personalities about us. Drop me a note, or 'phone me, giving me perhaps a choice of time, and I'll come in just for the meeting. You wrote once of a yacht club, I think it was, overlooking the East River where the ships pass. Perhaps that would be all right——or the Park Lane garden. I associate the Chatham now with sheer confusion!

1. Sara Teasdale (1884–1933), known for her poems that evoke mood rather than meaning.
2. *The Best Poems of 1936*, ed. Thomas Moult (New York: Harcourt, Brace, 1937).

. . . .

292. MEP to MKR (TLS: UF, 1 p.)

June 25, 1937

Dear Marjorie:

I just got your letter. Thanks ever so much. I shall call you up Monday to make an appointment.

Always yours,

. . . .

293. MEP to MKR (TLS: UF, 2 pp.)

July 23, 1937

Dear Marjorie:

Last night in the Grand Central I encountered Herschel Brickell and beguiled him to drink a cocktail with me since there was fifteen minutes before train time. He told me he had had a letter from you, and that you were glad to be back in Florida,- and I hope you found a not too trying kind of weather there. He said he had great hopes for the book, and we talked about you exclusively while we drank. He is a very pleasant person to be with I always did think. I hope I shall see him occasionally under the same circumstances since he takes my train twice a week.

The Korean I told you about, Younghill Kang,[1] is coming in this afternoon with the last of his proof and I am impatient to see him in order to discover whether he has done what I felt he really must do, but had refrained from on account of some Oriental reticence,- that is, to let the reader know at the end of the book that he married the girl Tripp. I have been trying to get this done ever since the manuscript first came in, but he cannot be brought to it.

Let me know how the work goes now that you have got back to it.

Always yours,

1. Younghill Kang (1903–1972), *East Goes West* (New York: Scribners, 1937).

....

294. MEP to MKR (TLS: UF, 2 pp.)

Aug. 18, 1937

Dear Marjorie:

I had been hoping to hear from you, just to know that everything was all right,- and not to bother you about the book. I know you have reached the stage where you may have to go rather slowly. And there is plenty of time before Spring publication, but I would like to know that you found things the way you wanted them when you got back.

Everything goes on here as usual except for the—thank Heaven—unusual incident of the literary quarrel in my office.- But the Times said that Mr. Eastman ought to be accustomed to having his nose in the book, and Mr. Hemingway to being bent over a desk.[1]

Send me just a line if you can.

Always yours,

1. The famous confrontation took place on August 11, 1937, provoked by Max Eastman's statement in "Bull in the Afternoon": "Come out from behind that fake hair on your chest, Ernest." Both writers ended up on the floor, and both claimed victory (see "Hemingway Slaps Eastman in Face," *New York Times*, August 14, 1937, 15). MEP wrote to Fitzgerald of the incident: "I think Eastman does think that he beat Ernest at least at a wrestling match but in reality Ernest could have killed him, and probably would have if he had not regained his temper" (see *Dear Scott/ Dear Max*, ed. John Kuehl and Jackson R. Bryer [New York: Scribners, 1971], 238–40).

....

295. MKR to MEP (TLS, I p.)

Cross Creek
August 22 [1937]

Dear Max:

I was tempted to wire you "You have my sympathy in your great sorrow", but I was afraid it might not, at the moment, strike you funny. It seems to me the honors are all Eastman's. Hemingway very definitely proved Eastman's contention. I have found that all truly big people are gentle, because they can afford to be. I know how you must have hated being mixed up in it.

Mrs. Grinnell sent me clippings on the fracas, with this amusing and trenchant comment:

"There are many more versions, but these mention your be-loved Max. Does he have a time with his men and women? He DO. First he takes a woman off the streets in the early morning to the quiet sanctity of his home——then he has to separate two beef-eating bulls to decide if the hair on the chests is genuine or false——and incidentally to raise in my childish mind the question of what constitutes manliness. I never would have dreamed of asking any gentleman to show me the hair on his chest before I labeled him as a man and a gentleman. Well, all this comes of being old-fashioned and not keeping up with the speed of the world. I am to meet a gentleman from Washington tonight whom I have admired greatly——but I will have nothing of him until he shows me whether or not he has hair on his chest. I will NOT be behind the times."

My silence does not mean that I am not progressing. The work, by the grace of God, has gone forward with a slow steadiness in spite of many obstacles. I found the grove in good shape, everything as it should be. The book will be finished by the middle of September. I think two weeks will do for revision. There will be very little editing necessary on the new portion. I have swung back into the tone for which I aimed. If the POST does not take it——and no one else would want it——we can count on winter publication——possibly we can anyway.

. . . .

296. MKR to MEP (ALS, 2 pp.)

Cross Creek
Sept. 15 [1937]

Dear Max:——

"The Yearling" is moving along on the home-stretch, right on schedule. Ten days to two weeks will see the end of the first draft. I may be over-optimistic but I don't think revision and editing will be too difficult—————two weeks for that.

I can't thank you enough for the Kang book. I'll write you about it when I strike a hiatus.

Maxwell Perkins in the 1920s. By permission of Princeton University Library.

297. MEP to MKR (CC, I p.)

Sept. 16, 1937

Dear Marjorie:

I was delighted to get your letter with the good news about "The Yearling". I figure then, that I shall be able to read it in about a month. I certainly look forward to it.

Always yours,

. . . .

298. MKR to MEP (ALS, 3 pp. frag.)

Cross Creek
Monday
[September 27, 1937]

Dear Max:——

You are a dear to send the stimulating non-fiction along at a time, when with your wizard's understanding, you know that it comforts me and gives just the right sort of distraction.

I reached, on schedule, the number of pages that I [page or pages missing] telescope, and get two or three incidents done quickly off-stage. Now I must go back and do them over again, directly, first-hand, in Jody's own experience. There is no alternative. And if it's dull, we'll just have to cut portions. The method itself cannot be hurried.

If I can keep up the rhythm——which, over a long period of time, becomes inevitably broken by nervous exhaustion——I shall still have the actual writing done in a week or ten days. I am at the critical point of weaving together the human threads, and when that is done, the ending will be a labor of purest love, for it [remainder of letter missing]

. . . .

299. MEP to MKR (TLS: UF, 2 pp.)

Sept. 29, 1937

Dear Marjorie:

Thanks ever so much for writing. I suppose the truth is that you are at the very hardest point in the book and will have to work it out, but I wouldn't worry much about its length. And if cutting has to be done, we can talk of it later. You will have at least one reader who will not object however long it may be. We can wait the additional time that you need to finish it.

We have just published a new edition of Marcia Davenport's "Mozart".[1] You may already have read it, but if you have not, it might well be a book that you would like at present, and so I am sending it.

Always yours,

1. Marcia Davenport (1903–1996), *Mozart* (New York: Scribners, 1937).

. . . .

300. MKR to MEP (ALS, I p.)

Hawthorn, Fla.

Oct. 20 [1937]

Dear Max:—

Finished the writing last week-end and am well into the editing.

It will go quite rapidly, I think, as what seems to be needed is lots of blue pencil, and a change here and there of tone, rather than revision.

. . . .

301. MEP to MKR (CC, I p.)

Oct. 28, 1937

Dear Marjorie:

I sent you what you may think is a very interesting book,- "From These Roots" by Molly Colum.[1] It is full of ideas.

I am looking forward eagerly to getting the whole manuscript soon.

Always yours,

1. Molly Colum [Mary G. Maguire] (1887?–1957), *From These Roots* (New York: Scribners, 1937).

. . . .

302. MKR to MEP (ALS, 2 pp.)

[Cross Creek]

[November 1937]

Dear Max:——

Copying the manuscript for some reason is a nightmare. It goes as slowly as walking in quicksand, and I am getting something of the same desperate feeling.

I don't remember that copying either of the other two was such a chore.

Of course this is half again as long, and I think perhaps I am making more changes as I go along, which slows me up. I expected to revise the others, you see, after you saw them, and I am trying to put this in shape right now. Pray for my sanity another week or so! I came within a breath today of throwing the whole thing in the open fire.

. . . .

303. MEP to MKR (CC, 1 p.)

Nov. 19, 1937

Dear Marjorie:

A man came in here the other day who said you were to be in New York about the middle of November.- And so I thought maybe you were, and that you were bringing the manuscript. You didn't come and overlook us, did you? <Anyhow, I hope the manuscript will come soon, even if you do not.>

This time I am sending you a really good book, and a best seller— "America's Cook Book".[1]

Always yours,

1. *America's Cook Book,* compiled by the Home Institute, *New York Herald Tribune* (New York: Scribners, 1937).

. . . .

304. MKR to MEP (ALS, 2 pp.)

[Cross Creek]
Monday
[November 22?, 1937]

Dear Max:——

You must certainly have known some strange authors, if you thought for a moment I was capable of coming to New York with a manuscript that owes its instigation directly to you, without coming near you————

The man who talked with Miss Wyckoff is a Florida friend who was in New York, knew that I should be about through with the book, and thought *possibly* [underlined three times] I had come up with the manuscript, and didn't want to miss me if I was there. He was here yesterday.

Don't ever again believe me capable of such perfidy!!!!

. . . .

305. MKR to MEP (TLS, 1 p.)

Hawthorn, Fla.
December 2, 1937

Dear Max:

Have just sent "The Yearling" to you by the noon express. Don't remember whether your week-end begins Friday or Saturday, but thought you would want to know it would be arriving certainly no later than Saturday morning, so that you could arrange to get it and read it over the week-end.

It is going American Express, and will reach New York about 3 P.M. tomorrow, Friday the 3d., but don't know whether you can expect delivery the same afternoon or not.

There are several things I want to take up about it, but in order not to start you off with too many preconceived prejudices, will speak of only two. Please watch for, and check, spots where it gets, simply, off-key. I have pruned out much of the——sappiness, is the only word that comes to me——but here and there is a taint of it. If a phrase, or bit of dialogue, makes you *uncomfortable,* it will be that. Please check. Again, I'd suggest you ask whether any of the hunting incidents seem purposeless and uninteresting and dragged in by the heels. Most of them are part of the fabric, others may not be.

I am sending Carl Brandt a carbon at the same time. It won't take long to find out whether the *Post* is interested. They would be the only ones who could make it worth my while to serialize. No one else would find it useable in any case.

Hope you find the book reasonably good.

. . . .

306. MEP to MKR (CC, 2 pp.)

Dec. 3, 1937

Dear Marjorie:

I have just received your letter saying that the manuscript had been sent by express. But I may not get it in time for this week-end because I have got to go to Boston on a five o'clock train. It is the last train that will get me there on time, and I won't be back until Monday.- But even so, I shall read "The Yearling" eagerly and quickly.

I never thought you would let us down in any kind of way, but only that you might possibly have come to New York to see that lady fisherman,[1] or something like that, and not have had time to come in.- Even then you would have telephoned.

I hope that express company does deliver before I have to leave, for then I would enjoy the five-hour journey.

Always yours,

1. Mrs. Oliver Grinnell.

Dec. 10, 1937

Dear Marjorie:

I am only writing you to tell you that I am reading "Yearling" with the very greatest pleasure, but it did not get here until Wednesday, and I shall probably not be able to write you about it until Monday. I have read 300 pages though, and haven't the slightest doubt about it in any serious sense. I am eager to go on with it.

Always yours,

P.S. I still think that the first visit to the Forresters is not right,- is somehow unreal. But if that is so, it can easily be made real.

. . . .

Dec. 13, 1937

Dear Marjorie:

I have read the whole book, and with constantly growing interest, and taken all in all, I think the last half is better than the first, and that the book gets increasingly good.- But the very beginning now is perfect, it seems to me, and of course the father and mother, and all about that life, and Jody's on the island, are as good as can be. When you come to the Forresters, I think there gets into it—especially in that first scene—a slight element of theatricality or romanticism, or something not quite true. Couldn't you make Lem show some of his meanness in that scene even—well, he did in his reference to Oliver,— but more of it. They are very tough people, and the toughness ought to be more evident, even though they seemed fine to Jody.- And I think you ought to cut out the unseemly performance of the old lady, because there was nothing else in the book like it, and no need to be, and it would prevent the book from getting a sale that it might easily get to younger people in the end, because all the libraries and the schools would object violently to it. I would not suggest taking it out if it were in any way essentially true to the book, but it almost seems to me as if it were a little the reverse.

I think Grandma Hutto is now a first rate character, but that there does get to be an element of unrealness in everything else when Jody goes to see her. For instance, Oliver never becomes very real,- he seems romanticized. He was romantic, of course, to Jody's eyes.- But this really is not important, for he is in the book very little as a person, and more as a sort of symbol.

All the hunting, all the nature, is superb, and the whole meaning of people living in that way with so much to fight is, and the development of Jody and its outcome, is beautifully done.- I would only suggest cutting out the next to the last paragraph. I may think of other things to tell you, but the book is ready to go into type, and ought to. It is long,- 163,000 words. It might be tightened up some, but whenever I thought of taking out anything, I hated to do it.- And I think any such question better wait until we both read it in type, and get that new view of it that comes from seeing it in a new form. It is a very beautiful book, and I greatly enjoyed every minute of it. Otherwise I would have read it faster. The better a book is, the slower I go.

Always yours,

. . . .

309. MEP to MKR (TLS: UF, 2 pp.)

Dec. 17, 1937

Dear Marjorie:

I remembered that you asked me some questions in your letter of December 2nd, written when you sent the manuscript. As to the off-key quality, the points I did speak of in my letter were in regard to that element, and I think there were perhaps a few little places of that kind, but too small to give consideration except in the proof. I did also think that in relation to the whole there might have been too much hunting, and perhaps that all that that followed the flood might be reduced.- But it was so good in itself that I disliked to suggest it, and thought of that too, that it could be looked at again in the proof. I did put marks against a number of little passages in reading the manuscript, and they will be queried in the proof too. But the truth is the book is so very fine that it seemed to me there was nothing of any major importance to be criticized. The whole flow and development is wonderfully successful.- And it was a mighty hard problem too, to bring Jody through to such an ending and such complete success.

Always yours,

. . . .

310. MEP to MKR (TLS: UF, 2 pp.)

Dec. 23, 1937

Dear Marjorie:

You will be hearing soon from Edward Shenton,[1] for we have asked him to do head pieces for the chapters on "The Yearling". I had lunch with him yesterday, and I think he understands the book completely, and certainly is in love with it. He ought to do better work than he ever has, and he has done very fine work, as in the case of Hemingway's "Green Hills". We must give this book individuality so that it will stand apart, and not be thought of as just the ordinary novel. We are therefore making it also a larger size than "South Moon Under" or "Golden Apples", and this, with the decorations, will give it distinction.

After completing such a book which shows no signs of effort, but certainly must truly represent an enormous amount of it, you ought to have a merry Christmas and a happy New Year, and I hope you may.

Always yours,

1. Edward Shenton (1895–1977), artist who did the illustrations for the trade edition of *The Yearling*.

. . . .

311. MEP to MKR (CC, 1 p.)

Dec. 28, 1937

Dear Marjorie:

A beautiful box of fruit came from you, and everyone was delighted with it at my house.

We gave a big party several weeks ago for Mollie Colum whose book "From These Roots" I sent you. When "The Yearling" comes out, why don't you come up and let us give one for you.

Always yours,

. . . .

312. MEP to MKR (CC, 1 p.)

Dec. 29, 1937

Dear Marjorie:

I meant to have sent you when I last wrote, the copies of the contract for "The Yearling". I enclose them herewith.

I hope you have heard from Shenton, and I am looking forward anxiously to see what he does. But his feeling for the book was so strong, and so true, that I felt sure he would do well.

Always yours,

Hawthorn, Florida

December 29, 1937

Dear Max:

The overwhelming relief of your liking the book——. And with no criticism that involves re-arrangement. The liberation is so great that my habitual winter catastrophes seem entirely trivial.

I am delighted that Shenton is to do head pieces. His stuff will have exactly the quality that I meant to express. I hope he will do the cover, too. The jackets of the other two books made me very unhappy. I should like to have the boy and the yearling deer side by side, the boy's arm across the young deer's neck, the two looking out with the same expression of big-eyed wonder, and behind or over them the type of vegetation, of forest, that Shenton does so beautifully. Perhaps only a magnolia tree, with its big stiff leaves, rather stylized. I think this type of illustration for the cover would in itself illuminate the title. It would certainly indicate at least that the yearling in question was a yearling deer and not a yearling bull, as might be <commonly> otherwise supposed. And the connotation might register that the boy was a yearling, too. It seems to me too that black and white, or black and white with, somehow, a luminous April green, would be effective. I know I am supposed to have nothing to say about this angle of it, but I did suffer over the other jackets. And I can see so plainly what Shenton could do. I had meant to beg that either Shenton or the wood-cut artist, J. J. Lankes,[1] do such a cover. And Shenton has a certain mystic quality that would be revelatory.

You are right, of course, about the "unseemly incident". I take a perverse pleasure in putting in such things that I know perfectly well are going to have to come out. <By> eliminating that part and probably the impromptu dancing, will perhaps clear up the whole Forrester unreality.

My feeling about the hunting incidents is that their inclusion or elimination should be determined solely by the answer to the question: Does the reader recognize the beginning of another hunting episode with pleasurable anticipation, or is he bored at the thought of another, and impatient to be on with the narrative? Everyone's reaction would not be the same, and we can ask that question of the several people who have already read the manuscript.

I have not heard yet from Carl about the POST's reaction. But that needn't slow us up in any way, however it comes out.

I have waited to see whether the POST was interested, to ask for an advance, because if money should come in that way, I prefer to let royalty payments all come later. But I actually cannot get along without money more than another

Marjorie Kinnan Rawlings with her pointer Pat, in the late 1930s. By permission of
Princeton University Library.

week. I had picked and sold not much more than a hundred dollars' worth of my citrus——and my crop was short this year, too——when that vicious freeze came in. I fired my young grove two nights in succession. It was very beautiful. There was a fat-wood bonfire in the center of each square, that is, one fire to each four trees. The light from the fat pine is a rich orange, and the grove seemed to be full of bivouac fires, as regular as a geometric design. They illuminated the sky to a Prussian blue, with the palm tops against it. Facing away from the fires, the light gave my low rambling house, the orange trees and palms around it, a flat silver-gold wash, most theatrical. The cold sky was absolutely sequined with stars. It was so beautiful that it was almost worth what it cost me. Then the next two nights I was ready to fire, but at four in the morning knew I did not have to. I was up with my crew of nine men the four nights. I kept them in food and coffee and liquor, and two of the boys sang almost all night long. I saved the young grove, raising the temperature from three to seven degrees. At first all of us in the section thought our mature fruit was not injured to speak of, but as the days passed, the damage became increasingly obvious, and just before Christmas the inspectors condemned carloads of fruit, including some of mine, and inspection is now very rigid. It is hoped that within a week or two the frozen fruit will rot and fall from the trees, and the good fruit be left on for profitable picking. But sometimes it all clings tenaciously, and there is no way to ascertain the damage without cutting the individual orange. So the winter funds that I had counted on drifted into that cold night air——and the Golden Apples money has long since gone with the wind! Finances don't worry me much any more, but I must have money within a week. We can wait and see about the POST a few days, then if there is no sale ——and I almost wish there won't be——I must have an advance, much as I dislike it. I actually need a thousand dollars, for I have notes of eight hundred to be met, and a few other bills. And since I have no money to go on just now, I really should have fifteen hundred. My fruit salvage at best will not be more than two or three hundred dollars.

All kinds of small unexpected expenses have popped up. A transient worker split his foot open with an axe while cutting wood for me, and since he had nothing, and I could not let him die, and since he had lost so much blood by the time they got him to me, and I was afraid of the time it would take to get him entered as a charity case at the hospital, I simply took him to my own doctor for the necessary surgery, X-rays and dressings, and have paid the bills myself. This sort of thing does not bother me, for I have increasingly the feeling that nothing tangible belongs to us. I have supported, with work and assistance, several poor neighbors, all summer and fall, people who are too proud to go on relief and anxious to work, and it seems to me that it doesn't make a scrap of difference whether the few hundred dollars involved are in my pocket or theirs.

There will be a chapter on the freeze in the grove, and the firing, in the book I shall do some day, CROSS CREEK: A CHRONICLE. I have accumulated quite a few chapters. I write up things from time to time with that in mind. But that will be several years away.

The freeze is why I sent you grapefruit instead of oranges. With their thick skins, they are not injured by our cold. And oddly, here and there tangerines, for all their delicacy, were not hurt.

I have a more hopeless feeling about Fitzgerald since his story recently in *Esquire,* about himself, of course, and the bitter refusal of his publisher to think he is done for. He seems sunk in subjectivity. Egoism, rather. His very laughing at himself is unhealthy.[2]

Thank you for your good letters. Yes, the book did take a prodigious effort, and I can't understand it, for I knew just what I wanted to do and where I was going. But I thought I should never get it out. Toward the end, I was a little insane. But I feel marvelously now in every way. It seemed a waste of time at the moment, but I believe that going to New York when I did, and making a fresh start, was a life saver.

[Postscript] I have forgotten to thank you for all the good books. It was grand to have them. I can't see the Colum book at all, however. It seems not only arrogant and biased, but very dull. Usually I love such books.

1. J. J. Lankes (1884–1960), artist and illustrator.
2. F. Scott Fitzgerald, "In the Holidays," *Esquire* 8 (December 1937): 82, 184, 186.

1938

314. MKR to MEP (TLS, 2 pp.)

Hawthorn, Florida
January 5, 1938

Dear Max:

No word from Carl Brandt as to the POST, so I judge there is no sale. Much as I need the money, I shall be a bit relieved not to go through with the distress of serialization.

It is nice of you to want to give a publisher's party for me when the book comes out, and I should enjoy coming up then very much. Personal publicity is apt to be dangerous to any writer's integrity; for the moment he begins to fancy himself as quite a person, a taint creeps into his work. But I have no illusions about my stuff, as you know, and am grateful for any and all understanding and appreciation, and am not disturbed by it, any more than I am unduly disturbed by criticism, for I am more sharply aware of my limitations than anyone else on the outside could possibly be. The party would be a real pleasure, because of the kind of people who would be there, and it is most gracious of you to want to do it.

Have you decided yet on the publication date?

I have not heard from Edward Shenton, but I have the greatest confidence in his approach and certainly should not expect even to have any suggestions for him, except that I do visualize, as I wrote you, the cover design that seems to me effective. Of course some one else may have a better idea, and I should have an open mind about it.

I shall be especially glad to come to New York, in order to talk with you about the book that both tempts and terrifies me. It is very nebulous as yet, for I have not dared let myself go about it, for fear of getting started on the wrong track. It is a book that will have to be very good, to be good at all. It is full of pit-falls, worse even than "Golden Apples", and I am not at all sure that I am equipped to do it.

· ·

315. MEP to MKR (TLS: UF, 2 pp.)

Jan. 7, 1938

Dear Marjorie:

I am sending the first fifteen galleys today. I have really had a happy time reading them, and I have more on my desk,- up to twenty-three. We cannot fix a date of publication until the serial matter is settled, and as I understood a few days ago, the manuscript is still at the Cosmopolitan which I think had some sort of an option on it. I know Carl felt that he had to send it there before he sent it to the Post. If the way were clear, I think we would publish about the middle of March, but we cannot tell yet.

If the serial question is settled unfavorably so that you want the advance, we should gladly send it.

I have just got to the Forresters. I'll finish that first encounter with them in the galleys now here,- but I rather think that your solution is all that is necessary. It is probably the dancing that seemed unreal.

Always yours,

· ·

316. MEP to MKR (TLS: UF, 2 pp.)

Jan. 10, 1938

Dear Marjorie:

I am sending you quite a few more galleys today. As for the Forresters, I think you have the right idea about them. I think perhaps you also lay on their qualities of bigness, etc., a little too heavily, and that it will be well if you can, to cut out the adjectives "great" and "big".- Sometimes, so as to reduce the emphasis. Even before you actually get to them they have been fixed pretty well in the minds of the reader.

Another thing.- I do not know whether you ever did state the age of Jody, but I think he could easily be twelve, and I think the older you could make him without making him too old, the better, in a way. I have an idea that he was intended to be ten but wouldn't twelve do just as well? Or in fact is it necessary ever to specify his age?

It is all very fine, and the information about the way a skilled hunter acts which I suppose you acquired from that old hunter you told me about, is wonderfully interesting. Penny Baxter is a splendid character.

Always yours,

. . . .

317. MKR to MEP (TLS, 1 p.)

Hawthorn, Fla.

January 10, 1938

Dear Max:

Here is the signed contract for the YEARLING. I puzzled over the added clause at the end, providing a reduction in royalty if after two years the book sold less than five hundred copies. The difference involved is so trivial that it makes no difference to me, but I can see that the difference multiplied by a whole list of writers would be considerable from the publishing end. Yet I thought there were not many authors on each publisher's list who received the full fifteen per cent. If this is a clause being applied to everybody, to help absorb mounting publishing costs, and doesn't represent a "demotion" in your opinion of my work, I don't mind in the least, for it is certainly reasonable.

Also, in case Carl Brandt does put through a serial sale, or sale of individual chapters, before book publication, I am assuming that such sale ante-dates this contract. Of course, after publication, then some publisher-author division is only fair.

While we're on business matters, I'd like to clear up a couple of minor things.

In going over some papers recently, I found a charge against me that should not have been made, of $23.03 for excess corrections on GOLDEN APPLES. You wrote me May 28, 1935, suggesting that the book be put into proof, and changes made then, "we to bear the expense". My royalty report for April 4, 1936, deducted the above item, and I did not notice it at the time.

Also, "Benny and the Bird Dogs" has appeared several places of which no notice was given me, and "Varmints" was in "Scholastic Magazine", without notice.[1] I am wondering if no fee was paid for these, or if the small amount usually due had been over-looked.

Also, what has happened about the 75¢ edition of GOLDEN APPLES?

---

1. "Benny and the Bird Dogs," *Scholastic Magazine* 2 (March 1935): 4–6, 10; and "Varmints," *Scholastic Magazine* 31 (December 1937): 26–32, 84–85.

318. MKR to MEP (wire)

1938 JAN 11 AM 11 57
MAXWELL E PERKINS—
597 FIFTH AVE—
CANNOT WAIT ON SERIAL OUTCOME ANY LONGER PLEASE AIR MAIL AD-
VANCE TODAY MAILED SIGNED CONTRACT YESTERDAY MANY THANKS
CHARGE THIS WIRE TO MY ACCOUNT—

. . . .

319. MEP to MKR (TLS: UF, 2 pp.)

Jan. 11, 1938

Dear Marjorie:

Here is the fifteen hundred.- I think "The Yearling" did get to the Post, but that they could not use it. It is not really in the nature of a serial.[1]

I found the place where you told the age of Jody as twelve, so what I said on that point is of no consequence. If there is any fault that should be rectified, it might be that the first part of the book is in some way a little soft,- that is, up to when Jody and Penny return from Volusia. There is no definite way that this could be changed,- there is, too, an advantage in the change that comes because it accompanies Jody's experience with life. The first part ought to be happy, but it almost seems idyllic at times. Perhaps there are little things that could be done here and there that would change this if you agreed with it. Anyhow, it is the only adverse criticism I can possibly think of making, and so I do it, but only for your consideration. I do not feel much confidence in it myself, and Shenton, a very good judge, only agreed in respect to the Forresters which you are changing.

Always yours,

1. Upon the immense success of The Yearling, the editor of the New York Post changed his mind, and the novel was serialized from June 5 to July 25, 1939.

. . . .

320. MKR to MEP (ANS at bottom of a letter from Brandt and Brandt, 1 p.)

Editor's note: MKR sent MEP a letter she received from Carl Brandt dated January 10, 1938. In the letter Brandt told Rawlings of the Post's "reluctant" rejection of The Yearling for serialization. Brandt informed MKR of future plans he had for serializing the novel, but admitted that it was unlikely. He added that he did not want to interfere with MEP's plans for publication. The following is at the bottom of the Brandt letter.

[Cross Creek]

[January 1938]

Dear Max:—

Let's hurry right ahead on the book, ignoring serialization. I can't think of any other magazine which would consider the book without drastic cutting, and I should not agree to that at any price. So go ahead. I am really relieved about this.

. . . .

321. MKR to MEP (ALS, 3 pp.)

[Cross Creek]

[January 1938]

Dear Max:—

I know just what you mean about the "softness" of some of the early part of the book. It's the quality, or rather, lack of quality, that I asked you to watch for, and I was hoping you would put your finger on the specific passages or lines that did the damage, as you did in other respects in criticizing my first draft of *South Moon Under*.

It is devilishly hard to get rid of, and a certain amount of it is unquestionably desirable and necessary, for contrast with the approaching tragedies and attendant maturity for the boy.

Let me keep the proofs as long as you possibly can, so that I can work on this carefully.

. . . .

322. MEP to MKR (CC, 3 pp., draft)

Jan. 17, 1938

Dear Marjorie:

The reduction of royalty after two years to 10% on any printing of less than 500 copies is something that we now put in all our contracts where a 15% royalty is paid, so that when we get to small printings in which the cost per copy is, of course, increased, we can still afford to make them instead of having to let the book go out of print as we formerly did. We used, when books got to the point where printings were too small, to write to the authors and make a new agreement to reduce the royalty.- But there never was an instance where an author did not agree for the sake of keeping the book in print, and we thought it simpler to make it a part of the regular agreement in advance.

I shall have the $23.03 added to the February royalty report. The charge went through in the regular routine and I had forgotten all about our agreement.

As to the reprinting of "Benny and the Bird Dogs" and "Varmints" I shall have to inquire of the magazine. There certainly must have been a fee. I shall let you know.

I am sending the last of the galleys today, but I have not read beyond 104 myself. I am reading the rest in duplicate, and will send on anything that I think of.- But I do think that the next to the last paragraph of the book is unnecessary and that the effect is better without it.- That I marked.

Shenton is coming in tomorrow with some of the drawings.

Always yours,

· ·

323.　　MEP to MKR (CC, 3 pp., frag.)

Jan. 17, 1938

Dear Marjorie:

The reduction of royalty after two years to 10% on any printing of less than 500 copies is something that we now put in all our contracts where a 15% royalty is paid, so that when we get to small printings in which the cost per copy is, of course, increased, we can still afford to make them instead of having to let the book go out of print as we formerly did. Recently, when books got to the point where printings were too small, we wrote to the authors and made a new agreement with the reduced royalty. But there never was an instance where an author did not agree for the sake of keeping the book in print, and we thought it simpler to cover the point in advance by making it a part of the regular agreement.

I shall have the $23.03 added to the February royalty report. The charge went through in the regular routine and I had forgotten all about our agreement. A report on the sales of the 75¢ edition of "Golden Apples" is due in January.

As to the reprinting of "Benny and the Bird Dogs" and "Varmints" I shall inquire of the magazine. There certainly must have been a fee. I will let you know.

I am sending the last of the galleys today, but I have not read beyond 104 myself. I am reading the rest in duplicate, and will send on anything that [remainder of letter missing]

Editor's note: This version of the letter, while similar to the draft preceding it, contains substantive differences.

. . . .

324. MEP to MKR (TLS: UF, 2 pp.)

Jan. 18, 1938

Dear Marjorie:

The trouble is, I am afraid of hurting the story. Now here are a couple of places marked which I noticed at the beginning, but hated to point out. Perhaps you could find something else to have him say instead of that about the little boy, on galley four. Then on galley six, about being pretty.- I think it is all a little too idyllic, and a little soft.- And yet it is part of such excellent dialogue. But you might fix it and take out the softness, and not lose anything.- One of the men who read the book here said that he thought it was practically flawless.

But we must not get the book out late, so don't keep the proofs long.

Always yours,

. . . .

325. MEP to MKR (TLS: UF, 3 pp.)

Jan. 22, 1938

Dear Marjorie:

I had meant to write you sooner that I have read all the rest of the proof, and that I found nothing to say except in praise, so far as Jody and Penny's story goes. It did seem to me the burning of the Hutto house was told hurriedly, and not very fully or satisfactorily explained. Was Oliver there to see it? It would not seem like him not to make some effort to prevent it. This instance seemed hurried and perhaps you could do some good there.- But even that is off the main story, and the main story is splendid, and when the trouble begins with Flag, it is simply masterly,- the whole episode which led up to the shooting, and the shooting, and what Jody did afterward, and the ending.

We have eight of the chapter headings from Shenton, and they look very good, I think.

Always yours,

P.S. I hate now to begin on the side of publishing that hasn't to do with the intrinsic qualities of the story, but with business, but such great harm is done a book if it comes out late. So I have to urge you to get the proofs back. I am sorry to do it, but it is so important.

· ·

326. MKR to MEP (TLS, with holograph additions, 2 pp.)

Hawthorn, Florida

January 23, 1938

Dear Max:

I have finished corrections on the proofs, and now I am going back over them again with as cold an eye as possible, to eliminate as much as I can of the flaccid quality to which you and I are both so sensitive. Isn't it odd that a writer can put down things that he would not tolerate in another's writings?

But in reading the whole thing as a unit, I realize that the quality, almost an indefinable one, is pervasive of the complete book, for the reason that that quality was actually a salient ingredient in my own feeling. And to a certain degree, I intended that quality, and meant to do it that way. What actually happened was that the boy became a very real boy, and less of a symbol of the transition from childhood into manhood, which was the thing I wanted to express. The first chapter, which is idyllic, is keyed as I intended, originally, to key the whole thing. I was disturbed when I found the boy becoming so actual, fearing disharmony. Whether the quality of actuality is more valuable than the idyllic quality, is perhaps a debatable question. But I do see the story, within myself, poetically, and I am afraid there is no getting away from it, even when there is too much of it. But there are many places which need a greater stiffness, and I shall supply it whenever I can.

Oddly, the two spots that you pointed out, at my request, I intended humorously, especially <his> the boy's saying that his mother was "purtiest" with a dish in her hand, because I meant to portray her as anything in the world but a pretty woman! I never intended him to think she was pretty. But if the effect is as it was on you, that settles it. Out it goes. But I was amazed to have you pick out what I meant facetiously, as instances of the thing we agreed should be eliminated.

I shall have to take an extra day, too, to go to see the [old] hunter, the only one alive of the two old men who gave me so much valuable hunting lore, to check two or three technical matters.

Unfortunately, I have to take Tuesday off to go to St. Petersburg, where I am giving a short talk at the meeting of the Florida Historical Society on the use of Florida historical material for creative writers. I felt obligated to accept the invitation, as I expect to use the Society ruthlessly in gathering material, if I do the book I have in mind.

But I can promise to have the complete set of proofs in your hands next Monday morning, Jan. 31. Would it be of much advantage to have me send on the galleys as I go over them again? Because of my trip to see the old hunter, only a couple of days would be saved.

I have no new photographs, but will try to have something taken in St. Petersburg. I never got around to having any done in New York. Why plaster a woman's face over very much of the advertising, anyway? It's not that I'm modest, probably the opposite, for I like to think that my work is more attractive than my face——certainly than my figure. So few writers express in their faces the best of their work.

I can't emphasize too strongly the necessity of the jacket's revealing the meaning of the title. Once the book has been read, there's no question but that "The Yearling" expresses it exactly, and with a desirable over-tone. But beforehand, it doesn't register any too well, I'm sorry to say. One man, an English professor, who inquired the title, asked if I wasn't afraid it would seem to indicate a yearling bull, which people think of first.[1]

Shall I see the Shenton drawings? I can't help wondering what he will do about suggesting the type of vegetation, which is so peculiar to the section. And since I have been at great pains to be accurate about physical details, any foliage or trees used, as Shenton uses them so beautifully, should certainly be true to the locale. He may know Florida, but it is different in different regions, and the vegetation of the scrub is like nothing anywhere. I can't help feeling uneasy, on that account only.

1. Clifford Lyons, chair of the English Department at the University of Florida.

. . . .

327. MEP to MKR (TLS: UF, with holograph postscript, 2 pp.)

Jan. 26, 1938

Dear Marjorie:

I have seen a lot of Shenton's pictures, about fifteen. At any rate they are the very best work he ever did, there is no doubt about it. They won't, of course, be in any sense literally accurate, for they are not intended to be, but wholly impressionistic.

I thought that where he said his mother was the purtiest with a dish in her hand, was fine. The place I meant to mark was where he said, "I'm purty, Ma." That too was humorous, of course, on his part. I knew that, but I thought the effect might be wrong a little, in intensifying the idyllic quality of the first part.

Everyone here who has read the book, and now a good many have, is very enthusiastic about it.

The best thing you could do to hasten the proof would be to send it back as you read it, no matter how little at a time.

Always yours,

. . . .

328. MEP to MKR (TLS: UF, 3 pp.)

Jan. 28, 1938

Dear Marjorie:

A great part—over eighty galleys—has come back, and I think you have done nothing but good in the corrections.- You won't lose the symbolic quality of the book at all on account of them, and you ought not to, but the reader ought to get that sense unconsciously, or almost.- And I think probably he will.

About the fire: it doesn't need much change, but one feels as if you hurried over it as if it were a necessary part of the scaffolding of the story. It is important only in that way really, but the reader ought not to be conscious of that.

We have now had twenty of Shenton's pictures,- very good too—with some thirteen or so to come.

Always yours,

[Postscript] I'll tell you what The Yearling has done for me. You know how much there is to worry about when one goes to bed *these* nights.- But I [my] mind often goes to The Yearling;- the country, people, & hunts- & then all is good & happy. Now, that's a test of how good a book is. Max

CHARLES SCRIBNER'S SONS
PUBLISHERS
597 FIFTH AVENUE, NEW YORK

Jan. 28, 1938

Dear Marjorie:

A great part--over eighty
galleys--has came back, and I think
you have done nothing but good in the
corrections.- You won't lose the
symbolic quality of the book at all
on account of them, and you ought not
to, but the reader ought to get that
sense unconsciously, or almost.- And
I think probably he will.

About the fire: it doesn't
need much change, but one feels as
if you hurried over it as if it were
a necessary part of the scaffolding
of the story. It is important only
in that way really, but the reader

No. 328 (MEP on *The Yearling*). By permission of University of Florida Libraries.

ought not to be conscious of that.

We have now had twenty of
Shenton's pictures,- very good too
--with some thirteen or so to come.

Always yours,

Max

To Mrs. Marjorie K. Rawlings

I'll tell you what The Yearling has done for me. You know how much there is to worry about when one goes to bed these nights. — But I mind often goes to the Yearling; — the country, people, & hunts — & then all is good & happy. Now, that's a test of how good a book it is

Max

329. MKR to MEP (ALS, 3 pp.)

> [Cross Creek]
> Monday
> [January 31, 1938]

Dear Max:—

Your note, hurrying the proofs, just received. I have helped the first part a great deal in many minor changes and deletions, and I'll get off a good batch of proofs to you tomorrow.

I am tempted to pass up making a check with the old hunter, as I don't really believe I have any errors of consequence. Most of the woods and animal lore I used was already more or less familiar to me anyway.

I am also cutting down on my time in St. Petersburg, planning to arrive there just in time for my talk, then leaving immediately.

I guess I had a false feeling of hastelessness in not digging in hard on the proofs earlier.

[Postscript] I'll try to fix the Hutto house burning better, but I don't think much should be made of it. I'll make it clear that Oliver was not there.

. . . .

330. MKR to MEP (ALS, 2 pp.)

> Hawthorn, Fla.
> Feb. 2, 1938

Dear Max:—

I am struggling with the house-burning episode. It is much easier to edit than to add, at this stage!

The rest of the corrections are made, and as soon as I get that other fixed up, today or tomorrow, I'll get the rest of the proofs right off to you.

Will you mark a "Stet" beside the moot sentence, "That's the way you're purtiest," if you want it in. I had deleted it before you wrote that it was all right.

The things you write about the book are most comforting.

[Postscript] *Please* [underlined three times] let me see the jacket design, or tell me about it.

[Cross Creek]
[February 1938]

Dear Max:

You were right about the bad psychology in having Oliver Hutto take the house-burning lying down. It was absolutely not in character. It would, however, I believe, be entirely in character for Grandma Hutto to use her head to get him out of greater tragedy, as I have had her do in the insert. I do hope you will think it is now handled properly.

On page 3 of the insert for galley 102, where Penny says to Grandma, "Ol' lady," he said. "Ol' lady—— Did I have the sense you got——" I haven't had time to decide whether I want to leave off the "Did I have the sense you got——". If you want that out, delete it for me.

. . . .

FEB. 3, 1938
MRS. MARJORIE K. RAWLINGS
ISLAND GROVE, FLORIDA
GALLEYS RECEIVED THROUGH ONE HUNDRED ONE. WILL THE OTHER
SEVENTEEN COME SOON?

. . . .

1938 FEB 3 PM 3 18
MAXWELL E PERKINS—
597 FIFTH AVE—
REMAINING GALLEYS BEING AIR MAILED TODAY—

. . . .

Feb. 4, 1938

Dear Marjorie:

I shall try to describe the jacket. I'll send it to you as soon as we can get the right colors. The background is yellow, but at present it is too lemon a yellow, and we must get it like one of those yellow flowers you would know the name of. The title is strong in black, and your name. In the center is a panel with a green background which shows Jody carrying the baby fawn, and behind him the house and sheds etc., small, and a background of pines of the Southern sort. On each side of this panel, faintly rendered in white, are flamingoes, some in flight, and others about to fly. I shall send you the jacket though, once we have the colors right.

The last proofs haven't yet come but I suppose they will any moment.

Always yours,

. . . .

335. MKR to MEP (ALS, 7 pp.)

Hawthorn, Fla.

Feb. 6, 1938

Dear Max:—

I cannot understand your not having received the last galley proofs by Friday noon. They went out Thursday afternoon air-mail special delivery on a train that connects easily with the N.Y. mail plane that gets into New York at 8 the following morning. If you do not have them, wire me at once.

The Shenton drawings are very lovely. I like particularly the heading for the second chapter, and the one showing Ma Forrester among her sons. Jody looks too dainty for my conception, and of course the sink-hole isn't quite right, but it would be impossible for Rembrandt or Corot to please me completely <without having seen the country>, which is too unique to be done from the imagination, or from any second-hand knowledge. But I am sure no one but myself could find any serious fault. The deer, somehow, doesn't look like a Florida deer. The ears and tail aren't right.

But the quality of the drawings is everything exquisite. Certainly it is better to have them so beautiful, than to have mere factual sketches. I can only wish Shenton could have come down. He could have made the trip itself for $50 to $75, and then been my guest. He would be immensely stirred by places I could have showed him. However, nothing is too seriously wrong. You think I'm needlessly fussy about my use of fact in fiction, but after all, nobody would put a Baltimore oriole in a drawing of Alaska. And while the book is (we hope) literature, and straight fiction, the details and the setting are true, as I think they should be. The Florida Historical Society has put both my other books in their library, which is amusing when you remember the howl first made of my "libeling" Florida when "Cracker Chidlings" appeared.

I left an unraveled end in Grandma Hutto's admirer, Easy Ozell, and am enclosing a brief insert to take care of him.

I have formed what I hope is a real friendship with Robert Frost and his family. They are in Gainesville for the winter. I spent the day with them yesterday, and I was shocked, as he had been, at the news that Thomas Wolfe went to Harper's for a large advance.[1] No wonder you thought me capable of coming to New York and not coming near you! I didn't realize how truly I spoke when I snapped at you that you must have known some very strange authors. Robert Frost and I both take it as a very menacing sign for Wolfe himself.

No advance could make up for losing you as an editor and critic. Then the damned advance has to be earned, and that's like paying for a dead horse. I did hate to have to ask for one, myself, for that reason. And after all Wolfe owes you——. His artistic future certainly hangs in a perilous balance.

The weather is heavenly, the orange trees just coming into bloom, and the yellow jessamine all over the woods, red-birds singing—— I'll be glad when the book is really out of the way and I can get on the lakes and rivers and in the woods, with a free mind.

I do think the physical make-up of the book is very impressive.

1. Wolfe moved to Harpers at the end of 1937.

. . . .

336. MEP to MKR (TLS: UF, 4 pp.)

Feb. 9, 1938

Dear Marjorie:

The proof got here in good time, anyhow. I was mystified that air mail didn't travel faster on that occasion, but it has all ended rightly. I thought the change you made about the fire and Oliver was excellently done.- In fact, I think in all your corrections you did nothing but good throughout. I was mighty glad and relieved too, to hear that you liked the pictures.- For I liked them a great deal, but knew that they must be far from literally accurate. Now we are going into page proof fast.

As to Tom: the note in Time was very unfair to him. He could have had the same advance from us, and knew it. There was nothing mercenary in what he did, and I don't think that he or I or anybody, really understands why he did it. He has a chaotic mind, and what rule<s> him are subconscious forces. But there were these three elements in it: the libel suit which he always strangely thought we got him into, although it seemed to us that he got us into it, and we had to pay for it; the desire which was very strong, to use us as material in a book,- and this may have been the largest influence upon him; and also a really fine and subconscious desire which I sensed, to tear himself loose from a state of dependence which he had got into toward us, and which wasn't right. We did not bring this about, but it just naturally developed out of his nature and circumstances, and he resented the fact that he had become so dependent, and I think that this was a very strong motive in what he did,- a kind of desperate tearing himself loose in order to stand up alone.- And of course that is what he ought to do, in fact, and must do, if he is to become a really great writer. Naturally the whole thing was a very bitter experience for me, and harmful in many ways (at the same time, it freed me from a burden that I never realized was so great until it was gone) but I can easily imagine a biography of Tom written twenty years from now that would ascribe this action to this instinctive and manly determination to free all his bonds and stand up alone. Anyhow—apart from the writing about people—Tom never does anything that is consciously mean. He has a magnificent equipment for rationalization, but he would never act on a sheer mercenary basis.

By the way, he won his lawsuit with the manuscript agent which had been tormenting him for the last two years. It was tried yesterday. I met Tom at his hotel to go over with a couple of others who were to be witnesses and he was just all full of worry and agony and resentment against the cruelties of fate, much the way he was when you saw him last summer. But the trial really was a foregone conclusion. The agent was simply annihilated,- it was really tragic for him. He had no support at all.- So then we went up to Cherio's[1] and celebrated the victory.-

Well, the next thing I must let you know is when we expect to publish, and then we can plan for the tea.

Always yours,

1. Cherio's, a New York restaurant where MEP lunched almost daily.

· ·

337. MKR to MEP

Hawthorn, Florida
Wednesday
[February 16, 1938]

Dear Max:

I've let Dr. Holt rope me in again to read on the Animated Magazine at Rollins College this coming Sunday.[1]

Would you consider it good or bad policy to read an incident from "The

Yearling"? The audience is always about 3500 people. If you think it is all right, and not against customary publishing policy, would you read the dog and gun trading incident, or one of the more idyllic incidents?

I'll appreciate your giving me your opinion by return air mail so that I can wire Rollins <my> the title of the reading.

Thanks a lot. I'll write you at length in a day or two, and the rest of the proofs will reach you Friday and Saturday.

Editor's note: At bottom of letter in MEP's hand: "Bk of mo Club / tea April 1 / front matter."

1. MKR read from *The Yearling;* reported in *Animated Magazine* 11 (February 20, 1938): 1–4.

....

338. MEP to MKR (TS for wire)

FEB. 17, 1938

MRS. MARJORIE RAWLINGS

ISLAND GROVE, FLORIDA

REJOICE WITH YOU THAT BOOK OF MONTH CLUB HAS TAKEN YEAR-LING FOR APRIL. PLEASE RUSH BACK PAGE PROOF AND PREPARE FOR TEA AROUND THE END OF MARCH.

....

339. MKR to MEP (TLS, 1 p.)

Hawthorn, Fla.
Feb. 18, 1938

Dear Max:

The book of the month selection is a most pleasant surprise. I had never even thought of that possibility. We are really very lucky to have it happen.

I am delighted with the Shenton drawings. He got a marvelous quality in the one showing Jody cajoling his mother, and the bear cubs are enchanting. Do tell him for me how happy I am to have my text interpreted so beautifully.

Max, are you tired of being told that you are a truly wonderful person? Your letter about Wolfe's desertion revealed, not only his character, which you intended, but your own nobility. It is an impressive document. But poor Tom ——. Doesn't he even suspect that he can't run away from himself? The only salvation for any of us is in fighting our particular battles on the spot.

The last of the page proofs went air mail yesterday. They should reach you today. I imagine that the others that were delayed were carelessly handled on the mail train to Jacksonville and went on to New York parcel post.

I know you will be wanting something in the way of a useable picture. I'll send you tomorrow the negative of an informal snapshot with my two hunting dogs that perhaps you can use, and I'll try to get you a formal picture next week.

. . . .

340. MEP to MKR (TLS: UF, 4 pp.)

Feb. 18, 1938

Dear Marjorie:

The proof has all come back.- All we need now is the front matter, and we shall send you proof of that today, and of course that won't take you any time at all.

I hope the telegram I sent you yesterday gave you great pleasure.- It certainly did me. It is wonderfully good fortune because it assures the book the success it could only have missed by not getting the word of mouth advertising necessary.- But with the distribution of between seventy and ninety thousand copies, we are sure of that. We were always sure of the book being loved if it had readers, and now we know that it will. It was also great good fortune that they took it for April.- They might have taken it for May or June, which would not have been nearly so favorable. But now we have to work fast because of the large printing, certainly more than 100,000 copies.

I think it excellent policy to read from "The Yearling" and I think if you just asked me what to read—assuming that a considerable part of the audience is masculine—I should have said the visit of Penny and Jody to the Forresters, and the swapping of the dog for the gun. I think it would be better, but if you could read two, perhaps the next best would be that episode which ended with Penny and Jody seeing the flamingoes dance.- That would be one of the best pieces that could stand by itself.- Of course the whole final bear hunting would be fine, but the significance of Slewfoot would not be known except to one who read the book right through.- But I would say the best of all was the one you named. If you are introduced, as I suppose you will be, I think it would be wise to have it said that the publication date was April first, and that the book had been selected from a couple of hundred offerings by the Book of the Month Club.- And by the way, they are after us for pictures. Did you have some done? This personal publicity is simply one of the penalties of such success, and has to be borne.

Will you come up for a tea on April first, which is a Friday?

Always yours,

P.S. The press is asking for the galley proofs which did not come back with the pages. Will you send these along?

. . . .

341. MEP to MKR (ANS: UF, 1 p.)

[February 18?, 1938]

Dear Marjorie:-

I'd meant to put in my letter that Shenton did a fine bear to take the place of the other one. Shenton said The Yearling was such a book as Mark Twain would have written if he'd been a good enough writer.- Max

. . . .

342. MKR to MEP (TLS, with holograph addition, 2 pp.)

Hawthorn, Florida

February 21, 1938

Dear Max:

The reading at Rollins seemed to go well. It was a magnificent day and the outdoor audience was over 5,000. I felt afterward that I had made a tactical error in using the dog-trade incident instead of something more representative of the over-tones of the book, for by the time I had pruned it into ten minutes' reading time to make a complete unit of it, my own reaction to it was of something faintly cheap. It seemed to me a sort of *manufactured* humor. Yet the very serious things have never seemed to me to go over at those affairs. When the visiting preachers go religious, and the visiting dramatists go solemn, and the visiting poets go lyric, the effect is somehow embarrassing and blatant. <lengthy illegible excision> Every time I do a vaudeville act, I swear it's the last time——. (I deleted an unkind remark about such performances.)

The things all of you write me about The Yearling, and the Book of the Month Club choice, make me very happy and very humble. The only reason I can accept it as even remotely deserved, is that I all but sweat blood in doing it. I do not see how any writer could work in greater agony and effort than I did on it, and this is strange to me, for no writer could ever have a clearer conception than I did of what I wanted to do and where I was going. But to make the intangible tangible, to pick the emotion out of the air and make it true for others, is both the blessing and the curse of the writer, for the thing between book covers is never as beautiful as the thing he imagined.

April first will be all right for the tea.

I suppose the front matter was only for me to see. I shouldn't know how to correct it in any case. The cover drawing is lovely.

Your Mr. Burke[1] in a very generous letter says that he thinks the book should have a good sale in England. Will you see that we don't get mixed up this time and that Faber and Faber pass on their verdict so that Carl Brandt can take over the English rights if they don't want it? I always thought that Carl could have placed Golden Apples in England if we had been informed that Faber and Faber weren't publishing, while the book was still doing moderately well in this country.

I wish you could be in Florida now. It is so beautiful that it is almost unbearable. The orange bloom is heavy this spring, so that the trees are white with it, and the fragrance, especially at night or just after a rain, is overwhelming. The yellow jessamine is in blossom in the hammocks, and the red-birds have begun to sing again. I am glad I don't have to leave it all to come to New York just yet. I think I shall drive up, and by that time the north should be having the first of its own spring. I hope there will be lilacs in bloom when I come. I have missed them more than anything else in the tropics.

Editor's note: At top of letter in Perkins's hand: "*Eng. Publ.* / List for the tea."

1. W. J. Burke, an editor at Scribner.

. . . .

343. MKR to MEP (TLS, 1 p.)

[Cross Creek]
Tuesday
[February 22, 1938]

Dear Max:—

Will have some photographs in your hands Saturday morning that I think will be all right. Discovered a very fine photographer who took formal poses today and is coming to my place in the morning for pictures in my garden etc.

Feb. 23, 1938

Dear Marjorie:

The front matter came back, so now the way is entirely clear.- We have already cast about half the pages, and shall soon be printing.

The English publication is being looked after, and by Brandt & Brandt. I sent Miss Baumgarten a set of the page proof some days ago, but told her that it was not final because you had not then returned the reader's set.- But I imagine that the English publisher—and I am sure you will have one—will set from a finished copy.

One thing you ought to do: make out a list of your friends in this neighborhood, or anywhere else for that matter, who should be invited for the first of April. I am glad it is so lovely in Florida. It will be nothing approaching it in April here, but some of the drive up will be beautiful, even perhaps until you get as far as Washington.

Yours always,

. . . .

[Cross Creek]
Thursday
[February 24, 1938]

Dear Max:—

Have just chosen proofs on the photographs and there are several I think you will really like. The prints will be sent air-mail tomorrow and should reach you Saturday morning. Please don't let anybody use again the awful one used in the Shop Talk.

. . . .

March 1, 1938

Dear Marjorie:

I am enclosing a check for five thousand dollars which represents your half of the payment made by the Book of the Month Club. It may be that "The Yearling" will go so well that you will receive a further payment later. I thought you might want us to take out the fifteen hundred advance from this, but it seemed safer to send you the full amount. It makes no difference to us: the advance will be easily covered anyway on publication in the regular trade orders.

I thought some of the photographs were very good indeed, and we shall probably be able to use all of them in one way or another. I am most impatient to see a finished book, but we won't get one until the 15th, and then I shall send you a copy by air mail.

Don't forget to send me a list of people who ought to come to the tea.- And will you have a place to stay? We can arrange for one if you want us to, and we are all looking forward to seeing you.

Always yours,

. . . .

347. MKR to MEP (TLS, 2 pp.)

Hawthorn, Florida
March 2, 1938

Dear Max:

Hope you aren't disappointed in the pictures I sent. I thought I looked very kind and intelligent, which is as much as we could hope for, and I did think the photographer got some good background effects at my place. He was interested in the job, and made very cheap prices, so I had him make up glossy prints of anything I thought usable, to give you a choice. The ducks in the one picture are wild Mallards, and I think it is not usual for them to become so tame that they will eat out of anyone's hand, not to say lap. Their wings have never been clipped, and while they fly back and forth across my house——always once or twice during the night!——and through the grove, they make no move to leave, and sleep on the grass outside my bedroom window. It almost kills me to eat them, and I usually have a slice of bacon instead when I serve them, but when there is a preponderance of drakes, I have to kill them off, for they are terribly lusty and almost kill the duck-hens, when there is more than one drake to three ducks. The brutes did kill one lovely pale blonde duck, who seemed to be the favorite.

If the picture is used showing me stooping by a patch of daisies in my garden, the circles under the eyes should be touched up on the negative.

It doesn't particularly matter now that I am to be free financially again, but shouldn't the pictures be paid for as advertising? Heaven knows, I should never have had any for my own amusement. I enclose my receipts, and if you think this should be done, reimbursement can be made me on my next report.

I did not receive my February report. Isn't there somebody except you I should bother about these details?

Whitney sent me the ad in the Publisher's Weekly,[1] and it did not look to me as though my full name appeared on the end of the book, the part that shows from a book-case. This is my one peculiarity, I think, or vanity, whatever you want to call it, of wanting the full name, for you know I always regretted not having used just "Marjorie Kinnan" to write under, and I want the middle name used always where it shows. I spoke of this for "Golden Apples" and must really insist on it.

Perhaps the cut of the jacket as used in this ad is just a drawing. But even if printing has begun on the jacket, I must have it that way. I'm hoping it's already all right.

I'll send you friends' names for the tea in a day or so. There will be only a few, no more than ten, perhaps less, for there is no reason to invite anyone who does not have literary interests, as I know it will be writers and editors etc. who will be there.

I noticed in Canby's very fine review that he calls the period "the decades after the Civil War before Florida became what Florida is now."[2] I shall be interested in seeing which reviewers notice that the period is actually one year, almost to the day——the year in the boy's life, which, through its happenings, takes him across what Penny calls "the state line" from boyhood into incipient maturity.

1. *Publishers' Weekly* 133 (January 29, 1938): 605.
2. Henry Seidel Canby, "*The Yearling,*" *Book-of-the-Month Club News* (March 1938): 1–2.

. . . .

348. MEP to MKR (TS for wire)

MARCH 3, 1938

MRS. MARJORIE RAWLINGS

ISLAND GROVE, FLORIDA

SATURDAY REVIEW ANXIOUS TO PRINT FIRST BEAR HUNT[1] STOP CIRCULATION INSIGNIFICANT BUT STANDING HIGH AND SUPPORT OF STAFF FOR BOOK VALUABLE STOP PAY ONLY THIRTY DOLLARS BUT ALL YOURS STOP THINK IT DESIRABLE ALL THINGS CONSIDERED [STOP] PLEASE WIRE

1. "Bear Hunt," *Saturday Review of Literature* 17.20 (March 12, 1938): 10–12.

349. MEP to MKR (CC, 2 pp.)

March 3, 1938

Dear Marjorie:

I think we ought to pay for the pictures too, and will see that it is done, and that you are repaid when the next royalties come due. I did like the pictures,- but you had not got my letter saying so.

The name was omitted from the back of the book, because it is the custom only to use one name there. But we shall make the correction and no copies will go out except with Marjorie Kinnan Rawlings wherever the name occurs. We have used that cut of the cover without the name, but we shall correct that as soon as the cover is made right, and the jacket, and we can make a new photograph.

Always yours,

P.S. I enclose a memorandum about the reprinting of stories, from the Magazine.

. . . .

350. MEP to MKR (TLS: UF, 2 pp.)

March 4, 1938

Dear Marjorie:

I am sending you the royalty report herewith and also a check for the amount due, including the cost of the photographs and a cancellation of the charge for corrections in "Golden Apples". We are working on the ads now. On the day of publication there will be one of about one-third of a page, and in the following week, a full page. If the Book of the Month Club had not taken the book, we might have reversed the order so as to give the biggest push at the beginning, but we thought we would get better value by letting the Book of the Month Club subscribers have time to get into the book and begin talking about it,- that the full page with the backing of publicity from the distribution would count for more.

Always yours,

351. MKR to MEP (wire)

1938 MAR 5 PM 12 38
MAXWELL PERKINS—
597 5 AVE—
MY OWN FEELING IS THAT NO EXCERPT FROM THE YEARLING WOULD
CONVEY ANY VERY REPRESENTATIVE OR FAVORABLE IMPRESSION OF
BOOK AS WHOLE STOP FOR MY SELF SHOULD REJECT PROPOSAL STOP
IF YOU PERSONALLY FEEL CERTAIN ENOUGH OF VALUE GO AHEAD AS
YOUR JUDGEMENT WOULD BE BETTER THAN MINE—

Editor's note: Single word, "EXCERPT," appears at bottom of telegram.

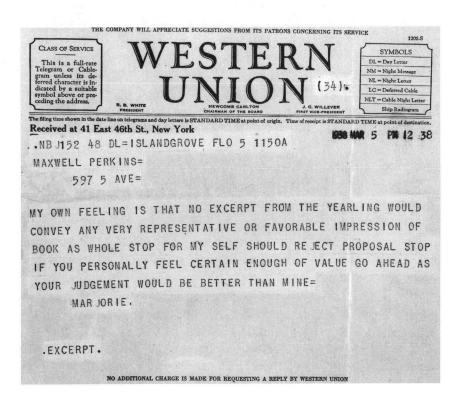

No. 351 (response to no. 348). By permission of Princeton University Library.

April 7, 1938

Dear Marjorie:

You got away just in time.- It began to snow Tuesday night and everyone took it for a joke. But there were four inches of snow on the ground this morning. It was the wintriest day of 1937–8. You left your cigarette case in the office of May Cameron[1] at the New York Evening Post, and it will be sent to you as soon as we are sure you are home, either by her or by us. I hope you didn't worry, but I don't think you do any worrying about possessions anyhow.

Indications for "The Yearling" are good,- little reorders are appearing. I am enclosing herewith an extremely fine and discerning review. James Gray[2] is one of the best reviewers there are, though sometimes erratic, I have thought.- This is very fine, and you ought to read it.

Always yours,

1. May Cameron, book reviewer at the *New York Post.*
2. James Gray of the *St. Paul Dispatch.* Review not seen.

. . . .

Hawthorn, Florida
April 23, 1938

Dear Max:

A wire from Carl Brandt says he has sold "The Yearling" to Metro Goldwyn Mayer[1] for thirty thousand. I think he was wise to do it, for the field is limited at best of such a story, especially one that hinges on a young boy.

It is heavenly to be home again. I found everything in fine shape, the dogs in splendid condition, the young grove thriving. There has been no rain for three weeks, however, and my bean crop that I have on shares will be a loss. But the weather is "prosperous for a rain" and it is amazing what growing things can do with one good wetting. My flower garden had been well cared for and my shabby farmhouse is so full of flowers that Goldfarb's would look like a dime store beside it. It is our loveliest time of the year and there's no place in the world I'd rather be at this moment.

I did have a gorgeous time in New York, and in Louisville, too, but something in me is increasingly restless on streets and within walls. I loved seeing some few of you, and meeting some few others. I had a beautiful note from Malvina Hoffman. I have the feeling that our paths will cross again and that perhaps we shall be friends. Something of the quality of her work is in her personality.

If anything could tempt me away again soon, it would be an invitation that came this morning from my brother. As I think I told you, he is building up a system of guided hunting and fishing expeditions in Alaska. He has four yachts under charter. He is leaving soon for from one to three months, to make a colored film of the places where he will go, a film that will be shown at such places as the Explorers' Club, and he wants me to go with him. He is using a small fast boat and says it will be hard going, but of course fascinating. The picture-hunt would be more to my taste than a shooting expedition. Yet it makes me unhappy to go too long without working, so I shall try to resist the temptation to join him, and settle down to a hard summer's work, instead.

The publisher of the OCALA BANNER, a small newspaper which covers Ocala and the rural territory, wrote asking for a copy of "The Yearling" for review. I think it would be worth while to send it to him. Harris Powers, editor and publisher, OCALA BANNER, Ocala, Fla. It was he who took up the cudgels for me against the STAR, when I was accused of writing about people who didn't exist——.

I want to pass on to you the nicest compliment I've had about the book. The twelve-year-old son of my Louisville friends[2] was half-way through it. He said to his mother, "Mom, she expresses it so good." His mother said, "Expresses what?" He said, "She expresses so good the way I feel."

That seemed to me praise from headquarters. He was finishing the book when I was there, and said he couldn't bear to have it end. He wanted it to go on forever. I guess there's no question but that boys will read it. Did the review in the Jacksonville Sunday Times-Union come to your attention?[3] It was most generous, and should make a noticeable difference in Florida sales.

How was Hemingway's play?[4] I can't help mistrusting it, in his present violently partisan mood.

So many thanks for all the lovely things you did for me.

Editor's note: At top of letter in MEP's hand: "*Income Tax.*"

---

1. Metro-Goldwyn-Mayer began filming of *The Yearling,* starring Spencer Tracy, in 1941. The filming was scrubbed. In 1946, it was produced starring Gregory Peck and Jane Wyman.
2. J. Edward Hardy and Lois Hardy.
3. Richard P. Daniel, "Beauty in the Florida Backwoods," *Jacksonville Times-Union,* April 3, 1938.
4. Ernest Hemingway, *The Fifth Column,* in *The Fifth Column and the First Forty-nine Stories* (New York: Scribners, 1938).

April 26, 1938

Dear Marjorie:

Your letter just came and I am glad you are back and found everything right.- I got worried because mail we forwarded was returned to us, and yet I thought you were to be home long ago.

I think the movie sale was first rate in the circumstances. Carl called me up today to say you had spoken about the income tax question, and had suggested the payment by the movie company be partly in 1939. He said, as he has told you, I guess, that he would not leave any money with a movie company that long, or any longer than necessary. But we published on April first and render the royalty report six months later,- that is, on October first. But we do not make payment until four months after that, which is February first.- So all the royalty will go into 1939, and so will any further payments from the Book of the Month.- And if you wanted to, after receiving the movie payment, you could send back all, or any part, of the first Book of the Month Club payment. It would be perfectly proper because we are not required by the contract to make any payment on this book until February first. Anyhow, you can depend on us to help in every way you want in this regard.

"The Yearling" was fifth in the Herald Tribune list of best sellers last week. Of course that list is always two or three weeks behind the facts. It was first last week in Chicago, and according to the Times it was second in New York, and it was doing well almost everywhere. In distant and quiet places like New Orleans, results come more slowly, but everything looks well.- I never knew a book that had such universal liking. I just got a letter from Scott in which he says:

> "The Marjorie Rawlings book fascinated me. I thought it was even better than 'South Moon Under' and I envy her the ease with which she does action scenes, such as the tremendously complicated hunt sequence, which I would have to stake off in advance and which would probably turn out to be a stilted business in the end. Hers just simply flows; the characters keep thinking, talking, feeling, and don't stop, and you think and talk and feel with them."

Hemingway's play is very fine, and it is extremely significant with regard to what is happening to him, whatever it is. The play is about a man Philip in the Intelligence Service of the Loyalists. The action is almost all in a Madrid hotel, and many bombardments and such violent things occur. This Philip is carrying on an affair with a rather frivolous girl named Dorothy. At the end, after Philip has gone through all kinds of horrors, he says to his side-partner,

"There's no sense babying me along. We're in for fifty years of undeclared wars, and I've signed up for the duration. I don't exactly remember when it was, but I signed up all right." And then later the girl, who has disgusted him by turning up with a silver fox cape bought for innumerable smuggled pesetas, tries to persuade him to marry her, or anyhow to go off with her to all the beautiful places on the Riviera and Paris and all that. And Philip says finally, "*You* can go. But I have been to all those places and I have left them all behind, and where I go now I go alone, or with others who go there for the same reason I go." You will see what I mean, that Ernest is going from where he was, somewhere else, and into larger fields.

Always yours,

. . . .

355. MEP to MKR (TLS: UF, 1 p.)

May 3, 1938

Dear Marjorie:

Katharine Boyd,[1] who is the wife of James Boyd, sent me this letter she wrote to the Nation. I haven't seen the review there, and probably you haven't, but you know how they always do test everything by the Marxian philosophy. As I suppose the letter may never be printed, you had better return this copy to me sometime, for Katharine may want it. I knew she and Jim would delight in "The Yearling".

Always yours,

1. Katharine Boyd, "Books in Brief," *Nation* 146.17 (April 23, 1938): 483–84, who said, "*The Yearling* will be remembered longest as a rather tragic story of childhood."

. . . .

356. MKR to MEP (TLS, 2 pp.)

Hawthorn, Florida

May 14, 1938

Dear Max:

My secret fear about "The Yearling" has just been allayed. I was so afraid the old-guard hunters and woodsmen would find flaws. I know you think I put too much emphasis on the importance of fact in fiction, but it seems to me that this type of work is not valid if the nature lore behind it is not scientifically true in every detail. I saw a letter to the old man[1] who told me so much, from the hunter who was with us on several of our hunts and prowls, and who knows his lore backward and forward. He wrote the old man that the book was a masterpiece, and that he not only read it but studied it. He said it made him so hungry for the scrub that he was ready to throw over his job and get back to it; that he could almost see old Slewfoot's tracks beside the branch. So now everything's all right.

People's response to the book amazes me. I am getting the most wonderful and touching letters. Readers themselves, I think, contribute to a book. They add their own imaginations, and it is as though the writer only gave them something to work on, and they did the rest. It is fine to have the book stirring as many people as it seems to, but as I wrote Whitney, the so-called "success" seems to have nothing to do with me.

I haven't been able to get down to work yet. I was really tired at the end of my trip.

That was really noble of Mrs. Boyd to write to the *Nation* so forcefully. I want to write her. I don't know when I have liked a couple as much as I did the Boyds. I almost stopped off in Southern Pines on my way up, to call on them, but was afraid it might seem an intrusion.

I was tempted to jump on Lewis Gannett[2] for questioning my *provable* nature incidents in his otherwise very generous review, but I don't think a writer ever gets anywhere with any sort of protest, no matter how right he is. It's a different matter when someone else does it, like Mrs. Boyd.

I'm glad the Hemingway play is good, and that he seems to be maturing. If someone could only wash out his mouth with soap, now, he might become the truly adult artist he should be. If he only knew the real he-men who object to his little-boy-dirtiness——. Of course he is an adult artist, a magnificent artist, but he has that funny defensive, arrogant quirk, that expresses itself in a completely unoriginal and puerile offensiveness.

Mrs. Grinnell is in Bimini on her yacht, and I expect to join her for a week in June when she cruises the Bahamas in general just for pleasure. I saw a careless fishing article of hers in some Miami publication, and she really writes awfully well. If she will ever do something about fishing, or Bahaman lore, it ought to be worthwhile. The Bahamas tempt me, too, as material. The poor people on some of the islands are up against the same primitive struggle as the scrub people, except that the sea and the wind are the adversary, instead of the land. I like to see people bucking something solid, instead of their own neuroses. Of course, neuroses have become something to reckon with——. I suppose it is too late for humans to turn back to the basic simplicities, the soil, the prehistoric struggle for food, and so forth. The answer is probably an advance outward, toward a cosmic perception, so that on the ultimate day when the earth burns out, or freezes solid, there will be a natural migration to some other planet, and some way of life more psychic, more electrical, than our unsatisfactory dependence on the physical.

I want to write Louise[3] a very nice letter soon. She is very sweet and a little pathetic, and I understand her. You are so much wiser than she——you must not be intolerant. The Catholic matter will probably fade away. I don't mean to be presumptuous in speaking so. But you know that.

Editor's note: Enclosed in MEP's hand is a list of people to whom *The Yearling* is to be sent:[4]

Katherine Bent   \<Louise>
Jim Boyd
Ernest Hemingway
Scott Fitzgerald   *Roger* [underlined three times] Burlingame
Constance Skinner 449
Eliz Lemmon
Nancy Wertenbaker
\<James B>
Marcia Davenport
Camilla Winship NC
Mrs Watson Lee New Canaan
Leonard Merrick.
[At bottom of list, circled] "Send / The Yearling."

1. Barney Dillard.
2. Louis S. Gannett, "Books and Things," *New York Herald Tribune* (April 1, 1938): 1.
3. Louise S. Perkins, wife of MEP.
4. Katherine Bent (not identified); Constance L. Skinner (1879–1939), Canadian-born novelist; Elizabeth Lemmon; Nancy Wertenbaker [Nancy Hale] (1908–1988), writer; Camilla Winship (not identified); Isabel Dwight Lee, wife of Watson Lee, advertising manager for Woman's Home Companion; Leonard Merrick (1864–1939), novelist and critic; Roger Burlingame (1889–1967), historian and biographer.

. . . .

357. MEP to MKR (TLS: UF, 4 pp.)

May 20, 1938

Dear Marjorie:

I am enclosing a very good review from the Atlantic Monthly,- the June issue just about to come out.[1] It should have effect in that medium. Anyhow, after two weeks in second place on the Tribune best seller list, it comes to first place on the list of the 29th.

I suppose when you do get to work, it is likely to be on the dramatization of "South Moon".[2] Couldn't you plan, however, for a book of stories for early 1939? But I do think we ought to have in it "Jacob's Ladder" and one or two others that do not strictly belong with the "Benny and the Bird Dogs" group. The best possible time for a book of stories would be closely after "The Yearling". But I think that is likely to have a long sale in considerable numbers, and so a book of stories this fall would be rather crowding it.- But next spring would be the best opportunity.

I hope you will have a fine cruise with Mrs. Grinnell. I should think she could write a book on fishing, and I do not know of one by a woman.- Probably she would not like to think of that as an element of importance in it, but it would be one of interest anyhow. I had a good letter from Hemingway yesterday which suggests that he will soon be home for a time, and in Key West. If so, he will probably be over among the Bahamas before very long.- He said nobody in Spain had any social standing now unless he had swum the Ebro.

We are out in New Canaan, and I hope for good. I never want to live in this city again.- And Louise has got greatly interested in planting trees and making fish ponds, etc. on our very small place.- And she finds several interesting churches in the neighborhood.- I don't want that interest to wear off,- that is what I am afraid it may do,- that it may be a disappointment. When the Protestants get under too much attack—although I have no particular interest in their churches—I cannot help speaking up for them. I think old Martin Luther was a most detestable man, but truly a great one.

In view of what you say about the human race never turning back, I am sending you a book we published several years ago and without success.- But it seemed to me extraordinarily interesting and menacing. It is called "Lest Ye Die" by Hamilton.[3]

Always yours,

P.S. I find we no longer have "Lest Ye Die" in stock, and so I am lending you our library copy.

1. Frances Woodward, "*The Yearling*," *Atlantic Monthly* 161 (June 1938): n.p.
2. MKR made plans for a script for a dramatization of *South Moon Under* with the actor Samuel Byrd. The project was abandoned.
3. Cicely M. Hamilton (1875–1952), *Lest Ye Die* (New York: Scribners, 1928).

Hawthorn, Fla.

May 21, 1938

Dear Max:

I just can't let you pay this personal charge. It was for pressing clothes and "beautifying". You WILL have your lawyer informing you that you've made yourself liable!

It is beastly hot and dry and I can't get down to work. Am considering taking my dogs and my nigger gal and going to one of the beaches until the summer rains begin, to cool things off.

Before I forget it again, I have a bet up with Louis Untermeyer[1] about the jacket design of "The Yearling". He says it is by some other artist than Shenton, and I wouldn't bet on that myself. He also says it is by Rockwell Kent,[2] and I bet him it was not. Please let me know, as I have his anthology coming to me if I'm right.

The Ocala Banner editor did not receive a copy of The Yearling. You didn't mention it after I suggested that it was worth while to send him a review copy.

Max, what a blessing we didn't cut the book any. Half the letters I receive complain that it isn't long enough, that they wanted it to go on and on. Of course, they don't know what they're talking about, as that feeling is exactly what any writer would want them left with. But it proved right to leave it alone.

I have been most unhappy about my seeming——perhaps actual——impertinence in commenting on your personal matters. My comment was really an impersonal and abstract thing. I see such a thing, aside from my interest in your mental welfare, from a detached and clinical viewpoint. I had never thought that I had any gift for understanding complex people, or civilized ones, but I have come to believe that I do have a certain clarity of insight into the relations between men and women. I have a friend who is a leading Florida physician,[3] and head of a large private hospital, who goes in for the psychology of such relations, and he insists that some day I must write about the things I know along this line. The subject does not appeal to me, but perhaps it will before I am done. He is writing a book on the subject, and is using an essay I read to a group of men, "Letter to a Lady",[4] which dealt with one phase of the thing, i.e. the jealous, female-spider-like possessiveness of the inferior female who tries to absorb a superior male——and, nine times out of ten, succeeds. So please consider me in this respect a casual analyst, and not an intruder——.

1. Louis Untermeyer (1885–1977), novelist, poet, and biographer.
2. Rockwell Kent (1882–1971), artist and illustrator.

3. Dr. T. Z. Cason, brother of Zelma Cason, who later brought a lawsuit against MKR for invasion of privacy.

4. Not identified.

· ·

359. MKR to MEP (TLS, I p.)

Hawthorn, Florida

May 21, 1938

Dear Max:

I imagine that radio interviews under the proper auspices are considered desirable and legitimate publicity.

I don't know a thing about this man. May I trouble you to have his proposition inquired into? I'd hate to find myself advertising underwear for Worcester's Popular Department Store. Whatever you advise me, I'll do.

Editor's note: At bottom of letter in MEP's hand: "*Jan Schimek / Columbia Broadcasting Co.*"

· ·

360. MKR to MEP (TLS, 2 pp.)

Hawthorn, Florida

May 22, 1938

Dear Max:

The book you sent, "Lest Ye Die", is painfully disturbing. I haven't finished it. I got so upset I had to stop for a while. It would be a fine book to re-print now, except that somehow you can't get people to read books like that. Something about it is too fierce and true to be artistic or even readable. What is upsetting, is recognizing at this moment that the mass symptoms are the same as in the pre-war days——and "pre-war" is all too accurate, for that one will seem like little boys playing, to another generation. And beyond that, is the horror of admitting that we have powers in our hands that our brains and hearts do not have the ability or the humanity to use and direct——. Yet somehow, the individual is all right——. No human being, if you understand him, but wants peace and loving and being loved. And at the same time, as Hamilton says, hate is natural. What a long fight this man-infested planet has ahead of it——. To achieve the civilization we have so smugly assumed we already possessed——.

The necessary business of doing one's own work and making one's own living seems trivial. For myself, I often have the feeling of hiding out; of cheating, by burrowing deep into an out-moded way of life, and living out of the times, with no concern for them. And I feel, guiltily, a smugness, in that in the event of a cataclysm, I can exist more safely than most, not so much in knowing a little the secret of the land, as in having a mental independence of poverty. Even, though one never knows until the actual moment of contact, of death.

And with the world on the edge of Hamilton's Ruin, I go ahead with research on north-east Florida in the period from 1790–1840! Oh well——.

About the 1939 book of stories, to be immediate. I think decidedly that Benny and Bird Dogs and Varmints should be kept for a book of Quincey Dover stories. This cannot be too hurried, as if I try to write stories around her telling of them, just for the purpose of getting enough for a volume, they are more than likely to be mechanical. While if they build themselves up, they will make a unified character study, as well as a group of humorous stories.

But a book containing Jacob's Ladder, Gal Young 'Un——which everyone seems to like except you and me——A Crop of Beans, the Pardon——possibly Alligators, would almost be long enough as it stood. There are unwritten stories in the back of my mind, and I shall try to get some of them out. Do you think those stories can stand on their own feet now that The Yearling has been so well liked? Reading over them, I am conscious of an emotional sincerity, but also of a lesser artistry. Better not to bring out anything at all, than to disappoint people.

I really believe the South Moon dramatization will go very fast. I wrote plays in college, and the form will give me no trouble. I just finished reading South Moon with a detached eye, with my mind on the possible dramatic unity, and it came very clearly to me. It will almost certainly be a study in inherited and inherent fear, with the theme of a man's being helpless in the sweep of forces beyond his will or understanding. The characters will only be Lant and Cleve, Piety and Kezzy, and Kezzy's step-father, (Piety's brother Zeke.) Whether Lant's alien sweetheart Ardis will enter I'm not sure. She may be necessary for counter interest and for adding to the theme of the fear that comes from betrayal. The texture of the dialogue will have a great deal of humor, and I think that makes a desirable drama. The overtone of tragedy can hang over the easy, humorous naturalness just as effectively as over a humorless Tolstoian type of thing.

I've gotten out of my agreement to give a course at the University summer school, so shall have the whole summer to work in. And if the heat or insects or what-not get on my nerves, I can always clear out to the Carolina mountains, where I can work equally well.

May 26, 1938

Dear Marjorie:

So far as I can make out by inquiring among radio people, the broadcast proposed to you by Mr. Lucas-Fisher[1] would not really be worthwhile. I think broadcasting under the right auspices is very advantageous, but I do not think there is any occasion for your going out of your way with regard to it now.- And this particular proposal does not seem to have much importance. I am returning the letter.

Edward Shenton did do the jacket for "The Yearling", not Rockwell Kent. I am sending the Ocala Banner a copy of "The Yearling". I don't know how I failed to do it before. Everything goes well with it.

Did you read "Lest Ye Die"? Yesterday Louise and I went to a tea given by Ellen Glasgow (we are publishing a limited edition of her works) and Louise and Miss Glasgow had a fine time because each one of them had a grandfather who was president of William and Mary College.

Always yours,

1. Not identified.

. . . .

Hawthorn, Florida
Friday
[June 3?, 1938]

Dear Max:

I did finish Lest Ye Die, and am returning it. I don't think I have ever read anything that disturbed me so. The Post editorial fits in with it. But what cure is there for human stupidity? Education, so-called, seems to have destroyed the individual power to think, rather than to have accelerated it. The idea of the non-inevitability of progress is cataclysmic. The only hope, to me, lies in the relative youth of the human race on earth. Figured in ratio to the probable life of our planet, a cosmologist pointed out to me that we are only a few hours old. Just as a child grows, and makes mistakes, and slips back, and goes on again, so perhaps in the end we may achieve a cosmic maturity. And to what end? You can go mad thinking about it.

I have always had a cosmic awareness. I am conscious most of the time of the universe of which we are a small part. But I have only lately become aware, so that it strikes deep into me, of the moment's earthy turmoil. I hate it. And it seems as though the whole plunge into ruin were a tangible cohesion of evil superimposed on the reasonable and kind and peace-loving individual. Each of us asks only to breathe without pain, to love and be loved, to work for the daily bread, without interference.

Editor's note: Enclosed is the following note:

> Will someone induce the Herald-Tribune BOOKS to spell my name correctly? They ran it "Margaret" three times and I finally asked them to correct it. This is on the "What America is Reading" list.
>
> Last week they had it "Margery" instead of "Marjorie". Silly to be fussy about such a thing, I suppose, but I imagine it bothers anyone to have his name mis-spelled.

[Following, in MEP's hand] *"OK."*

. . . .

363. MEP to MKR (TLS: UF, 2 pp.)

June 8, 1938

Dear Marjorie:

We'll leave the story question aside for the time then, and you must tell me how matters develop. It may be that you will write a couple of other stories, but I do think that if we can manage it, we ought to bring out a volume in the Spring. "The Yearling" goes on very well, and I think it will go on for a very long time.

I think it is much better for people who are sufficiently out of the turmoil to forget about it, and I ought not to break into your comparative quiet and peace with rumors of wars and revolutions, but I could not help sending you the enclosed editorial from the Saturday Evening Post. It may be that all kinds of things go in cycles and that people have got into such a way of life and thought that they do not any longer value independence and are willing to let what they had to fight for for centuries slip out of their hands.- Then later they will have to get it back again.

I hope you have gone on with "Lest Ye Die" because you won't get the real point unless you finish it.- Unless you realize that it is a novel of the past or of the future.- The only pleasing aspect of it is that it does suggest that the world's great age begins anew, but we won't be here to be in it.

Always yours,

Hawthorn, Florida

June 8, 1938

Dear Max:

I'm in for a rather serious operation that may sound like bad news, but that actually should prove to be a fortunate thing, for after a series of X-rays, I have finally run down the source of a condition that has kept me half-sick all my life. To explain it briefly, a section of the lower intestines must be removed. If the surgeon finds no inflammation, he will finish the whole job at the time and I'll be out of the hospital in two weeks. But he thinks it probable that it will be impossible to close things at once, and in the latter case I shall have to be in the hospital between three and four months. My appendectomy six or seven years ago——(you may remember that I was ill when "Cracker Chidlings" came out, and while I lay on my porch, convalescing, Harry Barnes' mother[1] drove up and down all day, sending word that she was coming in to whip me to death ——) took out a perfectly good appendix, just because no doctor had ever found the source of my attacks, and the peritonitis I had at the time proves now to have been caused by the intestinal condition——with which, as a matter of fact, I was born. There is a mass of twenty-five or thirty diverticulae, they call them. The immediate danger is of a peritonitis that might get out of control. The ultimate danger would be of malignancy setting in.

I go into so much detail so that if I am laid up a long time you will know why.

I sha'n't mind the thing in the least. I shall be in competent hands, and I have so much vitality, with nothing else wrong, that there is no reason for anything but quick and complete recovery. If by chance I should not come out of it, I do wish I could make it clear to you and to everyone else interested in me for whatever reason, that it would be the sort of death that would not matter. Some deaths do matter. The death of a young and promising person, the death of a young mother, seems unjust. The death of one of two devoted lovers, matters. But in my particular case, I have lived so full and rich a life, with so much more than my share of everything, that I feel indebted to life, instead of life's still being indebted to me. The next book that I have in mind is an uncertain proposition, as I have warned you. If I am big enough, I can make something of it. But the material itself is treacherous. The ultimate book, "Cross Creek: a Chronicle", will be a beautiful book, for its <material> substance is both sound and profound. It is the only thing about which I should feel that something was undone.

To be completely practical, for there is no point in being ostrichlike in the face of any possible danger, my brother is my heir and executor. He is Arthur

H. Kinnan, 403 Fourth and Pike Bldg., Seattle, Washington. In case of my death, he would go over all my papers, with authority to dispose of them as he wished. But I can assure you that I have nothing that you would want saved. Even the sketches for the "Cross Creek" are in the unpolished form that can be so bad with me, as you know. There is nothing there ready for publication.

I'm going to St. Joseph's Hospital, Tampa. I have every confidence in my surgeon, also a personal friend, Dr. John Boling. A close friend, Norton Baskin, Marion Hotel, Ocala, will have charge of my affairs if I am in for a long siege.[2] If I should not be able to scribble to you, you can get word of me at any time from him. I am not letting my brother know anything, as he leaves tomorrow for his Alaskan trip to make colored films, and there's no point in his being worried about me, when I am more than likely to be dancing on the fourth of July.

I go into the hospital this coming Monday, and Dr. Boling will operate on Wednesday the 15th. I'll ask Mr. Baskin to drop you a note toward the end of the week giving you news of me.

I should be able to go ahead with the South Moon Under dramatization most comfortably while I convalesce. I can't work on the story I had in mind, as I needed to do some more prowling and go to some backwoods cock fights first.

I'm missing my trip to the Bahamas with Mrs. Grinnell. She wired me last night to join her at once, but of course I couldn't make it.

I'll be glad to have you write me one of your good notes now and then. St. Joseph Hospital, Tampa, until further notice.

Please give Louise the enclosed, and please read it yourself. This is something I had meant to take up with you.

1. Henry Barnes was a Cracker boy whom MKR wrote about in "Cracker Chidlings." Barnes's mother, initially offended, later became a friend of MKR.
2. Norton S. Baskin, hotelier, whom MKR later married, on October 27, 1941.

. . . .

365. MEP to Norton Baskin (TLS: UF, 2 pp.)

June 10, 1938

Dear Mr. Baskin:

I have just had a letter from Marjorie Rawlings telling me she must go to the hospital in Tampa for an operation and describing the situation in such a way as to make me fear it may be very serious. At any rate, she tells me you are a close friend, and that you will be informed about her, and I beg you to inform me as soon as you possibly can. We here are her publishers, but that has nothing to do with it. It is for personal reasons that I am concerned and I hope you will wire me as soon as you can after you hear the result of the operation and all. I should be most grateful if you would. I do not like to trouble you, but I do not know to whom else I could turn, and I shall feel most anxious until I hear.

Ever sincerely yours,

. . . .

366. MEP to MKR (ALS: UF, 2 pp.)

[June 10, 1938]

Dear Marjorie:-

I'm so sorry that you have all that to go through with, & the news took me completely by surprise. I've read your letter over & over. I've always thought of you as well & strong in every way, & in fact I can't think of you otherwise. I've known of two such cases well, one much more difficult & uncomfortable than the other but each immensely improved as a result. I shall pray that all will go smoothly this time. Even if I had never seen you, & we had done everything by letter I should be profoundly concerned because the privilege—which is what it was—of cooperating with you as an Editor has been one of the happiest & most satisfying experiences I have ever had,- & ever shall–& I am most grateful for it.- So now I have nothing to say except to wish you luck. You'll not be out of my mind a moment. I'll write you often

Always yours

. . . .

367. MKR to MEP (wire)

1938 JUN 13 AM 12 04
MAXWELL PERKINS—
597 FIFTH AVE NYC—
OPERATION POSTPONED FOR FURTHER X RAY CHECK   PLEASE TELL
CARL BRANDT I WILL NOTIFY YOU DEVELOPMENTS LATER—

. . . .

368. MEP to MKR (TLS, 1 p.)

June 13, 1938

Dear Marjorie:

I got your telegram. Anyhow, I'll keep Carl Brandt informed, and do anything else in the world that you can think of that you want done. Thanks ever so much for your letter of Friday.

Always yours,

MAXWELL EVARTS PERKINS
597 FIFTH AVENUE
NEW YORK

Dear Marjorie :— I'm so sorry you have all that to go through with, & the news took me completely by surprise. I've read your letter over & over. I've always thought of you as well & strong in every way, & in fact I can't think of you otherwise. I've known of two such cases well, one much more difficult & uncomfortable than the other but each immensely improved as a result. I shall pray that all will go smoothly this time. Even if I had never seen you, & we had done everything by letter I should be profoundly concerned because the privilege— which is what it was— of co-operating with you as an editor has been one of the happiest & most satisfying experiences I

MAXWELL EVARTS PERKINS
597 FIFTH AVENUE
NEW YORK

have ever had,— & ever shall— & I am most grateful for it. — So now I have nothing to say except to wish you luck. You'll not be out of my mind a moment. I'll write you often   Always yours
Max

No. 366 (MEP on MKR's illness). By permission of University of Florida Libraries.

Hotel Marion
Ocala, Florida
June 14, 1938

Mr. Maxwell E. Perkins,
Charles Scribner's Sons,
Publishers,
New York City.

Dear Mr. Perkins:

I have your letter concerning Marjorie Rawlings and I am happy to be of any little service to you or her.

Several of us convinced Marjorie that it would be smart to have another doctor diagnose her condition and see if he agreed with the Tampa doctor.

Consequently, she has canceled her trip to the Tampa hospital and at present is in Jacksonville at Riverside hospital undergoing another examination.

It may be that they will agree with the first diagnosis and the operation will be performed right away. In that case I will be glad to keep you informed as to Marjorie's condition. If there is any disagreement, I imagine Marjorie will go either to Hopkins or to the Mayo clinic and really get a check-up.[1] In that case I am sure she will write you herself.

With kind regards, I am

Sincerely,
Norton Baskin

1. Johns Hopkins Hospital, Baltimore; Mayo Clinic, Rochester, Minn.

. . . .

[Jacksonville]
Wednesday
[June 15, 1938]

Dear Max:—

A hurried note just to say that I'm leaving the hospital tomorrow and will be home tomorrow night.

Treatments etc. have been reasonably successful, though I shall have to continue with them at home. It's a joke on me, who has never been methodical in my life, to be up against a type of thing for which the only palliative is daily, even hourly, care and caution. It would be much easier for one of my temperament to go through the most painful experience, so long as it had an end to it. Wasn't one of my bromides in "Golden Apples", "Only endlessness is torture"?

I'll write you decently when I'm home——and will you pass this on to Whitney Darrow with apologies for not writing direct.

The "[title illegible]" and "Dynasty of Death" reached me safely, but the book about a fox you said Charlie Scribner was sending, didn't come. Hadn't someone better check it? Maybe it was sent to Hawthorn?

. . . .

371. MEP to Norton Baskin (CC, 2 pp.)

June 17, 1938

Dear Mr. Baskin:

I am most grateful to you for your letter about Marjorie. I am glad she was persuaded to have examinations from another source. I had felt like suggesting this myself, but it seemed as if it might make her anxious and confused in a time of crisis to have anyone interfere from this distance. I had thought of even urging her to come up to Baltimore or New York, but on inquiry, I found that the Tampa hospital and the staff were admirable. I do not know just where Marjorie is now, or what to expect, but if you could send me another line soon, I could not thank you too much. Her book is doing wonderfully well.

Ever sincerely yours,

. . . .

372. MKR to MEP (TLS, 2 pp.)

Hawthorn, Florida
June 17, 1938

Dear Max:

Well, I got out of a devil of a mess by the skin of my teeth. I can't be positive of being through with it, but a reprieve is something. The three musketeers who are like brothers to me, got together and practically refused to allow me to go ahead with the operation without a corroborative diagnosis. I put up a fight, for the X-rays looked incontrovertible, and if I don't make up my mind quickly and stick to a decision, I suffer too much in vacillating. But I gave in at the last minute and they took me to Jacksonville, where the head of a fine private hospital, also a friend, put me through everything again.

The diagnosis was confirmed, but three good men there agreed that [an] operation was the last thing in the world to try, that it should be done only as a last resort or in an emergency, as could occur. It seems the mortality for that particular operation is 40%. Even if it is ever necessary, the Jacksonville man said there was no one in Florida competent to do it, and that I should go to Johns Hopkins or to Dr. Abell[1] in Louisville, president of the American Medical Association. But they believe that a rigid, though not at all unpleasant diet, will remove the toxic condition, and the danger, and make me feel all right.

The Jacksonville doctor friend[2] said that the Tampa surgeon had made utterly inadequate preparations. The restricted diet should come first in any case, and in the second place, my blood should have been typed and two donors ready the moment the operation was done, as transfusions are invariably necessary. So with the mortality so high even when a top-notch man does it, I can see that the Tampa man was going at it blindly, and the Jacksonville man was probably right, when he dismissed me yesterday, saying, "If you'd done it, you'd have been cavorting with the angels just about now."

So it was really a pretty close call. I wasn't at all afraid, but I did have the feeling that I probably shouldn't come out of it.

What I regret is getting several of you disturbed about it. I usually don't speak of difficulties until they are over, but expecting to be laid up so long, at best, there seemed to be no alternative but to communicate with you and two or three others who would have no explanation for my not communicating later. But I am so sorry to have worried anyone. But we can only do what seems wise at the moment.

Sam Byrd is coming to Florida next week and we will go over the South Moon Under dramatization plans.

1. Dr. Irvin Abell, president of the AMA in 1938 and professor of surgery at the University of Louisville.
2. Dr. T. Z. Cason.

· ·

373. MEP to MKR (TLS: UF, 1 p.)

June 20, 1938

Dear Marjorie:

Many thanks for writing me, and I am delighted things turned out that way. I felt anxious about the Tampa hospital, but I inquired of my son-in-law[1] and others, and they all seemed to think that everything was of the best there. But anyhow you don't have to worry, at least for the present. I do hope everything will go well. All goes very well with "The Yearling".

Always yours,

1. Dr. Robert King, husband of Louise "Peggy" Perkins.

June 29, 1938

Dear Marjorie:

I was talking to Carl Brandt yesterday, and he had just heard from you and told me what you said, which went a little further than I know. So I suppose now you are settled down to a diet, but I should not think that would be bad if there were enough variety in it. "The Yearling" goes on beautifully, only several hundred copies short of 45,000. And today the orders looked better than ever. All ages and all types of people like it.

We have been having a very cool summer so far, not more than three really hot days. And today it is almost cold. My daughter, with her new baby, is now with us in New Canaan.

I have just read a very fine manuscript of a novel about the pioneers going over the Oregon Trail in 1850.[1] It accomplishes the miracle of giving you a really intense individual story, a love story, and yet at the same time an acquaintance with many characters and a sense of the magnitude of the whole migration, and of the wonders of new and changing countries. It is by Archie Binns.- And Jim[2] has written an almost perfect book about the West in the seventies.- I am waiting impatiently for him to turn up for we always have a good time when he comes through New York.

Let me know how things go.

Always yours,

1. Archie Binns (1899–1971), *The Land Is Bright* (New York: Scribners, 1939).
2. James Boyd, *Bitter Creek* (New York: Scribners, 1939).

. . . .

July 7, 1938

Dear Marjorie:

These letters do not amount to much, but they were sent to me by the Book of the Month Club, and so I am forwarding them.

How are you getting on? We are confronted now with an operation in the family,- one of my daughters.- I don't know how serious it is.

We are planning quite a burst of advertising for "The Yearling". It is going on splendidly.

Always yours,

Hawthorn, Florida

July 11, 1938

Dear Max:

I am just back from a week in Bimini with Mrs. Grinnell. She was trying for a blue marlin five hundred pounds or better, so we fished hard in all kinds of weather, but without luck. I came home to do some work, planning to join her in about ten days to cruise the Bahamas, going to all the smaller islands, including San Salvador, where, as the colored boy who was going to guide us said, "Columbus sot foot." Incidentally, he swears that the foot-prints of Columbus are still there. The shore is of a cement-like marl or clay, and under proper weather conditions, he says that all prints in it remain indefinitely. However, a wire from Mrs. Grinnell today says that she has been obliged to cancel the cruise. I am sorry, for it was a chance to see strange places favorably, but perhaps now I can get some work done.

We are having a lovely summer, occasionally a hot day, but almost always afternoon showers to cool things. Today we are having a slow straight rain and the temperature is 72. I have an armful of Egyptian lotus blossoms on my veranda, and I have never seen anything so exotic. They look like a cross between a magnolia and a water lily, but the color is a pale lemon yellow, with deeper stamens, and the buds and half-opened flowers are a chartreuse. They have long stems and as <they> the blossoms spread wider and wider the huge petals drop with a sound like a large bird fluttering in a tree. They grow in a marsh near here, and little nigger boys will pull all you want for a dime. Something in me is completely passive and lethargic, and all I really want to do is lie on the veranda and watch the lotus petals fall——. A dozen magazines have been tormenting me for stories and articles, and I hate it. I balk against coercion, and I cannot and will not write to order. But if they don't leave me alone, I shall have difficulty in writing the things I want to.

I am not feeling any better, but since I was to report back for X-rays in five or six months, it is of course too soon to expect results from the diet. There seems to be improvement to the extent that I have skipped an occasional day without the rise in temperature.

Sam Byrd, the actor, is coming here this week to talk over South Moon Under play plans. I do hope I can make something of it for him.

I'm sorry you're having the operation in your family. I think we mind such things for others much more than for ourselves.

[Postscript] I'm very happy that the Boyd book is good. I look forward to it tremendously. I had a lovely letter from Mrs. Boyd asking me to visit them in October and I hope to go.

. . . .

377. MEP to MKR (TLS: UF, 3 pp.)

July 15, 1938

Dear Marjorie:

I am glad everything is so pleasant down where you are.- We have had a very hot and wet time lately. My daughter came through as well as she could, but had some very uncomfortable days.- The only danger is that she might have a recurrence of the same thing. She will be out of the hospital though in little more than a week, and maybe everything will go well.- Everything is going beautifully with "The Yearling". The sale now is only a very few copies short of 60,000. We shall have a fine page advertisement in the Times next week.- We are also planning a series of advertisements in the magazine, Time.

I have just heard that Tom Wolfe has been very ill.- He has been on a long tour in the Northwest, and was in Seattle and got pneumonia, but they say he has passed the crisis and that everything ought to go along well. The trouble is that Tom won't do as he should after he gets out. He should go somewhere with a mild climate and rest for six or eight weeks for the sake of his heart and his lungs.- I cannot see him doing it though.

Jim Boyd was here a while ago, and ought to be back again. We are thinking of getting Shenton to do decorations for his book,- and will if Jim approves of it. The book has a good deal of plot. It is about a boy who runs away, like so many in the 80's, to the West. It is to be serialized in the Post and I guess not much more than the plot will be in the serial.- But in reality the book is about the great young West when it was ruled by young men and was all new. That is what it ought to be presented as being; but being about the West, and having a lot of action in it, it runs so much risk of being thought of as "a western" and especially after serialization in the Post.- Now Shenton would understand exactly what Jim was about, and he would give that atmosphere and quality in the decorations.- So I hope Jim will approve of the plan.

Always yours,

378. MEP to MKR (TLS: UF, 2 pp.)

July 26, 1938

Dear Marjorie:

Novels do not often get any notice from the great sports writers, but "The Yearling" has from Joe Williams of the World Telegram.[1] I am enclosing what he says, even though he got your name wrong. Yesterday the R E A[2] called up about an interview with you, and even when we said you were in Florida, they wanted to send one of their correspondents there to see you. We generally refuse addresses, but we thought that you would not have to see this one unless you wanted to, and so gave them Hawthorn.

Tom Wolfe has been mighty sick with pneumonia in Seattle, and it is hard to make out now how he stands. He was all alone wandering around the Northwest, and he is in some sort of a private hospital, and has been for some time, and though it is said he is out of danger, he seems very far from well.- And when he does get well, he probably won't take care of himself, as he should after so deadly a thing as pneumonia.

Bing Crosby talked about "The Yearling" on the radio, I was told.- That is very unusual too.[3] I hope the diet is not too trying and is doing you good. All of us are well again.

Always yours,

1. Not seen.
2. R E A: Rural Education Association.
3. Bing Crosby praised *The Yearling* on the *Kraft Music Hall* radio program in July 1938.

. . . .

379. MKR to MEP (ALS, I p.)

[Jacksonville]
Thursday
[July 28, 1938]

Dear Max:—

I am at the Riverside Hospital, Jacksonville, for ten days of rest and rigid diet, etc. I'm anything but ill, but the temperature persists so I'm just being sensible. If they can clear up the present irritations they say I should go indefinitely without another attack.

Have you a good book?

July 29, 1938

Dear Marjorie:

I am sending you "Dynasty of Death"[1] which won't come out until September 16th.- But Charlie Scribner is sending you a really beautiful little book about a fox. The woodcuts alone will give you quite a lot of pleasure. I should not think ten days rest in a hospital would be so bad if it is not too hot.- But it can't be any hotter than it is here.

I cannot find out much about old Tom except that he is still very ill. But it seems that he only began to be ill about two weeks ago, and that is not too long a time for pneumonia.

Always yours,

1. Taylor Caldwell [Janet M. Holland] (1900–1985), *Dynasty of Death* (New York: Scribners, 1938).

. . . .

Aug. 10, 1938

Dear Marjorie:

I have just got an English copy of a book I am sure you would like very much.- "The Captain's Chair" by Bob Flaherty.[1] It may be too quiet a book to succeed more than moderately. Our copies are not ready because it was set up in England some time ago, and we are making it by offset from the English book. Some twenty years ago, Bob Flaherty, then unknown, came in and told about his life around Hudson Bay and talked about doing a book on it. He was in bad shape then for he had made a film, and then just before leaving the North, and examining it with a lighted pipe, he set it on fire with a spark, and lost the whole thing in a minute, and pretty nearly lost his hands too. They were bandaged when he came in.

One could see right away, that he was *somebody*, and I begged him to do a little of the book, and said I thought from that we might get somewhere definite, and he did bring in about 25 pages of the manuscript (they are still in the safe here) which I thought were extraordinarily fine, and I urged him to go on, all but promising to publish. I had no doubt we would, but he never did go on. I used to write him letters every month or so, and then when I saw him, I pressed him, but after a time it got to be embarrassing, and then he got going in the making of pictures. He is an Irishman, and careless, and I thought there was nothing to be hoped for until I heard he was doing this book, and planning to follow it. I think it is your kind of a book.

I wish I knew more about you and how everything was going, and whether it was very boring in the hospital there.

As for Tom, it seems as if there were every reason to think he was safe enough now. It was bronchial pneumonia he had, which is not as deadly as the other kind. In some ways I think though it might take longer to get over.

We have now made a[nother] printing of "The Yearling" which brings the total slightly over 200,000, including the Book of the Month Club. It does look as if it were "The Yearling"'s year.

Always yours,

1. Robert J. Flaherty (1884–1951), *The Captain's Chair* (New York: Scribners, 1938).

. . . .

382. MKR to MEP (TLS, 2 pp.)

Hawthorn, Florida

August 30, 1938

Dear Max:

I read our rival, "My Son, My Son", while I was in the hospital, and if it beats us, I for one sha'n't mind, as it is a very fine book.[1] It is not a classic, and will not, I think, be too long remembered, but there is something old-fashioned and satisfying about it, like a cross between Dickens and Arnold Bennett.[2] You have the feeling of really feeding on it, of going away with some substance in your stomach. Most of the "modern" books——Rebecca West's "The Thinking Reed"[3] is a supreme example——leave you with the same empty and frustrated and betrayed feeling that you get from a cheap baker's cream puff.

I have been much interested in the reviews of the Virginia edition of Ellen Glasgow and mean to read the prefaces as soon as I get a chance——without paying your fancy price.[4] Who buys such an expensive edition? It was a life-saver to my conscience to come across a statement quoted from one of her prefaces, in which she said that the writer must wait between books for the well of the sub-conscious to fill. I haven't been able to understand why I couldn't get to work, when on the surface at least I thought I wanted to. I have not felt much psychic exhaustion, and not too much physical enervation, in spite of the hospital's treatments, etc. having taken a good bit out of me——but the work just would not come. I imagine you wish I'd stop pouncing on other writers' theories and deciding they explain everything——I remember that I got very excited about James' "The Art of the Novel" and you warned me not to go off the deep end about his ideas. But the Glasgow theory is profoundly true.

For another thing, I do not believe a writer can go ahead with a new piece of work until he is entirely free of the old. And as long as one book is in the news, and is selling, and being talked about, so that everywhere the writer goes, questions are asked about it and comments made, and letters come in every mail about it——the writer is not free. I have to feel forgotten, and very private and isolated, to submerge myself in a new thing. Yet the good sales of "The Yearling", and the generous things people write and say, are remote, too, and I am ready to detach myself completely from the book as soon as I am allowed to. I suppose I am only rationalizing my periodic laziness and inertia——. Be patient with me, as always. You know I do get a lot done once I am really into anything.

I am feeling only moderately well, but reconciled to the slowness of everything.

How good you are to worry so about Tom Wolfe. The poor fumbling Behemoth will never again have the unselfish interest that you gave him.

1. Howard Spring (1889–1965), *My Son, My Son* (New York: Grosset and Dunlap, 1938).
2. Arnold Bennett (1867–1931), British novelist, playwright, and journalist.
3. Rebecca West [Cecily Andrews] (1892–1983), *The Thinking Reed* (London: Hutchinson, 1936).
4. Ellen Glasgow, *Works*, Virginia ed., 12 vols. (New York: Scribners, 1938).

. . . .

383. MEP to MKR (TLS: UF, 3 pp.)

Sept. 2, 1938

Dear Marjorie:

Every time I begin to get worried about you, not having heard, and write to inquire how things go on, my letter seems to cross yours. I hope it will this time too, and that the news you give me will be good.

I am enclosing an issue of "Shop Talk", designed for booksellers, which shows how "The Yearling" progresses.[1] If you see any other books described in it that would interest you, tell me and I shall send them.- I did send you Flaherty's book, I am pretty sure, "The Captain's Chair". That is really a very fine narrative. I know for sure you will like that. Do you think we could look forward to publishing stories next Spring,- say in March? "The Yearling" will have been out all but a year by then, and it should go on selling well up to that time too.- But that would be a very wise time to bring out a book of stories. I do hope it can be managed.

Hemingway was here two days this week.- On the morning of the second day he almost missed a boat for Paris, but not quite.- And then I and his sister-in-law, Jinny,[2] almost missed the gangplank, and so barely escaped going down the harbor and coming back with the pilot. Hemingway was really in better shape mentally, physically, and morally, than I have seen him in years. He has a very interesting plan for writing too, which he expects to do in Paris.- Too many Associations, etc., keep after him here on account of his activities in behalf of Spain.

I do think there is one book here you will enjoy, perhaps not to read all through, but on account of its subject and its pictures, and of a good deal of its writing too. That is, "The World Is [Was] My Garden: the Autobiography of a Plant Explorer".[3]

Yours always,

1. *Shoptalk,* the promotional publication at Scribner.
2. Jinny Pfeiffer, sister of Pauline Pfeiffer Hemingway.
3. David Fairchild (1869–1954), *The World Was My Garden: The Autobiography of a Plant Explorer* (New York: Scribners, 1938).

. . . .

384. MKR to MEP (ALS, 2 pp.)

[Cross Creek]
Tuesday
Sept. 5[?], [1938]

Dear Max:

Yes, I had answered your unasked questions, as does so often happen.

Then I began a letter to Whitney to go in the same mail, for he gets so touchy when I write other people and don't write him——and I was interrupted and held up your letter until I could finish his. I despise your saying what you did when you were asked if I was surprised at the "success" of The Yearling. I wish you had said it about someone else. It would be more accurate to say that neither failure nor success surprises me.

. . . .

385. MEP to MKR (TLS: UF, 3 pp.)

Sept. 8, 1938

Dear Marjorie:

I really do not think anyone ever said so many enlightening things about novel writing as Ellen Glasgow did in those prefaces, and I am going to send them to you. I have just found a way of getting proofs. Maybe you had better return them some day because they are part of our press records, but not until you are ready to. I am sure you will enjoy them very greatly. I read them as they came in and was amazed at their value, and I always meant to read them again all together.- Some day I shall.

I did not mean to be pressing you on to write at all. I know that is true about letting the reservoir fill up. It has to be done. I just thought that between now and this time next year you might have been able to write enough stories so that we could publish a book of them. "The Yearling" goes on beautifully. We just printed 10,000 more, making 211,000 in all.

You saw my sardonic remark about writers not being surprised by success in that "Shop Talk". I do not know why in the world they put it in there anyhow. A man came in to talk over the Fall books, he said, and I did not realize he was going to print anything, and then that statement appeared in the World-Telegram. I have a sardonic turn anyhow, and I said that not because of you at all, though you were the occasion, but because of a writer whose book had failed and who was very much upset about it, and thought us at fault,- although when we took it we said it was of a sort that could only be successful by a miracle, and the writer at that time was very grateful that we took it at all. What I really said was: I never knew a writer to be surprised by success, but only by failure, which seemed odd to the simple minded in face of the fact that there were at least 100 failures to every success. So please forgive me.

You ought to read "The Captain's Chair" for it is a very fine book.

Always yours,

· ·

386. MEP to MKR (TLS: UF, 1 p.)

September 19, 1938

Dear Marjorie:

I opened the enclosed by mistake. The word <"stupid"> 'stoop' you know, is used all over New England and New Jersey and all those places where I have lived.

You will have read of old Tom's death.[1] Louise and I went down to his funeral yesterday. I thought you might like to see the last thing that Tom ever wrote. It was done in Seattle before the trouble with his brain developed.

Yours always,

1. Wolfe died on September 15, 1938.

Hawthorn, Florida
September 21, 1938

Dear Max:

I have grieved for you ever since I heard of Tom's death. I grieve, too, for the certain loss of the work he would unquestionably have done, for his very touching letter to you shows a chastening and mellowing of that great half-mad diffusive ego, that would have been a guarantee of the literary self-discipline we all so wanted for him. It seems that each of us can go only so far in wisdom and in insight, and then for one reason or another we are done. And no one can take up where another leaves off. No one can profit by all that Tom had come to learn, with so much torture to himself and to others. Just as civilizations never learn from other civilizations, but must build up agonizingly, making the same mistakes over and over, with never any *cumulative* progress.

I know how glad you must be that you never withdrew your personal goodness from Tom, even when others were bitter for you.

It is not strange that so vibrant and sentient a personality as Tom knew or guessed that he had come to the great wall. He must have felt far beyond most of us that withdrawing of the cosmic force from his individual unit of life. I felt the thing this summer for myself, knowing——and I still know——that if I had done the thing I planned I should not have come through. I felt the reprieve, too, and I am still puzzled. It is like the hurricane scheduled for the Florida coast the other day, that suddenly swerved from its path and swept on elsewhere. It is all accidental and incidental, and yet why is it so often one knows in advance?

I have thought of you a great deal since hearing, and I hope it is something you can accept without too much pain.

. . . .

Oct. 21, 1938

Dear Marjorie:

I have wanted very much to write you, but have not been able to get the time, with all the things that have fallen upon me lately. I am enclosing an advertisement which you probably have seen anyhow, showing that we have now printed 220,000 of "The Yearling" in all. For the last couple of weeks it had been tied with "My Son" for best seller, but in the next couple of weeks it goes distinctly to the top again.

I was most grateful for what you wrote about Tom.- One of my difficulties now is that being his executor—and I could not see how I could rightly evade that—I have an enormous number of things to do, and the tremendous collection of manuscript material to look through. Tom kept everything, and it is a good thing he did, in some ways, but troublesome in others.

Are things going well with you? I don't want you to feel that you have to write a letter.- A postcard would do. I only want to know how things are going.- Jim Boyd has been hereabouts, but now he is somewhat ill. I think not seriously at all. Even so, he is working on with his book, which could be considered finished now. I hope you won't read any of it in The Saturday Evening Post, for it has been cut to pieces there. It is a truly beautiful book in fact.

Always yours,

. . . .

389. MEP to MKR (ANS: UF, on the front cover of *Carolina Magazine*)

[October 1938]

Dear Marjorie:-

I'm sending this on with hesitation, but you felt so much about Tom & his writing & I made this futile & hasty effort to show what he was like.[1]

1. In "Scribner's and Tom Wolfe," *Carolina Magazine* 58.1 (October 1938): 15–17, Perkins wrote of Wolfe: "He was wrestling as no artist in Europe would have to do, with the material of literature. . . . He knew that the light and color of America were different. . . . It was with this that he was struggling, . . . to reveal America and Americans to Americans. That was the heart of Tom's fierce life" (15).

. . . .

390. MEP to MKR (ALS: UF, 4 pp.)

Nov. 2, 1938

Dear Marjorie:

I just went up to see Copey (formerly Professor of Harvard) a while ago. He spoke in the highest terms of "The Yearling" and asked many questions about you. He is as keen as ever about literature, though he is now seventy-six years old. I have always been trying to get him to write his memoirs, and now he says he will, bit by bit. He told me plainly that all I knew about books and writing came from his instruction,- which is about true. What's more, I gather that he did not think I knew much anyhow. I got him into the Copley-Plaza for lunch in place of a dreadfully dreary restaurant across from his Cambridge apart-

No. 389 (MEP on Thomas Wolfe). By permission of University of Florida Libraries.

ment, but I could not persuade him to have a drink at the Merry-Go-Round bar. He always insists on seeing me alone "to talk business",- we published "The Copeland Reader"[1] some twelve years ago, and later "The Copeland Translations". The last time I went up there Louise wanted to go to Boston anyhow, and though I told her she could not see Copey whom she very much enjoys. But when I left the hotel to go to see him, she went back on the agreement, or tried to.- So when I saw Copey I said Louise had come to Boston and that when I went to see him she had said, "Am I a little fox terrier, to lie on the floor with my nose at the crack of the door to wait until you come back?" So then Copey immediately telephoned to the hotel and she came out, and we had lunch all together.- So no business was talked, and I must come again alone, though no business was talked that time either, or ever is, really.

I am getting the North American Review. I had not seen it.

I am very glad that you can do the two more stories, and we can make up the collection, and I think that using the Quincey Dover stories in this book would not make a separate volume later impossible. When there are enough for that, we might make something special, perhaps with some kind of decorations like Shenton's in "The Yearling". Ninety thousand words would be enough, though one hundred would be better.

Marjorie, the only time I ventured an important criticism of a Hemingway book, he uttered one of those expletives that sometimes get into print, and followed it with "Why don't you get Tom Wolfe to write it for me?"- This is confidential.

Always yours,

1. Charles T. Copeland, *The Copeland Reader* (New York: Scribners, 1926).

. . . .

391. MEP to MKR (TLS: UF, 2 pp.)

Nov. 22, 1938

Dear Marjorie:

I thought you would like to see the first English review. I think Mr. Reid flatters himself when he says he is like Jody, but anyhow he likes "The Yearling" even though he does not wholly grasp it, and I thought you might like to see what the formidable Spectator said.[1]

We think next Fall we should have an illustrated edition of "The Yearling" and we are considering carefully who should do the pictures. They ought to be in color. The general opinion at present seems to be that the best man would be N. C. Wyeth, who would certainly be completely sympathetic with the book, and would probably want to go down and look over the country, and would do the work with enthusiasm, but though he does as good work as he ever did, as that book called "Men of Concord, Selections from Thoreau" distinctly shows, his greatest day is past.[2]

I hope all goes well with you. What about the dramatization of "South Moon Under"? I hope it is going on, and yet that it won't occupy you for too long.

Yours always,

1. Forrest Reid, "Fiction," *Spectator* 16 (November 11, 1938): 824.
2. N. C. Wyeth (1882–1945), painter and illustrator. The edition illustrated by Wyeth was published in 1939. *Men of Concord and Some Others as Portrayed in the Journal of Henry David Thoreau* (Boston: Houghton Mifflin, 1936).

. . . .

392. MKR to MEP (TLS, 1 p.)

Hawthorn, Florida
[December? 1938]

Dear Max:

This will introduce my very good friend, Robert Camp——one of the three friends who saved my life by refusing to let me be operated on without further diagnosis. I may have spoken to you of his work——he is an artist, one of whose paintings was among the ten to represent Florida art at last year's exhibit at Rockefeller Center. I have the highest opinion of his ability—he has a very great gift with tropical vegetation.

Since I don't know the personnel of the new Scribner's Magazine, may I trouble you to make any contacts for him there that might be helpful? It would be a personal favor to me.

. . . .

393. MEP to MKR (CC, 2 pp.)

Dec. 6, 1938

Dear Marjorie:

Here is another English review, from the Sunday Times.[1] I had hoped you would write me about the illustrated edition which we want to have for the Fall, and I suppose you will when you can get around to it. Have you had a chance to work on stories at all?

I am now sending you a book by another publisher, although written by one of our regular authors, Struthers Burt.- It is in that River series, and a brief examination of it makes me think it is something you would like.[2]

What in the world do you want to give lectures for? I would think your time was far too valuable for that. Please tell me how everything goes.

Always yours,

1. Doreen Wallace, "A Success in America," *London Times* (November 20, 1938): 9.
2. Maxwell Struthers Burt, *Powder River* (New York: Farrar and Rinehart, 1938).

. . . .

394. MKR to MEP (TLS, 6 pp.)

Hawthorn, Florida
December 6 [1938]

Dear Max:

I'm afraid I haven't thanked you for two or three books——the Goya,[1] which, however authentic, I considered an utter hodge-podge from a literary standpoint——and the Hemingway, which I am, to my surprise, mad about.[2] The play, I think, is only so-so——yet he holds you and you can't get away. But the stories——taken in bulk that way, one perfect thing after another, you recognize him as probably our only contemporary master of the short story. I have even had to forgive him a little for his absorption with morbid and perverse subjects, for a memory suddenly came back to me of some very beyond-the-pale things of my idol, de Maupassant. I remember a story of his about a veterinary who delivered a woman he loved of her child (not his), and another as sickening as anything Hemingway turns out, about a soldier starving to death, and a woman whose breasts were about to burst with milk, her child having died——. Hemingway never thought of anything any worse——. Yet for power and emotion and technique, the two men stand side by side.

I was very much pleased in looking over the lists of the year's "enjoyed" books by writers, to find The Yearling so often mentioned. Out of curiosity, I checked. Van Doren's Benjamin Franklin was listed 8 times, The Yearling 6 times, Rebecca 5 times, Listen, the Wind! 4 times, and no other more than 3.[3] There is naturally much more satisfaction in appealing to the people who know how hard it is to do, than the woman's-club buyers-of-any-best-sellers, who don't know what it is all about. Then on the other hand, I get a tremendous pleasure out of appealing to the hard-boiled hunters and people like that, who read one book every five years.

I'm waiting on Whitney's report to come to a final conclusion about the two months lecture tour next fall under Keedick.[4] I loathe everything about it except the money, and since I don't actually need that, it seems pretty much like prostitution. But it is a chilly world in which to be too lofty, isn't it?

Max, I simply can't get down to work. The long treatments probably are mostly to blame, for I still have to go to Gainesville twice a week——was going every other day until lately——for them, and anything like that, and adjusting yourself to a diet, is disorganizing. Also, the doctor told me my whole chemistry would change. Then the last six weeks I've been having repairs made on my house in the slowest and most inefficient way, almost literally running the termites down one by one.

December 8

Your note with the London Times review just came. I shouldn't wait so long to write you, because then there is so much to catch up with.

About the illustrated edition for next fall. I think it is a fine idea, and will begin to establish the book on the adolescent lists, also serve as a gift book at that time. But I can't quite see Wyeth. Everything that I remember of his is so delicate of line, almost ethereal, that I can't conceive of it conveying the robustness I like to think the book possesses. What about turning Shenton loose, with plenty of time, and letting him see the country? Does he ever work in color? I don't think you said so, but I got the impression it was color you had in mind. Thomason does more the sort of thing I think we want than Wyeth, yet somehow his stuff is so *sketchy* that it doesn't carry as well as Shenton. I don't think Shenton could be improved on. Everyone thinks, as I do, that he "got" the whole thing, pictorially.

To finish my tale of why I haven't worked——. The repairs have finally been finished on my old shack, and then it has had to be painted, and it will be another week before that is done, and I can settle the house. And my house-girl⁵ got married, and I took the man to keep her, and have had to break him in to the grove work. So all in all living has been too broken up to get anything done. But I long for a quiet and orderly routine once more, and feel sure that after Christmas I can settle down to it. One of the stories is shaping up in my mind and there is no question but that I shall have a couple for the collection by spring.

My ex-husband showed up last week, on his way to Tarpon Springs for the winter, and sent out a messenger to ask if I would see him. I didn't want to, but decided it made less of a point of it to see him than to refuse, so went through with it. His feelings obviously have never changed, but I simply can't help it. I put in a hellish fifteen years trying to make him happy, and I think fifteen years of sheer sadism <is> are enough to take. It upset me less than I thought it would, to see him. I knew it would happen sooner or later and I'm glad it's over with.

You ask why in the world I want to lecture. I don't, but Keedick has tormented me about it, and \$8,000 for 8 weeks' work looks like a lot of money to anybody at Cross Creek.

1. Charles Poore (1902–1971), *Goya* (New York: Scribners, 1938).
2. *The Fifth Column and the First Forty-Nine Stories.*
3. Carl Van Doren (1885–1950), *Benjamin Franklin* (New York: Garden City Publishing, 1938); Daphne du Maurier (1907–1989), *Rebecca* (New York: Doubleday, Doran, 1938); Anne Morrow Lindbergh (1906–), *Listen! The Wind* (New York: Harcourt, Brace, 1938).
4. Lee Keedick of the Lee Keedick Bureau, which managed author lecture tours.
5. Adrenna Mickens, daughter of Martha Mickens.

. . . .

395. MEP to MKR (CC, 2 pp.)

Dec. 8, 1938

Dear Marjorie:

We are all very much for beginning immediately on the full color illustrations for "The Yearling" and we are all agreed now, after examining Wyeth's last work, that he is the man to do them. To try anyone else would be very risky and experimental, and truly his work is very fine now. I rather think finer than any he ever has done. And we are confident he would have the deepest sympathy with "The Yearling". In order to show you what his pictures are now like, I am sending you a copy of Kenneth Roberts' "Trending into Maine".[1]

We have now printed the two hundred and sixty thousandth.

Always yours,

1. Kenneth Roberts (1885–1957), *Trending into Maine* (Boston: Little, Brown, 1938).

. . . .

396. MEP to MKR (CC, 1 p.)

Dec. 9, 1938

Dear Marjorie:

I am enclosing a copy of a telegram which came to our Mr. Chapin[1] who brought up the *possibility* of his illustrating "The Yearling". I hope the Maine book with his latest pictures will get to you soon. We must decide quickly and give him plenty of time, and I do not think we could get a safer—and after seeing the Maine pictures, a better—man, or in fact anyone anywhere near so good. Please send me some word when you can.

Yours always,

1. Joseph H. Chapin, head of the Art Department at Scribner.

397. MEP to MKR (TS for wire)

DEC. 10, 1938
MRS. MARJORIE K. RAWLINGS
ISLAND GROVE, FLORIDA
WILL YOU ATTEND LUNCHEON SOUTHERN WOMEN'S DEMOCRATIC
ASSOCIATION JANUARY TWENTY-EIGHT. AWARD HUNDRED DOLLARS
FOR BEST BOOK OF THE YEAR BY SOUTHERN WRITER BUT SHE MUST
BE PRESENT. THINK NOT VERY IMPORTANT BUT HOPE YOU CAN DO
IT AS EVERYONE WANTS TO SEE YOU. GENERAL EFFECT ADVANTA-
GEOUS. PLEASE WIRE.

. . . .

398. MKR to MEP (wire)

1938 DEC 10 PM 4 06
MAXWELL PERKINS—
597 FIFTH AVE—
OK IF YOU SAY SO—

. . . .

399. MKR to MEP (wire)

1938 DEC 11 PM 11 46
MAXWELL PERKINS—
597 FIFTH AVE NYC—
CHANGED MIND WONT COME FOR DEMOCRATIC WOMENS AWARD IF
THEIR CONVICTIONS ABOUT BEST BOOK BY SOUTHERN WRITER
ARENT SINCERE ENOUGH TO MAKE AWARD IN ABSENTIA I DONT WANT
IT I NEVER WILL GET ANY WORK DONE IF INTERRUPTIONS DONT
STOP—

. . . .

400. MEP to MKR (TLS: UF, 2 pp.)

Dec. 12, 1938

Dear Marjorie:

You put your finger on the weak point. It does not really matter much anyhow, but I hoped it might be the occasion for your coming on, and then we
could have talked things over.- But do please write me about the illustrated

edition because the longer Wyeth has to work on it, the better the result ought to be. And we want to make a truly beautiful thing of it.

I am just sending herewith our juvenile list to show you that "The Yearling" is included in it too. And it is mentioned also in the circular letter that goes with it.

I think your work ought to come before anything else in the world, and I was puzzled by your thinking of lecturing because of that. It is very exhausting and unrewarding, and would take you away from what is truly important, it seems to me.

Always yours,

. . . .

401. MKR to MEP (wire)

1938 DEC 12 PM 11 32
MAXWELL PERKINS—
597 FIFTH AVE—
TREMENDOUSLY ENTHUSED WYETH FOR YEARLING AFTER SEEING MAINE ILLUSTRATIONS WRITING—

. . . .

402. MKR to MEP (ALS, 5 pp.)

[Cross Creek]
December 14 [1938]

Dear Max:—

There doesn't seem to be a chance in the world of finishing this decently and saying all the things I had in mind, so I will mail it off anyway.

The Wyeth illustrations in the Maine book are stunning, and I take back everything I said about his too-great delicacy. Somewhere I have seen some pale, colored, line-drawings of his that were insipid. But these things are almost art, (several probably are) and certainly most effective. So you have my blessing if you decide to use him.

I am swamped and tormented with detail——The Yearling correspondence, requests to do this and that from organizations——my grove work is exacting now——orange-picking time——I'm breaking in new grove help—and my repaired and being-painted house is upside down. I shall almost certainly pass up the lecture trip for next year at least.

The Arthur Train book looks delightful. My one joy at present is reading good things when I go to bed at night. I've liked lots of things lately Mann's "Joseph in Egypt"— Esther Forbes' "The General's Lady"— the Hemingway etc.[1]

Made a week-end trip to Durham N.C. for the Pitt-Duke game & had a brief call on James and Catherine Boyd. Hated not seeing more of them. They are so lovely. I'm anxious to see his book.

Thanks for everything. Will try to write soon again.

Editor's note: Pages of letter are numbered 7–11. Pages 1–6 probably destroyed by MKR.

1. Arthur C. Train, *Old Man Tut* (New York: Scribners, 1945); Thomas Mann (1875–1955), *Joseph in Egypt* (New York: Knopf, 1938); Esther Forbes (1894–1967), *The General's Lady* (New York: Harcourt, Brace, 1938); Hemingway, *The Fifth Column and the First Forty-Nine Stories.*

· ·

403. MEP to MKR (TLS: UF, 2 pp.)

[Cross Creek]
Dec. 20, 1938

Dear Marjorie:

I sent you another book yesterday because I knew you would like it,- a book of photographs by Walker Evans.[1] I don't know what it is that makes them so good, but they certainly are good. You must not bother to write me about these things, or even about anything else at all, unless you have time and inclination. I only want to know that everything is going along all right.- If you just promise to tell me if it isn't, that would be enough. Otherwise just write me when you feel like it. I know how trying all these little interruptions are when one wants to work.

As for Wyeth, he can do mighty vigorous pictures, and will get the strong masculine qualities into those Forresters, and he will make something of Penny that will delight people. And he can do the delicate pictures too. He is much better than he used to be,- and what a satisfaction that must be to a man of his age.

There is one novel <you> we are doing that you will not be able to resist.- That is Jim Boyd's "Bitter Creek". It has a sad beauty all through it. I'll send it along when it comes, though Jim will probably send you a copy himself.

Always yours,

1. Walker Evans (1903–1975), *American Photographs* (New York: Museum of Modern Art, 1938).

404. MKR to MEP (wire)

1938 DEC 21 AM 11 50
MAXWELL PERKINS—
597 FIFTH AVE—
WHAT IS CHARLES SCRIBNERS HOME ADDRESS WANT TO SEND
ORANGES—

. . . .

405. MEP to MKR (TS for wire)

DEC. 21, 1938
MRS. MARJORIE RAWLINGS
ISLAND GROVE, FLORIDA
CHARLES SCRIBNER'S ADDRESS ONE TWO FIVE EAST SEVENTY-
SECOND NEW YORK CITY

. . . .

406. MEP to MKR (TLS: UF, 2 pp.)

Dec. 22, 1938

Dear Marjorie:

We had a good talk with N.C. Wyeth today, and arranged with him to do the pictures, and I am sending him also a copy of "South Moon Under" to read. He was most enthusiastic about "The Yearling". We'll reproduce, as was done in the book on Maine that I sent you, by offset.

Wyeth must go down now and see the country and all the scenes that can be shown him. How had this better be arranged? He thought that he could get the time to do it about the second week of January. He wants, of course, to see and talk with you, and I thought that you might be able to turn him over to some one person or to various people who could take him about. You would know what would be needed. Is that old huntsman still available? At any rate I am telling you the situation. I do not want you to take on too much of a burden, of course, nor would he. Maybe everything will be simple and you will know what to suggest.

Always yours,

Dec. 29, 1938

Dear Marjorie:

Now I have to bother you again.- Irita Van Doren called me up to urge me to cooperate with her in beguiling you to come to the Book and Author luncheon of February 14th when Fadiman presides, and the booksellers' award for the favorite booksellers' book is given.- And presumably to you, and this time, whether you come or not.[1] This award is on the level,- but did it occur to you that by not coming to the other luncheon you put an award that would have been on the level, off it.- If it had been given to you it would have been genuine, but since you could not be there, it was not. I thought of that later, but anyhow it makes no difference, and you were right in principle.

I think it highly probable that you ought not to come up here to New York with all the difficulties that are besetting you. The most important thing is your work, and so it is the one thing you should think of seriously. And if you think you ought not to come, I shall tell Mrs. Van Doren and make it all right. We do not think it important that you should come, but we would like to see you ourselves, and if you want to do it—and don't do it if your instinct is against it—we should like to pay the expense of it. But I truly mean it when I say don't do it if you should not. All you have to write me is Yes or No,- and something about Wyeth's visit. Don't feel that you must undertake any obligations in connection with it except to see and talk to Wyeth. What we expect is to bring out this edition with fourteen colored pieces in it and on it, at a fairly high price, and then in the next year, to put "The Yearling" into the Illustrated Classics series that contains Jim Boyd's "Drums" for one, and Stevenson's books, etc.,[2] when it will begin to sell more especially to young people.

For no reason in particular, I am sending you a little book about the War that we printed privately.

Always yours,

1. Irita Van Doren, book review editor of the *New York Herald Tribune;* Clifton Fadiman (1904–), writer, critic, and book editor at the *New Yorker.*
2. James Boyd, *Drums* (New York: Scribners, 1928); Robert Louis Stevenson, *Kidnapped* (New York: Scribners, 1933).

Dec. 30, 1938

Dear Marjorie:

I think I have a right to quote to you from a letter from Ellen Glasgow.- I told her for one thing, that you had nominated her Prefaces as one of the three things you had most enjoyed reading during the year, and I had told her also how much you liked them before that.- And she says: "I am very much pleased by what you say of Marjorie Rawlings and her liking for my prefaces. Few books have ever moved me more deeply than 'The Yearling'. The tragedy of the end seemed to me almost too intense to be borne. It is a perfect thing of its kind, with the accent of inevitability that tempts me to use the word 'genius'. And genius as a term in literary criticism does not often appeal to me."

I thought this from her might please you.

Always yours,

1939

409. MKR to MEP (TLS, 4 pp.)

Hawthorn, Florida
January 2, 1939

Dear Max:

Again, many thanks for the books. It is good of you to bother.

About Wyeth. I'll take him over most of the territory myself to start with. It would be best for him to make his headquarters at the Marion Hotel in Ocala, at least when he first arrives. There may be a place where he would be comfortable at Silver Glen, which is in the heart of the territory, but I'll have to check on that. My friend who was more or less the prototype of Lant in South Moon,[1] could be engaged, if Mr. Wyeth wishes, to take him wherever he wants to go. He has an old but infallible car and an outboard motor and knows all of the scrub and of course makes the perfect guide. My old hunter friend[2] would be glad to be of any help he could, but he does not drive a car so would not be very useful. The young man is doing carpenter work these days and works for $4 a day. You see the distances are considerable through there and the roads are mostly hard going. But I'll get Mr. Wyeth started and then help him make whatever other arrangements seem desirable after he has seen the terrain.

I don't know what to say about the February trip to New York. I just have no desire to leave home this time of year. Let me think about it a little, if you don't mind.

My domestic arrangements have been again disturbed by another of the explosions that seem always to occur here. "So much happens at Cross Creek". One darkey shot my new man, who was proving most satisfactory. My house-girl married him mostly to get me a man on the place. He was shot three times in the abdomen and back and chest with a shotgun and his condition is critical. I have him in the Gainesville hospital but it will be a week or so before we know what will happen, if he lives that long. He was perfectly innocent in the whole thing.[3] I am of course much upset about it, not only because of the chaos to the work and my comfort, but because they are good decent colored people and my girl and I are devoted to each other.

Did the oranges reach you all right? I assumed you would be in your town house this time of year. Got a check for $334.00 for 1200 boxes—it's a good thing The Yearling has taken care of me. Haven't had a report yet on my other fruit, about 1500 to 1800 boxes, but know it will be no better. I can't understand the poor returns to the grower of so many agricultural products. I know oranges are never dirt cheap in the cities, especially the good ones, such as we grow in this section. People dependent on grove returns will simply have to abandon their groves in many cases. One small grower plans to sell his grove for enough to pay his fertilizer bill.

I'll write you again about the trip.

1. Leonard Fiddia.
2. Barney Dillard.
3. Adrenna was married to B. J. Sampson, MKR's grove manager, who was shot by his brother-in-law Henry Fountain. MKR describes this incident in *Cross Creek,* chapter 16.

. . . .

410. MEP to MKR (CC, 2 pp.)

Jan. 4, 1939

Dear Marjorie:

Mr. Chapin had a letter today from Wyeth and then yours came, and I told Chapin what you said, which is just what is needed. So no doubt you will be hearing from Wyeth yourself. I am sure you will like him.

As to the trip to New York, if you do not want to make it, I would say trust your instinct and don't do it. I do not think there is any advantage in it at all, and I should think that such an incident as that of the shooting you tell about would be exceedingly disturbing. It is too bad.

I had meant to tell you that the oranges did come safely, and were greatly appreciated. I had heard from a man in New Canaan, who is in some kind of export and import business, that the situation was very bad from an economic standpoint as to the orange crops this year. He explained it all to me, but I could not very well understand it. I suppose it must be over-production at bottom.

Always yours,

411. MEP to MKR (TS for wire)

JAN. 11, 1939
MRS. MARJORIE RAWLINGS
ISLAND GROVE, FLORIDA
MARJORIE I HATE TO RUSH YOU BUT IRITA VAN DOREN AND BOOK-
SELLERS KEEP AFTER ME FOR YOUR ANSWER STOP BUT DON'T COME
IF YOU OUGHT NOT TO STOP AWARD ALMOST CERTAIN

. . . .

412. MKR to MEP (wire)

1939 JAN 12 PM 5 48
MAXWELL PERKINS—
—597 FIFTH AVE—
WIRING VAN DOREN REFUSAL PLEADING NEED OF NONINTERRUPTION
TO WORK—

. . . .

413. MKR to MEP (TLS, 2 pp.)

[Cross Creek]
January 16, 1939

Dear Max:

I hope I haven't made things difficult or unpleasant for you, or done any damage, by refusing the invitation to New York at this time. But to come just now would put me off my stride again for an indefinite period.

I have only now smoothed out my domestic routine and taken care of local and personal commitments so that I see hope of settling down to work for two or three solid months. There is something peculiarly disrupting in a long trip, in public speaking and above all, in public attention. I think that only a writer concerned with sociological or economic phases of writing can do it without harm, and of course such contacts are stimulating for such a one. But anything of value that I may have comes out of long quiet and isolation, and while I enjoy most social contacts as much as anyone, just now I do think it desirable to do two or three stories with the volume in mind, and to do the South Moon Under script, which has had to go entirely by the boards. So forgive me if I seem perverse.

I have abandoned all idea of the lecture tour next fall. Some day, perhaps when I am at loose ends, with no new thing in mind, I should enjoy it. But not for two or three years.

My grove man who was shot is home from the hospital and recovering rapidly, and his wife, (my house-girl) and the family are all so grateful for what little I was able to do for them, that they have all settled down to making life pleasant for me. I had a rather impressive experience when I brought my girl home from Gainesville, where she stayed with an elderly relative to be near the hospital. The old woman, whom I had happened never to have seen, came marching out to my car with what seemed almost like belligerence. She was an immense but handsome and immaculate woman of the old-school type I thought no longer existed.

She called, "That the white woman?" My girl said, "Yes." The old woman shouted, "I want to see her face." I thought I had done something that had displeased her. She came to the car window and looked directly at me for some seconds. I said, "Good morning," and she made no answer. Finally she said slowly, "I want to look in the face of the white woman, got such sympathy for the black one." She nodded her head. She said, "I got you in my prayers. Say your name." I said, "Mrs. Rawlings", and she repeated it. She said, "When I take the case to the Lord, I want to carry your name natural." And she turned and marched away. I had the uncanny feeling of the tangible value of such purposeful meditation——.

. . . .

414. MKR to MEP (ALS, 1 p.)

Hawthorn, Fla.

Jan. 21, 1939

Dear Max:—

I am lending my brother $4500.—(forty-five hundred dollars). May I trouble you to send *at once*, air-mail, special delivery, a certified or cashier's check for that amount, out of my royalties due February first, to:—

Arthur H. Kinnan

505 First Avenue North

Seattle, Wash.

Sorry to bother you, but would appreciate your seeing that this is done immediately.

(using full signature by way of authorization)

Jan. 25, 1939

Dear Marjorie:

Charles Scribner wrote you about the check for your brother, which was attended to instantly.

We have told the American Mercury[1] that they can put out an edition of "Golden Apples" even though it is already in the reprints.- But Grosset was willing to allow this because these paper bound books go to a certain list of subscribers and otherwise are sold in a way which does not interfere at all with the ordinary cheap edition market. But I stipulated that since the book would have to be considerably abridged, you should have an opportunity to see it after they had cut it, or if you wished, to abridge it yourself. The books are small and look well, and as one is issued each month, its life is only about that long. They pay an advance of $250, and they sell them for 25¢ a copy, and pay a royalty of 1¢ a copy. It seemed to me that there was some advantage in doing this, as keeping the book in circulation.- I am trying to arrange to have them do one of Scott Fitzgerald's books for the same reason. It is somewhat the same kind of an idea as Omnibook which seems to further the sale of the books contained in it.

That was a wonderful picture you gave of the old negress.- I have known two like that, even up here in the North.- Women of magnificent character and dignity. They could make a boy who did wrong more ashamed of themselves than his own grandmother.

I went up to Windsor (where these old negresses used to be) last week and saw the terrible destruction to all the woods we cared for by the hurricane.- For some strange reason it would leave a fringe of pines wherever there was a grove of them, and lay low every single one inside.- One can hope though, that there won't be another hurricane for over a hundred years and then it may not strike Windsor.[2]

Yours always,

1. This deal for paperback publication by Mercury Books did not materialize.
2. Windsor, Vermont, the family home of MEP's grandfather.

. . . .

Feb. 7, 1939

Dear Marjorie:

Mr. Chapin got from N. C. Wyeth a letter, very enthusiastic, about the country and the people, and about the help you have given him.- From his account it seemed as if—he having seen a bear and heard a panther—things were now just about the way they were at the time of "The Yearling". He has evidently got his whole heart in the work.

I am sending you the abridgment about which I wrote you of "Golden Apples". Of course no abridgment is right, or anywhere near right, but these paper books have so brief a life that they really amount to the same kind of publication as occurs in syndication in newspapers, or in Omnibook, or in fact in some of the regular popular magazines.- They cut Jim's story frightfully close for the Saturday Evening Post.[1] I hope you did not read it there, for though it was greatly liked even then, it could not compare with what it will be.

We shall have to wait now for your consent, but I think that this publication will be somewhat advantageous in keeping "Golden Apples" to the front, and perhaps advancing its chances for a movie sale.

Yours always,

1. James Boyd, "*Bitter Creek*," *Saturday Evening Post* 211.16–23 (October 15–December 3, 1938).

. . . .

417. MEP to MKR (TLS: UF, 1 p.)

Feb. 10, 1939

Dear Marjorie:

Pretty soon you will get a very beautiful book, and one that you will love, I think. We published it in a limited edition, getting the copies from England, and they were all sold before publication. That made reviews unimportant and I was able to corral one of the review copies, and it is going on to you.

I am delighted about the Institute.- I had secret information that that was in progress some time ago, but I should not have had it, and so I did not say anything.[1] You will have to come on now for the dinner.

Always yours,

1. MKR was elected to the National Institute of Arts and Letters.

. . . .

418. MEP to MKR (TLS: UF, 2 pp.)

Feb. 16, 1939

Dear Marjorie:

We have a letter from a Mr. Bott, Superintendent of the Bay Springs Schools in Mississippi. He says he has your permission to include "The Pardon" in an anthology of Contemporary Southern Short Stories,[1] but that you have suggested that he ask permission of us also. The story is, of course, entirely yours, since it has not been in any book published by us, and publication in the magazine establishes no claim beyond that. At the same time, it seems to us that you are entitled to a fee, and if you would like us to write directly to Mr. Bott, as we should do anyhow in answer to his letter, we could require one and collect it, and put it to your account. We think that as high a fee as fifty dollars would be reasonable. We could make this request without any embarrassment to you as he evidently feels that as your publishers, we have some proprietary interest in the story too,—though in fact we have not, because it has not appeared in book form. If you will just send me a line to say that you approve of our doing this, I shall do it.

Always yours,

1. Not identified.

. . . .

419. MEP to MKR (TLS: UF, 2 pp.)

Feb. 16, 1939

Dear Marjorie:

I only just today got off "Wild Chorus".[1] It is a little bit damaged because the covers have somewhat warped. But it is the inside that counts, and that is all right. It was a review copy we had given to a store to exhibit before the book was out, and we had a hard time getting it back. I know you will like the pictures in it.- They are better than the text, but the text is good too.

I hope everything goes well. I suppose I shall see Evans[2] pretty soon, and he will tell me about his visit.- How is it these English publishers always get spoiled by authors, and not the Americans!

Always yours,

1. Peter Scott (1909–1989), *Wild Chorus* (London: Country Life, 1939).
2. C. S. Evans of William Heinemann, London.

. . . .

420. MKR to MEP (TLS, 5 pp.)

Hawthorn, Florida
Feb. 22, 1939

Dear Max:

That "Wild Chorus"! It is so beautiful I almost cried. It was wonderful of you to send it to me——one of the loveliest gifts I've ever had. I hate to disturb the volume, but shall probably have to have one or two of the color plates framed. Scott has caught the wild ducks and geese as I have never seen it done before. And his settings are superb in themselves. What he couldn't do with this Florida country!

Young Wyeth[1] did some stunning water colors while he was here with his father. He works very fast, direct from the landscape, without sketching, and does not work on the pieces again. He has the genius to get away with it. I wanted to buy one in particular, that he did up the road from my place, a marsh scene, but he gets a hundred and fifty dollars for all his things, and the Scotch in me rebelled against that price for an hour's work from a twenty-one year-old boy, which is an asinine way to look at it! Then, too, the piece clashed violently with the two flower paintings in oil done by my friend Robert Camp, who called on you, and I would not be willing to move them from my living room.

I can tell you why English publishers are spoiled. My dear Max, they spoil themselves, and the poor authors can do nothing about it. I have never been quite so floored as by Evans' *adoption* of my domicile. I thought of course he was coming for business reasons, and to see what one of their American authors was like, and to see the background of "The Yearling". He didn't give a damn about any of those things——he was simply having himself a Florida vacation. When, after two days, I found that he had no intention of stirring, I was aghast. The second day I took him over the Yearling territory, and then on to Daytona Beach, in which all foreigners are interested, because of the auto speed trials. Coming home——I was exhausted——he leaned back comfortably in the car and said, "Tomorrow, if it's fine, I shall just sit in your garden and absorb the sun." I had visions of his being here until spring, and thought desperately that perhaps he would go home if I recited very movingly, "Oh, to be in England, now that April's there." I think he would still be here if at an opportune moment I hadn't been able to impart the information that my doctor was much concerned about my avoiding nervous strain. Since I kept him going at a pace that would have worn down a jitterbug, he named, reluctantly, a date for his departure—six days after his arrival. He was bent on getting a tan, it seemed——.

He was a perfectly nice person, and actually it was all right, but who but an English publisher would descend on a perfect stranger for six days?

And you, whom I have begged to come for six or sixty days, you accuse me of flower-strewing the welcome mat for a foreigner!

Max, I am going to refuse permission to publish "Golden Apples" in that emasculated form. It is inharmonious enough as it stands, and I am not willing to have my name appear over a mere piece of melodramatic plot. I don't want, as readers, the kind of people who might like the book in that mere-story form; and I don't care to alienate, with it, the people who would like my regular type of writing. The thing would do me infinitely more harm than good. So it is definitely "No" on the whole proposition. *Everything* that I cared about saying is cut out in the version you sent me.

With the Booksellers' award going to "Rebecca", I feel very smug about having *not* come to New York to talk above the clatter of dishes. You get the feeling of being thrown in with the food, with the chance of being blamed for any consequent indigestion.

I read "Rebecca" last night, and it is indeed fascinating. I couldn't put it down, once I had begun. The style is beautiful. Unfortunately, she cheapens it at the end by making a trick plot, with a regular detective story ending. If she had kept it as a psychological study, it would have been a fine and permanent book, but as it stands, it will be forgotten within a year.

I have read Faulkner's "Wild Palms", too.[2] He is a magician. It is a pity that he deals in black magic. It is hard to dissociate his real power from the morbid eroticism that holds you just as when you were a child and peeked in doctors' books.

I shall be so happy when this winter season is over. Today I am expecting two Northern guests for a few days. Monday I go to Rollins College for the silly business of receiving an honorary degree.[3] Then, God willing, there will be all of March and April to work in, before I take my jaunt to the Kentucky Derby, with the Columbus talk on the side. My place is heavenly now. The orange bloom is just beginning, and my garden is perfection, and my poor shot-up black Sampson will soon be able to do his regular work again. The shooting episode is not ended, for the white neighbor who employed the darky who did the shooting, slipped the black rascal out of jail by connivance with the local state's attorney, who plays petty politics with no concern for such trivialities as justice. There will be no peace at Cross Creek until the other nigger is shut up, for he has made trouble here from the beginning. I find that it was he who drove off my previous good man. I mean to take the matter to the governor if I cannot force the state's attorney to put through a Grand Jury investigation. Testimony was never even taken from the man who was shot, nor from the only eye-witness of the shooting, and the attorney dismissed the case without bringing it before the Grand Jury "for lack of evidence"!

Max, the theme that begins to shape itself in my mind for the next novel, the one about the planter who was a slave trader and married, legally, the African princess, is that of the conflict between the world of the imagination and the world of reality. This man would have lived a hard and ruthless life, and his establishment of a black woman as mistress of his household would have been taken as a further indication of his callousness to ordinary living. Actually, the woman's gentleness would be the one point of contact between that lovely world where all is gentle and beautiful, and the true world——that, and his attempt to make an earthly Paradise, physically, of his plantation on the river. Few of us ever align the dream world with the true one, and it is a universal theme. There would of course be a white woman in the story, who could have offered him the same thing as the black one, but he would have turned to the black gentleness as a refuge from all he had known of harsh and predatory women. This is all entre nous, for I am not ready to talk of the book. The background in time, 1790–1840, is a most picturesque one in Florida history.

I didn't like "Abe Lincoln in Illinois".[4] It seems to me pretentious and stuffy. But I can't thank you enough for "Wild Chorus."

1. Andrew N. Wyeth (1917–), son of N. C. Wyeth.
2. William Faulkner, *The Wild Palms* (New York: Random House, 1939).
3. MKR received a Doctor of Letters from Rollins College in February.
4. Robert Sherwood (1896–1955), *Abe Lincoln in Illinois* (New York: Scribners, 1938).

. . . .

421. MEP to MKR (CC, 2 pp.)

Feb. 28, 1939

Dear Marjorie:

I was delighted to get your letter and very much amused by some of it.- I know the way Englishmen do settle down on one. An English author once came to us for a weekend and spent the whole winter, with brief excursions for lectures.

About the young Wyeth I did not know anything. I'll look up his pictures. N. C. Wyeth works at a very different pace and I only wish he went fast so that we could see what he will do for "The Yearling".

I am writing now especially to enclose a letter from Spivak,[1] to whom I wrote the moment your letter came. I don't suppose it would be worth your while to cut "Golden Apples" even if you were willing to do it. But the truth is I never knew any harm would come from these subsidiary ways of publishing, although for years I was against them and thought they must be damaging. Even in first serials the popular magazines cut a novel to pieces, but the book public never knows anything about it.- So at last I had got to thinking of all these things as simply a way of bringing in a little revenue, and being in some degree a kind of publicity that might enlarge a writer's public.

Yours always,

1. Lawrence Spivak, editor and publisher.

March 11, 1939

Dear Marjorie:

I have been thinking about the novel you are planning. It does offer a hard problem, but it also has very great possibilities, and I hope you will do it. There is the practical question you raise about miscegenation. You had thought this much more serious than I when you spoke of it. But how serious it is depends a good deal on the whole quality of the book. Perhaps it could be somewhat reduced anyhow by making the woman partly white, an octoroon, or something like that. My sense of what you are doing comes entirely from what you once told me in Chatham Gardens. Isn't there a chance that we can sit there again when Spring actually comes. I had thought your election to the Institute would bring you here by necessity, but Arthur told me that they give only one dinner a year, and that the next one won't be until the Fall. You will have to come for that, but I do wish you were coming sooner. It seems a very long time since I have seen you.

We are to have another daughter married this month, and to a very nice fellow and an able one.- But so gentle that I am afraid of her tyrannizing over him. Zippy's husband had his one-man show and it seems to have been very successful, and even to be likely to result in the sale of several pictures. I wish you could have seen it.- Perhaps you have seen the reproduction of Tom's portrait which was one of its main features.- But the portrait loses much more than is usual in a reproduction. There is something in the color values in that picture that is totally lost in a photograph. My oldest daughter's husband is building up a real practice as a doctor in New Canaan.[1] Louise has been very well this winter, and gets great pleasure out of the Catholic Church. I am looking forward though to the days when she is no longer a convert, but an old Catholic because I have observed that the old Catholics do not take it nearly so hard. Louise goes to church every single day, and it seems as if she spent most of Sunday there. But on the whole it has all been a good thing.

Always yours,

Editor's note: Written in left margin of p. 3 of letter, in MEP's hand: "I don't often send you novels but I thought you would like to see Jim's.[2] Tell me sometime how you like it. I'm sending Pent House of the Gods.[3] M.P." At the top of p. 3: "Over". On p. 4, in MEP's hand: "Have you a new, informal picture,- for general publicity, like those you sent before,- We're planning a considerable drive at the time The Yearling becomes one year old. Max."

1. Louise E. "Peggy" Perkins married Robert King, M.D.; Elisabeth "Zippy" Perkins married Douglas Gorsline, an artist; Bertha Perkins married John Frothingham, M.D.
2. James Boyd, *Bitter Creek.*
3. Theos Bernard, *Penthouse of the Gods: A Pilgrimage into the Heart of Tibet* (New York: Scribners, 1939).

. . . .

423. MEP to MKR (CC, 3 pp.)

March 26, 1939

Dear Marjorie:

"The Yearling" has been out for all but a year, and during that time we have been constantly pressed about second serialization,- that is, serialization in the newspapers. Often that is allowed from three months to six months after publication, but in this special instance we have refused to discuss it seriously. But soon the time will come when it should be done, if it is to be done, and I am writing to ask you how you feel in the matter. Most authors take it as a matter of course, and of little consequence, regarding it as profitable in a small way, and as having a certain advertising value. The newspapers often feature their serials, and that indirectly advertises the book. And the public that reads serials apparently is not a book-reading public. Certainly I never knew any second serialization to have any harmful effect, and in some cases—as with Kenneth Roberts' "Northwest Passage"——it definitely stimulates the sale.[1] There is no doubt that that was true in Philadelphia after second serialization began in the Inquirer there, with its concomitant advertising. We have a very good man through whom we do all this syndication that is done, Ralph Graves, and I must tell him whether he can count upon releasing "The Yearling" for the papers at some time in the not distant future.

I hope everything is right with you. I see in my last letter that I used a very wrong word. Fortunately not as wrong a one as Creole. What I meant to say was that the woman in the novel you project might be a mulatto, which I believe may mean only a small degree of whiteness, but doesn't arouse the same animosity as no whiteness at all. I think an octoroon is only one-eighth negro. Or is it only one-eighth white? That would be all right.

Always yours,

1. Kenneth Roberts, *Northwest Passage* (New York: Doubleday, Doran, 1937).

March 29, 1939

Dear Marjorie:

I thought you would like to see this ad taken from the Times at the beginning of the second year of "The Yearling". Maybe you will write me before long about the second serialization question.

If you see the Virginia Quarterly Review, there is a really excellent article in it about Tom, with plentiful quotations from his letters.- The best thing that has been done about him.[1]

We had a third wedding in our family Saturday, and a very gay time.- Second girl to marry a doctor, this one a surgeon.

Yours always,

1. Review of *The Web and the Rock,* by Wilbur L. Schramm, "Careers at Cross Roads," *Virginia Quarterly Review* 15.3 (Summer 1939): 627–33.

. . . .

April 6, 1939

Dear Marjorie:

I just wanted to tell you that Wyeth brought in two of the illustrations yesterday,- one the lining paper. The regular illustration was of old Slewfoot when first Penny and Jody caught up with him. It was excellent, I thought,- gave you the very feel of the country. And Jody was fine, with his tow head. The lining paper showed Jody and Flag walking, he a little ahead, over sand, with all the tropical growth around them, the moss on the trees, etc. I think we shall have a fine book out of it. Wyeth told stories about the blind bear who ripped off the man's boot, and of the panther being loose in the enclosure when he and Lant were in it, though they did not know it.

Always yours,

P.S. Younghill Kang asked me, as his friend, to try to help him become an American citizen. He ought to be one. He knows this country better than most Americans, and loves it more too. There is to be a private bill introduced to make him a citizen, and if you have time and inclination—he has the greatest admiration for you—would you write a letter in his favor addressed to the Hon. Members of the House of Representatives, and send it either to me or to him? If it comes to me, I'll give it to him. Even a line would count for much if you wrote it.

Hawthorn, Florida
April 17, 1939

Dear Max:

What a strange feeling it must be to live a good part of a life-time with five children, and then have them fade into the outer world. Or don't they fade? Do you have, instead, the feeling of enlarging your own world? I've often wondered.

Between endless interruptions I've finally written a very short story, but it's no good and I have to do it all over again. The idea is all right. I hope that every week the influx of visitors, known and unknown, will stop. Cross Creek proves, after all, not to be sufficiently remote.

The MGM movie people were in Florida doing a Tarzan picture, and while here their camera man was commissioned to take shots of The Yearling country. They gave me a set, and I'm sending them for you to forward to Wyeth *as a loan.* Please emphasize that I want them back.

I enclose also a negative of a picture they took of me that is as good as any I've had. Thought you might like to have some prints made in case you still need a new picture. I had none at the time you asked. Would appreciate either having the negative back, or several prints for friends here.

About the newspaper serialization. You wouldn't plan to do it until after the Wyeth edition, would you? I should think it would hurt sales, but perhaps newspaper readers don't buy books enough to matter. After my other experience with cutting, I am a bit of a fanatic, and would want the stipulation of no cutting. But if you think the serialization is desirable, I don't mind.

Have done a story, but it's no good and will have to do it over. Idea's all right.

Had a lovely note from Ellen Glasgow asking me to stop in Richmond and talk with her the next time I go north. It will be summer anyway before I get anywhere near, but I should gladly go far out of my way to meet her.

I'll be away from April 30 to May 10. Think I told you I'm going to the Kentucky Derby May 6th, and giving a lecture (well paid) in Columbus the same week.

Am feeling fine again.

[Postscript] The small pictures are of Lant and Piety, and their place. The large pictures are of the abandoned clearing where I lived and where I laid The Yearling. Other large pictures of the Yearling territory.

Editor's note: At top of p. 2 of letter in Joseph Chapin's hand: "19 small / 18 large / to Wyeth / apr. 24/39 / asked him / to return / them."

April 20, '39

Dear Marjorie:-

I just saw the jacket design for the illustrated Yearling,- an all around jacket that shows Jody, Flag, Penny, & the Mother–& the dogs too–against the background of their home;- & very effectively both for a jacket & a poster.[1]

I'll write you lots of news if you'll soon send me a postcard. Have you scratched the old Fox off your list altogether that you won't answer his letters?!

1. Dust jacket for the trade edition of the Pulitzer Prize Edition. For a publishing history of MKR's works, see Rodger L. Tarr, *Marjorie Kinnan Rawlings: A Descriptive Bibliography* (Pittsburgh: University of Pittsburgh Press, 1996).

. . . .

May 3, 1939

Dear Marjorie:

I suppose wherever you were, you were promptly informed in some way, that you had won the Pulitzer prize. We were all ready for the news and are making the most of it we can. We are getting out copies of "The Yearling" already, with a band around them, and we plan to take the painting Wyeth did for the jacket of that edition for the cover of our Fall List. It will run all around, front and back. We now have wonderful support for an illustrated edition. In fact, everything about and to do with "The Yearling" seems to turn out rightly.- It must be a great pleasure to you to have written such a book,- one that must become an American classic.

The pictures came, and we sent all of them on to Wyeth "as a loan". But the excellent one of you sitting under a tree—the best we have had—we had on hand in time for the Saturday Review of Literature to use on its cover when it came out yesterday.[1]

Your friend Mr. Miller[2] came in after his return from Florida, and he told me how well you seem now.- He told me a good deal too about the country and Lant, etc. He is a mighty nice man. He cannot write novels though. Maybe the book he is talking of about old days up the Hudson might work out.

There is one business matter I should have taken up with you. The Wyeth edition is extremely expensive both on account of the large payment we must make him, and because of the color plates and printing, and I had assumed that you would accept, as is the general practice with reprint editions of that kind, a royalty of 10% throughout. I shall soon, I think, be able to send you proofs of the pictures.- They promise to be excellent. Wyeth called up when he heard that you had won the Pulitzer, to express his delight.

Always yours,

1. *Saturday Review of Literature* 20.2 (May 6, 1939). Contains note on the Pulitzer Prize for *The Yearling* on pp. 7–8.
2. Not identified.

....

429. MKR to MEP (TLS, 2 pp.)

Upper River Road
Louisville, Kentucky
Monday
[May 8, 1939]

Dear Max:

Thought I might hear from you here, as I knew Miss Wyckoff must have my Louisville address from last year. Am anxious to know if Wyeth found the photographs helpful.

Had a grand time over the Derby weekend, without too much damage to the body, soul or pocket-book. The Columbus lecture went off swimmingly, but the nervous tension is so great that I doubt if I should ever dare try a real lecture tour. Was glad to try it as an experiment for that reason.

I'm terribly anxious to get home and settle down to a summer's work. Leave here Wednesday and get home Friday.

I'm enclosing a drawing that came from my young artist friend whom you met, Robert Camp. He clipped my awful face evidently from a newspaper and drew his libelous lines around it. The portraits unfortunately are all accurate, especially of my faithful black Adrina [Adrenna], but he is not quite fair to my aristocratic pointer dog. It is so funny, though, that I thought you and Whitney and Charlie Scribner might get a laugh. Be sure and send it back to me.

....

430. MEP to MKR (TLS: UF, 3 pp.)

May 9, 1939

Dear Marjorie:

I wish I had thought to look for your Louisville address. I did not remember that we had had it. I read about the Kentucky Derby and thought of you as being there. As for lecturing, I hope you never will do it. I know it must be dreadfully trying, and you have so much to do. One thing you might do too, is to write a book about the region of Florida you are in as it is,- a book of description and incident which would put the place, and the life, and the beauty of the country and all, before a reader. This might be easier to do than fiction, and perhaps could be done, if you thought well of it, from time to time, as a relief from the difficulty of what is more strictly speaking, creative writing. It would make a beautiful book, and could be illustrated, perhaps with photographs or with pictures by such a one as Shenton. You could put into it such anecdotes as you have told me,- the one about the old negress, for instance.

But I did not mean to begin by bringing up such a matter as that. I enjoyed the picture you sent, and so did Charlie and all of us, and I am returning it.

I believe you will *have* to come up here for the Pulitzer dinner on the 22nd, for you are the most conspicuous winner. Bob Sherwood cannot be there, for he is abroad. The novel is the most important prize, and next to that the play.

You will find a letter awaiting you that I wrote after the Pulitzer prize was announced, though I knew you could not get it until the 10th.

Always yours,

. . . .

431. MKR to MEP (TLS, 4 pp.)

Hawthorn, Florida
May 13, 1939

Dear Max:

Your suggestion about the non-fiction book is actually uncanny. I had decided to do the "Cross Creek" book as soon as I finish the two or three new stories, and before I tackle the novel. The decision was made for two reasons: I have enough material for a perhaps not-too-thick book, some of the chapters being already written, as I mentioned to you last spring; and there is no reason why, if the book is any good and is at all liked, there should not be one or two companion books over a long period of years. The other reason is a feeling of uncertainty about the novel, which I have learned to trust. It is simply not properly shaped in my mind——I don't know quite where I am going on it—— and it would be absurd to begin it until it is as clearly defined as was "The Yearling". I learned from that, that it works out best for me to know exactly what I want to do, even though that makes the actual writing a thousand times harder, and almost joyless, from feeling with every paragraph that I'm not doing it. Yet the final result is bound to be better.

I had begun struggling with myself as to whether to tell you what I had decided. I was afraid you would be dubious; even, and this is an intimate confession, whether you would think the Pulitzer award and all the momentary fuss had thrown me off balance, so that all I could do was to jabber, without knowing what I was really about. But now that you have read my mind, it seems, and have the same feeling that I do about it, the way is clear.

I mean to do it as a succession of sketches. Most will be coordinated episodes, almost complete stories, except that they will be true, and I shall do only a faint coloring or pointing up here and there for dramatic or harmonious effect. Some will be literally sketches. Then when it is done, if it seems too uncoordinated to us, we can consider the possibility of my working the material into a true narrative. But as I see it now, the way I have in mind should be able to stand. And you know how little afraid I am of work, so that if it isn't right, we needn't feel discouraged.

I am almost ready to do one of the longer humorous stories, one of the Quincey Dover series. I shall surely have two or three stories ready for the collection next spring, if you still plan that schedule. Then a year or possibly in the fall or winter after the stories, "Cross Creek" should be ready. *Definitely* ready, if we don't change the form.

I had a nice wire from Wyeth. His enthusiasm is grand, isn't it.

. . . .

432. MKR to MEP (TLS, with holograph postscript, 4 pp.)

Hawthorn, Florida

May 17, 1939

Dear Max:

I have just returned the manuscripts in the '38–9 Hopwood Contest at the University of Michigan, for which I acted as one of the three judges.[1]

Among the novel entries, was one so startlingly good, to my notion, that I have asked the Director of the Hopwood Awards for permission for Scribner's to contact the author, to consider the book for publication.

The book is called "Loon Totem", and was signed with the nom-de-plume "Molly Beaver".[2] It is the only thing I have seen from the inside of the Indian mind. It is laid in the Wisconsin, Illinois and Michigan Indian country from 1804 to about 1830, and is told in the first person as though by an elderly woman——the daughter of the great Tecumseh.

The book is of as rare a beauty as I have encountered in many a day. Paragraph after paragraph, sentence after sentence, brought the tears that come in response to anything beautiful. The style is superb, and exquisitely simple. The

Indian lore, and the woods lore, are coordinated threads in a lovely tapestry. Many of the simple similes, drawn from nature, take you off your feet with their perfection. The story itself is absorbing, with all the characters real and vital. The narrative moves forward without flaw. The dialogue is almost as restrained as Hemingway's. The only possible criticism I could make is of the writing at the dramatic climax. It tends to melodrama, but with the author's gift for restraint, could easily be toned down in keeping with the rest of the writing.

Do trust my reaction to the book to the extent of having the manuscript sent you for reading.

I should suggest that you write to:

R.W. Cowden
Director of Hopwood Awards
Hopwood Room
University of Michigan
Ann Arbor, Michigan

The contestants are all Michigan students, but since graduate students, and applicants for master's and doctor's degrees are permitted to compete, it seems likely that "Molly Beaver" is beyond undergraduate age. Certainly there is no trace of immaturity in her work.

[Postscript] I should have copied excerpts from the book for you, but I was pressed to meet the dead-line because of the scant time left me on my return from Kentucky.

1. Named after the dramatist and Michigan graduate Avery Hopwood (1882–1928).
2. Molly Beaver [Iola Fuller Goodspeed], *The Loon Feather* (New York: Harcourt, Brace, 1939).

. . . .

433. MEP to MKR (TLS: UF, 4 pp.)

May 22, 1939

Dear Marjorie:

Thanks very much for writing about "Loon Totem". I have written to Mr. Cowden, with whom we have had to do previously. The book sounds mighty good from what you say, and I hope we can get the first chance to read it.

As to your novel, I am sure you are right in waiting until you feel eager to write it. I know you did not feel satisfied as yet, and while I hope it won't be so very long before it has all matured in your mind, so that you can do it, I know that we must wait,- that you must not hurry yourself, and that we must not urge you. The work will all go on in your mind, even without your being conscious of it.

I am mighty glad that you are planning for the non-fiction book too, and I shall expect the stories for the Spring. I had hoped the Pulitzer dinner would come off, and that you would attend it, and while I have heard nothing to the contrary, neither have I heard anything of developing plans. Maybe they have given it up. They generally announce the winners at a dinner, and that gave it its great interest. They gave that up, I guess because the invitations inevitably led to a revelation of the winners in advance.

I went up to Windsor yesterday, and for the first time really saw what damage had been done to all the woods we cared so much about, by the hurricane of last Fall. It was not as bad as it might have been. While it destroyed everything on the first ridge, and around what we always called the Plain—and it used to seem to us a great upland prairie—it did really not so much damage everything back of there. Large parts of it are still as they used to be, and a boy could have as much pleasure out of it all as we used to have.

That Mr. Miller came in on Friday with some chapters of a book of reminiscences, and they seem to me very well done, though perhaps not sufficiently important to justify publication. He cannot write fiction though. He wanted me to let him know when we had some of the Wyeth pictures here for "The Yearling". He said he would come in any time to look at them.- And I would like him to see the originals because they are inevitably better than the most careful reproduction, of course.

Always yours,

. . . .

434. MKR to MEP (TLS, 1 p.)

Hawthorn, Fla.
June 5 [1939]

Dear Max:

My guess was right about the maturity of the author of the very beautiful Indian manuscript. Do hope you get hold of it for a reading. Cowden wrote me that the other judges were as impressed with it as I was. Nothing else in the contest is worth a moment of your time.

I've forgotten to write you about the question of my royalty on the illustrated edition of the Yearling. You know I'm not mercenary, and will agree to whatever is right, but offhand, the question arises in my mind as to why I should be the one to take a cut. I know Wyeth is high priced, and that such an edition would be very expensive to print, but I assumed the selling price would cover everything, without reducing my royalty rate. Of course the pictures and printing will sell the book, but after all there wouldn't be an edition without my text! You have never mentioned what the retail price of the book will be, or how large the edition, or to what extent the sales will absorb sales of the regular edition. I'd appreciate a little more information, and more details as to why I should be the one not to profit.

Probably my English contract has spoiled me, as on anything over 5,000 copies I get 20%. Of course their selling price is lower than ours, and there are all kinds of commissions and a British government tax, but 20% even so on anything that sells is a grand rate. Evans[1] was sure it would go 50–60,000.

People have been lovely about the Pulitzer. It would be awful to have a general lament go up over such an award!

Please pray for peace for me, so I can work.

Editor's note: At top of page in MEP's hand: "8000 / copies / 7000 plant / same as present."

1. C. S. Evans.

. . . .

435. MEP to MKR (CC, 4 pp.)

June 7, 1939

Dear Marjorie:

I am most grateful to you for writing about Mrs. Goodspeed's novel. As soon as I got your letter I telegraphed, and followed the telegram with a letter, and just this morning came a letter from Mrs. Goodspeed saying she had sent the manuscript by express although she had had telegrams from other publishers.- And so it will be read the moment it gets here, and acted upon with all speed, and I think it was mighty good of you to help us.

I'll tell you exactly now how matters stand about the Wyeth edition. What we call the plant of the book,- all basic expenses that is, before printing comes to seven thousand dollars. This is more than five thousand dollars more than the usual plant. We expect to publish the Wyeth edition at $3.50. If we paid you a royalty of 10% you would be getting the same amount as you get now on the regular edition of "The Yearling". But we would get nothing at all until we had sold 8,000 copies because it would take that sale to pay for the investment in the plant. If we paid a 15% royalty, we should not get a return per copy that would give us the necessary margin of profit even after the plant was all paid for. Those are the plain facts, and I could show you all of the figures, and I am pretty sure you could understand them.- We are counting upon this $3.50 edition having a good sale at the price but later we should expect to put it in as one of the classics for young readers in a somewhat different sized book, but printed from the same plates, and with all the Wyeth illustrations.- But if we did do that, we should have to sell it, as we do Jim Boyd's "Drums" and all the other books in that group, at $2.50, and then we could not possibly pay more than 25¢ a copy,- that is still 10%. But on the first Wyeth edition you would be receiving 35¢ a copy, and getting a renewed sale. I truly think this is a fair proposition, and it is the usual one in the circumstances,- in fact, I should think the invariable one.

You know, of course, that the English royalties always run higher than ours because they give only a 33% discount, while we often give not far from 50%, and because all publishing expenses here are much higher, including manufacturing and transportation, salesmanship and advertising.

But won't you be coming up here before very long at all? We simply will not make any arrangement with you that does not satisfy you, but we could talk about it more fully and easily if you were here, and you run no risk of my putting anything over, because I am not any good that way.

I am going to jump at "Loon Totem" the moment it comes. Mr. Miller was just in here. He is a most companionable man. I always like to talk to him. He is going to Maine, and I told him he must look up old Waldo Peirce.[1]

Always yours,

1. Waldo Peirce, painter, MEP's classmate at Harvard University.

. . . .

436. MEP to MKR (CC, 3 pp.)

June 19, 1939

Dear Marjorie:

After much anxious thought and great difficulty, I decided against "Loon Totem". I got two others here, Jack Wheelock and Wallace Meyer,[1] to read it first, but they felt as I did, that beautiful as its underlying spirit, its expression of Indian lore, and that profound love of all the phenomena of nature were, it *did* fail as a novel. I therefore thought that if we published it, we should not do well with it and the writer would be disappointed. It was a mighty hard decision because looked at in one way it seemed a betrayal of an unusual talent. But I have had to learn the bitter lesson that if one publishes a book without success the author is disappointed, and the publisher too. And in these times of economic stress, a publisher cannot ignore the economic factor to the extent that he would wish. I dealt with the manuscript just as fast as I possibly could, reading it all in one day, and getting the others to do the same, and I simply felt in the end that hard as it was, I was compelled to act upon my convictions.- When I see you, I'll tell you all the details of why the book seemed to me not to succeed as fiction.- What an awful tragedy that was of the American Indian and such as Tecumseh, and what's more, it never has been told so people can realize it.- Or was it in Parkman?[2] I never did read him, always meant to. Years ago we had here a collection of the speeches of some of those great, simple, noble leaders. They were magnificent, and opened my eyes for the first time fully. What a cruel fate the Indians met! Caroline Gordon is writing a novel about the Cherokees.[3] She feels deeply the whole story of the Indians, and I am in hopes that that will do what she wants it to.

Jim Boyd was just here, and I hope he will come back at 4:30 when we can go out and talk comfortably. He does not look very well, but he does seem to be in good spirits. I always enjoy being with him.

Always yours,

1. John H. Wheelock and Wallace Meyer, Scribner editors.
2. Francis Parkman (1823–1893), noted for his histories of Native Americans.
3. Caroline Gordon, *Green Centuries* (New York: Scribners, 1941).

. . . .

437. MEP to MKR (TLS: UF, 3 pp.)

June 28, 1939

Dear Marjorie:

I thought I had better ask you if you wished to read the proof of "The Yearling" for the Wyeth edition.- It is made up into pages at the start, and I can have it read carefully here, and then we should gain time. The only reason for your reading it would be the possibility that you might wish to change a word or two here and there, but I can't imagine why. Let me know.

Fritz Dashiell called me up to tell me that the Reader's Digest wanted very much to print a part of "The Yearling" somewhat cut.- I told him that you were very much averse to abridgement, but since he knew you so well I thought he was entitled to put the matter before you and to write you himself, and suggested his doing it. There is one thing sure, no injury is done to the sale or reputation of the book by that kind of thing if it is skillfully done. Reprinting does not seem to have any effect unless a favorable one. The syndication of "The Yearling" has not reduced the sale, and it almost appears to have helped it. Another point is that the Wyeth edition will not so much sell to new readers of "The Yearling" as to those who love it and want it in a beautiful form, and to those who will take advantage of its form to give it to those who have not yet read it or whom they know to love it.- And on that account the more widely its fame is spread, the more people who are acquainted with it to greater or less degree, the better.

Have you read Tom's book?[1] I'll send you a copy if you haven't one already. I think the lady in it did great service to Tom, especially in believing in him firmly when he was, as he almost always was, desperate and losing faith in himself.- And yet Mrs. Wolfe[2] told me at great length yesterday how if it had not been for that Tom would have married a nice simple girl and had a large family and lived a domestic life!

Always yours,

1. Thomas Wolfe, *The Web and the Rock* (New York: Harper, 1939).
2. Julia E. Wolfe.

. . . .

438. MKR to MEP (CC of letter to Dashiell, with holograph addition, 4 pp. frag.)

Hawthorn, Florida
June 29, 1939

Dear Mr. Dashiell:

It is indeed pleasant to be discussing manuscripts with you again. I do not think any psychologist has ever quite explained the peculiar comfort that comes in a recurrence of the familiar; a repetition of something that has been done before.

I am writing you about the proposed condensation of "The Yearling" in a brief moment of courage. If I do not do it now——the ultimate answer would have to be the same——I shall put it off for many unhappy days. I cannot possibly allow the condensation. But few refusals have made me so unhappy, for I am overcome with the gift for analysis, the editorial genius, of whatever members of your staff have done this remarkable job of skeletonizing. No better job could possibly have been done, certainly not by me, in reducing the motif of the story to its essential elements. It makes me almost ill to think of wasting so much really brilliant editing. But the answer is irrevocably "No" to any such "digest", and I shall try very hard to explain the necessity for the negative.

I think it comes down, basically, to the *effect* of style. My style, for better or for worse, is my own. All my writing life I have struggled for a compromise between a lushness that is natural to me, and an admiration for stark simplicity. No one knows how many composite sentences I have broken up into shorter direct ones, like the convict at hard labor "making little ones out of big ones" on the rock pile. But the short, simple and direct sentences by themselves are monotonous and without color, and so, with a conscious effort toward a certain *rhythm,* I allow myself to explode, deliberately, into longer and richer sentences, definitely poetic, that come as a reward to myself and to the reader for our asceticism.

In reducing "The Yearling" to its basic story, there was no alternative but to use the short, plain sentences that carry the narrative forward. Standing by themselves, these sentences produce an almost puerile effect. The style of the condensation is that of one "writing down" to a juvenile audience. I could imagine the proposed form as a desirable one for very young children. I cannot visualize it with any appeal to the adult mind.

In the second place, the cumulative effect of the condensation strikes me as one of painful sentimentality. The story of the boy and the fawn, by itself, is vapidly idealistic. No background is provided of the lonely conditions of the boy's life that make a companion something more than a childish luxury. No true study is given of the desperate straits of such a life as the Baxters', that makes an interference with daily subsistence a tragedy, and not an inconvenience. I was telling, not only the story of a boy's precipitation from adolescence into maturity, but the story of all Penny Baxters, fighting against odds, but hoping that the beloved younger generation might be spared a little of the pain of an inevitably uneven fight. None of this struggle is apparent in the condensation, from lack of space in which to express it. I like to think that there is meaning in the full story. There is sentimentality, but little meaning, in the abbreviated form. Unless one is conscious of the desperate impositions of living, the tale of a boy's disappointment is a trivial one.

I think that anyone who had read "The Yearling" would not be offended by the remarkable simplification. I am convinced that anyone who had not read it, would be left with an ineradicable sense of juvenile sentimentality. Since the appeal of all material in the "Reader's Digest" is to those who have not read the original in its full form and would not otherwise know it, I feel that I cannot allow myself to be judged, as a creative writer, by this emasculated version, no matter how well done from the editorial point of view. I could guarantee that the reaction of the new reader would be, "This is very sweet. There are flashes of beauty. But the sweetness is insipid. The result is nothing." There is no *substance* behind the little tale. Take away from me that substance, and you have negated all that life has beaten into me.

You see, I am not a professional writer. Even when I was in desperate financial circumstances, merely selling things was not good enough. I could always have made my living as a journalist——as a cook! Nothing has mattered in my writing except the expressing, as best I might, my cumulative reaction to life, and in especial, to life in this place, with the particular appeal to my sympathies. I have used a section and a people that I loved, and, strangely, understood, as a medium for the things I wanted to say about all people and all living. The condensed version of "The Yearling" does not say those things, and no possible arrangement in 15,000 words could say them. <illegible excision> If I were to try to tell that story in so brief a medium, I should have done it, technically, in quite different fashion.

There is no financial inducement in the proposed "digest." I should have to be much more desperate than when you paid the fabulous amount of $700 for "Jacob's Ladder" to agree to appearing before new readers in a form abhorrent to something very deep inside me. I do not believe I could be hungry enough to do it. <illegible excision>

So I must ask you to respect a deeply seated integrity about my work, and to forgive me for refusing permission to use a beautiful piece of editing that, after all, violates that integrity. [remainder of letter missing]

Editor's note: The above letter is a copy of a letter from MKR to Fritz Dashiell. MKR sent it to MEP with this handwritten message at the top: "Dear Max:— Here's a copy of the letter I wrote Dashiell about the condensation for the Digest. You would agree with me if you read it."

. . . .

439. MEP to MKR (TLS: UF, 3 pp.)

July 7, 1939

Dear Marjorie:

I read with great interest the letter you wrote to Fritz Dashiell.- It seems to me the most absolutely complete and convincing and considerate answer that could be given. I infer what actually was done, though from what Fritz told me I had thought they had taken some one episode from the book and had not made much change in it. Of course you cannot shorten up the sentences without ruining the whole effect. That is plain enough, but I don't know that Fritz is very sensitive to that sort of thing. It would have been rather embarrassing to me if you had accepted the proposal, as a matter of fact, because I have been fighting off Omnibook for months in their determination to beguile us and you into allowing them to make an abridgement.

This Spring has been a very bad one for sales, mostly, it is thought, on account of repeated war scares. But this morning, in spite of a new scare on the horizon, we have an order from Baker & Taylor for 2,500 Yearling, from Wanamaker for 100, from Speigel, Inc. [*sic*] in Chicago for 100, and a good many 5s and 10s.- I am assuming that you would not require to read the proof of the Wyeth edition, and am having it read carefully here. I do not think there is any reason why you should read it.

Are you getting on with stories? Carl Brandt said something to lead me to think you were.

Always yours,

. . . .

440. MKR to MEP (TLS, I p.)

[Cross Creek]
July 23, 1939

Dear Max:

The Wyeth edition of "The Yearling" promises to be very handsome. I like the type and make-up very much. I am torn between admiration and disapproval of the illustrations themselves, but don't let that comment go any farther, as there is no point in upsetting Wyeth about it. The color, the backgrounds, the animals, the action, are superb. I can't see the characterizations at all. They are as far removed from Cracker types as possible. The expression on Jody's face is very sweet and appealing, but that mop of yellow hair offends me. Penny is fair. Ma Baxter is not right at all. Shenton got her absolutely in the drawing in which Jody is cajoling her. Wyeth's Ma looks to me like a Pennsylvania Dutch farm woman. However, my reaction would be the last one in the world to pay any attention to, and if outside people like the characterizations, that's all that matters. My friends here who have seen the advance make-up do not like them, either. But there is no point in saying anything about this. I am sure that the magnificent color and settings and dramatic action will carry the thing, and that the effect of the book will be striking, which is all that matters. What do people up there think about the characters?

If you trust the proof-reading there, there's no need of my doing it, though I sha'n't mind if you think it safer.

I've done two stories, but they're not right and I have to do them over again.

I have almost decided to abandon the material for the novel, and it is terribly upsetting. I shall go ahead with research on that plantation period, for the background is fascinating, and something may work out eventually.

We're having a nice summer, rain every day, so that we've been comfortable. No, I haven't "The Web and the Rock" and somehow dread it, for the reviewers all say it shows no progress. Of course, we know that if there was to have been progress, it would have come after Tom's illness.

. . . .

441. MEP to MKR (TLS: UF, 4 pp.)

July 28, 1939

Dear Marjorie:

To tell you the truth, I do agree with you about Ma Baxter. She does look like a Pennsylvanian, or a Delaware farmer's wife. That is true, but everyone here who does not know the Cracker type—and none of us here do—were very much taken with the pictures, though of course they would not, and could not, be what the creator of these characters really meant. I do not think Wyeth is that kind of an illustrator. I have only seen the first several pictures. Wyeth is sending the others directly to the engraver but two came not long ago and I was in Baltimore at the time. We have read the proof very carefully, and I am sure it is right.

Well, don't read "The Web and the Rock",- although in the first half of it are some of the very best stories Tom ever did, including that one he called "Tiger Tiger". It is as good narrative as anyone ever did. But it is true that the last half of the book—the love affair—is and always was not what it ought to be. It should have been written fifteen years later maybe.- And there was Tom's predicament. He had caught up to himself in time, and when he wrote about things too near, he could not make them what they should have been. It was a real predicament, and I don't know what could have come of it.

But we are publishing a collection of his poetical passages from the earlier books to be called "The Face of a Nation"[1] and Shenton has done magnificent decorations for it, and Jack Wheelock has written a fine introduction. I'll send you a copy of that. It is in proof now.

Perhaps that novel will take a long time before you can write it and some other one, not so psychologically difficult, may come first. But the book of stories should be the next thing anyhow, and I know you will have to struggle hard to get them right. That can't be helped.

You are lucky for having rain. We are having a drought they say, though I personally rather enjoy it.

Always yours,

1. *Face of a Nation: Poetical Passages from the Works of Thomas Wolfe* (New York: Scribners, 1939).

Hawthorn, Florida
July 31, 1939

Dear Max:

Just to give you my address for the month of August:

c/o Poole[1]

Crescent Beach R.F.D.

via St. Augustine

Florida

I've rented a delightful modern cottage right on the ocean for the month, in complete isolation, which I wasn't getting at Cross Creek, and think I'll really get some work done. My hope is to get in shape the two stories I've done— one of them, if it turns out any good, suitable for the spring collection. Then I'd like to get at least a first draft of the South Moon dramatization. Sam Byrd has started production on the Roark Bradford negro musical, "John Henry", with Paul Robeson, the New York opening due the last of December.[2] It would be fine if I could have South Moon ready for him to go into as soon as he's ready after that.

Every now and then I do something for the "Cross Creek". As soon as I have a representative assortment in shape to suit me, I'll send you some of the sketches, and you can get an idea of the book, and perhaps know whether the episodic form is going to carry. I see no alternative at the moment, as the material is so varied, for one thing, and to put it in narrative form——preferable, of course, if possible——would make it difficult to tell a connected story, especially as I do not want to make a truly personal thing of it.

I am writing on a canopied terrace overlooking the ocean, and it is grand and cool.

[Postscript] The Poole cottage belongs to someone you may know. Ralph Poole is a nephew of Ernest Poole, and his wife was a Kitty Forsythe who worked for Scribner's——I think the publishing house, not the magazine.[3]

1. Ralph Poole of Scribners, who owned the cottage that MKR finally bought.
2. Roark Bradford (1896–1948), *John Henry* (New York: Harper, 1939). Paul Robeson (1898–1976), African-American singer and actor.
3. Ernest Poole (1880–1950), novelist and social critic. Kitty Forsythe Poole, wife of Ralph Poole.

August 11, 1939

Dear Marjorie:

I know the girl whose house you have rented, and though I saw little of her, I thought she was not only very attractive, but very intelligent.- But I suppose you won't have any particular contact with her beyond paying the rent.

I hear that you are to come up anyhow in December,- though December is difficult to imagine in the present state of the temperature and climate. But when you do, we can talk everything over as to the novel if you will be willing. I have been skimming through "Jacob's Ladder". What a fine piece that was, and it revealed a very great wealth of material in Florida still unused excepting there.

We were talking about the Wyeth edition, and when I came back from a prolonged lunch—the lady was very late in reaching here anyhow—I found that Mr. Scribner, off for a weekend, had left this memorandum, and I enclose it. But I did not say you were dissatisfied with the royalty. But only that I had felt a little doubtful because you had made no specific answer as yet. But anyhow, this memorandum puts the case all complete before you, I think, and so I'll just send it along.

Always yours,

Editor's note: Enclosed, a memorandum from Charles Scribner to Perkins dated August 11, 1939:

Memorandum for Mr. Perkins:

I understand that the royalty arrangements with Mrs. Rawlings on the Wyeth Edition of "The Yearling" have never been definitely settled and that Mrs. Rawlings thought that our offer of 10% was not altogether fair, as it meant receiving 35¢ royalty on each copy whereas she receives 37 1/2¢ on the regular edition. I would like to see her entirely satisfied but at the same time it is next to impossible to pay a straight 15% on the $3.50 volume—10% having been as much as we have been able to pay under similar circumstances.

The new edition certainly ought to stimulate the sale of "The Yearling" and should help to establish it over the years to come. This was our reason for issuing it and as the cost of the new plates for the text, plus Wyeth's fee and the plates of the illustrations, amounts to over $8,000.00 we will be very lucky if we get our money back within a year, and it must be regarded as an investment for the future rather than a way of getting a quick return.

I wonder, therefore, if Mrs. Rawlings would not accept 37 1/2 cents a copy which would insure her not losing any money on the sale of the new edition as opposed to the sale of the regular edition.

The limited edition of the *Wyeth* appears to be still somewhat in doubt. We had hoped that this edition would make a considerable contribution toward the cost of the new plant but we are only planning to print 750 copies for sale at $10.00 per copy, and if they are not unusually attractive it is not worth while printing them, but this costs considerable money and the total return they will bring towards helping to pay for the plant will not be more than approximately $2,000., provided Mrs. Rawlings accepts a royalty of $1.00 on each of these copies sold. If she is unwilling to do this it is hardly worth while to gamble on making the edition, although I do think that a number of people would appreciate a fine copy of "The Yearling" with Mrs. Rawlings's signature and that it would add a certain lustre to the book.

. . . .

444. MKR to MEP (TLS, 4 pp.)

Hawthorn, Florida
August 14, 1939

Dear Max:

The royalty arrangement suggested by Mr. Scribner is perfectly all right. I certainly should not expect to collect anything extra on the strength of the illustrations, but on the other hand I do think it is fair to pay me what I get on the regular edition. The $1. royalty is also all right on the limited edition.

I have almost finished the first draft of the new Quincey Dover story, and have done the first draft of another long story. Both are very bad, but since so much of my stuff is literally impossible when it first emerges, I am trying not to let it bother me, but to keep myself at the re-writing.

I have had a strange fight to get myself going again. I always have an inertia to combat, then once I am past that, I work very hard. In this instance, I have been forced to wonder whether, *subconsciously*, I had been working all my life toward what is known as "success", and since "The Yearling" was undeniably that, whether something in me was satisfied. It would embarrass me to believe this, yet if it is true, it is necessary to admit it——and go on from there. I should certainly hate to think that, ego having been satisfied, I was an empty box. A more self-complimentary theory would of course be Ellen Glasgow's, and that more than usual had been taken out of me in doing "The Yearling", and that "the well of the subconscious" had needed this much time in which to fill again. And I do know that it is true that the so-called success of the book has forced many worldly contacts on me, in correspondence and so on, that have interfered with the sense of being alone with my thoughts and my material.

I really do find it much easier to work over here in the cool freshness and the absolute isolation. I hate to have to run from my own home, for you know my feeling that we never run from conditions and circumstances but from ourselves, as Wolfe did, so that actually we make no escape. But there are times when it doesn't hurt us to yield a bit, as long as we are not deceiving ourselves too greatly.

I was reading a bit from Katherine Mansfield's diary,[1] in which she said that she was convinced that once a story was thought out, nothing remained but the labor. That is not entirely true, unless in the connotation of the word "labor" she included that fixation of the mind and emotions, whereby things are made to emerge clear and true and colorful. That is what the two stories lack, that I have done. The "plot", the point, is there, technically correct. But the breath of life is in neither one of them. Carl Brandt bullies me a bit, as is natural, but I shall not let him have them until I am reasonably satisfied.

Max, several friends have asked me for copies of that last picture I sent you, the one taken by the movie people, sitting under a tree with my dog. You may remember that I asked you to send back the negative, or to send me some copies of the picture for this purpose. Will you, please?

I should like very much to talk about the novel, for some approach may occur to us.

1. Katherine Mansfield (1888–1923), *Journal* (New York: Knopf, 1930).

. . . .

445. MEP to MKR (CC, 1 p.)

August 15, 1939

Dear Marjorie:

Here is the first English review of GOLDEN APPLES[1] and although it's inaccurate it is also very good in some respects.

Yours,

1. Forrest Reid, "[*Golden Apples*]," *Spectator* 163 (1939): 232.

August 17, 1939

Dear Marjorie:

I am sure that your situation at present is explicable only by the Ellen Glasgow theory which everybody who has had to do with writers or any artists knows to be a true one. The other theory could be true of some people but not of a real writer. No one who has done a work that you have could possibly fit into that category. Then, too, your illness and the treatment of it must have taken away a good deal of energy for quite a long time, probably for longer than you realized.

We understand now then that we are to pay a royalty of 37 1/2 cents a copy on the Pulitzer Prize Edition of THE YEARLING with the Wyeth illustrations, and $1.00 a copy in royalty on the Limited Edition, each copy of which is to be signed by you. Later on we shall undoubtedly wish to issue THE YEARLING as one of our Illustrated Classics for Younger Readers. It would then have to be priced at $2.50 and we couldn't possibly pay more than a royalty of 10% as is the case of all the other books in that group. But we needn't take that matter up until we come to it. The type page then would be just as it is in the Pulitzer Prize Edition but the size of the book itself would be larger a little.

We are having a very bad run of weather, unlike what August is supposed to provide.- That and the series of war scares make me more than ever envious of people who can live in such pleasant places as you are in.

Always yours,

P.S. If the enclosed memorandum seems to you correct, will you sign it and send it back so that we can attach it to the regular contract.

[Enclosure, page 1]
   Memorandum of Terms for the Publication
   of the Pulitzer Prize Edition of
   "The Yearling," illustrated by N. C. Wyeth
[page 2]
   It is agreed that on this edition a royalty of 37 1/2¢ a copy shall be paid.
   It is also agreed that on a limited edition to be signed by the author a royalty of $1.00 a copy shall be paid.

   Memorandum of Terms for the Publication
   of the Pulitzer Prize Edition of "The Yearling"
   illustrated by N. C. Wyeth

   It is agreed that on this edition a royalty of 37 1/2¢ a copy shall be paid as long as the price remains $3.50, but if later on an edition in the same typogra-

phy and with the same illustrations were published at $2.50 some new arrange-
ment as to royalty would be necessary.

It is also agreed that on a limited edition to be signed by the author a royalty
of $1.00 a copy shall be paid.

. . . .

447. MKR to MEP (TLS, 2 pp.)

Riverside Hospital
Jacksonville, Fla.
August 29, 1939

Dear Max:

Getting the stories done is like walking up a windy hill in a nightmare. I
finished the first drafts of three new stories, and seemed to be feeling fine,
planning to get the revising done by the end of this week. A perfectly vicious
intestinal attack hit me, and after ten days of acute pain——thinking each day it
would end of itself——I came to the Hospital in Jacksonville. An X-ray showed
that one area of the colon was in rags and tatters, with one diverticulum so
thin-walled that puncture seemed a matter of hours. I was popped into bed,
put on water for two days and just liquids since, and things have quieted down
enough so that I can be driven home by a friend Thursday.

However, my doctor,[1] the head of the hospital, feels that something in our
treatment has not been right, and that there should either be an alteration in
tactics, or an operation in that one small area considered. So after a few days at
home, he is sending me to Boston by train to the Lahey Clinic, which he considers the best in the world for such things. For abdominal things he likes it
better than Johns Hopkins. He doesn't like Mayo's at all, having been a patient
there himself——says it is the most depressing place he has ever been in.

I hate to worry you with all these intimate symptoms, but if I am going to
have to be dilatory about my work, you should know why. However, even if
operation should be recommended——and my doctor says that the danger
from an operation is infinitely less now that the trouble is so localized——I
think I can get the stories revised before then and get them off to Carl, with
copies to you. If you don't mind, will you call Carl and tell him about the delay,
but encourage him, too, as I am sure I can get them in shape regardless.

I'm not particularly upset or discouraged about this, but I am mad as hell!
Just as I seemed "in the groove" again, and apparently a lot better, and my plans
for work, and a few very profitable lectures in places I wanted to go to anyway,——oh well.

But it will all work out somehow.

I will let you know, from Cross Creek, when I go to Boston. Don't feel up to stopping off in New York coming or going. Will make a quick easy trip of it.

Don't be concerned about this, but thought you should know.

1. T. Z. Cason.

. . . .

448. MEP to MKR (CC, 1 p.)

Sept. 1, 1939

Dear Marjorie:

Thank you ever so much for writing me. I am awfully sorry about it, and I hope I can keep in touch with you right along. I have a sister in Boston whom you would greatly like, and know various people connected with the medical profession there. I have called up Carl and told him about the stories and of the probability of your going to Boston, and explained what you said. I do hope everything will go well, and that I can be kept informed.

Always yours,

. . . .

449. MKR to MEP (TLS, 3 pp.)

Hawthorn, Florida
Sept. 7, 1939

Dear Max:

A large box of sheets from the Wyeth "Yearling" came, and I assume that I am to sign the left-hand side. No instructions came, but perhaps they will be in tomorrow's mail. Unless you have already given me complete directions, let me know in about what part of the page the signature should go; whether I am to leave room or not for Wyeth's signature; and whether I am supposed to do the numbering from 1 to 750, myself.[1]

I had a bad attack while in the hospital, and didn't come home until Sunday. My plans are changed about the consultation. I am staying home for this month, spending a good deal of time in bed on a liquid diet. If able, I am keeping an Oct. 4 lecture date in Louisville and Oct. 11 at the University of Chicago. Between those dates, I am to meet one of my doctors from the Riverside Hospital, with my set of X-rays, for a consultation with Dr. Rankin at Lexington, Ky.[2] He was the alternative to the Lahey Clinic in any case. Then if his suggested treatment does not give results, or we don't like his suggestions, I can still go to the Lahey Clinic when I come to New York. This will be earlier than planned if the Thanksgiving change is definite, as the teachers have their

Council during their Thanksgiving recess. That would put me in New York probably Nov. 24. I shouldn't have chosen so much time in New York just then——my Columbia University date is Dec. 5—but if I do go to Boston then it will work out all right.

I am still in bed, but feeling infinitely better and think I can manage the story revision all right.

I've been much amused at the British press on "Golden Apples". It would be impossible to get a more contradictory one. One reviewer was overcome with the complete humanity and credibility of all the characters, the next found them all unreal. One found it "even better" than "The Yearling", another, "disappointing after 'The Yearling'." "It is a great novel." "It is completely mediocre." The bulk of them, though, <were> was very generous, but making exactly the criticism that you or I would make——the artificiality and melodrama of the "outside" characters in contrast with the native ones. Frank Swinnerton[3] wrote a criticism so acute that I think I shall have to write him, verifying his guesses. He was the only one to recognize it as probably having been written before "The Yearling," before I learned where co-ordination lay, for me.

1. On October 30, 1939, 770 copies of the Pulitzer Prize Limited Edition were published, 750 of which were for sale.
2. Charles M. Rankin.
3. Frank Swinnerton, "[*The Yearling*]," *London Observer* (January 1, 1939).

. . . .

450. MEP to MKR (CC, 2 pp.)

Sept. 11, 1939

Dear Marjorie:

I think you must have got a letter from Miss Beam[1] explaining all about the signing of the sheets for the illustrated edition, but just for safety's sake I enclose a copy. I do not think that we shall number the edition at all, but anyway, you need not bother about that matter. All we need is your signature.

I am mightily interested in the English reviews of "Golden Apples". The only one I had seen I sent you. But Weber, who looks over the English reviews from time to time, will show me the others.

I do hope everything will go well, and that you may avoid the operation. I only wish whatever is required could be done quickly, but of course you can only act according to what the doctors say.

Always yours,

1. Gwenneth Beam of Scribners' Art Department.

451. MKR to MEP (ALS, 1 p.)

Hawthorn, Florida

[September 1939]

Dear Max:—

Please return these——and don't forget that picture I asked to have returned.

Have completed revision on the new stories as well as I can for the time being. Am reasonably satisfied with 2 out of the 4. Will get them off to Carl within a few days.

. . . .

452. MEP to MKR (TLS, 2 pp.)

Sept. 18, 1939

Dear Marjorie:

We never had the negative of that picture, but I am sending all the prints we have. I am keeping the original and we can make more, and probably shall in the natural course. Could you sometime just send me a postcard to tell what has become of the sheets we sent for your signature for the illustrated edition,- whether you have sent them to Wyeth, or when you are likely to? The reason I ask is that he is moving from one place to another and we must keep him posted, and we do not want to lose any time we can save.

I hope you have more strength of mind than I, and can keep off the radio. It is futile to listen to it and yet impossible not to.

I shall read the clippings you sent with great interest, and then I shall send them back. May all go well with you.

Always yours,

. . . .

453. MKR to MEP (ALS, 1 p.)

Hawthorn, Florida

Sept. 20 [1939]

Dear Max:—

I signed the sheets and sent them, express prepaid, to Wyeth at Chadds Ford just about a week ago. Miss Beames (sp.?) gave me that address for him, and since I got them done very quickly, I did not question the address. I did not notify Wyeth, but had no report from Express Co.

Editor's note: Written at top of letter in MKR's hand: "The enclosed letter may interest you as a response to the Wyeth edition."

Sept. 20, 1939

Dear Marjorie:

I have read all the English reviews, and I am returning them herewith. What I had feared was that English reviewers would say the character of Tordell was not that of an Englishman. English reviews almost always do that when there is an English character of importance in a novel. These cuttings are rather a mixed lot. English reviewing is different from American, but I do not think it is much better.

I hope I shall hear from you about the signed pages for the limited soon, because we must keep in touch with Wyeth and have him do his part as quickly as he can.

I am sending you "The Face of a Nation: Poetical Passages from the Writings of Thomas Wolfe".

Always yours,

. . . .

Hawthorn, Florida

Sept. 30, 1939

Dear Max:

I think your Miss Beames (sp. ?) was a bit careless in her orders for forwarding of the signed sheets to Mr. Wyeth. I had a letter from him last week from Maine, but he did say it was his last week there. I broke my neck to get the sheets signed and sent off to Chadds Ford, Pa., as per instructions. She should have made certain of his address and given me dates for reaching him. Only hope the box hasn't been sitting out in the rain on a station platform all this time. Let me know as soon as you get a check-up on it.

Of the four stories I sent Carl Brandt, the only definite report I have is that the *Post* was delighted with the new Quincey Dover story, and bought it at once.[1] It is definitely suitable for the collection. Length about 8,000 words. Of the four, there was only one, titled "The Enemy"——also, I hoped, right for the collection——that I did not question.[2] Carl, however, questions my having made my point. It is now with Cosmopolitan, and he seemed to think it would come back. I do not agree with his analysis of it, but if there is anything wrong with it, I myself can't put my finger on it. I have asked him, if it comes back from them, to send it at once to you for your criticism. Since it is meant for the collection I felt it was not out-of-the-way to ask you to give me your critical opinion. If he sends it to you, I will appreciate your sending me your criticism direct——not with a view to making it saleable, but to working out its artistry for book use.

I leave tomorrow, Oct. 1, for Louisville and Chicago. My address from Oct. 2 to 10, care of J. Edward Hardy, Brinly-Hardy Plow Co., Louisville, Ky. Home again after Oct. 14.

So many thanks for the Tom Wolfe poetical passages. That was a grand idea, and seems perhaps the finest way to read Wolfe. The Shenton drawings are superb. They are so good, that damn it, why didn't you have him do a different heading for each section instead of repeating? If we illustrate "Cross Creek", it must certainly be Shenton.

1. "Cocks Must Crow," *Saturday Evening Post* 212 (November 25, 1939): 5–7, 58, 60, 62–64.
2. "The Enemy," *Saturday Evening Post* 212 (January 20, 1940): 12–13, 32, 36, 39.

· ·

456. MEP to MKR (CC, 3 pp.)

Oct. 5, 1939

Dear Marjorie:

I greatly hope that I may hear from you pretty soon from Louisville or Chicago, so as to know better how you are now.- But your letters sound first-rate.

As to the signed sheets, all is well with them.- They have gone to the press. I don't think that Miss Beam was to blame. It was that Wyeth did not keep us fully informed as to his plans. But everything is straight now.

I am glad to know about the story, and don't ever feel that anything you have written would be other than a pleasure to me to read. Nobody's writing could interest me more deeply.- And in these dreadfully anxious days your way of writing does one great good. I'll never forget how much I owe "The Yearling" in that regard,- how I was able to think about it and re-live the episodes in it when nothing else would take my mind away from the perplexities of the time. Now they are much worse, though in some ways certainty is better than apprehension.

Now I am enclosing your royalty report for October 2nd, but I am also enclosing a revised report for October 1, 1938. There was a thousand dollars that should have then been reported and was not, so that it is now carried forward to the new report,- which may perhaps have a practical advantage in the matter of income tax, because unless you want it sooner, it won't be paid until 1940.

I do hope that that story will come.- And "Cross Creek" certainly should have decorations by Shenton.

Always yours,

Oct. 13, 1939

Dear Marjorie:

Please do write me and tell me how things are. I know that Carl Brandt placed the stories readily. But I mean about yourself and what your plans are now.

I have sent six copies of the Wyeth edition.

Always yours,

. . . .

Hawthorn, Florida
October 18, 1939

Dear Max:

Every time I leave home, and return, I swear I sha'n't leave again. It is perhaps only the illusion of peace that I find here, but that is good enough.

I really enjoyed Louisville, as I always do. I have some grand friends there, among them the Mark Ethridges. He is managing editor of the Courier Journal——the first "czar of radio", etc., and one of the finest characters I've ever known. I always come back from Louisville feeling like the Queen of Sheba. Unfortunately, I came home via my lecture at the University of Chicago, and the contrast in loving care and hospitality was so awful that I left Chicago feeling like the lowliest of Sheba's slaves. The lecture itself went off all right. I had a good time warming them up. Percy Boynton,[1] who did the introducing, said he had never seen an audience so spell-bound. The poor devils hadn't been talked to by a human being probably since Robert Herrick's day, and they simply wouldn't leave. I finally told them I wasn't going to tell any more stories and they might as well go home. So that made up for Chicago's icy atmosphere.

Had a funny experience in Louisville. A businessman said to me, "I should think there'd be a big market right now for war stories. They're the easiest kind of trash in the world to write, aren't they?" I said, "I wouldn't know. I never wrote trash on purpose."

Had my consultation with Dr. Rankin in Lexington. He is a grand soul, and restores one's faith in the integrity of the medical profession. He looked at my X-rays and said, "That certainly is a mess. What do you expect me to do about it?" The gist of it is, that I can only go on as I have been doing, and try to avoid any acute attacks which might result in a perforation. He said the operation is simply not an elective one. He does it only when there are complications and he has to go in anyway. However, I stand an even chance of never having a perforation, and I have learned the danger signs of an attack, and simply go to bed at once on a liquid diet. His skill and prestige and integrity are so great that I shall go no further for advice. I feel so well so much of the time that I am going to dismiss the whole thing from my mind and never discuss it again. And when hostesses offer me things to eat that are taboo, instead of embarrassing myself and them by saying that I am on a diet, I shall ignore the forbidden food when allowed to, and when pressed, shall announce loftily that I don't like it! My diet is so generous that it doesn't bother me, especially when at home. So unless an attack interferes with my work so that I have to tell you, we sha'n't mention my insides again.

Carl has sold three of the four new stories, to the Saturday Post, the New Yorker, and Collier's.[2] The Post one is the new Quincey Dover, quite long, about 9,000 words, and I am sure you will want it for the collection. The other two, very short ones, I do not consider suitable. The New Yorker one is a perfectly evil, subtle thing that I had a swell time doing, and actually didn't think anyone would take it. It is good in its way, but it is so far out of my regular line that we should not want to include it. The Collier's one I do not consider good enough. It is a trick ending story, and as Katherine Mansfield described some of her stuff, it is "once removed from reality". The story still in the hands of Cosmopolitan, who have not given their decision yet, is the one I may need help on, but it is basically good and true, and will in the end work out for the collection.[3] It, too, is long, over 8,000. Don't you think that will make enough? I hope to do, soon, one more story that should be suitable. I think the collection will tide us over nicely. Lots of people have asked about the possibility and said they would like to have my stories. Of course, there wouldn't be any really popular sale.

By the way, "The Yearling" is the passion of Dr. Rankin's 12-year-old son, and he refused to charge me a consultation fee! So I want one of the first copies of the $10. limited edition to go to the boy, and enclose the name and address. Don't know whether any of the expensive edition come to me gratis, but if not, just charge my account with it.

I am so anxious to see the completed Wyeth. You'll send me a copy as soon as possible, won't you? I had a grand letter from him, and the angelic creature is going to make me a present of one of the originals, after the sale. Isn't that wonderful?

I am negotiating for the purchase of the very lovely modern cottage south of St. Augustine where I stayed this summer. Hope it goes through. Have reason to think my very low offer will be accepted, as the owner is moving back north. It would give me a grand place to slip away to when things get too complicated here. It's only 70 miles away, which on our good roads means only a hour and a quarter drive.

Did you know that Harcourt, Brace are publishing that "Loon Totem" I was so crazy about? I hope, for once, you were wrong!

1. Percy H. Boynton, professor of English literature at the University of Chicago.
2. "Cocks Must Crow"; "The Pelican's Shadow," *New Yorker* 15 (January 6, 1940): 17–19; and "In the Heart," *Collier's* 105 (February 3, 1940): 19, 39.
3. "The Enemy."

. . . .

459. MEP to MKR (CC, 2 pp.)

Oct. 26, 1939

Dear Marjorie:

Thanks ever so much for the letter. It must have crossed one I wrote you, as almost always happens between us.

As to the limited you asked us to send Charles M. Rankin, it is yours and will not be charged, and I am sending you two other copies of the limited which are also yours. Ed Shenton was in here yesterday, and somewhat to my surprise was very much pleased with the Wyeth pictures. He knows Wyeth's work well, of course, from the beginning, and allows for its limitations, but he thought the pictures would be extremely popular, and that the colors and backgrounds and all were very fine indeed. He did say that he thought in this new method Wyeth had, and has used in recent years, he has lost something of his skill in draftsmanship.

Any time you are willing to send me the stories that will be in the book, I'd love to read them, if only just for the pleasure of it. And it would then enable me to think about the book better, and plan for it. But don't do it until you want to. Carl told me he had sold the last of the stories you sent him, and to the Post. This is first rate.

Always yours,

. . . .

460. MEP to MKR (TLS: UF, 3 pp.)

October 26, 1939

Dear Marjorie:

Carl Brandt sent me a set of the proofs of "The Enemy" which the Post has taken,- and I read it with very great pleasure. I think Carl must have written you that the Post people thought what I think anyone would think, that the future of Milford, who had done something pretty rough, would have to be accounted for in some way.- The reader would want to know what retribution would follow his killing of the cattle or why none did. Would you let me write you as to this, and some other points, in the idea that bringing them up may have some value to you in correcting the proofs? Even if my suggestions are dumb, they may result in suggesting something better to your mind. At any rate, Carl seemed to think you wanted me to see this story. I guess it is the one you did talk of in a letter.

I thought that Milford was made to be quite a man. He had courage and his own idea of what was right, and he had authority. I thought he would not just have acquiesced without a word in Tom walking off to see Dixon. And if he did try to intervene by jumping up and stepping toward Tom, and if the other prevented him by blocking him off, and Tom still walked on, and if he shouted after him something to the effect that he was done with him, that would strengthen the presentation of Milford, and it would also make stronger the reason for Tom feeling free to take Doney and leave him. I do not think it would weaken the story in any way.

Then for a detail, when Doney comes in and finds Tom with Dixon, there is one phrase she uses which did not seem to me in her character. It may really have been, but I do not think the reader would find it so.- It is "My love, my love". It did not seem right that she should use those words, and I do not know that it would be any weaker if she used none at all. Her emotion is plentifully expressed—at least it would be in a book—by her actions.

But none of this overcomes the objection that the matter of Milford is left up in the air. Couldn't Tom quite naturally say to Dixon at the end of their talk, that he wished he could make him understand about Milford's attitude,- that Milford had lived always in the old way, and that it all seemed wrong to him that the land was taken? And couldn't Dixon then say that he <had> would overlook<ed> what Milford had done? I do think in some way you must cover that point.

The most difficult matter to my mind is the conclusion, and you may think I am all wrong about this. I think it would be much better if the three paragraphs almost at the end, beginning with "The road turned" and ending with "like the blackness of the forest" were omitted, or at least were very much shortened. I think they explain too much, and that it is as if the author were doing it, a little. I think that if you did that, and then also took out in the third paragraph from the end the sentence, "The enemy rode past her like an alien horseman", the way Doney felt, while not stated so explicitly, would yet be emotionally understood. And if it would be, it would be felt by the reader more deeply. I know this is a question, and I do not want to have any influence that would weaken the story. It is generally true that in a popular magazine there is much more danger of under-doing than of over-doing. But if you did take out those paragraphs, you might find some brief way of getting in the statement that life was the enemy, and yet not at any such length. If it could be done that way, I think it would be better.

I feel as if I might seem to be intruding myself into this matter, but I thought from what Carl said on the phone, that you wanted me to give my impressions. Anyhow, I believe the story will be immensely liked.

Always yours,

. . . .

461. MKR to MEP (TLS, 3 pp.)

Hawthorn, Florida

Oct. 28, 1939

Dear Max:

Our letters would have crossed again, except that I did not mail the one I wrote you two or three days ago. On re-reading, it seemed needlessly disagreeable about something you couldn't do anything about, in any case. I refer to an inexcusable mess on page 196 of the Wyeth Yearling. My eye just happened to light on it—it is a misplacement of a whole line, so that even I had difficulty in making sense out of most of the page. It is infuriating to a writer to work until he is almost insane, trying to get the effect he wants and convey the meaning, and then have a goddamned proof-reader or printer present something completely unintelligible. I haven't looked through the whole book and don't know whether there are other pieces of bungling or not. The edition is almost completely ruined for me. I hope this error, and any others, will be corrected at the first opportunity. An easily deciphered proof-reader's error is bearable, but not one that makes for chaos of the sense.

Shenton's opinion on the Wyeth paintings is most interesting, and corroborates my own feeling. The Wyeth Jody is not my Jody, and is not the Jody of others who have seen my copy, but I am certain that the illustrations as a whole will have a great appeal. There is an immensely exciting quality about many of them. I believe they will seem especially thrilling to anyone who has not already read the book, and so will make for new sales. I think they guarantee the success of the book for adolescents, for they have a certain magic, over which young people can pore and pore.

Knowing nothing of the technique of art, I feel a lack of artistry, of drafts-manship, in the paintings, and think I understand this. I think Wyeth was much stirred by the material and the country, and felt that he wanted to give a freer and less restrained and precise interpretation than is or has been his custom. Many of the paintings in "Drums" have the peculiarly contained and rounded quality of fine stained glass, or of certain types of work in enamel and porce-lain. "A Sea-Captain's Daughter" in "Trending into Maine" has this quality, and I loved it. Then in some of the sea things in the same book, you can see him breaking moulds, as it were, and striving for a looser expression. In the Yearling, I think he felt that the material required an almost complete abandonment of any classic or precise technique. I think "The Storm" and "The Burial of Fod-der-wing" are effective in this manner, but I prefer the paintings more in his earlier style, particularly "Penny Tells the Story of the Bear-Fight." That is sim-ply grand. And I am mad about "The Forresters Go to Town".[1] The humor in these two is delicious.

It is pure impudence for me to write like this, yet I do think that an eye-minded, descriptive writer of my type has very much the painter's point of view. And I do really believe you could not have found more effective illustra-tions from a salable standpoint.

I am struggling in the usual torment to make my point convincing in the fourth new story.[2] The Post accepted it as is, but is not satisfied with the end-ing. It may happen not to be possible to make the point artistically right, and yet satisfy the Post's idea of a story, and a story-ending. But if I can get it so that it suits you and me, the Post can go to the devil. I am very happy when a story happens to sell, but I will not try to please or placate the professional market. If I write trash, it won't be on purpose!

In the other story the Post took, the Quincey Dover story,[3] I had Quincey say that she boiled up hotter than a Presbyterian hell. The Post queried the "Presbyterian" on the proofs, so I just wrote on the margin: Author's note. Fix the fires of hell to suit the Post's religion.

When I have done what I can with the other story, I'll send it to you and we'll see what we can do.

I don't have carbons of the other stories, or decipherable first copies, but will ask Carl to try to get me proofs from the magazines to send you.

1. These are the titles given to Wyeth's illustrations in *Drums, Trending into Maine,* and *The Yearling.*
2. "The Enemy."
3. "Cocks Must Crow."

462. MEP to MKR (TS for wire)

OCT. 30, 1939

MRS. MARJORIE RAWLINGS

ISLAND GROVE, FLORIDA

ERROR PAGE 196 FOUND LAST WEEK AND CORRECTED IN GREATER PART
OF EDITION. EVEN BOUND COPIES CAN BE CORRECTED. WILL SEND YOU
SIX MORE.

....

463. MEP to MKR (TLS: UF, 2 pp.)

Oct. 30, 1939

Dear Marjorie:

The proof was read carefully. The mistake was made after it went back to
the press. It is really inexplicable in full, but it was caused by taking out a line to
make a correction and then inserting the wrong line.- But anyhow, we had
found it, I discovered, and have corrected it in all unbound copies, and can
correct it in bound copies.- And if you will send back those two copies of the
limited I sent, we shall do it there. The six copies of the regular edition with the
correction will go to you immediately.

I won't write you anything further about the Post story until I hear from
you again. I read it quickly and wrote in a rush because it was in proof, and I
thought the Post was probably in a hurry. Your letter does not sound as if it
was. I supposed they had set it up very far in advance of publication so that
you will be able to correct as much as you please.

I agree with you almost entirely as to which are the best pictures, and the
Storm and the Burial and the Forresters Going to Town were among the ones
that Shenton most liked too.

Always yours,

....

464. MKR to MEP (TLS, 2 pp.)

[Cross Creek]
Nov. 2, 1939

Dear Max:

I am at my wit's ends as to how to make the story, "The Enemy", as clear to
readers as it is (I think!) to me. My own thinking may——must be——muddled.
Let me state my intentions, and perhaps you can give me more help.

My prime purpose was to make it Doney's story. I wanted to give a very touching picture of a simple and profound love. The girl has, literally, nothing but her love for the young, kind husband. In that, she feels secure. The life under Milford's roof that would be unbearable otherwise, is accepted as perfectly all right and normal. Tom's enemies are her enemies, and because Milford is Tom's father, and so, a part of him in her mind, the old man's enemies are her enemies. Then, through the cataclysm of the cattle impasse, her world is suddenly turned upside down, and she is asked to renounce something that has been a part of her love for Tom, and in an instant to switch her loyalty to Dixon——previously "the enemy"——and away from the old man. She is unable to accept this, and in her attempt to make sense out of a situation so confusing and unreasonable to her, she recognizes that the angry and quarreling men are victims of circumstance, of the general necessity for making a living, which makes an enemy of whatever menaces <that living> the livelihood. <it is of course> She recognizes that there is very little abstract "right". It is as relative as enmity is relative. This of course must come into her mind in very simple and basic terms. It is of course nothing new or startling to recognize that life is the enemy. But the oldest idea becomes, or should become, immediate and personal and freshly true, when it is expressed through a character who has been made to seem true and real and moving to the reader, so that whatever happens to that character is as new and as important as whatever happens to one's own self. So, facing one of what might be called the fatal facts of life, I meant it to be very poignant that the girl should turn with a desperate clinging to the young husband, realizing the *compensatory* fact that her love——as embodied, quite by accident, in him,——is "a lean, frail bulwark against the foe."

Is that sequence sound in itself? I think it is. The greatest fault is undoubtedly in the end<, and> of the story as written, and as usual, it is over-writing rather than under-writing that has done most of the damage.

But aside from that, I am wondering if the frustrated and inconclusive feeling that the reader evidently gets from <it> the story as it stands, is from my not having made Doney real and moving enough. The greatest interest and sympathy seem to be with Milford, whom I meant to be, however real and vital and compelling, only the instrument of the precipitation of the girl into a tragic realization, with, after that, the poignant and beautiful "lift" of feeling from her recognition of love, however "lean and frail", as a bulwark.

As to "solving" Milford's personal predicament, I meant it definitely to be unsolved, by the man's own nature. I meant to imply that he would go right ahead with his own private war against Dixon. How they come out is no concern of this story, although there is the implication of Milford's fighting a losing battle——as he should, for, however much sympathy one has for him, he *is* wrong, as far, again, as abstract wrong can be determined. So if the reader's concern is not with Doney, but with what happens to Milford, I have failed somehow to put the emphasis where I wanted it.

If you accept my basic conception, will you give me your ideas along that line?

Editor's note: In left margin of p. 1 of letter in MEP's hand: "Insert ¶ / When he goes."

. . . .

465. MEP to MKR (CC, 4 pp.)

Nov. 8, 1939

Dear Marjorie:

Your letter came while I was away. Otherwise, I would have answered it instantly. The story is Doney's story. I think that is perfectly clear. She is a quiet passive character, as she should be, but perhaps you can find ways of emphasizing her attitude somewhat more,- though I think any discerning person would understand it. Certainly the completeness of her devotion to Tom is plain enough. I have no longer the proofs of the story, but in my remembrance of it, nothing was said of the effect upon her of Tom's decision to go to see Dixon. She would not have interfered, of course, but maybe her expression and behavior when he marched off, should be brought out distinctly. As it is, he sets out, then there is a space, and then she is seen on the road going to him. Perhaps there need not be so much of a break. Perhaps after he goes you could begin by telling what she did in the interval and how she could not help it but just naturally followed him in the end. If this were done, her confusion about the whole thing could be brought more distinctly to the reader before the end, and then the end would be plainer to him. But anyone would know it was Doney's story and it seems to me the actual ending itself is completely effective without most of those paragraphs I suggested omitting. I do think that that phrase, "life was the enemy" should come in somehow, but those two paragraphs tell too much, and while without them a reader might not be able to express the precise meaning of the story, he would feel it emotionally, which is the right way.

As for Milford, if he is in the story he must act in character, and the reader cannot be left in the dark about what is likely to happen to him. The fact is, he has done something that might have sensational results, and a reader cannot help wondering about him because of the possibilities. By leaving the reader in the dark you do divert his mind from the heart of the story to a character with whom he has no sympathy anyhow, simply because of the mystery about his future.- And I think he ought to put up some interference with John's going simply because he was the kind of man who would have done it. There is no doubt of the nature of Doney, or of her being the principal character. It may be that more ought to be told about her here and there in the story, for the sake of accentuation,- and in particular at the time when John starts off for Dixon, and between then and when she finds him.

Always yours,

. . . .

466. MKR to MEP (TLS, 3 pp.)

Hawthorn, Florida

Nov. 14, 1939

Dear Max:

Thank you for the new, corrected copies. I am sending back the two copies of the Limited for correction. It was cruel of me to be snappish about it, for I know that a publishing house like yours must take such errors even more seriously than do the authors.

Having raised the devil about it, I'd better not waste any more time confessing to my own mischievousness. I thought someone in the plant would notice what I did, but the limited edition evidently went through so mechanically that no one caught me at my tricks. Here is the story of my sin:

My name is so long, and I write so "sprawly", that signing all those eight hundred odd sheets of the limited edition was a frightful chore. I felt also a sense of pretentiousness in signing such an edition. I became more and more annoyed with myself as I went on with the signing, and I wished I had never heard of "Marjorie Kinnan Rawlings", "Marjorie Kinnan Rawlings"——. I reached what I thought was the bottom of the pile, and said to myself that I wouldn't sign "Marjorie Kinnan Rawlings" again for the ransom of India. And there was one more sheet——.

So I signed it "Dora Rolley Dooflickit."

The "Dora Rolley" is a joke among my friends here. I met some strangers at a big gay party, and as the festivities wore on, a woman wobbled up to me and said, "Please, may I call you 'Dora'?" I said, "Why, certainly, but don't be surprised if I don't answer, as it isn't my name." "Oh dear," she sighed, "I guess I'd just better go on calling you 'Mrs. Rolley'." So my friends call me "Dora Rolley" a great deal of the time, especially for the half of my schizophrenic personality that doesn't behave as well as the other half.

I thought I would hear something from this, and finally wrote Wyeth asking him if he had caught the odd signature, and if so, what he had done about it. My private wager was that with his artist's eye he would see it at once, and would add a flippant signature of his own. He answered me that he still hadn't gotten over the shock after some eight hundred MKR's, but that instantly he had caught my mood. So, he said, under "Dora Rolley Dooflickit", he wrote, "I always suspected she did."

He said that he knew you would not see the sheets, but that he had hoped "some bright Scribner menial" would see it and bind the copy for me, but that probably it had now fallen into the hands of some puzzled and disgruntled reviewer.

Heaven knows where it has gone. If you get a protest from some solemn and irate buyer, I shall be glad either to swap a respectable copy for the offending one, or to write a note of explanation which the buyer could paste near the naughty pair of autographs.

Scold me if you must——I am Dora Rolley at just the wrong moments, and I can't help it.

. . . .

467. MKR to MEP (TLS, with holograph postscript, 1 p.)

[Cross Creek]

[November 1939]

You will see, aside from the ending, what I have done. I have taken away all violence from Dixon, so that it is in keeping for him to be lenient with old Milford.

I have made Milford consistently violent, with no hope of compromise, when Tom leaves.

And perhaps most important, instead of having Doney think of Tom as a lean, *frail* bulwark against the foe, I have her think of him or rather, more definitely, her love, as a lean, *hard* bulwark against the foe, so that the "triumph of love" (do you know that God awful picture by Watts[1] by that title in the British Museum?) is complete.

As far as I am concerned, I think I have covered the unanswered questions about Milford and have taken care of any vagueness at the end. I am writing Carl that I have sent my revision to you, and that it can go on to the Post (who wants the story at once to schedule) *only* if you approve my changes. Otherwise, send it back to me with your suggestions.

[Postscript] If the revision seems O.K. to you, please send it on to the Post.

1. George Frederic Watts (1817–1904), British painter and sculptor.
2. Adelaide Neall, fiction editor at the *Saturday Evening Post.*

. . . .

468. MEP to MKR (CC, 1 p.)

Nov. 15, 1939

Dear Marjorie:

I think you did magnificently in your corrections. I read the story and mailed it off to the Post, putting on it "Attention of Adelaide Neall" whose name was given to me by Carl Brandt. The story now does certainly what you aimed to do, and I think you managed the changes with great skill, all of them.

Always yours,

. . . .

469. MEP to MKR (TLS: UF, 2 pp.)

Nov. 20, 1939

Dear Marjorie:

I am returning the two copies in the limited edition with the correction made. I wonder if we will ever hear about your aberration in signing the last copy.- Maybe it will turn out in the end to give it a collector's value, for the book is destined to be a classic. I was tempted to send out a literary note about it, but it would be better to let it lie and see what comes.

Now we ought to begin to prepare for the book of stories, and I wish you would tell me all about it that you can, and if possible send me what I have not seen, in duplicates.- But I think "The Enemy" turned out beautifully.

Always yours,

. . . .

470. MKR to MEP (TLS, 5 pp.)

Hawthorn, Florida
Dec. 14 [1939]

Dear Max:

The grove and the farmhouse are as lovely as I remembered them! Each time I go away and come back, I wonder if I will see them with more exact or exacting eyes, and find them ugly or inadequate——and it never happens.

Yet I did really have a good time in New York. The trouble is, that a part of me is drawn to the sophisticated life, to the *thinking* life as against the simple emotionalism of my relation to this place, and it takes some time to draw back again.

The Fairchild book[1] came today, and I am delighted to have it. The book opened itself to the section on chayotes——a tropical squash that I grew this summer with great success——and that I could not find in any dictionary. I had the pronunciation but not the spelling. If I were not quite so far north in the state, I should love experimenting with the tropical fruits and flowers and vegetables. While I was away, frost killed my fine border of poinsettias. My Adrina cut the blooms when she realized that covering would not save them, so I had a large tub of them that will last in water for a couple of weeks.

I leave tonight for a quick trip to Atlanta for the premiere of Gone With the Wind.[2] It will be a riotous occasion——may the Lord keep my stomach strong. As soon as I return and catch up with correspondence, I'll go right at the editing of the stories. If we use the title, "When the Whippoorwill——", I don't see how we can lead off with the completely farcical "Benny and the Bird Dogs". I think, too, that any sales for the collection will come from the more serious "Yearling" readers, who will look to the book for something of the thing they found in that story. That quality is much more in "Jacob's Ladder" and the more serious stories. I think the appeal should be made to such readers, and no attempt made to throw a sop to casual readers by starting off the collection with an almost ridiculously funny story. We will make a separate appeal to the less earnest readers, later on with the Quincey Dover collection. I have had some grand letters about the last story.

I enjoyed seeing you. I hope you were only joking, in my case, when you spoke of the business department taking writers away from you. I think you must know how conscious I am of the special quality of our relationship. It existed from the beginning, in my recognition and appreciation of your great critical gift, and I cannot conceive of its being changed by anything. I should expect you to have the same patience with me, the same understanding of what I try to do, if the results were completely unsalable. And you must surely know that no material returns from my work could possibly be as important to me as the doing of the work; and that there is more satisfaction in your verdict of approval than in that of any best-seller list. When I have done the best I can with any piece of writing, and you say it is all right, then I am done with it. What happens in the way of money and awards and what-not, is remote, and has no more connection with the work itself than would an inheritance from someone I had never heard of. My mental contact with you is a basic thing. I shall need it and want it and feel free to ask for it as long as I write. I could not imagine your withholding it, and you must not ever imagine for one moment that I could put other things ahead of it, or fail to appreciate it.

Editor's note: Enclosed are two notes regarding corrections for the Wyeth edition of *The Yearling,* one dated December 13, 1939, and the other December 14.

1. David Fairchild, *The World Was My Garden.*
2. MKR and Norton Baskin were Margaret Mitchell's guests for the premiere of the motion picture on December 15, 1939.

. . . .

471. MEP to MKR (CC, 2 pp.)

Dec. 19, 1939

Dear Marjorie:

I think you are quite right in what you say of the general principles of arranging the stories.- I would rather though, if possible, begin with a short story, and not one as long as "Jacob's Ladder". But we really do not have to determine a final order until we get into the galley proof which we shall do as fast as we can, as soon as you send back the material.

I hope you will come up to New York in the summer. It is really pleasanter then, at least I always thought so. I think your life is the right life, and not the kind we have to live here. You are living the way people were supposed to. But it was mighty pleasant to have you around for a few days,- and that everyone thought who saw you. Being a Yankee, I am not very expressive, but I am mighty glad that you do value my opinions.

By the way, I had meant to suggest to you that sometime when you are in an interval and can't get on to a larger and more important piece of work, you might write a real juvenile, perhaps a short one, about a girl of the hammock country. I am sure it would sell beautifully, but not only that.- Some of the very best books in the world have been written specifically for children. And if one has a gift for that way, there is every reason to use it.

Yours,

P.S. I am enclosing a letter that was sent on to me.

472. MKR to MEP (wire)

1939 DEC 20 PM 5 05
MAXWELL PERKINS—
597 FIFTH AVE—
PLEASE SEND CHECK ONE THOUSAND DOLLARS IMMEDIATELY SAM BYRD[1]
ONE THIRTY WEST FORTY FOURTH   CHARGE FEBRUARY ROYALTIES—
MARJORIE KINNAN RAWLINGS.

1. MKR's investment in Roark Bradford's play *John Henry*.

. . . .

473.   MEP to MKR (CC, I p.)

Dec. 27, 1939

Dear Marjorie:

   I suppose you have found it a considerable piece of work to edit the stories. Could you though, on receipt of this, return whatever has been done, and I hope that will be most of them. We ought to get the book out in good season, and that means we should begin setting immediately. Even now the order does not have to be determined. The main thing is to get them in type fast.

Always yours,

. . . .

474. MKR to MEP (wire)

1939 DEC 29 PM 1 24
MAXWELL PERKINS—
597 FIFTH AVE—
HAVE LIGHT FLU CANT SEND ANYTHING FOR FEW DAYS—

1940

[Cross Creek]
January 2, 1939 [1940]

Dear Max:

Here are the stories that are ready to go into proof. I am going slow on the others, for I am still undecided about the delicate matter of modifying and unifying the Cracker dialect, which I handled more loosely in some stories than in others. Once I have decided such things as whether to use "keer" for "care", "sich" for "such", and things of that sort, it will be a tedious but not too long a job to do the editing.

"The Enemy" comes out in the January 20 issue of the Post, and that will be ready to go into proof as it stands.

I have recovered from my flu and feel top-notch again. I was at home only a few days before putting in several more or less riotous days in Atlanta at the GWTW premiere, then Christmas festivities followed, with lots of company, and I finished myself off with a duck-hunt the last day of the season, sitting absolutely frozen in a duck blind from six in the morning until one, in almost freezing weather with a drizzling rain. I knew I had no business going out, as tired as I was, but staging the shoot was a moral necessity, for the reason that my white grove man was giving me a duck-hunt as my Christmas present. When I gave him his Christmas boxes, he said, "You do so much for me, and even if I had the money, I wouldn't know what to give anybody like you. But there's one thing I can give you. You get your crowd together, and I want to give you a day's duck-shooting." He got small boats to use as individual blinds, hired a helper and a motor, and put <us> the party in position and then kept circling the lake to keep the ducks in motion. It was a pleasure I couldn't deny him if it killed me.

I will be damned if I'll write a juvenile about a girl of the hammock country. I did Allie in "Golden Apples" and she made me sick at my stomach.

P.S. About "Alligators". As I read it over, I realized that some credit would have to be given Fred Tompkins. As far as I am concerned, the appended note takes care of everything, if you think it is not "off key" in any way. Also, I think it would be right to pay him the $25. customarily paid for inclusion of a story in a volume.

. . . .

476. MEP to MKR (TLS: UF, 3 pp.)

Jan. 5, 1940

Dear Marjorie:

Although I suppose you must manage the dialect—though it is hardly that—according to some general principles of your own, I put in a plea for "sich". Everyone is familiar with that word in that spelling, and will have no difficulty with it at all. I do think there are people who might trip on as obvious a spelling as "keer" though.

It is good to know that you got through the flu comfortably.- So many people do not, that I am always worried to hear of people having it.

The only time I ever shot ducks was with Hem during a week on the White River in Missouri, just before Christmas. I spent some of the coldest hours of my life in doing it, but yet had a mighty good time of it too. My first surprise was to be awakened in the pitch dark by Hem who had told me when we went to bed that we must get up at daybreak. I always supposed the sun got up at daybreak, and tried to argue that with Hem, but to no avail. It was still at its darkest when we headed up the river. I never said anything more about it to Hem, because he is not the man to argue such matters with, but it seemed to me that we got just as many birds at high noon, in fact more, and that we might just as well have slept what I call the night out. But it was on that river toward evening once that we heard a great uproar around the curve, and suddenly a regular old Huckleberry Finn steamboat with the two parallel funnels and the side wheels, came down toward us. It was much smaller than the old Mississippi steamboat, of course, but everything otherwise was exactly of that time, even the clothes of the captain and the crew.

By the way: did you ever return to me the Ellen Glasgow prefaces? And if not, can you? I think I could get them back for you later on if you still want them, but I promised Brace, of Harcourt, Brace, who publish her now, to try to make them available for him, without expense. He proposed to buy the entire limited set, and I suppose I ought to have let him.

Always yours,

· ·

477. MEP to MKR (CC, I p.)

Jan. 15, 1940

Dear Marjorie:

How are you getting on with the manuscript? I know, of course, that you are doing the best you can, but I would like to hear. I cannot help being nervous for fear we shall get out "Where the Whip-poor-will" so late as to lose considerable advantage. The press thought the two stories you did send me, even with the one about to appear in the SEP, were too few to begin on, unless they had a specific date for the arrival of the remainder.

Ever sincerely yours,

· ·

478. MKR to MEP (ALS, first eight words typed, I p.)

[Ocala]
Monday

Dear Max:

Had a relapse from the flu, and when I got good and down, all my help got sick too. Have someone to take care of them but no one to take care of me, so came in to the Marion Hotel in Ocala[1] where all runs smoothly and the doctor is handy. Am perfectly all right, nothing serious, but just "down".

Am sending on something & if I don't get O.K. in a few days will send everything & let you have it set up, making the minor corrections in proof.

1. Norton Baskin was the hotel manager.

· ·

479. MEP to MKR (CC, 2 pp.)

Jan. 23, 1940

Dear Marjorie:

I do hope that the flu has worn off completely, and that everything is right with you. I got the copy of the Post and cut "The Enemy" out of it, so we now have all the stories except three: "Jacob's Ladder," "A Crop of Beans," and "A

Plumb Clare Conscience". I hope to send you some of the proof very soon, and I suppose these three stories will be in our hands before long.

Did you realize that even though it was its second year of publication "The Yearling" was the seventh best seller for the year? I didn't until I saw the announcement.

Always yours,

. . . .

480. MEP to MKR (CC, 2 pp.)

Feb. 2, 1940

Dear Marjorie:

I sent you the first of the proof a couple of days ago, but of course that story will not be the first story. I'll rush the proof along to you as fast as I can for it is getting late in the season, and as soon as you can determine the right order, let us know it. I am just studying a list to see if I can make any suggestion as to what should come first. "Jacob's Ladder" would be excellent to lead with excepting that I thought a shorter story might be more suitable.- Perhaps there isn't much in that idea though. Then, the Quincy Dover stories should, I suppose, be separated from each other, for we do not want to emphasize them too much in this book.

Always yours,

. . . .

481. MEP to MKR (TLS: UF, 2 pp.)

Feb. 6, 1940

Dear Marjorie:

I am enclosing your royalty report herewith. It shows that "The Yearling" sold in all editions something over 22,000 copies. I did hope even in the face of previous experience that "South Moon Under" would come in for a renewed sale for it is a beautiful book and never had anything like the public it was entitled to. The luck was all against it. But it is a strange fact that older books do not seem to be affected by a great success very much. They are in libraries, but the attention of booksellers is so much on the new books always, that it does not extend to the bookstores.

I feel as if I were always harassing you, but I do hope you are getting along with the proof for we ought to be pushing forward as fast as we can.

Always yours,

482. MKR to MEP (ALS, 3 pp.)

Hawthorn, Florida
[February 1940]

Max:——

Am returning the first proofs. The last few Mss. pages of "Varmints" are not in proof. It seems to me "Jacob's Ladder" is all right for the first story. "A Crop of Beans" is short and has been liked, but seems not to have been read much. It would set the key.

"Benny" would be good for 2^d story, then sort of alternate heavy and lighter things.

· ·

483. MKR to MEP (TLS, 1 p.)

Hawthorn, Florida
[February 1940]

Dear Max:

I have had so many letters about the story in Collier's, that I think you had better at least read it for consideration in the collection. I myself do not consider it artistic, and there is no way to make it so. It has an artificial construction, and while it is good technically, it is not the sort of thing I should choose to do. But so many people have had an emotional reaction to it, that I feel you should consider it.

I have returned two parcels of corrected proofs. Another came from you today and I'll take it to Miami with me and try to do the corrections there at the hotel.

· ·

484. MKR to MEP (ALS, 2 pp.)

Hawthorn, Florida
[February 1940]

Dear Max:

I hate to be ugly, but after dealing with proof-readers on magazines, it seems to me that the Scribner proof-reading department is the most careless and inefficient I have ever come across. I have noticed that if I don't catch the typographical errors, they just don't get caught. I started to say this on the first proofs, then tore up the letter, but <so> I don't think it is right for the mechanical responsibility to be on the writer, when you pay people to do this work.

After I sent in the last proofs I realized I had been inconsistent in my spelling of "heered" and "heerd", using one in one story and one in another. Will you have a good reader go over this and unify it. I think I have used "heerd" the most, and I prefer it.

Try to hold up the use of any of my old photographs——I'll try to get a decent new one. Because of not having felt well, I dreaded trying it again, as I am likely to get a bad picture at best.

Editor's note: At top of letter in MEP's hand: "Rush too—." Enclosed is a 23-line acknowledgment by MKR of Fred Tompkins's contribution to the short story "Alligators." Written at top of acknowledgment in MEP's hand: "(Use this note in italics to precede the start of story 'Alligators.' — MEP)."

. . . .

485. MEP to MKR (CC, 3 pp.)

Feb. 15, 1940

Dear Marjorie:

I am enclosing a list of the stories arranged in an order that seemed to me to be pretty satisfactory. In truth I do not think that order is very important after the start, because people do not presumably read a book of stories consecutively and certainly they do not generally continue to read one immediately after finishing another. I think the main problem is to separate the Quincy Dover stories, then to have a strong story near the end. That is the idea with which these are arranged, but if you wish to move them about, it will be easy to do it.

I have read "In the Heart" but I think it is a story you could make better than it is, and that it had better be held over for a later volume.

I don't know exactly how we ought to handle the note for "Alligators". I have held it out. I think the best way would be to set it at the start of the story in italics, and perhaps to follow it with the words, "Author's Note". I'll take care of it.

I was very much worried about getting out "When the Whippoorwill" in good time and so I urged them on at the press to work fast when the copy came. And this fact, I am afraid, accounts for the four typographical mistakes. They would have been caught in the next reading, and I enclose herewith a note from the manager of the press with regard to the matter.

But when it comes to the variations in dialect, I do not think that the press can be held responsible. It is a different matter in the case of one story with a magazine. In the first place, a magazine has its own style, and the author is not given anything like the leeway he is in a book where his own preferences are regarded to a greater degree than in a periodical. I do not think that in truth a typesetter, or a proofreader, can be asked to do otherwise than simply follow the copy,- although Cadmus[1] says that with these proofs he will see that uniformity is given through a careful special reading.

I have many things to tell you about but I do not want to delay this letter because we must settle upon the order soon. I do hope all goes well.

Ever yours,

1. Not identified.

. . . .

486. MKR to MEP (TLS, 4 pp.)

Hawthorn, Florida
Feb. 20, 1940

Dear Max:

I've gotten cold feet, just as you did, about opening the book of stories with too long a story. I say, let's begin with "A Crop of Beans", then "Benny and the Bird Dogs", then "Jacob's Ladder". I suggest also not putting "The Pardon" and "The Enemy" right together, as they are perhaps the heaviest and gloomiest. And if you want to end with a strong story, I say by all means use "Cocks Must Crow" at the end instead of "Varmints", as it has been infinitely better liked. I think the subject matter, as well as the general tone, makes a good note to end on. I enclose your list with the sequence numbered according to these changes.

Dr. Clifford Lyons, a Johns Hopkins man who has been the head of the Dept. of English at the University of Florida for two or three years, absolutely *begs* us to include "Hyacinth Drift". He thinks it is wrong not to include it in a collection of my short things, even though it is not fiction. Of course, Cracker Chidlings is almost non-fiction, and A Plumb Clare Conscience is not much fictionized. Aside from flattering things about style, quality, etc., he thinks it has a great fascination. It is in the anthology he uses at the U. of Florida. I hate not to include it if it is <all> at all reasonable to do so. You will have to be the judge of its suitability, but I should be very pleased to have it used if you think it is right. I can think of no future volume where it would fit in. It won't do for "Cross Creek", as I mean to keep that here entirely.

I don't think anything can be done to the Collier's story, and I'm glad to have it go into limbo.

Did you by chance ever see the vicious thing I had in the Jan. 6 New Yorker?[1] I loved doing it. Needless to say, it has no place in any of my books! Lee Smith of the Miami Beach News Service wrote me that he "relished" it, saying it was his idea of a horror story——

I enclose some photographs he sent me, taken when I was there last week. I look as big as a house, but the one sitting down in the beach chair doesn't seem too bad to me. If you want to use it, don't know whether you need their permission or not.

My fine big orange crop is a total loss. I got your Conn. address late, meaning to send you fruit, and the freeze came before I could do it.

The failure of Roark Bradford's "John Henry" has silenced Sam Byrd about my dramatizing South Moon Under, which suits me. I look forward to May, when the last of my lectures are over, and all the winter coming-and-going and festivities, which are fun, but I simply cannot work. I'll be at my quiet beach cottage practically all summer and hope to get "Cross Creek" done.

I shall speak probably in October at my own university,[2] and then I am *through* with the lectures. I am so thankful I didn't get signed up for a beastly tour. It would have made a total wreck of me.

Am looking forward to the Scribners' stop here. Wish you were coming too.

Editor's note: Enclosed is MEP's list showing a preliminary order for the stories in *When the Whippoorwill—*. In MKR's hand to the left of each title is a number indicating her preferred order.

1. "The Pelican's Shadow."
2. University of Wisconsin.

. . . .

487. MEP to MKR (TLS: UF, 3 pp.)

Feb. 23, 1940

Dear Marjorie:

I think you have made the order better. It is wiser to begin with a shorter story, and "A Crop of Beans" is a fine one.- But while I don't suppose anyone in the world could have thought "Hyacinth Drift" as magical as I did, and loved it more, I do not think we should put it in this book. I think that bringing in material that does not strictly belong to fiction, would give the impression that we were trying to put everything in, for effect. There is no kind of necessity of doing that.

You know what I wanted to do a year ago was to publish Hemingway's stories under the title "The First Forty-Nine" as a volume alone, and to publish "The Fifth Column", his only play, separately. He would not do it. He thought that the more you put into a book, the more the public would think it was getting for its money. It would have been wiser if he had done the other way.- It did seem as if we were trying to put in everything because we thought the book was not strong enough. We did very well with the book, but we would have done equally well with each of the two books separately. He impaired the effect by the addition of "The Fifth Column" because it wasn't a natural part of the volume. It is somewhat that way that I feel about adding "Hyacinth Drift" to this book, and time can't injure it, and the occasion will come for publishing it with other pieces.

Charlie is about to push off, and will soon be where you are.

Always yours,

Editor's note: Enclosed is a list entitled "Final Order for Rawlings's Stories."

. . . .

488. MKR to MEP (TLS, 4 pp.)

Hawthorn, Florida

Feb. 27, 1940

Dear Max:

I'll get off the proofs I have, today or in the morning. I can't remember exactly, but it seems to be the last of it.

I expect you are right about "Hyacinth Drift." Now Max, for almost the same reason that you don't want it in, I want to leave out "Cracker Chidlings." But I want to leave them out for even more important reasons. They seem to me to have no place in a collection of presumably creative work. They are almost straight journalism, and the difference in style could not help but puzzle a reader. I think the average reader would be puzzled, and the critical or literary reader would get an off-key feeling. They give me, myself, a terribly embarrassed feeling. They have no pretense at artistry. They are only regional studies, saying, "Aren't these people amusing!" If I had never progressed beyond "Cracker Chidlings" in my use of the Florida material, I could make no claim to being a creative writer.

Two or three of the sketches can probably go in "Cross Creek".

They seem to amount to about 12 pages, and I don't think the size of the book would suffer noticeably in leaving them out. The quality as a whole would be immensely lifted. I have worried in silence about this, and it does not represent any sudden impulses or revulsion. I am very certain about the rightness of my feeling, and hope and pray you will agree with me.

Again, because of the intrusion of the journalistic element, we just cannot use that prefatory note to "Alligators". It can stand on its own feet as a humorous narrative. I know that you feel that this is a personal problem that I have to solve, and so it is. I want to do the right thing by my friend Fred Tompkins, but I certainly don't want to spoil the effect of a whole book by making any unnecessary gesture.

My understanding with him when I wrote and sold the story was that I would divide what I received from the magazine. I did this only because he was too intelligent a person to *trap* into talking, as I do with so many of the interesting characters. I just wanted to have the cards on the table and have him know that when I made him talk about alligators, I meant to use the material, and was willing to pay for cooperation. The yarn, as a yarn, is of course mine. So if it's all right with you, we'll leave out the note and any mention of him. Then I'd like you to write him a letter, saying that the story "Alligators" in which I used some of his tales, is to be included in a collection of my stories, and that I expressed a wish that he be paid the customary fee for inclusion of a story in a volume, $25. You can take the $25 out of my account if you prefer.

The Scribners arrived Sunday morning, and Charlie and Vera left Monday morning. I enjoyed having them here so much, although poor Vera was ill Sunday with one of her vicious headaches. Julia is here with me for the week and I'm enjoying her tremendously. She is a most unusual person.[1]

1. Charles Scribner, III; Vera Scribner, his wife; and Julia Scribner (Mrs. Thomas Bigham), his daughter. MKR became close friends with Julia, who later was named the executor of MKR's estate.

. . . .

489. MEP to MKR (TLS: UF, 2 pp.)

March 4, 1940

Dear Marjorie:

I suppose you are right about "Cracker Chidlings" and I have removed them. I thought there was an incongruity myself, but I had a sentimental feeling toward those pieces as being the beginning. But you could more properly, I should think, use parts of them in "Cross Creek". Anyhow, they are out, and so is the note about "Alligators". As a matter of fact, writers pick up stories from all kinds of people, and I do not truly think you are under any further obligation in that regard. But when the book comes out, we can do as you suggest.

I am sorry to hear that Vera was laid up when she was with you. I know that Julia is an unusual person and I think it will be mighty good for her to talk to you.

We are having very stormy weather. In our house there is no heat, no light, no telephone. It is an ice storm and it looks as though it were going to continue for now it is snowing, even in New York. The whole of Connecticut is littered with trees and branches.

Yours always,

March 11, 1940

Dear Marjorie:

I thought since these stories had already been in type, and you had read the galleys—and we are verifying all the corrections, and are asking for a special reading also at the Press—that you would not need to see page proof. I hate to lose the time that would be required in sending it all, and also to put you to this trouble that seems avoidable. So we'll take great care and will go ahead as fast as possible to publication.

I hope that Malvina Hoffman will find you. I felt sure you would want to see her, of course, and I gave her your address and your telegraph address. She left yesterday for Sarasota and means to be away a month. She really is a most interesting person. I very much enjoyed my talk with her of two or three afternoons ago. I think there is no doubt but she will in the end have a fine book. But I guess she is one of those who must do it in her own way, that her own instinct is the best guide.

I just had a letter from Charlie from Havana where he has been with Hemingway.- He read all of the manuscript that is in type, and Hemingway read him the rest of it.[1] Charlie thought that he had done something truly magnificent, that it showed that he had moved forward very distinctly. The chapters he sent me made me feel this too, but they were too little to judge by, and one of them was so *terrible* that I feared the book might be an ordeal to the reader. At the same time, it was an astonishing piece of writing. One would never forget it.

Always yours,

1. *For Whom the Bell Tolls* (New York: Scribners, 1940).

. . . .

March 28, 1940

Dear Marjorie:

Julia Scribner came back with no specific information, but great promises of what you were going to do, and in the form of a novel. But she said you would tell nobody, and so I won't ask any questions. I only know for sure that if you feel sure of your plan, it is right.

I want now to put myself on record for true consideration of you. My daughter and a friend in Vassar went to Florida, and they were both excited at the possibility of seeing you, and I did not do anything to further it. I wanted this daughter to see you, and I wanted you to see her, but I knew you were crowded with all kinds of visitors,- especially after what Charlie told me. These girls were going to Palm Beach, and I realized that if they did go to Hawthorn they would have to spend the night, and it would be too much.- It would be a different question if they could motor down and then get back the same day.

"When the Whippoorwill" is now on press, and I hope very soon to be able to send you copies.

I am in a very hard piece of work, and have gone through the usual abysses of despair over it.- But I have done that so often that although I always feel it just as much, I do now know that there is generally some way out, and often a mighty good way too. I know the hopelessness of an author writing a book is much greater.- Maybe what I suffer is similar to what they call sympathetic whooping cough. That is what people sometimes get when their children have whooping cough. I got it, and it did me plenty of harm too, and I think it was the real thing.

Won't something bring you up here in the Spring when it is possible to sit outside and drink a planter's punch maybe?

Always yours,

. . . .

492. MKR to MEP (TLS, with holograph postscript, 2 pp.)

Hawthorn, Florida
April 1 [1940]

Dear Max:

I keep waiting to write you a decent letter, and the leisure doesn't come, and I have to dash off a hurried note again. I leave in the morning for 12 days, speaking in Shreveport, La. (Washington-Youree Hotel April 4 and 5), Nashville, Tenn. (Hermitage Hotel April 8 and 9), Chattanooga, Tallahassee—home April 13. I am furious at myself for leaving now, for Florida is sheer perfection. My flower garden is a mass of the choicest flowers, the orange grove is in full bloom, and I am getting buckets of cream from the two perverse cows, who came fresh within two days of each other, after I had battled the wrong bulls and tried to make a match with the right one so that one cow would be six or eight months ahead of the other. I am getting cured so fast of the lecture idea that I'll do well not to walk out on my contracts.

I think the book Julia was talking about was the Cross Creek. I did speak of the plantation novel and abandoning the original idea, with the hope some day of writing about the place and period from some other angle. But there is no novel in mind now.

I am genuinely sorry about your daughter and your detouring of her. The wrong people are considerate of me! The only trouble with the winter's comings and goings is that while almost each person has been more than welcome, the long steady stream of callers and visitors has left me feeling rather drained. Julia's visit was pure joy, with no effort about it in any way, and it was grand to have Miss Hoffman here for a couple of days. But hardly a day passes without strangers calling, and that is terribly wearing.

I never saw the way in which you used the quotation, "When the whip-poor-will calls, it's time for the corn to be in the ground."[1] It seems to me that is all that is needed, on a separate page at the beginning. I should not think it desirable or necessary to add "Florida backwoods saying", or anything of that nature, and hope you have used only the quotation alone. Did you check the hyphenating of whip-poor-will? I see the title announced without hyphens. Or is this optional?

Charlie said the jacket is "not bad". Hope it's a little better than that!

If the book is ready, would enjoy having a copy at one of the addresses I gave you between now and the 13th.

No, I don't think I shall leave Florida again this spring or summer. I am desperate for peace and quiet and hard work.

[Postscript] Bernice Baumgarten reports surprisingly good sales of "The Yearling" (Il Cucciolo) in Italy and Bompiani is publishing "Golden Apples" there![2]

1. MKR originally titled the book *When the Whippoorwill Calls,* but the title was shortened to *When the Whippoorwill—* at the suggestion of Carl Brandt.
2. *Il Cucciolo,* trans. Carlo Coardi (Milan: Bompiani, 1939); *Le mele d'oro,* trans. Bruno Maffi and Edoardo Canali (Milan: Bompiani, 1945).

. . . .

493. MEP to MKR (CC, 2 pp.)

April 10, 1940

Dear Marjorie:

I sent off six copies of "When the Whippoorwill" yesterday. People seem to think it looks very well, and I hope you will agree.

Now, after bragging about how I resisted the temptation to send Jane[1] down to visit you, I spoil it by fulfilling a promise to Walter Gilkyson that I would write to say that in the course of the next six or seven weeks he and his wife,

Bernice, who has written some excellent poems in the course of the last ten years or so, would stop in to see you.[2] But I am dead sure you will like Walter. He is a most intelligent and perceptive man, and a real man too.- He could rival John L. Lewis[3] for eyebrows. But they won't come to stay, I think, but just to try to have tea with you, or something like that. I believe you will like both of them, but I am sure about Walter.

Hem is sending up the greater part of his manuscript very soon. In fact it must be on the way now.

Always yours,

1. Jane Perkins, later Mrs. George Owen.
2. Walter Gilkyson, novelist, and Bernice Gilkyson, poet and editor at Scribners, who wrote under the name Bernice Kenyon.
3. John L. Lewis, American labor leader.

. . . .

494. MKR to MEP (TLS, with holograph header, 2 pp.)

[Cross Creek]
April 17, 1940

Dear Max:

The copies of When the Whippoorwill—were here when I returned, and I think the book looks very well indeed. I like the jacket immensely, and while I haven't read all the stories through, have noticed only one minor proofreader's error. The make-up and type seem very attractive to me. Of course, we can't expect much of a book of stories, but perhaps it will do better than I think. But "Cross Creek" will be liked, if I can beat it into shape. I did a chapter today, and while the style is not right, the essence is there and it is only a matter of hard work to get it in key. It is infinitely harder, as I found with "The Yearling", to do a job when you know precisely the effect you want.

Carl Carmer[1] is in St. Augustine, I suppose monkeying around with his erotic material. I was asked to a party with him the day I returned, but I don't want to meet him, for I know exactly the type of mess he is going to make of my lovely country, and if I had too many drinks, I should tell him so. Which gets no one anywhere.

I had a really lovely trip, through the best of the southern spring. Stopped over in Natchez and was fascinated with it. It has ante-bellum glamor as you expect to find it only in books. And the Mississippi there looks just as it should.

I have meant to ask you why in God's name you published that Maine book, "Be Thou the Bride".[2] The book is well written in parts, but it seemed to me an utter waste of print paper. A book that begins with congenital idiots doing embarrassing things in a cage and goes on to a school boy's rape of a school teacher, with nothing further to say than that "People can be a lot worse than you think, but they can't possibly be much better", has no excuse for existence unless there is a magnificent style and a terrific luminosity, neither of which this thing possessed. The woman who wrote it is obviously a bitter and disgruntled Lesbian and it is a pity that Scribner's or any house other than Macauley[3] should encourage her. She has force, but so does a city sewer. I am anything but a prude, but I like my dirt to be gutsy and Rabelaisian. "Dirt" should spring from human lustiness, not from human frustrations.

I am all agog to see the new Hemingway book.[4] Charlie writes me that it is the best <it> he has done, and that Hemingway attributes it to being happy while he worked. I have wondered and wondered about that. I don't get as much work done when I am happy, but the work done in a tranquil or ecstatic mood is very possibly a little sounder than work done out of suffering. I really don't know. But if Hemingway has done a top-notch job, Pauline, from what little I have heard of her, is well sacrificed. It seems to me the most delicious irony that after stealing him from under his first wife's nose, she should catch the same thing this late in the day.[5]

Since I began this, a letter from a Jacksonville friend who first called to my attention and turned over to me the original material on the planter-slave-trader-negress-marriage says he spent a day with Carl Carmer taking him over the territory and lending him some of the original papers. He said that Carmer told him he meant to do a book on famous slave traders. If that is true, he couldn't possibly interfere with me if I ever use the material.

I know you don't get much time to read anything but manuscripts, but if you can, do read "River of Earth" by a friend of mine, a Kentucky poet, James Still.[6] I think it will interest you in every way.

Editor's note: At top of letter in MKR's hand: "If you haven't sent Wyeth my stories, please send him a copy on my account, compliments of the author."

1. Carl Carmer (1893–1976), novelist and historian.
2. Christine Weston (1904–1989), *Be Thou the Bride* (New York: Scribners, 1940).
3. Macaulay and Co., publishers.
4. *For Whom the Bell Tolls.*
5. Pauline Pfeiffer married Hemingway in 1927 and they divorced in 1940. Hemingway's first wife was Hadley Richardson; they married in 1920 and divorced in 1927.
6. James Still (1906–), *River of Earth* (New York: Viking, 1940).

495. MEP to MKR (CC, 2 pp.)

April 18, 1940

Dear Marjorie:

Mr. Watson just brought me your letter with regard to the use of "Gal Young Un" in an anthology in preparation by Mr. Fidler of the University of Alabama.[1] When the original request came in, he brought it to me as he generally does with requests for permission, and we both of us thought that $25 was too little for such a story. There is no fixed fee for permissions and we gauge them according to the importance, and also the length, of what is asked for. "Gal Young Un" ought to bring $50, and even that would not be high. For many long stories we get as much as $100,- stories by Hemingway, Lardner, Thomas Wolfe, etc. I think you would come out better if you would simply refer any future requests made for the use of the stories or passages from the novels, to us. But in this case Mr. Watson had already written Fidler that in view of your acceptance of the offer, we would also accept it, and so the charge is understood to be $25.

I hope the weather where you are is not so unseasonable as it is here. It is still cold, and we rarely see the sun. Even at that the buds have somehow managed to get out on some of the trees.

Always yours,

1. Watson, not identified. William Perry Fidler and Richmond Croom Beatty, eds., *Contemporary Southern Prose* (New York: Heath, 1940).

. . . .

496. MEP to MKR (CC, 1 p.)

April 24, 1940

Dear Marjorie:

Here are the two important reviews (Times and Tribune), and good ones, too.[1] They have just come in, and I am getting them off at the end of the day.

Just had another grandson,- Zippy's second boy.[2]

Always yours,

1. Edith Walton, "Tales of the Florida Crackers," *New York Times* (April 28, 1940): 6; and review of *When the Whippoorwill—, New York Herald Tribune* (April 28, 1940): 4.
2. Jeremiah, son of Elisabeth Perkins and Douglas Gorsline.

May 2, 1940

Dear Marjorie:

We have had a considerable number of reviews of "When the Whippoor-will", all very favorable, but I don't suppose you care much about seeing most of them, but here is an exceptional one from the Atlantic Monthly.[1]

You don't like cats, do you? We have published a mighty good book about them called "The Science and Mystery of the Cat"[2] and I would send it except that I knew you liked dogs and most people do not like both.

Always yours,

1. "When the Whippoorwill—," *Atlantic Monthly* 165.6 (June 1940): n.p.
2. Ida M. Mellen (1877–), *The Science and the Mystery of the Cat* (New York: Scribners, 1940).

· ·

Hawthorn, Florida

May 14, 1940

Dear Max:

The Gilkysons came by, and had Sunday dinner with me. He is just as jolly as can be, and I enjoyed them a lot. Bernice explained the Scribner proof-reading system to me, and it does explain why there is so much trouble. As I understand it, it is really no one's in particular business, that the editorial department does not have a definitely assigned proof reader. In future, unless this gap is filled meantime, I shall simply take responsibility for the proofs myself.

I should love to have the cat book. I like them almost as well as dogs.

I am delighted that the reviews of the stories are so kind. I had been dread-ing "Time",[1] and it was grand to have them say that the book had good claim to being a better book than "The Yearling". I should think that would be desirable for quoting, considering its source.

Had a lovely note from James Branch Cabell, whom I met in St. Augustine, sending me a copy of the rare pamphlet he wrote as a portrait of Ellen Glasgow, signed by her "With tremendous admiration".[2] I was overcome. In <it> the pamphlet he said that she admired only two women writers, one of them Jane Austen, and the other he agreed with her about. You don't suppose it would possibly have been the Yearling he was speaking of, do you? The pam-phlet was written in 1938, but the month was not given. He embarrassed me when I met him by asking, "How does it feel to be a great writer" and I couldn't tell whether or not he was pulling my leg. He told me that when I was elected to the National Institute of Arts and Letters, he had never known such unanimous accord on an election, and that the man who proposed my name said, "Of course, you realize that this woman's work will be known after everyone in this room is forgotten". Cabell is so frightfully sarcastic and a best-seller must seem such a horrible thing to him, that I felt dubious about his feelings.

Did I write you that I met Thornton Wilder[3] in St. Augustine and he came down to my cottage at the beach and had lunch with me? He is a grand person and coming up against his mind was tremendously exciting. We seemed to begin talking where we had left off. But such scholars make me feel positively illiterate. If I manage to stick life out, I shall devote my old age to my education.

[Postscript] I need 6 copies, please, of "Whippoorwill."

Editor's note: Typed at top of p. 1 of letter: "Your family is increasing so that some day I expect to see one of those immense group photographs of Sire Perkins and progeny ——"

1. "Crackers Collected," *Time* 35 (May 13, 1940): 100. Review of *When the Whippoorwill—*.
2. James Branch Cabell, *Of Ellen Glasgow: An Inscribed Portrait* (New York: Maverick, 1938).
3. Thornton Wilder (1897–1975), American novelist and playwright.

. . . .

499. MEP to MKR (CC, 3 pp.; UF has copy fragment)

May 16, 1940

Dear Marjorie:

Thanks ever so much for your letter. I am immediately sending the cat book and six copies of "The Whippoorwill". "The Whippoorwill" by the way, is doing excellently, even in these troubled times when people can hardly put their attention on anything but the war.

I knew in some way, that Cabell had a great admiration for your writings, and of course Miss Glasgow has, but then there are few who have not. None that I know of now. Many people have spoken to me about "The Whippoorwill" as if it surprised them, even after "The Yearling".

I am glad the Gilkysons turned up, and I am looking forward to having them tell me all about their whole trip, and especially that part of it. Bernice is all wrong about the proof reading question. Proof reading is a purely mechanical thing, and has to be done by a person with an eye, and knowledge of punctuation, spelling, etc. The kind of person who reads in the way that an editor would, critically, and with enjoyment, will not see typographical errors with any certitude. I don't think Bernice knows much about this matter anyhow, but we won't go into that. The fact is that our proof readers at our own press read every book twice in galley proof, then in page proof, then in foundry proof. It is the same with every press, and every press does unsatisfactory proof reading nowadays, and largely because the union situation is such that one cannot have complete control of who the readers are. They must be union men. In the old days they were not. That mistake which occurred in the Pulitzer edition of "The Yearling" where a line was lost and another repeated, could not have been caught by a proof reader. It occurred in the handling of the type just before it had been cast, after the foundry proof had been read. As a matter of fact, every book you ever published here has also been proof read in this office. The only one which I did not read through in the proof was "The Whippoorwill" because I knew the stories so well for the most part, and they had already been in type. It would be absurd for an editor to do the proof reading in the mechanical sense. If he did that, he could never do anything else. He does do the proof reading in the critical sense but in the case of these stories, that would have been superfluous. I have just been reading the proofs on Thomas Wolfe's "You Can't Go Home Again,"[1] as Executor, and with a view to libel and such things as that.- I have seen innumerable typographical errors in it. But I know for a certainty that I have not seen all there are because one reading for sense makes the optical correction with the eye. His mind is not on the mechanical error. It cannot be on both. Theoretically, the author's copy is supposed to be perfect, excepting that each press has certain different rules of uniformity.- But, of course, an author is supposed also to read both galley and page proof. But the author will not catch all the typographical errors. He will read for sense and effect, and not in the mechanical way. As a matter of fact, each editor here in charge of a particular book does read at least the galley proof, excepting with a few authors who are known to be very careful themselves.- Well, say one like President Butler for whom we have published for so many years, and who is completely aware of the whole situation. He is perhaps the only author whose books go through un-proofread in the editorial department.

You are dead right about Thornton Wilder. He is a true scholar. Like the scholars of the middle ages, like Erasmus,[2] he has all the feelings and perceptions of the scholar. I always thought that he should be only a teacher. That that was his real vocation. He is a true creative teacher. He loves the thing, for itself,- and to do that is what makes somebody some good. You do, with another thing, too.

Always yours,

1. Thomas Wolfe, *You Can't Go Home Again* (New York: Harper, 1940).
2. Desiderius Erasmus (1466–1536), Dutch philosopher.

May 22, 1940

Dear Marjorie:

I thought the enclosed list of comments on "The Whippoorwill" would interest you,- even though you do so wisely disregard the sales and advertising question. All of my family adore the book. I went over to see a daughter last night who was reading it—she was reading "Jacob's Ladder"—and she wouldn't even stop to talk to me.- But you will have plenty of letters from people who adore the book.

I had today the first letter in a long long time—aside from brief notes— from Scott Fitzgerald. It was a sombre letter, but yet it sounded good, as if he were under the control of himself again.- Well, he is supposed to have been that for a good while, but one cannot help worrying over him. Of course he was dreadfully upset about the war, but still he had his plans, and he had had the stimulation of directing the production of one of his own stories, one of his best too,- "Babylon Revisited".

Malvina Hoffman came in yesterday, and partly to let me hear, as I greatly enjoyed doing, little pieces from a letter you had written her.

There were a few little straws of good news in the afternoon papers anyhow. The very fact that the French could catch footing and strike back is encouraging.

Always yours,

. . . .

[Cross Creek]

May 24, 1940

Dear Max:

Thanks so much for the cat book. It's tremendously interesting. Actually, I like any animal book. I think what fascinates me most is seeing where animal and human characteristics overlap. And thanks too for both letters and the Times ad. It is a great relief to me not to have the book of stories dismissed as a trivial matter.

I am just back from a week at the beach cottage where I just about finished a story. The cottage is such a grand place to work, but all the time I had one of my black feelings. Part of that is the work, and part turned out to be that when I returned home with old Martha, who had "spelled off" Adrina, I found that

Adrina had eloped with a worthless nigger, half her age, to St. Petersburg.[1] She will be back eventually, for her new mate was only after her accumulated savings, but meantime my physical comfort will be non-existent. Old Martha, her mother, is a great spiritual satisfaction to me, but can't even make a decent cup of coffee. Martha is more crushed than I by Adrina's delinquency, for it is a reflection on her training! I shall have to console her more than she does me. When she finished the work Adrina had left undone, I said, "Bless you, Martha", and she said, "The same to you, Sugar." I suppose that sort of thing is more helpful than a well-made bed——.

I think we had perhaps the first American war-scare at the cottage Saturday. <I was having> Adrina and Martha were cleaning the cottage and there was a pogy boat seining in very close to shore. About twenty men were in the surf, pulling a seine very slowly. Adrina called out, "Lord have mercy, Mama, you reckon that's the Germans?" Told this to a friend who had seen an almost identical incident in the New Yorker.

I am not satisfied with the sketch form of "Cross Creek". If I could think of a way to do it in narrative form, it would almost certainly be better. Yet it seems impossible to tell a personal narrative no matter how objectively and yet elide the gaps where I don't want to speak personally. I'll get some more done the way I've begun and send it to you and let you see what you think.

I had a strange and lovely gift the other day. James Still, the young Kentuckian whose poetry I have so loved——"Hounds on the Mountain"[2]— and whose novel "River of the Earth" is so fine——sent me a dulcimer. He had it made for me by the only man living, as far as I know, who still makes them. Still visited me this winter and said, "Your place is lovely, but it isn't complete. You don't have a dulcimer." It is an exquisite instrument, long and slim, of pale maple wood, and I <should> hope I can learn to play it. It is used as a soft accompaniment to all the sad and plaintive mountain and old English songs, many of which are still sung in the southern backwoods.

May 25

My friend Leonard (Lant of South Moon)[3] just came by, and it took him about two minutes to figure out the dulcimer. He said, "Now that's the way the gentleman works". He said, "It ain't intended for no fancy playing. Just to carry the tune, and the chords right along with it, for them old mountain songs." He gave me a lesson and it is going to be very simple, even for one who can play nothing else. He even showed me how to get the Hawaian [sic] effect. "That-a-way you get kind of a whine in it. You want the whine." He said, "I wish Nettie Hall's blind brother could get a-holt of this. He plays an auto-harp, and I mean he covers the ground. Nettie Hall's brother could cold-out get music out of this gentleman." I read him some of James Still's poems that mention the dulcimer and he was very much affected by one of them.

1. Martha Mickens, mother of Adrenna Mickens, MKR's maid. Adrenna did return, but MKR refused to rehire her.
2. James Still, *Hounds on the Mountain* (New York: Viking, 1937).
3. Leonard Fiddia.

. . . .

502. MEP to MKR (CC, 2 pp.)

June 3, 1940

Dear Marjorie:

I am enclosing the check for the royalties due according to the last report. I think the cheap edition[1] of "The Yearling" is going to look mighty well.- You have seen the wrap in some early form, but even so you will be surprised, I think, at how well it looks when printed.

The blitzkrieg has certainly hurt the book business for the time being anyhow. But there are reorders for "The Whippoorwill". Weren't the British astounding and magnificent in getting out of Flanders? Military men that I knew had no idea that it was even a possibility. The strangest thing, how national characteristics seem to persist,- how the British are always at their best when licked. But you ought to try not to think about the war, for it does no good, and it may be possible to forget it in your country.

I am most eager to see any part of "Cross Creek" that you can send.

Always yours,

1. Popular Edition.

. . . .

503. MKR to MEP (TLS, 2 pp.)

Hawthorn, Florida
June 6, 1940

Dear Max:

Just as a curiosity, and to add to my collection of translations, I should like to get two copies of the Japanese edition of "The Yearling".[1] I wonder if your office would mind taking care of it for me? With the feeling of not being able to trust the Japanese even to the extent of their swapping books fairly, will you have this done whichever way is most likely to get me the copies——either paying them outright and billing me, or sending them the two American copies. Thanks a lot.

No, it is impossible to ignore the war, even at Cross Creek. The Ivory Tower long since became the Leaning Tower, and finally crashed to earth. It does disturb my work, for it is hard to present my simple matters of the moment in personal writing, even though one knows that in the long run it is those things, and not empires, that have an element of the timeless. Perhaps I can say a little of that. I am more depressed than I can tell you.

1. *The Yearling*, trans. Kaku Arai (Tokyo: Shigen-sha, 1939).

. . . .

504. MEP to MKR (TLS: UF, 3 pp.)

June 26, 1940

Dear Marjorie:

I am enclosing a copy of a letter furnished me by Stanley Rinehart who is in charge of the project in behalf of the various publishers referred to. You will know what good may come of this syndication without my adding anything more but this: nobody has expressed the American way as you have,- those things inherent in Americans, or in some of them, that are truly ours, or were. Nobody therefore could do this thing better. I am only writing at the moment to two others,- Ernest Hemingway and Arthur Train, though I think we shall later try to get Bob Sherwood, and possibly James Truslow Adams.[1] But you and Hemingway immediately occurred to me as indispensable, and you were the first ones spoken of by other people concerned.

I'll get you the Japanese edition referred to in the end, but it may take a long time. Yesterday I had lunch with Walter and Bernice Gilkyson. They were delighted by your hospitality, and by everything connected with their visit to you.

Of course I really know you could not truly get yourself separated from all these things that are going on in the world, but your work is greatly important, and it is important too in the direction of making Americans know themselves, and what is good in themselves again.

Always yours,

1. Stanley Rinehart, cofounder of Farrar and Rinehart publishers, and James T. Adams (1879–1949), historian. MKR's involvement in an article on the perils facing democracy and the entrance of the United States into World War II is not known. The project was syndicated by the Newspaper Enterprise Association.

[Cross Creek]

[July 1940]

Dear Max:

I have suffered and struggled over the article suggested, tearing up page after page. When one has trained oneself to write objectively, saying things always through a character, it is immensely difficult to write in the first person.

This is the best I can do, and I am sending it to Stanley Rinehart, with a copy to you. I hope you think it is all right.

. . . .

July 8, 1940

Dear Marjorie:

Many thanks for sending the little article. It made me feel mighty good to read it. It is true. We have our own special quality, if we can only realize it, and live up to it,- and it is shown nowhere better than in the characters in your book.

Always yours,

. . . .

[Cross Creek]

July 22 [1940]

Dear Max:

I can't thank you enough for the Gertrude Stein.[1] It is a beautiful piece of work, tremendously moving, very funny, and exquisitely written. The old gal really has the touch.

When your note came, saying that you liked the article, I was about to wire you telling you it wouldn't do at all. I am not at all satisfied with it, yet it is the best I could do. There are so many things that I feel that had no place in such an article——that democracy, actually, is a failure——the very individualism entailed makes for chaos——and above all, the fact that individual and national and racial greed and selfishness make the whole outlook entirely hopeless.

The only point I could emphasize was that we do <the> really believe, whether we practice it or not, in a basic kindliness, and consideration for the rights of the individual. It's probably time to begin preaching, a la Ortega,[2] the responsibilities and obligations of the individual! We've all been concerned with what we thought was coming to us, rather than what we could contribute to the general welfare.

Had something on my mind to mention to you and have been interrupted and can't think what it is. Can't be very vital.

Will soon send you enough samples from "Cross Creek" for you to give an opinion as to whether the episodic form I am using will be effective or not. I should immensely like straight narrative, but cannot see how I can make a consecutive thing of it.

1. Gertrude Stein, *Paris France* (New York: Scribners, 1940).
2. José Ortega y Gassett (1883–1955), Spanish philosopher.

· ·

508. MEP to MKR (CC, 3 pp.)

July 23, 1940

Dear Marjorie:

I know you like fine pictures and so I am sending you "The Fire Ox and Other Years",- and it may take your mind away from the troubles of the present for a time to look it over.[1]

But I must now write you to ask if in a sustaining program on a large network, providing all the other circumstances are satisfactory, such as the people who participate, you would allow a sort of dramatic presentation from "The Yearling". It may be that your moving picture contract will not allow this. That is a point to be watched, but I can check up on it with Carl Brandt very easily. I am writing tentatively to ask if you would be willing to have it done. It is the project of a young man who seems to be truly enthusiastic about books and about drama, and he has the interest of a number of good publishers.- But the practical value is only that of publicity.

I would like to know your general attitude. If you consented, we would not consent until we knew for a certainty that everything would be done in a suitable way.

I sent you some time ago with some hesitation, a copy of Gertrude Stein's "Paris France". It seemed a sad time to read it, but apparently the public does not feel so for it is selling extremely well. I was afraid when Paris fell, just before it appeared, that people would feel too badly about it all to want to think of Paris as it was, or the French.

If you want to read a truly great book, that might make it possible to take a calmer view than is possible for me anyhow, I'll send you "The Dynasts" by

Thomas Hardy.[2] You may have read it, but hardly anyone has. It is about the Napoleonic wars. When you are through with it[,] it is as if you had watched the whole world of that time from a cloud that hung above it. The reason people don't read it, I think, is that it is in the form of a poem, and it runs to about 1100 pages. If you haven't read it, you would be glad when you had.

Always yours,

1. (Charles) Suydam Cutting (1889–1972), *The Fire Ox and Other Years* (New York: Scribners, 1940).
2. Thomas Hardy (1840–1928), *The Dynasts* (London: Macmillan, 1903).

. . . .

509. MEP to MKR (TLS: UF, 4 pp.)

July 26, 1940

Dear Marjorie:

I must say I myself feel desperate about democracy. You cannot have it without a very strong sense of the thing now detested, "duty" and a sense that material success is a lower form than that of service. These things got to be regarded as hypocrisy, and I suppose the truth is people became hypocritical about them. But they were not that in my boyhood. The Yankees really believed them. We always were taught that in a community like Windsor, the truly important men were the school teacher, the newspaper editor, and the clergyman. The doctor too was more respected than the business man. These people were supposed to have made a sacrifice because they cared more to serve their professions and what they meant, than for money. I know that my father,[1] who practiced in New York and never made more than a good living for a big family out of it, nor left a penny, always thought that he was doing something more important than that, that he was advancing the idea of justice. And I know that when I was in college and saw so many old Boston people that were friends of my grandparents—and I admit there was some element of unconscious hypocrisy about them—they were obviously somewhat ashamed of wealth, and acted as if they did not have it, in a way. For instance, hardly any of them had men servants. They all had middle-aged, aproned maids with pompadours, who had been in the family from early youth. They soft-pedalled wealth. They didn't think that was supposed to be the point. And business men who were presumably working only for wealth were looked down upon, though not their grandchildren! But anyhow, it certainly is true that we cannot have what we meant to have without a different point of view from the present one, without a deep sense of responsibility.

I am delighted that some of "Cross Creek" will come soon. It cannot come too soon. A large part of yesterday I spent reading the last third of Ernest Hemingway's novel.[2] To prove to you how deeply absorbing and how large it is in meaning, I'll tell you that I read it with great concentration even though most of the time Ernest was standing behind my chair and reading it over my shoulder.- But I think I have told you what the nature of it was already.

I think the piece you did for the syndicate was admirable, and so did John Farrar.[3]

Always yours,

1. Edward Clifford Perkins was a lawyer. Charles Callahan and Frances D. Perkins were the paternal grandparents of MEP.
2. *For Whom the Bell Tolls.*
3. John Farrar, cofounder of Farrar and Rinehart publishers.

. . . .

510. MKR to MEP (TLS, 2 pp.)

[Cross Creek]
August 6, 1940

Dear Max:

The work is going quite steadily, but it does not seem good. I had planned to have each sketch, incident, etc. "a little gem of prose". Yet most of the material is so informal that the natural style for it seems to be a conversational one. At least that is the form it is taking. If it makes for good reading, it will perhaps be better than something formal and "exquisite", but I cannot judge. It seems to me totally undistinguished. That, it must not be.

When I send you some samples, you must promise not to show them to a soul——not to Charlie or *anyone.* I feel that you are the only one who could see through any bad writing to my ultimate aim. You will know whether I am on the right track or not. If not, the sooner I know, the better. If so, you can make allowances for the miracles that re-writing and editing can do for me. Everything I send will be *first drafts.* I sha'n't bother now with even the simplest editing. Altogether, in *very rough form,* I have nearly 200 book pages of copy. My notes are in hand for as much more as we need. A book of this type, if you feel that my scheme is effective, should probably not be too long——300 pages, perhaps, of print, with whatever of illustrations seem desirable. All plans are tentative, for I am most unhappy about the style.

You might keep this for a memorandum when the samples come in to you. I just felt like talking about it.

I enjoyed "The Fire Ox"——liked it much better than Theos Barnard's book of the same territory and people.[1] Suydam Cutting's gentleman-explorer narrative is so honest and sincere, and Barnard is an egoistic, hypocritical show-off.

I should like to have "The Dynasts". It is one of the things I have always meant to read.

August 19

The combination of not being pleased with my work, and countless interruptions, has me much depressed. Had to go back to my grove on business, had a dear friend from California spend a week——so glad to have her, an old college friend——but it doesn't advance the damn book. Also had a very ill week, and my substitute maid (the regular one who eloped not having returned) faked an illness so she wouldn't have to come back to the cottage with me, and I am without help, and not enjoying myself a bit. Must get some samples of Cross Creek to you soon, so that we can perhaps decipher a straight line for me. I can stand anything when I feel the work is on the right track.

Can't wait to see the new Hemingway. Am so glad that something top-notch came out of his emotional crisis. Would like to see him mop up with the carping critics who have been sticking pins in him.

Be patient with me. "Cross Creek" has the possibilities and I've just got to stay with it to get them out.

1. Theos Bernard (1908–), *Heaven Lies Within Us* (New York: Scribners, 1939).

. . . .

511. MEP to MKR (TLS: UF, 2 pp.)

August 7, 1940

Dear Marjorie:

I am just sending you the royalty report due August first, and you will see that "The Yearling" has sold over 6,000 copies in the two editions. I wish something could happen to make people realize what a beautiful book "South Moon Under" is. I don't know whether you took note of it, at the time, but it nearly broke my heart that it had to come out at the beginning of the bank holiday.- Well, maybe sometime we'll be able to get out a subscription set of your books, but you will have to have written enough to make ten volumes to do that.

By the way, I think probably that plan for radio dramatization has fallen through, for I have heard no more about it. It was supposed to be a sustaining program, and I was afraid all the time that it would seem to the radio people to be on too high a level. But anyhow, you had better tell me so I may be prepared, what you would think of it.

We have had a harried and feverish week with Ernest in town. In some miraculous way he went through his entire manuscript revising it while we were setting it up, and while his room was full of newspapermen, soldiers, bobbed haired bandits, etc.- And I spent a large part of the week there. This is a novel you will want to read, and anyhow now you are working on non-fiction. I'll send you the very first copy I can get.

Always yours,

. . . .

512. MEP to MKR (CC, 1 p.)

August 12, 1940

Dear Marjorie:

We got you the Japanese edition, and I am sending two copies now. I am hoping soon to see some of the "Cross Creek".

Always yours,

. . . .

513. MEP to MKR (CC, 3 pp.)

August 22, 1940

Dear Marjorie:

In case you have wondered, as you must have done, why the syndicate feature containing your article has not begun to appear I am quoting from a letter of the NEA who runs it,-

"As you know, we're terribly anxious that material of this importance should not be overlooked by any vacation-minded or heat-weary editors, so — acting upon the advice of a number of our important client newspapers — we decided on a late summer release for the series.

Everyone to whom we have talked in connection with the enterprise is tremendously enthusiastic.

Sorry that extra duties which have fallen upon me, trips out of town, office vacation problems, the acceleration of the war, and a head cold could have combined to prevent me from being in closer contact with you and your office in the last couple of weeks."

As to Cross Creek everything is all right and I'll just wait but I am sure you are simply going through the regular process of finding out the right way to do what you mean to do and that you will find it.

I haven't heard from Charlie et al about the discussions over the inclusions of THE YEARLING in the series of <literature> illustrated classics.- You know, in my mind it is the very best thing in the world that THE YEARLING appeals also to children. I always thought that. Most of the books in that series are adult books. Most of the best books in the world are read both by children and adults,- and that goes for such as GULLIVER'S TRAVELS and a large part of Rabelais and DON QUIXOTE—abridged mostly for the sake of shortening it— and many of the other great books. And of course it goes for all of Scott and much of Dickens including even PICKWICK. This is a characteristic of a great book, that it is both juvenile and adult and that is the thing that assures it a long life.

I know that all this is superfluous and that you are working it all out with Charlie, but I thought my saying something about it too, might reassure you. The best books have universal appeal, of course, and,- and [sic] THE YEAR-LING certainly has that.

> Always yours,

. . . .

514. MKR to MEP (TLS, 1 p.)

> [Cross Creek]
>
> Sept. 3, 1940

Dear Max:

I am sending you these samples most unhappily, for they are not at all what I want. It is all a matter of style, and these simply have none. But if we can agree on where I am going on it, it will be easier to continue, and I can take more pains with each section as I do it. These have all been the roughest of first drafts, just to get down the subject matter and the ideas.

Since these samples are so far from my goal, I sha'n't attempt to raise specific criticisms. But when Miss Wyckoff is back, so that you don't mind dictating a long letter, I wish you would point out anything that occurs to you. There are so many pitfalls to avoid. The style cannot be facetious. There must not be condescension or patronage as to the people written about. And so on and so on. But I hope you will be able to see through to the picture of living that I want to give.

And above all, I want you to decide whether this episodic form will carry, or whether you can see any possible way in which a connected narrative could be made of the material. I myself do not see how it could be managed, for any consecutive and chronological history could not avoid personal elements that

I do not wish to include. In this sketch form, the fact that I began life at Cross Creek with a husband and two brothers in law and then had none, need not enter. I want in any case just to give my own reactions to the people and the life around me——an objectively personal document.

I am checking the sketches that are nearest to what I want to do. But not a single one is right.

The first item, "Cross Creek", is the roughest sort of effort at what would be my introduction. I just wanted to put down on paper the point of my neighbor's saying "So much happens at Cross Creek."

Anyway, see what you think the potentialities are.

. . . .

515. MEP to MKR (TLS: UF, 2 pp.)

Sept. 16, 1940

Dear Marjorie:

You have splendid material for a book, and for just such a book as I think you could do better than anyone.- I don't mean that you could do it better because nobody else knows that material, of course, but that the kind of book it should be is one you would excel in. I have read it all and enjoyed doing it, and I think I do see the problem. I have too, my ideas of how it should be met, but before writing you at length about it, I want to go over the material again so that perhaps I can speak more definitely than now. But I am sure you can master the problem and do the book. Maybe what I say will seem to you wrong and maybe it will only result in bringing your own ideas into shape.- But if it does that, no more will be needed anyhow.

What delayed me, to my great regret too, was that I had to go away over two separate weekends on business.- And weekends is when I read. No time in the office.

Always yours,

. . . .

516. MKR to MEP (TLS, 3 pp.)

Hawthorn, Florida
September 19, 1940

Dear Max:

I can't tell you how relieved I am to hear from you, and to know that you don't consider the material hopeless. I shall wait to do any more work until I hear from you at greater length, for if you have hit on any better approach, I should prefer to make a fresh start. My mind is very open on the matter, and I shall be most receptive to anything that occurs to you.

However I handle it, the material is such that I can work through interruptions, as I cannot with fiction, and I look forward to settling down to a long good autumn and winter.

I remembered that I never answered your question about the radio use of "The Yearling". Anything that you considered desirable would be all right with me, but I have an idea that you will find the movie contract quite restrictive about such things. Carl will know about that.

I enjoyed Julia Scribner's visit immensely. She is most unusual and very mature.

My trip to Madison, Wisconsin will be a brief one just for the one lecture for the benefit of the Alumni Scholarship Fund. I am going at my own expense. It seems little enough to do for one's own college. I think I shall go by train instead of driving so that it will not take so much time.

Needless to say, I am most anxious to hear from you in detail, but because I do want your reaction in detail, please take your time.

We had an unexpected and very jolly meeting here with Ernest Hemingway and Martha Gilhorn.[1] I was entertaining over the week-end for Julia and our party was at Marineland at dinner. I recognized Hemingway at a nearby table and spoke to him. They joined us for drinks and then came up to the cottage and stayed much later than was wise for them, as he was trying to make time going west. He is obviously in a much better frame of mind than when I met him in Bimini, and we all liked Martha immensely. Do send me as early a copy of the book as you can. He spoke as though he might be coming through here in the fall and I offered him the use of the cottage, as I shall only come over here, after October first, for occasional week-ends. If he speaks of it, tell him the offer was not just drunken hospitality, and I should be glad to have him and Martha make a stay here. They would not be bothered by anyone.

Editor's note: Enclosed is a list of word counts for the stories in *When the Whippoorwill—*.

1. Martha E. Gellhorn (1908–1983), a journalist, married Hemingway in 1940 and was divorced from him in 1945.

September 20, 1940

Dear Marjorie:

What you say of the style is true—though there is in nothing you send me any condescension of which I think you are incapable—but it will all come right if you will look at the book as a whole, as a unit. Then the tone of what you do, or the style will fall into that conception and take care of itself,- and anyhow there are beautiful pieces here like the Storm, and The Pecan Tree, which, developed, are in the right tone.

But in writing you how I think it should be I must be cautious, and you still more so. For you only can write the book, and you must—and I know you will—do only what you are convinced of;- and what I say must be no more than suggestion and just "for example".

I think the book must give the neighborhood and its characters so that it will have a kind of completeness.- And the material to do that is here, or is implied.- But none of it is sufficiently developed.

I don't think the book should be episodic in the sense of being just a series of episodes in chronological or some other order, but it could and even must be organized around episodes which should be developed to stand out as the big events in a novel do. And all these episodes should also serve to develop a sense of community, to contribute to building up a total picture of the scene. And this really is not difficult. It is only a matter of your attitude toward the material. I think that the book should be a narrative varied somewhat by description, and by reflection,- to use a figure, it should be a single piece of string with knots in it, the knots being the episodes, but each connected with the other by the incidents, etc. I think you could use the talk of your negroes largely to make the connection and to prepare for the incidents in a natural way.- No one does negroes so sympathetically and so well, themselves and their talk.

Take an example at random,- or perhaps more because I liked the character and his possibilities so much: Mr. Marsh Tucker. He's grand. He was part of that community, a live and picturesque figure. But the reader should have known about him as on the landscape before these things happened, and in a way to be made curious about him,- maybe only by your passing him on the road and by someone telling of him,- for instance Martha. Who was she? Did she work for you? Those negresses should be used more to prepare for events and for their own sake too.- Like Adrina. She was in your household and should figure as a person before that fine incident of the storm.

Or take "The Pig Is Paid For". Wonderful.- But how much intensified in its qualities if both Mr. Martin and Mr. Higginbotham had been seen long before, or heard of from Adrina or someone, just incidentally. Perhaps just as a figure on the large scene in Martin's case. Anyhow, it seems to me that there ought to be some characters that recur a good many times in the course of the narrative, and that the reader ought to look forward to seeing them again.

Now, taking up these different pieces you have sent, some are episodes and should be developed as such, and some are just incidents and should only fill out the general scene and contribute to the total effect. I think "The Pig Is Paid For" should be one of the knots,- but we have spoken of that. The adventures in the mist is another,- but oughtn't you to give more about Uncle Barney and old Ca[l] Long, especially old Ca[l] Long.[1] Perhaps you plan for that. It seems to me that you should have a real hunt in this book because I know you were in them and it was part of the life. And I know old Ca[l] Long was a grand character. You couldn't develop the hunt part of this particular piece without destroying the effect you want which is about the mist, but I think you could develop the piece into more of a knot on the string. Another of the knots could be Mr. Marsh Tucker. I am only giving these for examples, but if they were the ones that most was made of—and all could be developed—I think that the characters in them should have been known of by the reader before they appear for that would strengthen the effect of the action in these pieces.

Then there are the incidental pieces such as that of "The Pound Party". The Townsends are grand and they themselves could be made more of at that party. But couldn't you have something said there about someone or something which was to form one of the knots in the string and so arouse the reader's expectations and prepare him?

Take as a similar instance, "The Catch Dog". It can be made a first rate little piece, part of the atmosphere and quality of it all, and yet a sort of story in itself, but couldn't it somehow connect itself with something that follows? "The Dime" is a good incident, but Bernie Bass ought to be somewhere in the book in other places, and it would have been better to have had her in earlier, just so people know she existed, and something about what she was like. And this is true too of the incident of old Boss. Old Jib should have been hanging around on the scene before you developed him to the point you do in the piece of that name, and so should old Joe, the mule, before he died. And who was Snow? If Willie Higgins appeared, he should perhaps be just seen and say what he did on the road as you passed him in going somewhere.[2]

Then there are the other pieces which you do most beautifully, about the sound of the frogs and the insects, and all that, and such as in "The Pecan Tree" and one could hardly have too much of that kind of writing.- But I have a possible suggestion that will bear on that kind of thing later. As matters stand, there aren't enough knots for the string.- But what about "Cracker Chidlings"? You meant to get them in, and they ought to be in. And what of that most lovely "Hyacinth Drift"? It was part of that world. Maybe it isn't strictly "Cross Creek" but you don't have to be too rigidly geographical. I swear I think you ought to have that in the book.

As to the beginning, it is on the right lines, in my opinion. I don't think it should be more than eight or ten pages long, and it seems to me that the little piece "The Road" could be in it, and that walking along that road could enable you in the most natural way to give at the start, a conception of the neighborhood.

I have not spoken about everything, of course, but I am afraid even now I may have spoken too definitely. I am always frightened to death of doing that. You must not take what I say as definite at all ever, but all as by way of example only. The whole thing might perhaps be done in some quite different way, and what I say are only suggestions toward the final effect. The ways and means to it may be very different from what I have used to illustrate.

Now there is another possibility, and I think it ought to be considered. You are taking a reader into a place, and you want him to get all its qualities, and to know the people. You write most beautifully of nature and of the changes of the seasons. Suppose you divided this book into four groups,- Spring, Summer, Autumn and Winter? The material would be the same as if you didn't do that, or almost the same, but the ordering of it would be different. The knots in the string would each fall into a part according to the season they came into. And you could lead into each section by telling what the season was like and how it came in the beautiful language you use.

I could go into all of this at greater length but it is better not to do it. I am almost afraid I have said too much, and may tend to throw you off the track instead of putting you on it.- But I am sure it ought to be one thing, that the characters should, to some degree anyhow, reappear. It can make a beautiful book.

There are very few true writers, and they vary widely, but I have at last discovered that those few share one trait. You would never suspect it,- you would think they would be the very ones with supreme confidence. In fact they do have a subconscious confidence, I think. But when they begin a big piece of work they have vastly less confidence than these men who just follow the trade of writing and who always know just where they are going and go there like business men,- those that we publish to keep the business going because the real ones are so few. I think, in truth, all you lack at this moment in regard to this book is confidence. I wish I could give you that, for I am sure you could make it a lovely book, and one full of the truth of life. One of these pieces began by saying that you sometimes felt as if you should be using your talent for the issues of the day. Sometime your talent might have occasion to fit into some issue. But unless that happened, I would forget about the day. In this depression men have gone to ruin because they were so tempted to forget their vocation and turn their material to an immediate purpose.- In a way that was one of the issues between me and Tom, and I kept telling him that what he felt would come through his writing even though not specifically stated.- And yet he wanted at that time to be a Communist, the last thing that he truly was, as his last book shows. With you too, what you mean comes through your writing, and don't let anything tempt you into the lists of controversy. I don't know who these people are who talk to you, but there are lots of people of high intelligence who respond to literature too, and yet haven't the faculty of exactly understanding where it comes from.- They just think a writer who is good can turn anyway he is asked to. It isn't true, and we know it. You, as well as I. But there is this pressure, and I hope you will resist it.- And as for what I have said in this letter, I only hope for it that it may give you an idea, and not that you will follow it closely, but that it will suggest a way.

Always yours,

P.S. If you adopt the seasonal arrangement, which is in no way artificial or forced in this particular book but quite natural to it, you could open each part in a way that would make the reader feel the coming of the new season. All that about frogs and all (Marjorie, I wasn't really able in the over-worked state of my eyes, to read much of "Toady-Frogs, Snakes, Varmints and Antses" because of the pale copy, as it seemed to me) could be worked in beautifully at the beginning, or near it, of each section. You have plenty of that.

1. Barney Dillard's and Cal Long's oral yarns and hunting prowess provided the backdrop for *The Yearling*.
2. Snow Slater and Old Boss Brice, residents of Cross Creek. Old Jib is a cat.

. . . .

518. MEP to MKR (CC, 2 pp.)

Oct. 8, 1940

Dear Marjorie:

The $2.50 illustrated edition of "The Yearling"[1] has just come from the press, and I am sending you two copies. I think we put the most effective picture on the cover of the book. The choice for the box picture was made on account of the coloring. It was necessary to print in black, and so we needed a light surface. But that picture does have the virtue of having both Jody and Flag in it.

I hope the Hemingway book got to you safely for I know you will wish to read it. Did my letter disturb you in seeming to ask too much? I don't really think that it is a complicated matter, but simply one of method.

Hoping you will soon write, I am,

Always yours,

1. The Illustrated Classics edition, illustrated by N. C. Wyeth.

. . . .

519. MKR to MEP (TLS, 3 pp.)

Hawthorn, Florida
October 26, 1940

Dear Max:

It was good to see you, if only so briefly. We manage to come to our understandings very nicely by letter, but there is always somehow a reassurance in the personal contact.

The way to go at "Cross Creek" is almost definite now. I can feel the beginning, and the key, taking shape. I think I shall be happy in the actual writing——that is, happier than in the torment of creative fiction——and as happy as it is possible to be when the words never seem quite to say the secret and lovely things behind them.

I found everything at the grove going well, in spite of a bad drought. But the orange trees are amazingly hardy and can stand extremes of all sorts.

Your shipping department went hay-wire on the books you sent me. Instead of the new illustrated edition, they sent me two copies of the old Shenton edition. The Hemingway was not here at all. Alan Villiers was here,[1] and I am very glad to have him, but the absence of the Hemingway is most distressing, for the reason that when I reached Washington I had still not had a chance to read him——knew the other copy would be waiting for me here——and blithely gave away the copy you gave me in New York to a friend who admires Hemingway immensely——

So here I am without the bell tolling, and in a cold fury at not having this great treat at hand——.

Do get me another copy post haste, billing me——but I suppose it won't be a first edition now. I am cold to most "firsts", but when you have loved and followed an author a long time, it is nice to have an early copy. I am so happy at the reception the book is getting, and at Hemingway's justification of our claim for him to genius.

The Ernest Thompson Seton[2] came in this morning, and I am delighted to have it.

You will send me back my manuscript soon, won't you? With the new approach in mind, I want to coordinate my material before I begin writing. I think I shall never again work any way except as I did with "The Yearling"—— knowing precisely where I am headed.

1. Alan J. Villiers, *Sons of Sinbad* (New York: Scribners, 1940).
2. Ernest Thompson Seton (1860–1946), *Trail of an Artist-Naturalist* (New York: Scribners, 1940).

. . . .

520. MKR to MEP (ALS, 1 p.)

[Cross Creek]
November 25, 1940

Dear Max:

I am having a perfectly evil time with the book. I finally have the preface, or first chapter, or introduction or whatever it is, more or less to suit me, but am having the devil's own time getting the main chronicle going. Have torn up half a dozen beginnings. The main difficulty is the one I have known all along I should have, if I tried to make a narrative of it——to give anything like a consecutive effect, a story moving along smoothly that includes the high spots of the incidents, it is almost impossible to avoid more of a personal touch than I want. Also, so many of the incidents that are complete little stories in themselves, cannot be told chronologically, as often the end, or the thing that gives them point, does not come until after a lapse of some years' time. The time element is for that reason very difficult to handle. I am in a furious mood. A perfectly unprecedented freeze came in a week or so ago, and in spite of firing my young grove across the road, it is a brown, hopeless looking mess, and I loathe looking out at the damage. Not for any money reasons, but because something beautiful and satisfying is now hideous and depressing.

However, I shall keep at the damn book until I do figure out a way to get it, for it can be done. And if the grove gets me down, I can go over to the cottage and work, where the ocean at least doesn't freeze. I don't like to leave, for things get in an awful tangle when I'm away too long, the help all gets to fighting among themselves, and I have only now gotten them straightened out after my summer's absence.

Don't mind my sputtering. I have learned that I always feel this way when I'm working something out, but God it is torment. Send me everything to read that you can. I read about a book a night.

. . . .

521. MEP to MKR (TLS: UF, 2 pp.)

Nov. 28, 1940

Dear Marjorie:

I can easily imagine that the difficulties of shaping the material are great, but that is part of the inevitable process.- Of course you need not be strictly bound by fact.- In such a book you can move things around rightly so long as you give the poetic truth.- But you know all about that anyhow.

I did send you a couple of books that make pretty good reading, and tomorrow I'll send you one of good pictures—and good reading too for that matter—John Thomason's "Lone Star Preacher".[1] He cares so much about the Army of Northern Virginia and its leaders, that I think he has his best work in these drawings.

Hem has arrived here today and is soon to come in. It would be hard to imagine a greater success than "The Bell" has had.

If ever you feel like sending me any part of the book as you go along, I would be eager to read it.

Always yours,

1. John Thomason, *Lone Star Preacher* (New York: Scribners, 1941).

. . . .

522. MEP to MKR (TLS: UF, 2 pp.)

Dec. 3, 1940

Dear Marjorie:

Forgive me for having neglected to send you the enclosed royalty report. I think that in view of the strong prejudice in the trade, and I suppose in the public too, against short stories, the outcome is really very satisfactory. What's more, "The Whippoorwill" continues to sell.

I hope you like John Thomason's book. For years he has been working on a book called "Lee's Men"[1] and that will be his great work, both in drawing and writing, and this little book is a sort of by-product.

Mabel Wolfe[2] wrote me about visiting you, with great enthusiasm.

Charlie Sweeney,[3] the soldier of fortune, just came back from England where he had organized an American air force of some kind, and to my astonishment he was very hopeful. He is generally most discouraging, and in spite of greatly liking him I used to almost wish he would stay away during the French campaign, and even after it. But he says England will surely win the war,- though I suspect he thinks we shall have to be fighting along side of them.

I hope you may feel like sending me some piece of manuscript sometime soon.

Always yours,

1. Douglas S. Freeman, *Lee's Lieutenants*. See note 2, letter 616.
2. Mabel Wolfe Wheaton, Thomas Wolfe's sister.
3. Colonel Charles Sweeney (1882–1963), soldier and writer, later the author of *Moment of Truth* (New York: Scribners, 1943).

1941

523. MEP to MKR (TLS: UF, 4 pp.)

Jan. 4, 1941

Dear Marjorie:

Thanks ever so much for remembering us again. We'll all enjoy the oranges.

I know that you must have felt very badly to read of Scott's death,[1] and the very worst of it is that he was doing what I think was a book of great importance and interest, and he was on the home stretch with it.- But he did die instantly, and at a time when he was happier, and calmer, and much more hopeful than in many years. I am trying hard to think of some kind of publication that will do him honor.- He suffered by having become too wholly identified with the age he gave a name to. He wrote many stories that had no dependence upon the lost generation.- And by the way, the papers attribute that phrase to him, or give the impression that it was his. It wasn't, of course. It was Hem who promulgated it, but Gertrude Stein who first uttered it.[2] Scott's despair didn't come upon him until the depression began, and then it was more a matter of drinking and personal disaster.- But now Zelda seems to be in pretty good shape, and is living normally in her old home, Montgomery, Ala.[3] The first two pieces on the first page of the current New Yorker about Scott are good, and so was the editorial in the Times.[4]

Hem left here about two weeks ago, and he told me that you had written him a letter that gave him great pleasure.- So it could not have been inadequate, as you thought. Now shortly Martha is heading for the Burma Road and Hem will also sail for the East, and they will meet somewhere or other. While they were here everything was very exciting, as it always is when he is about. He lives too hard. Dawn Powell[5] said when she saw him and he told her Martha was going to the Burma Road, he reminded her of a *wife*.- She asked him if he was going too, and he said he guessed he would because even that was better than staying at home and worrying.

I think Charlie has some plan for going to Florida before long.- As for me, I am afraid to death I may have to go to California for one day, to qualify as an executor for Scott. But I may get out of it,- I can do just as much in his interests without being executor, and there is some confusion in the Will. I wish you had known Scott in the old days. I suppose you are still struggling with your material, but that is the way the good writers do. In a kind of melancholy way, it was nice to hear from Scott's friend, Sheila Grahame [*sic*],[6] to whom he was talking happily at the moment of his death, that on that very day he had done one of the hardest parts of the book, and got it right. That was something. His last feeling was that wonderful one of satisfaction.

We'll be having some interesting books before long, and I'll send them on. We are in a lull now, of course.

I hope all goes well.

Yours always,

1. Fitzgerald died in Hollywood, California, on December 21, 1940. At the time of his death, he was working on *The Last Tycoon* (New York: Scribners, 1941).
2. Gertrude Stein once remarked to Hemingway, "You are all a lost generation," which he later used in his preface to *The Sun Also Rises* (New York: Scribners, 1926).
3. Zelda Fitzgerald (1900–1947), writer, wife of F. Scott Fitzgerald.
4. *New York Times* 23 (December 1940): L19; *New Yorker* 16.47 (January 4, 1941): 9.
5. Dawn Powell (1897–1965), novelist.
6. Sheilah Graham, a Hollywood columnist, was Fitzgerald's companion for the last three and one-half years of his life.

. . . .

524. MKR to MEP (TLS, 2 pp.)

[Cross Creek]
[January 1941]

Dear Max:

Had this sheet in the typewriter ready for making the ninth or tenth beginning of "Cross Creek". I still don't know why I can't find the right approach, but it will surely hit at any minute. I have torn up pages and pages. There is some key to coordination that I have not yet stumbled on, but it will come, and when it does, I know the work will go fast, because it is all piled up, dammed, ready and waiting to pour out. I shall be so happy when I really get going. The introduction, or preface, is still approximately right. The "light" approach proved very wrong. Or did I speak of that in a letter I began to you, and mislaid and never sent. I was writing you about some of the books you had sent. Please send me anything you can.

The news about Scott made me very sad, though his life was more tragic than his death. The tragedy came, I think, from having a spectacular success too early, and on top of that, valuing the wrong things in living. It is difficult enough to be happy when one takes satisfaction from the simple and infallible things, but it is an R.S.V.P. invitation to disaster to <to> depend on the quicksands of the treacherous things that to him represented the "gloria mundi". But as you say, it was not fair to attribute to him personally all the shallowness and stupidity of the people he wrote about. The very fact that he could write about them with that bitter irony, put him beyond them. But people in general are totally unable to detach the person of a writer from the products of his thinking.

The holiday season has been a round of more or less asinine parties that I felt obliged to go to, because of many visiting friends. I'm hoping things will be quieter now, and I am getting more ruthless about dodging people. And my perfectly grand well-educated new colored maid[1] makes everything domestic very pleasant and easy for me, so that when I do have company I enjoy it too.

My good colored man[2] came mournfully yesterday morning to give notice. It seemed he had sat down, quite unlike the average darky and <and> checked over his year's progress and decided there just wasn't any. When he got sympathy over such a sad but common state of affairs, he cheered up at once and poured out his year's sorrows, which consisted mostly of discouragement over having all his wages go to pay his fat lazy wife's doctor bills. The last doctor told her she needed more exercise and less laxatives, so under the unexpected, I presume, stimulus of my understanding, he decided to plant a cash crop for himself in one of my vacant fields and make his wife work in it. We agreed that this stood a good chance of bettering both their conditions, and he has been so happy today over the new hope that he has almost run me out of the house by piling joyous and unnecessary wood on all my hearth fires.

I continue to get a flood of literature asking for money and cooperation for everything connected with the world's mess——China's Children, Exiled Writers, Committee for Aiding the Allies, Committee for Keeping Us Out of the War, Hoover's Committee to Feed Europe, somebody else's committee to block such feeding. I send checks to a few and just tear up the rest of the stuff. If a creative worker needed any lesson in minding his own business, he would find it in Edna Millay's new book of so-called poetry, "Make Bright the Arrows."[3] Of all the tripe——. If an artist wants to do something practical like giving money or doing nursing, well and good, but he serves no purpose by so abandoning his art.

1. Idella Parker. See Idella Parker, *Idella: Marjorie Rawlings' "Perfect Maid"* (Gainesville: University Press of Florida, 1992), for a full account of the relationship.
2. "Little Will" Mickens.
3. Edna St. Vincent Millay (1892–1950), *Make Bright the Arrows* (New York: Harper, 1940).

. . . .

525. MKR to MEP (TLS, I p.)

[Cross Creek]
Jan. 17, 1941

Dear Max:

Know you will be glad to know that I have finally hit my approach and set, I think, the proper keynote. It is still a constant battle to keep on key, and this morning I find that yesterday's work was off. Yet the general trend is going right. And I am determined, since I know so exactly the final effect that I want, to work slowly and correctly as I go, so that I hope the question of revision will not have to enter too much in. It is the way I worked on "The Yearling", and while it is infinitely harder at the moment, I believe it is the best way in the end.

I want quite a bit done before I send you anything.

. . . .

526. MEP to MKR (TLS: UF, I p.)

Jan. 21, 1941

Dear Marjorie:

That is first rate. Of course I knew you would strike the note in the end, but I know it is a great struggle to find it. I guess now everything will go well, and all the quality of the material will be the better for the great effort.

Yours,

. . . .

527. MEP to MKR (TLS: UF, 2 pp.)

Feb. 11, 1941

Dear Marjorie:

I feel as if I had somehow by pressure of events got entirely cut off from you. Is the book going on well? I think it must be if you have got started right, and you would know for sure if you had.

I am sending you two books about England[1] which may make rather melancholy reading, but the point isn't to read them, but to look at the pictures. I know you will like to do that.

Is it your idea that when "Cross Creek" is ready, Shenton should do decorations for the chapter heads? I would think that he should.

Mabel Wolfe has been here for quite a long time. One of my daughters asked her for tea when her husband, and her sister and her sister's husband would be there, and others. And I stayed in for the afternoon since it was Saturday, because of some apprehensions about her.- You know her weakness. She never did turn up that day. The next Saturday my daughter asked her again, when only her sister was there. Mrs. Wolfe came along too, and Mabel said—I thought most pathetically, to her mother—"How is it that these two frail girls have children when a great big strong woman like me can't?" I think that if Mabel only had, she would not have been overcome by John Barleycorn. It's too bad.

Always yours,

1. J. M. Barrie (1860–1937), *Peter Pan and Wendy* (New York: Scribners, 1941), and Denis G. Mackail, *Barrie: The Story of J. M. B.* (New York: Scribners, 1941).

. . . .

528. MKR to MEP (TLS, 2 pp.)

Hawthorn, Florida
March 3, 1941

Dear Max:

No, my silence comes not from progress, but from being stopped again. I had quite a good deal done, when it seemed to me that it was still coming in too episodic a form. I began all over once more and the type of re-creation or re-visualization of the life and people and happenings, went so slowly because of the great concentration necessary——and I still could not tell whether it would work out that way——that I went into a temporary paralysis and thought it best to leave it alone a while. I am going back to both manuscripts in a day or two and hope that I will know, on re-reading, what is right.

It is difficult to explain the problem, but it is one principally of *time*. If I tell a direct, almost, in a way, day to day narrative, so many of the details of the stories of the people have no interest and no meaning. That is, it may have taken many of the years I have been here for enough details, with point to them, to accumulate about any one person or family. Their stories are sometimes only valid as completed stories. Doing it this way, as I was, it was necessary to write as of the moment, looking back to something completed. As I said, this seemed to me to make a choppy narrative. It also damaged that flowing sense of following a scene or a person, so that the reality is *immediate*. This is very important. It is not enough for good anecdotes to be told, either humorous or moving. The sense of knowing a particular place and people with a deep, almost Proustian deepness and intimacy and revelation, with my own feeling about things back of it, is what I want. Also, the way I was going, it went too glibly. It was easy to fall into a superficial narrative style that was almost journalistic. To do it as I have begun the last time, is more like doing hard creative fiction. I can call less on facts and true details, and must project myself painfully and slowly into years and scenes and feelings that I have actually forgotten, and must re-create. I would say that I cannot do it, except that I know by working hard enough, it is possible. And there is always that problem of making something of trifles that are not in themselves interesting, but must lay the ground for the point of incidents, to be resolved and completed long later.

Does this help make you see the peculiar difficulty? We cannot talk of illustrations or any publishing matters. The book can only be done right, no matter how long it takes. If it is right, it will be good and if it is not right it will not be worth publishing.

. . . .

529. MEP to MKR (TLS: UF, 2 pp.)

March 3, 1941

Dear Marjorie:

I am sending you at the same time, the February 1st royalty report, and the check in accordance with the first report on "The Whippoorwill". I hope the weather hasn't been too bad for you. I have been told it has been a cold winter in Florida.- But maybe one doesn't mind that who lives there all the time and is prepared for it,- though the oranges must mind it.

I am having a mighty good time now, both on my own account and on that of my grandson, aged six. I am actually reading him "The Yearling" and am seeing things in it that show how well contrived it was which I hadn't noticed or had forgotten.- But the real fun is to see the pleasure the boy takes in it. He asks innumerable questions. I simplify the language a little, but really not very much, and sometimes I skip a little bit. I told him that his hair and his eyes were like Jody's and that when he got out into the sun he would get freckled too. He is skeptical about the freckles, but somewhat hopeful.

Always yours,

530. MKR to MEP (ALS, 2 pp.)

[Cross Creek]
March 13, 1941

Dear Max:—

I have just finished reading over the "Cross Creek" manuscript on which I had done a good deal. I do not believe I was as far off as I thought. I went astray mostly in the last chapter I had done — in fact the writing itself is not too bad, but I think I plunged into the incidents too abruptly.

I am going back now and take up where I left off and continue more or less in the same vein. Then when I have a few more—chapters done, I'll send it all on to you and you can give me your opinion.

I feel much encouraged, and think my job is just not to let a careless narrative style run away with me.

. . . .

531. MEP to MKR (TLS: UF, 1 p.)

March 14, 1941

Dear Marjorie:

I was delighted with your penciled letter that just came this moment. I had been on the point of writing you. I know that the struggle is inevitable, of course, and I also realize that this is almost as creative a thing as fiction. But I really was certain that you would master it. It is a creative job because of the person who is doing it. Some of these writers, and some of them who are very successful, would make nothing much of it but entertainment. Thanks for the good news which is not plentiful these days.

Yours,

. . . .

532. MEP to MKR (TLS: Tarr Rawlings Collection, 3 pp.)

April 11, 1941

Dear Marjorie:

I hope when you opened this letter you didn't think to yourself, here comes that fellow again to urge me on with the book. It isn't for that purpose I am writing, and I realize that the book must develop naturally, and I don't mean to disturb you over it. This is about the educational edition of "The Yearling".[1] I have just been looking over a lot of tests on "The Yearling" from various schools, and by the representatives of various races and conditions in life. They are very interesting, though the tests seem in themselves to be rather foolish. They show though, that there is likely to be very great interest in the educational edition, and Mr. Lord[2] here is anxious to get on to publication. But a very important element in this edition should be a preface by you. It needn't be long, two and a half or three pages, say, unless you were inclined to do more. And I should think that it might simply be some account of how the idea of this book was formed in your mind from the life of the natives of that region of Florida. It might tell how actual people that you had known, for instance, suggested some of the characters. Any little narrative of the way the book came into being, would greatly interest the high school children and might add to their understanding of the story.

I think Charlie wrote you about this some time ago in a general way, and once discussed with you the question of terms:- the highest royalty possible on an educational book we would, of course, give, but it sounds low,- 10% on the price at which the books are sold, which involves invariably a 25% discount. But there are possibilities in the educational field of very large sales, and very long continued ones. I am sorry to interrupt you in the work you are engaged in with this matter, but in truth nothing could be of more advantage to "The Yearling" in furtherance of its influence and its sale than this educational publication of it. Could you do the preface soon?

Always yours,

1. The School Edition, published October 1, 1941. This edition contains a preface by MKR on the writing of *The Yearling*.
2. Edward Thomas Lord, head of the Educational Department at Scribner.

. . . .

533. MKR to MEP (TLS, 1 p.)

[Cross Creek]
May 6, 1941

Dear Max:

I did a Preface for the educational edition of The Yearling, but don't like it. I will try again in a day or two and send something on for your criticism.

I am going ahead steadily on "Cross Creek." It does not please me, for the most part, but I couldn't stand the frustration so have gone on and let it have its head. Most of it is more informal than I thought I wanted, but so much of the material is light or humorous that there may be no alternative. It means almost certainly a complete job of re-writing, but at least when the first draft is done, we shall know better what we have to work with. There is no question, barring something unforeseen, but that I shall have the first writing done before the summer is over. But I don't want to make any plans at all until you have seen all of what we shall just call the material.

About the educational edition. Since you and Charlie say that only a ten percent royalty is possible, all right, but I think there should be an agreement that if sales pass a certain point, I should have a higher royalty. If the book should become something of a text or standard required reading, you would be past the initial high expense of selling and so on. This might not come about at all, or perhaps only in the far future, but I think provision should be made for the possibility.

The movie people are hard at work here. I have met "Jody" and he is really charming. A little too delicate for my conception, but otherwise very acceptable. "Ma Baxter" is tall and thin, where I imagined a big heavy woman, but otherwise seems a good type.[1] I haven't watched them working on the set yet. I don't want to distract myself just now from my work by getting involved or even interested.

I am feeling marvelously, physically.

1. This film version of *The Yearling* was abandoned after the shooting of only a few scenes because of the hot and rainy weather, which led to cost overruns and unhappy actors. Spencer Tracy was to star as Pa, Anne Revere as Ma, and Gene Eckman as Jody.

. . . .

534. MEP to MKR (TLS: UF, 3 pp.)

May 20, 1941

Dear Marjorie:

I suppose the little introduction will come along soon.- And when you get the manuscript of "Cross Creek" done in the way you are doing it, I should be most delighted to read it and to try to help. I rather think it will turn out to be in much better shape than it seems to you as if it would. It is generally the books that worry good authors that do turn out to be the best ones.

As for the preface to the school edition, don't make too hard a job of it. It is the quality of it that counts for the most, and that just naturally gets into it if you do it. It ought to be somewhat personal. The educational people are anxious to see it, but we still have a good margin of time. The royalty question seems to be one that can hardly be disputed. There simply isn't margin enough to pay more than what we propose, nor is it ever done. In fact you are the gainer on account of our having a school book department. If we didn't have, there either could be no such edition, or else it would be done by another publisher, like a reprint, which in a way it is, and you would receive then a much lower royalty. A reprint at a low figure never brings more than 10¢ through the regular reprint houses, and that amount is divided between publisher and author invariably. I have talked again to Mr. Lord, but there seems to be no avoiding of it. We could easily show you why in figures.

Charlie has been having a very bad time because of a sort of neuritis from his shoulder up his neck. It has been very painful. He has stayed home for about ten days, and is getting better. Rest is supposed to be the right cure, but how a man can rest even with a little pain, is more than I can see.

Always yours,

. . . .

535. MEP to MKR (TLS: UF, 2 pp.)

May 29, 1941

Dear Marjorie:

I am enclosing herewith our check for the royalties now due in accordance with the last report.

Is everything right with you? We are having our first bad spell of heat. Hem is back from China, and in town, to be joined today by Martha Gellhorn.- Then he is heading for Key West and the Gulf Stream. Charlie is supposed to be improving, but he certainly does look pulled down and tired, and very thin. He would be mighty pleased if you wrote him a letter.

Always yours,

P.S. It is very pleasant indeed to go out of this building and see a window filled with "The Yearling" again. It is so principally because of a "coming attractions" announcement in the movies of the picture.- They even came up here and had me at my desk pretending to read "The Yearling" manuscript, and they took a picture of the library—for what reason I don't know—and one of the window on Fifth Avenue from across the street.

. . . .

536. MEP to MKR (TS for wire)

JUNE 6, 1941
MRS. MARJORIE RAWLINGS
ISLAND GROVE, FLORIDA
HOPE IT WILL BE POSSIBLE TO SEND PREFACE SOON. TIME GETTING
DANGEROUSLY SHORT. SORRY TO BOTHER.

537. MEP to MKR (CC, 1 p.)

June 13, 1941

Dear Marjorie:

   This is just to tell you that we are all of us very much pleased with the preface. Many thanks, and good luck.

Yours,

. . . .

538. MKR to MEP (TLS, 1 p.)

Hawthorn, Florida
June 23, 1941

Dear Max:

   May I have 3 When the Whippoorwills, 1 Yearling $1.29 edition, 1 Yearling Wyeth $2.50.

   And do send me anything to read, fiction or anything. The Nostradamus[1] was fascinating.

   "Cross Creek" goes steadily, though much of it is bad, but the thing to do is to get it down on paper. Barring accidents, I should have the first draft ready by the end of August, and then I think I'd like to bring the manuscript to you and discuss it with you, and take a week or two's vacation before I go at the editing and re-writing.

   I am at the Creek just for a couple of days and my address the rest of the summer will be Crescent Beach. RFD St. Augustine. Fla.

1. Stewart Robb, *Nostradamus on Napoleon, Hitler, and the Present Crisis* (New York: Scribners, 1941).

. . . .

539. MEP to MKR (TLS: UF, 1 p.)

June 30, 1941

Dear Marjorie:

   I think "Cross Creek" will be a very fine book indeed, and it will certainly be wonderful to see you in late August, so do bar accidents and come.

   I sent you a few books, and now we'll be getting more out and I'll try to keep you supplied. It is frightfully hot here.

Always yours,

July 6, 1941

Dear Marjorie:

I hope you are quite well now.- Whatever the trouble was that caused you to go to the hospital.— Darrow told me he had heard from you that you were just out of one and that everything seemed to be right. But there is one trouble here: the educational department is perfectly desperate to get that map that Miss DeVey[1] [*sic*] sent you in the hope that you would mark on it the area in which the story of the Yearling was set and list the names of various places that ought to be indicated. I have to urge you to send this. We don't need much to go by. The indications could be made roughly. We could work it up.

Yours always,

1. Elizabeth DeVoy, an assistant in the Art Department at Scribner.

. . . .

541. MKR to MEP (TLS, 3 pp.)

Hawthorn, Florida

July 8, 1941

Dear Max:

Thanks so much for the books. The Barrie was most revealing and interesting for a third or a half of the way, then it seemed to me to bog down completely under colds and duchesses. I can't conceive of the declining years of Shakespeare warranting that trivial personal detail. Mackail was too close to his subject, too impressed with the latter-year devotion of Lady Cynthia, too full of self-consciousness at being called on to do a definitive biography of one whose contemporary "greatness" had filled him with satisfaction in being close to it. I found his broken sentences annoying, and an occasional prissy quaintsy-waintsy style as well. But the first part was good reading, and the book had the merit, in my need, of being long.

The Nature and Destiny of Man[1] looks fascinating and provocative, and the mystery books will help to fill my non-working time.

I had to take a week out to be ill in the hospital, but the work has gone as usual this week and last, though part of it is done in bed. A certain nervous tension inevitably builds up under concentrated mental work, and this happens to have a fatal effect on my mixed-up and inadequate insides. I expect to have to go to bed at the end of a book, but I begrudge the time in the middle of it. By being careful, I think I can finish the first draft without any serious physical effects.

The Mackail book's fault brought again the horror of offering detail fascinating to oneself, but stupid to the reader. Yet a great amount of minute detail helps to give the reader an atmosphere, and properly done, works an enchantment on him. The trick is in drawing the line.

I want to use just a little of the "Cracker Chidlings" and find I have no copy at all. I seem to remember sending the pages from my one magazine copy when we thought we should use them in the book of stories. Can you lend me a copy for a short time?

Also, I have misplaced a letter from a Miss Elizabeth something in the educational department, saying she was sending a map and wanting me to mark locations in The Yearling.[2] My mail has been forwarded back and forth and the map has not reached me. I got out a Florida road map but it is one too small a scale to make it possible to mark the scrub area. Will you ask her to send another? The request irks me for two reasons: I begrudge time to anything but "Cross Creek"; and it has been so long since I wrote the Yearling that I don't remember a lot of the topography as I imagined it. The book was not documentary in fact or as to terrain, and I have dismissed all that part from my mind.

1. Reinhold Niebuhr (1892–1971), *The Nature and Destiny of Man* (New York: Scribners, 1941).
2. The map, once part of the Margaret A. Levings Rawlings Collection, is now at the University of Florida. Before Levings purchased the map, it hung on the wall of the Yearling restaurant at Cross Creek.

. . . .

542. MKR to MEP (ALS, 1 p.)

> Crescent Beach RFD
> St. Augustine, Florida
> Monday
> [July 14, 1941]

Dear Max:

The map that finally reached me was the very kind I had, and rejected because of the small scale. On this I can't do more than indicate the general area. I thought that an indication of the hunts and so forth was wanted, but evidently just a general idea is all.

I am sorry to be such a nuisance about details, but I have left behind, at the Creek, the proofs on the Preface. I had read them over and saw no errors, so perhaps you can get along without them. If you must have them, I can telephone a friend to go and get them.

I expect to be here at the cottage now until the first draft of the book is finished.

[Postscript] I enjoyed the Leslie Ford[1] mystery book *immensely.* It is delightful reading.

Editor's note: At top of letter, return address in MKR's hand on her Hawthorn stationery, with "Hawthorn" marked out.

1. Leslie Ford (1898–1983), *The Murder of a Fifth Columnist* (New York: Collier, 1941).

. . . .

543. MEP to MKR (CC, 1 p.)

July 18, 1941

Dear Marjorie:

This is to tell you that the map you sent back with the indications of areas is just what we wanted, and we are proceeding with it successfully.

Pretty soon I am going to send you some more Nostradamus, and then a book of prophecies.

I think the preface is very very fine, and so does Lord.

Yours,

. . . .

544. MKR to MEP (TLS, 1 p.)

[Crescent Beach]
July 23, 1941

Dear Max:

Just a line to say that the end of the first draft is coming within sight. I have only four more chapters to do. The "mileage" as far as I have gone is about 117,000 words, and the total will run about 134,000. That gives us plenty of room for cutting, if some of the material, as I think, is irrelevant and uninteresting. I shall do some editing here, but shall not make any great effort at it, as I want your feeling first. I want to do the copying myself, as I always make a great many changes while I am doing it. Barring accidents, I shall be ready for you to see it before the end of August. If you will be there at that time, I think I'll send the manuscript on to you, then drive up to talk about it.

I promised Carl Brandt a copy when I sent you yours, but I am going to cheat a little and wait until you have seen it first, at least. I am so afraid of his doing as happened with "Golden Apples" and pouncing on something that I'm not through working with. I should much prefer just to have it come out in book form only——provided it is worth publishing at all! It is very simple and homely, of course, and if I haven't managed to get any charm in those qualities, there just won't be any!

I haven't read it over lately so can't even give my own opinion at this time. But I thought you would be encouraged to know that we shall soon have something to work with.

· ·

545. MEP to MKR (CC, I p.)

August 1, 1941

Dear Marjorie:

I was delighted to hear by your letter of the 23rd that you would probably send the manuscript before the end of August, and you know how eagerly I'll read it. I think you are wiser in not letting Brandt get it until you have it exactly as you want it, without any consideration of the serialization.- But I would be much surprised if some considerable part of it were not serializable. I knew it would all come out well in the end.

Yours,

· ·

546. MKR to MEP (TLS, I p.)

Crescent Beach
RFD St. Augustine, Florida
[August 1941]

Dear Max:

I shall go at my last chapter, a short one, in the morning. I have a few items to add to the manuscript, and this actual writing will take me the rest of the week. Then I shall go at the copying. It runs now about 140,000 words. I can't tell for the life of me whether others will find it readable. There are several questions I shall want to raise, but we will go into that when I send you the manuscript.

You did not answer me when I asked if you had a copy of Cracker Chidlings in any form. I don't need much from it, but there are a couple of the sketches I want to incorporate, and as I wrote you, I have no copy at all. If you have an office copy, I can return it very shortly.

I have suffered so in doing this job, yet now that the material is in form, I almost wish I were beginning again. There is that dreadful feeling that a better job could have been done. But I shall try not to fret too much until you have seen it as it stands now.

. . . .

547. MEP to MKR (CC, I p.)

August 7, 1941

Dear Marjorie:

I'll send you tomorrow a photostat of "Cracker Chidlings" taken from the bound copy of the magazine. I had hoped to find a copy, but none is available.- But if at any time you should want other copies, we can have them made in the same way.

I think you have really done splendidly in pushing on with the book in the last month, and the manuscript will be most welcome here.

Yours,

. . . .

548. MEP to MKR (CC, I p.)

Aug. 8, 1941

Dear Marjorie:

Herewith is the photostat of "Cracker Chidlings". I thought you wouldn't mind it being white on black since it saved a little time to send you the negative;- and herewith also is your royalty report for sales in the last six months. All of the books are having good continued sales in one way or another,- but I shall never get over my disappointment about "South Moon Under" and the bank holiday.

Yours,

. . . .

549. MEP to MKR (TLS: UF, I p.)

August 19, 1941

Dear Marjorie:

The School Edition is completed and I am sending six copies. We tried to make the drawings of you, but we could not get anywhere near to your expression in them and so we did what was better still, and used a halftone.

This edition will still more firmly establish "The Yearling" as an American classic, and there are mighty few of them.

Always yours,

550. MKR to MEP (TLS, I p.)

Crescent Beach RFD
St. Augustine, Florida
August 25, 1941

Dear Max:

I am well into my copying and should have the first draft ready for you in a week or ten days at the most. Would have been through by this time, but went under again and was very ill for nearly two weeks. It is just a matter now of staying with the typewriter.

I notice on my royalty report an item of $12.50 to Ralph Graves for newspaper serialization of South Moon Under. Surely this is an error. Why on earth would serial rights be sold for this amount, even if the advertising was considered valuable? A newspaper syndicate recently offered me sixty dollars for newspaper rights on one of my very short New Yorker stories.

May I trouble you to pass on to the book store my order for two copies of Golden Apples, regular edition. Thanks.

Editor's note: At the bottom of the letter in MEP's hand: "8/27/41 / *Send.*"

. . . .

551. MEP to MKR (CC, 2 pp.)

Sept. 11, 1941

Dear Marjorie:

I sent you a couple of books the other day, but the general confusion of the times has upset authors a great deal, and we are rather late in getting into the full autumn swing. In a little while I'll have some good ones for you to read.

As to that item for syndication the price paid was $25.00. We receive only half of it on the regular syndicate basis. It does seem insignificant, I know, but so even do the top prices for syndication. But this sale was made for a paper in the little city of Watertown which is a manufacturing city with few book readers in it, and no real bookstore at all. Whatever value syndication has in a publicity sense—and that is really why publishers indulge in it—is especially applicable to such a case as that. It does familiarize people who can't be reached in the usual ways with your writing and your name. That is the only point in it.

Always yours,

[Crescent Beach]
Saturday
[Sept. 13, 1941]

Dear Max:

Will write you tomorrow about the manuscript, along with the various questions in my own mind about it.

Think it will be best in any case for you to read it unprejudiced by my own ideas.

Editor's note: This letter was included with the manuscript sent to Perkins.

. . . .

553. MEP to MKR (CC, 1 p.)

Sept. 15, 1941

Dear Marjorie:

The manuscript has come, and I'll take it home with me.

Always yours,

. . . .

554. MKR to MEP (TLS, with holograph header, 3 pp.)

[Crescent Beach]
Sept. 15, 1941

Dear Max:

I expressed you the first draft of "Cross Creek" on Saturday, and it should reach you today. I consider it only a draft, and I did hate to send it when I am so dissatisfied with many aspects of it. But it was making me so nervous not to have it in your hands, and I knew you must be anxious, too, that it seemed better to send it on without making any further effort at the moment to get it right. If you have not already finished reading it, I feel it will be better for you to do so *before* you read the following questionings.

The first and perhaps the most important question is whether there is even approximately sufficient fluidity of narrative. Now that you have the material in hand, I think you will understand why it seemed to me *impossible* to provide *straight narrative*. There was no one hook on which to hang anything approximating a *story*. There was not even the movement of a travel or adventure story, such as in Peter Freuchen's Arctic adventure,[1] or even my Hyacinth Drift.

I did not want to tell a story of myself, particularly. I did not want anything like an autobiography of these past thirteen years. I wanted the thing objective, the only subjectivity consisting of my personal reaction to the Creek, its natural aspects and its people. I came as close as possible to a thread, in more or less dealing with the growth of my knowledge of place and people. If I had tried to use Martha as more of a hook, for instance, I could not use much of the subjective material that seemed to me important. Also, to use her that way would be spurious, for I have exaggerated her importance as it is, just to keep a thread moving through the whole thing.

Now perhaps you may see a way in which I can make a stronger thread of the growth of my knowledge. I myself can not see one.

It seems to me that much of it carries along fairly well as something of a consecutive chain of events. Up to the chapter that I called "Residue," it does not seem to me too spotty. I have the feeling that that chapter, in spite of its uniting theme, is terribly episodic and jerky. The individual character studies are not woven into anything at all. I am hoping that you can see where they could be worked in more smoothly. I think on further consideration I might be able to use some of those people in that chapter in a less thrown-at-your-head manner.

Now for questions.

Is Martha sufficiently interwoven into the episodes, after my initial claim for her of something of a dusky Fate?

I wanted to avoid all reference to the family life that preceded my years alone at the Creek, yet I was not there alone at the beginning, and it seemed to me I needed some indication of the other life, so mentioned briefly the three brothers "for whom the pattern proved within a year not the right one", this in the chapter "The magnolia tree." Does this seem valid to you, and not offensive to the "three brothers?"

Now I have used true names in practically every instance. I have tried not to put things so that anyone's feelings would be hurt. These people are my friends and neighbors, and I would not be unkind for anything, and though they are simple folk, there is the possible libel danger to think of. What do you think of this aspect of the material?

Do you consider it bad taste for me to have mentioned my books and stories by name as I have done? In so many cases they were a part of something I was telling and I did not see how to avoid it. Yet it is very necessary not to seem to be blowing one's own horn, as it were. I also raise this question of good taste about my mention of kindnesses I have done for people at the Creek. There is a danger there of setting a reader's teeth on edge.

There is of course the very serious question of when details are interesting to others and when they are not. You will have to judge that.

Do you think it is desirable or otherwise to use chapter headings? In some cases the heading clarifies the material, but on the whole it may be that it would accentuate any possible jerkiness or episodic quality.

I find that there is a sharp variance of style between the serious nature or philosophic portions and the humorous incidents. I think I have too flippant or facetious a style in dealing with the humorous things. I can take care of that myself to an extent, but I wish you would check on the manuscript the places where the style is offensive.

There are places where I get too "preachy"—please indicate the places where you feel this, too.

I think the actual ending is nauseating. After giving a picture of struggle and strife, suddenly to go into the cosmic love angle is revolting. That passage just happens to be a favorite of mine, and I wound up with it, but I think it is out of keeping. I think things could end with the "there are only people" idea, phrased better.

As a minor detail, in the "Winter" chapter, I think the death of the mule should precede the Old Boss episode. It is absurd to grieve over Old Boss' dying wife and then follow with a dying mule.

There is really no reason for me to talk with you personally in New York about the material, for we do just as well by letter, but I need a change and plan to come up anyway, perhaps the end of this week or the beginning of next. I want to go to [the] Medical Center or somewhere for a physical check, for I have had more trouble than is reasonable with my insides. I will probably be here at the beach until Thursday, then at Hawthorn from Thursday to Saturday. Please give me a wire on your general feeling about the possibilities of the book.

Editor's note: Written at the top of the page: "*Through Thursday wire Western Union* [underlined twice] / Phone Crescent Beach 4, / St. Augustine. / After Thursday, <Hawthorn> Island Grove."

1. Peter Freuchen (1886–1957), *Arctic Adventure* (New York: Farrar and Rinehart, 1935).

555. MEP to MKR (TS for wire)

SEPT. 16, 1941
MRS. MARJORIE K. RAWLINGS
WESTERN UNION
PHONE CRESCENT BEACH 4
ST. AUGUSTINE, FLORIDA
HAVE READ ONLY FIRST PARAGRAPH OF LETTER. MUST HAVE WEEK-
END TO GIVE FULL AND QUIET READING TO MANUSCRIPT BUT AM
GREATLY ENJOYING IT. WILL WRITE YOU MONDAY.

. . . .

556. MEP to MKR (TS for wire)

SEPT. 22, 1941
MRS. MARJORIE K. RAWLINGS
ISLAND GROVE
FLORIDA
THINK CROSS CREEK WILL MAKE VERY FINE AND UNUSUAL BOOK. RE-
VISION NOT DIFFICULT BUT NEEDS SOME DAYS STUDY. WILL WRITE
FULLY.

Editor's note: Copy of telegram in MEP's hand included.

. . . .

557. MKR to MEP (TLS, 2 pp.)

Hawthorn, Florida
Tuesday
[Sept. 23, 1941]

Dear Max:

What a wonderful relief to have your wire and find you think the book is possible, with revision not too difficult. I shall be eager for your suggestions. Another reason why I could not weave some of the individual stories, such as the one about paying for the pig, and about Mr. Marsh Turner, into the thread of the narrative, such as it is, was because the one isolated story was all there was to tell about some of the people. And in some cases, it took the complete length of my time here for some of the incidents to be rounded out. At no one time was there anything interesting enough to be told from day to day, and it seemed confusing to introduce unimportant people without meaning, except as the completed tale about them had meaning.

In looking at the chapter "Residue" again, I think it holds up fairly well as a study of characters, except for the shiner's wife, the preacher's daughter, and Grampa Hicks. Unless these three studies can be woven inconspicuously in, somewhere else, I think it will be better to drop them altogether. The story of the village of defeat, we can drop altogether, too, if you think best. Perhaps it could be worked in better, if you like it at all, in one of the earlier chapters dealing with the country as a whole.

I think there is far and away too much literary theorizing before I tell about "Antses in Tim's breakfast." A small part of the relevant points will do.

You may find other places where too much irrelevant theorizing is distracting.

The worst trouble with the last chapter, "Who owns Cross Creek", aside from dragging in the Biblical love quotation, is in arrangement of material. I should say what I want to, in summing up, about the people at the Creek, then end up with the ownership question, and leave that as the final point.

No one knows better than I that it is a *queer* book. If we can get it right, I would hope that its effect on readers would be to take them into a totally strange world, and that they should feel a certain delight and enchantment in the strangeness. And of course the use together of straight humor and serious ideas is risky business.

Thanks a thousand times for wiring.

. . . .

558. MEP to MKR (TLS: UF, 4 pp.)

September 29, 1941

Dear Marjorie:

"Cross Creek" may be queer, but it is lovely, and it is human. I went through it again over the weekend. After my first reading I had tried to think of some rearrangement or revision which would make it more on *conventional* lines—we are all too prone to be guided by precedents—but on my second, I was delighted that circumstances had made you depart from the regular consecutive narrative. I think it is a very rare book, and that while you will, of course, improve it in a revision, you have nothing to feel anxiety about. It is a great pleasure to read such a book in such times. The whole quality of it, the implied philosophy, makes one feel better. It is a book that will stand all by itself, as the finest books do.

Just to clear everything up in so far as possible, I will answer your questions first:- Martha is grand. She serves the purpose, but if she could be emphasized here and there, it would be as well.- But of course what really binds the book together is the author. It is with the author that one becomes identified. At any rate, the book is sufficiently bound together and will be more so, I think, if some of the introductory paragraphs to chapters which generalize and philosophize and are perhaps a little sententious, are omitted. These are somewhat essay-like and tend rather to separate than connect.

"The Magnolia Tree" is excellent and serves its purpose. It gives part of the necessary background that grows throughout the book.

As to the question of libel, I doubt if there is any real danger because of the character of the people. When you speak of the trial, you speak of the lawyer in a way that might hold him up to contempt and ridicule, but that can be amended. I don't think any of the people of the book would bring a suit, but you are the one who must be the judge. If they did, it would not be done because of any injury, but out of meanness,- which is not indicated to be in them.

I do think at the beginning of some of the chapters you have been a little "preachy", a little sententious. But you have never been in the least egoistic, and the references to your writings could offend nobody at all.

I do agree that the mule story should precede Old Boss's tragedy.

Now here are a few scattered comments:

It did occur to me that the Magnolia Tree might be moved somewhat deeper into the book, but perhaps it is necessary to get what it does done at the start. I only thought if you could get to the Pound Party sooner, you would sooner get into a narrative part. Zelma and the census-taking is grand. I did have my doubts about the outhouse.- Thousands of people who love your writings might not like it, just because of what it is.

When you come to chapter 7, I should omit all, or most of the first three pages. I think here that you do go into the writing matter too much, and that it is an interruption of the book in a way. I think if you begin that chapter on page 68, with, "I have used factual background, etc." it would be better. But it is most interesting to see where the idea of Allie came from.- But chapters 7, 8, 9, 10, and 11 are all about the help, excepting that you do enliven them with other characters. I was wondering if possibly there could be some arrangement that would vary this group, or some reduction in its extent. I think Black Shadows is too long and rambling, for instance. Perhaps "A Pig Is Paid For" could be put within this group and so vary it.- And by the way, speaking of the help, although he is very amusing, I think Kellogg in chapter 18 might be omitted.- He does not fit into Spring at the Creek very well anyhow.- But it is rather that there has been too much about the servants.

I completely agree with you about the chapter "Residue".- I think the shiner's wife, and the preacher's daughter could go anyhow. The book is 160,000 words, which is perhaps somewhat too long.- And I would also sacrifice the story of "The Village of Defeat".

In chapter 13 I think there is a little too much of the essay material, and that the first several sentences should be omitted so that it would begin "Sometimes there are friendships".- I have also marked for omission two paragraphs on page 147 which delay the narrative more than need be, and a passage on 148. And I do not think that you need tell nearly as much in connection with Moe about "Golden Apples" and the trip to England, but only about the trip to New York.

To return to chapter 14, which is "Residue" it begins with some reflections which I think are not necessary, and hold you up. They take you out of Cross Creek. You ought always to stay in it,- excepting that whole thing has many implications for outside, of course.

Chapter 15, "Toady-Frogs, Etc." I think here you should cut your introductory paragraph and begin it with, "I do not profess to know all that is known about frogs, etc."- This gets you right into the chapter and keeps you at Cross Creek.

Then you come to "Our Daily Bread". I think you should omit that first paragraph, and start with "Cookery is my vanity." But I would by no means seriously cut that chapter further. It is delightful reading, almost better than eating.

Chapter 18 is Spring. I think that should begin at the bottom of the second page, "Here in Florida the seasons move in." I would leave out the general reflections before that. And as I have said, I would be inclined to let Kellogg go.

Summer seems to me to require some cutting in detail if possible.

When you come to the lovely "Hyacinth Drift" I would be inclined to begin it, "Once I lost touch with the Creek." I think that everything you should keep that is in the first two paragraphs, is conveyed. I would not think of referring to Hitler and his "Mein Kampf" in this book.

As for the ending, I think it should be "The disagreements are important, and the union vital." Or else perhaps the sentence before that, "We know above all that work must be beloved."- Otherwise there may be a certain amount of shortening and the last paragraph of the present chapter it seems to me should be omitted.

I am writing all this in a hurry, so that it will reach you before you leave. When you come we can talk matters over, but truly the book needs no special or serious revision, in my opinion, only the revision you would naturally give it.

It is grand that you are coming.

Always yours,

. . . .

559. MKR to MEP (ALS, on Hotel New Weston stationery, 3 pp.)

Hotel New Weston
34 East 50th Street
New York, NY
[Oct. 12, 1941]
Columbus Day—
damn it.

Dear Max:—

Put off my leaving with Julia Scribner on our trip until this afternoon, in order to see you—and find New York is celebrating the tactless discovery of America.

I will telephone you late Wednesday afternoon from wherever we are, in case any urgent message has come in.

I plan to leave for Florida next Monday or Tuesday, Oct. 20 or 21, and will plan to see you Monday—so save me some time then—it need not be for luncheon.

Am feeling very rested. The Medical Center verdict is that nothing can be changed or helped physically, but that I must ease up on nervous tension. The diagnostician said I had an engine too big for the chassis.

"The English Are Like That"[1] *infuriated* [underlined twice] me!

1. Philip Carr (1874–1957), *The English Are Like That* (New York: Scribners, 1941).

. . . .

560. MKR to MEP (ALS, 3 pp.)

Crescent Beach RFD
St. Augustine, Fla.
Oct. 27 [1941]

Dear Max:

Think I can get the editing done this week.

As you will know by this time, Norton Baskin and I are being married this morning. I am terribly happy about it.

I talked with Robert Camp about doing a Creek painting for the jacket and he would love to do the job. He has some fine ideas and will submit sketches at once. He wants information as enclosed.

He made the Pittsburgh National Exhibit——only 400 paintings chosen for exhibit from 4,500, submitted from all over the country.

He understands that this jacket is not a commission, and is subject to refusal, but I think he is just the man.

. . . .

561. MEP to MKR (ANS: UF, I p.)

[October 29, 1941]

Dear Marjorie:

Anything that makes you happy makes me happy. I hope someday I'll see Norton Baskin for I'm sure I should like anyone who loved you, & should have much in common with him too. All good fortune to you both

Yours Always

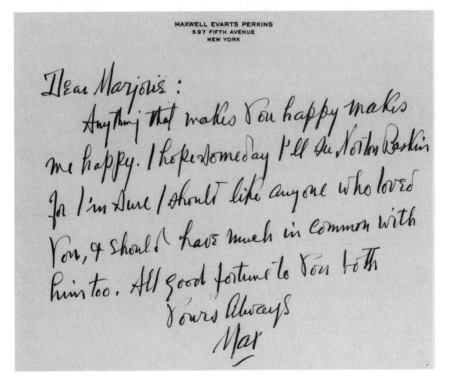

No. 561 (MEP on MKR's marriage). By permission of University of Florida Libraries.

562. MKR to MEP (ALS, 2 pp. frag.)

Crescent Beach RFD
St. Augustine
Oct. 30 [1941]

Dear Max:—

I expect to do some work when the material gets in proof. If it's all right with you, am sending back the first half with cutting and some rearrangement done, and by the time proofs are ready on it, will have the rest of the Mss. returned.

Chapter order is still flexible,

Toady-frogs etc.

The ancient enmity

Black Shadows (well separated *this way from other servant material).*

I need more help from you on The Black shadows, which I agree is too long and rambling.

Is it in the Kate and Raymond episode, or the story of Adrenna and the trial, that interest lags—or both?

Please make any suggestions and send this chapter back to me.

In "Residue" I have left [remainder of letter missing]

. . . .

563. MEP to MKR (CC, 1 p.)

Nov. 5, 1941

Dear Marjorie:

This is to tell you that the first part of the manuscript has come, and I'll go over it immediately. Everything seems to have worked out well with Shenton, and I believe he will do the best work he ever did.

Always yours,

. . . .

564. MEP to MKR (CC, 2 pp.)

Nov. 12, 1941

Dear Marjorie:

All of the manuscript has come, but there is one matter that is disturbing. The first chapter "For This is an Enchanted Land" stops short on page 14, with the beginning of the sentence, "Tom and his wife were not of the breed to accept an evil." There are presumably four pages missing. Couldn't you send duplicates?

I have gone through "Black Shadows" again, and it does read mighty well, and you have shortened it somewhat. Let's let it go and see how it reads in the proof. I was somewhat worried in reading it, in respect to libel. You libel anybody if you say they committed perjury, even if they did it like a gentleman. So I struck out the words "and in perjury" but I think the best thing to do is to set it up now and read it again in proof. Nobody who has read the manuscript thinks that the book is in any respect too long, and when you see it in type you see it afresh. I do hope everything will go successfully in the matter of illustrations.

With my regards to your husband whose picture I was most interested to see, I am,

Always yours,

. . . .

565. MEP to MKR (TS for wire)

NOV. 25, 1941
MRS. NORTON BASKIN
CRESCENT BEACH R.F.D.
ST. AUGUSTINE, FLORIDA
MISSING PAGES FOUND. THOUGHT NEW PHOTOGRAPHS BEAUTIFUL.
SHENTON DELIGHTED WITH VISIT.

. . . .

566. MEP to MKR (TLS: UF, 1 p.)

Dec. 5, 1941

Dear Marjorie:

I am sending you up to galley 23. I am having a wonderful time reading your proofs. One is made happy and contented in reading them, and also greatly entertained. I think you are most blessed to be able to give people such a book as this, and they are blessed thereby.

Always yours,

. . . .

567. MEP to MKR (CC, 2 pp.)

Dec. 9, 1941

Dear Marjorie:

Having read again last night the Court Room scene where you refer to one lawyer as shady, and to the judge as corrupt, etc., the terrible old libel fear that besets a publisher came back upon me. You know the ground so intimately, and the whole situation, that you are the best judge, but I do think it is very dangerous to characterize a lawyer in the way you do, and still more a judge, even when there is humor in it. Of course too, a good many other people are technically libeled in the book, but I don't suppose there is much risk that any of those would think of bringing a suit, or if it were suggested to them, would do it. But you might think it better to change some names, if they are real names. It would do no harm, and would be safer. The whole spirit of the book is such that nobody could really be harmed except the lawyer or the judge— but some things are libelous per se.

Always yours,

. . . .

568. MKR to MEP (TLS, 1 p.)

Crescent Beach RFD
St. Augustine, Fla.
Dec. 12, 1941

Dear Max:

Proofs through galley 59 are here, and I am working hard on them. I too have done a great deal of worrying about the libel possibilities. I am making a great many minor changes and deletions that will take care of much of the problem. It is simply impossible to tell how people will accept being written about. The negroes, Snow, Old Boss, the Glissons, the Bernie Basses, Zelma the census taker, are perfectly all right. The Townsends I'm sure would never sue under any circumstances, and I doubt if anything I said would register on them sharply enough to hurt their feelings. Mr. Storey's feelings might be hurt, but he is so trivial a character among us that I think I shall just change the name. George Fairbanks would not sue but I don't know whether he would be offended or not. The one most likely to give trouble would be Mr. Martin. He feels indebted to me, as he was very ill all summer and lived on nothing but milk that I sent him every day and would not let him pay for. But he would be angry if anyone would.[1]

I am going to the Creek tomorrow and plan to take the chapter about him and the pig and read it to him, asking him if there is anything I have said that he objects to.

Please question drastically anything that you think is dangerous, as it is always possible to make a point without being offensive. I didn't know that the use of fictitious names obviated this danger. I thought that if anyone was recognizable in his own neighborhood, he could still claim libel.

The lawyer and judge business I can take care of easily.

I am so happy over the things you say about the book. The general effect is not as heavy as I was afraid of, seeing it in print. There are some too-long sentences and some of the long paragraphs need breaking.

1. MKR's opinion proved to be incorrect. Zelma Cason did sue her for libel. MKR was found not guilty. However, the Florida Supreme Court overturned the jury verdict and found MKR guilty of invasion of privacy. See Patricia Acton, *Invasion of Privacy: The Cross Creek Trial of Marjorie Kinnan Rawlings* (Gainesville: University of Florida Press, 1988).

. . . .

569. MKR to MEP (TLS, with holograph addition and header, I p.)

> Crescent Beach RFD
> St. Augustine, Fla.
> Dec. 15, 1941

Dear Max:

When I went to the Creek Saturday I had a very pleasant meeting with Mr. Martin. He and his wife and Mrs. Joe Mackay's boy, "C. J." sat down with me in his living room and I read the chapter "A Pig is Paid For" from the proofs. I told him that my new book was called "Cross Creek" and told <of> <him> of the seasons, the life and the people and that we were all in it, and that our experience over his pig that I shot had always tickled me and I had used it to make a chapter. I said that I wanted to be sure he thought it was all right.

His wife chuckled all the way through, but he sat stonily with his hat in his hands. I fully expected him to rise from his rocker and say, "I don't someways like that. I can't agree." A couple of times he let out only an explosive "Hah!" that sounded much more angry than amused. Once was when I read the part where Tom Glisson told me that Mr. Martin had put out the word he was a man wouldn't be trifled with and had notches on his gun. When I came to the part about Mr. Higgenbotham he smiled broadly. I told him that I had changed the end a little, to make a good story of it, that it made it much more amusing if the sow took and was accepted for the debt. Actually, he didn't accept the sow and I paid him for my pig in cash. When I finished, he said, "He never did pay me for the use of the boar."

Then he got up to go out and said, "That's all right."

We talked of other things, and he said he was out of fish and frog-legs but usually had some, and I must be sure to stop by for a mess when I wanted any. He thanked me for a bucket of pecans I had brought and offered to pay for them. I said I didn't sell them, that I just gave them to my friends, and he nodded. I said again that I hoped he thought our story was as cute as I did, and I hoped he approved of my using it.

He said, "It's perfectly all right."

I feel much relieved. I have always found that complete frankness with these people makes them entirely cooperative.

Editor's note: At the top of the page in MKR's hand: "Galleys 52–56, I want to spell Samson's name in / the Biblical way. Am not sure of spelling—— / please check."

In the right margin in MKR's hand: "By the way, the judge in the negro case is dead."

. . . .

570. MEP to MKR (TLS: UF, 2 pp.)

Dec. 17, 1941

Dear Marjorie:

I was mighty glad to get the first fifty-nine galleys back, and I hope to send you what you haven't yet had before the end of the week. As a matter of fact, I thought Mr. Martin behaved like a gentleman in the pig episode anyway. He ought to feel complimented. But it's good you got his consent even to the notches on his gun. I thought also that you had done all that you could do about the trial, and the fact that the judge is no longer is an advantage. I should think everything was right. Samson spells his name without a "p".

Shenton sent us two of the illustrations, and they are very fine,- better than he ever did before, it seemed to me. One of the sticks region. We hope to have a number more this week.

Always yours,

. . . .

571. MKR to MEP (TLS, 1 p.)

[Crescent Beach]
Monday
[Dec. 22?, 1941]

Dear Max:

I will try very hard to get the rest of the proofs back to you by Friday.

Will you check back on some of the early galleys for me? On Galley 2, I don't think I <fixed up> changed, as I should have, and as you had indicated, a "whom" to "who", where I had "whom can be counted on for what."

On galley 6, you questioned '*til*, suggesting *till*. I thought the former was correct as an abbreviation for *until*.

Ask the proof-reader to check throughout for syrup and sirup. Ashamed to say I find I used both spellings. All should be *syrup*.

In changing chapters around, I lost track of chapter numbers. Please have someone see that these go through in proper order. I forget to check the changing after 17, I think.

On galley 56, are you sure I want to leave in Martha's comment on my being the new boss——along with the dog——at the Creek? Does it sound as though I were bragging or being arrogant?

Use the suggested enclosed insert for galley 60, or not, according to whether you like it.

Editor's note: At the bottom of the letter in MEP's hand: "Foreign / Facts & Figs / [line] / Col. Wm Donovan / Co. Ord of Inf / 270 Madison Ave. / (37th St.)."[1]

1. William "Wild Bill" Donovan, head of the OSS (Office of Strategic Services), later the CIA, in World War II.

. . . .

572. MEP to MKR (CC, I p.)

Dec. 26, 1941

Dear Marjorie:

I checked over the galleys in accordance with your letter, and I think everything is now right, and that the insert you enclosed for galley 60 ought to be there. I thought Martha's comment as to the Boss was good, and not in the least the way you thought it might be interpreted. Shenton's pictures are mostly in, and they are very fine indeed.

Always yours,

. . . .

573. MKR to MEP (ALS, 3 pp.)

[Crescent Beach]
Dec. 27 [1941]

Dear Max:——

Just had to do some Christmas preparing and couldn't finish the proofs any earlier.

My wonderful pointer dog Pat was run over and killed at the Creek Christmas eve. Idella and I have wept on each other's shoulders ever since. As Idella says, "He wasn't a dog. He was somebody."

On galley 50—please have someone call Abercrombie & Fitch or some expert and ask what a likely calibre would be for a Winchester big game rifle that would carry a telescopic sight. I'm not sure I have the right size.

Galleys 78 & 79, does the account of fighting the fruit fly seem boring? I am dubious about it. I wrote it originally as a separate sketch in the present tense, and such transpositions are often unsuccessful.

Galley 99, did you notice that I added an incident not in the published version? So many friends have been amused by the story of the yacht owner and his angry wife that I interpolated it. Take it out if you don't think it's suitable or amusing.

· ·

574. MKR to MEP

1941 DEC 30 AM 10 43
MAXWELL PERKINS—
597 5 AVE—
PLEASE WIRE BY WESTERN UNION IMMEDIATELY YOUR FEELING ABOUT
ATLANTIC PROPOSITION.[1] HOW LONG WOULD IT HOLD UP BOOK PUBLI-
CATION. AND DO YOU CONSIDER THEIR PRESTIGE SUFFICIENTLY VALU-
ABLE TO WARRANT DELAY. PRICE THEY OFFER SEEMS A PITTANCE.
SHENTON SAID BOOK SEEMED TO HIM A NATURAL FOR BOOK OF MONTH
CLUB. HAVE THEY NIBBLED OR ALREADY REJECTED IT.

Editor's note: Written at top of telegram in MEP's hand: "Crescent Beach #4 / Norton Baskin." Written at bottom in MEP's hand: "She has declined this MP."

1. The *Atlantic Monthly* offered to publish parts of *Cross Creek* and eventually published "Who Owns Cross Creek?" *Atlantic Monthly* 169 (March 1942): 439–50; and "Here Is Home," *Atlantic Monthly* 169 (April 1942): 277–85.

1942

Jan. 2, 1942

Dear Marjorie:

"Cross Creek" is now all in pages and most of the cuts are in the pages. We have made it up with great speed for the sake of presenting it most effectively to the Book of the Month Club judges. Let us remember how heavy the odds are in this Book of the Month Club question, but really the book is a most rare and fine one.- I took the chapter "Black Shadows" home because I cannot help but be worried about the libel aspect there in particular, and two of my daughters read it with the greatest pleasure. I do think that in reading the pages you ought to have the libel question in mind. I am thinking now of the negroes. It is impossible for anyone not in the region to know what the dangers are, but I am not sure that in some cases it might not do good to change the names. For instance, Samson might be prevented from getting jobs perhaps by the way he is represented here, but if that is his real name, and it were changed, no one would recognize him except in that particular region where he is no longer. How about Adrenna? I am only afraid, of course, of some lawyer like the one who represented Henry seeing a chance. Otherwise I would almost think that these people—if they knew they were in the book—would be pleased by it. Anyhow, have the question in mind. We'll be sending the page proofs the moment we have read them.

Always yours,

[Crescent Beach?]

Jan. 2, 1942

Dear Max:

I have not at any time been satisfied with the actual ending of "Cross Creek." I seem to have said about what I wanted to say, and I can't seem to find any better writing of it. It seems to me that I should be better satisfied with a transposing of the few last pages.

What would you think of going from the bottom of galley 101 directly to the paragraph at the bottom of galley 102, "I suppose there are a hundred other places where I might have found," etc., continuing on to what stands now as the end, then moving up what is practically all of galley 102, so that the end would be the part that begins "The question once arose, 'Who owns Cross Creek?'", and goes through to "Cross Creek belongs to the wind and the rain, to the sun and the seasons, to the cosmic secrecy of seed, and beyond all, to time."

It seems to me that perhaps that section makes a better summary of the feeling of the book, and that the important last line has more substance and beauty.

I am in favor of this rearrangement if it strikes you the same way. If so, please make the transposition for me before the galleys get into page proof. I know how much work it makes to make changes after the pages are blocked off.

I do hope someone is doing careful proof-reading. I was obliged, feeling rather hurried, to read for sense and sound, and in going over my duplicate set of proofs the last few days, have found six or eight typographical errors that I know I did not catch on the corrected proofs. Here are the corrections that I am not sure of:

galley 17, last line, Florida for Flordia.

gal. 21, first line, if not too much trouble, delete "of those". It repeats from a few lines before.

gal. 21, if not too much trouble, about two-thirds down the sheet, change listless air to listless manner. (I used "detached air" just two lines later.)

gal. 25, line 7, a ' should be added before the final ".

gal. 32, about 2/3 down, "Mis wife thought the illness" should be "His"

gal. 32, 3d par. from bottom, "I could not get out Moe out of"——delete first "out".

gal. 38, first line of Grampa Hicks story, "palmetto-lag" should be "log".

gal. 45, line 4, "he stopped" should be "be stopped."

gal. 50, 7th line of 2d par., "he Creek" should be "the Creek."

gal. 51, not quite 2/3 down, "My giggles impresed" should be "impressed."

gal. 52, line 23, "Kate patcked their suitcase", should be "packed."

gal. 52, line 64, "detest" should be "detect".

gal. 59, line 3, "down" should be "dawn."

59, half-way down, par. beginning "The old <fool> hen's a fool", "I just sell and out", delete the "and".

gal. 62, end of 7th par., "us mean mortals" should be "us modern mortals".

62, 12th line from bottom, "refuges" should be "refuge".

gal. <63> 63, 22d line from bottom, "bits and fish *are*" should be "*is*".

gal. 70, line <6> 5, "unforunate" should be "unfortunate."

gal. 83, first line of chapter "Fall", "propertly" should be "properly."

gal. 85, 21st line from bottom, "hurricance" should be "hurricane."

gal. 89, 8th line from bottom, "Guthrie road" should be "Guthrie place."

Some of these corrections were undoubtedly made on the other proofs, but some I am sure were not, so I included all of which I was doubtful. The original proofs seemed to me an unusually good and accurate job of type-setting.

. . . .

577. MEP to MKR (CC, 1 p.)

Jan. 5, 1942

Dear Marjorie:

We are in page proofs, and a good many of them go to you today. But to change the order at the end is not difficult, and I am inclined to think you are right in the suggestion of transposition. I think that makes the end more effective, but I'll study it over a little bit while the reading of the rest of the page proof goes along. We verified about half the corrections you indicated. We had found other typographical mistakes too, but I think we'll catch all of them.

Yours,

. . . .

578. MKR to MEP (ALS, 4 pp.)

[Crescent Beach?]

Jan. 12, 1942

Dear Max:—

I am mailing today page-proofs through page 212, and will have all the rest in your hands by Friday.

I really am sure there is nothing to be concerned about along the libel line as far as Adrenna and Samson are concerned. Adrenna and all her family are positively all right. Samson was called by everyone "B. J." I was the only one who ever called him by his last name. He is not anywhere around and I feel certain nothing I have said would do him any harm in any case. Also, no case of libel by a negro against a white would even reach a southern court.

Satisfy yourself completely about the whites involved as to "never having been in a court of justice less touched by truth and honesty", that applies to no one in particular, especially with the judge dead. I had been implying "imaginative fabrications" by the negroes, and no one will object to that.

I am delighted with most of the Shenton drawings that have been used so far—but the magnolia tree (Ch. 3) is so far off that it really upsets me. It doesn't look anything like a magnolia tree. If there is time for Shenton to look up a picture of one somewhere and do it over, I wish he could.

A magnolia tree is never thin and spindling like that. It has large, *broad* waxy leaves, and not fine feathery leaves as he has given it. All his Fla. things are so accurate and good, think the magnolia must have been the one thing he didn't make either drawn or mental notes on.

Also notice that the cut used with the Chapter "Spring at the Creek" should probably go with "Summer." It seems to be intended for the little colored boy gathering lotus, which is in the Summer chapter. But he is holding *water lettuce,* and not lotus. [Rawlings inserts a drawing of a lotus.] I like all others tremendously.

Editor's note: In upper left corner, in MKR's hand: "Better use 'Castle Warden / St. Augustine' for future / address."

. . . .

579. MKR to MEP (ALS, 1 p.)

> Castle Warden
> St. Augustine, Florida
> [January 1942]

Dear Max:—

The front pages are lovely. Is there a reason for using copyright by just Marjorie Rawlings, instead of using the full name?

Assume I may keep the proofs on heavy paper.

Editor's note: Written at top of letter in MEP's hand: "Send her: [Brace] Burt, / Gade, / Moran." At bottom of letter in MEP's hand: "Also send Hem [Brace]

Gade, / Moran, / [two words illegible]"[1] At the left of signature in MKR's hand: "Atlantic / 1942 / Scribner's Hyacinth."

1. Maxwell Struthers Burt; John Gade, a writer; Lois Moran, an actress.

. . . .

580. MEP to MKR (ALS: UF, 2 pp.)

Jan. 14, 1942

Dear Marjorie:

You know, sometimes the Book of the Month Club makes what they call a dual selection. That is, they take two books. They are doing that for the month of April, and one of the books is "Cross Creek",- the other is a short novel by Steinbeck. We had to give an instant decision, and we did not mind doing it for there was no question in our minds as to the wisdom of consenting. It would have been not inconsiderably better in remuneration if they had taken "Cross Creek" alone, but even so, you will be getting as much in this case—or very close to as much—as you did on "The Yearling" because the terms are now better. Besides, it will give us a great leverage in regard to the regular sale,- especially since "Cross Creek" is a book all its own, and with no direct competitor such as any novel must have in other novels.

Another good thing is that we shall be able to publish in the middle of March.- What we had feared was that they would take "Cross Creek" but as say a May book, which would have been bad. Herewith is a memorandum as to the terms, etc., from Whitney Darrow.

So now three of your books, out of four, have been taken by the Book of the Month Club, and I don't believe that has happened to anyone else.

Always yours,

. . . .

581. MEP to MKR (TLS: UF, 2 pp.)

Jan. 15, 1942

Dear Marjorie:

I think you were right in the idea of rearranging the very last of "Cross Creek" and have so indicated on the page proof. It won't be difficult mechanically. The first lot of pages through 212, have arrived and gone to the press.- The two pictures you don't like we'll try to correct. I myself felt dubious about the magnolia tree, but I thought maybe you had some different species down there. I hope, and think, there will be time to make this, and the other, right.

I know you had a very great struggle with this book, but it was worth it.-
And now its prospects look very fine indeed.

Yours,

. . . .

582. MKR to MEP (TLS, 3 pp.)

Castle Warden
St. Augustine, Florida
[March 1942]

Dear Max:

I feel as though I had lost you. All the business of the book publishing has so little to do with the book itself. But it is gratifying to have such a generous reception for so queer a book. I still wish, in a way, that I had done an entirely serious book with the "classic" touch——but the human stories were irresistible.

My colored maid Idella finished the book when we were at the Creek last week. She came to the door and twisted her apron, and said, "I had a speech all ready to say to you about the book, and now I've forgotten it." I said, "Never mind the speech. Just tell me what you thought of it." She burst out, "Oh, it's a beautiful book! When I read it, it seemed to me we ought to come back to the Creek to live."

I am slowly making an adjustment to the life in St. Augustine, but it is difficult. I had thought——and hoped——that perhaps I had wrung dry the backwoods section and living, but there is something there from which I cannot seem to tear away. My husband is so completely lovely a person, and it grieves me to see him grieved when I simply have to clear out and go back to the Creek. Actually, there is a whole new literary field before me in the old town of St. Augustine, and I really hope that in time I shall be able to sink myself into it.

I know that Whitney must be deep in his new marriage plans, which seem to me very nice and wise, so will ask you please to have sent, with compliments of the author of Cross Creek to Mrs. Sigrid Undset,[1] Hotel Margaret, Brooklyn.

Also copies to Edward Lawrence
        Frank Whitbeck
        Spencer Tracy
        Victor Fleming[2]
all care of Metro-Goldwyn-Mayer
        Culver City
        California
cards, compliments of the author.

I don't know whether I have you or Charlie to thank for the several good books sent me. I know the son of Gade who did the very good "All My Born Days."[3] The son, Herman Gade, lives in Jacksonville, and is a lovely person.

1. Sigrid Undset (1882–1949), Norwegian novelist.
2. Edward Lawrence and Frank Whitbeck, producers, and Victor Fleming, director at MGM.
3. John A. Gade, *All My Born Days* (New York: Scribners, 1942).

. . . .

583. MEP to MKR (CC, 2 pp.)

March 27, 1942

Dear Marjorie:

I know your husband is as you describe him, for everyone says so. I should think that that hotel[1] would develop<e> into a great success,- if the war doesn't harm it.- And it is true that St. Augustine presents real writing possibilities. Van Wyck Brooks went there some several years ago and thought it was a wonderful place. He stayed most of the winter.

I am sending "Cross Creek" to the people you named, "with the compliments of the author." Every soul who has read that book loves it, including every member of my family. It is going very well too, as I guess Whitney will have told you. We shall soon have printed 400,000 copies,- 300,000 for the Book-of-the-Month Club.

I do hope you will keep a hold on Cross Creek, though it will be more difficult to get to and fro as the tire problem increases.- Wasn't I smart to buy a house right next to the railroad station?

Always yours,

1. Castle Warden Hotel, owned by Norton Baskin.

. . . .

584. MEP to MKR (CC, 2 pp.)

April 7, 1942

Dear Marjorie:

I know you don't pay much attention to such things, but I thought you might be interested to see the page ad. that is coming out in the Times.

I had a letter this morning from a man named Harry Evans, just in praise of "Cross Creek": "It is completely charming, one of the most delightful books I have ever read." I know you get hundreds of letters to that effect, but this man who was in college with me, goes frequently to Cross Creek,- to Crescent Lake, to visit a man named Walter Oakman, and if Walter goes there next winter I do want him to meet you.[1] He is one of the best ever, and I know that you would like him too.

Always yours,

1. Henry Evans and Walter Oakman, classmates of MEP at Harvard.

. . . .

585. MKR to MEP (TLS, 2 pp.)

Hawthorn, Florida
April 18, 1942

Dear Max:

Whitney writes that you like the idea of "Cross Creek Cookery" and I'm so glad, as I shall enjoy doing it tremendously. He said that you had some ideas as to the form it should take, and since he wants a portion as soon as possible, will you write me immediately?

The recipes themselves will of course be practical and complete. I shall myself test any for which I do not already have exact proportions. Would you print the recipes in the orthodox set-off way, or do you visualize them incorporated in the text, as in the chapter in Cross Creek? And how much comment would you use? It gives a grand opportunity for gay comment. Bob Camp is enthused at the idea of doing black and white [—]humorous black and white[—] line drawings——he has been doing them for his own amusement for some time——and has already suggested some intriguing things——all very simple as to technique. Whitney wants the jacket very soon if possible. Bob suggested a black and white drawing of old Martha in her bandanna. Does that appeal to you?

Also, the Readers' Digest has written, wanting to do a 15,000 word condensation of "Cross Creek". The book certainly lends itself to this, and I should not have any objections, as I did to their condensing "The Yearling". The question is whether this would help regular book sales, or at least not harm them. I know nothing about this. They wrote that publishers felt it helped sales. Let me have your reaction to this right away, too.

April 21, 1942

Dear Marjorie:

Carl Brandt called me up this morning about the Reader's Digest condensation of "Cross Creek" and I told him that we did not think it would be injurious to the book sale, and were in favor of it.- In fact, I had known that the Digest was interested for some time, and when the other day Fritz Dashiell called me up about it, I said that I thought the best way to proceed would be for him to write you directly.- Carl seems to think someone else did, but I knew you would remember him from the old days, and would be glad to hear from him.

I am delighted you are all prepared for "Cross Creek Cookery". I thought it a splendid idea for a time when you were not engaged in any other book. It will fill in part of the necessary interval, and should be a very appealing little volume. I had no very clear idea as to the form, except that I did think there might be quite a little narrative in it. The recipes should stand out formally, and clearly, themselves, but I thought that you might be able to make some little story about each one, or else about certain ones,- in connection with how you first discovered the particular dishes. I also thought the moment Whitney talked about the book, that old Martha ought to be worked into it,- what she had to say about cooking, etc. There might be quite a long introduction in the vein of "Cross Creek" which would lead into the book itself, and that too could have narrative. Then the book would be a pleasure to read as well as to use. I'll think about the whole thing some more, but I am glad Robert Camp is so keen about it, and I rather think that a drawing of old Martha in a bandanna might be just the thing for the jacket.

Yours always,

. . . .

May 5, 1942

Dear Marjorie:

Two of our customers have asked us if you would be willing to autograph copies of "Cross Creek" for them. I thought you would be, and so I am having two copies sent to you, together with a self-addressed and stamped wrapper for their return to us.

Always yours,

Castle Warden
St. Augustine, Florida
June 19, 1942

Dear Max:

I do hope you are perfectly satisfied to let the Readers' Digest use 10,000 words of Cross Creek, for I am convinced that people who read excerpts or condensations do not buy the book. I hope I am wrong! People who wrote me after reading the parts in the ATLANTIC thought they had read the book. One man spoke of seeing it in a book shop window and said, "Of course I could not be a cash customer, as I had read it in the ATLANTIC." I think perhaps if you would make a personal request to Dashiell to have it made very clear at the beginning of their condensation, that it was less than a tenth of the book, he might cooperate. The Digest's 5 million readers and the Book of the Month's 500,000 certainly absorb the literary market. Wonder if the Digest would hold up their use a few months?

I have had a very heavy fan mail, much more so than on "The Yearling". Most letters speak of the food chapter. So many letters were addressed just to Cross Creek, Fla., which of course has no post office, that the Jacksonville postmaster wrote me asking for the proper address. Now they reach me all right.

I'm working on the cook-book. Think I really have some good and unusual recipes.

I've taken a fearful ribbing on an error in "Cross Creek". Is there ever any chance to make simple corrections? I had originally, in writing of trying to milk the cow, "I tightened my fingers around her teats." You questioned this in the margin of the proofs. I didn't know whether you were questioning the word teats, as being offensive, or whether you knew that one did not grasp all four teats at once. So I hurriedly changed it to "around two of the udders." Now as I knew perfectly, teats is the one correct word. There is no other. The udder is the bag, and there is only one. A great many people have called me on this.

Norton has put in a cocktail lounge and that has helped his business, especially with the army officers and their wives. The regular tourist travel dropped off to nothing because of the gas rationing. We are both fire wardens and are going to take our turns at airplane spotting. We have the dim-out and are very close to the war in general.

There are half a dozen huge magnolia trees on our grounds here, as tall as the hotel, and they have been covered for six weeks with blossoms. The trees and view from our apartment help make the hotel life bearable for me. I think I shall never get used to it or like it, but I think too I should have been very unhappy marooned alone at the Creek during the war.

. . . .

589. MEP to MKR (CC, 3 pp.)

June 23, 1942

Dear Marjorie:

You don't know how glad I was to get a letter from you. I have been buried for months in two huge books, and shall be for several months yet, more or less.- But it does look as if they were coming out well. But for all the interest of it, it has cut me off from anything pleasant, and you have seemed very, very remote.

As for the Reader's Digest, it has always been the theory that it helped the book sales,- and there are instances where books were those of information, when it unquestionably has helped them greatly. Anyway, I don't think it will hurt in the case of "Cross Creek".- But you are right about the Book of the Month Club. It is sponging up the whole market.

I only questioned the milking business because I didn't think it was being done quite rightly,- had no objection whatever to the word, but in fact there is good authority for the meaning you gave to the word you used. I would have thought it correct, and I still think it defensible according to the Century dictionary.- But we shall have a chance to make corrections like that, and if you have a number of them, send them to me and we'll change the plates for the next printing.- And I think there will be many more printings. It seems to me it is a book to live.

I am glad the cookery book is going along well. I read what you sent very hastily, and thought highly of it except on one point: you begin very skilfully, but I think it would be better if you could find some other way of leading in rather than the Gourmand and Gourmet. It isn't only that they have been talked about too much, but that somehow these French words do not seem compatible with Cross Creek, and the kind of cookery book this is to be. It is all right enough if there is no other way, but I thought you might find some more appropriate and indigenous introduction.

The cocktail lounge, and the magnolias even more, sound very enticing.

Do you plan before so very long to write more Quincey Dover stories?

Always yours,

[Crescent Beach]
July 15 [1942]

Dear Max:

I am staying at my cottage for a couple of weeks, and making rapid progress on the cook-book. I should say that I have finished three-fourths at least. I want to do some re-writing, as the introduction and many bits do not suit me. Now what should be the *actual deadline* for you to receive the material, both mine and Bob Camp's sketches? I see no reason why I should not meet any deadline necessary. But please don't move it up on me, "just to make sure", for I can promise not to be late. But I think it will be safer if I give Bob a date a week early. He brought me several more sketches to see, the other day, and they were most attractive. I think his combination of wash and line drawings proved very effective in the dummy.

I am wondering if you and Charlie have different ideas as to what the key-note of the book should be? Charlie wrote that he thought Bob's original jacket was too poor and countrified-looking, since a great many of the recipes are actually pretty fancy. On the other hand, you did not like my talk in the introduction about gourmands and gourmets, as being too sophisticated and removed from the simplicity of Cross Creek. I myself think it best to emphasize the Cross Creekified angle, although, while I seldom serve a really formal meal, some of the dinners are anything but plain or rural. But let's agree on the key-note.

I had my wild Mallard duck dinner Monday here at the cottage for several friends, and it was really delicious. Iced honeydew melon with lime juice, roast wild duck, wild rice, carrot souffle, fresh lima bean croquettes, whole small braised white onions, tiny cornmeal muffins, kumquat jelly, celery hearts instead of a salad, fresh mango ice cream and, most superfluously (because one of the men is crazy about it) devil's food cake. I had a heavenly time cooking it!

Editor's note: In left margin in MEP's hand: "*Mid August.*"

. . . .

July 20, 1942

Dear Marjorie:

The sooner we get the manuscript and the pictures, the better.- But I do think that the latest deadline I could safely set would be August 15th. Later than that, the season would have become too crowded by the time of publication.

I don't think that Charlie and I see the book differently. He says not. He only thought that the original jacket did not connote a very appetizing contents for the book. It was just because the first thing you see is the jacket, and you want it to produce the right impression. He thought as I did about the gourmand and the Gourmet. It isn't that we want to over-emphasize the rustic element in the book, but largely that those two, the gourmand and the gourmet, have been talked and written about so much. You did it very well, but if they could be avoided we thought it would be better.

Yours,

. . . .

592. MKR to MEP (ALS, 3 pp.)

[Crescent Beach]
July 23, 1942

Dear Max:

I am certain that I can beat the Aug. 15 deadline for the cook-book by at least a week, perhaps more. I talked on the phone with Bob Camp this morning and he said he has most of his material done now. He too is sure that he will be finished ahead of time. He spent yesterday at Cross Creek, he said, sketching. We will go over our material together today or tomorrow.

I never meant the original Preface to go through. I was doing a rush job to help Whitney with his merchandising of "the product", so just wrote as an idea came to me. He said I could do another later. I just wanted to be sure we all saw eye to eye on the keynote.

It is perfectly amazing, the number of letters about "Cross Creek" that comment on the foods. I believe that a fair percentage of "Cross Creek" readers will be interested in the cook-book. A great many people, too, write that now they mean to go back and read "The Yearling", and sometimes others of the earlier books. I think the $1.39 Yearling edition in the fall should do fairly well.[1]

Whitney wrote, asking me to try to think of a name for the $1.39 edition—— did not want to call it the Cross Creek edition for fear of confusion. <At the low> I am not writing him today, as I haven't yet thought of anything entirely satisfactory, but you might suggest to him the one idea that occurs to me. At the low price, what about calling it the Home Edition, or even, if not too pretentious, the American Home Edition? There is a tie-up, certainly, in the fact that the book presents American home life in simple and courageous aspects——and in the fact that people are going to be doing more home reading, and at the low price a family gets reading matter for all members. I thought of American Way or American Life Edition, emphasizing the basic Americanism of the individualistic Baxter family, but feel that is both too pretentious and capitalizing commercially on all the rather revolting and obvious "American" propaganda——which this country *does not need*. But Home Edition or American Home Edition seems rather logical. Anyway, please pass it on to Whitney until I can do some more thinking along the line.

Florida has been having a heat wave, and it was 100 in St. Augustine yesterday, and 104 in some other Florida cities—the hottest weather for Florida in 59 years. It has never been over 83 at the cottage, where I am working, and many days during the hot spell has been 72 when it was 90 in town. I tried to work in our apartment at the hotel, but just could not.

This part of the coast has become practically a military zone, and now passes are necessary to use the ocean road that leads to the cottage. I have black-out shades and it is rather creepy alone here at night, with no traffic on beach or highway, convoys going by, bombers overhead, and the thought of the saboteurs who land on isolated beaches. Twice a submarine has been seen from the airplane spotting post where Norton and I do duty, but the sub was gone by the time planes could reach the spot. We hear mysterious explosions out at sea, and never know the cause.

I have suffered over the requests of the Treasury Board and the War Writers' board, on which I agreed to become a member, and tried to write things, but have decided two things: the forced "Americanism" is both disgusting and unnecessary (the simplest people are aware of the danger and the need for concerted action); and I can do no more than write as I always do. A basic Americanism is implicit in what I write, and the inferred is always more effective than the obvious. An astonishing percentage of my letters about "Cross Creek" is from men in the service. I may have written you what one man in the Army said: "You are writing about the simple things for which we in the Army are fighting". A flier wrote from Cairo that space was at a premium in his duffel-bag in leaving Egypt, and he was tempted to leave "Cross Creek" behind, but did not, as it meant something valuable to him that he wanted to hang onto. I *cannot* turn out the sort of thing that Wrigley's chewing gum and Pepsi-cola use on the radio for "morale".

A week or so ago I had a call from a private with the Texas Division, a young chap who had been a clerk in a large book-store. He was an aesthete, almost a sissy, but with such a receptive mind that he was finding Army life fascinating. He said that he had roamed over old St. Augustine, alone, and said to himself, "Well, this is worth fighting for." You don't need "propaganda" when people feel that way. And the other day when Norton and I were doing our airplane spotting, a very tough and drunken soldier borrowed our binoculars and talked with us. He said, "I'm raring to go. I'm ready to shed my life's blood."

Now that sort of thing could be "worked up" into a radio skit or bit of newspaper propaganda——but it shouldn't and needn't be.

1. The Palmetto Edition.

. . . .

593. MKR to MEP (ALS, with holograph header, 1 p.)

[Crescent Beach]

August 6, 1942

Dear Max:

This turned out not to be too simple a job! I found out that it was difficult to engage in chit-chat, along with the practical listing of the recipes. If there seem to be places where too many recipes follow dully together, indicate them and I'll think up some yarns or comments for interspersing.

Please check for any trace of the smug or the sententious, on the one hand, and for too much flippancy on the other. Be as critical as you like with the preface. Would you prefer to title it in a lighter vein, such as "Scratch a Cook"?

Do you think it is all right and in good taste to tell the story about marrying Norton, and the friend's comment about his taking Pat's place and his saying that he just hoped nothing happened to Dora?[1] It is an awfully engaging story, I think, yet a cook book is hardly a good place to announce a marriage!

As you will notice, I couldn't resist the story about the elegant Kellogg and the collard greens and cornbread and the cows, that we took out of "Cross Creek". It seemed to fit here.

At the very end, I think there should be some bit of narrative to taper off on, rather than ending bluntly with a list of recipes. I'll do that while the rest is being worked on at your end.

Since I'm anxious to get this in right away, I'm not copying the menus. I have made a couple of changes.

Do you want me to do the Index? Bob Camp on the phone today said his sketches are practically ready.

Editor's note: At top of page, in MKR's hand, excised: "I don't think Carl Brandt needs a carbon / now—he has placed something of it with Woman's / Home Companion—he'll send / for it if he needs it."[2]

On back of letter is a memo in MEP's hand: "How many / characters to line / —— / How many lines on p. / .. .. .. of a / New Chap."

1. Pat, the pointer, recently killed by a car, and Dora, the milk cow.
2. "Cross Creek Breakfasts," *Woman's Home Companion* 69 (November 1942): 72–73.

594. MEP to MKR (CC, 4 pp.)

Aug. 10, 1942

Dear Marjorie:

On page 2 of the Preface, you use the phrase "The corpulent corporal." It is too obviously alliterative. But anyhow, a man can weigh 220 pounds and not be at all corpulent,- look at a modern football team.

This seems a silly little matter at the beginning of a letter about a book, but the truth is it is the only criticism I have to make. For the rest, I think you have done a wonderfully fine piece of work,- that the book as a whole is delightful, and something altogether new. And Louise,[1] whom I began to question on various points of cooking, took the manuscript and read it straight through with the very greatest pleasure. You have been wonderfully ingenious in blending the practical directions with the anecdotes, and in a way which sets all against the background. It is a most charming book. And Kellogg absolutely belongs. He delighted Louise who had not before encountered him. I am glad you found a use for that good material. I should have said, if you had not, that you required some bit of narrative to taper off with, or some kind of conclusion to round the book out. But I don't doubt you will find it. There was one word in the Preface, "drooling" which I do not like myself, but they tell me I am too fastidious. Still, you might easily avoid it perhaps. As for telling about marrying, it comes in very neatly and is perfectly right, including the friend's comment.

For the title of the preface, I prefer, "To Our Bodies' Good," and the phrase, "Scratch a Cook" comes in better with the text.

You do make the practical parts good reading in themselves, as when you tell of making the doughnut hole in the Hush Puppies.

I hope the pictures will come soon. As for an index, I don't know that one is needed if we make a very full table of contents. That we should have, and if we have that, I do not know that very much should be added, practically speaking, by an index.- It would be better if you did one if one were to be done, but let's see how the galley proof looks.

I'll wait for your corrected manuscript.

Always yours,

1. Louise Perkins, MEP's wife.

Box 550
St. Augustine, Florida
August 21 [1942]

Dear Max:

I'm so glad that you find the Cookery good reading. I'll fix the details you mentioned. I too dislike the word "drooling" and used it almost unconsciously because so many of the letters to me, from plainly very nice people, used that word.

I am getting *so many* letters from men in the Service. Some ask where others of my books can be bought. One asked if I had any of my "old books or stories" I could send, as the library was meagre. Now, can you find out how many libraries there are for both soldiers and sailors? If there are not too terribly many, I'd like to send copies of my books to all of them.

Almost every letter I have had in connection with the Digest's condensation[1] has said that the reader now intended to buy the book, so I guess it is as you said, that it helps sales.

I have had four very vicious letters, two anonymous, calling me a low evil woman for writing about the disgusting sex relations of animals, but they were plainly from the kind of peculiar Puritan who, himself or herself, has the dirtiest kind of mind. <No> The other letters have been simply beautiful. Several from ministers, two of whom used bits of the book as texts for sermons. One used the part, "Sift every man through the sieve of circumstance, and you get the residue," etc. Also had a four-page dictated letter from an executive of the Aetna Life Insurance Co, who said he had handled $100,000,000 of mortgages of the "Okies," and trying to explain the capitalist's point of view! He said that "powerful writers like you and Steinbeck, whose written word is taken as law, should at least know the other side of the picture." Evidently something I said about property got under his skin!

Please tell Whitney that two instances have come to my attention where "Cross Creek" is being sold for $2.75 instead of $2.50. One was Salisbury, Md. (possibly a Baltimore store, I don't know), the other was Appleton, Wisconsin. This may have been from a Madison, Wis. store. Don't you try to avoid a higher price than the list one?

I thought Bob Camp's sketches were delightful. If you need more small, casual, humorous ones, he can turn out some more immediately.

One of my old maid aunts, about whom I have told you many tales, wrote me, "I just don't know what to think about your writing a *cook book.* Somehow, it doesn't seem at all *classical* or *literary.*"[2]

So it isn't, but Lafcadio Hearn's "Creole Cookery"[3] commands an unbelievable price and is a very rare collector's item. There was an essay about it in a recent Atlantic Monthly.

Norton has just had a fine business "break". The Coast Guard has just taken over the huge Ponce de Leon hotel in St. Augustine as a training school, and probably the two other good hotels, the Monson and the Bennett. Norton's Castle Warden had too few rooms for their purpose, and the Lieutenant Commander who looked at his place told him it was lucky, as his place was much too nice for such a purpose. It means that Norton is bound to have a splendid business, both from visiting families, officers, and the St. Augustine elderly Old Guard who come for the winter and just sit——since his will be the only good hotel open to private business. I am enough of a cynic to believe it will probably mean that now he is all set in a business way, he will be drafted! He applied for the officers' training school, but is not a college man, so was not eligible and will just wait for the draft.

My friend General Lange told him that if he is drafted, he will certainly be put in a place where his particular experience will be used. I think he could easily be entered in the officers' training school for draftees, as he is widely read and passes intelligence tests about 40% higher than I do!

We had a delightful week-end at Cross Creek. We had as guests seven army doctors, Majors, who have been coming from Camp Blanding to his place and have had their families there. They are Boston men, who organized their own unit of 50 so that they will go into action as a group——top-notch surgeons, plastic surgeons, brain surgeons etc. We went to Silver Glen in the Scrub Saturday, fishing for blue crabs. Sunday we had dinner at the Creek, <Crab N> baked sherried grapefruit, Crab Newburg, also plain crab with mayonnaise, raised rolls, guava jelly, carrot souffle, tomato aspic with artichokes, Dora's peach ice cream and orange cake. I didn't have enough good white wine for that many people so served a good Burgundy, and it went very well with the Newburg. One of the men said, "This meal was a symphony". Another said, "I don't know about that, but it's the best Goddam dinner I ever ate." So in spite of Auntie's qualms, there is certainly artistry in a perfect meal.

1. "Cross Creek," Reader's Digest 41 (August 1942): 149–76.
2. Wilmer Kinnan.
3. Lafcadio Hearn (1850–1904), Le Cuisine Creole (New York: Coleman, 1885), a collection of New Orleans creole recipes.

AUG. 21, 1942

MRS. NORTON BASKIN

CASTLE WARDEN

ST. AUGUSTINE, FLORIDA

CAN WE SET FROM MANUSCRIPT YOU SENT ME? I INFERRED YOU WOULD
SEND A SECOND CORRECTED COPY BUT THIS ONE SATISFACTORY.

. . . .

597. MKR to MEP (TLS, 1 p.)

> Box 550
> St. Augustine
> [August 1942]

Dear Max:

Sorry you misunderstood me about the second copy of the manuscript.
That was only the carbon, which I intended originally to send to you, for Carl
Brandt to send for. Then I realized that having sold a piece of it to the Woman's
Home Companion, he was in no hurry, so instead of sending it air mail along
with your copy, I just sent it to him by regular mail. I thought I crossed out
where I said I was sending you another copy.

Anyway, it was just Carl's carbon copy. I have no other correct copy.

. . . .

598. MKR to MEP (TLS, 2 pp.)

> Hawthorn, Florida
> August 31, 1942

Dear Max:

I want your opinion on a matter of taste, as well as policy. If you agree that
my plan is all right, you can take it up with Whitney or Charlie for an OK.

The enclosed letter is self-explanatory. My first impulse was to refuse, since
I do not care to be associated with strictly commercial writing, or to be paid to
"sponsor" anything at all.

Then the thought occurred to me: many of my best dishes in "Cross Creek
Cookery" are prepared with wine, and on many of the menus I suggest the
wine that I use with them for table use. I have written Mr. Rumrill[1] that with

Scribner's permission, I should be willing to have them use twelve menus straight from "Cross Creek Cookery", provided they used the caption for each one, "From 'Cross Creek Cookery', by Marjorie Kinnan Rawlings. By special permission of Charles Scribner and Sons."

I named a sizable fee, so that it would be worth my while to do this.

Their booklet and the first of the advertisements in their campaign would be out not much ahead of the book itself, and from a purely advertising viewpoint, I imagine that Scribner's would consider the plan acceptable, even desirable.

It seems to me that the arrangement I suggested is legitimate, and frees me of any embarrassment in writing menus and recipes *for* a wine company.

Let me have your reaction right away.

1. Charles L. Rumrill of Rumrill and Co., a wine distributor.

. . . .

599. MKR to MEP (wire)

1942 SEP 1 AM 11 57
MAXWELL PERKINS—
597 FIFTH AVE—
WHEN WILL PROOFS BEGIN COMING IN AND HOW FAST AM PLANNING
MAGAZINE ARTICLE FOR THE FORESTRY SERVICE[1] WHICH INVOLVES TRIP
THROUGH SOUTHEAST OF WEEK OR TEN DAYS WANT TO FIT TRIP IN
WITH PROOF READING PLEASE ADVISE BY WESTERN UNION—

1. "Trees for Tomorrow," *Collier's* 117 (May 8, 1943): 14–15, 24–25.

. . . .

600. MEP to MKR (TS for wire)

SEPT. 1, 1942
MRS. NORTON BASKIN
CASTLE WARDEN
ST. AUGUSTINE, FLORIDA
WILL SEND FIRST PROOF BY SEPTEMBER FOURTH. LAST PROOF TENTH
FIRST-CLASS MAIL. <[ILLEGIBLE WORD] PLANS YOU PREPARE FOR>

September 2, 1942

Dear Marjorie:

There are difficulties about that Rumrill & Company proposal, but apart from that, we should think your plan would be right enough. They expect to bring out their booklet several weeks ahead of "Cross Creek Cookery" which would not only greatly reduce the advertising value for us, but would impair the copyright on the recipes they use. If they should copyright their booklet, we could use their copyright line, but that would be objectionable.- You know our contempt for alcoholic beverages! Do you think they could defer their publication until the Cookery was out? I doubt it, but we must protect the copyright on the recipes and we cannot take it out until the book is published. If a way can be managed to let them use the material, perhaps I had better get in touch with the so appropriately nominated Mr. Rumrill.

That expedition you are to go on sounds wonderfully pleasant, and I hope my telegram which said that the last of the proofs would go to you on the 10th, will make it easy to plan.

I do think the Reader's Digest helped. Most certainly it did not hurt "Cross Creek" and should tend to increase your public, not only for the Cookery, but for all later books.

A company named The Crown Publishers got Hemingway to agree to write a preface to an anthology of war stories.[1] *I* would not have asked him to do it because I would think it so important that he should not be diverted from his own work, but both he and I got very much interested in the anthology, and it ended by his virtually making it.- It would have been an ill-favored thing but for him. His interest in it grew to such an extent that he really edited it, even cutting some of the stories, and then yesterday came the Introduction, and it is one of the finest pieces of writing I ever read. Every soldier ought to read it. The best medicine they could take. I'll send it to you in some form as soon as I can. Hem was sorry that we were not the ones to do the book, and so was I, of course, and even got to wishing he was not involved in it at all except that I was so interested myself and made many suggestions. But now when I see the superb utterance for the war, and for literature, I am glad he did it. I'll send you the book anyhow.

And there is another book here that is absolutely fascinating, though the idea will bore you;- for it is another attempt to prove—and it does prove—that Shakespeare was not the Poet, and that someone else was. The title is "Will Shakspere and the Dyer's hand".[2] I'll send you that book, and if you start reading it, you will finish it.

I was very much interested to hear about the hotel. That is a bit of good that was blown by an ill wind, or rather a hurricane.

Always yours,

P.S. Although it would be complicated, we could, with the cooperation of Mr. Rumrill, have his copyright transferred to us, and although it is doubted if this does give actual protection, it would give practical protection, and might serve.

1. Ernest Hemingway, *Men at War* (New York: Crown Publishers, 1942).
2. Alden Brooks, *Will Shakspere and the Dyer's Hand* (New York: Scribners, 1943).

. . . .

602. MKR to MEP (ALS, 5 pp.)

Castle Warden
St. Augustine, Florida
[September 1942]

Dear Max:—

I don't have the original dummy of the Cookery at hand, but I seem to remember a much more attractive type and set-up than is used on these proofs.

The large-face blunt type used for these recipe headings doesn't look very appealing.

The headings are all at the left, instead of centered. I suppose all that will be fixed on page proofs.

I see also that cups and tablespoons and teaspoons are written out instead of using the conventional C., T., and t. That is o.k.

It seems as though there should be a spacing, after a set of recipes and chit-chat, before a new set begins. It seems all to run in together too much.

Also, the chapters—Soup—Hot Breads—Vegetables—are not indicated, but assume that will come on page proofs too.

The Hemingway introduction sounds very exciting. Will look forward to the book. Where is he, and Martha? Would like to have them stop off and visit me if they pass through Florida.

The wine company deal is off, and it suits me just as well. They gave some other reason, but I know it was the size of the fee I asked that threw it out.

[Postscript] Can take care of the proofs as fast as they come—

And what about the menus? They are not with the proofs so far. I corrected the menus on the original booklet and clipped them to the manuscript when I sent it to you.

603. MEP to MKR (CC, 2 pp.)

Sept. 9, 1942

Dear Marjorie:

I have been sending the proofs to you very rapidly, and with only a skimming in order to expedite your plans, but don't worry about the typography. It will be just as it was in the dummy. The headings now are merely put in to indicate what they will say. The ones in the book are hand set and will be properly inserted.

I am confused about the menus, for I never saw them in copy, and I do not think you sent them back with the manuscript you sent me and from which we are setting. But anyhow, you would have to go over them again to insert the page references which can only be done when you have page proof, or else when you have complete galley proof,- for then you can indicate what galley and at what point in the galley the references come. So I think you had better make any corrections on the enclosed proof and return it with indications for the references.- I take it you won't want to read page proofs for that would delay your trip.

I am sending you "The Prodigal Woman" by Nancy Hale and "A Time to Be Born" by Dawn Powell.[1]

Always yours,

1. Nancy Hale, *The Prodigal Woman* (New York: Scribners, 1942), and Dawn Powell, *A Time to Be Born* (New York: Scribners, 1942).

. . . .

604. MKR to MEP (wire)

1942 SEP 11 AM 11 40
MAXWELL PERKINS—
—597 FIFTH AVE—
GALLEYS 33 TO 38 JUST RECEIVED NEVER RECEIVED 22 TO 33—

. . . .

605. MEP to MKR (TS for wire)

SEPT. 11, 1942
MRS. NORTON BASKIN
CASTLE WARDEN
ST. AUGUSTINE, FLORIDA
THINK MISSING GALLEYS WILL ARRIVE. SENT FIRST CLASS BUT MAILING DUPLICATES FOR SAFETY.

[St. Augustine]

Sept. 16 [1942]

Dear Max:—

Galley 44 is missing.

I find that on galley 25, already sent in, *1 tablespoon flour* should be added to the recipe for lamb kidneys, sherry gravy. It can go just behind the 1 tablespoon butter in the recipe.

Also, on galleys 3 (Cream of Peanut Soup & Cream of Cucumber Soup) and on galley 20, where I inserted a lobster recipe, chef *Houston* should be spelled *Huston.* Please make deletion for me.

Within the next two or three days, I'll write a little something in the narrative line to make a conclusion.

May possibly begin my Forestry Trip a little later than Sept. 21. Would really like to see page proofs if convenient, out of curiosity.

The type-setters have done an amazingly accurate job on this difficult work. Please compliment them.

[Postscript] Julia just arrived.

. . . .

Sept. 18, 1942

Dear Marjorie:

Would it be hard for you to go over the galleys of the menus again? I simply cannot find your corrections. Is it possible that they have already been made?

The other galleys have now all come back, and I have made the additional corrections you wrote about.

Tell Julia her brother is now an Ensign in the U.S. Navy.[1]

I think it is desirable that you should see the page proof. A dummy has just been very carefully prepared, but it was necessary to do a little moving about for the sake of make-up. I think you will approve, but it is only right that you should have the chance to disapprove.

Yours,

1. Charles Scribner, Jr.

[St. Augustine]

[September 1942]

Dear Max:—

I think the section "Potatoes, Rice, Grits", should come *ahead* [underlined twice] of meats and salads. It could come either before or after "Vegetables". This section begins on galley 34.

I *did* [underlined twice] send in the corrected menus with the original manuscript. I corrected them on pages from the printed dummy, and have no other copy of the corrections.

. . . .

609. MEP to MKR (CC, 2 pp.)

Sept. 29, 1942

Dear Marjorie:

I think the ending is good, and I have sent it over, but I changed your quotation, for apparently it should be, "Better the dinner of herbs where love is, than a stalled ox and hatred therewith." But the next chapter but one of Proverbs has another quotation which might seem more apt, "Better is a dry morsel and quietness therewith, than an house full of sacrifices with strife." That is, I never quite understood about the stalled ox, whether it was that his presence indicated prosperity, or that he was supposed to be ready for the slaughter. The quotation you gave was best, but apparently it does not exist, and I should judge that you must have put two together in your memory.

I think we'll get everything right now.

Always yours,

. . . .

610. MEP to MKR (CC, 2 pp.)

Oct. 2, 1942

Dear Marjorie:

I am sending you a proof of the additional piece,- the human angle. You will see I changed the quotation according to the King James version. But when I read your copy again your version seemed to be much better for the purpose, and I tried to find it. I could not, in the three versions of the Bible in our bookstore, including the Catholic one. But they are all widely different, and probably you have quoted rightly still another version. Let's go back to it. It says what is wanted, and it would appear to be as accurate a translation from the actual original as any of the others.

We'll soon be sending you page proof and a complete dummy.

I was writing this letter when Mrs. Strakosch[1] came in, and I enclosed her letter which tells the whole matter. I think that this would be splendid publicity for the cook book, and hope you will be willing to let her come. I am sending a copy of the Post of September 5th which has one of those picture stories by Pope on page 26.[2] I have seen a rough outline of the text, and it is all right. It quotes one of your menus, and it tells about how turtles and alligators are caught, and all that sort of thing. It is almost entirely about the various kinds of food in the neighborhood of Cross Creek, and how to get them.

Hoping your trip was a great success, I am,

Yours always,

1. Frances Maria Strakosch, feature writer.
2. Vernon Pope and Paul Dorsey, "Island of Navy Wives," *Saturday Evening Post* 215.10 (September 5, 1942): 26–27, 68–69.

· ·

611. MEP to MKR (CC, 1 p.)

Oct. 5, 1942

Dear Marjorie:

I am sending you now the page proof, and with it a dummy.- Don't be worried about the headings after the first third perhaps, because they will be in the right hand-set type. In several places you are asked if we can get another spot, but we are so late with the book that I do not think we ought to wait for Mr. Camp to do more. We can readily improvise spots from the pictures he has done. As they say now about military matters, "Time is of the essence",- so please read proof as fast as you can, and return it first-class.

Always yours,

· ·

612. MEP to MKR (TS for wire)

OCT. 8, 1942
MRS. NORTON BASKIN
CASTLE WARDEN
ST. AUGUSTINE, FLORIDA
HOPE PAGE PROOF AND DUMMY ARRIVED SAFELY AND WILL SOON COME BACK. COULD YOU WIRE ABOUT MRS. STRAKOSCH'S STORY? THINK IT WOULD BE WONDERFUL PUBLICITY FOR THE BOOK.

613. MKR to MEP (wire)

1942 OCT 8 PM 5 33
MAXWELL PERKINS—
597 FIFTH AVE—
PROOFS REACHING YOU MONDAY   STRAKOSCH STORY OK   WRITING—

. . . .

614. MKR to MEP (TLS, 4 pp.)

[St. Augustine]
Oct. 10, 1942

Dear Max:

I think the cook book looks very promising. I wish there were more small illustrations scattered through it, but the way it stands, it looks quite business-like, which is probably a good idea. Although you said there was not time for more spots, I took a chance and phoned Bob Camp this morning, telling him the exact places where a spot was called for, and he said he could easily do them this afternoon and would send them air mail this evening or tomorrow, so that if he does do it, they should reach you at the same time as this, and it may be possible to rush them through. They really are badly needed. The spots he is doing are:

p. 14——sketch of a soft-shelled cooter

p. 46 — sketch of a rum omelet, blazing

If you do wait for the new spots, in this instance the recipe for pecan patties should be moved up, so that the rum omelet comes last.

p. 66——There is perhaps not room at the top of the page for a spot, but each chapter should certainly have some illustration to begin with. He is doing a sketch of a platter of stuffed baked potatoes.

p. 155—sketch of cross-section of watermelon cake

p. 215— sketch of assorted jellies and marmalades, with fruits

p. 217—some little decorative sketch, a centerpiece of flowers with perhaps a plate and crumpled napkin, showing the meal is over

There are several places where, in order to make things come out even as to pages, the arranger has put some sauce that should go with a particular dish, in among some other irrelevant recipes, etc. In most of these, arranging them properly will not bring things out unevenly, but even in a place where it does throw things out of kilter, I am afraid the changes will simply have to be made. These are:

p. 9——last paragraph (There are countless pages, etc.) should be moved up earlier, either ahead of "Not far from Tampa", on p. 8, or ahead of recipe "Mrs. Chancey's Spanish bean soup" on p. 7

ps. 123–125. Recipe for dumplings on p. 125 must follow after recipe for chicken and dumplings on p. 123

ps. 156–158. Recipe for Seven-Minute Frosting on p. 158 must follow recipe for Devil's Food Cake on ps. 156–7.

p. 10——recipe is correct, but title is a duplicate. Title should be "Chef Huston's Cream of Cucumber Soup". Notice this is correct in proofs, but not in dummy.

ps. 14–15. A spot is asked for. Didn't Bob Camp do one——I am sure he did——of a crab? It would be suitable here.

p. 38. Shouldn't each new chapter have an illustration to begin with? I was sure Bob did one for each chapter. Please check.

p. 42——spot of basket of vegetables seems most inappropriate here. <Bob is doing the blazing rum omel[ette]> Haven't you something else that could go here? Basket of vegetables should go with vegetables or salad. However, it can be left here if not practical to change.

p. 66. Chapter should have illustration heading. If not room for the sketch of *baked stuffed potatoes,* would suggest that the 2-page spread, ps. 70–71, be made the beginning of the chapter, and the illustration p. 65 which ends the vegetable chapter be moved back to p. 64, after "as though by giant forks."

p. 79. Note correction on proofs.

p. 86. Note correction. Hand-set heading does not use accent acute and has two "e's."

p. 147. Illustration not at all suitable to immediate subject. It should go in with the ice creams.

p. 207. Do you think the illustration, full page, on p. 209 should be moved up to p. 207 to make chapter heading?

I almost forgot to do the index.

Have just finished it, but am too tired to copy it, so will send it in air mail tomorrow.

Someone will have to check the page numbers of the recipes where changes had to be made in the page arrangement, because of moving such things as Seven Minute Frosting etc. that were out of place.

[Postscript] Page numbers should be checked very carefully, especially where changes have been made in order of recipes.

[Postscript] Dear Max:

The Index from the office came in just as I was going to mail the one I worked up. I find an index annoying that is not in alphabetical order, and if you agree, I suggest using mine, which is in order.

. . . .

615. MEP to MKR (CC, 2 pp.)

Oct. 13, 1942

Dear Marjorie:

We think we ought to stick to the conventional order of a table of contents which sets down the chapters and the headings, etc., in the order in which they come. What you have done is a kind of combination between a Contents and an Index, but since we decided there should be an index at the end of the book, and have made a good one, we do not think that the contents should try to be also an index, or that it need be. We do think we should follow the conventional method which is what people expect. I am sorry about this confusion. When I concluded that there should be an index, I never meant to suggest that you should do it. Miss Beam here is an expert on indexes, and she did it. So will you forgive us if we follow our contents which gives the main topics in the order in which they come, and let the index which is full, and alphabetical, do the rest? We are mighty glad to get the proofs back too, and now the way seems all clear.

Always yours,

. . . .

616. MKR to MEP (TLS, 2 pp.)

Hawthorn, Florida
Monday
[October 1942]

Dear Max:

I am overdue with thanks for all the good books you have been sending me—books of such varying quality. "A Time to be Born" is clever and cannot be put down, but it is a trivial thing. "The Prodigal Woman" is better, but again, none of the people matter. But I have just this minute finished "The Valley of Decision",[1] and I think I have never read a more magnificent American book. It has everything. It is as exciting as "Gone With the Wind", and is a thousand times better in so many ways, one being that some of the characters are not only strong but good, good in the most profound sense.

I have read only a couple of reviews of the book, but they do not seem to me to do it justice. And why on earth did not the Book of the Month take it? You don't always answer my questions. Tell me why the Book of the Month did not take it.

I have not yet read "Lee's Lieutenants"[2] but am looking forward to it. After I have read it, I hope you won't mind my sending it to a present-day Southern Colonel who is a great student of military history and who will go overseas any day. He will not only read and enjoy it himself, but will pass it on to other Army men equally interested.

I have been deep in finishing my article presumably for the Saturday Evening Post on the matter of our American forests. I guess I wrote you that I took a two-weeks' trip with the U.S. Forest Service, covering nearly 5,000 miles through the south-east, to gather material. I don't think I am the person to do such an article, but have done the best I could.

Even when I don't write, do know how much I appreciate your sending me books. I also didn't mean to imply that I didn't enjoy "The Prodigal Women". It was simply enthralling, but when you had finished, you felt it just didn't matter. I do hope "Valley of Decision" does as well as it deserves to. Thanks for everything.

1. Marcia Davenport, *The Valley of Decision* (New York: Scribners, 1942).
2. Douglas S. Freeman, *Lee's Lieutenants* (New York: Scribners, 1942).

. . . .

617. MKR to MEP (TLS, 1 p.)

Castle Warden
St. Augustine, Florida
Nov. 13, 1942

Dear Max:

I think I might have been sent at least one copy of the cook book before it reached the stores! Was amazed to have the bookshop woman here bring over an armfull [*sic*] for signing——had had them nearly a week——and I hadn't seen a copy. I don't think the jacket is effective. It all blurs in together. The inside looks very well. A mistake must have been made at the last minute in the hand-set heading type. The very last recipe in the book is supposed to be Loquat Preserves, and it is marked Loquat Chutney. The Index has it correctly.

In addition to the six copies due me, I need twelve copies more to give away.

Would it be too awfully much trouble for each of the twelve to be wrapped and mailed separately, so I could sign them and mail them on again? Would be glad to pay any extra expense.

Well, hope we get some decent Christmas sales out of the book. Wish it looked more striking. Also was surprised to see $2.50 as price. It was advertised at $2 to begin with——a much better gift price, of course.

Editor's note: In left margin in MEP's hand: "11/16/42."

. . . .

618. MEP to MKR (TLS: UF, 4 pp.)

Nov. 13, 1942

Dear Marjorie:

Well then, I'll send you a very good book indeed now,- "Cross Creek Cookery" six copies.

"The Valley of Decision" came very close to being adopted by the Book-of-the-Month Club, but there were two judges who did not think highly of it. Schurman,[1] head of the Club, told me that he was very sorry indeed that it was voted down. But the whole publishing of that book was amazing and miraculous. Six months before it appeared the author was for scrapping it. When she turned it over to me it was the most chaotic manuscript I ever saw in my life. I had it at home for a long time, and once Louise said—not knowing what it was, but recognizing it by the yellow paper as the same thing that I had been working on weekends and evenings—"Why do you put so much time on that?" And I said—thinking that it would never be anything more than publishable—"Because I am a damned fool." I had thought it was only worth the time because it would not do to allow Marcia to fail on this big undertaking. It might ruin her career to get beaten that way. She was so completely entangled in the underbrush of the book that she could not manage it. So I wrote a commentary on the whole thing, and then when she agreed to the general principles, I wrote a commentary on each chapter, suggesting the right organization of it. Would you ever think that good results could be got that way? I thought the outcome would be bound to be perfunctory writing. The most amazing thing happened. Marcia virtually rewrote the whole book, and with great speed and great skill. She is a woman of character and determination, and she had always a firm conception of what she wanted the book to accomplish. But she did need help. As she tells it, it was a case of Trilby and Svengali.[2] I ought not to have been telling this, but I am telling you confidentially. Still,

Marcia is telling everybody. In fact, she told the World Telegram in an interview which fortunately was crowded out of the last edition.

As to the Nancy Hale, that too was a great triumph because she had published three failures. "The Prodigal Woman" started with a rush. It had very great beauty in it though, quiet little places like where Leda is alone in the pullman compartment leaving New York, and sees the snow beginning to fall, and it is astonishingly revealing, I thought, of feminine character,- how glamorous life seems to young girls. I don't remember any book that was so successful in that respect. And she also had Boston dead right,- much better than Marquand.[3]

Everyone here is very much pleased with everything about the Cookery book. And people I have given it to have been delighted by it.

Now will you be settling down to another big piece of work, or is there a chance of your doing some Quincey Dover stories?

Always yours,

1. Harry Scherman, cofounder and president of the Book-of-the-Month Club.
2. Svengali, the mesmeric musician; see George du Maurier (1834–1896), *Trilby* (New York: Harper, 1894).
3. J. P. Marquand (1893–1960).

. . . .

619. MEP to MKR (TLS: UF, 2 pp.)

Nov. 23, 1942

Dear Marjorie:

Because you liked Marcia Davenport's book so much, I thought you might like to know how much she liked yours. I gave her a copy, and this is what she said:

"I have already devoured Cross Creek Cookery at one gulp, as if it had been a meal cooked by Marjorie Rawlings herself. She has the most fantastic gift for making every word she writes warm and tantalizing and intimate. I think she is an extraordinary artist. Gastronomically I disagree with her predilection for fruit and sweet-potato dishes to be served with meat, but I would indeed defend to death her right to make them, serve them, and write about them!

"Incidentally, this is the most beautiful looking book I have ever seen. The binding is so breathtaking a surprise, and so exquisitely designed and executed that you should all be strutting with pride around there."

By the way, her book is all but the best seller.

The reason you didn't get copies sooner was that the book came out late in the season and we did not have the interval between its complete manufacture and publication that is usual,- nor anything like it, and we were anxious to get copies to the trade as fast as we possibly could. I hear there is a very good review in next week's Tribune.[1]

Always yours,

1. Sheila Hibben, "Hopping John and Poke Green," *New York Herald Tribune* (November 29, 1942): 8.

1943

620. MEP to MKR (TLS: UF, 2 pp.)

Feb. 5, 1943

Dear Marjorie:

I had meant to write you how sorry I felt about the lawsuit,[1] for I know how dreadfully worrying those things are,- how unpleasant even when not serious. I showed the passage to Arthur Train, and he said that if it were in New York, it could easily be laughed out of court, but that he knew nothing about the character of Florida juries. Anyhow I hope that all goes well.

I am very much puzzled about Edith Pope's book,[2] but I promised her I would go through it and make comments. It does really need some serious reorganization. The most interesting thing is that she actually has handled a subject generally regarded as repellent and even taboo in a way which makes it completely unobjectionable. But she should have made it tragedy. It is all mixed up with other things now. Anyhow, I enjoyed very much my talk with her, and I hope I can help her.

Always yours,

1. *Cross Creek* lawsuit brought by Zelma Cason.
2. Edith Pope, *Colcorton* (New York: Scribners, 1944).

. . . .

621. MKR to MEP (TLS, 2 pp.)

Cross Creek

April 13, 1943

Dear Max:

It's dreadful of me not to have written you before and I have no excuse at all. I have simply been in a completely passive state, which is probably desirable, as my assigned period of convalescence is over, with a few reservations, and I feel perfectly normal.

I have the feeling that it won't be too much longer before I know what I want to tackle next, and how. But I sha'n't hurry it. I am terribly restless to get to work. Carl will harry me for stories, I know, and I just don't feel like stories.

It has been heavenly at the Creek. I have loved every minute of it. I am caught in the middle in a serious war between Old Boss Brice and Tom Glisson and while trying to stand for abstract justice, am also trying to keep on good terms with both sides——and I'm even enjoying the row! These Creek battles are the most complicated I have ever known.[1]

Edith Pope wrote me that you thought I stayed nobly at the Davenports in order not to offend the poor Negro, but I stayed only because it was all so interesting. I couldn't leave at the moment at which Wendell Willkie had driven the Japs back from St. Louis to Denver![2] There were no ill effects, other than a slight hangover the next morning.

I'm going to St. Augustine tomorrow to spend a week with my neglected husband, then will come back here again if he doesn't act too pitiful.

Do you think Edith will be able to whip her book into shape? I am so anxious to know whether she can profit by your help.

Please send me any books you can. I have been driven back on the Bible for reading matter.

1. W. R. "Old Boss" Brice and Tom Glisson once nearly came to blows over a cattle gap. MKR settled the dispute.
2. Marcia and Russell Davenport, the latter the campaign manager for Wendell L. Willkie, Republican candidate for President in 1940.

. . . .

622. MEP to MKR (TLS: UF, 3 pp.)

April 15, 1943

Dear Marjorie:

I didn't think you should have written me. I have been blaming myself ever since our drive back to the hospital, that I did not put down the seat in front and get you to put your feet on it, because I could see you were exhausted.

I did send you a book today, to St. Augustine,- Tom's letters to his mother. I am so glad you have been passive, which is the right way to be. Nancy Hale, who is still here in New York resting, had the very same thing that you had, so I am told by Marcia. Her doctor told her that she would know when she was well, when she was bored. She is not yet bored,- although I should be bored with one hour in any hotel suite that I ever saw.

Tomorrow I shall be able to send you John Thomason's ". . . and a Few Marines".[1] We have two such wonderful books coming along, but they won't be ready for several months. One is called "Indigo" by Christine Weston, about India.[2]

Poor Edith Pope has measles, but she did send me back the first chapter very greatly improved, and I have just this moment received the second chapter. I think she is on the right track, but I had to stop in my work until I saw how far she could go along with me on these first chapters.

Since you left, Russell Davenport has had appendicitis,- and I thought he looked very badly the night we were there, and since all went well in the operation, he may now be much better;- and Marcia came mighty close to pneumonia, and was pretty ill for a time. She took some of the sulpha drugs which cured her, but were unpleasant.

I am delighted you are beginning to think you could start in on a big piece of work. If it came to stories, what I would hope would be what I have spoken about a good many times, and I think you were the first to speak of it,- more of those told by Quincey Dover. Then we would have a book of them.

Yours,

P.S. I am also sending you Nancy Hale's short stories.[3]

1. John Thomason, —*And a Few Marines* (New York: Scribners, 1943).
2. Christine Weston (1904–), *Indigo* (New York: Scribners, 1943).
3. Nancy Hale, *Between the Dark and the Daylight* (New York: Scribners, 1943).

· ·

623. MKR to MEP (TLS, 3 pp.)

Hawthorn, Florida
June 17, 1943

Dear Max:

The chances are I shall see you soon, and I hope so, as the book I want to do seemed suddenly to take <complete> shape.[1] It is a milieu I had never dreamed of using, and I may be on the wrong track. But I can see it as so complete a unit that there seems a certain inevitability about it. The basic character stems from my grandfather, the one who had the Michigan farm. If you will look up the book VOGUE'S FIRST READER, you will find a sketch there, FANNY, YOU FOOL, which gives you some idea of these two.[2] I should use them both only as a starting point, developing them for my particular purpose. I think it was Arnold Bennett who said that character, or characterization, is the essence of a good book, and the set of characters that came to mind seem to lend themselves to something almost a cross between Dickens and some of the Russian novels. It would not be a farm book, nor a "novel of the soil", but the wonderful farm life would be the background. You asked me once if I ever thought of using the details of my childhood, and I said that I should <so do> do so only objectively and creatively, and it would be so in this. The things one has known and loved lend themselves to richness of detail, I think. I shall want to talk with you about the whole plan when I see you. Don't say anything to anyone, as no one but you understands a superficial outline.

What will probably bring me to New York is a rather distressing matter. Norton has signed up with the American Field Service and leaves for overseas within the month. It is a dangerous branch of service, as they operate their ambulances in the front line of battle. In the last war their casualties were twice the ratio of Army casualties. I feel utterly flattened out about it, yet I respect Norton immensely for doing something he did not have to do. I knew nothing about it until he was practically in. It is the type of decision a man has to make for himself and about which a woman has nothing to say.

I think they always sail from New York, and if so I'll go up with him and wait with him for his final orders.

Many thanks for the books you have sent.

1. *The Sojourner* (New York: Scribners, 1953).
2. "Fanny—You Fool!" *Vogue* 100 (July 15, 1942): 42. Reprinted in *Vogue's First Reader* (New York: Messner, 1942), 319–21.

. . . .

624. MEP to MKR (TLS: UF, 2 pp.)

June 21, 1943

Dear Marjorie:

I certainly do look forward to seeing you, even though the occasion be a sad one,- But I suppose it is just impossible to keep a Southerner out of a war if he can qualify to get into it somehow. I hope the hotel will go on all right.

I remember "Fanny, You Fool," in so far as its quality and character went, but I did get it and read it again. I think you are very much on the right trail, and I hope we may soon have a talk,- By the way, if Edith Pope can carry through the most difficult chapters of her book as well as she has the earlier ones and the greater part of the book, she will come out very well indeed. I am suggesting that she change the title from "Abby" —which is rather trivial and narrow—to "Colcorton".

Maxwell Perkins. By permission of University of Florida Libraries.

Give my remembrances to your husband. There is no need to tell him that I respect his action, for any man would.

Yours always,

. . . .

625. MKR to MEP (TLS, 6 pp.)

Note summer address:

Crescent Beach, Star Route

St. Augustine, Fla.

Aug. 2, 1943

Dear Max:

Home again, after a more or less satisfactory hegira. I got along fairly well until I headed for Florida, then have been increasingly depressed at coming back to——no Norton. That's one trouble with having an almost perfect husband——anything that happens is too awful. I was delighted to find two letters from him, mailed en route. It seems possible that he is on the *Queen Mary.* Each man in the unit has his own cabin and private cabin boy, and he was enjoying everything immensely. He said that the first night out he heard three torpedoes swish by and just miss the boat. In the morning he found out that it was someone flushing the toilet——.

He wrote: "We all talk like Hemingway characters. Now and then an eight-letter word creeps in, but then you realize it is made up of two four-letter words." His sense of humor will be a life-saver through the mess he is going into. He said he was by far the oldest of the unit, "but they show me no respect." He is crazy about all the men but one, who is a stinker, loathed jointly by all the others.

"Aunt Ethel"[1] proved a fount of knowledge of the rich days on the farm, and had in her possession, to boot, the most fascinating family letters dating back as far as 1822. I spent most of my time reading them, box after box, and studying the old ledgers and account books. It was intriguing to re-create the personalities from the correspondence. Great-aunt Elsie,[2] writing to my great-grandmother, wrote the best letters of the lot, and was up on all current movements and ideas. She asked in 1869 what her sister thought about the women's suffrage convention, the first one ever held. She wrote, "On this subject, I myself am greatly in its favor, and mean to exercise every privilege offered me."

The information I got on my own grandfather,[3] the prototype of the principal character in my book, did not fit in with what I plan to do. My grandfather was much better educated than I realized, much more articulate. This need not throw me off from my original conception of the character I have in mind. I

549

found that he was passionately devoted to music, especially the violin, but was not allowed by his fanatically religious mother to study the instrument. He kept a violin in the hay-loft and slipped off there to play by himself. I shall probably use this angle, as it fits in with my idea of a frustrated artist and man of thought. I was amused and a little shocked to find that both my great-grandmother and her sister, who married my great-grandfather after my great-grandmother's death, were inveterate writers of poetry. I had thought that all my annoying urge-to-expression came from the intellectual Kinnan side, but find I am doubly damned. Out of the welter of religious poetry written by my great-grandmother, there were some telling phrases. Speaking of her own weariness, she wrote, in a verse, "The Savior's heart and hands were weary, too." And she wrote to a grieving sister, "Do not let your sorrow drink your blood"——which is vivid enough for anybody!

They may not enter in my scheme——as I haven't decided yet how far back I shall take the story——but there were marvelous letters from my grandfather's brother, who died in the Civil War. He had a brilliant mind and gave a picture of the war, from the Northern angle, and all its implications, that Douglas Freeman could well have used. And great-aunt Elsie, the politically minded one, wrote my great-grandmother in 1864, I think it was, that prices were high (inflation), and that the copperheads were saying that if Old Abe was elected again, things would be worse. "What do you think of that for sound reasoning!" she wrote.

You will remember that one of the keynotes of my book was to be the consciousness of the principal character of the cosmic set-up. I all but fainted when I found a receipt among my great-grandfather's accounts for a book on astronomy, which my grandfather must have read in detail. I am putting in an order with the Argus Bookshop (Chicago), which has gotten me many rare books, for this one, for it will give me just the slant I want on the principal character's thoughts along cosmic lines. It does seem a strange coincidence, doesn't it? I feel more than ever that what I want to do is "a natural". Yet I know that my bones will have to go through a duck-press to squeeze out the essence of the thing I want to do.

Edith Pope has been spending the week-end at the cottage with me. Entertaining her proved no problem, for a box of new books was delivered, and we have spent our time at opposite ends of the davenport, reading up a breeze.

Please send me any reading matter you can lay hands on.

1. Ethel Traphagen Riggs.
2. Elsie Traphagen.
3. Abram Traphagen.

626. MEP to MKR (TLS: UF, 2 pp.)

Aug. 10, 1943

Dear Marjorie:

Charlie just brought in your telegram about the lawsuit,- so that is off your mind. I know how worrying such things are, how almost impossible they make it for a writer to work,- although I realize, of course, that Tom Wolfe was an extreme example.

What you tell of Norton's observations is very amusing and makes an editor wonder if he might not in the end produce a really human, and humorous, piece of writing on this whole adventure. And if only things go well, a year isn't long. That may be a pity, but it's true.

I am delighted with what you say about all you found in Michigan. What you tell suggests splendid material,- and it is odd that the prototype of your character actually did buy the book on astronomy,- and good that he played the violin. Maybe there is some intuition in this of which you are unconscious.

I ought to get a letter soon from Edith Pope, but I judge she is no longer with you.

It was grand to see you here, and looking so well.

Always yours,

. . . .

627. MKR to MEP (ALS, I p.)

Crescent Beach, Star Route
St. Augustine, Florida
Aug. 11, 1943

Dear Max:

Here is Zora Neale Hurston's letter, which I should like returned.[1]

From lack of a maid (I have a good one coming this week)[2] and business to be taken care of, I haven't settled down to the book yet, but it shapes daily in my mind.

I am at the cottage, and shall be until into October. Do send me books, even fiction.

Wasn't that fine news about the lawsuit? My lawyer says they will probably offer an amended declaration, but he thinks the same judge will almost automatically accept our demurrer. Then they can present it to the Florida Supreme Court——and I have no qualms once it goes that high.

1. Zora Neale Hurston (1903–1960), novelist, close friend of MKR.
2. Sissie Fountain, Martha Mickens's daughter.

551

628. MEP to MKR (CC, I p.)

Aug. 13, 1943

Dear Marjorie:

Herewith is your royalty report,- and it is good to see that all the books are doing well. Our great tragedy was that "South Moon Under" came out at the moment it did and never got its due, but now in the cheap edition it is selling in considerable numbers.

Always yours,

. . . .

629. MEP to MKR (CC, I p.)

Aug. 16, 1943

Dear Marjorie:

Thanks ever so much for letting me read Zora Hurston's letter. She certainly writes good letters, and is obviously a very unusual person. I hope some day you can go on that trip with her. I am returning the letter herewith,- And I am sending you some novels now,- I would have sent them sooner except that I knew you generally avoided fiction when you were about to write, or were writing. I hope you will soon get to it.

Always yours,

. . . .

630. MKR to MEP (TLS, 3 pp.)

Crescent Beach, Star Route
St. Augustine, Florida
Aug. 26, 1943

Dear Max:

Many thanks for all the good books. The James Truslow Adams[1] seems to top them all.

The book you gave me in New York, the one then called "Lest They [Ye] Die,"[2] annoyed me very much. I thought it frightfully cheap. It read like a poor detective story, with no reality, no conviction, no sense of truth or honesty. I think it was the kind of book that suffered from collaboration. Nothing so intimate can be "written up" by outside hack writers.

The Col. Scott book was amazingly good.[3]

It looks as though Norton would reach India or the Middle East in time for Lord Mountbatten's Burmese push.[4]

The office may do it anyway, but will you please have them send me the statement of what my 1943 income will be, approximately?

I have a tentative title for my book——not the final one, but I like to have something to work under and toward. Have been unable to get to work yet, but once I get the income tax thing off, think I can settle down. I finally got a maid to come to the cottage. And what do you think? When I wrote Zora Neale Hurston, thanking her for her letter, I happened to mention that my wonderful maid Idella, whom she knew, had "gone Harlem" and I was in difficulties, as I needed all my energy for a book I was beginning. She wrote back that she was working on a book of her own, but if I got too desperate and found myself losing my stride, she would drop her own writing and come and keep me comfortable until I finished my book. That seems a truly big thing to me. Usually the first thing a Negro does who advances in the world, is to put anything "menial" behind him. It shows a great character in her, I think.

She wrote that she had thought Idella more intelligent, and that she would have recognized a privilege. She said, "But people like you will always be chunking their jewelry into hog pens"——a most engaging version of pearls before swine!

1. James T. Adams (1878–1949), *The American* (New York: Scribners, 1943).
2. Cicely M. Hamilton, *Lest Ye Die.*
3. Peter Scott, British naturalist and explorer.
4. Louis Francis Albert Victor Nicholas, Lord Mountbatten (1900–1979), head of the Southeast Asia Command, commanded the Allied operations against the Japanese in Burma.

· ———————— ·

631. MEP to MKR (CC, 2 pp.)

Aug. 30, 1943

Dear Marjorie:

I am sending you another book though it is a little one,- But soon we shall have some big ones that you will like.

I am writing quickly so that you can get your income estimate in. During the year we shall have paid you in all, $35,613.88. $4,765.06 of this is due on December 1st. The next royalty report will not be rendered until February 1st. Of the total I have given you, $21,128.94 represented royalties for the sale of "Cross Creek" in the last six months. As a matter of fact, you probably have royalty reports which account for all of the total except $55.40 which you wanted, I think, for tickets etc., when you left here after your last visit.

I was delighted to read what you say about the novel, showing that it is developing rapidly and that you were deeply interested in it. I am sure it will turn out well.

Always yours,

Nov. 1, 1943

Dear Marjorie:

Remembering your pleasure in Ellen Glasgow's Introductions, I am sending you a copy of "A Certain Measure"[1] containing those you have seen, and one other,- I hope you have not already bought the book.

I really think that Edith Pope's novel will turn out very well indeed. Other people here are reading it now, and with enthusiasm. She has truly made a character in Abby, the title is to be "Colcorton".

I am sure you are having a hard time,- not only because Norton is way off Heaven knows where, but also because you are going through those agonizing stages of trying to begin a novel,- And it isn't any consolation or encouragement, to one in that state, to remember that they have gone through it before and overcome all the problems. I am only writing in remembrance of how it is with you when you start, from remembrance of the earlier books and the processes of getting them done. I am not asking you any questions at all because I know all will come right in the end, and that it all has to go according to nature,- your nature.

A man who is in the Army in Alaska, a former instructor, sent me some of the poetical passages of Tom Wolfe put into verse form, and they are wonderful.[2] Here is one of them:

The plum-tree, black and brittle,
Rocks stiffly in winter wind.
Her million little twigs are frozen
In spears of ice.

But in the Spring, lithe and heavy,
She will bend under her great load
Of fruit and blossoms.
She will grow young again.

Red plums will ripen,
Will be shaken desperately upon the tiny stems.
They will fall bursted
On the loamy warm wet earth.

When the wind blows in the orchard
The air will be filled with dropping plums;
The night will be filled
With the sound of their dropping.

And a great tree of birds will sing,
Burgeoning, blossoming richly,
Filling the air also
With warm-throated, plum-dropping bird-notes.

I knew that such as this could be done, and before we published "The Face of a Nation" considered it.

But there is that strange repulsion with Americans to verse form. I thought we could do better by keeping "The Face of a Nation" in the form of prose,- Sometimes I wonder if I wasn't mistaken,- But we can and may still publish Tom's pure poetry in verse. I suppose everything must be very much upset down where you are. Louise and I have really had less trouble out of the war, apart from our children etc., than anybody. We have two nice old colored maids who wouldn't dream of working in plants, and a Scotch waitress who has a family and can't leave them, who comes in by the day. And as you know, we live right next to the railroad station and so don't care whether we have gas or not.

Have you had further word from Norton? I have always felt ashamed that terribly cold night when I had only a block to walk and he had only a raincoat, that I did not give him my overcoat.

Always yours,

1. Ellen Glasgow, *A Certain Measure* (New York: Harcourt, Brace, 1943).
2. John S. Barnes, *A Stone, a Leaf, a Door* (New York: Scribners, 1945).

. . . .

633. MKR to MEP (TLS, 2 pp.)

Cross Creek
Hawthorn, Florida
Nov. 13, 1943

Dear Max:

Your letter was a great consolation to me, and on the strength of it, I took myself by the nape of the neck, lifted myself by my boot-straps, and began the book. There is something most peculiarly wrong with it so far——not quite two chapters. It is stiff, it is stilted, it is cold. I can't tell whether the two characters so far, the man and his mother, come to life or not. I have begun it just before his marriage, and won't know until the end, perhaps, whether I should go farther back into his boyhood. But if I take him slowly through a long life, it seems at the moment better not to begin needlessly early. I shall do three or four chapters, then send them to you for your opinion as to what is wrong. I feel so incompetent, as though I were writing a book, writing anything, for the first time. I am probably trying to go too fast, and not squeezing it out word by word, as I have known I must do. But it is certainly better to have begun, for once I have something tangible to work with, I can re-write.

And don't send me any more modern fiction! I have been depressed by the numbers of *able* but *mediocre* books, and have a horror of contributing to the list. They all have approximately the same style, adequate and undistinguished. It is a pernicious style, too, and reading too much of it has a lethal effect.

I thought "Indigo" was a splendid job——it should never have been condensed for the *Atlantic*. I sent it to Norton in one of his Christmas boxes.

I can't tell you how happy I am that Edith Pope's book has come out well. Charlie writes me that he thinks it will have a good sale, too. I felt it was asking a great deal of you even to read it, to say nothing of working intensively with her. But I have always had a conviction that she has something of real genius, and I felt she was at a cross-roads <with> in her work, and if she was not helped at this moment, she would be lost forever as an artist. B[ut] doing something right, now, and having it well received, should start her on a career of tremendously fine work. Her insight into people is amazing. She needed only to develop the technique of transferring her own understanding to the written word. And I *knew* that if she had anything at all of value in the book to start with, <that> she could absorb your criticism as dry earth absorbs rain. She was parched and *ready* for just what you had to give.

After some hesitation, I passed on to Norton your suggestion that he might do something humorous about his experiences. I was afraid it might make him self-conscious, for his wit has always flowed as naturally as a spring bubbles. He tells a wonderful story of a woman who introduced him to her dowager mother, explaining what a famous wit and humorist <was> he was. She joined their hands together and said, "Now Norton, be funny for Mother."

His letters are perfectly delightful.

. . . .

634. MEP to MKR (TLS: UF, 2 pp.)

Nov. 22, 1943

Dear Marjorie:

Here is the royalty report on "Cross Creek Cookery" and you will accordingly in March receive a very considerable sum. What's more, I should think this would be a book that would continue to sell for a long time.

I am glad you sent "Indigo" to Norton for I suppose he is likely to go to India—I keep hearing of men in that service going there—and in that case it would be especially interesting to him.

I really enjoyed very much working on Edith Pope's manuscript,- which in the beginning seemed to me to be almost totally hopeless, but the reason was that she had not really made up her own mind which of several stories she was writing. Once that was determined, everything went well enough.

I agree with you about the run of even the better fiction now,- but I don't think I myself have sent you anything for many months except "Indigo".

As for your own book, I am eager to read whatever you can send me, and I look forward to receiving it. Of course this book would necessarily be even more of a struggle than any of the others, I should say.

Always yours,

. . . .

635. MKR to MEP (TLS, I p.)

Hawthorn, Florida
Nov. 23, 1943

Dear Max:

My work so far is such a mess there's no point in letting you see it. I have about come to the conclusion that I shall have to go back several years earlier in the man's life. One trouble seems to be that I find myself having to interrupt the narrative to explain too much about him, about his background, and why he is as he is, etc., matter that should come out more casually. It might be a good idea in any case to begin at the same age <of> as the grandson at the time the book ends——that would give a complete cycle, and one would have the sense of continuity of lives.

The work so far loses the sense of reality almost the moment I begin to establish it, and I think it is because the scene was never properly set, in advance.

1944

636. MEP to MKR (TLS: UF, 2 pp.)

Jan. 11, 1944

Dear Marjorie:

You did send us the most wonderful oranges ever, and the only reason Louise hasn't written you to thank you for them is that I keep forgetting to bring her your address, and never can quite remember it when I am home. I can remember it now, but I never can get a name when I want one,- although Professor Copeland, who remembered millions of names, said all you have to do is let down a bucket in your subconscious and bring it up. I know what he means, but I can't do it with names.

I do hope you are hearing from Norton and that his letters are as amusing as the pieces you quoted to me.

Edith Pope is in New York somewhere. She came in when I was away last week, and she saw Charlie.- But I want very much to talk to her and to see what she plans in writing. She really brought something very fine out of that last manuscript.- The trouble with it was simply that she did not know which of several stories she meant to tell, and once she agreed upon which one it was, all went very smoothly indeed. She has a talent.

How are things going now with the book? I am sure you will find the way to manage it, but I know you have got to go through a lot of suffering in the process. Whenever you want, we shall be eager to read any part of it.

Always yours,

Hawthorn, Florida
Jan. 13, 1944

Dear Max:

I have not written you, out of shame. I made a new beginning on the book yesterday, and while it is not as bad as the other, it is still anything but right. The book haunts me, I wake up in the night and think about it, and I do not know whether I simply am not ready, or whether my general mental distraction is to blame. I have never gone through a more mentally disorganized period in my life. I hope that I am about to come out of it.

For one thing, I think it has been necessary to shake free from the facts and true characters that first suggested the book to me. The truth was not making me free but was chaining me! I shall do better to keep to the basic conception and use more imagination in dealing with the characters. My subject matter is too big for me and my only salvation will be in working slowly and carefully. I seem to be faced with a great block of marble, from which I must chip out, fragment by fragment, my concept.

Thank you for the Santayana.[1] I read it in the Atlantic, probably cut, and have read it cursorily in the book form. I intend to read it again with great care, for I seem alone in considering it entirely trivial, compared with the bigness of the man's other work and general mentality. It has to me the great flaw of most autobiographies, a listing, for personal satisfaction, of utterly dull details. An autobiography must have either the abandoned subjectiveness of a Rousseau, or the same selective objectivity as fiction, to be effective. Santayana is neither frank and revealing, nor properly selective. Perhaps the next volume will be more so.

Martha Gellhorn's book,[2] for which I also thank you, is a most exciting job. It is not "literature", yet it has almost a Conradian quality and is as fascinating reading as I have met in many a day. I wish you had edited out a few Hemingway-isms——"He felt wonderful", etc. They are inconsistent with her generally very good and effective style. But it is really a splendid job and I am proud of her. The characterization of the girl is a fine and sensitive piece of work.

Norton is in actual battle action. He makes one five-hour trip a day alone, hauling wounded in his ambulance. I do not know where he is, but my guess is, near the India-Burma border. My inability to dismiss him from my mind for a moment is of course a great factor in not getting down to the proper concentration on my work.

My good maid Idella has returned to me from New York, so I am more comfortable.

I hope you have missed the flu.

1. George Santayana, *The Background of My Life* (New York: Scribners, 1944).
2. Martha Gellhorn, *Liana* (New York: Scribners, 1944).

. . . .

638. MEP to MKR (TLS: UF, 2 pp.)

Jan. 19, 1944

Dear Marjorie:

I am terribly sorry that you are having such a bad time. I can imagine how the truth could have chained you, and I should think that you were taking the right course. I can only hope all goes well with Norton,- and don't you think that humorous people are lucky in these kind of things? If they are, it is for a real reason, of course, and I don't know exactly what that would be, but it seems to me that it is true.- Not that I knew he was humorous, except by something in his looks at the time I met him. But Edith Pope was also telling me so. I had lunch with her a few days ago. I had meant to take her to a French restaurant on 53rd Street, and not to Cherio's because that negro writer, Roy Ottley, goes there—and I think he is greatly hurting the place—but there were too many waiting at the French place, and we did go to Cherio's and there was Roy Ottley with his back to us.[1] But Edith Pope said she did not mind, and said it convincingly. I do hope it was true. I guess it was.

Charlie Scribner had a bad fall, and broke a rib and maybe broke something else too. But he makes light of it on the telephone, and expects soon to leave on a vacation.

I'll have some books for you soon.

Always yours,

1. Roi Ottley (1906–1960), journalist and social historian.

. . . .

639. MEP to MKR (TLS: UF, 2 pp.)

March 15, 1944

Dear Marjorie:

How are you making out? I am sending you a quite amusing book about exploration. I think Edith Pope's book which I suppose she will have sent you, is going to be a distinct success. It has a most excellent review in the daily Times, and the editor of the Book Supplement is profoundly impressed by it.- He brought up the subject, not I. We have printed 15,000.- And naturally we are most grateful to you for having headed her in our direction.

I had lunch the other day with Marcia Davenport, who asked about you,- but I could not tell her much of anything. She has a very good idea for another novel, with large dimensions, but not so large as those of the Valley.[1]

I know you are not having any fun now, but I wish you could send me a line or two to say how things are.- I don't mean about the book, for you would tell me about that when you were ready, but about you and yours.

Always yours,

1. Marcia Davenport, *East Side, West Side* (New York: Scribners, 1947).

. . . .

640. MEP to MKR (TS for wire)

MARCH 22, 1944
MRS. NORTON BASKIN
ISLAND GROVE, FLORIDA
MUST COMMUNICATE WITH EDITH POPE. HAVE YOU HER ADDRESS?
SPLENDID REVIEWS IN SUNDAY'S TIMES AND TRIBUNE.

. . . .

641. MKR to MEP (wire)

1944 MAR 23 PM 4 39
MAXWELL PERKINS—
597 FIFTH AVE NEW YORK NY—
EDITH SHOULD REACH COLORADO TODAY AFTER FEW DAYS IN FLORIDA.
HER ADDRESS IS ONE ONE TWO SEVEN NORTH MAINE STREET PUEBLO
COLORADO[.] SUGGEST YOU SEND DUPLICATE MESSAGE CARE CAPT
VERLE POPE T A V A A B PUEBLO. AM UTTERLY THRILLED OVER HIGH
QUALITY AND SUCCESS OF BOOK[.] I TOO AM ILL ABOUT BOYD BUT DID
NOT KNOW ABOUT THOMASON—[1]

1. Verle Pope, Edith Pope's husband. Both James Boyd and John Thomason died in 1944.

642. MKR to MEP (ALS, 3 pp.)

Hawthorn, Florida
March 29, 1944

Dear Max:

I haven't written you, because I have been living in the damndest apathetic vacuum. Work has been impossible. This was fortunate as far as Julia's visit was concerned, for she stayed longer than was planned. I still long to be writing, and shall go back to my manuscripts shortly, to see what is possible. But I am afraid that I won't be able to write until Norton is safe home, or if that worst happens, for a year or two after——.

I have had news that is most disturbing, to put it mildly. American Field Service headquarters in New York, and a news item on page 14 of the Sunday N.Y. Times of March 26——please look it up, for complete information—— informed me that the unit to which Norton was attached was cut off by the Japs in Burma, was ordered to abandon ambulances and equipment and make their way back to the British lines as best they could. Five men walked down a river bed for two days, under constant fire by Jap snipers, one man being "slightly wounded" by shrapnel. The report said that "others were presumed to have reached stronger British forces in an isolated forward position." I have no way of knowing whether Norton was among the five, or was the one slightly wounded, or was one of those presumed to have reached the advanced British outpost and is not yet reported.

Later

A wire just came from A.F.S. headquarters in New York that they had just had a cable saying the men were all "presumed" to be safe——which still does not account for those supposed to have gone to the forward British post. But I *feel* that Norton is all right.

It is all too hideous.

The bright spot in life at the moment is Edith's book. I hope you will give it some advertising, as I think it needs only to be called to people's attention to be bought and read and enjoyed. It is a beautiful job, and I am proud of my modest share in it. I think you will find that Edith learned from working with you, as I did on "South Moon Under", and will never wander in a fog again, but turn out splendid work from now on.

I have just gone over the two separate drafts I began on the book, and they are worse than I remembered! I don't think the trouble is entirely my anxiety about Norton and the war. Something is deeply wrong with the material. I still feel that if I could get off on the right foot, I could work like mad. Sooner or later I'll hit on what is wrong——and what would be right——and go at it.

I am very well physically.

Please do send me two copies of Edith's book, one for me and one to send to Norton. She received only one of the six copies coming to her, and did not have one to give me. While she was in Florida for a few days I read her one copy, which she had signed for her husband.

· ·

643. MEP to MKR (TLS: UF, 2 pp.)

April 10, 1944

Dear Marjorie:

I hope you let me know anything you learn definitely about Norton. I have somehow got to feel as if I know him, and that he has become my friend even on the basis of one meeting and of what people have told me about him. I do hope the news will be good.- If only he did come out of that adventure safely, it will have been something to remember.

I have just had a letter from Edith Pope. Her letters are always very good, but she is hard to reach, though I got her promptly after your wire came. I can't make out whether it is that my letters are still trailing her, but she should answer me on some business matters, such as whom to have for an agent. Katharine Cornell[1] is very much excited about the book and has asked us not to dispose of the dramatic rights until we hear definitely from her. She is having someone put the book into play form. The sale goes on well. And Mrs. Pope expects to be back in St. Augustine about the 18th. Her plan for a novel is very interesting.

It is too bad you have to struggle so with this material,- partly, of course, because of the fact that it is so different from what you have used before. But I suppose it is possible you may hit your stride at any moment.

Always yours,

1. Katharine Cornell (1898–1974), American actress.

· ·

644. MKR to MEP (TLS, 1 p.)

Hawthorn, Florida
April 17, 1944

Dear Max:

Edith Pope was originally due here yesterday, but I did not hear from her, so I know she broke her trip by stopping off in Mississippi. I should have word from her today, and really expect her today or tomorrow. I'll set her right down and have her write you. I am sure that you can reach her here in the next few days. Toward the end of the week, we'll probably go to my cottage at St. Augustine, and care of Ocean Manor[,] St. Augustine[,] would be your best bet for reaching her after that. In case you haven't contacted her about it, I'll tell her that you wanted to know about an agent etc.

Norton is safe, at least for the moment. But the Burma news is so bad that his safety seems only a temporary reprieve. He writes that he will not re-enlist when his time is up September first, as when he went in he said he would be a one-year man, and he said that he feels he has been useful enough, and will be for the rest of the time, to salve his conscience as to his duty.

I wasn't too enthused about the profile of you in the *New Yorker*.[1] It didn't have the barbs they often let loose on their "profiles", but on the other hand, it missed a great deal that is interesting about you. It seemed to wander off into a discussion of the publishing business, instead of keeping to the warmer human element.

If the house guests ever stop coming, I really think I can get down to work. I always work best in the summer, anyway, probably because there are fewer interruptions, and I look forward to the months at the cottage, at work. The two beginnings I made before are still unbelievably bad, but an approach has come to me, a certain feeling about it, that may be right. The fact that in spite of both my disgust, and the fret and nag of my anxiety about Norton, the book haunts me and descends on me when I wake up in the night, must show that it is something I really want to do.

Thanks for your patience and understanding.

1. Malcolm Cowley, "Unshaken Friend," *New Yorker* 20.7 (April 1, 1944): 28–32, and *New Yorker* 20.8 (April 8, 1944): 30–34, 36, 39–40.

. . . .

645. MEP to MKR (TLS: UF, 4 pp.)

April 19, 1944

Dear Marjorie:

I am delighted to hear about Norton, and I hope he will stick to his decision and come back in September. I didn't realize that the time was so far off though. I had figured that his year was all but up now.

As to the Profile, I thought I got off pretty well, and was very glad that Cowley did wander off more or less into a discussion of publishing instead of me. It is making plenty of trouble though,- all kinds of manuscripts come in to me on the theory that I was created to put them into publishable shape.- And because of the remark that one can tell as much by seeing an author as by reading the manuscript, all sorts of authors insist on being seen as well as read. But it did one very fine thing.- Very old, and ill, Mrs. John Leal, the widow of the school teacher I mentioned, in Plainfield, N. J., was simply delighted, I am told. The Plainfield paper told of the Profile and of the fact that John Leal who was so much admired in the town, was referred to. I had always felt I let John Leal down, and I was glad of this.

My grandson, who is five, was looking at the illustrations in the original edition of "The Yearling" and asked me about the story, so I partly read, and partly told him a good deal of it, and when it came to how poor Jody had to shoot Flag, he was extremely distressed. He understood though, that they could not live if Flag was at large. He sat for a long time pondering the problem of confining Flag successfully, looking almost like an old man while in thought.- And then he suddenly brightened, and said, "They could keep him from jumping the fence with chicken wire stretched over a pen." But I told him Penny couldn't get chicken wire, even if there was any in those days, so then he sank back into thought, and finally he shouted, "They could get rope and stretch a net over." He thought that solved the problem, and it made it seem as if it had happened, to him, and he was happy again. I shouldn't have told him the story until he was old enough to read it all.

I am enclosing a copy of an ad of "Colcorton" which goes into The Saturday Review. We would advertise it more, much more, except that we are rationed in advertising too. You can't tell what you can get into the paper, but very little, comparatively.

I am simply delighted by what you said of your novel.

Always yours,

. . . .

646. MEP to MKR (TLS: UF, 1 p.)

May 2, 1944

Dear Marjorie:

I just now heard from Hamilton Basso of that terrible fire,[1] and I know how it must trouble you. I want to say how deeply sorry I am. It will grieve Norton too, but in a way I am glad he was not there when it happened.

Always yours,

1. At the Castle Warden Hotel, in which two people died.

Hawthorn, Florida
May 3, 1944

Dear Max:

I just had an amusing (to me) letter from my wild friend Dessie, the young woman who took the St. John's River trip with me. She is a lieutenant in the WACS, quite the perfect place for her, and she informed me that I was failing in my duty, not particularly to my country, but to literature. She wrote, "Kid, you're making the biggest mistake of your life, not getting into the war. You were able to write about Florida and the Crackers with such understanding, because you lived the life. You must get into the war, so that you'll understand all that is at stake, and then you must write about that." She stopped to see me a few weeks ago on her furlough, and damn near had me, Idella my colored maid, and Moe my bird-dog, in the WACS. She worked on me to join, and I said laughingly, "Oh, I couldn't leave Moe and Idella." She pointed out that Idella could join the colored WACS, and something could certainly be done about Moe. I have been expecting her to show up with an order from a General, designating Moe as a WAC mascot, leaving me no exit. It will be almost impossible to explain to Dessie that I should never write about war, except as an incidental influence on the people I should fictionize.

Edith Pope arrived at the Creek from Colorado when her husband left to go overseas. The bus she arrived on, which I met in Gainesville, was four hours late, having blown its tires and caught fire, en route. The first day she was here she wandered out in the yard and called to me, with her slow drawl, "Marjorie, what sort of snake has black and yellow and red bands? Goodness, it's pre-e-etty!" I answered casually, "Probably a ribbon, or garter, snake. If by chance it has a black nose, it's a coral snake." Edith is completely near-sighted, and I went out to the yard. She had her face with its beautiful big brown myopic eyes, practically in the face of——a coral snake. I called to Idella to bring my gun and shot its head off, and it was not only the largest coral snake I have ever seen, but the first I have seen around here in several years. The next evening we took a walk up the road, and she investigated a piece of rubber tubing that proved to be a small cottonmouth moccasin. I told her she'd better go home, as she was too dangerous to have around!

She has just had a cable that her husband has arrived safely—almost certainly in England. She is now in St. Augustine.

Max, I have never taken such a beating as in the last few weeks. I put in more than two weeks, not knowing whether Norton was dead or alive, and it almost floored me. I have heard from him directly, and he was one of the American

Field Service men who drove his ambulance through to an isolated forward British post. He got out by the skin of his teeth, with his ambulance loaded to the roof, and lost all his personal belongings. He wrote that he wondered what little yellow so-and-so was wearing the Tibetan lama's brocaded robe he had bought for me, to use as an evening wrap! On his furlough, just before the near-encirclement, he had been up near Tibet, in sight of Mt. Everest. His sense of humor, thank God, is still rampant, and in his last letter he said that after his day's run he had been playing poker at the base, and set out for his ambulance, half a mile away, "for censorable reasons", in the bright moonlight, <with> gaily swinging two bottles of American beer that had been issued. He said that the guards just now were very much on the alert, and he was suddenly halted and found himself looking down a rifle barrel. He couldn't remember the pass-word, but said, "This is a friend, friend. I can't remember the pass-word, but will two bottles of American beer do just as well?" The British Tommy guard said, "You're damn well right they will", and Norton said he continued on still gay, but swinging nothing.

I had no sooner caught my breath from his narrow escape, when I was called to St. Augustine. A disastrous fire swept through one wing of the Castle Warden, killing two women——the woman in whose room the fire started, where presumably she fell asleep with a lighted cigarette——and a dear friend of ours who was using our pent-house apartment. I wouldn't go through such a week again for a king's ransom. One other friend and I had to take care of all the details for the friend who died, and I had to keep the hotel manager, who was devoted to our friend, from going entirely to pieces, and had to take care of insurance details etc. It was a nightmare.

I suffered as to whether I should write Norton about it, but the A. P. sent the story all over the country, including New York and Chicago, and I was afraid someone would mention the catastrophe to Norton, in writing him, in such a way as to upset him worse than the truth, so I wrote him the details.

My lawyer wrote me that he was uneasy as to not having a decision in Zelma's law-suit from the Florida Supreme Court, and it seemed ominous to him, but his partner, a much older man, said he was sure the Court had already given us a favorable decision, and that the Judge assigned to write the verdict was engaged in producing a literary masterpiece in keeping with the literary tone of the suit! Well and good, but he could just as well be engaged in producing a literary masterpiece against us!

If life ever calms down a bit, I still think I can go ahead on the book. It is entitled, tentatively, "Earth and Sky." That title will probably not stand, but at the moment it covers my theme. Please tell Whitney and Charlie how thrilled I have been to see the good ads for "Colcorton", and I hope and believe they will pay off.

I think I was right in feeling that while Norton is a born narrator, he could not write consciously——or self-consciously. He had a story in the India publication of the Field Service, and while it was not bad, he would have written of the incident to me with much more natural vivacity. The other day he enclosed a story for me, of an experience of his youth and it was so bad that I was embarrassed. I wrote him that, so help me God, I should quit him if he came home writing stories. I said that it was hellish enough to be burdened with the delusion that *I* could write, without having him get off the boat, bringing, like a rat carrying the Bubonic plague, the delusion that *he* could write!

. . . .

648. MEP to MKR (TLS: UF, 3 pp.)

June 8, 1944

Dear Marjorie:

Edith Pope called me up yesterday, having just arrived in New York, and I am to have lunch with her today.- But she told me by phone that things were well with you on the whole, and that you had recently heard from Norton who, though disturbed about the fire, of course, was in good shape otherwise.- I had thought that perhaps even the fire would not much disturb him, for when a man gets into the Army all those civilian matters seem to drop out of his mind, and I hope that he was much less disturbed than he would otherwise have been. I can understand what you say as to his writing,- that when he comes to do it, with the consciousness that he is writing, he loses much that came spontaneously.

Anyhow, I am glad you are not a WAC, and I hope you can go ahead with the novel. I have a very fine book I should like to send you, but there is too much war in it for you to enjoy reading it now,- though I am sure you would greatly admire it.

Hemingway was here for about two weeks or so, and then flew to England. You probably read of his accident, but it seems likely only to have given him another scar,- and he looks better for his scars. He looks better too, for a magnificent gray beard, though he grew it only for protection against the sun and the wind, for he has been living the seafaring life apparently, for several years,- that is, coastal seafaring in tropical waters. He says he has absolutely got to get to writing soon, and he knows what he wants to write. He got out of the hospital after not more than a day or two, and cabled that he was back at work,- and just about in time for the invasion. Martha Gellhorn is also in England, also for Collier's. She went by convoy and wrote Charlie quite impressively about that form of travel in the midst of an endless fleet.

I am looking forward to lunch with Edith Pope, for she will be able to tell me more about how things are at Cross Creek. She is to be or perhaps already has been, interviewed for a feature story in the World Telegram.

Always,

. . . .

649. MKR to MEP (TLS, 3 pp.)

Crescent Beach, Star Route
St. Augustine, Florida
June 20, 1944

Dear Max:

I have agreed with Macmillan, short of signing a contract, to do for them in the indeterminate future a presumably definitive book on Florida, in a projected series they are planning, to be called "The Epic of America." I wrote them that I considered the scheme asinine, bombastic, juvenile and futile, but that no one had ever "done" Florida to suit me, and if time was no object, I should prefer to botch the job myself, to having someone else bungle it. I told them I had two books in mind that would take perhaps ten years altogether. I could conceive of enjoying doing such a book when I was at loose ends creatively. Does it sound reasonable to you?

I can draw a breath about Norton for a while, for he is on leave, and while he wrote June 5 from Calcutta, hoped to get up into the Vale of Kashmir. He thumbed a ride out of Assam on an American mail plane. He had to dodge a British Colonel, to get out; an amazing character of whom everyone stands in terror, but who corners Norton to tell him details of his frustrated life. He had been saving a bottle of choice whiskey for a session with Norton and said he would get him on a plane in a day or two to take his leave, but when Norton found an American pilot who knew a flyer friend of ours, he cleared out, waving good-bye to the astonished and still frustrated Colonel. I do hope he gets to Kashmir. He will have only July and August to put in, and with the monsoons in full force, I do not see how there can be much activity then.

Contrary to your expressed hope, the men in action seem to dwell more on home and personal elements than we do, and the news of our friend's death in the hotel fire made him literally ill.

I had been feeling that I had wasted my time for the past year, but I decided that it was the world that was wasting its time, and not I. I have done intensive thinking.

I moved over to my cottage on the ocean last week, and Crescent Beach, St. Augustine, will be my address for the rest of the summer. I plan to go to New York in the fall to meet Norton on his return, and will probably be there a couple of weeks before he arrives.

Edith Pope wrote me that the doctors had you on vitamins instead of cocktails. My sympathy!

. . . .

650. MEP to MKR (TLS: UF, 4 pp.)

June 23, 1944

Dear Marjorie:

There is this you should consider: your position as a writer is such that it is not an advantage to be in a series—as it is to lesser writers often, and very good ones—but only to the advantage of the series;- and a book by you on Florida would be much better all by itself, and could be, I should suppose, much more what you wanted to make it. I am simply telling you this because it is the truth,- for in general, we have always thought that a writer should be free in every respect to contribute a work to a series. Even when we have had options that could stand in the way of this, we have never used them.

I had quite an argument with Struthers Burt because he objected to a book on grounds of conventional morality, and when I told him that writers and editors should leave such matters to the clergy and others, because their allegiance was to talent, he said I was a sadist.- So maybe you will agree with him when I say that though I hate to think of your suffering about getting a book under way, and getting reoriented, I still do think that that suffering is good, and in the end productive to such a book. So perhaps I am not as sympathetic as I should be. I know good will come of it all in time.

Norton seems to have a gift for adventure, and I hope he does get to that place which always—mostly because of its name, alone—seemed to me more desirable than Paradise.- The Vale of Kashmir.

I am on vitamins,- but can have two cocktails a day, and I sometimes take three over weekends. Louise jockeyed me into a thorough going over, which I never would have consented to had I known what was planned. When I found what I was in for, I protested against it;- I said I would need a couple of weeks to get into good shape, which amused the nurses, who thought the time to see a doctor was when you were in bad shape. But to my astonishment, I seem to be remarkably O.K. in all the important things.- It was just—the doctor said—

that I was getting at least one-third of my nourishment from alcohol. It wasn't that I was really drinking heavily, but that I was not eating nearly enough, and wouldn't if I didn't cut down. I don't mind it anyhow. It was really with me just that two or three cocktails would make one less aware of the passage of time, and let one think and ponder in a leisurely way. Everything moves too fast nowadays, and John Barleycorn slows things up. I had always thought that if I got very old, I would take up hashish, which completely destroys the sense of time, so that you can sit in eternity.

Yours,

. . . .

651. MKR to MEP (TLS, 4 pp.)

Crescent Beach, Star Route
St. Augustine, Florida
July 10, 1944

Dear Max:

I know you will be glad that I am not going to do the book on Florida for the Macmillan series. I had a letter from Mr. Brett saying that Roderick Peattie[1] had been far off the beam in telling me there was no hurry, that the Florida book should be the first of the series, to keep the chronological order of the development of the United States. I wrote him that that eliminated me altogether, and I recommended three other Florida writers who, I felt, would do a good job. If he takes one of them, I shall feel all right about it. I was really only willing to do the job to keep from turning it over to someone like Theodore Pratt,[2] for instance, who would do superficial work.

I seem to be fated to be interfered with on my book. I made a third beginning that seemed much more closely keyed, in style and tone, to what I want, and felt I could really go ahead. I brought down a good stenographer to catch me up on the usual piles of correspondence, that nag at me when I want to give my mind to real work, and I had the slate clear.

The very next day the 84-year-old "adopted" aunt (the widow of my ex-husband's mother's uncle!) who has become my responsibility for the last ten or twelve years, solely because of the awful and exigent claim made by one who has nobody else at all and who clings to me and centers her life around my comings and goings, was asked to leave the very lovely small boarding house where she has been living, as the landlady wants to close the house for the summer and does not know her fall plans. Also, I am sure that "Aunt Ida" had driven her all but insane, as she does me. But there was nothing for it but to pack her up and bring her to my cottage.

The housing problem is serious here as everywhere, and I was in despair. By the grace of God, I have found a little apartment for her with which she is delighted and where she will be very happy, certainly as happy as any place away from me. (The landlady said to me, "I suppose you know what she really wants. She wants to live with you." I knew it, but will do anything for her *except* that.) Some repairs have to be made on the apartment, and I don't know how long it will take. I am hoping it will only be a couple of weeks. But it is getting so close to the time when Norton will leave India for home, and if he can come at least part-way by plane, may arrive in September, that I am afraid I won't be able to keep my mind on my work when I do get back to it.

It is impossible to work with the old lady in the house, for while she keeps saying, "Now, I'm not going to bother you," she can't resist interrupting me, usually to say something like, "Mrs. White made chili sauce and it was too sour, and now she has to take it all out of the jars and add sugar and cook it again and put it back." Since I have heard each such news item several times before, the irritation is extreme. She is a very amusing old lady in many ways, especially because of her Malaprop-isms. She informed me that a certain old man had finally died, after lying for a week in a semi-comma. Having often lain myself for a week in a semi-comma, I was all sympathy. Just now she is reading "Grapes of Wrath",[3] and she looked up from her book a few minutes ago to say, "This is a wonderful book for anyone to read, that's moving."

I agree with the nurses that it is very funny for you to want to get in good shape before a medical examination! I hope you're feeling all right.

1. G. P. Brett, Jr., president of Macmillan; Roderick Peattie, an editor.
2. Theodore Pratt (1901–1969), novelist, who once bragged that he had written twenty-two books about Florida.
3. John Steinbeck (1902–1968), *The Grapes of Wrath* (New York: Viking, 1939).

. . . .

652. MEP to MKR (TLS: UF, 3 pp.)

July 27, 1944

Dear Marjorie:

I know all about such a situation as that with regard to people who become dependent upon you, because it is always happening to Louise,- in fact that was one reason we moved away from New Jersey—and in truth it happens to some considerable extent with me. You get to like the people, and they are yours, or you are theirs. But anyhow, I hope you have established this adopted aunt in comfortable quarters outside your own.

I did get myself laid up, but not with anything painful, or apparently serious.- But it does seem to indicate that I ought to take a vacation. I did take two weeks because I had to, and I did an almighty lot of sleeping. I may try to take some more time in October and go out to my daughter in Ohio, whose husband has bought two saddle horses that need exercising. That's something I'd like to attend to,- the first idea of a vacation that has interested me for many years. This that I had was supposed to be due to fatigue, although I wasn't conscious of fatigue. I suspect it was largely due to the doctor's inducing me to change my habits. Arthur Train said, "Never change your habits."

I have a very good, long letter from Edith Pope, who is well established in Peterborough and very much pleased with it all,- has a cabin that suits her perfectly, in which she says she has spent most of her time sleeping. I daresay that after all the excitement and anxiety about her husband and everything, *she* needed a rest. But she is thinking of attempting the dramatization of "Colcorton" and I am afraid she may just waste her time, as so many, many writers have. The one who did do a scenario of it for Katharine Cornell, simply missed the entire book, and this made Mrs. Pope think she ought to try her hand. I advised her to go no further than the scenario herself, and I really would be glad to hear that she had given up the whole thing, and was planning and pondering about a novel.- And I think that is how it will end.

I am glad you have given up the Florida book, for if you did that, it should be entirely your own book and not in a series.

I hope you are getting good news from Norton. I suspect he is the sort who will find a way of flying back when he is through.

Always yours,

. . . .

653. MEP to MKR (TLS: UF, 1 p.)

Aug. 3, 1944

Dear Marjorie:

I am sending you the royalty report, which I think will please you, for it shows how well the books are continuing in general.

We have been having a terrible spell of heat here. It seemed to be about to end last night when it rained hard, but now it is as bad as ever again. I only hope it is not relatively as hot where you are.- It couldn't be. Whitney told me of your letter to him in which you spoke about Norton, and it would be grand if you should come up here at the beginning of September.

Always yours,

Hawthorn, Florida

Oct. 11, 1944

Dear Max:

Edith Pope arrived last night, in the middle of the night, as always. Her train got in at 2:15 A.M. Why I tell her that I will meet her, I do not know. She said that you were not taking an October vacation as you planned. I had been afraid that I might miss you when I came to New York, but Norton's return is so delayed and so uncertain, that I am sure you will be there if and when I do come.

I have been pulling all sorts of wires to arrange to have Norton flown home if the hospital will release him, and expect news momentarily. A newspaper man visited here yesterday who was a personal friend of the vice president of the Pan-American Airways and we phoned Washington just in case. The same man is expecting Ernie Pyle[1] to arrive in Florida tomorrow and I invited them to come to the Creek. Pyle is a nervous wreck from what he has seen in the war, and I think the peace and quiet of the Creek would be good for him.

Strangely, the death of my friend Wendell Willkie did not upset me. I had had a fatalistic feeling that he was "through", and I am sure he would have preferred to go out like a great light, instead of a small one. He made his impress on our generation, but it was not in the cards for him to do more.

My book will have to wait for some sort of security of my personal life before I can go ahead with it. I have done some short stories, one of which will be in the NEW YORKER soon.[2] Carl Brandt is stuck with another. He sent me the Cosmopolitan's note of rejection——and I could kill him for even submitting it to such people——in which the editor said that they loved the story, but it was too far out of line for them and "would shock the already sagging girdles off our matrons." The irony is that the story is completely moral and literally God-fearing——.[3]

Edith tells me the fascinating news that Martha Gellhorn was the blonde lady of the sonnets of "Rome Hanks".[4] What a joke if Martha picked the wrong genius——. But I was terribly disappointed in Rome Hanks, which you DID NOT SEND ME. It arrived nowhere. Good writing is not enough. There must be form, after the basic artistry, and Pennell does not have this, at least in that particular book. He must learn to be objective and not subjective if he is to be an important writer.

1. Ernie Pyle (1900–1945), journalist and war correspondent.
2. "The Shell," *New Yorker* 20 (December 9, 1944): 29–31.
3. "Miriam's Houses," *New Yorker* 21 (November 24, 1945): 29–31.
4. Joseph S. Pennell (1908–1963), *The History of Rome Hanks* (New York: Scribners, 1944).

Oct. 17, 1944

Dear Marjorie:

The only reason I did not send you ROME HANKS even before it came out was—though now that you do not care much for it, it doesn't matter—that it was too much about war for one whose husband was in the midst of war. I wanted to wait until Norton was safe and sound again. When he gets home let him read it. He has seen battle. I have never known anyone who had seen battle to read that book but they were immensely impressed. I know two who said it actually is war,- and added that that could be said of no other book. As for form, I know that is wanting, but there were reasons peculiar to the case which made its full achievement impossible.- And it has other things that are far less common. Anyhow, I am glad I never was much good in college because a number of the books that I have been peculiarly concerned in publishing would probably have got turned down by us as well as they were by other publishers because they lacked form.

I have realized that your situation was such as to make writing on a larger scale pretty nearly impossible, but I should think it must soon come about that Norton would be got home now. And I am glad you are doing stories anyhow. Won't you ever do one or two more Quincey Dover ones, for then we should have a book all about her.

I only saw Wendell Willkie that one night when you were at dinner at the Davenports too, but he was a real man. He did give a sense of power and depth.- But I would guess too that his career was really ended.

Right now I am laid up with the most idiotic and utterly unknown ailment. I am absolutely well, and just can't get around.- And what's more, I keep getting worse, and worse, and worse. I wish I could see you,- and I did greatly enjoy seeing Edith Pope. She has a quality that always was very rare, but is especially so today, but if I gave a name to it, it would sound silly because of the fashions of the times.

Always yours,

1945

656. MEP to MKR (TLS: UF, 2 pp.)

March 6, 1945

Dear Marjorie:

I have been on the point of writing you many times, and then I always felt as if I would give you the impression that I was checking up on you and your progress. I am not. I know you have had plenty of troubles and difficulties,- And I am writing now only to ask how things are with you and what you are planning. I've heard you made a broadcast from somewhere in the South but I never did get onto the radio well enough to hear any of the broadcasts that I should have heard. Are you likely to come to New York in the Spring? It seems ever so long since I had seen you.

I suppose you read about Hem and Martha,- and then that Hem was planning another marriage. And to a career woman, too,- head of the Paris office of TIME.[1] I have not heard from him since Christmas, and then he only told me about Martha.

Edith Pope has been here for some time, but I only saw her for five minutes,- We are to have lunch on Friday, and I am going to urge her to do that book and let the research go hang until later. She would be happier working, and once she got going I don't think she would find it hard.

The oranges were wonderful. Remembrances to Norton.

Always yours,

1. Hemingway met Mary Welsh Monks in May 1944, and divorced Martha Gellhorn Hemingway on December 21, 1945. He married Monks on March 14, 1946.

Hawthorn, Florida

April 11, 1945

Dear Max:

It was good to hear from you——and please don't ever not-write for fear I'll feel prodded. No one knows better than you, except another writer to whom it does not come easily, that sometimes one cannot be hurried, no matter how long the delay in getting to work.

In the winter, I made still another start on the book, and it was wrong, too. Part of the trouble, of course, is not having had freedom of mind, and also enough solitude. The rest is that something is still not right with my conception, and I shall never force a thing like that again, as I did with "Golden Apples." I woke up last night with something of a new slant, and while I rejected it, I had the feeling that I was coming closer to the road out.

I am moving to the cottage on the ocean at the end of April, and since Norton has taken over the management of the hotel, as the manager is leaving, and will be gone all day and sometimes evenings, too, I think I will have enough peace and privacy. I am staying alone at the Creek for a couple of weeks, and am hoping that I may be able to make my start here. I think that once I feel I have begun properly, I can work even with a few handicaps. I'll let you know.

No, I didn't know about Martha and Ernest until you wrote me. I have heard a little more about it since, but none of it makes too much sense. I was amazed that apparently it was Hemingway who strayed, for I had thought that he would not be able to hold Martha, and that she would be tired of him first. It is so expensive and nerve-wracking for a man to keep *marrying* women! And I do not see why he takes on another woman presumably deep in her own work. A man like Hem admires a woman who can hold her own with him intellectually, but <they> he also likes a domestic establishment run for <their> his sole benefit!

I gather that Julia's approaching marriage to the young clergyman has been a bomb-shell in the family. I know it has to Vera, who is selfishly putting Julia through a big formal wedding, which she hates. Edith Pope did not care for the man, and neither did a most attractive friend of mine of whom I had hopes for a romance with Julia, also an Episcopal clergyman, but a lieutenant-chaplain in the Navy now. They felt he was a bit of a stuffed shirt and had his eye on the main chance. However, I do trust Julia's judgment, for she has been cold to so many suitors, and she is very much in love and says that she and the man have a rare understanding.[1]

You did not say how you are feeling, <and> whether you are taking care of yourself. ? ? ?

Norton is reasonably well, though he tires easily and is upset by things that never disturbed him before. He does complain mildly that I have spoiled my dog Moe in his absence. He said that while he, Norton, is a scion of an old Southern family, and Moe is indubitably a son of a bitch, he thinks that I tend to confuse them——.

Infinite thanks for the new Santayana. It is all and more that one would wish for from him. I can only hope there will be at least three more volumes. I felt I could not get enough of it, and was desolée when "The Middle Span" ended.[2] I must go back to the first volume, which seemed dull. Yet it does seem to me that in the second one he felt more free, and allowed himself to make delicious philosophical observations, was objective, where in the first he was too absorbed in getting down rather meaningless items about his childhood and schooling.

Thank you, too, for the Ray Stannard Baker,[3] whom I know and admire very much as a person, but whose story, especially by the side of Santayana, is worthy and dull——as Hemingway said to me of the women who go in for game-fishing.

My best,

1. Julia Scribner married Thomas Bigham in June 1945. MKR preferred Lieutenant Bertram Cooper, but publicly supported Julia's choice.
2. George Santayana, *The Middle Span* (New York: Scribners, 1945), the second volume of the trilogy *Persons and Places*. Volume 1: *The Background of My Life* (New York: Scribners, 1944); volume 3: *My Host the World* (New York: Scribners, 1953).
3. Ray Stannard Baker (1870–1946), *American Chronicle* (New York: Scribners, 1945).

. . . .

658. MEP to MKR (TLS: UF, 3 pp.)

May 2, 1945

Dear Marjorie:

I know you will find the way in the end, and I know how hard it is for you to struggle toward it, or to wait to find it. When you have it, life will be pleasanter. But a book such as you will do must take quite a long time, even when you are well started. Isn't there a possibility that you might write two or three more Quincey Dover stories? She is a great character, and she should have a book, and it should be to some extent illustrated. I don't know how writing stories fits in with writing a novel, with you, but I wish that book could be done. It should be some day.

Ed Shenton was in here yesterday to show me sketches for illustrations he is doing for A SHROPSHIRE LAD,[1] and I thought them admirable, done in some combination of water color and line. I hope we shall get back to where we can illustrate books as was done in the old days,- and he was saying that such things should be made for CROSS CREEK. But of course I had to say not until after the war, at any rate.

Edith Pope brought in her juvenile about the lizard, the chameleon, and—I haven't seen it—it is thought to be very good, but expensive to make rightly.[2] She really should get at her novel though, and without further delay for research. She knows really what she needs to know, and the details of research are better done later. If they are done first, as sometimes they have to be because the writer knows too little to do anything without the research, the details tend to injure the book. I even thought that Jim Boyd overdid it somewhat with accurate detail in some of his chapters in both DRUMS and MARCHING ON.[3]

I had a very nice note from Martha Gellhorn lately. I think she regarded this episode *as* an episode. It was Hem who insisted on marriage. In fact, I think she has really behaved gallantly in that, and in other things,- I was all against her in the beginning, and was once very rude to her. She forgave that too, which showed generosity.

I am taking it for granted now that Norton is quite OK.

Always yours,

1. A. E. Housman (1859–1936), *A Shropshire Lad.* Apparently the project was not completed.
2. Edith Pope, *The Biggety Chameleon* (New York: Scribners, 1946).
3. James Boyd, *Marching On* (New York: Scribners, 1927).

. . . .

659. MEP to MKR (CC, 1 p.)

July 5, 1945

Dear Marjorie:

I am sending you an ad which, according to plan, will run in one issue of Collier's and one of Life. It seems to me that it is a good ad for three of your books and no more objectionable than any ad. Of course they do not think that the picture they have at the top is yours. They would get a picture from us. If you approve, sign both copies of the permission, and send them back to me. I'll see that the copy is corrected,- for instance, that CROSS CREEK is not called a novel.

The only good news I know is that Edith Pope has begun to write, and has found it goes easily.

My best to Norton.

Always yours,

Crescent Beach
St. Augustine, Fla.
July 18, 1945

Dear Max:

I never heard of anyone's rushing out to buy a book after seeing it mentioned in a wine ad, but if you think it's a good idea, why, all right. Don't they pay anything, or do they figure they are giving enough free publicity? It sort of gives me the creeps, but I suppose it is worth-while to keep a mention before people, especially so far in between books.

I have done several short stories that Carl Brandt and Bernice Baumgarten were enthusiastic about, and Carl hasn't been able to sell a one of them. The New Yorker reported that they felt what I was doing was "terribly experimental", which gives me the feeling that just possibly, it may be good! It is all stuff certainly very different from my Florida stories and books. When I have done a couple more, there would be enough for a book, including the three I have already had in The New Yorker, "The Pelican's Shadow", "Jessamine Springs", and "The Shell". (Did you see "The Shell" in the Dec. 9 New Yorker?) They also will publish soon a story they accepted a year or more ago, "Dark Secret". When I have enough, I'll send them on to you, published or not, for you to see how you like them, with a volume in mind.

I have done five chapters on my latest try at the book, and they are incredibly bad. But I felt my only salvation was to plough ahead, hoping to hit, sooner or later, the proper key. If that comes, it will be easier to go back and re-write the earlier portion. It is mostly a matter of style. I know exactly what I want to say, and so far, have been totally unable to say it in a style that suits me. I may break down and send you what I have done, just to see if you think the characters come to life, and seem worth following, to a reader. You wouldn't be able to help me, as it is all a question of manner and mood.

This morning I woke up wondering if I had a story there, after all. But I must have, or it could not have haunted me so.

By the way, when you provide the wine vendors with a picture, do pick out one with a reasonably pleasant face, not that grim one that is used too often.

Norton hardly gets to the cottage at all, as the help problem makes him uneasy about leaving the hotel. This is of course conducive to work but not to domestic felicity.

My wonderful maid Idella is coming back to me the first of August. She said she guessed we were meant to be together.

661. MEP to MKR (CC, I p.)

July 20, 1945

Dear Marjorie:

Those advertising people have kept calling me up to know about the ad I sent you on July 5th. But this has turned out advantageously because now they offer you a payment of $250.00.

Edith Pope came in the other day with her husband, who seems to have made the most of the war so far as experience is concerned. She will soon be back in your neighborhood.

I hope all goes well.

Always yours,

. . . .

662. MEP to MKR (TLS: UF, 2 pp.)

Aug. 6, 1945

Dear Marjorie:

I certainly did read "The Shell" and I think it is a beautiful story. "The Pelican's Shadow" I admired too, for it was extraordinarily effective. I'll look out for "Dark Secret" but I do think a book could be made of such stories in the end,- Of course, as you know, I have always hoped you would get Quincey Dover into a book. Won't you some time?

I delayed answering in the hope of sending you that check for $250.00, but it has not come. I'll see that it is paid to you.

If you do want to do it, I should be delighted to see the chapters that you have written, but I understand your trouble. The solution may come suddenly. Scott used to say that his always came in his sleep. Anyhow they cannot be got by any process of logic, or anything anyone knows how to control.

I showed the agent your postscript about the use of wine, and it seemed to impress them.

I'm glad that Idella is coming back.

Yours,

. . . .

663. MEP to MKR (TLS: UF, I p.)

Aug. 10, 1945

Dear Marjorie:

Here is the check from the advertising agents. But far better than $250 is the fact evinced in the enclosed letter, that you have made a warm friend of J. Walter Thompson Co. And so have I. Aren't advertising people wonderful!

Always yours,

Crescent Beach, Star Route
St. Augustine, Florida
Aug. 17, 1945

Dear Max:

No, I most certainly do not think advertising people are wonderful. I think they are horrible, and the worst menace to mankind, next to war; perhaps ahead of war. They stand for the material viewpoint, for the importance of possessions, of desire, of envy, of greed. And war comes from these things.

J. Walter Thompson was polite only because we played into their hands. We should not have done it, for profoundly moral reasons. Though the use of wine in cooking is beneficent rather than harmful. It doesn't particularly need advertising. There are people who try to cook well, and they know wine or will discover it; and there are people who do not try to cook well, and all the wine ads in the world will not change them.

I do not see how I can send you what is done on the manuscript. It is too very bad. But I am still plodding ahead, and if I don't burn it first, will eventually send it on to you.

Carl Brandt sold one of my "queer" stories.[1] One of the stories that was rejected was, of all things, a Quincy Dover story.[2] Carl and Bernice Baumgarten were enthusiastic about it and were amazed when Sat. Eve. Post turned it down. It did not have a typical happy ending, which to my notion was its salvation, for I did not care for it, but evidently that was enough for the Post, horrid sheet. They told Carl that the Quincy Dover angle was fine, but the rest of it did not ring true—and "the rest of it" was the true story of my friend Dessie, of "Hyacinth Drift", except for the ending! This only proves what I tell young writers, that the truth is artistically fallacious.

Well, the last time I was at Cross Creek, I was depressed by the condition of the place, the house not clean, since old Martha[3] can only keep up with the stock, making butter, etc., the yard a jungle. And the toilet would not flush. I used it for about eighteen hours, and Martha went to the bathroom to clean. She called out, "There's something in the toilet." I said yes, I knew, it wouldn't flush, and did she have any idea what it might be. "Yessum. Cottonmouth moccasin." It stuck its head up when she sifted in the Dutch cleanser, and stuck it up again when I peered in. I slammed down the lid and blocked the crevices with bath towels and went to Ocala on business. I had hoped to find Ross Allen, Florida's leading herpetologist, to come out and "bring it back alive." Ross was out of town. When I reached home, my good friend Leonard[4] ("Lant" of "South Moon Under") had been out to see me, and laughing like a hyena at

Martha's and my predicament, had speared the moccasin with an ice pick, hauled it out and killed it outside. It was four feet long, and thick enough in the middle to have blocked the toilet. He found a break in the drainage tile where it had gotten in, and fixed that.

Oh, when I told Martha how <said> sad I was at the state of the place, and the moccasin showed up in the toilet, she said, "Sugar, this is the wind-up."

This morning Idella found a small snake under the head of my bed at the cottage. I am reasonably sure it was harmless, though it had a black mask and was not familiar to me. I killed it with a poker.

1. "Miriam's Houses."
2. "Donnie, Get Your Gun!" Unpublished.
3. Martha Mickens.
4. Leonard Fiddia.

. . . .

665. MEP to MKR (TLS: UF, 2 pp.)

August 20, 1945

Dear Marjorie:

Anyhow, could I read the Quincy Dover story? I judge that you don't yourself think highly of it now, but I should like to see for myself if you have a copy handy. The opinion of the Post counts for nothing from our point of view.

As for advertising, I am in complete agreement with you. I was just trying to be sarcastic. I never can get away with that. I have praised people ironically only to hear later on that they had taken me in dead earnest, and were telling others what I had said. I think also that the advertising business is ruinous to the character of those who work in it,- "Subdued to that they work in."

Marcia Davenport finally got herself abroad, and is now, I think, in Czecho-Slovakia. She felt she must go before she could write.

That was an exciting letter. It made me shudder.

Always yours,

. . . .

666. MKR to MEP (TLS, I p.)

Hawthorn, Florida

Aug. 27, 1945

Dear Max:

I should have realized that you were joking about the advertising people. Your comment was so out of character that it was stupid of me not to "get it".

Edith Pope sent me some books from the Scribner shop, and characteristically did not give me an address. If you know where she is, please forward the enclosed, if not, she will drop in some day and you can give it to her.

Carl Brandt has the only decipherable copy of the Quincy Dover story, so you can ask him for it. It really is no good, although Carl and Bernice Baumgarten liked it. Carl said that the POST, in rejecting it, said that <while> where Quincy was involved, it rang true, but the girl did not seem real. It only proves my theory that the truth is unconvincing, for except for the ending, it is the true story of Dessie, of the river trip! I have two more Quincy Dover stories in mind. However, I think a book of my other stories is nearer ready. TOWN AND COUNTRY has taken one,[1] and I have done two more. I should hope for a small succes d'estime on them, but they might alienate some of the readers of the more sweetness-and-light books. Though I hope to God none of them are sloppy. (The s and l books.)

1. "Miss Moffett Steps Out," eventually published in *Liberty* 23.7 (February 1946): 31, 58–61.

. . . .

667. MEP to MKR (CC, 1 p.)

Aug. 29, 1945

Dear Marjorie:

We have Edith Pope's address and have forwarded your letter.

I'll get the story from Carl Brandt anyhow. I am glad you do plan to do others on Quincy Dover for some day we should make a book of her, whatever may come ahead of it.

Always yours,

. . . .

668. MEP to MKR (CC, 2 pp.)

Sept. 27, 1945

Dear Marjorie:

Income tax troubles, and such things as that, kept me from writing you sooner about DONNIE AND THE GUN, although I read it a good many days ago. It does not seem to me successful, though it starts off with great promise. Donnie as a child is good, but after she gets to be seventeen, it seems to me that she becomes less convincing, and in the latter part of the story completely unconvincing. She loses reality. Then too, Quincy Dover does not actually figure much in the story except as a spectator.

On the other hand, I think that BLACK SECRET is very moving indeed, and beautifully told.

Always yours,

(over)

P.S. I know you avoid fiction when you are writing a novel, but one of the books I am sending you, AND THE FIELD IS THE WORLD,[1] is something special, and I am sure you will be interested.

1. Dola DeJong (1911–), *And the Field Is the World* (New York: Scribners, 1945).

. . . .

669. MKR to MEP (TLS, I p.)

St. Augustine, Florida

October 4, 1945

Dear Max:

I knew you would agree with me about the so-called Quincy Dover story. I did hate to have you see it. Sometimes a thing is better than I think, but when I KNOW it is bad, it is bad.

I have done two more "queer" stories and so far Carl has not been able to sell them. One of them I think is all right.

I have laid by the book again, but without undue anxiety. It is truly bad as it stands and I cannot let you see it. Sooner or later the proper approach will come to me, and then it should go rapidly, as the characters and the outline are clear to me.

"Town and Country" took one of the queer stories. Counting the four stories that have been in "The New Yorker", there are seven that I should not be ashamed of, and when I have about ten, I should hope that you would like them well enough to make a book of them.

It is good to have Edith Pope home again. Her husband is out of the Army, and she has been able to work the last few days.

. . . .

670. MKR to MEP (TLS, I p.)

Crescent Beach

St. Augustine, Florida

Oct. 23, 1945

Dear Max:

I heard some ghastly news yesterday that I hope is not true——that N.C. Wyeth and a grand-child were killed at a Pennsylvania railroad crossing.[1] I

585

never knew a happier or more united family, and he was the pivot on which it swung. Do let me know. I remember now with horror the time I drove him back from the Scrub, at night, doing about 85 miles an hour.

I did like "And the Field is the World" so much, and was surprised at the minor reviews. It has a great poignancy and intensity, with something savage in it that is good and valid.

"Teresa"[2] is the type of thing I just don't care for, though it was entertaining after its fashion. I like a straight novel or pure biography, and any combination never seems successful, to my notion.

Editor's note: At bottom left in MEP's hand: "*Portable.*"

1. N. C. Wyeth died on October 19, 1945, at Chadd's Ford, Pa., when a train struck the car he was driving.
2. Austin K. Gray (1887?–1945), *Teresa* (New York: Scribners, 1945).

. . . .

671. MEP to MKR (TLS: UF, 2 pp.)

Oct. 26, 1945

Dear Marjorie:

You must know long before this that the news was true. It's too bad, but anyhow he had done, I suppose, his best work. It is almost worse to think of the grandson whom I had been told about because his mother wrote poetry, for he had not done anything at all. I asked Wyeth some years ago to write a kind of artist's autobiography for what we call "young people". I thought that using his own pictures as examples, pictures which any child could understand, he could begin to show them through what he had done in a way that would particularly interest them because of their fondness for his pictures, what it was to be an artist. I had been on the point of writing him again about that, which he really meant to do, when this news came.

I knew you would like AND THE FIELD IS THE WORLD. I believe it is going to have some very understanding reviews, but certainly the Times muffed it completely. The important thing is not the war, but the nature of the children, of course.

Always yours,

Hawthorn, Florida

Dec. 7, 1945

Dear Max:

In wiring Whitney that my lawyer Philip May[1] wanted a conference with him and Charlie, I did not suggest your joining them, as what he needs is the sales figures in sworn testimony, and I felt you didn't need to be bothered. However, Phil is an awfully nice little chap, and a true friend, and if you have any free time Tuesday morning when he has finished the business, I'd appreciate your having a [moment] for him to drop in just long enough to meet you. I have talked of you so much to him.

Also, I am wondering if Miss Wyckoff keeps carbons of the letters you write me. I have kept all your letters, and one I want now, I cannot find. It is a letter written me at Crescent Beach in the late summer or early fall of 1941, when you had first read the proofs on "Cross Creek", I think. In this letter you said something to the effect that Zelma the censustaker was a wonderful character, and we must have more about her, what she was like etc. It was in response to that, that I wrote the description of her to which she objected——or pretended to object. That letter would be a great help in the suit if you have a copy. Also a later letter saying that now Zelma was fine.

If Miss Wyckoff has it, please have her give it to Mr. May. He was taking the file on the case with him, to do some work on the train. The suit is due for trial in February. SURELY I can work again when that is over and done with!

Did you see a story of mine in The New Yorker a couple of weeks ago, "Miriam's Houses", and if so, did you like it? A rather short volume of stories of that type, "The Shell", "Black Secret", etc., might be interesting in a small way.

1. Philip S. May, Sr., of Crawford and May, Jacksonville, Fla., MKR's attorney and chief counsel for the *Cross Creek* trial.

. . . .

Dec. 18, 1945

Dear Marjorie:

I did read MIRIAM'S HOUSE, just the other day and by chance. It is certainly good. I wish the New Yorker would put the names of authors at the top of stories. I should have read it long ago if I knew it was by you, and I read it not knowing, but soon began to wonder. It is a good story, and I do think a volume of that kind of story should be published ultimately.

When your letter came telling me what I had said about Zelma, it seemed to me that I remembered saying all of it, and especially that we ought to have more of her. But when we searched through the letters, all I could find was the sentence, "Zelma and the census-taking is grand." I must have said the rest either verbally or on the margin of the proof. If it were on the proof, it is gone now forever. Could you tell me anything you remember? Did I see you in New York during the time the book was being written, and after I had read about Zelma? I could have sworn I said just what you say I said, but there is no typed record of it. Tell me what you can. Anyhow, that is what I thought,- One got a very affectionate feeling for the character who was very real, and she was the last character in the whole book I would have dreamed of as making any trouble.

Always yours,

1946

674. MEP to MKR (TS for wire)

MAY 28, 1946
MRS. NORTON BASKIN
C/O SCRUGGS AND CARMICHAEL
GAINESVILLE, FLORIDA
DEAR MARJORIE JUST LEARNED TRIAL IS ON. WE WISH YOU ALL SUC-
CESS IN THIS FIGHT FOR FREEDOM OF EXPRESSION. CHARLIE ABROAD
WANTS ME TO WIRE OUTCOME. MAY YOU WIN FOR US ALL.

. . . .

675. MEP to MKR (TS for wire)

MAY 29, 1946
MRS. NORTON BASKIN
ISLAND GROVE, FLORIDA
MANY THANKS FOR TELEGRAM. GREATLY RELIEVED AND PLEASED.

. . . .

676. MEP to MKR (TLS: UF, 2 pp.)

May 29, 1946

Dear Marjorie:

I didn't know the case had come to trial until Monday. Then Tuesday quite late, when I was reading a manuscript, came your telegram saying you had won. And I slept the better for that. Charlie managed to get off on Saturday, and he wanted to know the outcome, but I think I'll not wire him on the boat, but will write him air mail so that my letter will get to London before he does. I never thought this case could be lost. My brother Edward said that if it were, and went to a higher court, it would be turned down for sure. Just the same, one does worry about such a thing because of the seriousness of it if it should go wrong. I hope we shall hear the details, and perhaps we could use them through Bennett Cerf in The Saturday Review.[1] How dreadful are the law's delays. Think how long this thing has been hanging over! Now I think you will feel free, and be able to write as you want.

Always yours,

1. Bennett Cerf (1898–1971), editor and cofounder of Random House.

. . . .

677. MKR to MEP (TLS, 4 pp.)

Cross Creek
Hawthorn, Florida
June 5, 1946

Dear Max:

I have read the book you sent me, "I Chose Freedom",[1] with profound interest. I began it some time ago, and it sounded "ghost-written" to me, and I dropped it. Then the other night three professors from the University of Florida were here, and we were arguing about Russia, and capitalism, and so on, and one, who had been an administrator in Germany after the end of the war, until very lately, quoted the book. His thesis was that we are ignorant of what is going on in Russia, and of Russia's intentions, that is, of the intentions of the Soviet regime, that they are utterly dangerous, and that book gives the true picture. So I read it. I have been an apologist for the Soviet system, in total ignorance. If this book is true, the picture is so different from what we honest liberals have imagined, that it is most alarming.

I have been thrown off the track, like many others, because of the type of people who for the most part have damned the Soviet system, in ignorance equal to mine. I have considered these people, not only capitalistic but *materialistic,* which is both different and worse, as dangerous to the world, to humanity, as it is possible to be. They are the people with an overly-large and quite *unearned* share of material things, placing too great an emphasis on material things, and frightened to death that a world revolution would deprive them of

Marjorie Kinnan Rawlings. By permission of University of Florida Libraries.

trips to Palm Beach, etc. etc. etc. I still consider them dangerous, but they seem like small fry indeed in comparison with the menace this book portrays. I hope this man will be able to go further and give some idea of what can be done, in a tangible way. Of course, exploding the myth is of primary importance.

Thank you for your wires about the trial. I had begun to feel that I had been thrown to the wolves from the sleigh, so that the other occupants of the sleigh might make their escape. There was apparently nothing about the suit in the papers outside of Florida, and I am amazed at this, as it would seem to me obvious to all concerned with writing in any form that if I lost this case, no writer could be truly free. I know that I could have bought Zelma off for infinitely less than it has cost me, but I felt I should be betraying all writers if I took the easy way out. A thousand dollars at most, I am sure, would have stopped her and her lawyers, and it has already cost me about $4500, with the final lawyers' bills not yet presented. Phil May has charged me reasonably, <only> but it has been going on over three years, and he did not leave a stone unturned, in case we had to go to the Florida Supreme Court. As it turned out, we did not need the expense of the New York testimony, but he was taking no chances. He did read to the jury your testimony, Dr. Canby's and Bernice Baumgarten's. It came at the end of a long hard day and the jury was exhausted, and he was tempted not to use it, as he felt the jury had already decided to vote in my favor, but he was afraid not to get it into the record. (James Branch Cabell wrote me that, knowing juries, he would personally be afraid of a conviction if accused of killing Julius Caesar.) Phil and I were gratified to have the jury listen to that literary testimony as avidly as to the enemy's reading aloud of what they called "lewd, lascivious, lustful and salacious" passages from "Cross Creek". The enemy used Whitney's testimony for their side! They also entered Norton as their own witness, to his utter confusion and horror, but did not call him. I think they were just prepared to use Whitney's statements on sales, and to ask Norton about his finances, if my financial answer did not suit them. I was obliged to announce my net worth in money, from the witness stand.

After my experience, hard as it was, I think Tom Wolfe and any other writer ought to fight any such suit.[2] Perhaps Tom was getting old grievances off his chest, and so really had something to fear. It was clear to all that I had no grudge or malice in my brief writing of Zelma.

The charge of malice against me took equal place with the charge of invasion of privacy, and the very fair judge was obliged to instruct the jury that if malice was proved, there must be extra "punitive" damages against me. The trial was utterly vicious. We kept our side of it on as high a plane as possible, and even that was thrown in our teeth by the opposition. Because critics had written that what I wrote was literature, because I was in "Who's Who", because I was the only woman and only the second person ever to receive three honorary degrees from Florida universities, they said "Is there to be one law for the rich and famous and another for the poor and humble?" They said that only my vast wealth had enabled me to call fifty-one witnesses from the environs, and take depositions all over the country. This proved a boomerang, as the good, but extremely average jury could recognize that every person who testified for me, personally or in absentia, was motivated by genuine friendship.

Zelma had approached some of the Cross Creek people to help her, saying that if she won, they could sue me, too. They were already perfectly aware of this. Tom Glisson spoke for them all when he told her, "Friendship is worth more to me than any amount of money."

The trial vindicated, to me, two things: the democratic system, for I felt that if that most commonplace jury, none of whom had ever read anything I had written, could not see that something important was involved, there was no hope; and the loyalty and friendship of all the people, their integrity, of which I had written for so many years. There was an ovation in the court-room when the jury's verdict of "Not guilty" was announced.

But why, why, did the newspapers outside of Florida not understand what was happening?

The opposition ended their address to the jury with saying that it was exactly as though Joe Louis, the Negro champion, had stalked into Gainesville and knocked down a private citizen without provocation. "He might have done it with great finesse, gentlemen of the jury, as we admit that this woman handles language beautifully, but is that any reason for the public to applaud such a malicious attack?"

One of the most amusing incidents of the trial, to me, was when Zelma's lawyer was cross-examining me.[3] I could see the petty pit-falls he was trying to lay, and could anticipate him. He had asked me an inane question, and I said, "Now do you mean so and so, for the answer in that case would be one thing, or do you mean thus and so, in which the answer would be quite different," and so on. He floundered around, and Phil May jumped up and said, "Mr. Walton, what are you doing?" Walton said most plaintively, "I'm answering her question." Phil said, "Mr. Walton, you don't have to answer her question. She has no right to ask you questions." The court-room and the judge all but had hysterics.

Well, it is over, and I hope to get down to hard work. I still think it will have to be the book I have torn up so often.

1. Victor A. Kravchenko (1905–1966), *I Chose Freedom* (New York: Scribners, 1946).
2. In 1936, Thomas Wolfe was sued successfully by an individual who claimed to be damaged by a character in the story "No Door."
3. J. V. Walton and Kate Walton, his daughter, were the chief counsels for Zelma Cason.

. . . .

678. MEP to MKR (TLS: UF, 3 pp.)

June 10, 1946

Dear Marjorie:

I have just read with great amusement and interest the accounts of the trial in the St. Augustine paper which I guess Mr. May sent up to Whitney Darrow. We ought now to be able to get some literary publicity at any rate. We are sending the clippings over to the Publisher's Weekly, and we can use them elsewhere too. Don't you think that Zelma was put up to sue,- that she never would have done it on her own account?

I read to Mr. Kravchenko some of what you said about his book, and I told him that I thought the way you had felt about Russia and about attacks on Russia was the way 90% of our own most intelligent, tolerant people still did feel. They cannot believe that things are as they are. But I know of it from other sources than Kravchenko. Leigh White was over there as a correspondent a couple of years ago. He was very far to the left then, and he thought he was going to the Promised Land. He wrote a month or so back from Europe to ask if we would have the courage to publish a book he described, to be called TWO WORLDS.[1] He said that along side it Bill White's book[2] would seem like communist propaganda. And the reason for it is simply that a totalitarian country must become tyrannous,- must be a police state. Even if it starts with the best intentions and under the best men, it will end up that way. It is hard to see what we are coming to here, but the people who laid down the principles of our government realized the terrible danger of concentrated power, and set up a system for the diffusion of power. The idea was expressed by Lord Acton when he said, "Power always corrupts, and absolute power corrupts absolutely."[3] I think we are in an awful situation. But anyhow, you have this case off your mind, and better forget all such things as communism and totalitarianism, etc., and just write your own book. I remember well how many anxious nights I got through happily by just thinking about the YEARLING, and I hope for one more such experience.

I know how terribly hard is such a fight as you have gone through—how horrible all that has to do with law and courts is. If my father had not died when I was seventeen, I should probably have been a lawyer,- although even then, I did plan to be a newspaperman. But the family pressure was pretty strong the other way. I have always been grateful that I escaped the family fate. In the instance of Tom, he simply could not take it. It was for that reason that we settled the lawsuit, although we never did tell him so. He was so tormented that he could do nothing but drink and brood. It was absolutely necessary to get the thing out of the way, and this was only done with his apparently satisfied agreement. But afterward he did think that we had let him down.- So, after seeing him go through some preliminaries, I can well imagine the strain you have been under.

Yours,

1. Leigh White (1914–). *Two Worlds* was published with the title *The Long Balkan Night* (New York: Scribners, 1944).
2. William C. White (1903–1955), *Made in the USSR* (New York: Knopf, 1944).
3. John E. E. Dalberg, Lord Acton (1834–1902), British historian: "Power tends to corrupt and absolute power corrupts absolutely."

. . . .

679. MKR to MEP (TLS, 2 pp.)

Cross Creek
Hawthorn, Florida
June 18, 1946

Dear Max:

A friend of mine, Norman Berg,[1] who is Southern trade manager for Macmillan, out of Atlanta, Ga., wrote me that he was leaving for New York, and hoped to stop in at Scribner's and attempt to see you. He asked me to speak of him to you so that he would not be a total stranger. I think this is a bit presumptuous of him. I'll quote what he wrote me: "After twenty years in publishing I have been disappointed with most of the editors whom I have met and have sort of held him as an ideal. Any man who has handled a Rawlings, a Tom Wolfe and a Hemingway <at the same time> without going completely mad must be worth meeting."

Norman is an odd sort of egotist and it has not occurred to him to ask himself whether you would consider *him* worth meeting. However, as he really is a good friend of mine, I am doing as he asked. You probably won't understand a thing he says. He speaks in an extremely low voice and I have never heard anyone mumble so. His words come from the back of his mouth totally without articulation. Norton complains that he gets about one-tenth of what Norman says.

Norman and I quarrel violently. We quarreled over the Russian situation and I made him read the Kravashanko and he is still unconvinced. He is most thorough-going and now he has gone back to read Russian material of 1924 on, the ABC of Communism[2] and some biographies of Lenin and Stalin.

A scholarly friend of mine in Jacksonville wrote me that "I Chose Freedom" is a "must" for all Americans. Yet many people seem to have the question about Kravashanko in their minds that I did, some strange feeling that something is not quite right, faintly spurious. This friend for instance said that he was asking someone in a position to know more about it, to give him a check on K's "reliability". You yourself must feel perfectly satisfied about him, or you wouldn't have published the book.

Don't know whether I had mentioned it, but Zelma's lawyers filed a motion for a new trial. This will be heard by the judge July 15. Phil May thinks the judge will deny it, but that probably they will then appeal to the Fla. Supreme Court. He is no longer worried about it, he says. Did I write you that Phil said that Zelma's lawyer's zeal reminded him of Santayana's definition of a fanatic, "A person who redoubles his efforts after he has lost sight of his purpose."

I am beginning to feel a little better. I had rather a bad nervous and physical reaction for a couple of weeks. I don't mind, as long as I held out through the trial itself.

If Norman Berg does come in, tell him (this refers to his letter to me) that I have decided he is correct in his criticism of the last line in my story "Miriam's Houses". Also tell him that if and when we do have a complete collection of my queerer stories, it would be much more friendly of him to point out the instances of "good style" rather than of "bad style." If he cares to point out the spots of "bad style" in my stories *before* they are in book form, that would be kind, but after that, let him forever hold his peace.

1. Norman S. Berg later published under his own imprint *South Moon Under, When the Whip-poorwill—, Cross Creek,* and *The Sojourner.*
2. Nikolai Bukharin (1888–1938), *ABC of Communism* (New York: Workers Party of America, 1921).

. . . .

680. MEP to MKR (TLS: UF, 2 pp.)

June 20, 1946

Dear Marjorie:

I'm mighty glad to hear that you are feeling better. I knew that the trial had been a great strain upon you. Though you went through it beautifully, it must have been exhausting, and people who have that quality of rising to an occasion, do their suffering afterward.

When Norman Berg comes, I'd be mighty glad to talk to him, but I can see we are going to have an argument about the present regime in Russia. It is amazing how the whole United States has been deceived, partly by wishful thinking, but largely by the cunning of the Communist propaganda. I had a letter yesterday from a woman who had spent several years in Russia, as more or less of a prisoner during the war, and she said she thought Kravchenko, because he belonged to the upper class, had actually understated his case. We have had a number of letters to that effect. After all, it is the logic of history that when power becomes so concentrated, it must inevitably become tyranny. What happened in Russia had to happen.

As to the authenticity of the book, suspicion is thrown upon it in two ways. The first is that having been put into English and into form by a journalistic writer,- it reads more smoothly than it should, and the other is that all the Leftists and their publications tried to smear it. They are very clever and are all over the place. The Book-of-the-Month Club almost took this book twice. Before the second consideration, Canby went through all the material, the Russian original, the first rough translation, etc. and he carefully cross-examined Kravchenko with an interpreter. He was absolutely convinced.

Edith Pope is here and I am to have lunch with her in a day or two. Then I'll hear much more about the trial.

Always yours,

. . . .

681. MKR to MEP (TLS, 2 pp.)

Box 335
Blowing Rock, N.C.
Sept. 18, 1946

Dear Max:

I am most happily located in the mountains, to finish my expanding of the story "A Mother in Mannville" for M.G.M.[1] I only wish I had a creative job on hand, for it is a perfect place for work. The cottage is a mile away from the tourist town, and has a view of miles and miles of valley and mountain. My maid is with me, and my dog and cat, and Norton spent a few days.

The only books I brought with me were the Bible, Proust, and James' "The American Scene",[2] which you sent me. The James is a revelation. At first, the extremity of the involutions of his style <illegible excision> is exasperating. Then you realize that you have simply been reading too much stuff that was written as though the authors were rushing to meet a deadline on the MGM

$125,000 prize contest. It strikes you with embarrassment that you are forced to go as slowly as James, and to *think* along with him. It is the strangest "travel" book I have ever read, intensely subjective, and yet, when you have finished with one of his *discussions* as to how he was affected by a certain aspect of the scene, you have as objective a picture of that scene as though Thoreau had described it.

I had not realized, either, that James was so critical of the society with which I had always assumed he had snobbishly associated himself.

Many thanks indeed.

The story is going rapidly. Pray for and with me that when it is done, the right approach for my book will have come to me.

1. The story was expanded and given the new title "Mountain Prelude" and published as a serial in the *Saturday Evening Post* in April–May 1947. Scribner rejected it for publication as a novel with the title *A Family for Jock*. MGM hired MKR to write a "Lassie movie" and then used the spirit of the story for the hit musical *The Sun Comes Up* (1949), starring Jeanette MacDonald.
2. Henry James, *The American Scene* (New York: Harper, 1907).

. . . .

682. MEP to MKR (TLS: UF, 2 pp.)

Sept. 25, 1946

Dear Marjorie:

It wasn't until quite recently that I knew you were developing the story A MOTHER IN MANVILLE. Carol[1] told me. I got the impression that she thought I might be resentful that, partly through her, you had been diverted from the big novel. But I was not. I could see that this lawsuit and all, had made it impossible for you to completely give yourself to a full-size piece of work. And I thought that this diversion might be just the thing that you needed. What's more, I can hardly imagine that you will not have a book. It is a beautiful story. The only danger would be that having written it as a story first, you might not get into it the spontaneity you have always seemed to have. But I do not think it is likely you will have lost anything. The story itself is too good, and I certainly expect it will be a book. So does Carol.

I knew you would like the James book. I have looked forward for years to a peaceful decade or so after seventy or eighty, when I could slowly read Dostoievsky, Proust, and James.

By the way, a very interesting looking, and talking, English publisher, William Collins, was in here yesterday who, although he was supposed to be persuading us to take some of his books, spent most of his time expressing admiration for yours. He was not trying to get them for England either, which would be unethical. He was just enthusiastic.

I am glad you are in such a beautiful place.

Always yours,

1. Carol Brandt of Brandt and Brandt, MKR's agents.

. . . .

683. MKR to MEP (TLS, I p.)

Crescent Beach
St. Augustine, Florida
Oct. 31, 1946

Dear Max:

Whatever Carl Brandt's reaction to my boy-and-dog story for MGM may be, don't pay any attention to him. He seems to me rather hysterical on the subject, and I think it may be because this is the first movie deal he and his wife Carol have worked out together, since she gave up her own agency.

I should not object to the story's appearing in a magazine, but my opinion is that, in book form, it would do great damage to whatever literary reputation I may have. It is probably a "sweet" story, and Norton in reading it found himself often touched, but that is not enough. I trapped myself into doing it, because I could see how easily the original story "A Mother in Mannville" could be enlarged to make a movie story.

Editor's note: At bottom of letter in MEP's hand: "*Dora Chaplain / Schwartzchild.*"[1]

1. Dora Chaplain, wife of Duncan Chaplain.

. . . .

684. MEP to MKR (TLS: UF, 3 pp.)

Nov. 7, 1946

Dear Marjorie:

I do not think that A FAMILY FOR JOCK should be published as a book. It isn't written as you would have written it had you intended it to be a book. Besides, it did not originate in you, as all your other books have, but was written, one might say, by assignment,- and when it is that way, a book never does come up to the author's own level. That is what people would say of this when they thought of CROSS CREEK, and THE YEARLING, and SOUTH MOON UN-DER, etc. And they would not understand the reasons. But I rather think it is a super movie scenario, and that for its purpose you should have written it as you did. It goes much too fast for a book by you,- isn't even in your style. But it suggests a magnificent picture, and your response to the beauty of the mountains, and the qualities of the mountain people, and all that, would be carried into the picture itself. Besides the boy is very good and sound.

You were not writing a book, and so you did not write one. My first reaction when Carol told me of this plan, was that it could not result in a book that should be yours, but then when I thought of the dog and the boy, and all the elements, it did seem to me that you were likely to carry it off. But how could you write a scenario for the screen, and at the same time make it what you would make a book of your own?

I think with some enlargement, it might make a popular magazine serial. But I do not think it should be a book, which reviewers would inevitably compare with what you had done before. They would not know the reason for the difference.

Always yours,

. . . .

685. MKR to MEP (TLS, I p.)

Crescent Beach
St. Augustine, Florida
Nov. 9, 1946

Dear Max:

Your letter has just come about the movie story, and I must get off a note to you, to tell you how relieved I am that you see this as I do. If you had approved of book publication, it would have undermined all my confidence in your literary judgments, to say nothing of my own. But I was absolutely certain that we should agree.

Carl and M.G.M. are so starry-eyed about it, that I could not help being just a little worried. No author can ever be entirely trusted, or trust himself, to know what is right and what is not, yet there are times when, if one is wrong, too much is at stake. My blessings on you. I knew you would not fail me.

I shall probably be in New York shortly, and have plans to discuss with you.

1947

Cross Creek
Hawthorn, Florida
Jan. 20, 1947

Dear Max:

I don't know who is handling the business end of Whitney's former work,[1] so am writing you. I overlooked the enclosed request of months ago.

The arrangement is all right with me, if Scribner's approves. I believe this is the sort of thing that we have on a 50-50 basis, isn't it?

I think on my next contracts I shall not agree to this arrangement, though I know it is standard. But I consider it unfair and always have.

With the movie story revisions and proof-correcting for the Post out of the way, I have just about caught up on ordinary detail, and after I have entertained a few more relatives and friends, hope to be free to settle down to hard, uninterrupted work. If I am interfered with too much, I shall go back to the mountain cottage as early in the spring as it is habitable. I can really work there.

My best,

If you approve this thing, will you have it signed and sent on to Doubleday, Doran.

1. Whitney Darrow insisted that a travel book about Russia by Melvin A. Hall (1889–1962), *Journey to the End of an Era* (New York: Scribners, 1947), be pushed as the Scribner book of the year. The book did not succeed, and it has been described as Darrow's "last intervention." See Charles Scribner, Jr., *In the Company of Writers* (New York: Scribners, 1990), 47–48.

687. MEP to MKR (TLS: UF, 2 pp.)

Dear Marjorie:

Whatever you may think about it, we had attended to the request you enclosed a long time ago. It was not right. They offered you a certain payment for good, but it should have been on the basis of a certain number of copies, and provision should have been made for later printing. They finally found that we had published the story, and made the usual application to us, and we had a proper agreement drawn up as the publishers of the story. So the whole thing is settled, and to your advantage, in spite of the fact that Barabbas was a publisher.[1]

It really was wonderful to see you up here. I wish it had been more than once,- the second time was just a glimpse. Walter Gilkyson and Bernice expect soon to be down in your territory and are eager to see you. Hem was here for several furious days. I lost his fishing rod, but he had left it in my office for seven years. I don't know just what to do about it.

Always yours,

1. Barabbas, the robber whom Pilate released from prison instead of Jesus.

. . . .

688. MKR to MEP (TLS, 4 pp.)

Cross Creek
Hawthorn, Florida
Feb. 13, 1947

Dear Max:

I have been reading in the ATLANTIC the letters of Tom Wolfe to his teacher Mrs. Roberts.[1] They have been consistently moving, but the final ones in the February issue are truly great. They reveal the attitude, the necessities, of the artist, like nothing else I have ever read, not even Ellen Glasgow's wonderful Prefaces. It is rather sickening to find that even this most sympathetic woman, to whom he poured out so much of himself, was "hurt," and asked him to write his last book "as discreetly as possible." I mourned more than ever that, having reached such maturity as he shows here, he did not live to write more books.

In a way, of course, that maturity was more or less imaginary. In the earlier letters, he was often so sure that he was all through with his doubts and wonderings, and ready to do *the one* book, and then the years passed and he was as at sea as ever, from the standpoint of a *personal* adjustment to life. But the good books kept coming, and would have come.

For myself, I have never felt more inadequate. The time between books has been so unreasonably long that I feel a true writer would not, could not, have let it happen. I don't mean about "publication," etc., but about *working*. At any rate, I am going to Cross Creek early next week, to *stay* until I have my teeth into something. Norton is in the middle of his busiest season and does not get to the cottage for dinner, so I can leave him with a clearer conscience than at any time before.

I am torn between two or three things. Your suggestion that I let the child's story of the little Negro girl[2] develop as it would, reminded me of something I said in "Cross Creek," that "some day a poet will write a sad and lovely story of a Negro child." I have found that each of my books has developed out of something I have written in a previous book. Some thought evidently unfinished. I think I could do such a book now, and would prefer doing it, I believe, to the *terrible* chore of the book about the spiritual and inarticulate man who derived remotely from my own grandfather.

But if I do a book about a Negro child in a creative way, that leaves out entirely the child's book for which Robert Camp has already done all the paintings and drawings, and I hate to let him down. I could do a very simple text for this child's book, right now, easily and quickly, letting his really wonderful illustrations carry most of it, and then go on to the creative thing.

I have long tales to tell you <, which will> when I see you, which will probably be in April, if that is when Julia Scribner's baby is christened, when I will be a god-mother.

1. Thomas Wolfe, "Writing Is My Life," *Atlantic Monthly* 178.6 (December 1946): 60–66; 179.1–2 (January–February 1947): 39–45, 55–61.
2. Published posthumously as *The Secret River* (New York: Scribners, 1955).

. . . .

689. MEP to MKR (TLS: UF, 2 pp.)

Feb. 25, 1947

Dear Marjorie:

I believe you could write a sad and lovely story of a negro child. I don't see either quite why Robert Camp's pictures might not be adjusted to such a book,- I mean a really creative and developed one. But anyhow, I hope you will do such a book. If his pictures would only suit the first plan, couldn't the little book be deferred?

It was too bad that Mrs. Roberts failed Tom at that critical time, although only briefly. I think it was more on account of her husband, and perhaps her sister-in-law. Tom almost caricatured her husband, and I think it was because as a boy, though perhaps unconsciously, he was jealous of him because of his admiration of Mrs. Roberts. It isn't surprising she should have been resentful, and it wasn't for long. His whole family were shocked too, but they were completely loyal to Tom, even though they did not understand him, and for the most part they concealed any resentment, and supported him,- especially his mother did. They are grand letters.

Always yours,

. . . .

690. MEP to MKR (TLS: UF, I p.)

Feb. 27, 1947

Dear Marjorie:

I thought you might have missed this one.[1]

Always yours,

1. Subject not identified.

. . . .

691. MKR to MEP (TLS, 2 pp.)

Cross Creek
Hawthorn, Florida
March 18, 1947

Dear Max:

Here is the first draft of the child's story, to go with Bob Camp's paintings and drawings, which were sent off yesterday. It seems to me that I may have fallen between two stools. As you will see, there is a certain symbolism, a certain irony at the end, where the little colored girl assumes that the world will be a kind and beautiful place, and <our knowing> we know that she will not find it so. And whether the story is right for a definite age-group or not, I would not know. It may be too mature in its implications.

Having told the story in pretty much fairy-tale style, there was no temptation to do a longer or creative thing. If I ever do a creative book or long story about a colored child, I think the only element I might need, out of the present child's story, is having her potentially a poet. Yet that is risky in a serious piece, for when the author produces "potential poetry" for a character, it had damn well better be good! So it would probably be safer to give her a recognizably poetic nature. Recently I read for the first time Alain Fournier's "The Wanderer"[1] and I realized that its *mood* is about what I had in mind for the serious thing, if I ever do it. "The Secret River" could make a good title for it, though I should probably use a real river instead of an imaginary one, and there are always other titles. But in the present story, do you think perhaps it would be better to have Calpurnia find a real river, and not have the element of fantasy? Children love fantasy, so long as it is remotely intelligible.

If you like the general idea of the present story, Bob Camp will have to do a few more drawings or paintings to go with the latter part. He could do a really beautiful painting of the white crane flying across the moon, with the panther crouching, etc. Then perhaps just a black and white drawing of a bear, etc.

1. Alain-Fournier [Henri-Alban Fournier] (1886–1914), *Le Grand Meaulnes* [*The Wanderer*] (1913).

. . . .

692. MEP to MKR (TLS: UF, 1 p.)

March 28, 1947

Dear Marjorie:

I shall write you on Monday about "The Secret River". I know, or almost know, what I am going to say, but it is quite complicated, and I thought no harm would be done if I thought it over during the weekend,- especially since I haven't time to do it today. I think it is a little story of great charm and delicacy. There are lovely paragraphs in it. I think, though, that very considerable changes should be made, or that the ones I suggest may suggest to you better ones.

Always yours,

. . . .

693. MEP to MKR (TLS: UF, 3 pp.)

March 31, 1947

Dear Marjorie:

This is what I think about the SECRET RIVER. It should be a real river, though a little and deeply concealed one, which this child, Calpurnia, had never seen, but had heard of. In fact, I think the whole story should have the quality of enchantment, the magical quality that this draft of it does have, but yet it should be more realistic, if one could apply such a stern term to such a delicate thing. I think it should take Calpurnia a longer time to get to the river, because that would intensify the suspense and the anxiety which <the> a child would find in reading it or in having it read to <her> him. In other words, I think she ought to turn her head because of various other apparitions than the two mentioned, and keep on following her nose for a longer time.- In fact, I think the story ought to be more developed throughout, and that buggy horse should do more, or be kept more on the scene.

Then you have the bull frog talk. No other creature talks, nor do the trees. If one talks, all should talk, but then you would have a complete fairy story. It would become wholly fantasy. I think it should not do that, but rather verge the other way. I think that it ought to be said that when the frog croaked, it seemed to her as if he said what you have him say.- This would tend also to take the reader into the child's identity, which I think you have not done. I think the reader—though perhaps the child reader would not—looks upon Calpurnia too objectively, and without becoming her in this adventure.

By the way, I think the child's poems are admirable, though if a little of the negro quality could be got into the phrasing without its being actually dialect, I would be for that.- And in fact, I did not understand why you did not use the negro rhythm of speech and phrasing, which you know so well. To take a trifling example, when Calpurnia asks if she can go up to find the colored paper, or whatever it was, the mother says, "Of course, my dear child." I would suppose that a negress would say, "Of course, child."

In verging more toward reality, I would even dare to suggest that the bear and the panther should be changed to a raccoon and wild cat, which would be almost as interesting to child readers, and might seem exciting to Calpurnia, and dangerous too. Either one of them would have accepted a fish.

Now the way I am looking at the story is that the things in the story actually happened, but that it did not seem to Calpurnia that they were as they were. For one thing, she was a little child. Everyone as a child can remember coming upon some seemingly enchanted spot of incredible beauty, and a sort of unreality, where for the time everything was perfect and right. That does not only happen to a child either, but an adult does not believe actually in the magic of it. I remember for one instance, climbing up the cliffs beside a waterfall as a boy, and coming to the top where the brook had spread out almost into a little river and flowed peacefully, and the green meadows on each side. It was like entering fairyland. Everyone knows about this. I would have it that the adult reader would so understand, and yet you would have all the latitude you wanted. The bear and the panther could be thought of as almost imagined by Calpurnia. But in this interpretation, Madam Albirtha might presumably have given the advice, "Follow your nose," thinking the girl knew where she was and would soon get home, and then when she did turn up with the fish and Madam Albirtha said she would never see the river again, it would signify to the adult that she realized that this child had been through one of those magical experiences, and that while she might have others, this one would never recur. The river would never look to her as it had that time, even if she did see it again. Or it might mean, as seemed somewhat to be implied, that this was an instance where the child had thought the necessity was so great that she had, as people sometimes do in very great stress, over-reached herself, in the same way that one jumps some incredible distance across an abyss which never could have been normally done. But I think the first conception is the right one, and more in consonance with your narrative.

But there is one more thing, I do not think you ought to have Madam Albirtha the mistress of a beauty parlor in the forest. That seems to me facetious, almost. Couldn't you have her something more credible?

This is the hardest kind of thing to write about. It seems silly. It is like applying logic to ALICE IN WONDERLAND, but even in ALICE there is a kind of wild logic, and the foundation of that is a dream.

Always yours,

P.S. I am returning the first draft.

. . . .

694. MKR to MEP (ALS, 2 pp.)

Cross Creek
Hawthorn, Florida
April 4, 1947

Dear Max:

I have just read your good letter, and it gives exactly the sort of guidance that I hoped for. I think you are absolutely right about what should be the nature of the river, that the magic should be emotional rather than in the pure realm of faery.

I wanted you to see what I was getting at in a general way. And although you told me before not to bother about keeping it too short, I didn't want to develop it further until you could pass judgment on the skeleton of the story. I shall enjoy going ahead now and making Calpurnia and Buggy-horse seem more real to a child.

Now you know we do have bears and panthers in several sections of Florida, but I can see how a more charming effect could be obtained from using two smaller animals, and then perhaps having Calpurnia enlarge them in her mind, even doing another little poem about having placated a bear and a panther.

I did not use any trace of Negro dialect for two reasons. I wanted to give a complete dignity to all the Negroes in the story, with no "Uncle Remus" or "Little Black Sambo"[1] sort of stuff, with its humorous, often depreciatory effect. Calpurnia is only accidentally a little colored girl. The educated Negroes even down here talk just like anyone else. I feel so strongly about the so-called Negro "problem," and giving them self-respect, thinking of them and seeing them as human beings, with the color of the skin as incidental as it is with blonde Swedes and dark Italians, seems to me a most important thing. I deplore in the same breath the "comic" treatment of the Negro, and the unreasonable martyrdom, with emphasis on their tragedy of color and race, that is being assigned to them in a great spate of current books.

The first painting that Bob Camp made of Calpurnia was so exaggerated as to be almost a caricature, although it was really an enchanting and whimsical portrait, and although he does not share my feelings on the race question, he did agree with me that artistically it would be better to have a straight and more soulful portrait of the child, and he did another that is really a beautiful thing.

My second reason for not using dialect or even idiom is that I think such a story will be more effective if there is nothing of the sort to distract the attention from the tale itself.

Evidently you have not seen Bob's paintings and drawings, which I expressed to him just before I sent you the first draft of the manuscript. I regret this exceedingly as his work and mine supplement each other, and I did want you to see what he has done, in conjunction with my story. Please look at his things when I send you the next draft.

Thanks a lot, and I'll get to work at once.

1. Joel Chandler Harris (1848–1908), *Uncle Remus* (1881); and Helen Bannerman (1862–1946), *Little Black Sambo* (1899).

. . . .

695. MEP to MKR (TLS: UF, 2 pp.)

April 16, 1947

Dear Marjorie:

Bob Camp brought in his pictures. The original one of Calpurnia is wonderful, and the others are very promising though some of them do run too far toward the grotesque. But they are full of feeling, and Camp is willing, in fact anxious, to modify them or even make others to go with the spirit of the story. He, and in fact all of us, think that the work should be done in that way,- that illustrations ought to be made to fit the story, and not that the story should be made to fit the illustrations. I hope you will go on with Calpurnia as if it were wholly your own idea, and let it run to what it will. I understand how you feel about the Negro way of speech, and I was altogether for the avoidance of dialect. But the world will be robbed if the phrasings and rhythms of different peoples are avoided. They are part of the wealth of literature. The Irish, Scotch, and Welch, for instance, have all their own ways of expression.

By the way, we have just taken an option on Zora Hurston's next novel. All I had read of hers was that autobiographical book,[1] but she came in, and gave me the impression of somebody so full of life and emotion and intelligence that whatever she did should be good. She roused up the whole office by the vitality of her presence.

Always yours,

1. Zora Neale Hurston, *Seraph on the Suwanee* (New York: Scribners, 1948). The autobiographical book is *Dust Tracks on a Road* (Philadelphia: Lippincott, 1942).

. . . .

696. MKR to MEP (TLS, 2 pp.)

Cross Creek
Hawthorn, Florida
April 30, 1947

Dear Max:

I am delighted that you may publish Zora Neale Hurston's next book. I feel that she has a very great talent. You really should read her "Moses, Man of the Mountain."[1] She has not only the Negro gift of rhythm and imagination, but she is proud of her blood and her people, and presents her stories from the Negro point of view. I am very fond of her. And will you send me her address? I have been wanting to write her, but didn't know where she was.

I was just ready to go to work on Calpurnia again, when I wrecked my car seriously, myself and maid rather lightly, considering the fact that we turned over twice. Our road at the Creek had been oiled, without my knowing of it. It was raining hard, and we skidded. My only damages were beautiful multi-colored bruises, but Idella broke two ribs.

The delay will probably be to the good in re-writing the story, as I do need the perspective you suggested, of not trailing after Bob Camp's very engaging pictures. He made them all, before I had begun work, and they did have a great deal of influence on me. He and I had been talking about the book for several years.

I can't help wishing, in spite of the very high remuneration, that Carl Brandt had not sold that movie story to the POST. When I wrote it in narrative form for M.G.M., I really never expected it to appear in print of any sort. I read the first installment of the serial, and could have died of shame. It is even worse, from a literary standpoint, than I remembered.

My beloved friend Edith Pope is certainly rubbing it in. We were at a party with Owen D. Young,[2] and he asked her if she had read the first issue. She had, and gave him such a wan, comprehensive smile! Norton reports that the next night she and her husband were at his Marineland for dinner,[3] and she asked Norton if he had read it saying, "DON'T." I told Norton that I didn't mind Edith's high-hatting me about it, as I deserved it to begin with, and it might have a good effect on her, by making her think twice before she put down something sub-standard. But I am most embarrassed about it all.

I'll go back to "The Secret River" now, and we can only see what comes of it.

My best,

1. *Moses, Man of the Mountain* (Philadelphia: Lippincott, 1939).
2. Owen D. Young (1874–1962), lawyer, executive, and ambassador, who was from Van Hornesville, N.Y.
3. In 1946, Norton S. Baskin became manager of two restaurants at Marineland.

. . . .

697. MEP to MKR (TLS: UF, 1 p.)

May 29, 1947

Dear Marjorie:

This is just a line to say how deeply I sympathize with you in the outcome of the appeal.[1] It all seems utterly mysterious to me. I must get hold of the law and read it myself. It is very much too bad.

Always yours,

1. On May 23, 1947, the Florida Supreme Court found MKR guilty of "invasion of privacy" in the Zelma Cason lawsuit.

. . . .

698. MKR to MEP (TLS, 2 pp.)

Cross Creek
Hawthorn, Florida
June 7, 1947

Dear Max:

The ruling is truly idiotic, but it means that while I have not injured Zelma in any way whatsoever, the Florida Supreme Court is backing up some strange law on the Florida books, whereby I have automatically invaded Zelma's privacy.

I have written Whitney a long letter about details, and you might ask to see this.

As to what concerns you and me, I feel that I am ready to get to work on my book. My automobile accident and then this law business stopped short my re-working of the child's story. I have lost interest in it. I am also afraid that you expect me to do a much more creative job on it than I ever planned to do. I really saw no reason why I should not do a text to go with Bob Camp's drawings and paintings. However, I shall try to do a new version before I go at the novel, as it would be nice to have the child's book ready for the Christmas trade.

As I have written Whitney, I am leaving soon for Van Hornesville, N. Y., where Mr. and Mrs. Owen D. Young are lending me for the summer an old Dutch house, modernized, a woman to come in every day to do domestic details, a wonderful view, moderately isolated. This will be much better than my original idea of going to the Carolina mountains to work on my book, as the flora and fauna, the general terrain, will be much closer to the setting that I am using, of southern Michigan. Incidentally, don't ever mention the Michigan setting, as I wish to keep it vague. The book should be the sort where locale does not matter.

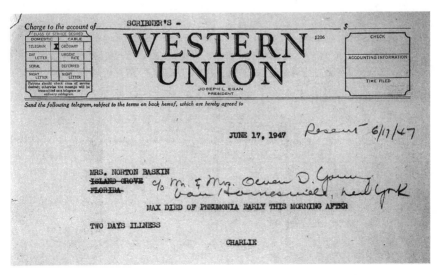

Charles Scribner's wire to MKR on the death of Perkins. By permission of Princeton University Library.

Maxwell Evarts Perkins died suddenly on June 17, 1947.

Marjorie Kinnan Rawlings died suddenly on December 13, 1953.

Index

Fountain, Henry, 384–85, 385n, 387, 392
Fountain, Sissy, 551, 551n
Frank, Waldo, 42, 42n, 43
Franklin, Benjamin, 375, 377n
Freeman, Douglas S., 205n, 476, 477n, 540, 540n, 550
Freuchen, Peter, 495, 497n
From these Roots (Colum), 305, 305n, 310, 314
Frost, Robert, 331
Frothingham, John, 395n
Furriner, The (*Golden Apples*), 162, 168–69

Gade, Herman, 517n
Gade, John A., 514, 515n, 517n
Galsworthy, John, 46–47, 48n, 140, 162, 162n, 240
"Gal Young Un" (Rawlings), 3, 50, 50n, 88–89, 130, 130n, 351, 453
Gannett, Lewis S., 46–47, 48n, 346, 347n
Garden Murder Case, The (Van Dine), 235n
"Gavotte, La" (Hoffman), 246, 247n
"'Geechee" (*Cross Creek*), 231
Gellhorn, Martha E. *See* Hemingway, Martha E. Gellhorn
General Grant's Last Stand (Green), 263–64, 264n
General's Lady, The (Forbes), 380, 380n
Gilkyson, Bernice, 20, 450–51, 451n, 454–55, 460
Gilkyson, Walter, 450–51, 451n, 454–55, 460
Glasgow, Ellen, 12–13, 104n, 235, 235n, 352, 366, 367n, 368, 383, 397, 414, 416, 439, 454, 455, 455n, 554, 602
Glisson, Mrs. Tom, 506–7
Glisson, Tom, 506, 545, 545n, 593
Golden Apples (Rawlings), 220, 238, 251, 254, 263, 316, 339–40, 359, 388, 439, 494, 501, 577; abridgment, 389, 391–93; alternate titles, 37, 160–62, 168–70; Book-of-the-Month Club, 177, 180–81, 229; contract, 180, 188, 204, 210, 221–22; film rights, 204, 212, 389; foreign rights and editions, 180, 202–3, 336, 450, 450n; illustrations, 311; publicity, 192–93, 197–98, 219–20, 233–34, 237, 393; reception and sales, 7,13, 21, 221, 225, 227, 231–32, 235–36, 240–42, 248, 253, 313, 317; reviews, 7, 223, 226–28, 232, 415, 419, 421; royalties, 7, 180, 186, 188, 239; serialization, 146, 163, 166, 168–69, 171, 186, 188, 190, 192–93, 195, 197–99, 202, 204, 211–12, 237, 491
—composition: planning, 5–6, 37, 38n, 40, 47, 89, 95, 101, 111–13, 117, 121–23, 237; writing, 6–7, 11, 132–35, 137–40, 143–44, 148, 150, 152, 154; revision, 7, 151–59, 161–65, 167–68, 171–89, 191–93, 195–96, 198–202, 206–10, 212–18, 220, 222, 228, 317
Goldfarb's, 342
Gone with the Wind (Mitchell), 435, 436n, 438, 539
Goodbye, Mr. Chips (Hilton), 251, 252n
Good Earth, The (Buck), 76, 76n
Goodman, Paul, 258, 259n
Goodspeed, Iola Fuller (Molly Beaver), 401, 402n, 403–5, 425
Gordon, Caroline, 163, 163n, 406, 406n
Gorsline, Douglas, 395n, 453n
Gorsline, Jeremiah, 453, 453n
Goya (Poore), 375, 377n
Goya, Francisco José de, 375, 377n
Grace Steamship Line, 111
Graham, Sheilah, 479, 479n
Granberry, Edwin, 284, 284n
Grand Canyon, 223
Grand Central Station, 300
Grandfather Orphanage, 260, 261n
Grant, Ulysses S., 263–64
Grapes of Wrath, The (Steinbeck), 18, 572, 572n
Graves, Ralph H., 395, 494
Gray, Austin K., 586n
Gray, James, 342, 342n
Grayson, David (Ray S. Baker), 578, 578n
Great Sea Mystery (Lockhart), 236, 236n, 237, 239
Green, Horace, 263, 264n
Green Centuries (Gordon), 406, 406n
Grey, Zane, 244, 247n
Grey Owl, 196, 197n
Grinnell, Mrs. Oliver Cromwell, 244, 244n, 295–98, 302, 307, 346, 348, 355, 362
Grosset and Dunlap, 203, 203n, 388
Grove Park Inn, 260
Gulliver's Travels (Swift), 467

Hale, Nancy (Nancy Wertenbaker), 347, 533, 533n, 539–40, 542, 545–46, 546n
Half Moon Under (*South Moon Under*), 53